THE TECHNIQUE OF FILM AND VIDEO EDITING

History, Theory, and Practice

FOURTH EDITION

KEN DANCYGER

ELSEVIER

AMSTERDAM • BOSTON • HEIDLEBERG • LONDON
NEW YORK • OXFORD • PARIS • SAN DIEGO
SAN FRANCISCO • SINGAPORE • SYDNEY • TOKYO
Focal Press is an imprint of Elsevier

Focal
Press

Acquisitions Editor: Elinor Acipis
Project Manager: Paul Gottehrer
Assistant Editor: Robin Weston
Marketing Manager: Christine Degon Veroulis
Cover Design: Eric DeCicco

Focal Press is an imprint of Elsevier
30 Corporate Drive, Suite 400, Burlington, MA 01803, USA
Linacre House, Jordan Hill, Oxford OX2 8DP, UK

 Recognizing the importance of preserving what has been written,
Elsevier prints its books on acid-free paper whenever possible.

Library of Congress Cataloging-in-Publication Data

Application submitted

British Library Cataloguing-in-Publication Data
A catalogue record for this book is available from the British Library.

ISBN 13: 978-0-240-80765-2
ISBN 10: 0-240-80765-0

For information on all Newnes publications,
visit our website at www.books.elsevier.com.

07 08 09 10   10 9 8 7 6 5 4 3 2 1

Printed in the United States of America

**Working together to grow
libraries in developing countries**

www.elsevier.com | www.bookaid.org | www.sabre.org

ELSEVIER   BOOK AID
International   Sabre Foundation

THE TECHNIQUE OF FILM AND VIDEO EDITING: HISTORY, THEORY, AND PRACTICE

FOURTH EDITION

*For the next generation,
and dedicated to my
contribution to that
generation,*

Emily and Erica.

CONTENTS

ACKNOWLEDGMENTS FOR THE FOURTH EDITION

Thanks to Elinor Actipis and Becky Golden-Harrell at Focal Press for their work on this edition. I'd also like to thank my students in the History of Editing class in the Film Department at TISCH School of the Arts, New York University. They have helped me convert that class into a laboratory where ideas about editing can by explored.

ACKNOWLEDGMENTS

Many people have been helpful in the preparation of this manuscript.

At Focal Press I thank Karen Speerstra for suggesting the project to me, and Sharon Falter for her ongoing help.

I'm grateful to the following archives for their help in securing the stills for this book: the British Film Institute, the French Cinematheque, the Moving Image and Sound Archives of Canada, and the Museum of Modern Art, New York.

For their generous financial support I thank the Faculty of Fine Arts, York University, and the Canada Council. This book could not have been written on the scale attempted without the financial support of the Canada Council.

This project was complex and challenging in the level of support services it required. From typing and shipping to corresponding with archives and studios on rights clearances, I have been superbly supported by my assistant, Steven Sills, in New York and my friend and colleague, George Robinson, in Toronto. I thank them both. Finally, I thank my wife, Ida, for being so good-natured about the demands of this project.

INTRODUCTION TO
THE FOURTH EDITION

The Technique of Film and Video Editing was first published in 1993. Much has changed as addressed in the second and third editions. With this fourth edition it's opportune to acknowledge all the changes since 1993.

First we need to acknowledge the digital revolution. Technology has transformed the technology of editing, the speed of editing and conceptually the aesthetics of editing. Both in production and post-production, the digital revolution has had a profound impact on sound and image. The goal of these two phases as well as pre-production is storytelling. Has the digital changes influenced storytelling? This is a primary issue in editions two through four.

A second issue that needs to be acknowledged is that this book has increasingly become a history of editing. It didn't start out that way. It began as a book intended to be helpful to directors. But as change accelerates, the need to be reminded where the changes came from has grown stronger. The seminal moments in the history of editing, Hitchcock's *Blackmail,* (1929), Welles' *Citizen Kane* (1941), Kurosawa's *Rashomon* (1951), Resnais' *Hiroshima, Mon Amour* (1960), Godard's *Breathless* (1959) and Fellini's *8 ½* (1963) have grown in importance.

New issues included in the second and third editions are the evolution of the MTV style and nonlinear editing. Both address these new issues. Another issue addressed in the third and now in the fourth edition is the number of phenomenological issues has entered the editing arena. In a digital age when an image can be amended, altered to look real, what is real and what is unreal? What reality determines editing choices? The documentary film increasingly has flirted with entertainment values just as the dramatic film has flirted with documentary values. When educational forms and entertainment forms adapt the values of the other, how does this influence editing choice? And in a world where novelty has become a value rather than a passing observation, how does this affect editing choices. The new chapters on long shots and close shots, sound, pace and the changes in documentary discuss these issues.

Much changes and nothing changes. History is a continuum and editing is informed by that history. I'm pleased that the subtitle of this book is now "History, Theory and Practice." That is my purpose in writing this fourth edition.

INTRODUCTION

It has been half a century since Karel Reisz, working with a British Film Academy committee, wrote *The Technique of Film Editing*. Much has happened in those 50 years. Television is pervasive in its presence and its influence, and cinema, no longer in decline because of television, is more influential than ever. The videocassette recorder (VCR) has made movies, old and new, accessible, available, and ripe for rediscovery by another generation. The director is king, and film is more international than ever.

In 1953, Reisz could not foresee these changes, but he did demonstrate that the process of film editing is a seminal factor in the craft of filmmaking and in the evolution of film as an art form. If anything, the technological changes and creative high points of the past 50 years have only deepened that notion.

Reisz's strategic decision to sidestep the theoretical debate on the role of editing in the art of film allowed him to explore creative achievements in different film genres. By doing so, he provided the professional and the student with a vital guide to the creative options that editing offers.

One of the key reasons for the success of Reisz's book is that it was written from the filmmaker's point of view. In this sense, the book was conceptual rather than technical. Just as it validated a career choice for Reisz (within 10 years, he became an important director), the book affirmed the key creative role of the director, a view that would soon be articulated in France and 10 years later in North America. It is a widely held view today. The book, which was updated in 1968 by Gavin Millar (now also a director), remains as widely read today as it was when first published.

It was my goal to write a book that is, in spirit, related to the Reisz-Millar classic but is up-to-date with regard to films and film ideas. I also refer to the technical achievements in film, video, and sound that have expanded the character of modern films and film ideas. This update illustrates how the creative repertoire for filmmakers has broadened in the past 50 years.

□ POINT OF VIEW

A book on film and video editing can be written from a number of points of view. The most literal point of view is, of course, that of the film editor, but even this option isn't as straightforward as it appears. *When the Shooting Stops-.-.-.-*, by Ralph Rosenblum and Robert Karen, is perhaps the most comprehensive approach to the topic by a film editor. The book is part autobiography, part editing history, and part aesthetic statement. Other editing books by film editors are strictly technical; they discuss cutting room procedure, the language of the cutting room, or the mechanics of off-line editing. With the growth of high-technology editing options, the variety of technical editing books will certainly grow.

This book is intended to be practical in the sense that editing an action sequence requires an appreciation of which filmic elements are necessary to make that sequence effective. Also needed is a knowledge of the evolution of editing so that the editor can make the most effective choices under the circumstances. This is the goal of the book: to be practical, to be concerned about aesthetic choices, but not to be overly absorbed with the mechanics of film editing. In this sense, the book is written from the same perspective as Reisz's book—that of the film director. It is my hope, however, that the book will be useful to more than just directors. I have enormous admiration for editors; indeed, I agree with Ralph Rosenblum, who suggests that if editors had a different temperament and more confidence, they would be directors. I also agree with his implication that editing is one of the best possible types of training for future directors.

One final point: By adopting the director's point of view, I imply, as Reisz did, that editing is central in the creative evolution of film. This perspective allows me to examine the history of the theory and practice of film editing.

□ TERMS

In books about editing, many terms take on a variety of meanings. *Technique, art*, and *craft* are the most obvious. I use these terms in the following sense.

Technique, or the technical aspect of editing, is the physical joining of two disparate pieces of film. When joined, those two pieces of film become a sequence that has a particular meaning.

The craft of film editing is the joining of two pieces of film together to yield a meaning that is not apparent from one or the other shot. The meaning that arises from the two shots might be a continuity of a walk (exit right for shot one and enter left for shot two), or the meaning might be an explanation or an exclamation. The viewer's interpretation is clarified by the editor practicing her craft.

What about the art? I am indebted to Karel Reisz for his simple but elegant explanation. The art of editing occurs when the combination of two or more shots takes meaning to the next level—excitement, insight, shock, or the epiphany of discovery.

Technique, craft, and *art* are equally useful and appropriate terms whether they are applied to visual material on film or videotape, or are used to describe a visual or a sound edit or sequence. These terms are used by different writers to characterize editing. I have tried to be precise and to concentrate on the artistic evolution of editing. In the chapters on types of sequences—action, dialogue, comedy, documentary—I am as concerned with the craft as with the art. Further, although the book concentrates on visual editing, the art of sound editing is highlighted as much as possible.

Because film was for its first 30 years primarily a silent medium, the editing innovations of D. W. Griffith, Sergei Eisenstein, and V. I. Pudovkin were visual. When sound was added, it was a technical novelty rather than a creative addition. Not until the work of Basil Wright, Alberto Cavalcanti, Rouben Mamoulian, and Orson Welles did sound editing suggest its creative possibilities. However, the medium continued to be identified with its visual character—films were, after all, called motion pictures. In reality, though, each dimension and each technology added its own artistic contribution to the medium. That attitude and its implications are a basic assumption of this book.

□ THE ROLE OF EXPERIMENTAL AND DOCUMENTARY FILMS

Although the early innovations in film occurred in mainstream commercial movies, many innovations also took place in experimental and documentary films. The early work of Luis Buñuel, the middle period of Humphrey Jennings, the cinema verité work of Unit B of the National Film Board of Canada, and the free associations of Clement Perron and Arthur Lipsett (also at the National Film Board), contributed immeasurably to the art of editing.

These innovations in editing visuals and sound took place more freely in experimental and documentary filmmaking than in the commercial cinema. Experimental film, for example, was not produced under the scrutiny of commercial consideration. Documentary film, as long as it loosely fulfilled a didactic agenda, continued to be funded by governments and corporations. Because profit played a less central role for the experimental and documentary films, creative innovation was the result. Those innovations were quickly recognized and absorbed by mainstream filmmaking. The experimental film and the documentary have played an important role in the story of the evolution of editing as an art, and consequently, they have an important place in this book.

□ THE ROLE OF TECHNOLOGY

Film has always been the most technology-intensive of the popular arts. Recording an image and playing it back requires cameras, lights, projectors, and chemicals to develop the film. Sound recording has always relied on technology. So, too, has editing. Editors needed tape, a splicer, and eventually a motorized process to view what they had spliced together. Moviolas, Steenbecks, and sophisticated sound consoles have replaced the more basic equipment, and editroids, when they become more cost-effective, may replace Steenbecks. The list of technological changes is long and, with the high technology of television and video, it is growing rapidly. Today, motion pictures are often recorded on film but edited on video. This gives the editor more sophisticated choices.

Whether technological choice makes for a better film or television show is easily answered. The career of Stanley Kubrick, from *Paths of Glory* (1957) to *Full Metal Jacket* (1987), is telling. Kubrick always took advantage of the existing technology, but beginning with *2001: A Space Odyssey* (1968), he began to challenge convention and to make technology a central subject of each of his films. He proved that technology and creativity were not mutually exclusive. Technology in and of itself need not be used creatively, but, in the right hands, it can be. Technology plays a critical role in shaping film, but it is only a tool in the human hands of the artists who ply their ideas in this medium.

□ THE ROLE OF THE EDITOR

It is an overstatement for any one person involved in filmmaking to claim that his or her role is the exclusive source of creativity in the filmmaking process. Filmmaking requires collaboration; it requires the skills of an army of people. When filmmaking works best, each contribution adds to the totality of our experience of the film. The corollary, of course, is that any deficit in performance can be ruinous to the film. To put the roles into perspective, it's easiest to think of each role as creative and of particular roles as more decisive, for example, the producer, the writer, the director, the cinematographer, the actors, and the editor. Sound people, gaffers, art designers, costumers, and special effects people all contribute, but the front-line roles are so pervasive in their influence that they are the key roles.

The editor comes into the process once production has begun, making a rough assembly of shots while the film is in production. In this way, adjustments or additional shots can be undertaken during the production phase. If a needed shot must be pursued once the crew has been dispersed and the set has been dismantled, the cost will be much greater.

The editor's primary role, however, takes place in the post-production phase. Once production has been completed, sound and music are added during this phase, as are special effects. Aside from shortening the film, the editor must find a rhythm for the film; working closely with the director and sometimes the producer, the editor presents options, points out areas of confusion, and identifies redundant scenes. The winnowing process is an intuitive search for clarity and dynamism. The film must speak to as wide an audience as possible. Sound, sound effects, and music are all added at this stage.

The degree of freedom that the editor has depends on the relationship with the director and the producer. Particular directors are very interested in editing; others are more concerned with performance and leave more to the editor. The power relationship between editor and director or editor and producer is never the same; it always depends on the interests and strengths of each. In general terms, however, editors defer to directors and producers.

The goals of the editor are particular: to find a narrative continuity for the visuals and the sound of the film, and to distill those visuals and sound shots that will create the dramatic emphasis so that the film will be effective. By choosing particular juxtapositions, editors also layer that narrative with metaphor and subtext. They can even alter the original meaning by changing the juxtapositions of the shots.

An editor is successful when the audience enjoys the story and forgets about the juxtaposition of the shots. If the audience is aware of the editing, the editor has failed. This characterization should also describe the director's criteria for success, but ironically, it does not. Particular styles or genres are associated with particular directors. The audience knows an Alfred Hitchcock film or a Steven Spielberg film or an Ernst Lubitsch film. The result is that the audience expects a sense of the director's public persona in the film. When these directors make a film in which the audience is not aware of the directing, they fail that audience. Individual directors can have a public persona not available to editors.

Having presented the limits of the editor's role in a production, I would be remiss if I didn't acknowledge the power of editors in a production and as a profession. The editor shares much with the director in this respect.

Film and television are the most powerful and influential media of the century. Both have been used for good and for less-than-good intentions. As a result, the editor is a very powerful person because of her potential influence. Editing choices range from the straightforward presentation of material to the alteration of the meaning of that material. Editors also have the opportunity to present the material in as emotional a manner as possible. Emotion itself shapes meaning even more.

The danger, then, is to abuse that power. A set of ethical standards or personal morality is the rudder for all who work in film and television. The rudder isn't always operable. Editors do not have public personae that force them to exercise a personal code of ethics in their work. Consequently, a personal code of ethics becomes even more important. Because ethics has played a role in the evolution of the art of editing and in the theoretical debate about what is art in film, the issue is raised in this book.

☐ ORGANIZATION OF THIS BOOK

This book is organized along similar lines to the Reisz-Millar book. However, the first section, the history section, is more detailed not only because the post-1968 period had to be added, but also because the earlier period can now be dealt with in a more comprehensive way. Research on the early cinema and on the Russian cinema and translations of related documents allowed a more detailed treatment than was available to Karel Reisz in 1952. Many scholars have also entered the theoretical debate on editing as the source of film art. Their debate has enlivened the arguments, pro and con, and they too contribute to the new context for the historical section of this book.

The second part of the book, on the principles of editing, uses a comparative approach. It examines how particular types of scenes are cut today relative to how they were cut 60 years ago. Finally, the section on the practice of editing details specific types of editing options in picture and sound.

☐ A WORD ABOUT VIDEO

Much that has evolved in editing is applicable to both film and video. A cut from long shot to close-up has a similar impact in both media. What differs is the technology employed to make the physical cut. Steenbecks and tape-splicers are different from the off-line video players and monitors deployed in an electronic edit. Because the aesthetic choices and impacts are similar, I assume that those choices transcend differing technologies. What can be said in this context about film can also be said about video. With the proviso that the technologies differ, I assume that what can be said about the craft and art of film editing can also be said about video editing.

☐ A WORD ABOUT FILM EXAMPLES

When Reisz's book was published, it was difficult to view the films he used as examples. Consequently, a considerable number of shot sequences from the films he discussed were included in the book.

The most significant technological change affecting this book is the advent of the VCR and the growing availability of films on videotape, videodisc, and now on digital versatile disc (DVD). Because the number of films available on video is great, I have tried to select examples from these films. The reader may want to refer to the stills reproduced in this book but can also view the sequence being described. Indeed, the opportunity for detailed study of sequences on video makes the learning opportunities greater than ever. The availability of video material has influenced both my film choices and the degree of detail used in various chapters.

Readers should not ignore the growing use of videodiscs and DVDs. This technology is now accessible for most homes, and more and more educational institutions are realizing the benefit of this technology. Most videodisc and DVD players come with a remote that can allow you to slow-forward a film so that you can view sequences in a more detailed manner. The classics of international cinema and a growing number of more recent films on videodisc can give the viewer a clearer picture and better sound than ever before technologically possible.

This book was written for individuals who want to understand film and television and who want to make film and television programs. It will provide you with a context for your work. Whether you are a student or a professional, this book will help you move forward in a more informed way toward your goal. If this book is meaningful to even a percentage of the readers of the Reisz-Millar book, it will have achieved its goal.

I

HISTORY OF
FILM EDITING

■

■

■

■

1

The Silent Period

■

Film dates from 1895. When the first motion pictures were created, editing did not exist. The novelty of seeing a moving image was such that not even a screen story was necessary. The earliest films were less than a minute in length. They could be as simple as *La Sortie de l'Usine Lumière* (*Workers Leaving the Lumière Factory*) (1895) or *Arrivée d'un Train en Gare* (*Arrival of a Train at the Station*) (1895). One of the more popular films in New York was *The Kiss* (1896). Its success encouraged more films in a similar vein: *A Boxing Bout* (1896) and *Skirt Dance* (1896). Although George Méliès began producing more exotic "created" stories in France, such as *Cinderella* (1899) and *A Trip to the Moon* (1902), all of the early films shared certain characteristics. Editing was nonexistent or, at best, minimal in the case of Méliès.

What is remarkable about this period is that in 30 short years, the principles of classical editing were developed. In the early years, however, continuity, screen direction, and dramatic emphasis through editing were not even goals. Cameras were placed without thought to compositional or emotional considerations. Lighting was notional (no dramatic intention meant), even for interior scenes. William Dickson used a Black Maria.[1] Light, camera placement, and camera movement were not variables in the filmic equation. In the earliest Auguste and Louis Lumière and Thomas Edison films, the camera recorded an event, an act, or an incident. Many of these early films were a single shot.

Although Méliès's films grew to a length of 14 minutes, they remained a series of single shots: tableaus that recorded a performed scene. All of the shots were strung together. The camera was stationary and distant from the action. The physical lengths of the shots were not varied for impact. Performance, not pace, was the prevailing intention. The films were edited to the extent that they consisted of more than one shot, but *A Trip to the Moon* is no more than a series of amusing shots, each a scene unto itself. The shots tell a story, but not in the manner to which we are accustomed. It was not until the work of Edwin S. Porter that editing became more purposeful.

□ EDWIN S. PORTER: FILM CONTINUITY BEGINS

The pivotal year in Porter's work was 1903. In that year, he began to use a visual continuity that made his films more dynamic. Méliès had used theatrical devices and a playful sense of the fantastic to make his films seem more dynamic. Porter, impressed by the length and quality of Méliès's work, discovered that the organization of shots in his films could make his screen stories seem more dynamic. He also discovered that the shot was the basic building block of the film. As Karel Reisz suggests, "Porter had demonstrated that the single shot, recording an incomplete piece of action, is the unit of which films must be constructed and thereby established the basic principle of editing."[2]

Porter's *The Life of an American Fireman* (1903) is made up of 20 shots. The story is simple. Firemen rescue a mother and child from a burning building. Using newsreel footage of a real fire, together with performed interiors, Porter presents the 6-minute story as a view of the victims and their rescuers. In 6 minutes, he shows how the mother and child are saved.

Although there is some contention about the original film,[3] a version that circulated for 40 years presents the rescue in the following way. The mother and daughter are trapped inside the burning building. Outside, the firemen race to the rescue. In the version that circulated from 1944 to 1985, the interior scenes were intercut with the newsreel exteriors. This shot-by-shot alternating of interior and exterior made the story of the rescue seem dynamic. The heightened tension from the intercutting was complemented by the inclusion of a close-up of a hand pulling the lever of a fire alarm box.

The inclusion of the newsreel footage lent a sense of authenticity to the film. It also suggested that two shots filmed in different locations, with vastly different original objectives, could, when joined together, mean something greater than the sum of the two parts. The juxtaposition could create a new reality greater than that of each individual shot.

Porter did not pay attention to the physical length of the shots, and all of the shots, excluding that of the hand, are long shots. The camera was placed to record the shot rather than to editorialize on the narrative of the shot.

Porter presented an even more sophisticated narrative in late 1903 with *The Great Train Robbery*. The film, 12 minutes in length, tells the story of a train robbery and the consequent fate of the robbers. In 14 shots, the film includes interiors of the robbery and exteriors of the attempted getaway and chase. The film ends very dramatically with an outlaw in subjective midshot firing his gun directly toward the audience.

There is no match-cutting between shots, but there are location changes and time changes. How were those time and location changes managed, given that the film relies on straight cuts rather than dissolves and fades, which were developed later?

Every shot presents a scene: the robbery, the getaway, the pursuit, the capture. No single shot in itself records an action from beginning to end. The audience enters or exits a shot midway. Here lies the explanation for the time and location changes. For narrative purposes, it is not necessary to see the shot in its entirety to understand the purpose of the shot. Entering a shot in midstream suggests that time has passed. Exiting the shot before the action is complete and viewing an entirely new shot suggest a change in location. Time and place shifts thus occur, and the narrative remains clear. The overall meaning of the story comes from the collectivity of the shots, with the shifts in time or place implied by the juxtaposition of two shots.

Although *The Great Train Robbery* is not paced for dramatic impact, a dynamic narrative is clearly presented. Porter's contribution to editing was the arrangement of shots to present a narrative continuity.[4]

□ D. W. GRIFFITH: DRAMATIC CONSTRUCTION

D. W. Griffith is the acknowledged father of film editing in its modern sense. His influence on the Hollywood mainstream film and on the Russian revolutionary film was immediate. His contributions cover the full range of dramatic construction: the variation of shots for impact, including the extreme long shot, the close-up, the cutaway, and the tracking shot; parallel editing; and variations in pace. All of these are ascribed to Griffith. Porter might have clarified film narrative in his work, but Griffith learned how to make the juxtaposition of shots have a far greater dramatic impact than his predecessor.

Beginning in 1908, Griffith directed hundreds of one- and two-reelers (10- to 20-minute films). For a man who was an unemployed playwright and performer, Griffith was slow to admit more than a temporary association with the new medium. Once he saw its potential, however, he shed his embarrassment, began to use his own name (initially, he directed as "Lawrence Griffith"), and zealously engaged in film production with a sense of experimentation that was more a reflection of his self-confidence than of the potential he saw in the medium. In the melodramatic plot (the rescue of children or women from evil perpetrators), Griffith found a narrative with strong visual potential on which to experiment. Although at best naive in his choice of subject matter,[5] Griffith was a man of his time, a nineteenth-century Southern gentleman with romanticized attitudes about societies and their peoples. To appreciate Griffith's contribution to film, one must set aside content considerations and look to those visual innovations that have made his contribution a lasting one.

Beginning with his attempt to move the camera closer to the action in 1908, Griffith continually experimented with the fragmentation of scenes. In *The Greaser's Gauntlet* (1908), he cut from a long shot of a hanging tree (a woman has just saved a man from being lynched) to a full body shot of the man thanking the woman. Through the match-cutting of the two shots, the audience enters the scene at an instant of heightened emotion. Not only do we feel what he must feel, but the whole tenor of the scene is more dynamic because of the cut, and the audience is closer to the action taking place on the screen.

Griffith continued his experiments to enhance his audience's emotional involvement with his films. In *Enoch Arden* (1908), Griffith moved the camera even closer to the action. A wife awaits the return of her husband. The film cuts to a close-up of her face as she broods about his return. The apocryphal stories about Biograph executives panicking that audiences would interpret the close-up as decapitation have displaced the historical importance of this shot. Griffith demonstrated that a scene could be fragmented into long shots, medium shots, and close shots to allow the audience to move gradually into the emotional heart of the scene. This dramatic orchestration has become the standard editing procedure for scenes. In 1908, the effect was shocking and effective. As with all of Griffith's innovations, the close-up was immediately adopted for use by other filmmakers, thus indicating its acceptance by other creators and by audiences.

In the same film, Griffith cut away from a shot of the wife to a shot of her husband far away. Her thoughts then become visually manifest, and Griffith proceeds to a series of intercut shots of wife and husband. The cutaway introduces a new dramatic element into the scene: the husband. This early example of parallel action also suggests Griffith's experimentation with the ordering of shots for dramatic purposes.

In 1909, Griffith carried this idea of parallel action further in *The Lonely Villa*, a rescue story. Griffith intercuts between a helpless family and the burglars who have invaded their home and the husband who is hurrying home to rescue his family. In this film, Griffith constructed the scenes using shorter and shorter shots to heighten the dramatic impact. The resulting suspense is powerful, and the rescue is cathartic in a dramatically effective way. Intercutting in this way also solved the problem of time. Complete actions needn't be shown to achieve realism. Because of the intercutting, scenes could be fragmented, and only those parts of scenes that were most effective needed to be shown. Dramatic time thus began to replace real time as a criteria for editing decisions.

Other innovations followed. In *Ramona* (1911), Griffith used an extreme long shot to highlight the epic quality of the land and to show how it provided a heightened dimension to the struggle of the movie's inhabitants. In *The Lonedale Operator* (1911), he mounted the camera on a moving train. The consequent excitement of these images intercut with images of the captive awaiting rescue by the railroad men again raised the dramatic intensity of the sequence. Finally, Griffith began to experiment with film length. Although famous for his one-reelers, he was increasingly looking for more elaborate narratives. Beginning in late 1911, he began to experiment with two-reelers (20 to 32 minutes), remaking *Enoch Arden* in that format. After producing three two-reelers in 1912—and spurred on by foreign epics such as the 53-minute *La Reine Elizabeth* (*Queen Elizabeth*) (1912) from France and *Quo Vadis* (1913) from Italy—Griffith set out to produce his long film *Judith of Bethulia* (1913). With its complex Biblical story and its mix of epic baffles and personal drama, Griffith achieved a level of editing sophistication never before seen on screen.

Griffith's greatest contributions followed. *The Birth of a Nation* (1915) and *Intolerance* (1916) are both epic productions; each screen story lasts more than two hours. Not only was Griffith moving rapidly beyond his two-reelers, he was now making films more than twice the length of *Judith of Bethulia*. The achievements of these two films are well documented, but it is worth reiterating some of the qualities that make the films memorable in the history of editing.

Not only was *The Birth of a Nation* an epic story of the Civil War, but it also attempted in two and one-half hours to tell in melodramatic form the stories of two families: one from the South, and the other from the North. Their fate is the fate of the nation. Historical events such as the assassination of Lincoln are intertwined with the personal stories, culminating in the infamous ride of the Klan to rescue the young Southern woman from the freed slaves. Originally conceived of as a 12-reel film with 1544 separate shots, *The Birth of a Nation* was a monumental undertaking. In terms of both narrative and emotional quality, the film is astonishing in its complexity and range. Only its racism dates the film.

The Birth of a Nation displays all of the editing devices Griffith had developed in his short films. Much has been written about his set sequences, particularly about the assassination of Lincoln[6] and the ride of the Klan. Also notable are the battle scenes and the personal scenes. The Cameron and Stoneman family scenes early in the film are warm and personal in contrast to the formal epic quality of the battle scenes. These disparate elements relate to one another in a narrative sense as a result of Griffith's editing. In the personal scenes, for example, the film cuts away to two cats fighting. One is dark, and the other is light gray. Their fight foreshadows the larger battles that loom between the Yankees (the Blues) and the Confederates (the Grays). The shot is simple, but it is this type of detail that relates one sequence to another.

In *Intolerance*, Griffith posed for himself an even greater narrative challenge. In the film, four stories of intolerance are interwoven to present a historical perspective. Belshazzar's Babylon, Christ's Jerusalem, Huguenot France, and modern America are the settings for the four tales. Transition between the time periods is provided by a woman, Lillian Gish, who rocks a cradle. The transition implies the passage of time and its constancy. The cradle implies birth and the growth of a person. Cutting back to the cradle reminds us that all four stories are part of the generational history of our species. Time and character transactions abound. Each story has its own dramatic structure leading to the moment of crisis when human behavior will be tested, challenged, and questioned. All of Griffith's tools—the close-ups, the extreme long shots, the moving camera—are used together with pacing. The film is remarkably ambitious and, for the most part, effective.

More complex, more conceptual, and more speculative than his former work, *Intolerance* was not as successful with audiences. However, it provides a mature insight into the strengths and limitations of editing. The effectiveness of all four stories is undermined in the juxtaposition. The Babylonian story and the modern American story are more fully developed than the others and seem to overwhelm them, particularly the St. Bartholomew's Day Massacre in Huguenot France. At times the audience is confused by so many stories and so many characters serving a metaphorical theme. The film, nevertheless, remains Griffith's greatest achievement in the eyes of many film historians. Because *The Birth of a Nation* and *Intolerance* are so often the subject of analysis in film literature, rather than refer to the excellent work of others, the balance of this section focuses on another of Griffith's works, *Broken Blossoms* (1919).

Broken Blossoms is a simple love story set in London. A gentle Chinese man falls in love with a young Caucasian woman. The woman, portrayed by Lillian Gish, is victimized by her brutal father (Donald Crisp), who is aptly named Battler. When he learns that his daughter is seeing an Oriental (Richard Barthelness), his anger explodes, and he kills her. The suitor shoots Battler and then commits suicide. This tragedy of idealized love and familial brutality captures Griffith's bittersweet view of modern life. There is no place for gentleness and purity of spirit, mind, and body in an aggressive, cruel world.

The two cultures—China and Great Britain—meet on the London waterfront and in the opium dens (Figures 1.1 and 1.2). On the waterfront the suitor has set up his shop, and here he brings the young woman (Figures 1.3 and 1.4). Meanwhile, Battler fights in the ring (Figure 1.5). Griffith intercuts the idyllic scene of the suitor attending to the young woman (Figure 1.6) with Battler beating his opponent. The parallel action juxtaposes Griffith's view of two cultures: gentleness and brutality. When Battler finishes off his opponent, he rushes to the suitor's shop. He is led there by a spy who has informed him about the whereabouts of the young woman. Battler destroys the bedroom, dragging the daughter away. The suitor is not present.

At home, Battler menaces his daughter, who hides in a closet. Battler takes an ax to the door. Here, Griffith intercut between three locations: the closet (where the fearful, trapped young woman is hiding), the living room (where the belligerent Battler is attacking his daughter), and the suitor's bedroom (where he has found the room destroyed). The suitor grabs a gun and leaves to try to rescue the young woman. Finally, Battler breaks through the door. The woman's fear is unbearable. Griffith cuts to two subjective close-ups: one of the young woman, and one of Battler (Figures 1.7 and 1.8). Battler pulls his daughter through the shattered door (Figure 1.9). The scene is terrifying in its intensity and in its inevitability. Battler beats his daughter to death. When the suitor arrives, he finds the young woman dead and confronts Battler (Figure 1.10), killing him. The story now rapidly reaches

Figure 1.1   *Broken Blossoms*, 1919. Still provided by British Film Institute.

Figure 1.2   *Broken Blossoms*, 1919. Still provided by Moving Image and Sound Archives.

Figure 1.3 *Broken Blossoms*, 1919. Still provided by British Film Institute.

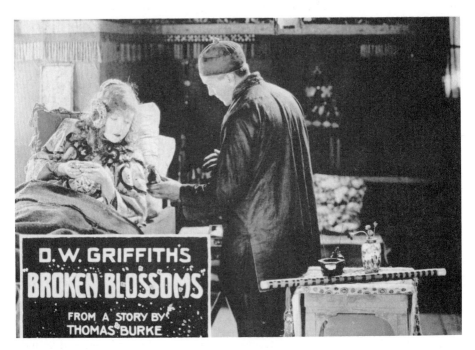

Figure 1.4 *Broken Blossoms*, 1919. Still provided by British Film Institute.

Figure 1.5   *Broken Blossoms*, 1919. Still provided by British Film Institute.

Figure 1.6   *Broken Blossoms*, 1919. Still provided by Moving Image and Sound Archives.

Figure 1.7 *Broken Blossoms,*
1919. Still provided by
British Film Institute.

Figure 1.8 *Broken Blossoms,* 1919. Still
provided by British Film
Institute.

Figure 1.9 *Broken Blossoms,* 1919. Still provided by British Film Institute.

Figure 1.10   *Broken Blossoms*, 1919. Still provided by British Film Institute.

its denouement: the suicide of the suitor. He drapes the body of the young woman in silk and then peacefully accepts death.

Horror and beauty in *Broken Blossoms* are transmitted carefully to articulate every emotion. All of Griffith's editing skills came into play. He used close-ups, cutaways, and subjective camera placement to articulate specific emotions and to move us through a personal story with a depth of feeling rare in film. This was Griffith's gift, and through his work, editing and dramatic film construction became one.

□ INTERNATIONAL PERSPECTIVES

There is little question that D. W. Griffith was the first great international filmmaker and that the drop in European production during World War I helped American production assume a far greater international position than it might have otherwise. It should not be surprising, then, that in 1918 Griffith and his editing innovations were the prime influence on filmmakers around the world. In the Soviet Union, Griffith's *Intolerance* was the subject of intense study for its technical achievements as well as for its ideas about society. In the ten years that followed its release, Sergei Eisenstein wrote about Griffith,[7] V.I. Pudovkin studied Griffith and tried to perfect the theory and practice of communicating ideas through film narrative, and Dziga Vertov reacted against the type of cinema Griffith exemplified.

In France and Germany, filmmakers seemed to be as influenced by the other arts as they were by the work of other filmmakers. The influence of Max Reinhardt's theatrical experiments in staging and expressionist painting are evidenced in Robert Wiene's *The Cabinet of Dr. Caligari* (1919) (Figure 1.11). Sigmund Freud's ideas about psychoanalysis join together with Griffith's ideas about the power of camera movement in F. W. Murnau's *The Last Laugh* (1924). Griffith's ideas about camera placement, moving the camera closer to the action, are supplemented by ideas of distortion and subjectivity in E. A. Dupont's *Variety* (1925). In France, Carl Dreyer worked almost exclusively with Griffith's ideas about close-ups in *The Passion of Joan of Arc* (1928), and he produced one of the most intense films ever made.

Griffith accomplished a great deal. However, it was others in this silent period who refined and built upon his ideas about film editing.

□ VSEVOLOD I. PUDOVKIN: CONSTRUCTIVE EDITING AND HEIGHTENED REALISM

Although all of the Soviet filmmakers were deeply influenced by Griffith, they were also concerned about the role of their films in the revolutionary struggle. Lenin himself had endorsed the importance of film in supporting the revolution. The young Soviet filmmakers were zealots for that revolution. Idealistic, energetic, and committed, they struggled for filmic solutions to political problems.

Perhaps none of the Soviet filmmakers was as critical of Griffith as V.I. Pudovkin.[8] As Reisz suggests, "Where Griffith was content to tell his stories by means of the kind of editing construction we have already seen in the excerpt from *The Birth of a Nation*, the young Russian directors felt that they could take the film director's control over his material a stage further. They planned, by means of new editing methods, not only to tell stories but to interpret and draw intellectual conclusions from them."[9]

Pudovkin attempted to develop a theory of editing that would allow filmmakers to proceed beyond the intuitive classical editing of Griffith to a more formalized process that could yield greater success in translating ideas into narratives. That theory was based on Griffith's perception that the fragmentation of a scene into shots could create a power far beyond the character of a scene filmed without this type of construction. Pudovkin took this idea one step further. As he states in his book,

> The film director [as compared to the theater director], on the other hand, has as his material, the finished, recorded celluloid. This material from which his final work is composed consists not of living men or real landscapes, not of real, actual stage-sets, but only of their images, recorded on separate strips that can be short-

Figure 1.11 *Dos Cabinet des Dr. Caligari*, 1919. Still provided by Moving Image and Sound Archives.

ened, altered, and assembled according to his will. The elements of reality are fixed on these pieces; by combining them in his selected sequence, shortening and lengthening them according to his desire, the director builds up his own "filmic" time and "filmic" space. He does not adapt reality, but uses it for the creation of a new reality, and the most characteristic and important aspect of this process is that, in it, laws of space and time invariable and inescapable in work with actuality become tractable and obedient. The film assembles from them a new reality proper only to itself.[10]

Pudovkin thereby takes the position that the shot is the building block of film and that is the raw material whose ordering can generate any desired result. Just as the poet uses words to create a new perception of reality, the film director uses shots as his raw material.[11]

Pudovkin experimented considerably with this premise. His early work with Lev Kuleshov suggested that the same shot juxtaposed with different following shots could yield widely different results with an audience. In their famous experiment with the actor Ivan Mosjukhin, they used the same shot of the actor juxtaposed with three different follow-up shots: a plate of soup standing on a table, a shot of a coffin containing a dead woman, and a little girl playing with a toy. Audience responses to the three sequences suggested a hungry person, a sad husband, and a joyful adult, and yet the first shot was always the same.

Encouraged by this type of experiment, Pudovkin went further. In his film version of *Mother* (1926), he wanted to suggest the joy of a prisoner about to be set free. These are Pudovkin's comments about the construction of the scene:

> I tried to affect the spectators, not by the psychological performances of an actor, but by the plastic synthesis through editing. The son sits in prison. Suddenly, passed in to him surreptitiously, he receives a note that the next day he is to be set free. The problem was the expression, filmically, of his joy. The photographing of a face lighting up with joy would have been flat and void of effect. I show, therefore, the nervous play of his hands and a big close-up of the lower half of his face, the corners of the smile. These shots I cut in with other and varied material—shots of a brook, swollen with the rapid flow of spring, of the play of sunlight broken on the water, birds splashing in the village pond, and finally a laughing child. By the junction of these components our expression of "prisoner's joy" takes shape.[12]

In this story of a mother who is politicized by the persecution of her son for his political beliefs, a personal approach is intermingled with a political story. In this sense, Pudovkin was similar in his narrative strategy to Griffith, but in purpose he was more political than Griffith. He also experimented freely with scene construction to convey his political ideas. When workers strike, their fate is clear (Figure 1.12); when fathers and sons take differing sides in a political battle, the family (in this case, the mother) will suffer (Figure 1.13); and family tragedy is the sacrifice necessary if political change is to occur (Figure 1.14).

Pudovkin first involves us in the personal story and the narrative, and then he communicates the political message. Although criticized for adopting bourgeois narrative techniques, Pudovkin carried those techniques further than Griffith, but not as far as his contemporary, Sergei Eisenstein.

□ SERGEI EISENSTEIN: THE THEORY OF MONTAGE

Eisenstein was the second of the key Russian filmmakers. As a director, he was perhaps the greatest. He also wrote extensively about film ideas and eventually taught a generation of Russian directors. In the early 1920s, however, he was a young, committed filmmaker.

Figure 1.12 *Mother*, 1926. Still provided by Museum of Modern Art/Film Stills Archives.

Figure 1.13 *Mother*, 1926. Still provided by Museum of Modern Art/Film Stills Archives.

Figure 1.14   *Mother*, 1926. Still provided by Museum of Modern Art/Film Stills
Archives.

With a background in theatre and design, Eisenstein attempted to translate the lessons of Griffith and the lessons of Karl Marx into a singular
audience experience. Beginning with *Strike* (1924), Eisenstein attempted to
theorize about film editing as a clash of images and ideas. The principle
of the dialectic was particularly suitable for subjects related to prerevolu-
tionary and revolutionary issues and events. Strikes, the 1905 revolution,
and the 1917 revolution were Eisenstein's earliest subjects.

Eisenstein achieved so much in the field of editing that it would be most
useful to present his theory first and then look at how he put theory into
practice. His theory of editing has five components: metric montage, rhythmic montage, tonal montage, overtonal montage, and intellectual montage.
The clearest exposition of his theory has been presented by Andrew Tudor
in his book *Theories on Film*.[13]

METRIC MONTAGE

Metric montage refers to the length of the shots relative to one another. Regardless of their content, shortening the shots abbreviates the time the audience
has to absorb the information in each shot. This increases the tension resulting from the scene. The use of close-ups with shorter shots creates a more
intense sequence (Figures 1.15 and 1.16).

Figure 1.15   *Potemkin*, 1925. Courtesy Janus Films. Still provided by British Film Institute.

Figure 1.16   *Potemkin*, 1925. Courtesy Janus Films. Still provided by British Film Institute.

RHYTHMIC MONTAGE

Rhythmic montage refers to continuity arising from the visual pattern within the shots. Continuity based on matching action and screen direction are examples of rhythmic montage. This type of montage has considerable potential for portraying conflict because opposing forces can be presented in terms of opposing screen directions as well as parts of the frame. For example, in the Odessa Steps sequence of *Potemkin* (1925), soldiers march down the steps from one quadrant of the frame, followed by people attempting to escape from the opposite side of the frame (Figures 1.17 to 1.21).

TONAL MONTAGE

Tonal montage refers to editing decisions made to establish the emotional character of a scene, which may change in the course of the scene. Tone or mood is used as a guideline for interpreting tonal montage, and although the theory begins to sound intellectual, it is no different from Ingmar Bergman's suggestion that editing is akin to music, the playing of the emotions of the different scenes.[14] Emotions change, and so too can the tone of the scene. In the Odessa Steps sequence, the death of the young mother on the steps and the following baby carriage sequence highlight the depth of the tragedy of the massacre (Figures 1.22 to 1.27).

OVERTONAL MONTAGE

Overtonal montage is the interplay of metric, rhythmic, and tonal montages. That interplay mixes pace, ideas, and emotions to induce the desired effect from the audience. In the Odessa Steps sequence, the outcome of the massacre should be the outrage of the audience. Shots that emphasize the abuse of the army's overwhelming power and the exploitation of the citizens' powerlessness punctuate the message (Figure 1.28).

INTELLECTUAL MONTAGE

Intellectual montage refers to the introduction of ideas into a highly charged and emotionalized sequence. An example of intellectual montage is the sequence in *October* (1928). George Kerensky, the Menshevik leader of the first Russian Revolution, climbs the steps just as quickly as he ascended to power after the Czar's fall. Intercut with his ascent are shots of a mechanical peacock preening itself. Eisenstein is making a point about Kerensky as politician. This is one of many examples in *October* (1928).

EISENSTEIN: THEORETICIAN AND AESTHETE

Eisenstein was a cerebral filmmaker, an intellectual with a great respect for ideas. Many of his later critics in the Soviet Union believed that he was too academic and his respect for ideas would supersede his respect for Soviet realism, that his politics were too aesthetic, and that his aesthetics were too individualistic.

Figure 1.17   *Potemkin*, 1925. Courtesy Janus Films Company. Still provided by British Film Institute.

Figure 1.18   *Potemkin*, 1925. Courtesy Janus Films Company. Still provided by British Film Institute.

Figure 1.19 *Potemkin*, 1925. Courtesy Janus Films Company. Still provided by British Film Institute.

Figure 1.20 *Potemkin*, 1925. Courtesy Janus Films Company. Still provided by British Film Institute.

Figure 1.21   *Potemkin*, 1925. Courtesy Janus Films Company. Still provided by British Film Institute.

Figure 1.22   *Potemkin*, 1925. Courtesy Janus Films Company. Still provided by Moving Image and Sound Archives.

Figure 1.23 *Potemkin*, 1925. Courtesy Janus Films. Stills provided by Moving Image and Sound Archives.

Figure 1.24 *Potemkin*, 1925. Courtesy Janus Films. Stills provided by Moving Image and Sound Archives.

Figure 1.25 *Potemkin*, 1925. Courtesy Janus Films. Stills provided by Moving Image and Sound Archives.

Figure 1.26 *Potemkin*, 1925. Courtesy Janus Films. Stills provided by Moving Image and Sound Archives.

Figure 1.27 *Potemkin*, 1925. Courtesy Janus Films. Still provided by British Film Institute.

Figure 1.28 *Potemkin*, 1925. Courtesy Janus Films. Still provided by Moving Image and Sound Archives.

It is difficult for modern viewers to see Eisenstein as anything but a committed Marxist. His films are almost as naive as those of Griffith in their simple devotion to their own view of life. In the 1920s, whether he was aware of it or not, Eisenstein discovered the visceral power of editing and of visual composition, and he was a master of both. He was dangerous in the same sense that every artist is dangerous: He was his own person, a unique individual. Today, Eisenstein is greatly appreciated as a theoretician, but, like Griffith, he was also a great director. That is the extent of his crime.

□ DZIGA VERTOV: THE EXPERIMENT OF REALISM

If Eisenstein illustrated an editing theory devoted to reshaping reality to incite the population to support the revolution, Dziga Vertov was as vehement that only the documented truth could be honest enough to bring about true revolution.

Vertov described his goals in the film *The Man with a Movie Camera* (1929) as follows: "*The Man with a Movie Camera* constitutes an experiment in the cinematic transmission of visual phenomena without the aid of intertitles (a film with no intertitles), script (a film with no script), theater (a film with neither actors nor sets). Kino-Eye's new experimental work aims to create a truly international film—language, absolute writing in film, and the complete separation of cinema from theater and literature."[15]

Pudovkin remained interested in bourgeois cinema, and Eisenstein was too much the intellectual. Neither was sufficiently radical for Vertov, whose devotion to the truth is exemplified by his documentary, *The Man with a Movie Camera*. Because the film was the story of one day in the life of a film cameraman, Vertov repeatedly reminds the viewer of the artificiality and nonrealism of cinema. Consequently, nonrealism, manipulation, and all of the technical elements of film become part of this self-reflexive (looking on the director's own intentions and using film to explore those intentions and make them overt) film. Special effects and fantasy were part of those technical elements (Figures 1.29 to 1.32).

Although on paper Vertov seems doctrinaire and dry, on film he is quite the opposite. He edits in a playful spirit that suggests filmmaking is pleasurable as well as manipulative. This sense of fun is freer than the work of Pudovkin or Eisenstein. In attitude, Vertov's work is more experimental and free form than the work of his contemporaries. This sense of freedom and free association becomes particularly important in the work of Alexander Dovzhenko in the Ukraine and Luis Buñuel in France.

In terms of editing, Vertov is more closely aligned with the history of the experimental film than with the history of the documentary. In terms of his ideas, however, he is a forerunner of the cinema verité movement in documentary film, a movement that awaited the technical achievements of World War II to facilitate its development.

□ ALEXANDER DOVZHENKO: EDITING BY VISUAL ASSOCIATION

In his concept of intellectual montage, Eisenstein was free to associate any two images to communicate an idea about a person, a class, or a historical event. This freedom was similar to Vertov's freedom to be playful about the clash of reality and illusion, as illustrated by the duality of the filmmaking process in *The Man with a Movie Camera*. Alexander Dovzhenko, a Ukranian filmmaker, viewed as his goal neither straight narrative nor documentary. His film *Earth* (1930) is best characterized as a visual poem. Although it has as its background the class struggle between the well-to-do peasants (in the era of private farms) and the poorer farmers, *Earth* is really about the continuity of life and death. The story is unclear because of its visual indirectness, and it leads us away from the literal meaning of the images to a quite different interpretation.

The opening is revealing. It begins with a series of still images—tranquil, beautiful compositions of rural life: a young woman and a wild flower, a farmer and his ox, an old man in an apple orchard, a young woman cutting wheat, a young man filled with the joy of life. All of these images are presented independently, and there is no apparent continuity (Figures 1.33 to 1.37). Gradually, however, this visual association forms a pattern of pastoral strength and tranquillity. The narrative finally begins to suggest a family in which the grandfather is preparing to die, but dying surrounded by apples is not quite naturalistic. The cutting is not direct about the narrative intention, which is to illustrate the death of the grandfather while suggesting this event is the natural order of things, that is, life goes on. The apples being present in the images surrounding him, takes away from the sense of loss and introduces a poetic notion about death. The poetic sense is life goes on in spite of death. The old man returns to the earth willingly, knowing that he is part of the earth and it is part of him.

The editing is dictated by visual association rather than by classical continuity. Just as the words of a poem don't form logical sentences, the visual pattern in *Earth* doesn't conform to a direct narrative logic. Initially, the absence of continuity is confusing, but the pattern gradually emerges, and a different editing pattern replaces the classical approach. It is effective in its own way, but Dovzhenko's work is quite different from the innovations of Griffith. It does, however, offer a vastly different option to filmmakers, an option taken up by Luis Buñuel.

□ LUIS BUÑUEL: VISUAL DISCONTINUITY

Surrealism, expressionism, and psychoanalysis were intellectual currents that affected all of the arts in the 1920s. In Germany, expressionism was the most influential, but among the artistic community in Paris, surrealism had

Figure 1.29   *The Man with a Movie Camera,* 1929. Still provided by British Film Institute.

Figure 1.30   *The Man with a Movie Camera,* 1929. Still provided by Moving Image and Sound Archives.

Figure 1.31   *The Man with a Movie Camera,* 1929. Still provided by Moving Image and Sound Archives.

Figure 1.32   *The Man with a Movie Camera*, 1929. Still provided by Moving Image and Sound Archives.

Figure 1.33   *Earth*, 1930. Still provided by Museum of Modern Art/Film Stills Archives.

Figure 1.34   *Earth*, 1930. Still provided by Museum of Modern Art/Film Stills Archives.

Figure 1.35   *Earth*, 1930. Still provided by Museum of Modern Art/Film Stills Archives.

Figure 1.36   *Earth*, 1930. Still provided by Museum of Modern Art/Film Stills Archives.

Figure 1.37   *Earth*, 1930. Still provided by Museum of Modern Art/Film Stills Archives.

an even greater influence. Salvador Dali and Luis Buñuel, Spanish artists, were particularly attracted to the possibility of making surrealist film. Like Vertov in the Soviet Union, Buñuel and Dali reacted first against classical film narrative, the type of storytelling and editing represented by Griffith. Like Eisenstein, Buñuel particularly viewed the use of dialectic editing and counterpoint, setting one image off in reaction to another, as a strong operating principle.

The filmic outcome was *Un Chien d'Andalou* (*An Andalusian Dog*) (1929). Buñuel particularly was interested in making a film that destroyed meaning, interspersed with the occasional shock. Suddenly, a woman's eye is being slashed, two donkeys are draped across two pianos, a hand exudes ants or caresses a shoulder (Figures 1.38 to 1.41).

The fact that the film has become as famous as it has is a result of what the film represents: a satirical set of shocks intended to speak to the audience's unconscious. Whether the images are dream-like and surreal or satiric remains open to debate. The importance of the film is that it represents the height of asynchronism; it is based on visual disassociation rather than on the classic rules of continuity. Consequently, the film broadens the filmmaker's options: to make sense, to move, to disturb, to rob of meaning, to undermine the security of knowing.

Figure 1.38 *Un Chien d'Andalou*, 1929. Still provided by Moving Image and Sound Archives.

Figure 1.39   *Un Chien d'Andalou*, 1929. Still provided by British Film Institute.

Figure 1.40   *Un Chien d'Andalou*, 1929. Still provided by British Film Institute.

Figure 1.41 *Un Chien d'Andalou*, 1929. Still provided by Moving Image and Sound Archives.

To frame Buñuel's contribution to film editing in another way, consider classic narrative storytelling as a linear progression. The plot begins with the character's achievement or final failure of achieving that goal. The plot follows the progress of the character in a linear fashion.

Buñuel, in undermining narrative expectations creates in essence a nonlinear plot. Character may be replaced by a new character or by a new goal for the old character. This nonlinearity can be frustrating for the viewer. But it also can open up the story to a new series of story options and consequent experiences for the audience.

In this sense, Buñuel creates at least philosophically a nonlinear experience for his audience. And he uses editing to do so.

Buñuel and Dali followed up *Un Chien d'Andalou* with a film that is a surreal narrative, *L'Age d'Or* (*The Golden Age*) (1930). In this film, a couple is overwhelmed by their passion for one another, but society, family, and Church stand against them and prevent them from being together. This is a film about great passion and great resistance to that passion. Again, the satiric, exaggerated imagery of surrealism interposes a nonrealistic commentary on the behavior of all. Passion, anger, and resistance can lead only to death. The film's images portray each state (Figures 1.42 to 1.46).

□ CONCLUSION

The silent period, 1885–1930, was an age of great creation and experimentation. It was the period when editing, unfettered by sound, came to maturity and provided a full range of options for the filmmaker. They included considerations of visual continuity, the deconstruction of scenes into shots, the development of parallel editing, the replacement of real time by a dramatic sense of time, poetic editing styles, the assertive editing theories of Eisenstein, and the asynchronous editing styles of Vertov and Buñuel. All of these became part of the editing repertoire.

One of the best examples of a filmmaker who combined the style of Griffith with the innovations of the Soviets was King Vidor. In his silent work, *The Big Parade* (1925) and *The Crowd* (1928), and later in his early sound work, *Billy the Kid* (1930) and *Our Daily Bread* (1934), he presented sequences that were narrative-driven, like Griffith's work, and idea- or concept-driven, like Eisenstein's. Both Griffith and Eisenstein were influential on the mainstream cinema, and their influence extended far beyond the silent period.

Figure 1.42   *L'Age d'Or*, 1936. Still provided by Moving Image and Sound Archives.

Figure 1.43 *L'Age d'Or*, 1936. Still provided by Moving Image and Sound Archives.

Figure 1.44 *L'Age d'Or*, 1936. Still provided by Moving Image and Sound Archives.

Figure 1.45 *L'Age d'Or*, 1936. Still provided by Moving Image and Sound Archives.

Figure 1.46 *L'Age d'Or*, 1936. Still provided by Moving Image and Sound Archives.

☐ NOTES/REFERENCES

1. The Black Maria was an irregularly shaped building with a movable roof that could be raised to allow natural light to enter. Inside, the building was draped in black to prevent light reflection. The only light source was the roof, which could be moved to accommodate the location of the sun.

2. Karel Reisz and Gavin Millar, *The Technique of Film Editing* (Boston: Focal Press, 1968), 19.

3. The history of the debate over which version is Porter's original is fully described by David A. Cook in *A History of Narrative Film* (New York: W. W. Norton, 1990).

4. Porter's contribution to crosscutting for pace remains open to debate.

5. The controversy about racism in his work stems from *The Birth of a Nation* (1915), but as a subject, it is notable from his first film, *The Adventures of Dolly* (1908). Griffith, a Southern gentleman, tended to be paternalistic and racist about slaves and slavery.

6. A full analysis of the 55-shot assassination sequence can be found in Cook, *Narrative Film*, 84–88.

7. See Sergei Eisenstein, "Dickens, Griffith and the Film Today," in *Film Form* (New York: Harcourt Brace Jovanovich, 1977), 195–255.

8. Pudovkin's ideas about editing are fully presented in his book, *Film Technique and Film Acting* (London: Vision Press, 1968).

9. Reisz and Millar, *Film Editing*, 27.

10. Pudovkin, *Film Technique*, 89–90.

11. Ibid., 24–25.

12. Ibid., 27.

13. Andrew Tudor, *Theories on Film* (London: Martin Secker and Andrew Warburg, 1974).

14. I. Bergman, "Introduction." *Four Screenplays of Ingmar Bergman* (New York: Simon & Shuster, 1960), xv–xviii, xxi–xxii. Reprinted in *Film, a Montage of Theories*, R. D. MacCann, ed. (E. P. Dutton & Co, New York, 1966), 142–146.

15. Annette Michaelson, ed., *Kino-Eye: The Writings of Dziga Vertov* (Berkeley: University of California Press, 1984), 283.

2

The Early Sound Film

■

A great many innovations in picture editing were compromised with the coming of sound. The early sound films have often been called *filmed plays* or *radio plays with pictures* as a result of the technological characteristics of early sound. In this period, however, there was an attempt to come to grips with the theoretical meaning of sound as well as an attempt to find creative solutions to overcome its technological limitations and to return to a more dynamic style of editing. It is to these early experiments in sound and picture editing that we now turn our attention.

☐ TECHNOLOGICAL LIMITATIONS

Although experiments in sound technology had been conducted since 1895, it was primarily in radio and telephone transmission technology that advances were made. By 1927, when Warner Brothers produced the first sound (voice) feature film, *The Jazz Singer* with Al Jolson, at least two studios were committed to producing sound films. The Warner Brothers system, Vitaphone, was a sound-on-disk system. The Fox Corporation invested in a sound-on-film system, Movietone. Photophone, an optical system produced by RCA, eventually became the industry standard. In 1927, though, Photophone had not yet been tested in an actual production, whereas Warner Brothers had used Vitaphone in *The Jazz Singer* and Fox had produced the popular Movietone news.

To use sound on film, several technological barriers had to be overcome. The problems revolved around the recording system, the microphone quality and characteristics, the synchronization of camera and sound disk playback, and the issue of sound amplification.

In the production process, the microphones used to record sound had to be sufficiently directional so that the desired voices and music were not drowned out by ambient noise.

A synchronization process was also needed. The camera recording the image and the disk recording the voice or music had to be in continuous synchronization so that, on playback, picture and sound would have a direct and constant relationship to one another. This system had to be carried through so that during projection the sound disk and the picture were synchronized. In sound-on-film systems, the sound reader had to be located on the projector so that it was read precisely at the instant when the corresponding image was passing under the light of the projector.

Finally, because film was projected in an auditorium or theater, the amplification system had to be such that the sound playback was clear and, to the extent possible, undistorted.

The recording of sound was so daunting a task that picture editing took second place. Dialogue scenes on disk could not be edited without losing synchronization. A similar problem existed with the Movietone sound-on-film movies. A cut meant the loss of sound and image. Until rerecording and multiple camera use became common, editing was restricted to silent sequences. Consequently, the coming of sound meant a serious inhibition for editing and the loss of many of the creative gains made in the silent period.

This did not mean that film and film production did not undergo drastic changes in the early sound period. Suddenly, musicals and their stars became very important in film production. Stage performers and playwrights were suddenly needed. Journalists, novelists, critics, and columnists were in demand to write for the new dimension of speech on film. Those who had never spoken, the actors and their writers, fell from favor. The careers of the greatest silent stars—John Gilbert, Pola Negri, Emil Jannings, Norma Talmadge—all ended with the coming of sound. Many of the great silent comedians—Buster Keaton, Fatty Arbuckle, Harry Langdon—were replaced by verbal comedians and teams. W. C. Fields and the Marx Brothers were among the more successful. It was as if 30 years of visual progress were dismissed to celebrate speech, its power, and its influence.

Returning to the editing gains of the silent period, it is useful to understand why sound and picture editing today provides so many choices. The key is technological development. Today, sound is recorded with sophisticated unidirectional microphones that transmit sound to quarter-inch magnetic tape. Recording machines can mix sounds from different sources or record sound from a single source. The tape is transferred to magnetic film, which has the same dimensions as camera film and can be edge-numbered to coincide with the camera film's edge numbers. Original sound on tape is recorded in sync with the camera film so that camera film and magnetic film can be easily synchronized. Editing machines can run picture and sound in sync so that if synchronization is lost during editing it can be retrieved. Finally, numerous sound tracks are available for voice, sound effects, and music, and each is synchronized to the picture. Consequently, when those sound tracks are mixed, they remain in sync with the edited picture. When the picture negative is conformed to the working copy so the prints can be struck, an optical print of the sound is married to those prints from the negative. The married print, which is in sync, is used for projection.

The modern situation allows sound and picture to be disassembled so that editing choices in both sound and picture can proceed freely. Synchronization in picture and sound recording is fundamental to later synchronization. In the interim phases, the development of separate tracks can proceed because a synchronized relationship is maintained via the picture edit. Projection devices in which the sound head is located ahead of the picture allow the optical reading of sound to proceed in harmony with the image projection.

□ TECHNOLOGICAL IMPROVEMENTS

This freedom did not exist in 1930. It awaited a wide variety of technological improvements in addition to the decision to run sound and film at 24 frames per second (constant sound speed) rather than the silent speed of 16 frames per second (silent speed of film).

By 1929, camera blimps were developed to rescue the camera from being housed in the "ice box," a sound-proofed room that isolated camera noise from the action being recorded. As camera blimps became lighter, the camera itself became more mobile, and the option of shooting sound sequences with a moving camera became realistic.

Set construction materials were altered to avoid materials that were prone to loud, crackling noises from contact. Sound stages for production were built to exclude exterior noise and to minimize interior noise.

Carbon arc lights, with their constant hum, were initially changed to incandescent lights. More sophisticated circuitry eventually allowed a return to quieter arc light systems.

By 1930, a sound and picture editing machine, the Moviola, was introduced. In 1932, "edge numbering" allowed sound and picture to be edited in synchronization. By 1933, advances in microphones and mixing allowed sound tracks to use music and dialogue simultaneously without loss of quality.

By 1936, the use of optical sound tracks was enhanced by new developments in optical light printers, which now provided distortionless sound. Quality was further enhanced by the development of unidirectional microphones in 1939.

Between 1945 and 1950, the use of magnetic recording over optical improved quality and permitted greater editing flexibility. Magnetic film began to replace optical film for sound editing.

Larger film formats, CinemaScope and TODD-AO, provided space on film for more than one optical track. Stored sound offered greater sound directionality and the sense of being surrounded by sound.

☐ THEORETICAL ISSUES CONCERNING SOUND

The theoretical debate about the use of sound was a deliberate effort to counter the observation that the sound film was nothing more than a filmed play complete with dialogue. It was an attempt to view the new technology of sound as a gain for the evolution of film as an art. Consequently, it was not surprising that the first expression of this impulse came from Eisenstein, Pudovkin, and Grigori Alexandrov. Their statement was published in a Leningrad magazine in 1928.[1]

Eisenstein, Pudovkin, and Alexandrov were concerned that the combination of sound and image would give the single shot a credibility it previously did not have. They worried that the addition of sound would counter the use of the shot as a building block that gains meaning when edited with other shots. They therefore argued that sound should not be used to enhance naturalism, but rather that it be used in a nonsynchronized or asynchronous fashion. This contrapuntal use of sound would allow montage to continue to be used creatively.

The next year, Pudovkin argued in his book *Film Technique and Film Acting* for an asynchronous use of sound. He believed that sound has far greater potential and that new layers of meaning can be achieved through the use of asynchronous sound. Just as he saw visual editing as a way of building up meaning, he viewed sound as an additional element to enrich meaning. In the early work of Alfred Hitchcock, Pudovkin's ideas are put into practice. We will return to Hitchcock later in this chapter.

Later, directors Basil Wright and Alberto Cavalcanti experimented with the use of sound in film. In the early 1930s, each argued that sound could be used, not only to counteract the realistic character of dialogue, but also to orchestrate a wide variety of sound sources—effects, narration, and music—to create a new reality. They viewed sound as an element that could liberate new meanings and interpretations of reality. Because both worked in documentary film, they were particularly sensitive to the "realism" affected by the visuals.

For the most part, these directors were attempting to find a way around the perceived tyranny of technology that resulted in the distortion of the sound film into filmed theatre. In their theoretical speculations, they pointed out the direction that enabled filmmakers to use sound creatively and to resume their attempts to find editing solutions for new narratives.

☐ EARLY EXPERIMENT IN SOUND— ALFRED HITCHCOCK'S *BLACKMAIL*

Alfred Hitchcock's *Blackmail* (1929) has many of the characteristics of the earliest sound films. It was shot in part as a silent film and in part as a sound film. The silent sequences have music and occasional sound effects. These sequences are dynamic—the opening sequence, which shows the apprehension and booking of a criminal by the police, is a good example. Camera movement is fluid, images are textured, and the editing is fast-paced. The sound sequences, on the other hand, are dominated by dialogue. The camera is static, as are the performers. The mix of silent and sound sequences of this sort typifies the earliest sound films. Hitchcock didn't let sound hamper him more than necessary, however. This story of a young woman (Anny Ondra) who kills an overzealous admirer (Cyril Ritchard) and is protected from capture by her Scotland Yard beau is simple on the surface, but Hitchcock treated it as a tale of desire and guilt. Consequently, these very subjective states are what he attempted to create through a mix of visuals and sound.

After the murder (Figures 2.1 to 2.3), Alice wanders the streets of London. A neon sign advertises Gordon's Gin cocktail mix, but instead of a cocktail

Figure 2.1 *Blackmail*, 1929. Still provided by British Film Institute.

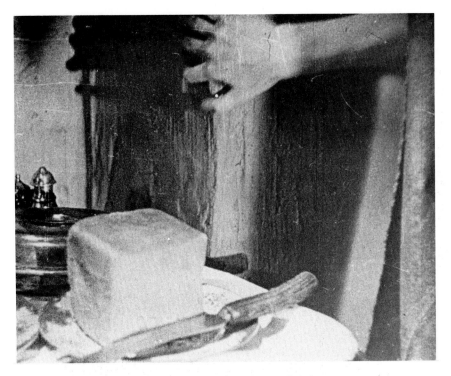

Figure 2.2 *Blackmail*, 1929. Still provided by British Film Institute.

shaker, Alice sees the stabbing motion of a knife. Later, this subjective suggestion is carried even further. She arrives home and pretends that she has
spent the night there.

Her mother wakes her for breakfast, mentioning the murder. She changes
and goes to the confectioner's store, where a customer begins to gossip about
the murder. The customer follows her into the breakfast room behind the
store, continuing to talk about the murder instrument. The dialogue begins
to focus on the word *knife*. The image we see is of Alice trying to contain
herself. The dialogue over the visual of Alice is as follows: ".-.-.-Never use
a knife-.-.-.-now mind you a knife is a difficult thing to handle-.-.-.-I mean
any knife-.-.-.-knife-.-.-.-knife-.-.-.-knife-.-.-." The word *knife* is now all that
we (and Alice) hear, until she takes the knife to slice the bread. As she picks
up the knife, the pitch and tone of the word changes from conversational to
a scream of the word *knife*, and suddenly, she drops the knife.

This very subjective use of dialogue, allowing the audience to hear only
what the character hears, intensifies the sense of subjectivity. As we identify
more strongly with Alice, we begin to feel what she feels. The shock of the
scream seems to wake us to the fact that there is an objective reality here

Figure 2.3 *Blackmail*, 1929. Still provided by British Film Institute.

also. Alice's parents are here for breakfast, and the customer is here for some gossip. Only Alice is deeply immersed in the memory of the murder the night before, and her guilt seems to envelop her.

Hitchcock used sound as Pudovkin had envisioned, to build up an idea just as one would with a series of images. In *Blackmail*, sound is used as another bit of information to develop a narrative point: Alice's guilt over the murder. This early creative use of sound was achieved despite the technological limitations of dialogue scenes and despite silent sequences presented with music and simple sound effects. It was a hindrance because the static results of sound recording—no camera movement, no interference with the literal recording of that sound, means literal rather than creative use of sound. In *Blackmail*, Hitchcock transcends those limitations.

□ SOUND, TIME, AND PLACE: FRITZ LANG'S *M*

Fritz Lang's *M* (1931), although made only two years after Hitchcock's *Blackmail*, seems much more advanced in its use of sound, even though Lang faced many of the same technological limitations that Hitchcock did. Like *Blackmail*, Lang's film contains both dialogue sequences and silent sequences with music or sound effects. How did Lang proceed? In brief, he edited the sound as if he were editing the visuals.

M is the story of a child murderer, of how he paralyzes a German city, and of how the underworld finally decides that if the police can't capture him, they will. The criminals and the police are presented as parallel organizations that are interested primarily in self-perpetuation. Only the capture of the child murderer will allow both organizations to proceed with business as usual. We are introduced to the murderer in shadow (Figure 2.4) when

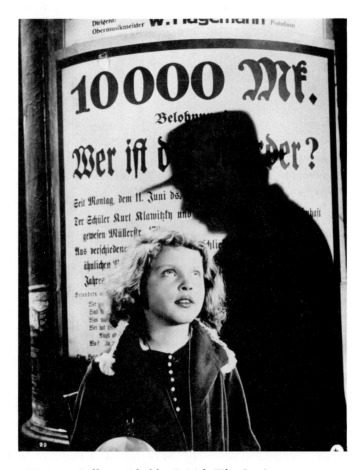

Figure 2.4 *M*, 1931. Still provided by British Film Institute.

he speaks to a young girl, Elsie Beckmann. We hear the conversation he makes with her, but we see only his shadow, which is ironically shown on a reward poster for his capture.

Lang then set up a parallel action sequence by intercutting shots of the murderer (Peter Lorre) with the young girl and shots of the young girl's mother. The culmination of this scene relies wholly on sound for its continuity. The mother calls out for her child. Each time she calls for Elsie, we see a different visual: out the window of the home, down the stairs, out into the yard where the laundry dries, to the empty dinner table where Elsie would sit, and finally far away to a child's ball rolling out of a treed area and to a balloon stuck in a telephone line. With each shot, the cries become more distant. For the last two shots, the mother's cries are no more than a faint echo.

In this sequence, the primary continuity comes from the soundtrack. The mother's cries unify all of the various shots, and the sense of distance implied by the tone of the call suggests that Elsie is now lost to her mother.

Later in the film, Lang elaborates on this use of sound to provide the unifying idea for a sequence. In one scene, the minister complains to the chief of police that they must find the killer of Elsie Beckmann. The conversation reveals the scope of the investigation. As they speak, we see visual details of the search for the killer. The visuals show a variety of activities, including the discovery of a candy wrapper at the scene of the crime and the subsequent investigation of candy shops. Geographically, the police investigation moves all around the town and takes place over an extended period of time. These time and place shifts are all coordinated through the conversation between the minister and the chief of police.

In terms of screen time, the conversation is five minutes long, but it communicates an investigation that takes place over many days and in many places. We sense the police department's commitment but also its frustration at the lack of results.

What follows is the famous scene of parallel action where Lang intercut two meetings. The police and the criminal underworld meet separately, and the leaders of both organizations discuss their frustrations about the child murderer and devise strategies for capturing him.

Rather than simply relying on visual parallel action, Lang cut on dialogue at one point, starting a sentence in the police camp and ending it in the criminal meeting. The crosscutting is all driven by dialogue. There are common visual elements: the meeting setting, the smoky room, the seating, the prominence of one leader in each group. Despite these visual cues, it is the dialogue that is used to set up the parallel action and to give the audience a sense of progress. Unlike Griffith's chase, there is no visual dynamic to carry us toward a resolution, nor is there a metric montage. The pace and character of the dialogue establish and carry us through this scene.

Lang used sound as if it were another visual element, editing it freely. Notable is how Lang used the design of sound to overcome space and time issues. Through his use of dialogue over the visuals, time collapses and the

Figure 2.5 *M*, 1931. Still provided by British Film Institute.

Figure 2.6 *M*, 1931. Still provided by British Film Institute.

Figure 2.7 *M*, 1931. Still provided by British Film Institute.

audience moves all about the city with greater ease than if he had straight-cut the visuals (Figures 2.5 to 2.7).

□ THE DYNAMIC OF SOUND:
ROUBEN MAMOULIAN'S *APPLAUSE*

As Lucy Fischer suggests, "Mamoulian seems to 'build a world'—one that his characters and audience seem to inhabit. And that world is 'habitable' because Mamoulian vests it with a strong sense of space. Unlike other directors of the period he recognizes the inherent spatial capacities of sound and, furthermore, understands the means by which they can lend an aspect of depth to the image."[2]

Applause (1929) is a tale of backstage life, and it creates a world surrounded by sound (Figures 2.8 and 2.9). Even in intimate moments, the larger world expunges the characters. To capture this omnipresent sense of sound, Rouben Mamoulian added wheels to the sound-proof booth that housed the camera. As his characters moved, so did the camera and the sound. He also recorded two voices from two sources simultaneously. This challenge to technological limitations characterizes Mamoulian's attitude

Figure 2.8 *Applause*, 1929. Still provided by British Film Institute.

Figure 2.9 *Applause*, 1929. Still provided by Moving Image and Sound Archives.

toward sound. Mamoulian realized that the proximity of the microphones to the characters would affect the audience's sense of closeness to the characters. Consequently, he used proximity and distance to good effect. Proximity meant that the characters (and the viewers) were surrounded and invaded by sound. Distance meant the opposite: total silence. Mamoulian used silence in Kitty's (Helen Morgan) suicide scene.

In this sense, Mamoulian used sound as long shot (silence) and close-up (wide open sound). It wasn't necessary to use sound and picture in synchrony. By using sound in counterpoint to the images, Mamoulian was able to heighten the dramatic character of the scenes.

This operating principle was elaborated and made more complex three years later in Mamoulian's *Dr. Jekyll and Mr. Hyde* (1932). The Robert Louis Stevenson novel was adapted with a Freudian interpretation. Repressed sexuality leads Dr. Jekyll (Frederic March) to free himself to become the uninhibited Mr. Hyde. The object of his desire (and later his wrath) is Ivey (Miriam Hopkins).

To create an interior sense of Dr. Jekyll and to enhance the audience's identification with him, Mamoulian photographed the first 5 minutes with a totally subjective camera. We see what Dr. Jekyll sees. Consequently, we hear him but don't see him until he steps in front of the mirror. Poole, Jekyll's butler, announces that he will be late for a lecture at the medical school. We hear Jekyll as if we were directly beside him. The microphone's proximity gives us, in effect, "close-up" sound. Poole, on the other hand, is distant from the audience. At one point, the drop in sound is quite pronounced, a "long shot" sound.

This sense of spatial separation and character separation is continued when Jekyll enters the carriage that will take him to the medical school, but now the reverse begins to occur. The "close-up" sound is of the driver, and it is Jekyll who sounds distant. This continues when he is greeted by the medical school attendant.

Jekyll is now in the classroom, and all is silence. Then whispers by students and faculty can be heard. Only when Jekyll begins to lecture do the sound levels become more natural. When the film cuts to a closer visual of Jekyll, the sound also becomes a "close-up." Consequently, what Jekyll is saying about the soul of man is verbally presented with as much emphasis as if it were a visual close-up.

Later, when Jekyll rescues Ivey from an abusive suitor, Mamoulian returns to this use of "visual" sound. He advises bed rest for her injuries. When she slips off her garter and her stockings, there is sudden silence, as though Jekyll were silenced by her sensuality. He tucks her into bed, and she embraces and kisses him just as his colleague, Lagnon, enters the room. Misunderstanding and embarrassment lead Jekyll and Lagnon to leave as Ivey, with one leg over the bed, whispers "Come back soon.

As Jekyll and Lagnon walk into the London night, Ivey and her provocative thigh linger as a superimposed image and the soundtrack repeats the whisper, "Come back soon." The memory of Ivey and the desire for Ivey are recreated through the sound. Throughout the film, subjectivity, separation, desire, and dreams are articulated through the use of sound edits.

□ CONCLUSION

In their creative work, Mamoulian, Lang, and Hitchcock attempted to overcome the technological limitations of sound in this early period. Together with the theoretical statements of Eisenstein, Pudovkin, and the documentary filmmakers, they prepared the industry to view sound not as an end in itself, but rather as another element that, along with the editing of the visuals, could help create a narrative experience that was unique to film.

□ NOTES/REFERENCES

1. Reprinted in Elisabeth Weis and John Belton, eds., *Film Sound: Theory and Practice* (New York: Columbia University Press, 1985), 83–85. An entire section of the book is devoted to sound theory; see pp. 73–176.
2. Lucy Fischer, "*Applause*: The Visual and Acoustic Landscape," in Weis and Belton, *Film Sound*, 232–246.

3

The Influence of
the Documentary

■

D. W. Griffith and his contemporaries were part of a growing commercial industry whose prime goal was to entertain. This meant that the ideas presented in their films were subordinate to their entertainment value. Griffith attempted to present conceptual material about society in *Intolerance* and failed. Although other filmmakers—such as King Vidor (*The Crowd*, 1928), Charlie Chaplin (*The Gold Rush*, 1925), and F. W. Murnau (*Sunrise*, 1927)— blended ideas and entertainment values more successfully, the commercial film has more often been associated primarily with entertainment.

The documentary film, on the other hand, has always been associated with the communication of ideas first and with entertainment values a distant second. Griffith was very successful in using editing techniques to involve and entertain. He was less successful in developing editing techniques that would help communicate ideas. Which editing theories and techniques facilitate the communication of ideas? How do ideas work with the emotional power implicit in editing techniques?

Because the documentary film was less influenced by market forces than commercial film was and because the filmmakers attracted to the documentary had different goals from commercial filmmakers, often goals with social or political agendas, the techniques they used often displayed a power not seen in the commercial film. Subsidized by government, these filmmakers blended artistic experimentation with political commitment, and their innovations in the documentary broadened the repertoire of editing choices for all filmmakers.

The documentary, or "film of actuality," had been important from the time of the Lumière brothers in France, but it was not until the 1920s that the work of the Russian filmmakers—Eisenstein, Pudovkin, and the National Film School under Kuleshov—and the release of Robert Flaherty's *Nanook of the North* (1922) prompted John Grierson in England to consider films of actuality and "purposive filmmaking."[1] As Paul Swann suggests, "Grierson was prompt to note Lenin's belief in 'the power of film for ideological propaganda.' Grierson's great innovation was to adapt this revolutionary dictum to the purpose of social democracy."[2]

Grierson was very affected by the power of the editing in *Potemkin* and the method Eisenstein used to form, present, and argue about ideas visually (intellectual montage). There is little question that a dialectic between form and content became a working principle as Grierson produced his own film, *The Drifters* (1929), and moved on to produce the work of many others at the British Marketing Board.

Grierson took the principle of social or political purpose and joined it with a visual aesthetic. Greatly aided by the coming of sound after 1930, the documentary as propaganda developed into an instrument of social policy in England, in Germany, and temporarily in the United States. In their work, the filmmakers applied editing solutions to complex ideas. Through their work, the options for editing broadened almost exponentially.

□ IDEAS ABOUT SOCIETY

The coming of sound was closely followed by shattering world events. In October 1929, the U.S. stock market crash signaled the onset of the Great Depression. Political instability led to the rise of Fascist governments in Italy and Germany. The aftereffects of World War I undermined British and French society. The United States maintained an isolationist position. The period, then, was unpredictable and unstable. The documentary films of this time searched for a stability and strength not present in the real world. The efforts of these filmmakers to find positive reinterpretations of society were the earliest efforts to communicate particular ideas about their respective societies. Grierson was interested in using film to bring society together. Working during the Depression, a fracturing event, he and others wanted to use film to heal society. In this sense he was an early propagandist.

ROBERT FLAHERTY AND *MAN OF ARAN*

Robert Flaherty's *Man of Aran* (1934) closely resembles a commercial film. In this fictionalized story of the Aran Islands off the coast of Ireland, Flaherty used actual islanders in the film, but he created the plot according to his goals rather than basing it on the lives of the islanders.

Man of Aran tells the story of a family that lives in a setting where they are dwarfed by nature and challenged by the land and sea. Flaherty used two shark hunts to suggest the bravery of the islanders, and the storm at the end of the film illustrates that their struggle against nature makes them stronger, worthy adversaries in the hierarchy of natural beings. People, not being supreme in the natural hierarchy, are shown to be worthy adversaries for nature when the challenge is considerable. In essence, a poetic interpretation of people's struggle with nature makes them look good.

This idea of the nobility of humanity and of its will to live despite the elements was Flaherty's creation. The Aran Islanders didn't live as he presented them. For example, the sharks they hunted are basking sharks, a species that is harmless to humans (the film implies that they are man-eaters). Of course, Flaherty's production of such a film in 1934 in the midst of the Great Depression suggests how far he roamed from the issues of the day. Like Griffith, he had a particular mythic vision of life, and he re-created that vision in all of his films.

In terms of its editing, *Man of Aran* is similar to the early sound films of Mamoulian and Hitchcock. Music and simple sound effects are used as sound coverage for essentially silent sequences. There is no narrative, and where dialogue is used, it is equivalent to another sound effect. The actual dialogue is not necessary to the progress of the story. The film has a very powerful visual character, which is presented in a very formal manner. Although the film offers opportunity for dialectical editing, particularly in the shark hunts, the actual editing is deliberate and avoids developing a strong identification with the characters. In this sense, the intimacy so vital to the success of a film like *Broken Blossoms* is of no interest to Flaherty (Figures 3.1 to 3.4). Instead, Flaherty tries to create an archetypal struggle of humanity against nature, and dialectics seem inappropriate to Flaherty's vision. Consequently, the editing is secondary to the cumulative, steady development of Flaherty's personal ideas about the struggle. The fact that the film was made in the midst of the Depression adds a level of irony. It makes *Man of Aran* timeless; this quality was a source of criticism toward the film at the time.

Figure 3.1   *Man of Aran*, 1934. Still provided by Moving Image and Sound Archives.

Figure 3.2   *Man of Aran*, 1934. Still provided by Moving Image and Sound Archives.

Figure 3.3   *Man of Aran*, 1934. Still provided by British Film Institute.

Figure 3.4   *Man of Aran*, 1934. Still provided by Moving Image and Sound Archives.

For our purposes, however, *Man of Aran* presents the documentary film in a form similar to the commercial film. Performance, pictorial style, and editing serve a narrative: in this case, Flaherty's version of the life of the Aran Islanders. It is not purposive filmmaking, as Grierson proposed, but nor is it the Hollywood film he so vehemently criticized.

BASIL WRIGHT AND *NIGHT MAIL*

Night Mail (1936), produced by John Grierson and the General Post Office film unit and directed by Basil Wright, was certainly purposive, and it used sound particularly to create the message of the film. The film itself is a simple story of the delivery of the mail by train from London to Glasgow, but it is also about the commitment and harmony of the postal workers. If the film has a simple message, it's the importance of the job of delivering the mail. The sense of harmony among the workers is secondary.

Turning again to the events of the day, 1936 was a dreadful time in terms of employment. Political and economic will were not enough to overcome the international protectionism and the strains of the British Empire. Consequently, *Night Mail* is not an accurate reflection of feeling among postal workers. It is the Grierson vision of what life among the postal workers should be.

For us, the film's importance is the blend of image and sound and how the sound edit is used to create the sense of importance and harmony. As in all of these films, there is a visual aesthetic that is in itself powerful (Figures 3.5 and 3.6), but it is the sound work of composer Benjamin Britten, poet W. H. Auden (who wrote the narration), and above all Alberto Cavalcanti (who designed the sound) that affects the purposeful message Grierson intended.

The sound of the train simulating a cry or the rhythm of the narration trying to simulate the urgent, energetic wheels of the train rushing to reach Glasgow create a power beyond the images themselves. The reading, although artificial in its nonrealism, acts as Dovzhenko's visuals did—to create a poetic idea that is transcendent. The idea is reinforced by the music and by the shuffling cadence of the narration. Together, all of the sound, music, words, and effects elevate the images to achieve the unifying idea that this train is carrying messages from one part of the nation to another, that commerce and personal well-being depend on the delivery of those messages, and that those who carry those messages, the workers, are critical to the well-being of the nation. This idea, then, is the essence of the film, and it is the editing of the sound that creates the dimensions of the idea.

Figure 3.5   *Night Mail*, 1936. Still provided by Moving Image and Sound Archives.

Figure 3.6   *Night Mail*, 1936. Still provided by British Film Institute.

PARE LORENTZ AND *THE PLOW THAT BROKE THE PLAINS*

A more critical view of society was taken by Pare Lorentz in *The Plow That Broke the Plains* (1936), a film sponsored by the Resettlement Administration of the U.S. government. Lorentz looked at the impact of the Depression on the agricultural sector. The land and the people both suffered from natural as well as human-made disasters. The purposive message of the film is that government must become actively involved in recovery programs to manage these natural resources. Only through government intervention can this sort of suffering be alleviated.

To give his message impact, Lorentz relied on the photojournalist imagery made famous by Walker Evans and others during the Depression. In terms of the visual editing, the film is imitative of Eisenstein, but the sequences aren't staged as thoroughly as Eisenstein's were. Consequently, the sequences as a whole don't have the power of Eisenstein's films. They resemble more closely the work of Dovzhenko in which the individual shots have a power of their own (Figures 3.7 and 3.8).

It is the narration and the music by Virgil Thomson that pull the ideas together. Lorentz has to rely on direct statement to present the solution to the government. In this sense, his work is not as mature propaganda as the later work of Frank Capra or the earlier work of Leni Riefenstahi. Lorentz was more successful in his second film, *The River* (1937). As Richard Meran

Figure 3.7   *The Plow That Broke the Plains*, 1936. Still provided by Moving Image and Sound Archives.

Figure 3.8   *The Plow That Broke the Plains*, 1936. Still provided by British Film Institute.

Barsam states about Lorentz, "While (his films) conform to the documentary problem–solution structure, these films rely on varying combinations of repetition, rhythm, and parallel structure, so that problems presented in the first part of the films are solved in the second part, but solved through such an artistic juxtaposition of image, sound, and motif that their unity and coherence of development set them distinctly apart."[3]

□ IDEAS ABOUT ART AND CULTURE

Flaherty, Grierson, and Lorentz had specific views about society that helped shape their editing choices. Other filmmakers, although they also held particular political views, attempted to deal with more general and more elusive ideas. How they achieved that aesthetic goal is of interest to us.

LENI RIEFENSTAHL AND *OLYMPIA*

It would be simple to dismiss Leni Riefenstahl's work as Nazi propaganda (Figure 3.9). Although Riefenstahl's *Olympia Parts I and II* (1938) are films of the 1936 Olympics held in Berlin and hosted by Adolph Hitler's Nazi government, Riefenstahl's film attempts to create a sensibility about the human form that transcends national boundaries. Using 50 camera operators and the latest lenses, Riefenstahl had at her disposal slow-motion images, microimages, and images of staggering scale. She presented footage of many of the competitions in the expected form—the competitors, the competition, the winners—but she also included numerous sequences about the training and the camaraderie of the athletes. *Part II* opens with an idyllic early morning run and the sauna that follows the training. Riefenstahl used no narration, only music, and she didn't focus on any individual. She focused only on the beauty of nature, including the athletes and their joy.

This principle is raised to its height in the famous diving sequence near the end of *Part II*. This 5-minute sequence begins with shots of the audience responding to a dive and shots of competitors from specific countries. Then Riefenstahl cuts to the mechanics of the dive. Gradually, the audience is no longer shown. Now we see one diver after another. She concentrates on the grace of the dive, then she begins to use slow motion and shows only the form and completion of the dive. The shots become increasingly abstract. We no longer know who is diving. She begins to follow in rapid succession dives from differing perspectives. The images are disorienting. She begins to fragment the dives. We see only the beginning of dives in rapid succession. Then the dives are in silhouette, and they seem like abstract forms rather than humans. Two forms replace one. She cuts from one direction to another, one abstract form to another. Are they diving into water or jumping into the air? The images become increasingly abstract, and eventually, we see only sky.

Figure 3.9 *Olympia*, 1938. Still provided by British Film Institute.

In 5 minutes, Riefenstahl has taken us from a realistic document of an Olympic dive (complete with an audience) to an abstract form leaping through space—graceful beauty in motion. Through the sequence, we hear only music and the splash of water as the diver hits the surface. Riefenstahl's ideas about beauty and art are brilliantly communicated in this sequence. No narration was necessary to explain the idea. Editing and music were the tools on which Riefenstahl relied.

W. S. VAN DYKE AND *THE CITY*

In the late 1930s, the American Institute of Planners commissioned a film about the future city to be shown at the 1939 World's Fair in New York City. W. S. Van Dyke and Ralph Steiner, working from a script by Henwar Rodakiewicz and Lewis Mumford (and an outline by Pare Lorentz), fashioned a story about the future that arises out of the past and present. The urgency of the new city is born out of contemporary problems of urban life. The images of those problems are in sharp contrast to the orderly prosperous character of the future city (Figures 3.10 to 3.12).

In *The City* (1939), ideas about politics are mixed with ideas about the culture of the city: urban life as a source of power as well as oppression. Unfortunately, the images of oppression are so memorable and so human that they overwhelm the suburban utopia presented later.

In the third section of the film, featuring the city of New York, Van Dyke and Steiner portray the travails of the lunch hour in the big city. Everyone is on the run with the inevitable congestion and indigestion. All this is portrayed in the editing; the pace and the music capture the charm and the harm of lunch on the run. This metaphor is carried through to the conclusion through images of the icons of the large city—the signs that, instead of giving the city balance, imply a rather conclusive improbability about one's future in the city of the present. This sequence prepares us for the city of the future.

As in *The Plow That Broke the Plains*, the American documentary structure follows a point–counterpoint flow that is akin to making a case for the position put forward in the concluding sequence, in this case, the city of the future. The film unfolds as a case for the prosecution would in a trial. It's a

Figure 3.10　*The City*, 1939. Still provided by Museum of Modern Art/Film Stills Archives.

Figure 3.11 *The City*, 1939. Still provided by Museum of Modern Art/Film Stills Archives.

Figure 3.12 *The City*, 1939. Still provided by Museum of Modern Art/Film Stills Archives.

dramatic device differing from the slow unfolding of many documentaries. As in the Lorentz film, music is very important. Another similarity is the strength of the individual shots. Van Dyke and Steiner, as still photographers, bring a power to the individual images that undermines the strength of the sequences. However, the film does succeed in creating a sense that the city is important as more than an economic center. The urban center becomes, in this film, a place to live, to work, and to affiliate and a cultural force that can shape or undermine the lives of all who live there. Van Dyke's city becomes more than a place to live. It becomes the architectural plan for our quality of life.

□ IDEAS ABOUT WAR AND SOCIETY

The shaping of ideas became even more urgent when the purpose of the film was to help win a war fought for the continued existence of the country. Grierson provided the philosophy for the propaganda film, and Eisenstein and Pudovkin provided the practical tools to shape and sharpen an idea through editing. In the 1930s, such filmmakers as Riefenstahi put the philosophy and techniques to the practical test. Her film, *Triumph of the Will* (1935), became the standard against which British and American war documentaries were measured. The work of Frank Capra, William Wyler, and John Huston in the United States and of Alberto Cavalcanti, Harry Watt, and Humphrey Jennings in Great Britain displayed a mix of personal creativity and national purpose. Their films drew on national traditions, and in their own way, each advanced the role of editing in shaping ideas effectively. Consequently, the power of the medium seemed to be without limit and thus dangerous. This perception shaped both the fascination with and the suspicion of the media, particularly film and television, in the post-war period.

FRANK CAPRA AND *WHY WE FIGHT* (1943–1945)

Frank Capra, one of Hollywood's most successful directors, was commissioned by then-Chief of Staff George C. Marshall to produce a series of films to prepare soldiers inducted into the army for going to war. The *Why We Fight* series (1943–1945), seven films produced to be shown to the troops, are among the most successful propaganda films ever made. As Richard Dyer MacCann suggests about the films, "They attempted (1) to destroy faith in isolation, (2) to build up a sense of the strength and at the same time the stupidity of the enemy, and (3) to emphasize the bravery and achievements of America's allies. Their style was a combination of a sermon, a between-halves pep talk, and a barroom bull session."[4]

Capra used compilation footage, excerpts from Riefenstahl's *Triumph of the Will*, re-created footage, and excerpts from Hollywood films to create a sense of actuality and credibility. To make dramatic points, Capra resorted to animation. Maps and visual analogies—such as the juxtaposition of two globes, a white earth (the Allies) and a black earth (the Axis), in *Prelude to War* (1942)—illustrate the struggle for primacy. Capra used the animation to make a dramatic point with simple pictures.

The narration is colloquial, highly personalized, and passionate about characterizing each side in terms of good and evil. The narration features slang, rather than objective language. Read by Walter Huston, it illustrates and deepens the impact of the images.

Picture and sound complement one another, and where possible, repetition follows a point made in a rapid visual montage. The pace of the film is urgent. Whether the scene has to do with the subversion necessary from within in the takeover of Norway or the more complex portrayal of French capitulation and Nazi perfidy and consequent glee (the repetitive shot of Hermann Göring rubbing his hands together), Capra highlighted victim and victimizer in the most dramatic terms (Figures 3.13 to 3.15).

Capra, then, used visual and sound editing in a highly dramatized way. A great deal of information is synthesized into an "us against them" structure. Eisenstein's dialectic ideas have rarely been used more effectively.

Figure 3.13 *Divide and Conquer*, 1945. Still provided by Museum of Modern Art/Film Stills Archives.

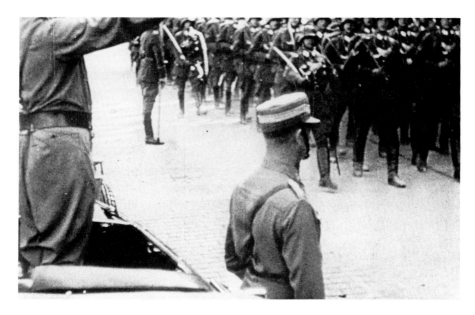

Figure 3.14 *Divide and Conquer*, 1945. Still provided by Museum of Modern Art/Film Stills Archives.

Figure 3.15 *Divide and Conquer*, 1945. Still provided by Museum of Modern Art/Film Stills Archives.

HUMPHREY JENNINGS AND *DIARY FOR TIMOTHY*

By the time he produced *Diary for Timothy* (1945), Humphrey Jennings had already directed two of the greatest war documentaries, *Listen to Britain* (1942) and *Fires Were Started* (1943). Whereas Capra in his films concentrated on the combatants and the war, Jennings, in his work, concentrated on the home front.

Diary for Timothy is a film about a baby, Timothy, born in 1944. The film speculates about what kind of world Timothy will grow up in. The film's tone is anxious about the future. As with all of Jennings's work, this film tends to roam visually, not focusing on a single event, place, or person. To create a sense of the society as a whole, Jennings includes many people at work or at home with their families. This general approach poses the problem of how to unify the footage (Figure 3.16).

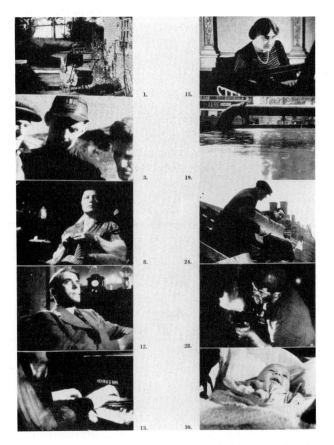

Figure 3.16   *Diary for Timothy*, 1945. Stills provided by British Film Institute.

In this film, the baby, at different ages, acts as a visual reference point, and the narration addressed to Timothy (read by Michael Redgrave, written by E. M. Forster) personalizes and attempts to shape a series of ideas rather than a plot.

The film contains six sections. Although there is a temporal relationship, there is no clear developmental character. Instead of a story, as Alan Lovell and Jim Hillier suggest, "*A Diary for Timothy* depends for its effect on highly formal organization and associative montage."[5] Within the montage sections, the sum is greater than the parts. Again quoting from Lovell and Hillier:

> With the wet reflection of a pit-head and "rain, too much rain," the film launches into a further sequence of images and events: Tim's mother writing Christmas cards, rain on Bill's engine, rain in the fields, Tim's baptism, Peter learning to walk again, Goronwy brought up from the pit on a stretcher. It is of course possible to attempt an intellectual analysis of the sequence of images but such analysis rarely takes us far enough. Jennings seems to have reached such a pitch of personal freedom in his association of ideas and shifts of mood that we lose the precise significance of the movement of the film and respond almost completely emotionally.[6]

This emotion is charged with speculation in the last sequence. Instead of a hopeful, powerful conclusion, as in *Listen to Britain*, or a somber, heroic conclusion, as in *Fires Were Started*, Jennings opted for an open-ended challenge. He put the challenge forward in the narration:

> Well, dear Tim, that's what's been happening around you during your first six months. And, you see, it's only chance that you're safe and sound. Up to now, we've done the talking; but, before long you'll sit up and take notice.-.-.-.-What are you going to say about it and what are you going to do? You heard what Germany was thinking, unemployment after the war and then another war and then more unemployment. Will it be like that again? Are you going to have greed for money or power ousting decency from the world as they have in the past? Or are you going to make the world a different place—you and all the other babies?[7]

□ CONCLUSION

Perhaps more than any other genre, the documentary has been successful in communicating ideas. The interplay of image and sound by filmmakers such as Riefenstahl, Capra, and Jennings has been remarkably effective and has greatly enhanced the filmmaker's repertoire of editing choices. These devices have found their way back into the fictional film, as evidenced in the work of neorealist filmmakers and the early American television directors whose feature film work has been marked by a pronounced documentary influence.

□ NOTES/REFERENCES

1. Paul Swann, *The British Documentary Film Movement, 1926–1946* (Cambridge: Cambridge University Press, 1989), 9.
2. Ibid., 7.
3. Richard Meran Barsam, ed., *Nonfiction Film: A Critical History* (New York: E. P. Dutton, 1973), 99–100.
4. Richard Dyer MacCann, "World War II: Armed Forces Documentary (1943)," in *Nonfiction Film: Theory and Criticism*, Richard Meran Barsam, ed. (New York: E. P. Dutton, 1976), 139.
5. Alan Lovell and Jim Hillier, *Studies in Documentary* (London: Martin Secker and Warburg, 1972), 105.
6. Ibid., 108.
7. Quoted from the shot-by-shot analysis of *Diary for Timothy* in Evan Cameron, "An Analysis of 'A Diary for Timothy,'" *Cinema Studies* (Spring 1967).

4

The Influence of
the Popular Arts

■

Film as a narrative form had numerous influences, particularly the popular novel of the nineteenth-century[1] and the theatrical genres of spectacle, pantomime, and melodrama.[2] The character and narrative conventions of those forms were adapted for film through editing. The types of shots required and how they were put together are the subject of Chapter 1. This chapter is concerned with the ongoing development in the popular arts and how they affected editing choices. In some cases (radio, musicals), they expanded those choices, and in others (vaudeville, theatre), they constrained those choices.

The interaction of these popular forms with film broadened the repertoire for film and eventually influenced other arts. However, film's influence on theatre, for example, took much longer. That influence was not apparent in theatrical production until the 1960s. In the 1920s and 1930s, it was the influence of theatre and radio that shaped film and film editing.

☐ VAUDEVILLE

In the work of Griffith and Vidor, narrative goals affected editing choices. In the subsequent work of Eisenstein and Pudovkin, political goals influenced editing choices. Vaudeville, as in the case of the documentary, presented yet another set of priorities, which in turn suggested different goals for editing.

Vaudeville, whether associated with burlesque or, later, with the more respectable theatre, offered a different audience experience than the melodramas and epics of Griffith or the polemics of the Russian revolutionary filmmakers. Vaudeville embraced farce as well as character-based humor and physical humor as well as verbal humor. As Robert C. Allen suggests, diversity was a popular characteristic of vaudeville programs: "A typical vaudeville bill in 1895 might include a trained animal act, a slapstick comedy routine, a recitation of 'inspirational' poetry, an Irish tenor, magic lantern slides of the wilds of Africa, a team of European acrobats, and a twenty-minute dramatic 'playlet' performed by a broadway star and his/her company."[3]

Vaudeville skits didn't have to be realistic; fantasy could be as important as an everyday situation. Character was often at the heart of the vaudeville act. Pace, character, humor, and entertainment were all goals of the act. In the early period, the audience for vaudeville, just like the early audience for film, was composed of the working class and often immigrants.[4] Pantomime and visual action were thus critical to the success of the production because routines had to transcend the language barrier.

We see the influence of vaudeville directly in the star system. Both Charlie Chaplin and Buster Keaton began in vaudeville. In their film work, we see many of the characteristics of vaudeville: the victim, the routine, the performance, and a wide range of small set-pieces (brief dramatized comic scenes) that are either stand-alone routines or parts of a larger story. What unifies the Chaplin and Keaton films is their characters and the people they represent: in both cases, ordinary men caught up in extraordinary situations.

In terms of editing, the implications are specific. First, the routine is important and must be clearly articulated so that it works. Second, the persona of the star—Chaplin or Keaton—must remain central; there can be no distractions from that character.

The easiest way to illustrate these principles is to look at Charlie Chaplin's films. Structurally, each film is a series of routines, each carefully staged through Chaplin's pantomime performance. Chaplin called *City Lights* (1931) "a comedy romance in pantomime." The opening sequence, the unveiling of a city statue on which Chaplin's character, "the little tramp," is sleeping, is both absurd and yet logical. Why is a man sleeping in the arms of a statue? Yet this very absurdity emphasizes the homelessness of the character. He is in every sense a public ward. This type of absurdity is notable in many of Chaplin's sequences, for example, the eating of shoelaces as spaghetti in *The Gold Rush* (1925) and the attempted suicide in *City Lights*. Absurdity is often at the heart of a sequence when Chaplin is making a point about the human condition. Perhaps the most absurd is the scene in *The Great Dictator* (1940) in which the dictator plays with a globe as if it were a beach ball. Absurdity and logic are the key elements to these vaudeville-like routines in Chaplin's films.

Perhaps no film by Chaplin is as elaborate in those routines as *Modern Times* (1936). The structure is a series of routines about factory life and personal life during the Depression. The first routine focuses on the assembly line. Here, the little tramp is victimized first by the pace and regimentation of the line and then by a lunch machine. He suffers an emotional breakdown, is hospitalized and released, and when he picks up a red flag that has fallen off a passing truck, he is arrested as a Communist. In jail, he foils a jail break, becomes a hero, and is released back into society. He meets a young woman, fantasizes about domestic life with her, and sets about getting a job to achieve that life. His attempt as a night watchman fails. When the factories reopen, he takes a job as a mechanic's assistant. A strike ends the job, but after another spell in jail, he gets a job as a singing waiter. He succeeds, but the young woman must flee for breaking the law. In the end, the tramp is on the road again, but with the young woman. Their life is indefinite, but he tries to smile.

Every scene in the film is constructed as a vaudeville routine. It has an internal logic and integrity. Each is visual and often absurd, and at its core is Chaplin portraying the little tramp. The scene in which Chaplin works as a mechanic's assistant presents an excellent example. Chaplin tries to be helpful to the mechanic (portrayed by Chester Conklin), but at each step, he hinders his boss. First, the oil can is crushed in the press, and eventually all of the mechanic's tools are crushed. Even the mechanic is swallowed up by the machinery (Figure 4.1). Now the absurdity twists away from the mechanic's fate; the lunch whistle blows, so the tramp attempts to feed the mechanic, who at this stage is upside down. To help him drink the coffee, he uses an oil spigot. He discards it for a whole chicken whose shape works as a funnel. As absurd as the situation seems, by using a chicken, the mechanic can be fed coffee. Finally, lunch is over and the mechanic can be freed from the machine. Once freed, however, the job ends due to a strike.

In terms of editing, the key is enough screen time to allow the performance to convince us of the credibility of the situation. The emphasis throughout the scene is on the character's reaction to the situation, allowing us to follow through the logic of the scene. In every case, editing is subordinate to setting

Figure 4.1 *Modern Times*, 1936. Still provided by British Film Institute.

and performance. Pace is not used for dramatic purposes. Here, too, performance is the key to the pacing.

If one looks at the work of Keaton, Langdon, or Harold Lloyd in the silent period or the Marx Brothers, Abbott and Costello, or other performer-comedians in the sound period, the same editing pattern is apparent. Editing is determined by the persona of the character, and affirmation of that persona is more important than the usual dramatic considerations for editing. In a sense, vaudeville continued in character in the films that starred former vaudeville performers. Beyond the most basic considerations of continuity, the editing in these films could take any pattern as long as it supported the persona of the actor. Within that range, realism and surrealism might mix, and absurdity was as commonplace as realism. This style of film transcends national boundaries, as we see in the films of Jacques Tati and Pierre Etaix of France and the Monty Python films of England.

□ THE MUSICAL

The musical's importance is underlined by the success of *The Jazz Singer* (1927), the first sound picture. As mentioned earlier, however, the early sound films that favored dialogue-intensive plots tended to be little more than filmed plays.

By the early 1930s, however, many directors experimented with camera movement to allow for a more dynamic approach, and post-synchronization (adding sound after production is completed) freed the musical from the constraints of the stage. As early as 1929, King Vidor post-synchronized an entire musical, *Hallelujah* (1929). However, it was the creative choreography of Busby Berkeley in *Gold Diggers of 1933* (1933) that pointed the direction toward the dynamic editing of the musical. Berkeley later became one of the great directors of the musical film.

The musical posed certain challenges for the editor. The first was the integration of a dramatic story with performance numbers. This was most easily solved by using dramatic stories about would-be performers, thus making the on-stage performance appear to be more natural. The second challenge was the vaudeville factor: the need for a variety of routines in the film, comedy routines as well as musical routines. This was the greater challenge because vaudeville routines could not be integrated as easily into the dramatic story as could a few musical numbers. Another dimension from vaudeville was the persona of the character. Such actors as Fred Astaire and Edward Everett Horton had to play particular characters. The role of the editor was to match the assembly of images to the star's persona rather than to the drama itself. Despite these limitations, the musical of the 1930s and beyond became one of the most dynamic and visual of the genres.

A brief examination of *Swing Time* (1936) illustrates the dynamism of the musical. The director, George Stevens, tells the dramatic story of performer-gambler Lucky Garnett (Fred Astaire) and his relationship to performer Penny Carroll (Ginger Rogers). The dramatic story reflects the various stages and challenges of the relationship. This dimension of the film is realistic and affecting, and the editing is reminiscent of *Broken Blossoms* or *The Big Parade*.

The editing of the musical numbers, on the other hand, follows the rhythm of Jerome Kern's music and highlights the personae of Astaire and Rogers. The scale of these numbers is closer to the Ziegfeld Follies than to vaudeville, and consequently, the editing of these numbers could have differed markedly from the editing of the balance of the film. However, because Stevens tended to be a more "realistic" director than Berkeley, these numbers are edited in a manner similar to that of the dramatic portion of the film. There is thus little dissonance between the performance and dramatic sections of the film.

All of the musical numbers—the dancing lesson, the winter interlude, the nightclub sequence, "Bojangles"—have a gentle quality very much in key with Kern's music. Other directors, notably Vincente Minnelli, George Sydney, Stanley Donen, and Gene Kelly, were more physical and assertive in their editing, but this style complemented the persona of frequent star Gene Kelly. Later, directors Robert Wise in *West Side Story* (1961) and Bob Fosse in *Cabaret* (1972) were even freer in their editing, but their editing decisions never challenged the rhythm of the music in their films. The scores were simply more varied, and where the music was intense, the director could choose a more intensified editing style, thus using editing to help underscore the emotions in the music.

The musical was a much freer form to edit than films such as *Modern Times*. The narrative, the persona of the performer-star, and the character of the music influenced the editing style. Together with the strengths of the director of the film, the editing could be "stage-bound" or free.

□ THE THEATRE

Like the musical, the theatre became an important influence on film with the coming of sound. Many plays, such as Oscar Wilde's *The Marriage Circle* (1924), had been produced as silent films, but the prominence of dialogue in the sound movies and the status associated with the stage provided the impetus for the studios to invite playwrights to become screenwriters. Samuel Raphaelson, who wrote *The Jazz Singer*, and Ben Hecht and Charles MacArthur, who wrote *The Front Page* (1931), are among those who accepted. Eugene O'Neill, Maxwell Anderson, and Billy Wilder were also invited to write for the screen.

There was, in the 1930s, a group of playwrights whose work exhibited a new political and social realism. Their form of populist art was well suited to the most populist of mediums: film. The works of Robert Sherwood,

Sidney Kingsley, Clifford Odets, and Lillian Hellman were rapidly adapted to film, and in each case, the playwrights were invited to write the screenplays.

How did these adaptations influence the way the films were edited? Two examples suggest the influence of the theatre and how the transition to film could be made. Kingsley's *Dead End* (1937) and Hellman's *The Little Foxes* (1941) were both directed by William Wyler.

Dead End is the story of adolescents who live in a poor neighborhood in New York. They can go the route of trouble and end up in jail, or they can try to overcome their environment. This naturalistic movie features an ensemble of characters: a gang of youths (as the Dead End Kids, the group went on to make a series of films), an adult who is going "bad," and an adult who is trying to do the right thing. No single character dominates the action. Characters talk about their circumstances and their options. There is some action, but it is very little by the standards of the melodrama or gangster genres. Consequently, the dialogue is very important in characterization and plot advancement.

The editing of this film is secondary to the staging. Cutting to highlight particular relationships and to emphasize significant actions is the extent of the editing for dramatic purposes. Editing is minimalist rather than dynamic. *Dead End* is a filmed play.[5]

In *The Little Foxes*, Wyler moved away from the filmed play. He was greatly aided by a play that is character-driven rather than polemical. The portrayal of the antagonist, Regina (Bette Davis), establishes the relationships within a family as the heart of the play. Behavior can be translated into action as a counterweight to the primacy of dialogue, as in *Dead End*. Because relationships are central to the story, Wyler continually juxtaposed characters in foreground–background, side frame–center frame variations. The editing thus highlights the characters' power relationships or foreshadows changes in those relationships. The editing is not dynamic as in a Pudovkin or an Eisenstein film, but there is a tension that arises from these juxtapositions that is at times as powerful as the tension created by dynamic editing.

Wyler allowed the protagonist–antagonist struggle to develop without relying solely on dialogue, and he used staging of the images to create tension. This method foreshadowed the editing and framing relationships in such Cinemascope films as *East of Eden* (1955).

Although its style of editing is not as dynamic as in such films as *M* nor is it as restricted as in such films as *Dead End*, *The Little Foxes* illustrates a play that has been successfully recreated as a film. Because of the staging and importance of language over action, character over event, in relative terms the film remains more strongly influenced by the conventions of the theatre and less by the evolving conventions of film than were other narrative sources with more dynamic visual treatment. Westerns and traditional gangster films are very visual rather than verbal.

□ RADIO

Whether film or radio was a more popular medium in the 1930s is related to the question of whether film or television is a more popular medium today. There is little question today that the influence of television is broader and, because of its journalistic role, more powerful than film. The situation was similar with radio in the 1930s.

Radio was the instrument of communication for American presidents (for example, Franklin D. Roosevelt's "fireside chats") and for entertainers such as Jack Benny and Orson Welles. In a sense, radio shared with the theatre a reliance on language. Both heightened (or literary) language and naturalistic language were readily found in radio drama. Beyond language, though, radio relied on sound effects and music to create a context for the characters who spoke that dialogue.

Because of its power and pervasiveness, radio was bound to influence film and its newly acquired use of sound. Perhaps no one better personifies that influence than Orson Welles, who came to film from a career in theatre and in radio. Welles is famous for two creative achievements: one in film (*Citizen Kane*, 1941), the other in radio (his 1937 broadcast of H. G. Wells's *The War of the Worlds*).

As Robert Carringer suggests,

Welles' background in radio was one of the major influences on *Citizen Kane*. Some of the influence is of a very obvious nature—the repertory approach, for instance, in which roles are created for specific performers with their wonderfully expressive voices in mind. It can also be seen in the exaggerated sound effects. The radio shows alternated between prestigious literary classics and popular melodrama.

Other examples of the radio influence are more subtle. Overlapping dialogue was a regular feature of the Mercury radio shows, as were other narrative devices used in the film—the use of sounds as aural punctuation, for instance, as when the closing of a door cues the end of a scene, or scene transitions in mid-sentence (a device known in radio as a cross fade), as when Leland, talking to a crowd in the street, begins a thought, and Kane, addressing a rally in Madison Square Garden, completes it.[6]

Indeed, from the perspective of narrative structure, *Citizen Kane* is infused by the influence of radio. The story is told via a narrator, a dramatic shaping device central to radio drama. Welles used five narrators in *Citizen Kane*.[7]

Although the story proceeds as a flashback from Kane's death, it is the various narrators who take us through key events in Kane's life. To put the views of those narrators into context, however, Welles used a newsreel device to take us quickly through Kane's life. With this short newsreel (less than 15 minutes), the film implies that Kane was a real and important man whose personal tragedies superseded his public achievements. The newsreel leaves us with an implicit question, which the first narrator, the newsreel reporter, poses: What was Kane's life all about? The film then shifts from newsreel biography to dramatic mystery. This is achieved through a series of radio drama devices.

In Movietone fashion, a narrator dramatizes a visual montage of Kane's life; language rather than image shapes the ideas about his life. The tone of the narration alternates between hyperbole and fact. "Xanadu, where Kublai Khan decreed his pleasure dome" suggests the quality of Kane's estate, and the reference to "the biggest private zoo since Noah" suggests its physical scale. The language is constantly shifting between two views of Kane: the private man and the public man. In the course of the newsreel, he is called "the emperor of newsprint," a Communist and a Fascist, an imperialist and a pacifist, a failed husband and a failed politician. Throughout, the character of language drives the narrative.

The music throughout the newsreel shifts the focus and fills in what is not being said. Here, too, Welles and composer Bernard Herrmann used music as it was used in radio.

The other narrators in the film—Thatcher, Leland, Bernstein, and Susan (Kane's second wife)—are less forthcoming than the newsreel narrator. Their reluctance helps to stimulate our curiosity by creating the feeling that they know more than they are telling. The tone and language of the other narrators are cautious, circumspect, and suspicious—far from the hyperbole of the newsreel. The implication is dramatically very useful because we expect to learn quite a lot if only they will tell us.

Beyond the dramatic effect of the narration device, the use of five narrators allowed Welles and screenwriter Herman I. Mankiewicz to tell in 2 hours the story of a man whose life spanned 75 years. This is the principle benefit of using the narrators: the collapse of real time into a comprehensive and believable screen time.

This challenge of collapsing time was taken up by Welles in a variety of fascinating ways. Here, too, radio devices are the key. In the famous Kane–Thatcher scene, the completion of one sentence by the same character bridges 17 years. In one shot, Kane is a boy and Thatcher wishes him a curt "Merry Christmas," and in the next shot, seventeen years later, Thatcher is dictating a letter and the dialogue is "and a Happy New Year." Although the device is audacious, the audience accepts the simulation of continuity because the complete statement is a well-known one and both parts fit together. Because Thatcher looks older in the second shot and refers to Kane's 25th birthday, we accept that 17 years have elapsed.

The same principle applies to the series of breakfast table shots that characterize Kane's first marriage. The setting—the breakfast table—and the time—morning—provide a visual continuity while the behavior of Kane and his wife moves from love in the first shot to hostility and silence in the last. In 5 minutes of screen time, Kane and editor Robert Wise collapse eight years of marriage. These brief scenes are a genuine montage of the marriage, providing insights over time—verbal punctuations that, as they change in tone and language, signal the rise and fall of the marriage. Here, too, the imaginative use of sound over image illustrates the influence of radio. See Figure 4.2.

Welles used the sound cut to amuse as well as to inform. As David Bordwell describes it, "When Kane, Leland and Bernstein peer in the Chronicle window, the camera moves up the picture of the Chronicle staff until it fills the screen; Kane's voice says 'Six years ago I looked at a picture of the world's greatest newspaper staff-.-.-.' and he strides out in front of the same men, posed for an identical picture, a flashbulb explodes, and we are at the Inquirer party."[8] Six years pass as Kane celebrates his human acquisitions (he has hired all the best reporters away from his competition) with sufficient wit to distract us from the artificiality of the device.

Finally, like Fritz Lang in *M*, Welles used sound images and sound cuts to move us to a different location. Already mentioned is the shift from Leland in the street to Kane at Madison Square Garden, in which Kane finishes the sentence that Leland had started. The sound level shifts from intimate (Leland) to remote (Kane), as the impassioned Kane tries harder to reach out and move his audience. The quality of the sound highlights the differences between the two locations, just as the literal continuity of the words spoken provides the sense of continuity.

Figure 4.2 *Citizen Kane*, 1941. ©1941 RKO Pictures, Inc. All Rights Reserved. Still provided by British Film Institute.

Another example of location shift together with time shift is the opera scene. Initially Kane's second wife, Susan Alexander, is seen being instructed in singing opera. She is not very good. Her teacher all but throws up his hands. Kane orders him to continue. Susan tries to reach higher notes, even higher in pitch than she has managed so far. In the next shot the orchestration of the music is more elaborate. Susan is reaching for an even higher note. And visually she is on stage surrounded by her fellow actors and singers. The opera is approaching its climax—the death scene.

Again, Welles has used sound to provide both continuity—Susan singing in training to Susan singing in the performance of the opera—and drama—the stakes are far higher in performance than in training. As we anticipate, both Susan and Kane are humiliated by the performance. Just as Kane did not accept the advice of the teacher, he vows not to accept the views of the audience and his main critic, Jed Leland. Only Susan is left trapped in humiliation.

In the opera scene, time and place change quickly, in a single cut, but the dramatic continuity of growing humiliation and loss demark another step in the emotional descent of *Citizen Kane*.

These radio devices introduced by Welles in a rather dramatic fashion in *Citizen Kane* became part of the editor's repertoire, but they awaited the work of Robert Altman and Martin Scorsese, more than 30 years later, to highlight for a new generation of filmmakers the scope of sound editing possibilities and the range that these radio devices provide.

□ NOTES/REFERENCES

1. Sergei Eisenstein, *Film Form: Essays in Film Theory* (New York: Harcourt, Brace and Company, 1949), 195–255.
2. A. Nicholas Vardac, *Stage to Screen* (Cambridge: Harvard University Press, 1949), 1–88.
3. Robert C. Allen, "The Movies in Vaudeville," in *The American Film Industry*, Tino Balio, ed. (Madison: University of Wisconsin Press, 1976), 57–82.
4. Russell Merritt, "Nickolodeon Theaters, 1905–1914: Building an Audience for the Movies," in Balia, *The American Film Industry*, 83–102.
5. The logical conclusion of the approach is the play filmed entirely in a single shot. Hitchcock attempted this in *Rope* (1948). He moved the camera to avoid editing.
6. R. L. Carringer, *The Making of Citizen Kane* (Berkeley: University of California Press, 1985), 100–101.
7. See the full discussion of the film's narrative structure in David Bordwell and Kristin Thompson, *Film Art: An Introduction*, 3d ed. (New York: McGraw-Hill, 1990), 72–84.
8. David Bordwell, "*Citizen Kane*," in B. Nichols, ed., *Movies and Methods: An Anthology* (Berkeley: University of California Press, 1976), 284.

5

Editors Who
Became Directors

■

One of the more interesting career developments in film has been the transition from editors to directors. Two of the most successful, Robert Wise and David Lean, are the subject of this chapter.

Is it necessary and natural for editors to become directors? The answer is no. Is editing the best route to directing? Not necessarily, but editing can be invaluable, as demonstrated by the subjects of this chapter. What strengths do editors bring to directing? Narrative clarity, for one: Editors are responsible for clarifying the story from all of the footage that the director has shot. This point takes on greater meaning in the following sampling of directors who have entered the field from other areas.

From screenwriting, the most famous contemporary writer who has tried his hand at directing is Robert Towne (*Personal Best*, 1982; *Tequila Sunrise*, 1988). Before Towne, notable writer-directors included Nunnally Johnson (*The Man in the Gray Flannel Suit*, 1956) and Ben Hecht (*Specter of the Rose*, 1946). All of these writers are great with dialogue, and their screenplays spark with energy. As directors, however, their work seems to lack pace. Their dialogue may be energetic, but the performances of their actors are too mannered. In short, these exceptional writers are unexceptional directors. This, of course, does not mean that all writers become poor directors; consider Preston Sturges, Billy Wilder, and Joseph Mankiewicz, for example. What it does imply, though, is that the narrative skill of writing doesn't lead directly to a successful directing career.

A similar conclusion can be drawn from cinematography. The visual beauty of the camerawork of Haskell Wexler has not translated into directorial success (*Medium Cool*, 1969); nor have William Fraker (*Monte Walsh*, 1970) or Jack Cardiff (*Sons and Lovers*, 1958) found success. Even Nicolas Roeg (*Don't Look Now*, 1973; *Walkabout*, 1971; *Track 29*, 1989) has a problem with narrative clarity and pace in his directed films, although he has won a following. There are, however, a few exceptions worth noting. Jan de Bout had great success with *Speed* (1994), and Barry Sonnenfield has been developing a distinctive style (*The Addams Family*, 1991, and *Get Shorty*, 1995).

Producers from David Selznick (*A Farewell to Arms*, 1957) to Irwin Winkler (*Guilty by Suspicion*, 1991) have tried to direct with less success than expected. Again, the problems of narrative clarity and pace have defeated their efforts.

Only actors have been as successful as editors in their transition to directors. From Chaplin and Keaton to Charles Laughton (*The Night of the Hunter*, 1955) and recently Robert Redford (*Ordinary People*, 1980) and Kevin Costner (*Dances with Wolves*, 1990), actors have been able to energize their direction, and for them, the problems of pace and clarity have been less glaring. Nor are actors singular in their talents. Warren Beatty has been very successful directing comedy (*Heaven Can Wait*, 1977). Diane Keaton has excelled in psychological drama (*Unstrung Heroes*, 1995), Mel Gibson has excelled in directing action (*Braveheart*, 1995). And Clint Eastwood has crossed genres, directing exceptional Westerns (*Unforgiven*, 1992) and melodrama (*The Bridges of Madison County*, 1995). Most notable in this area has been the work of Elia Kazan, director of *On the Waterfront* and *East of Eden*, who was originally an actor, and John Cassavetes (*Gloria*, 1980; *Husbands*, 1970; *Faces*, 1968).

The key is pace and narrative clarity. These concerns, which are central to the success of an editor, are but one element in the success of a director. Equally important and visible are the director's success with performers and crew, ability to remain on budget (shooting along a time line rather than on the basis of artistic considerations alone), and ability to inspire confidence in the producer. Any of these qualities (and, of course, success with the audience) can make a successful director, but only success with the building blocks of film—the shots and how they are put together—will ensure an editor's success. Again, we come back to narrative clarity and pace, and again these can be important elements for the success of a director.

Thus, editing is an excellent preparation for becoming a director. To test this idea, we now turn to the careers of two directors who began their careers as editors: Robert Wise and David Lean.

□ ROBERT WISE

Wise is probably best known as the editor of Orson Welles's *Citizen Kane* (1941) and *The Magnificent Ambersons* (1942). Within two years, he codirected his first film at RKO. As with many American directors, Wise spent the next 30 years directing in all of the great American genres: the Western (*Blood on the Moon*, 1948), the gangster film (*Odds Against Tomorrow*, 1959), the musical (*West Side Story*, 1961), and the sports film (*The Set-Up*, 1949). He also ventured into those genres made famous in Germany: the horror film (*The Body Snatcher*, 1945), the science-fiction film (*The Day the Earth Stood Still*, 1951), and the melodrama (*I Want to Live!*, 1958).

These directorial efforts certainly illustrate versatility, but our purpose is to illustrate how his experience as an editor was invaluable to his success as a director. To do so, we will look in detail at three of his films: *The Set-Up, I Want to Live!*, and *West Side Story*. We will also refer to *Somebody Up There Likes Me* (1956), *The Day the Earth Stood Still*, and *The Body Snatcher*.

When one looks at *Citizen Kane* and *The Magnificent Ambersons*, the work of the editor is very apparent. Aside from audacious cutting that draws attention to technique ("Merry Christmas-.-.-.-and a Happy New Year"), the breakfast scene and the opening introduction to the characters and the town stand out as tours de force, set-pieces that impress us. They contribute to the narrative but also stand apart from it, as did the Odessa Steps sequence in *Potemkin* (1925). Although this type of scene is notable in many of Wise's directorial efforts, the deeper contribution of the editor to the film is not to be intrusive, but rather to edit the film so that the viewer is clearly aware of the story and its evolution, not the editing.

The tension between the invisible editor and the editor of consciously audacious sequences is a tension that runs throughout Wise's career as a director. The equivalents of the breakfast scene in *Citizen Kane* emerge often in his work: the fight in *The Set-Up*, the dance numbers in *West Side Story*, and the opening of *I Want to Live!* As his career as a director developed, he was able to integrate the sequences into the narrative and make them revealing. A good example of this is the sampan blockade of the American ship in *The Sand Pebbles* (1966).

Another use Wise found for the set-piece is to elaborate a particular idea through editing. For example, in *The Day the Earth Stood Still*, Wise communicated the idea that every nation on Earth can be unified in the face of a great enough threat. To elaborate this idea, he cut sound and picture to different newsrooms around the world. The announcers speak different languages, but they are all talking about the same thing: an alien has landed, threatening everyone on the planet. Finally, the different nationalities are unified, but it has taken an alien threat to accomplish that unity. The idea is communicated through an editing solution, not quite a set-piece, but an editing idea that draws some attention to itself.

Wise used the same editing approach in *Somebody Up There Likes Me* to communicate the wide support for Rocky Graziano in his final fight. His family, his Hell's Kitchen friends, and his new fans are all engaged in "praying" at their radios that his fate in the final fight will mean something for their fate. By intercutting between all three groups, Wise lets us know how many people's dreams hang on the dream of one man. Here, too, the editing solution communicates the idea. Not as self-conscious as the breakfast scene in *Citizen Kane*, this sequence is nevertheless a set-piece that has great impact.

The principle of finding an editing solution to an idea surfaces early in Wise's career as a director. In *The Body Snatcher*, Wise had to communicate that Grey (the title character) has resorted to murder to secure a body for dissection at the local medical school. We don't see the murder, just the street singer walking through the foggy night-bound Edinburgh street. Her voice carries on. Grey, driving his buggy, follows. Both disappear. We see the street and hear the voice of the street singer. The shot holds (continues visually), as does the voice, and then nothing. The voice disappears. The visual remains. We know that the girl is dead and a new body will be provided for "science." The scene has the elements of a set-piece, an element of self-consciousness, and yet it is extremely effective in heightening the tension and drama of the murder that has taken place beyond our sight.

We turn now to a more detailed examination of three of Wise's films, beginning with *The Set-Up*.

THE SET-UP (1949)

The Set-Up is the story of Stoker Thompson's last fight. Stoker is 35 and nearing the end of his career; he is low on the fight card but has the will to carry on. He fights now in a string of small towns and earns little money.

This screen story takes place entirely on the evening of the fight. Stoker's manager has agreed to have his fighter lose to an up-and-coming boxer, Tiger Nelson. But the manager, greedy and without confidence in Stoker, keeps the payoff and neglects to tell Stoker he is to lose.

Struggling against the crowd, against his wife who refuses to watch him beaten again, and against his manager, Stoker fights, and he wins. Then he faces the consequences. He has been true to himself, but he has betrayed the local gangster, Little Boy, and he must pay the price. As the film ends, Stoker's hand is broken by Little Boy, and the fighter acknowledges that he'll never fight again.

The Set-Up may be Wise's most effective film. The clarity of story is unusual, and a powerful point of view is established. Wise managed to establish individuals among the spectators so that the crowd is less impersonal and seems composed of individuals with lives before and after the fight. As a result, they take on characteristics that make our responses to Stoker more varied and complex.

Like *Citizen Kane*, the narrative structure poses an editing problem. With *Citizen Kane*, two hours of screen time must tell the story of one man's 75-year life. In *The Set-Up*, the story takes place in one evening. Wise chose to use screen time to simulate real time. The 72 minutes of the film simulate those 70 or so minutes of the fight, the time leading up to it, and its aftermath. As much as possible, Wise matched the relationship between real time and screen time.

That is not to say that *The Set-Up* is a documentary. It is not. It is a carefully crafted dramatization of a critical point in Stoker's life: his last fight.

To help engage us with Stoker's feelings and his point of view, Wise used subjective camera placement and movement. We see what Stoker sees, and we begin to feel what he must feel. Wise was very pointed about point of view in this film.

This film is not exclusively about Stoker's point of view, however. Wise was as subjective about Stoker's wife and about seven other secondary characters or groups of characters and their points of view. All witness the fight, but some have a direct interest: the manager, his assistant, and Little Boy and his contingent. Five spectators are highlighted: a newspaper seller (probably a former boxer), a blind man, a meek man, an obese man, and a belligerent housewife. With the exceptions of the newspaper seller and the obese man, all have companions whose behavior stands out in contrast to their own.

The film introduces each of these spectators before the fight and cuts away to them continually throughout the fight. The camera is close and looks down or up at them (it is never neutral). Wise used an extreme close-up only when the housewife yells to Stoker's opponent, "Kill him!" All of the spectators seem to favor Nelson with much verbal and physical expression. If they could be in the ring themselves, they would enjoy the ultimate identification. Only when the fight begins to go against Nelson do they shift allegiances and yell their support for Stoker. The spectators do not appear superficially to be bloodthirsty, but their behavior in each case speaks otherwise.

Wise carried the principle of subjectivity as far as he could without drawing too much attention to it. He used silence as Hitchcock did in *Blackmail*. Before the fight, individual disparaging comments about his age and his chances are heard by Stoker. As he spars with his opponent, the two become sufficiently involved with one another that they can actually exchange words in spite of the din. Between rounds, Stoker is so involved in regrouping his physical and mental resources that for a few brief seconds, he hears nothing. Almost total silence takes over until the bell rings Stoker, and us, back into the awareness that the next round has begun. Sound continues to be used invasively. It surrounds, dominates, and then recedes to simulate how Stoker struggles for some mastery within his environment.

In *The Set-Up*, Wise suggested that Stoker's inner life with its tenacious will to see himself as a winner contrasts with his outer life, his life in society, which views him as a fighter in decline, one step removed from being a discard of society. So great is the derision toward him from the spectators that the audience begins to feel that they too struggle with this inner life–outer life conflict and they don't want to identify with a loser. These are the primary ideas that Wise communicates in this film, and by moving away from simple stereotypes with most of the people in the story, he humanizes all of them. These ideas are worked out with editing solutions. Both picture and sound, cutaways and close-ups, are used to orchestrate these ideas.

I WANT TO LIVE! (1958)

In *I Want to Live!*, Wise again dealt with a story in which the inner life of the character comes into conflict with society's view of that person (Figure 5.1). In this case, however, the consequences of the difference are dire. In the end, the main character is executed by society for that difference.

Barbara Graham enjoys a good time and can't seem to stay out of trouble. She perjures herself casually and thus begins her relationship with the law.

Figure 5.1   *I Want to Live!,* 1958. ©1958 United Artists Corporation. All rights reserved. Still provided by Museum of Modern Art/Film Stills Archives.

She lives outside the law but remains a petty criminal until circumstance leads her to be involved with two men in a murder charge. Now a mother, her defiant attitude leads to a trial where poor judgment in a man again deepens her trouble. This time she is in too far. She is sentenced to be executed for murder. Although a psychologist and reporter try to save her, they are too late. The film ends shortly after she has been executed for a murder she did not commit.

I Want to Live! is a narrative that takes place over a number of years. Wise's first challenge was to establish an approach or attitude that would set the tone but also allow for an elaborate narrative. Wise created the equivalent of a jazz riff. Set to Gerry Mulligan's combo performance, he presented a series of images set in a jazz club. The combo performs. The customers pair off, drink, and smoke. This is an atmosphere that tolerates a wide band of behavior, young women with older men, young men at the margin of the law. A policeman enters looking for someone, but he doesn't find her. Only his determination singles him out from the rest.

This whole sequence runs just over 2 minutes and contains fewer than 20 shots. All of the images get their continuity from two sources: the combo performance and the off-center, deep-focus cinematography. All of the images are shot at angles of up to 30 degrees. The result is a disjointed, unstable feeling. There is unpredictability here; it's a visual presentation of an off-center world, a world where anything can happen. There is rhythm but no logic here, as in a jazz riff. The pace of the shots does not help. Pace can direct us to a particular mood, but here the pace is random, not cueing us about how to feel. Randomness contributes to the overall mood. This is Barbara Graham's world. This opening sequence sets the tone for what is to follow in the next 2 hours.

After this prologue, Wise still faced the problem of a screen story that must cover the next 8 to 10 years. He chose to straight-cut between scenes that illustrate Graham's steady decline. He focused on those periods or decisions she made that took her down the road to execution. All of the scenes center around her misjudgments about men. They include granting ill-considered favors, committing petty crime, marrying a drug addict, returning to criminal companions, and a murder charge for being found with those companions. Once charged, she mistrusts her lawyer but does trust a policeman who entraps her into a false confession about her whereabouts on the night of the murder. Only when it is too late does her judgment about a male psychologist and a male reporter suggest a change in her perception, but by relentlessly snubbing her nose at the law and society, she dooms herself to death (this was, after all, the 1950s).

By straight-cutting from scene to scene along a clear narrative that highlights the growing seriousness of her misjudgments, Wise blurred the time issue, and we accept the length of time that has passed. There are, however, a few notable departures from this pattern—departures in which Wise introduced an editorial view. In each case, he found an editing solution.

An important idea in *I Want to Live!* is the role of the media, particularly print and television journalism, and the role they played in condemning Graham. Wise intercut the murder trial with televised footage about it. He also intercut direct contact between Graham and the print press, particularly Ed Montgomery. By doing this, Wise found an editing solution to the problem of showing all of the details of the actual trial on screen and also found a way to illustrate the key role the media played in finding Graham guilty. This is the same type of intercutting seen in *The Day the Earth Stood Still* and *Somebody Up There Likes Me*.

Another departure is the amount of screen time Wise spent on the actual execution. The film meticulously shows in close-up all of the details of the execution: the setting, its artifacts, the sulfuric acid, how it works, the cyanide, how it works, how the doctor checks whether Barbara is dead. All of these details show an almost clinical sense of what is about to happen to Barbara and, in terms of the execution, of what does happen to her. This level of detail draws out the prelude to and the actual execution. The objectivity of this detail, compared to the randomness of the jazz riff, is excruciating and inevitable—scientific in its predictability. This sequence is virtually in counterpoint to the rest of the film. As a result, it is a remarkably powerful sequence that questions how we feel about capital punishment. The scientific presentation leaves no room for a sense of satisfaction about the outcome. Quite the contrary, it is disturbing, particularly because we know that Graham is innocent.

The detail, the pace, and the length of the sequence all work to carry the viewer to a sense of dread about what is to come, but also to editorialize about capital punishment. It is a remarkable sequence, totally different from the opening, but, in its way, just as effective. Again, Wise found an editing solution to a particular narrative idea.

WEST SIDE STORY (1961)

Leonard Bernstein's *West Side Story* (1961) is a contemporary musical adaptation of Shakespeare's *Romeo and Juliet*. Instead of the Montagues and the Capulets, however, the conflict is between two New York street gangs: the Sharks and the Jets (Figure 5.2). The Sharks are Puerto Rican. Their leader is Bernardo (George Chakiris). The Jets are American, although there are allusions to their ethnic origins as well. Their leader is Riff (Russ Tamblyn). The Romeo and Juliet of the story are Tony (Richard Beymer), a former Jet, and Maria (Natalie Wood), Bernardo's sister. They fall in love, but their love is condemned because of the animosity between the two gangs. When Bernardo kills Riff in a rumble, Tony kills Bernardo in anger. It's only a matter of time before that act of street violence results in his own death.

West Side Story was choreographed by Jerome Robbins, who codirected the film with Robert Wise. Although the film is organized around a Romeo and Juliet narrative and Bernstein's brilliant musical score, the editing is audacious, stylized, and stimulating.

The opening sequence, the introduction to New York and the street conflict of the Sharks and the Jets, runs 10 minutes with no dialogue. In these 10 minutes, the setting and the conflict are introduced in a spirited way. Wise began with a series of helicopter shots of New York. There are no street sounds here, just the serenity of clear sightlines down to Manhattan. For 80 seconds, Wise presented 18 shots of the city from the helicopter. The camera looks directly down on the city. The movement, all of it right to left, is gentle and slow, almost elegant. Little sound accompanies these camera movements. Many familiar sights are visible, including the Empire State Building and the United Nations. We move from commercial sights to residential areas. Only then do we begin to descend in a zoom and then a dissolve.

The music comes up, not too loud. We are in a basketball court between two tenements. A pair of fingers snap and we are introduced to Riff, the

Figure 5.2 *West Side Story*, 1961. ©1961 United Artists Pictures, Inc. All rights reserved. Still provided by British Film Institute.

leader of the Jets, and then to another Jet and then to a group of Jets. The earlier cutting had no sound cues; now the cuts occur on the beat created by the snap of fingers. The Jets begin to move right to left, as the helicopter did. This direction is only violated once—to introduce the Jets' encounter with Bernardo, a Shark. The change in direction alludes to the conflicts to come.

The film switches to the Sharks, and as Bernardo is joined by his fellow gang members, they are introduced in close-ups, now moving left to right. When the film cuts to longer shots, we notice that the Sharks are photographed with less context and more visual entrapment. For example, as they move up alleys, the walls on both sides of the alley trap them in midframe. This presentation of the Sharks also differentiates them from the Jets, who appear principally in midshot with context and with no similar visual entrapment.

The balance of the sequence outlines the escalating conflict between the two gangs. They taunt and interfere with each other's activities. Throughout, the Jets are filmed from eye level or higher, and the Sharks are usually filmed from below eye level. The Jets are presented as bullies exploiting their position of power, and the Sharks are shown in a more heroic light. The sequence culminates in an attack by the Sharks on John Boy, who has been adding graffiti to Shark iconography. For the first time in the sequence, the Sharks are photographed from above eye level as they beat and maim John Boy. This incident leads to the arrival of the police and to the end of this 10-minute introduction. The conflict is established.

Because of the length of this sequence, the editing itself had to be choreographed to explain fully the conflict and its motivation and to differentiate the two sides. Wise was even able to influence us to side with the outsiders, the Sharks, because of the visual choices he made: the close-ups, the sense of visual entrapment, and the heroic camera angle. All suggest that we identify with the Sharks rather than with the Jets.

The other interesting sequence in *West Side Story* is the musical number "Tonight." As with the opera sequence in *Citizen Kane* and the fight sequence in *Somebody Up There Likes Me*, Wise found a unifying element, the music or the sounds of the fight, and relied on the sound carry-over throughout the sequence to provide unity.

"Tonight" includes all of the components of the story. Bernardo, Riff, the Sharks, and the Jets get ready for a rumble; Tony and Maria anticipate the excitement of being with one another, Anita prepares to be with Bernardo after the fight, and the lieutenant anticipates trouble. Wise constructed this sequence slowly, gradually building toward the culmination of everyone's expectations: the rumble. Here he used camera movement, camera direction, and increasingly closer shots (without context) to build the sequence. He also used a faster pace of editing to help build excitement.

Whereas in the opening sequence, pace did not play a very important role, in the "Tonight" sequence, pace is everything. Cross-cutting between the gangs at the end of the song takes us to the moment of great anticipation—the rumble—with a powerful sense of preparation; the song has built up anticipation and excitement for what will happen next. The music unifies this sequence, but it is the editing that translates it emotionally for us.

□ DAVID LEAN

Through his experience in the film industry, including his time as an assistant editor and as an editor, David Lean developed considerable technical skill. By the time he became codirector of *In Which We Serve* (1942) with Noel Coward, he was ready to launch into directing. As a director, he developed a visual strength and a literary sensibility that makes his work more complex than the work of Robert Wise. Lean's work is both more subtle and more ambitious. His experience as an editor is demonstrable in his directing work. Although Lean made only 15 films in a career of more than 40 years, many of those films have become important in the popular history of cinema. His pictorial epics, *Lawrence of Arabia* (1962) and *Doctor Zhivago* (1965), remain the standard for this type of filmmaking. His romantic films, *Brief Encounter* (1945) and *Summertime* (1955), are the standard for that type of filmmaking. His literary adaptations, *Great Expectations* (1946) and *Hobson's Choice* (1954), are classics, and *The Bridge on the River Kwai* (1957) remains an example of an intelligent, entertaining war film with a message. Lean may have made few films, but his influence has far exceeded those numbers. The role of editing in his films may help explain that influence.

To establish context for his influence, it is critical to acknowledge Lean's penchant for collaborators: Noel Coward worked on his first three films, Anthony Havelock Allan and Ronald Neame collaborated on the films that followed, and Robert Bolt and Freddie Young worked on *Lawrence of Arabia* and the films that followed (except *Passage to India*, 1984). Also notable are Lean's visual strengths. Few directors have created more extraordinary visualizations in their films. The result is that individual shots are powerful and memorable. The shots don't contradict Pudovkin's ideas about the interdependency of shots for meaning, but they do soften the reliance on pace to shape the editorial meaning of the shots. Lean seems to have been able to create considerable impact without relying on metric montage. That is not to say that there is no rhythm to his scenes. When he wished to use pace, he did so carefully (as he did in the British captain's war memories in *Ryan's Daughter* [1970]). However, Lean seems to have been sufficiently self-assured as a director that his films rely less on pace than is the case with many other directors.

To consider his work in some detail, we will examine *Brief Encounter*, *Great Expectations*, *The Bridge on the River Kwai*, *Lawrence of Arabia*, and *Doctor Zhivago*.

LEAN'S TECHNIQUE

Directors who are powerful visualists are memorable only when their visuals serve to deepen the story. The same is true about sound. Good directors involve us with the story rather than with their grasp of the technology. Editing is the means used to illuminate the story's primary meaning as well as its levels of meaning. By looking at Lean's style, we can see how he managed to use the various tools of editing.

Sound

In his use of sound, Lean was very sophisticated. He used the march, whistled and orchestrated, in *The Bridge on the River Kwai*, and in each case, its meaning was different. His use of Maurice Jarre's music in *Lawrence of Arabia*, *Doctor Zhivago*, and *Ryan's Daughter* is probably unprecedented in its popular impact. However, it is in the more subtle uses of sound that Lean illustrated his skill. Through an interior monologue, Laura acts first as narrator and then confessor in *Brief Encounter*. Her confession creates a rapid identification with her.

A less emphatic use of sound occurs in *Great Expectations*. As Pip's sister is insulting the young Pip, Lean blurred the insults with the sound of an instrument. The resulting distortion makes the insults sound as if they were coming from an animal rather than a human. She is both menacing and belittled by the technical pun.

A similar surprise occurs in an action sequence in *The Bridge on the River Kwai*. British commandos are deep in the Burmese forest. Their Burmese guides, all women, are bathing. A Japanese patrol happens upon them. The commandos hurl grenades and fire their machine guns. As the noise of murder grows louder, the birds of the area fly off frightened, and as Lean cut visuals of the birds in flight, the sound of the birds drown out the machine guns. At that instant, nature quite overwhelms the concerns of the humans present, and for that moment, the outcome of human conflict seems less important.

Narrative Clarity

One of the problems that editing attempts to address is to clarify the story line. Screen stories tend to be told from the point of view of the main character. There is no confusion about this issue in Lean's stories. Not only was he utterly clear about the point of view, he introduced us to that point of view immediately. In *Great Expectations*, Pip visits the graveyard of his parents and runs into a frightening escaped convict (who later in the story becomes his surrogate father). The story begins in a vivid way; the point of view subjectively presented is that of the young boy. Through the position of the camera, Lean confirmed Pip's point of view. We see from his perspective, and we interpret events as he does: The convict is terrifying, almost as terrifying as his sister.

Lean proceeds in a similar fashion in *Lawrence of Arabia*. The film opens with a 3-minute sequence of Lawrence mounting his motorbike and riding through the British countryside. He rides to his death. Was it an accident, or, given his speed on this narrow country road, was it willful? Who was this man? Because the camera is mounted in front of him and sees what he sees, this opening is entirely subjective and quite powerful. By its end, we are involved, and the character has not said a word.

In *Brief Encounter*, the opening scene is the last time that the two lovers, Laura (Celia Johnson) and Alex (Trevor Howard), will be together. Because of a chatty acquaintance of Laura's, they can't even embrace one another. He leaves, and she takes the train home, wondering whether she should confess all to her husband. This ending to the relationship becomes the prologue to her remembrance of the whole relationship, which is the subject of the film. We don't know everything after this prologue, but we know the point of view—Laura's—and the tone of loss and urgency engages us in the story. The point of view never veers from Laura. Lean used a similar reminiscence prologue in another romantic epic, *Doctor Zhivago*.

Subjective Point of View

The use of subjective camera placement has already been mentioned, but subjective camera placement alone doesn't account for the power Lean's sequences can have. The burial scene in *Doctor Zhivago* illustrates this point. In 32 shots running just over 3 minutes, Lean re-created the 5-year-old Yuri Zhivago's range of feelings at the burial of his mother.

The sequence begins in extreme long shot. The burial party proceeds. Two-thirds of the frame are filled by sky and mountains. The procession is a speck on a landscape. The film cuts to a moving track shot in front of a 5-year-old child. In midshot, at the boy's line of vision, we see him march behind a casket carrying his mother. He can barely see her shape. Soon, he stands by the graveside. A priest presides over the ceremony. Adults are in attendance, but the boy sees only his mother and the trees. When she is covered and then lowered into the ground, he imagines her under the ground, he sees her, he is beside her (given the camera's point of view), and he is aware of the rustle of trees. There is much feeling in this scene, yet Yuri does not cry. He doesn't speak, but we understand his depth of feeling and its lack of comprehension. We are with him. Camera, editing, and music have created these insights into the young Yuri at this critical point in his life.

The subjective point of view is critical if the narrative is to be clear and compelling.

Narrative Complexity

A clear narrative doesn't mean a simple narrative. Indeed, one characteristic of Lean's work that continues to be apparent as his career unfolds is that he is interested in stories of great complexity: India, Arabia, Ireland during troubled times. Even his literary adaptations are ambitious, and he always faces the need to keep the stories personally engaging.

The consequence has been a style that takes advantage of action sequences that occur in the story when they add to the story. The revolt of the army against its officers in *Doctor Zhivago* adds meaning to the goal of the revolution—the destruction of the class hierarchy—and this is central to the fate of Yuri and Lara. Can love transcend revolution?

The two sequences involving the capture of the convict-patron in *Great Expectations* also share complex narrative goals. In the first sequence, Pip is the witness to the soldier's tracking down the man to whom he had brought food. The sequence is filled with sky and the foreboding of the marsh fog. Later in the story, Pip himself is trying to save the convict from capture. He has come to view this man as a father, and he feels obligated to help. Now, at sea again, the escape is foiled by soldiers. The dynamism of this sequence is different from the first sequence, but it is horrifying in another way. It confirms the impossibility of rising above one's circumstances, a goal Pip has been attempting for 20 years of his short life. The action, the escape attempt, is dynamic, but its outcome is more than failure; it becomes a comment on social opportunity.

Pace

Lean did not rely on pace as much as other directors working in similar genres. That is not to say that the particular sequences he created don't rely on the tension that more rapid pace implies. It's just that it is rare in his films. One such sequence whose success does rely on pace is all the more powerful because it's a complex sequence, and as the climax of the film, it is crucial to its success: the climax of *The Bridge on the River Kwai*.

The group of three commandos has arrived in time to destroy the bridge as the Japanese troop train crosses it. They had laid explosive charges under the bridge that night. Now they await day and the troop train. The injured commando (Jack Hawkins) is atop the hill above the bridge. He will use mortars to cover the escape. A second commando (Geoffrey Horne) is by the river, ready to detonate the charge that will destroy the bridge. The third (William Holden) is on the other side of the river to help cover his colleagues' escape.

It is day, and there are two problems. First, the river's water level has gone down, and some of the detonation wires are now exposed. Second, the proud Colonel Nicholson (Alec Guinness) sees the wires and is concerned about the fate of the bridge. He is proud of the achievement. His men have acted as men, not prisoners of war. Nicholson has lost sight of the fact that his actions, helping the enemy, might be treason. He calls to Saito (Sessue Hayakawa), the Japanese commander, and together they investigate the source of the demolition wires. He leads Saito to the commando on demolition. The intercutting between the discovery and the reaction of the other commandos—"Use your knife, boy" (Hawkins) and "Kill him" (Holden)—leads in rapid succession to Saito's death and to the commando's explanation that he is here to destroy the bridge and that he's British, too. The explanation is to no avail. Nicholson calls on the Japanese to help. The commando is killed. Holden swims over to kill Nicholson, but he too is killed. Hawkins launches a mortar that seriously injures Nicholson, who, at the moment of death, ponders on what he has done. The troop train is now crossing the bridge. Nicholson falls on the detonator and dies. The bridge explodes, and the train falls into the Kwai River. The mission is over. All of the commandos but one are dead, as are Nicholson and Saito. The British doctor (a prisoner of war of the Japanese) comments on the madness of it all. Hawkins reproaches himself by throwing the mortar into the river. The film ends.

The tension in this long scene is complex, beginning with whether the mission will be accomplished and how. Who will survive? Who will die? The outcomes are all surprising, and as the plot turns, the pacing increases and builds to the suspenseful end.

Lean added to the tension by alternately using subjective camera placement and extreme long shots and midshots. The contrast adds to the building tension of the scene.

LEAN'S ART

Like all directors, David Lean had particular ideas or themes that recurred in his work. How he presented those themes or integrated them into his films is the artful dimension of his work.

Lean made several period films and used exotic locations as the backdrop for his stories. For him, the majesty of the human adventure lent a certain perspective that events and behavior are inscrutable and noble, the very opposite to the modern day penchant for scientific rationalism. Whether this means that he was a romantic or a mystic is for others to determine; it does mean that nature, the supernatural, and fate all play roles, sometimes cruel roles, in his films. He didn't portray cruelty in a cynical manner but rather as a way of life. His work is the opposite of films by such people as Stanley Kubrick for whom technology played a role in meeting and molding nature.

How does this philosophy translate into his films? First, the time frame of his film is large: 20 years in *Great Expectations* and *Lawrence of Arabia*, 40 years in *Doctor Zhivago*. Second, the location of his films is also expansive. *Oliver Twist* (1948) ranges from countryside to city. *Lawrence of Arabia* ranges from continent to continent. The time and the place always have a deep impact on the main character. The setting is never decorative but rather integral to the story.

A powerful example of Lean's use of time, place, and character can be found in *Lawrence of Arabia*. In one shot, Lawrence demonstrates his ability to withstand pain. He lights a match and, with a flourish, douses it with his fingers. As the flame is extinguished, the film cuts to an extreme long shot of the rising sun in the desert. The bright red glow dominates the screen. In the lower part of the screen, there are a few specks, which are identified in a follow-up shot as Lawrence and a guide. The cut from a midshot of the match to an extreme long shot of the sun filling the screen is shocking but also exhilarating. In one shot, we move five hundred miles into the desert. We are also struck in these two shots by the awesome, magnificent quality of nature and of the insignificance of humanity. Whether this wonderment speaks to a supernatural order or to Lawrence's fate in the desert, we don't know, but all of these ideas are generated by the juxtaposition of two images. The cut illustrates the power of editing to generate a series of ideas from two shots. This is Lean's art: to lead us to those ideas through this juxtaposition.

An equally powerful but more elaborate set of ideas is generated by the attack on the Turkish train in *Lawrence of Arabia*. Using 85 shots in 6 minutes and 40 seconds, Lean created a sense of the war in the desert. The visuals mix beauty (the derailment of the train) and horror (the execution of the wounded Turkish soldier). The sequence is dynamic and takes us through a narrative sequence: the attack, its details, the aftermath, its implications for the next campaign, Lawrence's relationship to his soldiers. When he is wounded, we gain an insight into his masochistic psychology. Immediately thereafter, he leaps from train car to train car, posing shamelessly for the American journalist (Arthur Kennedy). In the sequence, we are presented with the point of view of the journalist, Lawrence, Auda (Anthony Quinn), Sharif Ali (Omar Sharif), and the British captain (Anthony Quayle).

This sequence becomes more than a battle sequence; Lean infused it with his particular views about heroes and the role they play in war (Figure 5.3). The battle itself was shot using many point-of-view images, principally Lawrence's point of view. Lean also used angles that give the battle a

Figure 5.3 *Lawrence of Arabia.* Copyright © 1962, Revised 1990, Columbia Pictures Industries, Inc. All rights reserved. Still courtesy British Film Institute.

sense of depth or context. This means compositions that have foreground and background. He also juxtaposed close and medium shots with extreme long shots. Finally, Lean used compositions that include a good deal of the sky—low angles—to relate the action on the ground to what happens above it. Looking up at the action suggests a heroic position. This is particularly important when he cut from a low angle of Lawrence atop the train to a high-angle tracking shot of Lawrence's shadow as he leaps from train car to train car. By focusing on the shadow, he introduced the myth as well as the man. The shot is a vivid metaphor for the creation of the myth. This battle sequence of less than 7 minutes, with all of its implied views about the nature of war and the combatants, also contains a subtextual idea about mythmaking, in this case, the making of the myth of Lawrence of Arabia. This, too, is the art of Lean as editor-director.

David Lean and Robert Wise provide us with two examples of editors who became directors. To take us more deeply into the relationship of the editor and the director, we turn now to the work of Alfred Hitchcock.

6

Experiments in Editing:
Alfred Hitchcock

■

Few directors have contributed as much to the mythology of the power of editing as has Alfred Hitchcock. Eisenstein and Pudovkin used their films to work out and illustrate their ideas about editing, but Hitchcock used his films to synthesize the theoretical ideas of others and to deepen the repertoire by showcasing the possibilities of editing. His work embraces the full gamut of editing conceits, from pace to subjective states to ideas about dramatic and real time. This chapter highlights a number of set-pieces that he devoted to these conceits. Before beginning, however, we must acknowledge that Hitchcock may have experimented extensively with editing devices, but he was equally experimental in virtually every filmic device available to him.

Influenced by the visual experiment of F. W. Murnau and G. W. Pabst in the expressionist Universum Film Aktiengesellschaft (UFA) period, Hitchcock immediately incorporated the expressionist look into his early films. Because of the thematic similarities, elements of his visual style recur from *Blackmail* (1929) to *Frenzy* (1972). Particularly notable in the areas of set design and special effects are *Spellbound* (1945) and *The Birds* (1963). In *Spellbound*, Hitchcock turned to Salvador Dali to create the sets that represented the dreams of the main character, an amnesiac accused of murder. The sets represented a primary key to his repressed observations and feelings. Although not totally faithful to the tenets of psychoanalysis, Hitchcock's visualization of the unconscious remains a fascinating experiment. Equally notable for its visual experiments is the animation in *The Birds*. This tale of nature's revenge on humanity relies on the visualization of birds attacking people. The attack was created with animation. Again, the impulse to find the visual equivalent of an idea led Hitchcock to blend two areas of flimmaking—imaginative animation with live action—to achieve a synthesized filmic reality.

Hitchcock experimented with color in *Under Capricorn* (1949) and *Marnie* (1964). In *Rear Window* (1954), he made an entire film shot from the point of view of a man confined to a wheelchair in his apartment. Robert Montgomery experimented with subjective camera placement in *Lady in the*

Lake (1946), but rarely had subjectivity been used as effectively as in *Rear Window*. Hitchcock was less successful in his experiment to avoid editing in *Rope* (1948), but the result is quite interesting. In this film, camera movement replaces editing; Hitchcock continually moved his camera to follow the action of the story.

Turning to Hitchcock's experiments in editing, what is notable is the breadth and audacity of the experimentation. Ranging from the subjective use of sound in *Blackmail*, which was discussed in Chapter 3, to the experiment in terror in the shower scene in *Psycho* (1960), Hitchcock established very particular challenges for himself, and the result has a sophistication in editing rarely achieved in the short history of film. To understand that level of sophistication, it is necessary to examine first the orthodox nature of Hitchcock's approach to the storytelling problem and then to look at how editing solutions provided him with exciting aesthetic challenges.

☐ A SIMPLE INTRODUCTION: PARALLEL ACTION

Strangers on a Train (1951) is the story of two strangers who meet on a train; one is a famous tennis player (Farley Granger), the other is a psychopath (Robert Walker). Bruno, the psychopath, suggests to Guy that if they murdered the person who most hampers the progress of the other's life, no one would know. There would be no motive.

So begins this story of murder, but before the offer is made, Hitchcock introduced us to the two strangers in a rather novel way. Using parallel editing, Hitchcock presented two sets of feet (we see no facial shots). One is going right to left, the other left to right, in a train station. The only distinguishing feature is that one of them wears the shoes of a dandy, the other rather ordinary looking shoes. Through parallel cutting between the movements right to left and left to right, we get the feeling that the two pairs of shoes are approaching one another. A shot of one of the men walking away from the camera toward the train dissolves to a moving shot of the track. The train is now moving. The film then returns to the intercutting of the two sets of feet, now moving toward each other on one car of the train. The two men seat themselves, still unidentified. The dandy accidentally kicks the other and finally the film cuts to the two men seated. The conversation proceeds.

In this sequence of 12 shots, Hitchcock used parallel action to introduce two strangers on a train who are moving toward one another. As is the case in parallel action, the implication is that they will come together, and they do.

□ A DRAMATIC PUNCTUATION: THE SOUND CUT

Hitchcock found a novel way to link the concepts of trains and murders in *The 39 Steps* (1935). Richard Hannay (Robert Donat) has taken into his home a woman who tells him she is a spy and is being followed; she and the country are in danger. He is woken up by the woman, who now has a knife in her back and a map in her hand. To escape a similar fate, he pretends to be a milkman, sidesteps the murderers who are waiting for him, and takes a train to Scotland, where he will follow the map she has given him.

Hitchcock wanted to make two points: that Hannay is on his way to Scotland and that the murder of his guest is discovered. He also wanted to link the two points together as Hannay will now be a suspect in the murder investigation. The housekeeper opens the door to Hannay's apartment. In the background, we see the woman's body on the bed. The housekeeper screams, but what we hear is the whistle of the train. In the next shot, the rushing train emerges from a tunnel, and we know that the next scene will take place on the train.

The key elements communicated here are the shock of the discovery of the body and the transition to the location of the next action, the train. The sound carry-over from one shot to the next and its pitch punctuate how we should feel about the murder and the tension of what will happen on the train and beyond. Hitchcock managed in this brief sequence to use editing to raise the dramatic tension in both shots considerably, and their combination adds even more to the sense of expectation about what will follow.

□ DRAMATIC DISCOVERY: CUTTING ON MOTION

This sense of punctuation via editing is even more compelling in a brief sequence in *Spellbound*. John Ballantine (Gregory Peck) has forgotten his past because of a trauma. He is accused of posing as a psychiatrist and of killing the man he is pretending to be. A real psychiatrist (Ingrid Bergman) loves him and works to cure him. She has discovered that he is afraid of black lines across a background of white. Working with his dream, she is convinced that he was with the real psychiatrist who died in a skiing accident. She takes her patient back to the ski slopes where he can relive the traumatic event, and he does. As they ski down the slopes, the camera follows behind them as they approach a precipice. The camera cuts closer to Ballantine and then to a close-up as the moment of revelation is acknowledged. The film cuts to a young boy sliding down an exterior stoop. At the base of the stoop sits his younger brother. When the boy collides with his brother, the young child is propelled onto the lattice of a surrounding fence and is killed. In a simple cut, from motion to motion, Hitchcock cut from present to past, and the continuity of visual motion and dramatic revelation provides a startling moment of discovery.

□ SUSPENSE: THE EXTREME LONG SHOT

In *Foreign Correspondent* (1940), Johnnie Jones (Joel McCrea) has discovered that the Germans have kidnapped a European diplomat days before the beginning of World War II. The rest of the world believes that the diplomat was assassinated in Holland, but it was actually a double who was killed. Only Jones knows the truth. Back in London, he attempts to expose the story and unwittingly confides in a British politician (Herbert Marshall) who secretly works for the Nazis. Now Jones's own life is threatened. The politician assigns him a guardian, Roley, whose actual assignment is to kill him. Roley leads him to the top of a church (a favorite Hitchcock location), where he plans to push Jones to his death.

Roley holds a schoolboy up to see the sights below more clearly. The film cuts to a vertical shot that emphasizes how far it is to street level. The boy's hat blows off, and Hitchcock cut to the hat blowing toward the ground. The distance down is the most notable element of the shot. The schoolboys leave, and Jones and Roley are alone until a tourist couple interferes with Roley's plans. Shortly, however, they are alone again. Jones looks at the sights. The next shot shows Roley's outstretched hands rushing to the camera until we see his hands in close-up. Hitchcock then cut to an extreme long shot of a man falling to the ground. We don't know if it's Jones, but as the film cuts to pedestrians rushing about on the ground, a sense of anticipation builds about Jones's fate. Shortly, we discover that Jones has survived because of a sixth sense that made him turn around and sidestep Roley. For the moment that precedes this information, there is a shocking sense of what has happened and a concern that someone has died. Hitchcock built the suspense here by cutting from a close-up to an extreme long shot.

□ LEVELS OF MEANING: THE CUTAWAY

In *The 39 Steps*, Hannay is on the run from the law. He has sought refuge for the night at the home of a Scottish farmer. The old farmer has a young wife that Hannay mistakes for his daughter. When the three of them sit down for dinner, the farmer prays. Hannay, who has been reading the paper, notices an article about his escape and his portrayal as a dangerous murderer. As he puts down the paper at the table, the farmer begins the prayer. The farmer, suspecting a sexual attraction developing between his young wife and Hannay, opens his eyes as he repeats the prayer. Hannay tries to take his mind away from his fear. He eyes the wife to see if she suspects. Here, the film cuts to the headlined newspaper to illustrate Hannay's concern. The next shot of the wife registers Hannay's distraction, and as her eyes drift down to the paper, she realizes that he is the escaped killer. Hitchcock then cut to a three-shot showing the farmer eyeing Hannay and the wife now acknowledging visually the shared secret. These looks, however, confirm for the husband that the sexual bond between Hannay and the wife will soon strengthen. He will turn out this rival, not knowing that the man is wanted for a different crime.

In this sequence, the cutaway to the newspaper solidifies the sense of concern and communication between Hannay and the wife and serves to mislead the husband about their real fears and feelings.

□ INTENSITY: THE CLOSE-UP

In *Notorious* (1946), Alicia (Ingrid Bergman) marries Alex (Claude Rains) in order to spy on him. She works with Devlin (Cary Grant). Alex is suspected of being involved in nefarious activities. He is financed by former Nazis in the pursuit of uranium production. He is the leading suspect pursued by Devlin and the U.S. agency he represents. Alicia's assignment is to discover what that activity is. When she becomes suspicious of a locked wine cellar in the home, she alerts Devlin. He suggests that she organize a party where, if she secures the key, he will find out about the wine cellar.

In a 10-minute sequence, Hitchcock created much suspense about whether Devlin will find out about the contents of the cellar, whether Alicia will be unmasked as a spy, and whether it will be Alex's jealousy or a shortage of wine at the party that will unmask them. Alicia must get the key to Devlin, and she must show him to the cellar. Once there, he must find out what is being hidden there.

In this sequence, Hitchcock used subjective camera placement and movement to remind us about Alex's jealousy and his constant observation of Alicia and Devlin's activities. Hitchcock used the close-up to emphasize the heightened importance of the key itself and of the contents of a shattered bottle. He also used close-up cutaways of the diminishing bottles of party champagne to alert us to the imminence of Alex's need to go to the wine cellar. These cutaways raise the suspense level about a potential uncovering of Alicia and Devlin.

Hitchcock used the close-up to alert us to the importance to the plot of the key and of the bogus wine bottles and their contents. The close-up also increases the tension building around the issue of discovery.

□ THE MOMENT AS ETERNITY: THE EXTREME CLOSE-UP

There is perhaps no sequence in film as famous as the shower scene in *Psycho*.[1] The next section details this sequence more precisely, but here the use of the extreme close-up will be the focus of concern.

The shower sequence, including prologue and epilogue, runs 2 minutes and includes 50 cuts. The sequence itself focuses on the killing of Marion Crane (Janet Leigh), a guest at an off-the-road motel run by Norman Bates (Anthony Perkins). She is on the run, having stolen $40,000 from her employer. She has decided to return home, give the money back, and face the consequences, but she dies at the hands of Norman's "mother."

The details of this scene, which takes place in the shower of a cheap motel bathroom, are as follows: the victim, her hands, her face, her feet, her torso, her blood, the shower, the shower head, the spray of water, the bathtub, the shower curtain, the murder weapon, the murderer.

Aside from the medium shots of Crane taking a shower and the murderer entering the inner bathroom, the majority of the other shots are close-ups of particular details of the killing. When Hitchcock wanted to register Crane's shock, her fear, and her resistance, he resorted to an extreme close shot of her mouth or of her hand. The shots are very brief, less than a second, and focus on a detail of the preceding, fuller shot of Crane. When Hitchcock wanted to increase the sense of shock, he cut to a subjective shot of the murder weapon coming down at the camera. This enhances the audience's shock and identification with the victim. The use of the extreme close-ups and the subjective shots makes the murder scene seem excrutiatingly long. This sequence seems to take an eternity to end.

□ DRAMATIC TIME AND PACE

In real time, the killing of Marion Crane would be over in seconds. By disassembling the details of the killing and trying to shock the audience with the killing, Hitchcock lengthened real time. As in the Odessa Steps sequence in *Potemkin*, the subject matter and its intensity allow the filmmaker to alter real time.

The shower scene begins with a relaxed pace for the prologue: the shots of Crane beginning her shower. This relaxed pacing returns after the murder itself, when Marion, now dying, slides down into the bathtub. With her last breath, she grabs the shower curtain and falls, pulling the curtain down over her. These two sequences—in effect, the prologue and epilogue to the murder—are paced in a regular manner. The sequence of the murder itself and its details rapidly accelerate in pace. The shot that precedes the murder runs for 16 seconds, and the shot that follows the murder runs for 18 seconds. In between, there are 27 shots of the details of the murder.

These shots together run a total of 25 seconds, and they vary from half a second—12 frames—to up to one second—24 frames. Each shot is long enough to be identifiable. The longer shots feature the knife and its contact with Crane. The other shots of Crane's reaction, her shock, and the blood are shorter. This alternating of shorter shots of the victim and longer shots of the crime is exaggerated by the use of point-of-view shots: subjective shots that emphasize Crane's victimization. Pace and camera angles thus combine to increase the shock and the identification with the victim.

Although this sequence is a clear example of the manipulative power of the medium, Hitchcock has been praised for his editing skill and his ability to enhance identification. As Robin Wood suggests about the shower sequence, "The shower bath murder [is] probably the most horrific incident in any fiction film."[2] Wood also claims that "*Psycho* is Hitchcock's ultimate achievement to date in the technique of audience participation."[3]

□ THE UNITY OF SOUND

The remake of *The Man Who Knew Too Much* (1956) is commendable for its use of style to triumph over substance. If *Psycho* is the ultimate audience picture, filled with killing and nerve-wrenching unpredictability, *The Man Who Knew Too Much* is almost academic in its absence of emotional engagement despite the story of a family under threat. Having witnessed the killing of a spy, Dr. McKenna (James Stewart) and his wife Jo (Doris Day) are prevented from telling all they know when their son is kidnapped. The story begins in Marrakesh and ends in London, the scene of the crime.

Although we are not gripped by the story, the mechanics of the style are underpinned by the extensive use of sound, which is almost unmatched in any other Hitchcock film. This is best illustrated by looking at three sequences in the film.

In one sequence, Dr. McKenna is following up on information that the kidnappers have tried to suppress. McKenna was told by the dying spy to go to Ambrose Chapel to find the would-be killers of the prime minister. He mistakenly goes to Ambrose Chappell, a taxidermist, and doesn't realize that it is a false lead. He expects to find his son.

In this sequence, Hitchcock relies on a very low level of sound. Indeed, compared to the rest of the film, this sequence is almost silent. The audience is very aware of this foreboding silence. The result is the most tense sequence in the film. Hitchcock used moving camera shots of McKenna going warily toward the address. The streets are deserted except for one other man. The two eye each other suspiciously (we find out later that he is Ambrose Chappell, Jr.).

The isolation of McKenna, who is out of his own habitat in search of a son he fears he'll never see again, is underscored by the muted, unorchestrated sound in the sequence.

Another notable sequence is one of the last in the film. The assassination of the prime minister has been foiled, and the McKennas believe that their last chance is to go to the foreign embassy where they suspect their son is being held. At an embassy reception, Jo, a former star of the stage, is asked to sing.

She selects "Que Sera, Sera," a melody that she sang to the boy very early in the film. She sings this lullaby before the diplomatic audience in the hope of finding her son.

The camera moves out of the room, and Hitchcock began a series of shots of the stairs leading to the second floor. As the shots vary, so does the tone and loudness of the song. The level of sound provides continuity and also indicates the distance from the singer. Finally, on the second floor, Hitchcock cut to a door, and then to a shot of the other side of the door. Now we see the boy trying to sleep. His mother's voice is barely audible.

The sequence begins a parallel action, first of the mother trying to sing louder and then the boy with his captor, Mrs. Drayton, beginning to hear and to recognize his mother.

Once that recognition is secure, the boy fluctuates between excitement and frustration. His captor encourages him to whistle, and the sound is heard by mother and father. Dr. McKenna leaves to find his son; Jo continues to sing. We know that the reunion is not far off. The unity of this sequence and the parallel action is achieved through the song.

The final sequence for this discussion is the assassination attempt, which takes place at an orchestra concert at Albert Hall. This rather droll, symphonic shooting is the most academic of the sequences; the unity comes from the music, which was composed and conducted by Bernard Herrmann. In just under $12\frac{1}{2}$ minutes, Hitchcock visually scored the assassination attempt.

The characters of Hitchcock's symphony are Jo McKenna, her husband, the killer, his assistant, the victim, the prime minister and his party, conductor Herrmann, his soloist, his orchestra (with special emphasis on the cymbalist), and, of course, the concert-goers.

Hitchcock cut between all of these characters, trying to keep us moving through the symphony, which emphasizes the assassination with a clash of the cymbals. Through Jo, Hitchcock tried to keep the audience alert to the progress of the assassination attempt: the positioning of the killer, the raising of the gun. To keep the tension moving, Dr. McKenna arrives a few moments before the assassination, and it is his attempt to stop the killer that adds a little more suspense to the proceedings.

Hitchcock accelerated the pace of the editing up to the instant of the killing and the clash of the cymbals, which the killers hope will cover the noise of the gun being fired. Just before the clash, Jo screams, and the gunman fires prematurely. Her scream prompts the prime minister to move, and in doing so, he is wounded rather than killed by the shot. Although the death of the assassin follows after the struggle with Dr. McKenna, the tension is all but over once the cymbals clash. As in the other two sequences,

Figure 6.1   *North by Northwest*, 1959. ©1959 Turner Entertainment Company.
All Rights Reserved. Still provided by Moving Image and Sound
Archives.

the unity comes from the sound: in this case, the symphony performed in
Albert Hall.

□ THE ORTHODOXY OF THE VISUAL: THE CHASE

The famous cornfield sequence in *North by Northwest* (1959) is unembel-
lished by sound (Figure 6.1). Without using music until the end of the
sequence, Hitchcock devoted a $9\frac{1}{2}$-minute sequence to man and machine:
Roger Thorndike (Cary Grant) chased by a biplane. As usual in Hitchcock's
films, the death of one or the other is the goal.

In this sequence of 130 shots, Hitchcock relied less on pace than one might
expect in this type of sequence. In a sense, the sequence is more reminiscent
of the fun of the Albert Hall sequence in *The Man Who Knew Too Much*
than of the emotional power of the shower sequence in *Psycho*. It may be
that Hitchcock enjoyed the visual challenge of these sequences and his film
invites us to enjoy the abstracted mathematics of the struggle. The odds are
against the hero, and yet he triumphs in the cornfield and in Albert Hall. It's
the opposite of the shower sequence: triumph rather than torture.

In the cornfield sequence, Hitchcock used much humor. After Thorndike is dropped off on an empty Iowa road, he waits for a rendezvous with George Caplan. We know that Caplan will not come. Indeed, his persecutors think Thorndike is Caplan. Cars pass him by. A man is dropped off. Thorndike approaches him, asking whether he is Caplan. He denies it, saying he is waiting for a bus. Just as the bus arrives, he tells Thorndike that the biplane in the distance is dusting crops, but there are no crops there. This humor precedes the attack on Thorndike, which follows almost immediately.

Throughout the attack, Thorndike is both surprised by the attack and pleased by how he thwarts it. It is not until he approaches a fuel truck that the attack ends; but not before he is almost killed by the truck. As the biplane crashes into the truck, the music begins. With the danger over, the music grows louder, and Thorndike makes his escape by stealing a truck from someone who has stopped to watch the fire caused by the collision.

In this sequence of man versus machine, the orthodoxy of the visual design proceeds almost mathematically. The audience feels a certain detached joy. Without the organization of the sound, the battle seems abstract, emotionally unorchestrated. The struggle nevertheless is intriguing, like watching a game of chess; it is an intellectual battle rather than an emotional one.

The sequence remains strangely joyful, and although we don't relate to it on the emotional level of the shower scene, the cornfield sequence remains a notable accomplishment in pure editing.

□ DREAMSTATES: SUBJECTIVITY AND MOTION

Perhaps no film of Hitchcock's is as complex or as ambitious as *Vertigo* (1958), which is the story of a detective, Scottie (James Stewart), whose fear of heights leads to his retirement (Figure 6.2). The detective is hired by an old classmate to follow his wife, Madelaine (Kim Novak), whom he fears is suicidal, possessed by the ghost of an ancestor who had committed suicide. She does commit suicide by jumping from a church tower, but not before Scottie has fallen in love with her. Despondent, he wanders the streets of San Francisco until he finds a woman who resembles Madelaine and, in fact, is the same woman. She, too, has fallen in love, and she allows him to re-create her into the image of his lost love, Madelaine. They become the same, but in the end, he realizes that, together with Madelaine's husband, she duped him. They knew he couldn't follow her up the church stairs because of his fear of heights. He was the perfect witness to a "suicide." Having uncovered the murder, he takes her back to the church tower, where she confesses and he overcomes his fear of heights. In the tower, however, she accidentally falls to her death, and Scottie is left alone to reflect on his obsession and his loss.

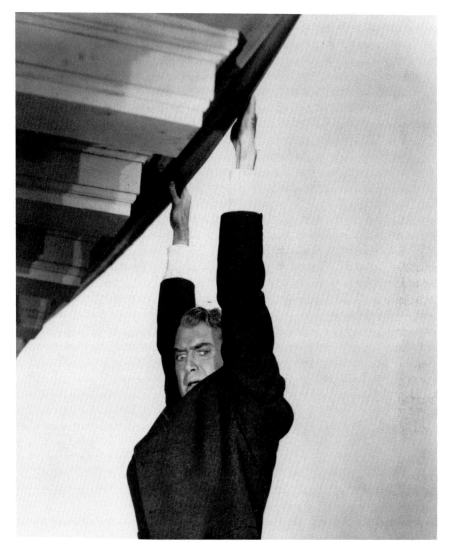

Figure 6.2   *Vertigo*, 1958. Copyright © by Universal City Studios, Inc. Courtesy
of MCA Publishing Rights, a Division of MCA Inc. Still provided by
Museum of Modern Art/Film Stills Archives.

This very dark story depends on the audience's identification with Scottie.
We must accept his fear of heights and his obsession with Madelaine. His
states of delusion, love, and discovery must all be communicated to us
through the editing.

At the very beginning of the film, Hitchcock used extreme close-ups and
extreme long shots to establish the source of Scottie's illness: his fear of

heights. Hitchcock cut from his hand grabbing for security to long shots of Scottie's distance from the ground. As Scottie's situation becomes precarious late in the chase, the camera moves away from the ground to illustrate his loss of perspective. Extreme close-ups, extreme long shots, and subjective camera movement create a sense of panic and loss in his discovery of his illness. The scene is shocking not only for the death of a policeman but also for the main character's loss of control over his fate. This loss of control, rooted in the fear of heights, repeats itself in the way he falls in love with Madelaine. Assigned to follow her, he falls in love with her by watching her.

Scottie's obsession with Madelaine is created in the following way. Scottie follows Madelaine to various places—a museum, a house, a gravesite—and he observes her from his subjective viewpoint. This visual obsession implies a developing emotional obsession. What he is doing is far beyond a job. By devoting so much film to show Scottie observing Madelaine, Hitchcock cleverly forced the audience to relate to Scottie's growing obsession.

A midshot, full face shot of Scottie in the car is repeated as the base in these sequences. The follow-up shots of Madelaine's car moving down the streets of San Francisco are hypnotic because we see only a car, not a close-up or a midshot of Madelaine. All we have that is human is the midshot of Scottie. With these sequences, Hitchcock established Scottie's obsession as irrational—given his distance from Madelaine—as his fear of heights.

Another notable sequence takes place in the church tower where Madelaine commits suicide as Scottie watches, unable to force himself up the stairs. Scottie's fear of heights naturally plays a key role. The scene is shot from his point of view. He sees Madelaine quickly ascend the stairs. She is a shadow, moving rapidly. He looks up at her feet and body as they move farther away. Scottie's point of view is reinforced with crosscut shots of Scottie looking down. The distance is emphasized. When he is high enough, the fear sets in, and as in the first sequence, the sense of perspective changes as a traveling shot emphasizes the apparent shifting of the floor. These shots are intercut with his slowing to a stop on the stairs. The fear grows.

The ascending Madelaine is then intercut with the slowing Scottie and the ascending floor. Soon Scottie is paralyzed, and rapidly a scream and a point-of-view shot of a falling body follow. Madelaine is dead.

Point of view, pace, and sound combine in this sequence to create the sense of Scottie's panic and then resigned despair because he has failed. The editing has created that sense of panic and despair. All that now remains is for *Vertigo* to create the feeling of rebirth in Scottie's increasingly interior dream world.

This occurs after Scottie has insisted that Judy allow herself to be dressed and made up to look like Madelaine. Once her hair color is dyed and styled to resemble Madelaine's, the following occurs.

From Scottie's point of view, Judy emerges from the bedroom into a green light. Indeed, the room is bathed in different colors from green to red. She emerges from the light and comes into focus as Madelaine reborn. Scottie embraces her and seems to be at peace. He kisses her passionately, and the camera tracks around them. In the course of this 360-degree track, with the two characters in medium shot, the background of the room goes to black behind them. Later in the track, the stable where Scottie and Madelaine originally embraced comes into view. As the track continues, there is darkness and the hotel room returns as the background. In the course of this brief sequence, love and hope are reborn and Scottie seems regenerated.

Because this is a Hitchcock film, that happiness will not last. The scene in the church tower quickly proceeds, and this time Judy dies.

In the sequence featuring Judy's make-over as Madelaine, Hitchcock used subjectivity, camera motion, and the midshot in deep focus to provide context. The editing of the scene is not elaborate. The juxtapositions between shots and within shots are all that is necessary.

☐ CONCLUSION

Hitchcock was a master of the art of editing. He experimented and refined many of the classic techniques developed by Griffith and Eisenstein. Not only did he experiment with sound and image, but he enjoyed that experimentation. His enjoyment broadened the editor's repertoire while giving immeasurable pleasure to film audiences. His was a unique talent.

☐ NOTES/REFERENCES

1. This statement could be challenged using the Odessa Steps sequence in *Potemkin* or the final shoot-out in *The Wild Bunch* (1969). All are sequences about killing, and their relationship to Eisenstein's ideas and films must be acknowledged. Which is the greatest seems to be beside the point; all are remarkable.
2. Robin Wood, *Hitchcock's Films Revisited* (New York: Columbia University Press, 1989), 146.
3. Ibid., 147.

7

New Technologies

■

The 1950s brought many changes to film. On the economic front, the Consent decrees of 1947 (antitrust legislation that led to the studios divesting themselves of the theatres they owned) and the developing threat of television suggested that innovation, or at least novelty, might help recapture the market for film. As was the case with the coming of sound in the late 1920s, new innovations had considerable impact on how films were edited, and the results tended to be conservative initially and innovative later.

This chapter concentrates on two innovations, each of which had a different impact on film. The first was the attraction to the wide screen, including the 35-mm innovations of Cinerama, CinemaScope, Vistavision, and Panavision and the 70-mm innovations of TODD-AO, Technirama, Supertechnirama, MGM 65, and, later, Imax. Around the world, countries adopted similar anamorphic approaches, including Folioscope. If the goal of CinemaScope and the larger versions was to increase the spectacle of the film experience, the second innovation, cinema verité, with its special lighting and unobtrusive style, had the opposite intention: to make the film experience seem more real and more intimate, with all of the implications that this approach suggested.

Both innovations were technology-based, both had a specific goal in mind for the audience, and both had implications for editing.

☐ THE WIDE SCREEN

To give some perspective to the wide screen, it is important to realize that before 1950 films were presented in Academy aspect ratio; that is, the width-to-height ratio of the viewing screen was 1:1.33 (Figure 7.1).

This ratio was replicated in the aperture plate for cameras as well as projectors. There were exceptions. As early as 1927, Abel Gance used a triptych approach, filming particular sequences in his *Napoleon* (1927) with three cameras and later projecting the images simultaneously. The result was quite spectacular (Figure 7.2).

In these sequences, the aspect ratio became 1:3. The impact of editing in these sequences was startling. How did one use a close-up? What happened when the camera moved? Was a cut from movement to movement so

Figure 7.1 Academy aspect ratio.

Figure 7.2 Triptych format.

jarring or awkward that the strength of these editing conventions became muted? The difficulties of Gance's experiment didn't pose a challenge for film-makers because his triptych technique did not come into wide use. Other filmmakers continued to experiment with screen shape. Eisenstein advocated a square screen, and Claude Autant-Lara's *Pour Construire un Feu* (1928) introduced a wider screen in 1928 (the forerunner of CinemaScope). The invention of CinemaScope itself took place in 1929. Dr. Henri Chretien developed the anamorphic lens, which was later purchased by 20th Century–Fox.

It was not until the need for innovation became economically necessary that a procession of gimmicks, including 3-D, captured the public's attention. The first wide-screen innovation of the period was Cinerama. This technique was essentially a repeat of Gance's idea: three cameras record simultaneously, and a similar projection system (featuring stereophonic sound) gave the audience the impression of being surrounded by the sound and the image.[1] Cinerama was used primarily for travelogue-type films with simple narratives. These travelogues were popular with the public, and at least a few narrative films were produced in the format. The most notable was *How the West Was Won* (1962). The system was cumbersome, however, and the technology was expensive. In the end, it was not economically viable.

20th Century–Fox's CinemaScope, however, was popular and cost effective, and it did prove to be successful. Beginning with *The Robe* (1953), CinemaScope appeared to be viable and the technology was rapidly copied by other studios. Using an anamorphic lens, the scenes were photographed on the regular 35-mm stock, but the image was squeezed. When projected normally, the squeezed image looked distorted, but when projected with an anamorphic lens, the image appeared normal but was presented wider than before (Figure 7.3).

The other notable wide-screen process of the period was VistaVision, Paramount Pictures' response to CinemaScope. In this process, 35-mm film was run horizontally rather than vertically. The result was a sharper image and greater sound flexibility. The recorded image was twice as wide as the conventional 35-mm frame and somewhat taller. For VistaVision, Paramount selected a modified wide-screen aspect ratio of 1:1.85, the aspect ratio later adopted as the industry standard.

Figure 7.3   CinemaScope. Aspect ratio 1:2.55 (later reduced to 1:2.35).

The larger 70-mm, 65-mm, TODD-AO, and Panavision 70 formats had an aspect ratio of 1:2.2, with room on the film for four magnetic soundtracks. Not only did the larger frame make possible a bigger sound, but it also allowed sharper images despite the size of the screen. Imax is similar to VistaVision in that it records 70-mm film run horizontally. Unlike Vista-Vision, which had a normal vertical projection system, Imax is projected horizontally and consequently requires its own special projection system. Its image is twice as large as the normal 70-mm production, and the resultant clarity is striking.

Of all of the formats, those that were economically viable were the systems that perfected CinemaScope technology, particularly Panavision. The early CinemaScope films exhibited problems with close-ups and with moving shots. By the early 1960s, when Panavision supplanted Cinema-Scope and VistaVision, those imperfections had been overcome, and the wide-screen had become the industry standard.[2]

Today, standard film has an aspect ratio of 1:1.85; however, films that have special releases—the big-budget productions that are often shot in anamorphic 35-mm and blown up to 70-mm—are generally projected 1:2.2 so that they are wider screen presentations. Films such as *Hook* (1991) or *Terminator 2* (1991) are projected in a manner similar to the early CinemaScope films, and the problems for the editor are analogous.[3]

In the regular 1:1.33 format, the issues of editing—the use of close-ups, the shift from foreground to background, and the moving shot—have been developed, and both directors and audiences are accustomed to a particular pattern of editing. With the advent of a frame that was twice as wide, all of the relationships of foreground and background were changed.

In Figure 7.4, two characters, one in the foreground and the other in the background, are shown in two frames, one a regular frame and the other a CinemaScope frame. In the CinemaScope frame, the characters seem farther apart, and there is an empty spot in the frame, creating an inner rectangle. This image affects the relationship implied between the two characters. The foreground and background no longer relate to one another in the same way because of the CinemaScope frame. Now the director also has the problem of the middle ground. The implications for continuity and dramatic meaning are clear. The wider frame changes meaning. The director and editor must recognize the impact of the wider frame in their work.

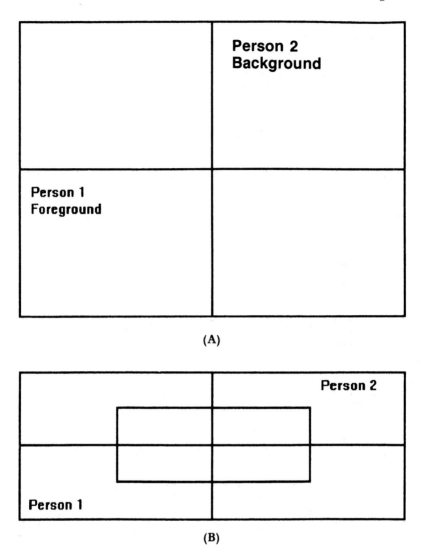

Figure 7.4 Foreground–background relationship in (A) Academy and (B) wide-screen formats.

The width issue plays equal havoc for other continuity issues: match cuts, moving shots, and cuts from extreme long shot to extreme close-up. In its initial phase, the use of the anamorphic lens was problematic for close-ups because it distorted objects and people positioned too close to the camera. Maintaining focus in traveling shots, given the narrow depth of field of the lens, posed another sort of problem. The result, as one sees in the first CinemaScope film, *The Robe*, was cautious editing and a slow-paced style.

Some filmmakers attempted to use the wide screen creatively. They demonstrated that new technological developments needn't be ends unto themselves, but rather opportunities for innovation.

CHARACTER AND ENVIRONMENT

A number of filmmakers used the new wide-screen process to try to move beyond the action-adventure genres that were the natural strength of the wide screen. Both Otto Preminger and Anthony Mann made Westerns using CinemaScope, and although Mann later became one of the strongest innovators in its use, Preminger, in his film *River of No Return* (1954), illustrated how the new foreground–background relationship within the frame could suggest a narrative subtext critical to the story.

River of No Return exhibits none of the fast pacing that characterizes the dramatic moments in the Western *Shane* (1953), for example. Nor does it have the intense close-ups of *High Noon* (1952), a Western produced two years before *River of No Return*. These are shortcomings of the wide-screen process. What *River of No Return* does illustrate, however, is a knack for using shots to suggest the character's relationship to their environment and to their constant struggle with it. To escape from the Indians, a farmer (Robert Mitchum), his son, and an acquaintance (Marilyn Monroe) must make their way down the river to the nearest town. The rapids of the river and the threat of the Indians are constant reminders of the hostility of their environment. The river, the mountains, and the valleys are beautiful, but they are neither romantic nor beckoning. They are constant and indifferent to these characters. Because the environment fills the background of most of the images, we are constantly reminded about the characters' context.

Preminger presented the characters in the foreground. The characters interact, usually in medium shot, in the foreground. We relate to them as the story unfolds; however, the background, the environment, is always present. Notable also is the camera placement. Not only is the camera placed close to the characters, but the eye level is democratic. The camera neither looks down or up at the characters. The result doesn't lead us; instead, it allows us to relate to the characters more naturally.

The pace of the editing is slow. Preminger's innovation was to emphasize the relationship of the characters to their environment by using the film format's greater expanse of foreground and background.

Preminger developed this relationship further in *Exodus* (1960). Again, the editing style is gradual even in the set-piece: the preparation for and the attack on the Acre prison. Two examples illustrate how the use of foreground and background sets up a particular relationship while avoiding the need to edit (Figure 7.5).

Early in the film, Ari Ben Canaan (Paul Newman) tries to take six hundred Jews illegally out of Cyprus to Palestine. His effort is thwarted by the British Navy. When the British major (Peter Lawford) or his commanding officer

Figure 7.5   *Exodus*, 1960. ©1960 United Artists Pictures, Inc. All Rights
Reserved. Still provided by Moving Image and Sound Archives.

(Ralph Richardson) communicate with the *Exodus*, they are presented in
the foreground, and the blockaded *Exodus* is presented in the same frame
but in the background.

Later in the film, Ari Ben Canaan is showing Kitty, an American nurse
(Eva Marie Saint), the location of his home. The scene takes place high atop
a mountain overlooking the Jezreel Valley, the valley in which his home is
located as well as the village of his Arab neighbors. In this shot, Ari explains
to the nurse about the history of the valley, and the two of them acknowledge
their attraction to one another. Close to the camera, Ari and Kitty speak and
then embrace. The valley they speak about is visible in the background.
Other filmmakers might have used an entire sequence of shots, including
close-ups of the characters and extreme long shots of the valley. Preminger's
widescreen shot thus replaces an entire sequence.

RELATIONSHIPS

In *East of Eden* (1955), Elia Kazan explored the relationship of people to
one another rather than their relationship to the environment. The film con-
siders the barriers between characters as well as the avenues to progress in
their relationships.

East of Eden is the story of the "bad son" Cal (James Dean). His father
(Raymond Massey) is a religious moralist who is quick to condemn his

actions. The story begins with Cal's discovery that the mother he thought dead is alive and prospering as a prostitute in Monterey, 20 miles from his home.

Kazan used extreme angles to portray how Cal looks up to or down on adults. Only in the shots of Cal with his brother, Aaron, and his fiancee, Abra (Julie Harris), is the camera nonjudgmental, presenting the scenes at eye level. Whenever Cal is observing one of his parents, he is present in the foreground or background, and there is a barrier—blocks of ice or a long hallway, for example—in the middle. Kazan tilted the camera to suggest the instability of the family unit. This is particularly clear in the family dinner scene. This scene, particularly the attempt of father and son to be honest about the mother's fate, is the first sequence where cutting between father and son as they speak about the mother presents the distance between them. The foreground–background relationship is broken, and the two men so needy of one another are separate. They live in two worlds, and the editing of this sequence portrays that separateness as well as the instability of the relationship.

One other element of Kazan's approach is noteworthy. Kazan angled the camera placement so that the action either approaches the camera at an angle or moves away from the camera. In both cases, the placement creates a sense of even greater depth. Whereas Preminger usually had the action take place in front of the camera and the context directly behind the action of the characters, there appears a studied relationship of the two. Kazan's approach is more emotional, and the extra sense of depth makes the wide-screen image seem even wider. On one level, Kazan may have been exploring the possibilities, but in terms of its impact, this placement seems to increase the space, physical and emotional, between the characters.

RELATIONSHIPS AND THE ENVIRONMENT

No director was more successful in the early use of the wide-screen format than John Sturges, whose 1955 film *Bad Day at Black Rock* is an exemplary demonstration that the wide screen could be an asset for the editor. Interestingly, Sturges began his career as an editor.

John McCready (Spencer Tracy) is a one-armed veteran of World War II. It is 1945, and he has traveled to Black Rock, a small desert town, to give a medal to the father of the man who died saving his life. The problem is that father and son were Japanese-Americans, and this town has a secret. Its richest citizen, Reno Smith (Robert Ryan), and his cronies killed the father, Kimoko, in a drunken rage after the attack on Pearl Harbor. The townspeople try to cover up this secret, but McCready quickly discovers the truth. In 48 hours, McCready's principal mission, to give the Medal of Honor to a parent, turns into a struggle for his own survival.

The characters and the plot of Sturges's film are tight, tense, and terse. In terms of style, Sturges used almost no close-ups, and yet the tension and emotion of the story remain powerful. Sturges achieved this tension through his intelligent use of the wide screen and his application of dynamic editing in strategic scenes.

Two scenes notable for their dynamic editing are the train sequence that appears under the credits and the car chase scene in the desert. The primary quality of the train sequence is the barrenness of the land that the train travels through. There are no people, no animals, no signs of settlement. The manner in which Sturges filmed the train adds to the sense of the environment's vastness. Shooting from a helicopter, a truck and a tracking shot directly in front of the train, Sturges created a sense of movement. By alternating between angled shots that demonstrate the power of the train breaking through the landscape and flat shots in which train and landscape seem flattened into one, Sturges alternated between clash and coexistence. His use of high angles and later low angles for his shots adds to the sense of conflict.

Throughout this sequence, then, the movement and variation in camera placement and the cutting on movement creates a dynamic scene in which danger, conflict, and anticipation are all created through the editing. Where is the train going? Why would it stop in so isolated a spot? This sequence prepares the audience for the events and the conflicts of the story.

After introducing us to John McCready, Sturges immediately used the wide screen to present his protagonist in conflict with almost all of the townspeople of Black Rock. Sturges did not use close-ups; he favored the three-quarter shot, or American shot. This shot is not very emotional, but Sturges organized his characters so that the constant conflict within the shots stands in for the intensity of the close-up.

For example, as McCready is greeted by the telegraph operator at the train station, he flanks the left side of the screen, and the telegraph operator flanks the right. The camera does not crowd McCready. Although he occupies the foreground, the telegraph operator occupies the background. In the middle of the frame, the desert and the mountains are visible. The space between the two men suggests a dramatic distance between them. As in other films, Sturges could have fragmented the shot and created a sequence, but here he used the width of the frame to provide dramatic information within a single shot without editing.

Sturges followed the same principle in the interiors. As McCready checks into the hotel, he is again on the left of the frame, the hotel clerk is on the right, and the middle ground is unoccupied. Later in the same setting, the sympathetic doctor occupies the background, local thugs occupy the middle of the frame, and the antagonist, Smith, is in the left foreground. Sturges rarely left a part of the frame without function. When he used angled shots, he suggested power relationships opposed to one another, left to right, foreground to background. When he used flatter shots, those conflicting forces faced off against one another in a less interesting way, but nevertheless in opposition. Rather than relying on the clash of images to suggest conflict and emotional tension, Sturges used the wide-screen spaces and their organization to suggest conflict. He avoided editing by doing so, but the power and relentlessness of the conflict is not diminished because the power within the story is constantly shifting, as reflected in the visual compositions. By using the wide screen in this way, Sturges avoided editing until he really needed it. When he did resort to dynamic editing, as in the car chase, the sequence is all the more powerful as the pace of the film dramatically changes.

By using the wide screen fully as a dramatic element in the film, Sturges created a story of characters in conflict in a setting that can be used by those characters to evoke their cruelty and their power. The wide screen and the editing of the film both contribute to that evocation.

THE BACKGROUND

Max Ophuls used CinemaScope in *Lola Montes* (1955). Structurally interesting, the film is a retrospective examination of the life of Lola Montes, a nineteenth-century beauty who became a mistress to great musicians and finally to the King of Bavaria. The story is told in the present. A dying Lola Montes is the main attraction at the circus. As she reflects on her life, performers act out her reminiscences. Flashbacks of the younger Lola and key phases are intercut with the circus rendition of that phase. Finally, her life retold, Lola dies.

Ophuls, a master of the moving camera, was very interested in the past (background) and the present (foreground), and he constantly moved between them. For example, as the film opens, only the circus master (Peter Ustinov) is presented in the foreground. Lola (Martine Carol) and the circus performers are in the distant background. As the story begins, Lola herself is presented in the foreground, but as we move into the past story (her relationship with Franz Liszt, her passage to England, and her first marriage), Lola seems uncertain whether she is important or unimportant. What she wants (a handsome husband or to be grown up) is presented in the middle ground, and she fluctuates toward the foreground (with Liszt and later on the ship) or in the deep background (with Lieutenant James, who becomes her first husband). Interestingly, Lola is always shifting but never holding on to the central position, the middle of the frame. In this sense, the film is about the losses of Lola Montes because she never achieves the centrality of the men in her life, including the circus master.

The wide-screen shot is always full in this film, but predominantly concerns the barriers to the main character's happiness. The editing throughout supports this notion. If the character is in search of happiness, an elusive state, the editing is equally searching, cutting on movement of the character or the circus ensemble and its exploration/exploitation of Lola. The editing in this sense follows meaning rather than creates it.

By using the wide screen as he did, Ophuls gave primacy to the background of the shot over the foreground, to Lola's search over her success, to her victimization over her victory. The film stands out as an exploration of the wide screen. Ophul's work was not often imitated until Stanley Kubrick used the wide screen and movement in a similar fashion in *Barry Lyndon* (1975).

THE WIDE SCREEN AFTER 1960

The technical problems of early CinemaScope—the distortion of close-ups and in tracking shots—were overcome by the development of the Panavision camera. It supplanted CinemaScope and VistaVision with a simpler system whose anamorphic projections offered a modified wide-screen image with an aspect ratio of 1:1.85 and in its larger anamorphic use in 35 mm or 70 mm, it provided an image aspect ratio of 1:2.2. With the technical shortcomings of CinemaScope overcome, filmmakers began to edit sequences as they had in the past. Pace picked up, and close-ups and moving shots took on their past pattern of usage.

A number of filmmakers, however, made exceptional use of the wide screen and illustrated its strengths and weaknesses for editing. For example, Anthony Mann in *El Cid* (1961) used extreme close-ups and extreme long shots as well as framed single shots that embrace a close shot in the foreground and an extreme long shot in the background. Mann presented relationships, usually of conflict, within a single frame as well as within an edited sequence. The use of extreme close-ups and extreme long shots also elevated the nature of the conflict and the will of the protagonist. Because the film mythologizes the personal and national struggles of Rodrigo Díaz de Bivar, the Cid (Charlton Heston), those juxtapositions within and between shots are critical.

Mann also used the width of the frame to give an epic quality to each combat in which Rodrigo partakes: the personal fight with his future father-in-law, the combat of knights for the ownership of Calahorra, and the large-scale final battle on the beach against the Muslim invaders from North Africa. In each case, the different parts of the frame were used to present the opposing force. The clash, when it comes, takes place in the middle of the frame in single shots and in the middle of an edited sequence when single shots are used to present the opposing forces. Mann was unusually powerful in his use of the wide-screen frame to present forces in opposition and to include the land over which they struggle. Few directors have the visual power that Mann displayed in *El Cid*.

In his prologue in *2001: A Space Odyssey* (1968), Stanley Kubrick presents a series of still images that, together, are intended to create a sense of vast, empty, unpopulated space. This is the Earth at the dawn of humanity. Given the absence of continuity—the editing does not follow narrative action or a person in motion—the stills have a random, discontinuous quality, a pattern of shots such as Alexander Dovzhenko used in *Earth* (1930). Out of this pattern, an idea eventually emerges: the vast emptiness of the land. This sequence leads to the introduction of the apes and other animals. From our vantage point, however, the interest is in the editing of the sequence. Without cues or foreground–background relationships, these shots have a genuine randomness that, in the end, is the point of the sequence. There is no scientific gestalt here because there is no human here. The wide screen emphasizes the expanse and the lack of context.

A number of other filmmakers are notable for their use of the wide screen to portray conflict. Sam Peckinpah used close-ups in the foreground and background by using lenses that have a shallow depth of field. The result is a narrowing of the gap between one character on the left and another character, whether it be friend or foe, on the right. The result is intense and almost claustrophobic rather than expansive. Sergio Leone used the same approach in *The Good, the Bad, and the Ugly* (1967). In the final gunfight, for example, he used close-ups of all of the combatants and their weapons. He presented the subject fully in two-thirds of the frame, allowing emptiness, some background, or another combatant to be displayed in the balance of the frame. Leone seemed to relish the overpowering close-ups, as if he were studying or dissecting an important event.

John Boorman, on the other hand, was more orthodox in his presentation of combatants in *Hell in the Pacific* (1968). The story, set in World War II, has only two characters: a Japanese soldier who occupies an isolated island and an American flyer who finds himself on the island after being downed at sea. These two characters struggle as combatants and eventually as human beings to deal with their situation. They are adversaries in more than two-thirds of the film, so Boorman presented them in opposition to one another within single frames (to the left and right) as well as in edited sequences. What is interesting in this film is how Boorman used both the wide screen and conventional options, including close-ups, cutaways, and faster cutting, to maintain and build tension in individual sequences. When he used the wide screen, the compositions are full to midshots of the characters. Because he didn't want to present one character as a protagonist and the other as the antagonist, he did not exploit subjective placement or close-ups. Instead, whenever possible, he showed both men in the same frame, suggesting the primacy of their relationship to one another. One may have power over the other temporarily, but Boorman tried to transcend the nationalistic, historical struggle and to reach the interdependent, human subtext. These two characters are linked by circumstance, and Boorman reinforced their interdependence by using the wide-screen image to try to overcome the narrative conventions that help the filmmaker demonstrate the victorious struggle of the protagonist over the lesser intentions of the antagonist.

Other notable filmmakers who used the wide screen in powerful ways include David Lean, who illustrated again and again the primacy of nature over character (*Ryan's Daughter*, 1970). Michelangelo Antonioni succeeded in using the wide screen to illustrate the human barriers to personal fulfill-ment (*L'Avventura*, 1960). Luchino Visconti used the wide screen to present the class structure in Sicily during the Risorgimento (*Il Ovottepordo*, 1962). Federico Fellini used the wide screen to create a powerful sense of the supernatural evil that undermined Rome (*Fellini Satyricon*, 1970). Steven

Spielberg used subjective camera placement to juxtapose potential victim and victimizer, human and animal, in *Jaws* (1975), and Akira Kurosawa used color and foreground–background massing to tell his version of King Lear's struggle in *Ran* (1985). Today, the wide screen is no longer a barrier to editing but rather an additional option for filmmakers to use to power their narratives visually.

□ CINEMA VERITÉ

The wide screen forced filmmakers to give more attention to composition for continuity and promoted the avoidance of editing through the use of the foreground–background relationship. Cinema verité promoted a different set of visual characteristics for continuity.

Cinema verité is the term used for a particular style of documentary filmmaking. The post-war developments in magnetic sound recording and in lighter, portable cameras, particularly for 16-mm, allowed a less intrusive filmmaking style. Faster film stocks and more portable lights made film lighting less intrusive and in many filmmaking situations unnecessary. The cliché of cinema verité filmmaking is poor sound, poor light, and poor image. In actuality, however, these films had a sense of intimacy rarely found in the film experience, an intimacy that was the opposite of the wide-screen experience. Cinema verité was rooted in the desire to make real stories about real people. The Italian neorealist filmmakers—such as Roberto Rossellini (*Open City*, 1946), Vittorio DeSica (*The Bicycle Thief*, 1948), and Luchino Visconti (*La Terra Trema*, 1947)—were the leading influences of the movement.

Cinema verité, then, was a product of advances in camera and sound recording technology that made filmmaking equipment more portable than had previously been possible. That new portability allowed the earliest practitioners to go where established filmmakers had not been interested in going. Lindsay Anderson traveled to the farmers' market in Covent Garden for *Every Day Except Christmas* (1957), Karel Reisz and Tony Richardson traveled to a jazz club for *Momma Don't Allow* (1955), Terry Filgate followed a Salvation Army parish in Montreal in *Blood and Fire* (1959), and D. A. Pennebaker followed Bob Dylan in *Don't Look Back* (1965). In each case, these films attempted to capture a sense of the reality of the lives of the characters, whether public figures or private individuals. There was none of the formalism or artifice of the traditional feature film.

How did cinema verité work? What was its editing style? Most cinema verité films proceeded without a script. The crew filmed and recorded sound, and a shape was found in the editing process.[4] In editing, the problems of narrative clarity, continuity, and dramatic emphasis became paramount. Because cinema verité proceeded without staged sequences and with no artifical sound, including music, the raw material became the basis for continuity as well as emphasis.

Cinema verité filmmakers quickly understood that they needed many close-ups to build a sequence because the conventions of the master shot might not be available to them. They also realized that general continuity would come from the sound track rather than from the visuals. Carrying over the sound from one shot to the next provided aural continuity, and this was sometimes the only basis for continuity in a scene. Consequently, the sound track became even more important than it had been in the dramatic film. Between the close-ups and the sound, continuity could be maintained. Sound could also be used to provide continuity among different sequences. As the movement gathered steam, cinema verité filmmakers also used intentional camera and sound mistakes, acknowledgments of the film-making experience, to cover for losses of continuity. The audience, after all, was watching a film, and acknowledgment of that fact proved useful in the editing. It joined audience and filmmaker in a moment of confession that bound the two together. The rough elements of the filmmaking process, anathema in the dramatic film, became part of the cinema verité experience; they supported the credibility of the experience.[5] The symbols of cinema verité were those signposts of the hand-held camera: camera jiggle and poor framing.

Before exploring the editing style of cinema verité in more detail, it might be useful to illustrate how far-reaching its style of intimacy with the subject was to become. Beginning with the New Wave films of François Truffaut and Jean-Luc Godard, cinema verité had a wide impact. What-ever their subject, young filmmakers across the world were attracted to this approach. In Hungary, Istvan Szabo (*Father*, 1966), in Czechoslovakia, Milos Forman (*Fireman's Ball*, 1968), in Poland, Jerzy Skolimowski (*Hands Up*, 1965) all adopted a style of reportage in their narrative films. Because the hand-held style of cinema verite had found its way into televi-sion documentary and news the style adopted by these filmmakers suggested the kind of veracity, of weightiness, of importance, found in the television documentary. They were not making television documentaries, though.

Nor were John Frankenheimer in *Seconds* (1966) or Michael Ritchie in *The Candidate* (1972), and yet the handheld camera shots and the allusions to television gave each film a kind of veracity unusual in dramatic films.[6] The same style was taken up in a more self-exploratory way by Haskell Wexler in *Medium Cool* (1969). In these three films, the intimacy of cinema verité was borrowed and applied to a dramatized story to create the illusion of reality. In fact, the sense of realism resulting because of cinema verité made each film resemble in part the evening news on television. The result was remarkably effective.

Perhaps no dramatic film plays more on this illusion of realism deriving from cinema verité than *Privilege* (1967). Peter Watkins re-created the life of a rock star in a future time. Using techniques (even lines of dialogue) borrowed from the cinema verité film about Paul Anka (*Lonely Boy*, 1962), Watkins managed to reference rock idolatry in a manner familiar to the audience.

Watkins's attraction to cinema verité had been cultivated by two documentary-style films: *The Battle of Culloden* (1965) and *The War Game* (1967). Complete with on-air interviews and off-screen narrators, both films simulated documentaries with cinema verité techniques. However, both were dramatic re-creations using a style that simulated post-1950 type of reality. The fact that *The War Game* was banned from the BBC suggests how effective the use of those techniques were.

To understand how the cinema verité film was shaped given the looseness of its production, it is useful to look at one particular film to illustrate its editing style.

Lonely Boy was a production of Unit B at the National Film Board (NFB) of Canada. That unit, which was central in the development of cinema verité with its Candid Eye series, had already produced such important cinema verité works as *Blood and Fire* (1958) and *Back-Breaking Leaf* (1959). The French unit at the NFB had also taken up cinema verité techniques in such films as *Wrestling* (1960). *Lonely Boy*, a film about the popular young performer Paul Anka, brought together many of the talents associated with Unit B. Tom Daley was the executive producer, Kathleen Shannon was the sound editor, John Spotton and Guy L. Cote were the editors, and Roman Kroitor and Wolf Koenig were the directors. Each of these people demonstrated many talents in their work at and outside the NFB. Kathleen Shannon became executive producer of Unit D, the women's unit of the NFB. John Spotton was a gifted cinematographer (*Memorandum*, 1966). Wolf Koenig played an important role in the future of animation at the NFB. Tom Daley, listed as the executive producer on the film, has a reputation as one of the finest editors the NFB ever produced.

Lonely Boy is essentially a concert film, the predecessor of such rock performance films as *Gimme Shelter* (1970), *Woodstock* (1970), and *Stop Making Sense* (1984). The 26-minute film opens and closes on the road with Paul Anka between concerts. The sound features the song "Lonely Boy." Within this framework, we are presented with, as the narrator puts it, a "candid look" at a performer moving up in his career. To explore the "phenomenon," Kroiter and Koenig follow Paul Anka from an outdoor performance in Atlantic City to his first performance in a nightclub, the Copacabana, and then back to the outdoor concert. In the course of this journey, Anka, Irving Feld (his manager), Jules Podell (the owner of the Copacabana), and many fans are interviewed. The presentation of these interviews makes it unclear whether the filmmakers are seeking candor or laughing at Anka and his fans. Their attitude seems to change. Anka's awareness of the camera and retakes are included here to remind us that we are not looking in on a spontaneous or candid moment but rather at something that has been staged (Figures 7.6 to 7.8).

The audience is exposed to Anka, his manager, and his fans, but it is not until the penultimate sequence that we see Anka in concert in a fuller sense. The screen time is lengthy compared to the fragments of concert

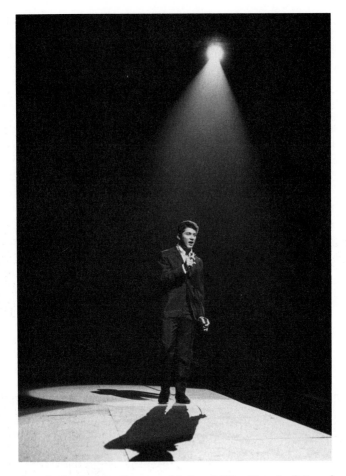

Figure 7.6 *Lonely Boy*, 1962. Courtesy National Film Board of Canada.

performance earlier in the film. Through his performance and the reaction of the fans, we begin to understand the phenomenon. In this sequence, the filmmakers seem to drop their earlier skepticism, and in this sense, the sequence is climactic.

Throughout the film, the sound track unifies individual sequences. For example, the opening sequence begins on the road with the song "Lonely Boy" on the sound track. We see images of Atlantic City, people enjoying the beach, a sign announcing Paul Anka's performance, shots of teenagers, the amusement park, and the city at night. Only as the song ends does the film cut to Paul Anka finishing the song. Then we see the response of his audience.

Figure 7.7   *Lonely Boy*, 1962. Courtesy National Film Board of Canada.

Figure 7.8   *Lonely Boy*, 1962. Courtesy National Film Board of Canada.

The shots in this sequence are random. Because many are close-ups inter-cut with long shots, unity comes from the song on the sound track. Between tracking shots, Kroiter and Koenig either go from movement within a shot, i.e., the sign announcing Anka's performance, to a tracking shot of teenagers walking—movement of the shot to movement within the shot. Again, overall unity comes from the sound track.

In the next sequence, Anka signs autographs, and the general subject (how Anka's fans feel about him) is the unifying element. This sequence features interviews with fans about their zeal for the star.

In all sequences, visual unity is maintained through an abundance of closeups. A sound cue or a cutaway allows the film to move efficiently into the next sequence.

In the final sequence, the concert performance, the continuity comes from the performance itself. The cutaways to the fans are more intense than the performance shots, however, because the cutaways are primarily close-ups. These audience shots become more poignant when Kroiter and Koenig cut away to a young girl screaming and later fainting. In both shots, the sound of the scream is omitted. We hear only the song. The absence of the sound visually implied makes the visual even more effective. The handheld quality of the shots adds a nervousness to the visual effect of an already excited audience. In this film, the handheld close-up is an asset rather than a liability. It suggests the kind of credibility and candor of which cinema verité is capable.

Lonely Boy exhibits all of the characteristics of cinema verité: for example, too much background noise in the autograph sequence and a jittery hand-held camera in the backstage sequence where Anka is quickly changing before a performance. In the latter, Anka acknowledges the presence of the camera when he tells a news photographer to ignore the filmmakers. All of this—the noise level, the wobbly camera, the acknowledgment that a film is being made—can be viewed as technical shortcomings or amateurish lapses, or they can work for the film to create a sense of candor, insight, honesty, and lack of manipulation: the agenda for cinema verité. The filmmakers try to have it all in this film. What they achieve is only the aura of candor. The film is fascinating, nevertheless.

Others who used the cinema verité approach—Allan King in *Warrendale* (1966), Fred Wiseman in *Hospital* (1969), Alfred and David Maysles in *Salesman* (1969)—exploited cinema verité fully. They achieved an intimacy with the audience that verges on embarrassing but, at its best, is the type of connection with the audience that was never possible with conventional cinematic techniques.

Cinema verité must be viewed as one of the few technological develop-ments that has had a profound impact on film. Because it is so much less structured and formal than conventional filmmaking, it requires even greater skill from its directors and, in particular, its editors.

□ NOTES/REFERENCES

1. A six-sprocket system also made the Cinerama image taller. The result was an image six times larger than the standard of the day.
2. Directors often shot their films with the television ratio in mind (the old Academy standard 1:1.33). The result was shots with the action centered in the frame. When projected on television, the parts of the frame outside the television aspect ratio were cut off. Filmmakers have abandoned shots framed with characters off to the side of the frame or have skewed the foreground–background relationship to the sides rather than to the center.
3. For the television broadcast of large-scale epics shot with a ratio of 1:2.2, the films were optically rephotographed for television. Optical zooms and pans were used to follow actions and movements of characters within shots. The results were aesthetically bizarre and questionable, but they allowed the television audience to follow the action.
4. An excellent description of the process is found in David Bordwell and Kristin Thompson, *Film Art: An Introduction*, 3d ed. (New York: McGraw-Hill, 1990), 336–342. The authors analyze the form and style of Fred Wiseman's *High School* (1968), a classic cinema verité film. With the Maysles brothers (*Salesman*, 1969; *Gimme Shelter*, 1970), Fred Wiseman epitomized the cinema verité credo and style.
5. For a full treatment of the attractiveness of the veracity and objectivity implicit in cinema verité, see Karel Reisz and Gavin Millar, *The Technique of Film Editing*, 2d ed. (Boston: Focal Press, 1968), 297–321.
6. The orgy scene in *Seconds* was filmed as if it were occurring.

8

International Advances

■

The year 1950 is a useful point to demarcate a number of changes in film history, among them the pervasive movement for change in film. Nowhere is this more apparent than in the growth in achievement and importance on an international level. Just as Hollywood experimented with the wide screen in this period, a group of British filmmakers challenged the orthodoxy of the documentary, a group of French writers who became filmmakers suggested that film authorship allowed personal styles to be expressed over industrial conventions, and young Italian filmmakers simplified narratives and film styles to politicize a popular art form. All sought alternatives to the classical style.

The classical style is best represented by such popular Hollywood filmmakers as William Wyler, who made *The Best Years of Our Lives* (1946). The film has a powerful narrative, and Wyler's grasp of style, including editing, was masterful but conventional. There were more exotic stylists, such as Orson Welles in *The Lady from Shanghai* (1948), but the mainstream was powerful and pervasive and preoccupied with more conventional stories.

By 1950, the Allies had won the war, and just as victory had brought affirmation of values and a way of life to the United States, the war and its end brought a deep desire for change in war-torn Europe. Nowhere was this impulse more quickly expressed than in European films. The neo-realist movement in Italy and the New Wave in France were movements dedicated to bringing change to film.

That is not to say that foreign films had not been influential before World War II. The contributions of Eisenstein, Pudovkin, and Vertov from the Soviet Union, F. W. Murnau and Fritz Lang of Germany, and Abel Gance and Jean Renoir of France were important to the evolution of the art of film. However, the primacy of Hollywood and of the various national cinemas was such that only fresh subject matter treated in a new and interesting style would challenge the status quo. These challenges, when they came, were of such a provocative and innovative character that they have profoundly broadened the editing of films. The challenges were broadly based: new ideas about what constitutes narrative continuity, new ideas about dramatic time, and a new definition of real time and its relationship to film time. All this came principally from those international advances that can be dated from 1950.

□ THE DYNAMICS OF RELATIVITY

When Akira Kurosawa directed *Rashomon* (1951), he presented a narrative story without a single point of view. Indeed, the film presents four different points of view. *Rashomon* was a direct challenge to the conventions that the narrative clarity that the editor and director aim to achieve must come from telling the story from the point of view of the main character and that the selection, organization, and pacing of shots must dramatically articulate that point of view (Figure 8.1).

Rashomon is a simple period story about rape and murder. A bandit attacks a samurai traveling through the woods with his wife. He ties up the samurai, rapes his wife, and later kills the samurai. The story is told in flashback by a small group of travelers waiting for the rain to pass. The film presents four points of view: those of the bandit, the wife, the spirit of the dead samurai, and a woodcutter who witnessed the events. Each story is different from the others, pointing to a different interpretation of the behavior of each of the participants. In each story, a different person is responsible for the death of the samurai. Each interpretation of the events is presented in a different editing style.

Figure 8.1   *Rashomon*, 1951. Courtesy Janus Films Company. Still provided by British Film Institute.

After opening with a dynamic presentation of the woodcutter moving through the woods until he comes to the assault, the film moves into the story of the bandit Tajomaru (Toshiro Mifune). The bandit is boastful and without remorse. His version of the story makes him out to be a powerful, heroic figure. Consequently, when he fights the samurai, he is doing so out of respect to the wife who feels she has been shamed and that only a fight to the death between her husband and the bandit can take away the stain of being dishonored.

The presentation of the fight between the samurai and Tajomaru is dynamic. The camera moves, the perspective shifts from one combatant to the other to the wife, and the editing is lively. Cutting on movement within the frame, we move with the combat as it proceeds. The editing style supports Tajomaru's version of the story. The combat is a battle of giants, of heroes, fighting to the death. The editing emphasizes conflict and movement. The foreground–background relationships keep shifting, thereby suggesting a struggle of equals rather than a one-sided fight. This is quite different from all of the other versions presented.

The second story, told from the point of view of the wife, is much less dynamic; indeed, it is careful and deliberate. In this version, the bandit runs off, and the wife, using her dagger, frees the samurai. The husband is filled with scorn because his wife allowed herself to be raped. The question here is whether the wife will kill herself to save her honor. The psychological struggle is too much, and the wife faints. When she awakes, her husband is dead, and her dagger is in his chest.

The wife sees herself as a victim who wanted to save herself with as much honor as she could salvage, but tradition requires that she accept responsibility for her misfortune. Whether she killed her husband for pushing her to that responsibility or whether he is dead by his own hand is unclear. With its deliberateness and its emphasis on the wife's point of view, the editing supports the wife's characterization of herself as a victim. The death of her husband remains a mystery.

The third version is told from the point of view of the dead husband. His spirit is represented by a soothsayer who tells his story: The shame of the rape was so great that, seeing how his wife lusts after the bandit, the samurai decided to take his own life using his wife's dagger.

The editing of this version is dynamic in the interaction between the present—the soothsayer—and the past—her interpretation of the events. The crosscutting between the soothsayer and the samurai's actions is tense. Unlike the previous version, there is a tension here that helps articulate the samurai's painful decision to kill himself. The editing helps articulate his struggle in making that decision and executing it.

Finally, there is the version of the witness, the woodcutter. His version is the opposite of the heroic interpretation of the bandit. He suggests that the wife was bedazzled by the bandit and that a combat between Tajomaru and the samurai did take place but was essentially a contest of cowards. Each man seems inept and afraid of the other. As a result, the clash is not dynamic but rather amateurish. The bandit kills the samurai, but the outcome could as easily have been the opposite.

The editing of this version is very slow. Shots are held for a much longer time than in any of the earlier interpretations. The camera was close to the action in the bandit's interpretation, but here it is far from the action. The result is a slow, sluggish presentation of a struggle to the death. There are no heroes here.

By presenting a narrative from four perspectives, Kurosawa suggested not only the relativity of the truth, but also that a film's aesthetic choices—from camera placement to editing style—must support the film's thesis. Kurosawa's success in doing so opens up options in terms of the flexibility of editing styles even within a single film. Although Kurosawa did not pursue this multiple perspective approach in his later work, *Rashomon* did show audiences the importance of editing style in suggesting the point of view of the main character. An editing style that could suggest a great deal about the emotions, fears, and fantasies of the main character became the immediate challenge for other foreign filmmakers.

□ THE JUMP CUT AND DISCONTINUITY

The New Wave began in 1959 with the consecutive releases of François Truffaut's *The 400 Blows* and Jean-Luc Godard's *Breathless*, but in fact its seeds had developed ten years earlier in the writing of Alexandre Astruc and André Bazin and the film programming of Henri Langlois at the Cinémathèque in Paris. The writing about film was cultural as well as theoretical, but the viewing of film was global, embracing film as part of popular culture as well as an artistic achievement. What developed in Paris in the post-war period was a film culture in which film critics and lovers of film moved toward becoming filmmakers themselves. Godard, Eric Rohmer, Claude Chabrol, Alain Resnais, and Jacques Rivette were all key figures, and it was Truffaut who wrote the important article "Les Politiques des Auteurs," which heralded the director as the key creative person in the making of a film.

These critics and future filmmakers wrote about Hitchcock, Howard Hawks, Samuel Fuller, Anthony Mann, and Nicholas Ray—all Hollywood filmmakers. Although he admired Renoir enormously, Truffaut and his young colleagues were critical of the French film establishment.[1] They criticized Claude Autant-Lara and Rene Clement for being too literary in their screen stories and not descriptive enough in their style. What they proposed in their own work was a personal style and personal stories—characteristics that became the hallmarks of the New Wave.

In his first film, *The 400 Blows*, Truffaut set out to respect Bazin's idea that moving the camera rather than fragmenting a scene was the essence of discovery and the source of art in film.[2] The opening and the closing of the film are both made up of a series of moving shots, featuring the beginning of Paris, the Eiffel Tower,[3] and later the lead character running away from a juvenile detention center. The synchronous sound recorded on location gives the film an intimacy and immediateness only available in cinema verité. It was the nature of the story, though, that gave Truffaut the opportunity to make a personal statement. *The 400 Blows* is the story of Antoine Doinel, a young boy in search of a childhood he never had. The rebellious child is unable to stay out of trouble at home or in school. The adult world is very unappealing to Antoine, and his clashes at home and at school lead him to reject authority and his parents. The story may sound like a tragedy that inevitably will lead to a bad end, but it is not. Antoine does end up in a juvenile detention center, but when he runs away, it is as rebellious as all of his other actions. Truffaut illustrated a life of spirit and suggested that challenging authority is not only moral, but it is also necessary for avoiding tragedy. The film is a tribute to the spirit and hope of being young, an entirely appropriate theme for the first film of the New Wave.

How did the stylistic equivalents of the personal story translate into editing choices? As already mentioned, the moving camera was used to avoid editing. In addition, the jump cut was used to challenge continuity editing and all that it implied.

The jump cut itself is nothing more than the joining of two noncontinuous shots. Whether the two shots recognize a change in direction, focus on an unexpected action, or simply don't show the action in one shot that prepares the viewer for the content of the next shot, the result of the jump cut is to focus on discontinuity. Not only does the jump cut remind viewers that they are watching a film, it is also jarring. This result can be used to suggest instability or lack of importance. In both cases, the jump cut requires the viewer to broaden the band of acceptance to enter the screen time being presented or the sense of dramatic time portrayed. The jump cut asks viewers to tolerate the admission that we are watching a film or to temporarily suspend belief in the film. This disruption can help the film experience or harm it. In the past, it was thought that the jump cut would destroy the experience. Since the New Wave, the jump cut has simply become another editing device accepted by the viewing audience. They have accepted the notion that discontinuity can be used to portray a less stable view of society or personality or that it can be accepted as a warning. It warns viewers that they are watching a film and to beware of being manipulated. The jump cut was brought into the mainstream by the films of the New Wave.

Two scenes in *The 400 Blows* stand out for their use of the jump cut, although jump cutting is used throughout the film. In the famous interview with the psychologist at the detention center, we see only Antoine Doinel. He answers a series of questions, but we neither hear the questions nor see the questioner.[4] By presenting the interview in this way, Truffaut was suggesting Antoine's basic honesty and how far removed the adult world is from him. Because we see what Antoine sees, not viewing the psychologist is important in the creation of Antoine's internal world.

At the end of the film, Antoine escapes from the detention center. He reaches the seashore and has no more room to run. There is a jump cut as Antoine stands at the edge of the water. The film jumps from long shot to a slightly closer shot and then again to midshot. It freeze-frames the midshot and jump cuts to a freeze-frame close-up of Antoine. In this series of four jump cuts, Truffaut trapped the character, and as he moved in closer, he froze him and trapped him more. Where can Antoine go? By ending the film in this way, Truffaut trapped the character and trapped us with the character. The ending is both a challenge and an invitation in the most direct style. The jump cut draws attention to itself, but it also helps Truffaut capture our attention at this critical instant.

Truffaut used the jump cut even more dynamically in *Jules et Jim* (1961), a period story about two friends in love with the same woman. Whenever possible, Truffaut showed all three friends together in the same frame, but to communicate how struck the men are upon first meeting Catherine (Jeanne Moreau), Truffaut used a series of jump cuts that show Catherine in close-up and in profile and that show her features. This brief sequence illustrates the thunderbolt effect Catherine has on Jules and Jim (Figures 8.2 and 8.3).

Figure 8.2   *Jules et Jim*, 1961. Courtesy Janus Films Company. Still provided by British Film Institute.

Figure 8.3 *Jules et Jim*, 1961. Courtesy Janus Films Company. Still provided by Moving Image and Sound Archives.

Whether the jump cut is used to present a view of society or a view of a person, it is a powerful tool that immediately draws the viewer's attention. Although self-conscious in intent when improperly used, the jump cut was an important tool of the filmmakers of the New Wave. It was a symbol of the freedom of film in style and subject, of its potential, and of its capacity to be used in a highly personalized way. It inspired a whole generation of filmmakers, and may have been the most lasting contribution of the New Wave.[5]

□ OBJECTIVE ANARCHY: JEAN-LUC GODARD

Perhaps no figure among the New Wave filmmakers raised more controversy or was more innovative than Jean-Luc Godard.[6] Although attracted to genre films, he introduced his own personal priorities to them. As time passed, these priorities were increasingly political. In terms of style, Godard was always uncomfortable with the manipulative character of narrative storytelling and the camera and editing devices that best carried out those storytelling goals. Over his career, Godard increasingly adopted counterstyles. If continuity editing supported what he considered to be bourgeois storytelling, then the jump cut could purposefully undermine that type of storytelling. If sound could be used to rouse emotion in accordance with the visual action in the film, Godard would show a person speaking about a seduction, but present the image in mid- to long shot with the woman's face totally in shadow. In shadow, we cannot relate as well to what is being said, and we can consider whether we want to be manipulated by sound and image. This was a constant self-reflexivity mixed with an increasingly Marxist view of society and its inhabitants. Rarely has so much effort been put into alienating the audience! In doing so, Godard posed a series of questions about filmmaking and about society.

Perhaps Godard's impulse toward objectification and anarchy can best be looked at in the light of *Weekend* (1967), his last film of this period that pretended to have a narrative. *Weekend* is the story of a Parisian couple who seem desperately unhappy. To save their marriage, they travel south to her mother to borrow money and take a vacation. This journey is like an odyssey. The road south is littered with a long multicar crash, and that is only the beginning of a journey from an undesirable civilization to an inevitable collapse leading, literally, to cannibalism. The marriage does not last the journey, and the husband ends up as dinner (Figures 8.4 and 8.5).

How does one develop a style that prepares us for this turn of events? In all cases, subversion of style is the key. A fight in the apartment parking lot descends into absurdity. The car crash, instead of involving us in its horror, is rendered neutral by a slow, objective camera track. In fact, once the camera has observed the whole lengthy crash, it begins to move back over the crash,

Figure 8.4 *Weekend,* 1967. Still provided by British Film Institute.

Figure 8.5   *Weekend*, 1967. Still provided by British Film Institute.

front to back. When a town is subjected to political propaganda, the propagandists are interviewed head-on. Later, in a more rural setting, the couple comes across an intellectual (Jean-Pierre Leaud) who may be either mad or just bored with contemporary life. He reads aloud in the fields from Denis Diderot. Eventually, when revolution is the only alternative, the wife kills and eats the husband with her atavistic colleagues deep in the woods. At each stage, film style is used to subvert content. The result is a constant contradiction between objective film style and absurdist content or anarchistic film style and objective content. In both cases, the film robs the viewer of the catharsis of the conventional narrative and of the predictability of its style and meaning. There are no rules of editing that Godard does not subvert, and perhaps that is his greatest legacy. The total experience is everything; to achieve that total experience, all conventions are open to challenge.

☐ MELDING PAST AND PRESENT: ALAIN RESNAIS

For Alain Resnais, film stories may exist on a continuum of developing action (the present), but that continuum must include everything that is part of the main character's consciousness. For Resnais, a character is a collection of memories and past experiences. To enter the story of a particular character is to draw on those collective memories because those memories are the context for the character's current behavior. Resnais's creative challenge was to find ways to recognize the past in the present. He found the solution in editing. An example illustrates his achievement.

Hiroshima Mon Amour (1960) tells the story of an actress making a film in Hiroshima. She takes a Japanese lover who reminds her of her first love, a German soldier who was killed in Nevers during the war. She was humiliated as a collaborator when she was 20 years old. Now, 14 years later, her encounter with her Japanese lover in the city destroyed to end the war takes her back to that time. The film does not resolve her emotional trauma; rather, it offers her the opportunity to relive it. Intermingled with the story are artifacts that remind her of the nuclear destruction of Hiroshima.

The problem of time and its relationship to the present is solved in an unusual way. The woman watches her Japanese lover as he sleeps. His arm is twisted. When she sees his hand, Resnais cut back and forth between a close-up of the hand and a midshot of the woman. After moving in closer, he cut from the midshot of the woman to a close-up of another hand (a hand from the past), then back to the midshot and then to a full shot of the dead German lover, his hand in exactly the same position as that of the Japanese lover. The full shot shows him bloodied and dead and the film then cuts back to the present (Figures 8.6 to 8.8).

The identical presentations of the two hands provides a visual cue for moving between the past and the present. The midshot of the woman watching binds the past and present.

Later, as the woman confesses to her contemporary lover, the film moves between Nevers and Hiroshima. Her past is interwoven into her current relationship, and by the end of the film, the Japanese lover is viewed as a person through whom she can relive the past and perhaps put it behind her. Throughout the film, it is the presence of the past in her present that provides the crucial context for the woman's affair and for her view of love and relationships. The past also comes to bear, in a less direct way, on the issues of war and politics and how a person can become immersed in them. The fluidity and formal quality of Resnais's editing fuses past and present for the character.

The issue of time and its relationship to behavior is a continuing trend in most of Resnais's work. From the blending of the past and present of Auschwitz in *Night and Fog* (1955) to the role of the past in the present identity of a woman in *Muriel* (1963) to the elevation of the past to the self-image of the main character in *La Guerre Est Finie* (1966), the exploration of editing solutions to narrative problems has been the key to Resnais's work.

Resnais carried on his exploration of memory and the present in *Providence* (1977), which embraces fantasy as well as memory. Later, he used the intellect, fantasy, and the present in *Mon Oncle d'Amerique* (1980).

Figure 8.6 *Hiroshima Mon Amour*, 1960. Courtesy Janus Films Company. Still provided by British Film Institute.

Figure 8.7 *Hiroshima Mon Amour*, 1960. Courtesy Janus Films Company. Still provided by British Film Institute.

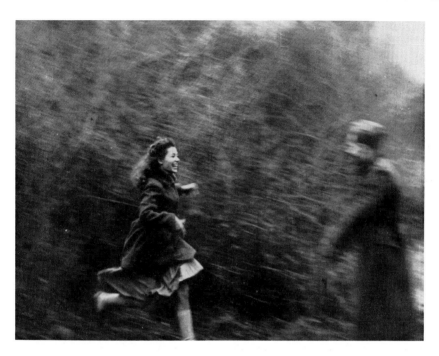

Figure 8.8   *Hiroshima Mon Amour*, 1960. Courtesy Janus Films Company. Still provided by British Film Institute.

The greater the layers of reality, the more interesting the challenge for Resnais. Always, the solution lies in the editing.

□ INTERIOR LIFE AS EXTERNAL LANDSCAPE

The premise of many of Resnais's narratives—that the past lives on in the character—was very much the issue for both Federico Fellini and Michelangelo Antonioni. They each found different solutions to the problem of externalizing the interior lives of their characters.

When Fellini made *8½* in 1963, he was interested in finding editing solutions in the narrative. In doing so, he not only produced a film that marked the height of personal cinema, he also explored what, until that time, had been the domain of the experimental film: a thought rather than a plot, an impulse to introspection unprecedented in mainstream filmmaking (Figure 8.9).

8½ is the story of Guido (Marcello Mastroianni), a famous director. He has a crisis of confidence and is not sure what his next film will be. Nevertheless, he proceeds to cast it and build sets, and he pretends to everyone that

Figure 8.9 *8½*, 1963. Courtesy Janus Films Company. Still provided by British Film Institute.

he knows what he is doing. He is in the midst of a personal crisis as well as a creative one. His marriage is troubled, his mistress is demanding, and he dreams of his childhood. *8½* is the interior journey into the world of the past, of Guido's dreams, fears, and hopes. For 2½ hours, Fellini explores this interior landscape.

To move from fantasy to reality and from past to present, Fellini must first establish the role of fantasy. He does so in the very first scene. Guido is alone in a car, stuck in a traffic jam. The traffic cannot be heard, just the sounds Guido makes as he breathes anxiously. The images begin to seem absurd. Suddenly we see other characters, older people in one car, a young woman being seduced in another. Are they dreams or are they reality? What follows blurs the distinction. The camera angle seems to indicate that she is looking straight at Guido (we later learn that she is his mistress). Suddenly, the car begins to fill with smoke. Guido struggles to get out, but people in other cars seem indifferent to his plight. His breathing is very labored now. Then he is out of the car and floating out of the traffic jam. We see a horseman, and Guido floats high in the air. An older man (we find out later that he is Guido's producer) suggests that he should come down. He pulls on Guido's leg, and he falls thousands of feet to the water below (Figure 8.10).

The film then cuts to neutral sound, and we discover that Guido has been having a nightmare. The film returns to the present, where Guido is being

Figure 8.10 8½, 1963. Courtesy Janus Films Company. Still provided by British Film Institute.

attended to in a spa. His creative team is also present. In this sequence, the fantasy is supported by the absurdist juxtaposition of images and by the absence of any natural sound other than Guido's breathing. The sound and the editing of the images provide cues that we are seeing a fantasy. This is a strategy Fellini again and again uses to indicate whether a sequence is fantasy or reality. For example, a short while later, Guido is outside at the spa, lining up for mineral water. The spa is populated by all types of people, principally older people, and they are presented in a highly regimented fashion. In a close-up, Guido looks at something, dropping his glasses to a lower point on his nose. The film cuts to a beautiful young woman (Claudia Cardinale), dressed in white, gliding toward him. The sound is suspended. Guido sees only the young woman. She smiles at him and is now very close. The film cuts back to the same shot of Guido in close-up. This time he raises his glasses back onto the bridge of his nose. At that instant, the sound returns, and the film cuts to a midshot of a spa employee offering him mineral water. Again, the sound cue alerts us to the shift into and out of the fantasy (Figure 8.11).

Throughout the film, Fellini also relies on the art direction (all white in the fantasy sequences) and on the absurdist character of the fantasies, particularly the harem-in-revolt sequence, to differentiate the fantasy sequences from the rest of the film. In the movement from present to past, a sound phrase—such as Asa-Nisi-Masa—is used to transport the contemporary Guido back to his childhood. Fellini also uses sound effects and music as

Figure 8.11 *8¹/₂*, 1963. Courtesy Janus Films Company. Still provided by British Film Institute.

cues. In *8¹/₂*, Guido's interior life is as much the subject of the story as is his contemporary life. Although the film has little plot by narrative standards, the concept of moving around in the mind of a character poses enough of a challenge to Fellini that the audience's experience is as much a voyage of discovery as his seems to be. After that journey, film editing has never been defined in as audacious a fashion (Figure 8.12).

Michelangelo Antonioni chose not to move between the past and the present even though his characters are caught in as great an existential dilemma as Guido in *8¹/₂*. Instead, Antonioni included visual detail that alludes to that dilemma. His characters live in the present, but they find despair in contemporary life. Whether theirs is an urban malaise born of upper-middle-class boredom or whether it's an unconscious response to the modern world, the women in his films are as lost as Guido. As Seymour Chatman suggests: "The central and distinguishing characteristic of Antonioni's mature films (so goes the argument of this book) is narration by a kind of visual minimalism, by an intense concentration on the sheer appearance of things—the surface of the world as he sees it—and a minimalization of exploratory dialogue."[7]

We stay with Antonioni's characters through experiences of a variety of sorts. Something dramatic may happen in such an experience—an airplane ride, for example—but the presentation of the scene is not quite what con-

Figure 8.12 *8½*, 1963. Courtesy Janus Films Company. Still provided by British Film Institute.

ventional narrative implies it will be. In conventional narrative, an airplane ride illustrates that the character is going from point A to point B, or it illustrates a point in a relationship (the airplane ride being the attempt of one character to move along the relationship with another). There is always a narrative point, and once that point is made, the scene changes.

This is the point in *L'Eclisse* (*The Eclipse*) (1962), for example. The airplane ride is an opportunity for the character to have an overview of her urban context: the city. It is an opportunity to experience brief joy, and it is an opportunity to admire the technology of the airplane and the airport. Finally, it is an opportunity to point out that even with all of the activity of a flight, the character's sense of aloneness is deep and abiding.

The shots that are included and the length of the sequence are far different than if there had been a narrative goal. Also notable are the number of long shots in which the character is far from the camera as if she is being studied by the camera (Figures 8.13 and 8.14).

L'Eclisse is the story of Vittoria (Monica Vitti), a young woman who is ending her engagement to Roberto as the film begins. She seems depressed. Her mother is very involved in the stockmarket and visits her daily to check on her health. Although Vittoria has friends in her apartment building, she seems unhappy. The only change in her mood occurs when she and her friends pretend they are primitive Africans. She can escape when she pretends.

Figure 8.13 *L'Eclisse*, 1962. Courtesy Janus Films Company. Still provided by British Film Institute.

One day, she visits her mother at the stock exchange. The market crashes and her mother is very bitter. Vittoria speaks to her mother's stockbroker, Piero (Alain Delon). He seems quite interested in her, and a relationship develops. The relationship seems to progress; the film ends inconclusively when she leaves his apartment, promising to meet in the evening. Her leave-taking is followed by a 7-minute epilogue of shots of life in the city. The epilogue has no visual reference to either Vittoria or Piero.

Whether one feels that the film is a condemnation of Piero's determinism and amorality or a meditation on Vittoria's existential state or her search for an alternative to a world dominated by masculine values, the experience of the film is unsettling and open. What is the meaning of the stock market? Vittoria says, "I still don't know if it's an office, a marketplace, a boxing ring, and maybe it isn't even necessary." Piero's vitality seems much more positive than her skepticism and malaise. What is the meaning of the role of family? We see only her mother and her home. The mother is only interested in acquiring money. The family is represented by their home. They are personified by the sum of their acquisitiveness. What is meant by all of the shots of the city and its activity without the presence of either character?

One can only proceed to find meaning based on what Antonioni has given us. We have many scenes of Vittoria contextualized by her environment, her

Figure 8.14 *L'Eclisse*, 1962. Courtesy Janus Films Company. Still provided by British Film Institute.

apartment, Roberto's apartment, Piero's two apartments, her mother's apartment, and the stock exchange. In these scenes, there is a foreground–background relationship between Vittoria, her habitat, and her relationship to others: her friends, Roberto, Piero, her mother. Antonioni alternated between objective and subjective camera placement to put the viewer in a position to identify with Vittoria and then to distance the viewer from Vittoria in order to consider that identification and to consider her state.

Space is used to distance us, and when Vittoria exits into the city, these spaces expand. Filmed in extreme long shot with a deep-focus lens, the context alternates between Vittoria in midshot in the foreground and Vittoria in the deep background dwarfed by her surroundings, by the human-made monuments, the buildings, and the natural monuments (the trees, the river, the forest).

Antonioni used this visual articulation, which for us means many slowly paced shots so that there is considerable screen time of Vittoria passing through her environment, rather than acting upon it as Piero does. What is fascinating about Antonioni is his ability in all of these shots to communicate Vittoria's sense of aloneness, and yet her sensuality (life force) is exhibited in the scene with her friends and in the later scenes with Piero. In these sequences, Antonioni used two-shots that included elements of the apartment: a window, the drapes. Because of the pacing of the shots, the film does not editorialize about what is most important or least important. All of the information, artifacts, and organization seem to affect Vittoria, and it is for us to choose what is more important than anything else.

If Antonioni's goal was to externalize the internal world of his characters, he succeeded remarkably and in different ways than did Fellini. Two sequences illustrate how the present is the basis for suggesting interior states in *L'Eclisse*.

When the relationship between Vittoria and Piero begins, Antonioni abandons all of the other characters. The balance of the film, until the very last sequence, focuses on the two lovers. In a series of scenes that take place in front of her apartment, at the site of his car's recovery from the river, in his parents' apartment, in a park, and in his pied-à-terre, Vittoria gradually commits to a relationship with Piero. Although there is some uncertainty in the last scene as to whether the relationship will last, the film stays with the relationship in scene after scene. There is progress, but there isn't much dialogue to indicate a direct sense of progress in the relationship. The scenes are edited as if they were meditations on the relationship rather than as a plotted progression. The editing pattern is slow and reflective. The final sequence with the characters ends on a note of invasion from outside and of anxiety. As Vittoria leaves, Piero puts all of the phones back on the hook. As she descends the stairs, she hears as they begin to ring. The film cuts to Piero sitting at his desk wondering whether to answer them. In a very subtle way, this ending captures the anxiety in their relationship: Will it continue, or will the outside world invade and undermine it?

The epilogue of the film is also notable. In the last shot of the preceding sequence, Vittoria has left Piero's apartment. She is on the street. In the foreground is the back of her hand as she views the trees across the road. She turns, looks up, and then looks down, and she exits the frame, leaving only the trees.

The epilogue follows: 7 minutes without a particular character; 44 images of the city through the day. Antonioni alternates between inanimate shots of buildings and pans or tracks of a moving person or a stream. If there is a shape to the epilogue, it is a progression through the day. This sequence ends on a close-up of a brilliant street lamp. Throughout the sequence, sound becomes increasingly important. The epilogue relies on realistic sound effects and, in the final few shots, on music.

The overall feeling of the sequence is that the life of the city proceeds regardless of the state of mind of the characters. Vittoria may be in love or feeling vulnerable, but the existence of the tangible, physical world objectifies her feelings. To the extent that we experience the story through her, the sequence clearly suggests a world beyond her. It is a world Antonioni alluded to throughout the film. Early on, physical structures loom over Vittoria and Roberto. Later, when we see Vittoria and Piero for the first time, a column stands between them. The physical world has dwarfed these characters from the beginning. The existential problem of mortal humanity in a physically overpowering world is reaffirmed in this final sequence. Vittoria can never be more than she is, nor can her love change this relationship to the world in more than a temporal way. The power of this sequence is that it democratizes humanity and nature. Vittoria is in awe of nature, and she is powerless to affect it. She can only co-exist with it. This impulse to democratization—identification with the character and then a distancing from her—is the creative editing contribution of Michelangelo Antonioni.

□ NOTES/REFERENCES

1. Just as Anderson, Reisz and Richardson railed against the British film establishment during this period, Truffaut, Godard, and Chabrol were critical of Claude Autant-Lara, Rene Clement, and the other established directors of the French film industry.
2. *Mise-en-scene*, or the long take, meant moving the camera to record the action rather than ordering the action by fragmenting and editing the sequence.
3. The personalized reference in this prologue is typical of the New Wave. One of the moving shots travels by the Cinémathèque, and the Eiffel Tower is in the background.
4. The jarring effect of the jump cut is softened in this sequence with dissolves.
5. The worldwide influence of the New Wave can be seen in the film movements of the last 30 years. It can be seen in the Czech New Wave, the work of Milos Forman and Jiri Menzel. It can be seen in Yugoslav film, particularly in the work of Dusan Makavejev. It can be seen in the work of Glauber Rocha in Brazil and in the work of Fernando Solanas in Argentina. The New Wave also influenced the work of Pier Paolo Pasolini and the Taviani brothers in Italy. In the United States, Arthur Penn and Mike Nichols were strongly encouraged to experiment by the success of the New Wave.
6. There is an excellent account of Godard's editing style in Karel Reisz and Gavin Millar, *The Technique of Film Editing* (Boston: Focal Press, 1968), 345–358.
7. Seymour Chatman, *Antonioni, or the Surface of the World* (Berkeley: University of California Press, 1985), 2.

9

The Influence of
Television and Theatre

■

□ TELEVISION

No post-war change in the entertainment industry was as profound as the change that occurred when television was introduced. Not only did television provide a home entertainment option for the audience, thereby eroding the traditional audience for film, it also broadcast motion pictures by the 1960s. By presenting live drama, weekly series, variety shows, news, and sports, television revolutionized viewing patterns, subject matter, the talent pool,[1] and, eventually, how films were edited.

Perhaps television's greatest asset was its sense of immediacy, a quality not present in film. Film was consciously constructed, whereas television seemed to happen directly in front of the viewer. This sense was supported by the presentation of news events as they unfolded as well as the broadcasting of live drama and variety shows. It was also supported by television's function as an advertising medium. Not only were performers used in advertising, but the advertising itself—whether a commercial of 1 minute or less—came to embody entertainment values. News programs, commercials, and how they were presented (particularly their sense of immediacy and their pace) were the influences that most powerfully affected film editing.

One manifestation of television's influence on film can be seen in the treatment of real-life characters or events. Film had always been attracted to biography; Woodrow Wilson, Lou Gehrig, Paul Ehrlich, and Louis Pasteur, among others, received what has come to be called the "Hollywood treatment." In other words, their lives were freely and dramatically adapted for film. There was no serious attempt at veracity; entertainment was the goal.

After television came on the scene, this changed. The influence of television news was too great to ignore. Veracity had to in some way be respected. This approach was supported by the post-war appeal of neorealism and by the cinema verité techniques. If a film looked like the nightly news, it was important, it was real, it was immediate.

Peter Watkins recognized this in his television docudramas of the 1960s (*The Battle of Culloden*, 1965; *The War Game*, 1967). He continued with this approach in his later work on Edward Munch. In the feature film, this style began to have an influence as early as John Frankenheimer's *The Manchurian Candidate* (1962) and was continued in his later films, *Seven Days in May* (1964) and *Black Sunday* (1977). Alan J. Pakula took a docudrama approach to Watergate in *All the President's Men* (1976), and Oliver Stone continues to work in this style, from *Salvador* (1986) to *JFK* (1991).

The docudrama approach, which combines a cinema verité style with jump-cut editing, gives films a patina of truth and reality that is hard to differentiate from the nightly news. Only the pace differs, heightening the tension in a way rarely seen on television news programs. Given that the subject, character, or event already has a public profile, the filmmaker need only dip back into that broadcast-created impression by using techniques that allude to veracity to make the film seem real. This is due directly to the techniques of television news: cinema verité, jump-cutting, and on- or off-air narrators. The filmmaker has a fully developed repertoire of editing techniques to simulate the reality of the nightly news.

The other manifestation of the influence of television seems by comparison fanciful, but its impact, particularly on pace, has been so profound that no film, television program, or television commerical is untouched by it. This influence can be most readily seen in the 1965–70 career of one man, Richard Lester, an expatriate American who directed the two Beatles' films, *A Hard Day's Night* (1964) and *Help!* (1965) in Great Britain.

Using techniques widely deployed in television, Lester found a style commensurate with the zany mix of energy and anarchy that characterized the Beatles. One might call his approach to these films the first of the music videos.

Films that starred musical or comedy performers who were not actors had been made before. The Marx Brothers, Abbott and Costello, and Mario Lanza are a few of these performers. The secret for a successful production was to combine a narrative with opportunities for the performers to do what they did best: tell anecdotes or jokes or sing. Like the Marx Brothers' films, *A Hard Day's Night* and *Help!* do have narratives. *A Hard Day's Night* tells the story of a day in the life of the Beatles, leading up to a big television performance. *Help!* is more elaborate; an Indian sect is after Ringo for the sacred ring he has on his finger. They want it for its spiritual significance. Two British scientists are equally anxious to acquire the ring for its technological value. The pursuit of the ring takes the cast around the world.

The stories are diversions from the real purpose of the films: to let the Beatles do what they do best. Lester's contribution to the two films is the methods he used to present the music. Notably, no two songs are presented in the same way.

The techniques Lester used are driven by a combination of cinema verité techniques with an absurdist attitude toward narrative meaning. Lester deployed the same techniques in his famous short film, *Running, Jumping and Standing Still* (1961).

Lester filmed the Beatles' performances with multiple cameras. He intercut close-ups with extreme angularity—for example, a juxtaposition of George Harrison and Paul McCartney or a close-up of John Lennon—with the reactions of the young concert-goers.

The final song performed in *A Hard Day's Night* is intercut with the frenzy of the audience. Shots ranging from close-ups to long shots of the performers and swish pans to the television control booth and back to the audience were cut with an increasing pace that adds to the building excitement. The pace becomes so rapid, in fact, that the individual images matter less than the feeling of energy that exists between the Beatles and the audience. Lester used editing to underscore this energy.

Lester used a variety of techniques to create this energy, ranging from wide-focus images that distort the subject to extreme close-ups. He included handheld shots, absurd cutaways, speeded-up motion, and obvious jump cuts.

When the Beatles are performing in a television studio, Lester began the sequence with a television camera's image of the performance and pulled back to see the performance itself. He intercut television monitors with the actual performance quite often, thus referencing the fact that this is a captured performance. He did not share the cinema verité goal of making the audience believe that what they are watching is the real thing.

He set songs in the middle of a field surrounded by tanks or on a ski slope or a Bahamian beach. The location and its character always worked with his sense of who the Beatles were.

A Hard Day's Night opens with a large group of fans chasing the Beatles into a train station. The handheld camera makes the scene seem real, but when the film cuts to an image of a bearded Paul McCartney sitting with his grandfather and reading a paper, the mix of absurdity and reality is established. Pace and movement are always the key. Energy is more important in this film than realism, so Lester opted to jump-cut often on movement. The energy that results is the primary element that provides emotional continuity throughout the film (Figure 9.1).

Lester was able to move so freely with his visuals because of the unity provided by the individual songs. Where possible, he developed a medley around parallel action. For example, he intercut shots of the Beatles at a disco with Paul's grandfather at a gambling casino. By finding a way to intercut sequences, Lester moved between songs and styles. He didn't even need to have the Beatles perform the songs. They could simply act during a song, as they do in "All My Loving." This permitted some variety within sequences and between' sequences. All the while, this variety suggests that anything is possible, visually or in the narrative. The result is a freedom of choice in editing virtually unprecedented in a narrative film. Not even Bob Fosse in *All That Jazz* (1979) had as much freedom as Lester embraced in *A Hard Day's Night*.

Lester's success in using a variety of camera angles, images, cutaways, and pace has meant that audiences are willing to accept a series of diverse images

Figure 9.1 *A Hard Day's Night*, 1964. Still provided by British Film Institute.

unified only by a sound track. The accelerated pace suggests that audiences are able to follow great diversity and find meaning faster. The success of Lester's films suggests, in fact, that faster pace is desirable. The increase in narrative pace since 1966 can be traced to the impact of the Beatles' films.

Not only have narrative stories accelerated,[2] so too has the pace of the editing. As can be seen in Sam Peckinpah's *The Wild Bunch* (1969) and Martin Scorsese's *Raging Bull* (1980), individual shots have become progressively shorter. This is nowhere better illustrated than in contemporary television commercials and music videos.

Richard Lester exhibited in the "Can't Buy Me Love" sequence in *A Hard Days Night*, the motion, the close-ups, the distorted wide-angle shots of individual Beatles and of the group, the jump cutting, the helicopter shots, the slow motion, and the fast motion that characterize his work. Audience's acceptance and celebration of his work suggest the scope of Lester's achievement—freedom to edit for energy and emotion, uninhibited by traditional rules of continuity. By using television techniques, Lester liberated himself and the film audience from the realism of television, but with no loss of immediacy. Audiences have hungered for that immediacy, and many filmmakers, such as Scorsese, have been able to give them the energy that immediacy suggests.

Lester went on to use these techniques in an uneven fashion. Perhaps his most successful later film was *Petulia* (1968), which was set in San

Francisco. In this story about the breakup of a conventional marriage, Lester was particularly adept at moving from past to present and back to fracture the sense of stability that marriage usually implies. The edgy moving camera also helped create a sense of instability (Figure 9.2). Lester's principal contribution to film editing was the freedom and pace he was able to achieve in the two Beatles' films.

□ THEATRE

If the influence of television in this period was related to the search for immediacy, the influence of theatre was related to the search for relevance. The result of these influences was a new freedom with narrative and how narrative was presented through the editing of film.

During the 1950s, perhaps no other filmmaker was as influential as Ingmar Bergman. The themes he chose in his films—relationships (*Lesson in Love*, 1954), aging (*Wild Strawberries*, 1957), and superstition (*The Magician*, 1959)—suggested a seriousness of purpose unusual in a popular medium such as film. However, it was in his willingness to deal with the supernatural that Bergman illustrated that the theatre and its conventions could be accepted in filmic form. Bergman used film as many had used the stage:

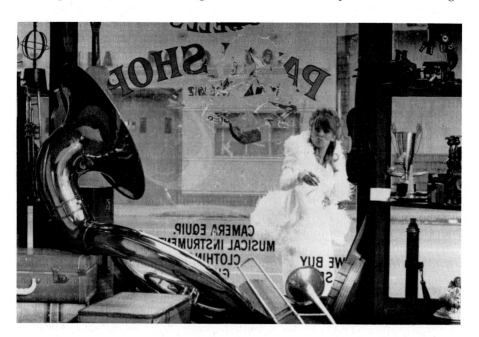

Figure 9.2   *Petulia*, 1968. ©1968 Warner Bros.–Seven Arts and Petersham Films (Petulia) Ltd. All Rights Reserved. Still provided by Moving Image and Sound Archives.

to explore as well as to entertain. Because the stage was less tied to realism, the audience was willing to accept less reality-bound conventions, thus allowing the filmmaker to explore different treatments of subject matter. When Bergman developed a film following, he also developed the audience's tolerance for theatrical approaches in film.

This is not to say that plays were not influential on film until Bergman came on the scene. As mentioned in Chapter 4, they had been. The difference was that the 1950s were notable for the interest in neorealist or cinema verité film. Even Elia Kazan, a man of the theatre, experimented with cinema verité in *Panic in the Streets* (1950). In the same period, however, he made *A Streetcar Named Desire* (1951). His respect for the play was such that he filmed it as a play, making no pretense that it was anything else.

Bergman, on the other hand, attempted to make a film with the thematic and stylistic characteristics of a play. For example, Death is a character in *The Seventh Seal* (1956). He speaks like other characters, but his costume differentiates him from them. Bergman's willingness to use such theatrical devices made them as important for editing as the integration of the past was in the films of Alain Resnais and as important as fantasy was in the work of Federico Fellini.

Bergman remained interested in metaphor and nonrealism in his later work. *From the Life of the Marionettes* (1980) uses the theatrical device of stylized repetition to explore responsibility in a murder investigation. Bergman used metaphor to suggest embryonic Nazism in 1923 Germany in *The Serpent's Egg* (1978). Both films have a sense of formal design more closely associated with the theatrical set than with the film location. In each case, the metaphorical approach makes the plot seem fresh and relevant.

At the same time that Bergman was influencing international film, young critics-turned-filmmakers in England were also concerned about making their films more relevant than those made in the popular national cinema tradition. Encouraged by new directors in the theatre, particularly the realist work of John Osborne, Arnold Wesker, and Shelagh Delaney, directors Tony Richardson, Lindsay Anderson, and Karel Reisz—filmmakers who began their work in documentary film—very rapidly shifted toward less naturalistic films to make their dramatic films more relevant. They were joined by avant-garde directors, such as Peter Brook, who worked in both theatre and film and attempted to create a hybrid embracing the best elements of both media. This desire for relevance and the crossover between theatre and film has continued to be a central source of strength in the English cinema. The result is that some key screenwriters have been playwrights, including Harold Pinter, David Mercer, David Hare, and Hanif Kureishi. In the case of David Hare, the crossover from theatre to film has led to a career in film direction. Had Joe Orton lived, it seems likely that he, too, would have become an important screenwriter.

All of these playwrights share a serious interest in the nature of the society in which they live, in its class barriers, and in the fabric of human relationships that the society fosters. Beginning with Tony Richardson and his film adaptation of Osborne's *Look Back in Anger* (1958), the filmmakers of the British New Wave directed realist social dramas. Karel Reisz followed with *Saturday Night and Sunday Morning* (1960), and Lindsay Anderson followed with *This Sporting Life* (1963). With the exception of the latter film, the early work is marked by a strong cinema verité influence, as evidenced by the use of reallocations and live sound full of local accents and a reluctance to intrude with excessive lighting and the deployment of color. This "candid eye" tradition was later carried on by Ken Loach (*Family Life*, 1972) until recently. The high point for the New Wave British directors, however, came much earlier with Richardson's *The Loneliness of the Long Distance Runner* (1962). Later, each director yielded to the influence of the theatre and nonrealism. Indeed, the desertion of realism suggests that it was the seriousness of the subject matter of the early realist films rather than the philosophical link to the cinema verité style that appealed to Richardson, Anderson, and Reisz. In their search for an appropriate style for their later films, these filmmakers displayed a flexibility of approach that was unusual in film. The result again was to broaden the organization of images in a film.

The first notable departure from realism was Tony Richardson's *Tom Jones* (1963). Scripted by playwright John Osborne, the film took a highly stylized approach to Henry Fielding's novel. References to the silent film technique—including the use of subtitles and a narrator—framed the film as a cartoon portrait of social and sexual morality in eighteenth-century England.

To explore those mores, Richardson used fast motion, slow motion, stop motion, jump-cutting, and cinema verité handheld camera shots. He used technique to editorialize upon the times that the film is set in, with Tom Jones (Albert Finney) portrayed as a rather modern nonconformist. In keeping with this sense of modernity, two characters—Tom's mother and Tom—address the audience directly, thus acknowledging that they are characters in a film. With overmodulated performances more suited for the stage than for film, Richardson achieved a modern cartoon-like commentary on societal issues, principally class. Tom's individuality rises above issues of class, and so, in a narrative sense, his success condemns the rigidity of class in much the same way as Osborne and Richardson had earlier in *Look Back in Anger*. The key element in *Tom Jones* is its sense of freedom to use narrative and technical strategies that include realism but are not limited by a need to seem realistic. The result is a film that is far more influenced by the theatre than Richardson's earlier work. Richardson continued this exploration of form in his later films, *The Loved One* (1965) and *Laughter in the Dark* (1969).

Karel Reisz also abandoned realism, although thematically there are links between *Saturday Night and Sunday Morning* and his later *Morgan* (1966) and *Isadora* (1969).

Morgan: A Suitable Case for Treatment tells the story of the mental disintegration of the main character in the face of the disintegration of his marriage. Morgan (David Warner), a life-long Marxist with working-class roots, has married into the upper class. This social and political layer to his mental collapse is largely a factor in the failure of Morgan's marriage, but it is his reaction to the failure that gives Reisz the opportunity to visualize that disintegration. Morgan sees the world in terms of animals. He sees himself as a gorilla. A beautiful woman on a subway escalator is a peacock; a ticket seller is a hippopotamus. When he makes love with his ex-wife, they are two zebras rolling around on the veldt. Conflict, particularly with his ex-wife's lover, is a matter for lions. Whenever Morgan finds himself in conflict, he retreats into the animal world.

Reisz may have viewed Morgan's escape as charming or as a political response to his circumstances. In either case, the integration of animal footage throughout the film creates an allegory rather than a portrait of mental collapse. The realist approach to the same subject was taken by Ken Loach in *Family Life* (sometimes called *Wednesday's Child*). Reisz's approach, essentially metaphorical, yields a stylized film. In spite of the realist street sense of much of the footage, David Mercer's clever dialogue and the visual allusions create a hybrid film.

The same is true of *Isadara*, a biography of the great dancer Isadora Duncan (Vanessa Redgrave). Duncan had a great influence on modern dance, and she was a feminist and an aesthete. To re-create her ideas about life and dance, Reisz structured the film on an idea grid. The film jumps back and forth in time from San Francisco in 1932 to France in 1927. In between these jumps, the film moves ahead, but always in the context of looking at Duncan in retrospect to the scenes of 1927 in the south of France.

Reisz was not content simply to tell her biography. He also tried to re-create the inspiration for her dances. When she first makes love to designer Edward Gordon Craig (James Fox), the scene is crosscut with a very sensual dance. The dance serves as an expression of Duncan's feelings at that moment and as an expression of her inspiration. Creation and feeling are linked.

The film flows back and forth in time and along a chronology of her artistic development. Although much has been made of the editing of the film and its confusion, it is clearly an expression of its ambition. Reisz attempted to find editing solutions for difficult abstract ideas, and in many cases, the results are fascinating. The film has little connection to Reisz's free cinema roots, but rather is connected to dance and the theatre.

Lindsay Anderson was the least linked to realism of the three filmmakers. *O'Dreamland* (1953) moves far away from naturalism in its goals, and in his first feature, *This Sporting Life*, Anderson showed how far from realism his interests were. This story about a professional rugby player (Richard Harris) is also about the limits of the physical world. He is an angry man incapable of understanding his anger or of accepting his psychic pain. Only at the end does he understand his shortcomings. Of the three filmmakers, Anderson seems most interested in existential, rather than social or political, elements. At least, this is the case in *This Sporting Life*.

When he made *If*-.-.-.-(1969), Anderson completely rejected realism. For this story about rebellion in a public boy's school, Anderson used music, the alternating of black and white with color, and stylized, nonrealistic images to suggest the importance of freedom over authority and of the individual over the will of the society. By the end of the film, the question of reality or fantasy has become less relevant. The film embraces both fantasy and reality, and it becomes a metaphor for life in England in 1969. The freedom to edit more flexibly allowed Anderson to create his dissenting vision.

Anderson carried this theatrical approach even further in his next film, *O Lucky Man!* (1973). This film is about the actor who played Mick in *If*.-.-.-.-It tells the story of his life up to the time that he was cast in *If*.-.-.-.-The film is not so much a biography as it is an odyssey. Mick Travis is portrayed by Malcolm McDowell, but in *O Lucky Man!* he is presented as a Candide-like innocent. His voyage begins with his experiences as a coffee salesman in northern England, but the realism of the job is not of interest. His adventures take him into technological medical experimentation, nuclear accidents, and international corporate smuggling. Throughout, the ethics of the situation are questionable, the goals are exploitation at any cost: human or political. At the end of the film, the character is in jail, lucky to be alive.

Throughout *O Lucky Man!*, Anderson moved readily through fact and fantasy. A man who is both pig and man is one of the most repellent images. To provide a respite between sequences, Anderson cuts to Alan Price and his band as they perform the musical sound track of the film. Price later appears as a character in the film.

The overall impact of the film is to question many aspects of modern life, including medicine, education, industry, and government. The use of the theatrical devices of nonrealism, Brechtian alienation, and the naive main character allowed Anderson freedom to wander away from the narrative at will. The effect is powerful. When he was not making films, Anderson directed theatre. *O Lucky Man!*, with its focus on ideas about society, is more clearly a link to that theatrical experience than to Anderson's previous film, *Every Day except Christmas* (1957).

Not to be overlooked in this discussion of British directors is John Schlesinger. He also began in documentary. He produced an award-winning documentary, *Terminus* (1960), went on to direct a realist film, *A Kind of Loving* (1962), and, like his colleagues, began to explore the nonrealist possibilities.

Billy Liar (1963) is one of the most successful hybrid films. Originally a novel and then a play by Keith Waterhouse and Willis Hall, the story of Billy Fisher is the quintessential film about refusing to come of age.

Billy Fisher (Tom Courtenay) lies about everything: his family, his friends, his talents. Inevitably, those lies get him into trouble, and his charm cannot extricate him. He retreats into his fantasy world, Ambrosia, where he is general, king, and key potentate.

The editing is used to work Billy's fantasies into the film. Schlesinger straight-cut the fantasies as if they were happening as part of the developing action. If Billy's father or employer says something objectionable to Billy, the film straight-cuts to Billy in uniform, machine-gunning the culprit to death. If Billy walks, fantasizing about his fame, the film straight-cuts to the crowds for a soccer match. Schlesinger intercuts with the potentate Billy in uniform speaking to the masses. Before the speech, they are reflective; after it, they are overjoyed. Then the film cuts back to Billy walking in the town or in the glen above the town.

Billy is inventive, charming, and involving as a main character, but it is the integration of his fantasy life into the film that makes the character and the film engage us on a deeper level. The editing not only gives us insight into the private Billy, it also allows us to indulge in our own fantasies. To the extent that we identify with Billy, we are given license to a wider range of feeling than in many films. By using nonrealism, Schlesinger strengthened the audience's openness to theatrical devices in narrative films. He used them extensively in his successful American debut, *Midnight Cowboy* (1969).

No discussion of the influence of theatre on film would be complete without mention of Peter Brook. In a way, his work in film has been as challenging as his work in theatre. From *Marat/Sade* (1966) to his more recent treatment with Jean-Claude Carriere of *Maharabata* (1990), Brook has explored the mediation between theatre and film. His most successful hybrid film is certainly *Marat/Sade*.

The story is best described by the full title of the play: *Marat/Sade (The Persecution and Assassination of Jean-Paul Marat as Performed by the Inmates of the Asylum of Charenton under the Direction of the Marquis de Sade).* The playwright Peter Weiss was interested in the interfaces between play and audience, between madness and reality, and between historical fact and fiction. He used the set as well as the dramaturgy to provoke consideration of his ideas, and he mixed burlesque with realism. He used particular characters to "debate" positions, particularly the spirit of revolution and its bloody representative, Marat, and the spirit of the senses and its cynical representative, the Marquis de Sade.

The play, written and produced 20 years after World War II, ponders issues arising out of that war as well as issues central to the 1960s: war, idealism, politics, and a revolution of personal expectations. The work blurs the question: Who is mad, who is sane, and is there a difference?

The major problem that Brook faced was how to make the play relevant to a film audience. (The film was produced by United Artists.)

Brook chose to direct this highly stylized theatrical piece as a documentary.[3] He used hand-held cameras, intense close-ups, a reliance on the illusion of natural light from windows, and a live sound that makes the production by the inmates convincing. Occasionally, the film cuts to an extreme long shot showing the barred room in which the play is being presented. It also cuts frequently to the audience for the performance: the director of the asylum and two guests. Cutaways to nuns and guards in the performance area also remind us that we are watching a performance.

In essence, *Marat/Sade* is a play within a play within a film. Each layer is carefully created and supported visually. When the film cuts to the singing chorus, we view *Marat/Sade* as a play. When it cuts to the audience and intercuts their reactions with the play, Marat/Sade is a play within a play. When Charlotte Corday (Glenda Jackson in her film debut) appears in a close-up, a patient attempts to act as Corday would, or the Marquis de Sade (Peter Magee) directs his performers, *Marat/Sade* becomes a film.

Because *Marat/Sade* is a film about ideas, Brook chose a hybrid approach to make those ideas about politics and sanity meaningful to his audience. The film remains a powerful commentary on the issues and a creative example of how theatre and film can interface.

☐ NOTES/REFERENCES

1. In the drama genre, young writers such as Rod Serling, Reginald Rose, and Paddy Cheyefsky, and young directors such as John Frankenheimer, Sidney Lumet, and Arthur Penn developed their creative skills in television. Writers such as Carl Reiner and Woody Allen came out of television variety shows, and many performers got their start in television comedy. This continues to this day: Bill Murray, Chevy Chase, John Belushi, Gilda Radner, and Dan Ackroyd all entered the movie industry based on their success in "Saturday Night Live."
2. In "Changes in Narrative Structure, 1960–80: A Study in Screenwriting," a paper presented at the Popular Culture Conference, March, 1984, Toronto, I noted that master scenes in *The Apartment* (1960) were 5 minutes long. By 1980, the length of the average master scene was 2 minutes.
3. Bob Fosse decided to direct Cabaret (1972) as film noir. He combined opposites—musical and film noir, theatre and documentary. This seems a contradiction, but in both cases, it works to clarify one medium by using another.

10

New Challenges to Filmic Narrative Conventions

■

The international advances of the 1950s and the technological experiments in wide screen and documentary techniques provided the context for the influence of television and theatre in the 1960s and 1970s. The sum effect was twofold: to make the flow of talent and creative influence more international than ever and, more important, to signal that innovation, whether its source was new or old, was critical. Indeed, the creative explosion of the 1950s and 1960s was nothing less than a gauntlet, a challenge to the next generation to make artful what was ordinary and to make art from the extraordinary. The result was an explosion of individualistic invention that has had a profound effect on how the partnership of sound and image has been manipulated. The innovations have truly been international, with a German director making an American film (*Paris, Texas*, 1984) and an American director making a European film (*Barry Lyndon*, 1975).

This chapter reviews many of the highlights of the period 1968–1988, focusing primarily on those films and filmmakers who challenged the conventions of film storytelling. In each case, the editing of sound and image is the vehicle for that challenge.

☐ PECKINPAH: ALIENATION AND ANARCHY

Sam Peckinpah's career before *The Wild Bunch* (1969) suggested his preference for working within the Western genre, but nothing in the style of his earlier Westerns, *Ride the High Country* (1962) and *Major Dundee* (1965), suggested his overwhelming reliance on editing in *The Wild Bunch*. Thematically, the passing of the West and of its values provides the continuity between these films and those that followed, primarily *The Ballad of Cable Hogue* (1970) and *Junior Bonner* (1972). Peckinpah's later films, whether in the Western genre (*Bring Me the Head of Alfredo Garcia*, 1974) or the gangster genre (*The Getaway*, 1972) or the war genre (*Cross of Iron*, 1977), refer back to the editing style of *The Wild Bunch*; theme and editing style fuse to create a very important example of the power of editing.

The Wild Bunch was not the first film to explore violence by creating an editing pattern that conveyed the horror and fascination of the moment of death. The greatest filmmaker to explore the moment of death, albeit in a highly politicized context, was Sergei Eisenstein. The death of the young girl and the horse on the bridge in *October* (1928) and, of course, the Odessa Steps sequence in *Potemkin* (1925) are among the most famous editing sequences in history. Both sequences explore the moment of death of victims caught in political upheavals.

Later films, such as Fred Zinnemann's *High Noon* (1952), focus on the anticipation and anxiety of that moment when death is imminent. Robert Enrico's *An Occurrence at Owl Creek* (1962) is devoted in its entirety to the desire-to-live fantasy of a man in the moment before he is hanged. The influential *Bonnie and Clyde* (1967), Arthur Penn's exploration of love and violence, no doubt had a great impact on Peckinpah's choice of editing style.

Peckinpah's film recounts the last days of Bishop Pike (William Holden) and his "Wild Bunch," outlaws who are violent without compunction—not traditional Western heroes. Pursued by railroad men and bounty hunters, they flee into Mexico where they work for a renegade general who seems more evil than the outlaws or the bounty hunters. Each group is portrayed as lawless and evil. In this setting of amorality, the Wild Bunch become heroic.

No description can do justice to Peckinpah's creation of violence. It is present everywhere, and when it strikes, its destructive force is conveyed by all of the elements of editing that move audiences: close-ups, moving camera shots, composition, proximity of the camera to the action, and, above all, pace. An examination of the first sequence in the film and of the final gunfight illustrates Peckinpah's technique.

In the opening sequence, the Wild Bunch, dressed as American soldiers, ride into a Texas town and rob the bank. The robbery was anticipated, and the railroad men and bounty hunters, coordinated by Deke Thornton (Robert Ryan), a former member of the Wild Bunch, have set a trap for Bishop Pike and his men. Unfortunately, a temperance meeting begins to march toward the bank. The trap results in the deaths of more than half of the Wild Bunch, but many townspeople are also killed. Pike and four of his men escape.

This sequence can be broken down into three distinct phases: the 5½-minute ride into town, the 4½-minute robbery, and the 5-minute fight to escape from the town. The pace accelerates as we move through the phases, but Peckinpah relies on narrative techniques to amplify his view of the robbery, the law, and the role of violence in the lives of both the townspeople and the criminals. Peckinpah crosscuts between four groups throughout the sequence: the Wild Bunch, the railroad men and the bounty hunters, the religious town meeting, and a group of children gathered on the outskirts of town. The motif of the children is particularly important because it is used to open and close the sequence.

The children are watching a scorpion being devoured by red ants. In the final phase, the children destroy the scorpion and the red ants. If

Peckinpah's message was that in this world you devour or are devoured, he certainly found a graphic metaphor to illustrate his message. The ants, the scorpion, and the children are shown principally in close-ups. In fact, close-ups are extensively used throughout the sequence.

In terms of pace, there is a gradual escalation of shots between the first two phases. The ride of the Wild Bunch into town has 65 shots in $5\frac{1}{2}$ minutes. The robbery itself has 95 shots in $4\frac{1}{2}$ minutes. In the final phase, the fight to escape from the town, a 5-minute section, the pace rapidly accelerates. This section has two hundred shots with an average length of $1\frac{1}{2}$ seconds.

The final sequence is interesting not only for the use of intense close-ups and quick cutting, but also for the number of shots that focus on the moment of death. Slow motion was used often to draw out the instant of death. One member of the Wild Bunch is shot on horseback and crashes through a storefront window. The image is almost lovingly recorded in slow motion. What message is imparted? The impact is often a fascination with and a glorification of that violent instant of death. The same lingering treatment of the destruction of the scorpion and the ants underscores the cruelty and suffering implicit in the action.

The opening sequence establishes the relentless violence that characterizes the balance of the film. The impact of the opening sequence is almost superseded by the violence of the final gunfight. In this sequence, Pike and his men have succeeded in stealing guns for the renegade General Mapache. They have been paid, but Mapache has abducted the sole Mexican member of the Wild Bunch, Angel (Jaime Sanchez). Earlier, Angel had killed Mapache's mistress, a young woman Angel had claimed as his own. Angel had also given guns to the local guerrillas who were fighting against Mapache. Mapache has tortured Angel, and Pike and his men feel that they must stand together; they want Angel back. In this last fight, they insist on Angel's return. Mapache agrees, but slits Angel's throat in front of them. Pike kills Mapache. A massacre ensues in which Pike and the three remaining members of the Wild Bunch fight against hundreds of Mapache's soldiers. Many die, including all of the members of the Wild Bunch.

The entire sequence can be broken down into three phases: the preparation and march to confront Mapache, the confrontation with Mapache up to the deaths of Angel and Mapache, and the massacre itself (Figure 10.1). The entire sequence is 10 minutes long. The march to Mapache runs 3 minutes and 40 seconds. There are 40 shots in the march sequence; the average shot is almost 6 seconds long. In this sequence, zoom shots and camera motion are used to postpone editing. The camera follows the Wild Bunch as they approach Mapache.

The next phase, the confrontation with Mapache, runs 1 minute and 40 seconds and contains 70 shots. The unpredictability of Mapache's behavior and the shock of the manner in which he kills Angel leads to greater fragmentation and an acceleration of the pace of the sequence. Many close-ups

Figure 10.1   *The Wild Bunch*, 1959. ©1959 Warner Bros.–Seven Arts. All Rights Reserved. Still provided by British Film Institute.

of Pike, the Wild Bunch, and Mapache and his soldiers add to the tension of this brief sequence.

Finally, the massacre phase runs 4½ minutes and contains approximately 270 shots, making the average length of a shot 1 second. Some shots run 2 to 3 seconds, particularly when Peckinpah tried to set up a key narrative event, such as the characters who finally kill Pike and Dutch (Ernest Borgnine). Those characters are a young woman and a small boy dressed as a soldier and armed with a rifle.

Few sequences in film history portray the anarchy of violence as vividly as the massacre sequence at the end of *The Wild Bunch*. Many close-ups are used, the camera moves, the camera is placed very close to the subject, and, where possible, juxtapositions of foreground and background are included. Unlike the opening sequence, where the violence of death seemed to be memorialized in slow motion, the violence of this sequence proceeds less carefully. Chaos and violence are equated with an intensity that wears out the viewer. The resulting emotional exhaustion led Peckinpah to use an epilogue that shifts the point of view from the dead Bishop Pike to the living Deke Thornton. For 5 more minutes, Peckinpah elaborated on the fate of Thornton and the bounty hunters. He also used a reprise to bring back all of the members of the Wild Bunch. Interestingly, all are images of laughter, quite distant from the violence of the massacre.

Rarely in cinema has the potential impact of pace been so powerfully explored as in *The Wild Bunch*. Peckinpah was interested in the alienation of character from context. His outlaws are men out of their time; 1913 was no longer a time for Western heroes, not even on the American–Mexican border. Peckinpah used pace to create a fascination and later a visual experience of the anarchy of violence. Without these two narrative perspectives—the alienation that comes with modern life and the ensuing violence as two worlds clash—the pace could not have been as deeply affecting as it is in *The Wild Bunch*.

□ ALTMAN: THE FREEDOM OF CHAOS

Robert Altman is a particularly interesting director whose primary interest is to capture creatively and ironically a sense of modern life. He does not dwell on urban anxiety as Woody Allen does or search for the new altruism à la Sidney Lumet in *Serpico* (1973) and *Prince of the City* (1981). Altman uses his films to deconstruct myth (*McCabe and Mrs. Miller*, 1971) and to capture the ambience of place and time (*The Long Goodbye*, 1973). He uses a freer editing style to imply that our chaotic times can liberate as well as oppress. To be more specific, Altman uses sound and image editing as well as a looser narrative structure to create an ambience that is both chaotic and liberating. His 1975 film, *Nashville*, is instructive.

Nashville tells the story of more than 20 characters in a 5-day period in the city of Nashville, a center for country music. A political campaign adds a political dimension to the sociological construct that Altman explores. He jumps freely from the story of a country star in emotional crisis (Ronee Blakley) to a wife in a marriage crisis (Lily Tomlin) and from those who aspire to be stars (Barbara Harris) to those who live off stars (Geraldine Chaplin and Ned Beatty) to those who would exploit stars for political ends (Michael Murphy). Genuine performers (Henry Gibson and Keith Carradine) mix career and everyday life uneasily by reaching an accord between their professional and personal lives.

In the shortened time frame of 5 days in a single city, Nashville, Altman jumped from character to character to focus on their goals, their dreams, and the reality of their lives. The gap between dream and actuality is the fabric of the film. How to maintain continuity given the number of characters is the editing challenge.

The primary editing strategy Altman used in this film was to establish the principle of randomness. Early in the film, whether to introduce a character arriving by airplane or one at work in a recording studio, Altman used a slow editing pace in which he focused on slow movement to catch the characters in action in an ensemble style. Characters speak simultaneously, one in the foreground, another in the background, while responding to an action: a miscue in a recording session, a car accident on the freeway, a fainting spell at the airport. Something visual occurs, and then the ensemble approach allows a cacophony of sound, dialogue, and effects to establish a sense of chaos as we struggle to decide to which character we should try to listen. As we are doing so, the film cuts to another character at the same location.

After we have experienced brief scenes of four characters in a linked location, we begin to follow the randomness of the film. Randomness, rather than pace, shapes how we feel. Instead of the powerful intensity of Peckinpah's *The Wild Bunch*, we sense the instability that random action and response suggests in Altman's film. The uneasiness grows as we get to know the characters better, and by the time the film ends in chaos and assassination, we have a feeling for the gap between dreams and actuality and where it can lead.

Altman's *Nashville* is as troubling as Peckinpah's *The Wild Bunch*, but in *Nashville*, a random editing style that uses sound as a catalyst leads us to a result similar to that of pace in *The Wild Bunch*.

Sound itself is insufficient to create the power of *Nashville*. The ensemble of actors who create individuals is as helpful as the editing pattern. Given its importance to the city, music is another leitmotif that helps create continuity. Finally, the principle of crosscutting, with its implication of meaning arising from the interplay of two scenes, is carried to an extreme, becoming a device that is repeatedly relied upon to create meaning. Together with the randomness of the editing pattern and the overcrowded sound track, crosscutting is used to create meaning in *Nashville*.

□ KUBRICK: NEW WORLDS AND OLD

Stanley Kubrick has made films about a wide spectrum of subjects set in very different time periods. Coming as they did in an era of considerable editing panache, Kubrick's editing choices, particularly in *2001: A Space Odyssey* (1968) and *Barry Lyndon* (1975), established a style that helped create the sense of the period.

2001: A Space Odyssey begins with the vast expanse of prehistoric time. The prologue proceeds slowly to create a sense of endless time. The images are random and still. Only when the apes appear is there editing continuity, but that continuity is slow and deliberate and not paced for emotional effect. It seems to progress along a line of narrative clarification rather than emotional intensity. When an ape throws a bone into the air, the transition to the age of interplanetary travel is established by a cut on movement from the bone to a space station moving through space.

As we proceed through the story, which speculates on the existence of a deity in outer space, and through the conflict of humanity and machine, the editing is paced to underline the stability of the idea that humanity has conquered nature; at least, they think they have. The careful and elegant cuts on camera movement support this sense of world order. Kubrick's choice of music and its importance in the film also support this sense of order. Indeed, the shape of the entire film more closely resembles the movements of a symphony rather than the acts of a screen narrative.

Only two interventions challenge this sense of mastery. The first is the struggle of HAL the computer to kill the humans on the spaceship. In this struggle, one human survives. The second is the journey beyond Jupiter into infinity. Here, following the monolith, conventional time collapses, and a different type of continuity has to be created.

In the first instance, the struggle with HAL, all the conventions of the struggle between protagonist and antagonist come into play; crosscutting, a paced struggle between HAL and the astronauts leads to the outcome of the struggle, the deaths of four of the astronauts. This struggle relies on many closeups of Bowman (Keir Dullea) and HAL as well as the articulation of the deaths of HAL's four victims. A more traditional editing style prevails in this sequence (Figure 10.2).

In the later sequence, in which the spaceship passes through infinity and Bowman arrives in the future, the traditional editing style is replaced by a series of jump cuts. In rapid succession, Bowman sees himself as a middle-aged man, an old man, and then a dying man. The setting, French Provincial, seems out of place in the space age, but it helps to link the future with the past. As Bowman lies dying in front of the monolith, we are transported into space, and to the strains of "Thus Speak Zarathustra," Bowman is reborn. We see him as a formed embryo, and as the film ends, the life

Figure 10.2 *2001: A Space Odyssey*, 1968. Copyright Turner Entertainment Company. All Rights Reserved. Still provided by British Film Institute.

cycle has come full circle. In Kubrick's view of the future, real time and film time become totally altered. It is this collapse of real time that is Kubrick's greatest achievement in the editing of *2001: A Space Odyssey*.

Barry Lyndon is based on William Thackeray's novel about a young Irishman who believes that the acquisition of wealth and status will position him for happiness. Sadly, the means he chooses to succeed condemn him to fail. This eighteenth-century morality tale moves from Ireland to the Seven Years War on the continent to Germany and finally to England.

To achieve the feeling of the eighteenth century, it was not enough for Kubrick to film on location. He edited the film to create a sense of time just as he did in *2001*. In *Barry Lyndon*, however, he tried to create a sense of time that was much slower than our present. Indeed, Kubrick set out to pace the film against our expectations (Figure 10.3).[1]

In the first portion of the film, Redmond Barry (Ryan O'Neal) loves his cousin, Nora, but she chooses to marry an English captain. Barry challenges and defeats the captain in a duel. This event forces him to leave his home; he enlists in the army and fights in Europe.

The first shot of Barry and Nora lasts 32 seconds, the second shot lasts 36 seconds, and the third lasts 46 seconds. When Barry and Nora walk in the woods to discuss her marriage to the captain, the shot is 90 seconds long. By moving the camera and using a zoom lens, Kubrick was able to follow the action rather than rely on the editing. The length of these initial shots slows down our expectations of the pacing of the film and helps the film

Figure 10.3   *Barry Lyndon*, 1975. ©1975 Warner Bros. Inc. All Rights Reserved. Still Provided by British Film Institute.

create its own sense of time: a sense of time that Kubrick deemed appropriate to transport us into a different period from our own. Kubrick used this editing style to re-create that past world. The editing is psychologically as critical as the costumes or the language. In a more subtle way, the editing of *Barry Lyndon* achieves that other-world quality that was so powerfully captured in *2001*.

□ HERZOG: OTHER WORLDS

Stanley Kubrick was not alone in using an editing style to create a psychological context for a place or a character. Werner Herzog created a megalomania that requires conquests in *Aguirre: The Wrath of God* (1972). Aguirre the Spanish conquistador is the subject of the film. Even more challenging was Herzog's *The Enigma of Kaspar Hauser* (1974), the nineteenth-century story about a foundling who, having been kept isolated, has no human communication skills at the onset of the story. He is taken in by townspeople and learns to speak. He becomes a source of admiration and study, but also of ridicule. He is unpredictable, rational, and animistic.

Herzog set out to create an editing style that simulated Kaspar's sense of time and of his struggle with the conventions of his society. Initially, the shots are very long and static. Later, when Kaspar becomes socialized, the shots are shorter, simulating real time. Later, when he has relapses, there are gaps in the logic of the sequencing of the shots that simulate how he feels. Finally, when he dies, the community's sense of time returns. In this film, Herzog succeeded in using editing to reflect the psychology of the lead character just as he did in his earlier film.

In both films, the editing pattern simulates a different world view than our own, giving these films a strange but fascinating quality. They transport us to places we've never before experienced. In so doing, they move us in ways unusual in film.

□ SCORSESE: THE DRAMATIC DOCUMENT

Martin Scorsese's *Raging Bull* (1980) is both a film document about Jake LaMotta, a middle-heavyweight boxing champion, and a dramatization of LaMotta's personal and professional lives. The dissonance between realism and psychological insight has rarely been more pronounced, primarily because the character of LaMotta (played by Robert Do Niro) is a man who cannot control his rages. He is a jealous husband, an irrational brother, and a prize fighter who taunts his opponents; he knows no pain, and his scorn for everyone is so profound that it seems miraculous that the man has not killed anyone by the film's end (Figure 10.4).

Figure 10.4   *Raging Bull*, 1980. Courtesy MGM/UA. Still provided by British
Film Institute.

That is not to say that the film is not slavish in its sense of actuality
and realism. Do Niro, who portrays LaMotta over almost a 20-year period,
appears at noticeably different weights. It's difficult to believe that the later
LaMotta is portrayed by the same actor as was the early LaMotta.

In the non-fight scenes, Scorsese moved the camera as little as possible.
In combination with the excellent set designs, the result is a realistic sense
of time and place rather than a stylized sense of time and place.

In the fight sequences, Scorsese raised the dramatic intensity to a level
commensurate with LaMotta's will to win at any cost. LaMotta is portrayed
as a man whose ego has been set aside; he is all will, and his will is relentless and cruel. This trait is not usually identified with complex, believable
characters.

The fight genre has provided many metaphors, including the immigrant's dream in *Golden Boy* (1939), the existential struggle in *The Set-Up* (1949), the class struggle in *Champion* (1949), the American dream in *Somebody Up There Likes Me* (1956), and the American nightmare in *Body and Soul* (1947). All of these stories have dramatic texture, but none has attempted to take us into the subjective world of a character who must be a champion because if he weren't, he'd be in prison for murder. This is Scorsese's goal in *Raging Bull*.

To create this world, Scorsese relies very heavily on sound. This is not to say that his visuals are not dynamic. He does use a great deal of camera motion (particularly the smooth handheld motion of a Stedicam), subjective camera placement, and close-ups of the fight in slow motion. However, the sound envelops us in the brutality of the boxing ring. In the ring, the wonderful operatic score gives way to sensory explosions. As we watch a boxer demolished in slow motion, the punches resound as explosions rather than as leather-to-flesh contact.

In the Cerdan fight, in which LaMotta finally wins the championship, image and sound slow and distort to illustrate Cerdan's collapse. In the Robinson fight, in which LaMotta loses his title, sound grinds to a halt as Robinson contemplates his next stroke. LaMotta is all but taunting him, arms down, body against the ropes. As Robinson looks at his prey, the sound drops off and the image becomes almost a freeze frame. Then, as the raised arm comes down on LaMotta, the sound returns, and the graphic explosions of blood and sweat that emanate from the blow give way to the crowd, which cries out in shock. LaMotta is defiant as he loses his title.

By elevating and elaborating the sound effects and by distorting and sharpening the sounds of the fight, Scorsese developed a dramatized envelopment of feeling about the fight, about LaMotta, about violence, and about will as a factor in life.

In a sense, Scorsese followed an editing goal similar to those of Francis Ford Coppola in *Apocalypse Now* (1979) and David Lynch in *Blue Velvet* (1986). Each used sound to take us into the interior world of their main characters without censoring that world of its psychic and physical violence. The interior world of LaMotta took Scorsese far from the superficial realism of a real-life main character. Scorsese seems to have acknowledged the surface life of LaMotta while creating and highlighting the primacy of the interior life with a pattern of sound and image that works off the counterpoint of the surface relative to the interior. Because we hear sound before we see the most immediate element to be interpreted, it is the sound editing in *Raging Bull* that signals the primacy of the interior life of Jake LaMotta over its surface visual triumphs and defeats. The documentary element of the film consequently is secondary in importance to the psychic pain of will, which creates a more lasting view of LaMotta than his transient championship.

☐ WENDERS: MIXING POPULAR AND FINE ART

Wim Wenders's *Paris, Texas*, written by Sam Shepard, demonstrates Wenders's role as a director who chooses a visual style that is related to the visual arts and a narrative style that is related to the popular form sometimes referred to as "the journey." From *The Odyssey* to the road pictures of Bob Hope and Bing Crosby, the journey has been a metaphor to which audiences have related.

Wenders used the visual dimension of the story as a nonverbal roadmap to understanding the characters, their relationships, and the confusion of the main character. This nonverbal dimension is not always clear in the narrative.

Because Wenders used a layered approach to the unfolding understanding of his story, pace does not play a major role in the editing of this film. Instead, the visual context is critical to understanding the film's layers of meaning. The foreground–background juxtaposition is the critical factor.

Paris, Texas relates the story of Travis (Harry Dean Stanton), a man we first meet as he wanders through the Texas desert. We soon learn that he deserted his family 4 years earlier. The first part of the film is the journey from Texas to California, where his brother has been taking care of Travis's son, Hunter. The second part concerns the father–son relationship. Although Hunter was four when his parents left him, his knowledge seems to transcend his age. In the last part of the film, Travis and Hunter return to Texas to find Jane (Nastassia Kinski), the wife and mother. In Texas, Travis discovers why he does not have the qualities necessary for family life, and he leaves Hunter in the care of his mother.

A narrative summary can outline the story, but it cannot articulate Travis's ability to understand his world and his place in it. The first image Wenders presents is the juxtaposition of Travis in the desert. The foreground of a midshot of Travis contrasts with visual depth and clarity of the desert. The environment dwarfs Travis, and he seems to have little meaning in this context. Nor is he more at home in Los Angeles. Throughout the film, Travis searches for Paris, Texas, where he thinks he was conceived. Later in the film, when he visits the town, it doesn't shed light on his feelings.

Wenders sets up a series of juxtapositions throughout the film: Travis and his environment, the car and the endless road, and, later, Travis and Jane. In one of the most poignant juxtapositions, Travis visits Jane in a Texas brothel. He speaks to her on a phone, with a one-way mirror separating them. He can look at her, but she cannot see him. In this scene, fantasy and reality are juxtaposed. Jane can be whatever Travis wants her to be. This poignant but ironic image contrasts to their real-life relationship in which she couldn't be what he wanted her to be.

These juxtapositions are further textured by differing light and color in the foreground–background mix. Wenders, working with German cameraman Robbie Muller, fashioned a nether world effect. By strengthening the visual over the narrative meaning of individual images, he created a line somewhere between foreground and background. That line may elucidate the interior crisis of Travis or it may be a boundary beyond which rational meaning is not available. In either case, by using this foreground–background mix, Wenders created a dreamscape out of an externalized, recognizable journey popular in fiction and film. The result is an editing style that deemphasizes direct meaning but implies a feeling of disconnectedness that illustrates well Travis's interior world.

□ LEE: PACE AND SOCIAL ACTION

As a filmmaker, Spike Lee has constantly experimented with narrative convention. In *She's Gotta Have It* (1986), Lee had the main character address his audience directly. The narrative structure of that film was open-ended and rather more a meditation on relationships than a prescription for relationships. The narrative structure of *Mo' Better Blues* (1990) is also meditative but does not parallel the earlier film. Rather its structure approximates the rhythm of a spontaneous blues riff. A film between the two is even more different. The narrative structure of *Do the Right Thing* (1989) is analogous to an avalanche rushing down a steep mountain. Racial bigotry is the first rock, and the streets of Brooklyn the valley inundated with the inevitable destructive force of the results of that first rock falling.

There is no question that Spike Lee has as his goal to reach first an African-American audience, then an American audience and an international audience. His themes are rooted in the African-American experience, from the interpersonal (*Crooklyn*, 1994) to the interracial (*Jungle Fever*, 1991) to the political (*Malcolm X*, 1992) to the politics of color (*School Daze*, 1988). He is concerned about man-woman relationships (*She's Gotta Have It*), about family relationships (*Jungle Fever, Crooklyn*). Always he is interested in ideology and education, first and foremost in the African-American community (Figures 10.5 and 10.6).

But Lee is also a filmmaker interested in the aesthetic possibilities of visual expression. Although we will focus on his experiments with pace to promote social action, he has also explored the excitement of camera motion (following the character he plays in *Malcolm X* across the streets of Harlem), the possibilities of slow circular motion in the interview scene in *Jungle Fever*, and the possibilities of distortion of color using reversal film as the originating material in *Clockers* (1995). He is always exploring the possibilities of the medium.

The greatest tool, however, that Spike Lee has turned to is pace. Given his agenda for social change, one might anticipate that he would be attratced to pace as he is in *Do the Right Thing* to raise public ire and anger about racism. Although he uses pace very effectively in that film to promote a sense of

Figure 10.5   *Crooklyn*, 1994. Courtesy Forty Acres and a Mule Filmworks/Spike Lee.

Figure 10.6   *Crooklyn*, 1994. Courtesy Forty Acres and a Mule Filmworks/Spike Lee.

outrage, it is actually his other less predictable experiments with pace that make his work so interesting.

Jungle Fever, his exploration of an interracial relationship between an African-American male and an Italian-American female, is notable in how Lee backs away from using pace to create an us-against-them, hero-villain sense in the film (Figure 10.7). In fact, he only resorts to the expected sense of pace around the excitement of the initial sexual encounter of the couple. After that, with family hostility to the relationship growing, we might expect a growing sense of tension with the arc of the interracial relationship. But it doesn't happen. Instead, the tension and consequent use of pace shifts to those around the two lovers. In the Italian community, Angela, the young Italian-American woman (Annabella Sciorra), is beaten by her father upon discovery of the relationship. Pace, as expected, is an important expression of the emotion in the scene. Later, when Angela's spurned boyfriend, Pauly, speaks for tolerance toward the the African-American community, the tension in his soda and newspaper shop is palpable. His customers are intolerant about the new black mayor of New York and Pauly asks politely if they voted. And when he is kind to a young African-American female customer, these same customers are filled with rage and sexual aggression. Pace again plays an important role in the scene.

With regards to the African-American lover (Wesley Snipes), his community also expresses its tension about his new relationship. Whether it is his

Figure 10.7   *Jungle Fever*, 1991. Copyright ©1991 Universal Studios, Inc. All rights reserved. Courtesy Forty Acres and a Mule Filmworks/Spike Lee.

wife's female friends' discussions about black men and white women, or his visit to the Taj Mahal crack house to retrieve his parents' color television from his brother, Gator, in both scenes pace plays an important role to create tension about the potential outcomes of interracial as well as interfamilial relationships.

In relative terms, the exercise of a slower pace in the scenes between the two lovers creates a sense of reason and tolerance that doesn't exist either in the Italian-American community nor in the African-American community. Although the relationship in the end fails, by using pace in a way that we don't expect, Lee has created a meditation on interracial relationships rather than a prescriptive statement on those relationships.

In *Crooklyn*, the focus is less on two people than on a family in Brooklyn. And Lee has a different goal in the film—to suggest the strengths of the family and of the community.

Pace can be used to create tension, to deepen the sense of conflict between individuals, families, or communities. Pace can also be used to suggest excitement, energy, power. It is this latter use of pace to which Lee turns in *Crooklyn*. He wants to suggest the energy and positive force of family and community. The opening fifteen minutes of *Crooklyn* are instructive here. Children play in the streets adjacent to their home. The day is bright and the feeling is positive. He cuts on movement to make the energy seem more dynamic and positive.

In the home proper, the Carmichael family includes mother (Alfre Woodard), the father (Delroy Lindo), their five children and a dog. The family scenes, whether they are meals together or watching television or sharing news about the future, are energetic and dynamic. The feeling of the scenes is directed by the way Lee uses pace. At times even the chaos seems appealing because of the way pace is used.

These domestic scenes intercut with the less stable elements of the community, strengthen the feeling of the importance of family, of having a mother and a father, even one where the parents have divergent views about discipline.

Throughout the opening scenes, pace is used to affirm a positive, energetic sense of the Carmichael family in the Brooklyn community they are part of. Here, pace is used to underline the values of family so often the sources of tension in *Jungle Fever*.

Family and its values are also at the heart of the narrative in *Clockers* (Figures 10.8 and 10.9). Because *Clockers* is in its form a crime story, in this case the murder of a fast-food manager, we expect the investigation and prosecution of the perpetrator to dictate a particular pace to the film. The expected pace is cut faster as we move to the climax, the exciting apprehension of the perpetrator of the crime. The baptism scene at the end of *The Godfather* is a classic example of the use of pace to create a sense of climax and release in such a scene.

Lee sidesteps the entire set of expectations we bring to the crime story. Instead he fleshes out the narrative of an African-American family, the eldest

Figure 10.8   *Clockers*, 1995. Courtesy Forty Acres and a Mule Filmworks/Spike Lee.

son having been accused of the crime; but it is the youngest son in the family, the son deeply involved in the traffic of drugs, who we expect is the real killer, and it is this son who is the focus of the police investigation.

In order to discourage his audience from the celebration of violence inherent in the crime film, in order to educate his audience about the real crimes—drugs, mutual exploitation, the increasingly young perpetrators of violent crime in our ghettoes—Lee turns away from pace as a narrative tool. Just as he replaces scenes of characterization for scenes of action, he more slowly cuts those scenes of action when they occur. He also focusses far more on the victims of emotional and physical violence and undermines the potential heroic posture for the perpetrators, the drug king (Delroy Lindo) and the police investigator (Harvey Keitel).

By doing so, Lee risks disappointing his audience, who are accustomed to the fast pace of the crime story. But by doing so, he is pushing into the forefront his educational goals over his entertainment goals. Social action, a new rather than expected action, this is Spike Lee's goal in *Clockers*. And pace, albeit not as expected, plays an important role in *Clockers*.

□ VON TROTTA: FEMINISM AND POLITICS

In the 1970s, Margarethe von Trotta distinguished herself as a screenwriter on a series of films directed by her husband, Volker Schlondorff. They

Figure 10.9   *Clockers*, 1995. Courtesy Forty Acres and a Mule Filmworks/Spike
Lee.

codirected the film adaptation of the Henrich Böll novel, *The Lost Honor
of Katharina Blum* (1975). In 1977, von Trotta began her career as a writer-
director with *The Second Awakening of Crista Klages.*

All of her work as a director is centered on female characters attempting
to understand and act upon their environment. Von Trotta is interesting
in her attempt to find a narrative style suitable to her work as an artist, a
feminist, and a woman. As a result, her work is highly political in subject
matter, and when compared to the dominant male approach to narrative
and to editing choices, von Trotta appears to be searching for alternatives,
particularly narrative alternatives. Before examining *Marianne and Julianne*
(1982), it is useful to examine von Trotta's efforts in the light of earlier female
directors.

In the generation that preceded von Trotta, few female directors worked. Two Italians who captured international attention were Lina Wertmüller and Liliana Cavani. Wertmüller (*Swept Away-.-.-.-*, 1975; *Seven Beauties*, 1976) embraced a satiric style that did not stand out as the work of a woman. Her work centered on male central characters, and in terms of subject—male-female relationships, class conflicts, regional conflicts—her point of view usually reflected that of the Italian male. In this sense, her films do not differ in tone or narrative style from the earlier style of Pietro Germi (*Divorce—Italian Style*, 1962).

Liliana Cavani (*The Night Porter*, 1974) did make films with female central characters, but her operatic style owed more to Luchino Visconti than to a feminist sensibility. If Wertmüller was concerned with male sexuality and identity, Cavani was concerned with female sexuality and identity.

Before Wertmüller and Cavani, there were few female directors. However, Leni Riefenstahl's experimentation in *Olympia* (1938) does suggest an effort to move away from a linear pattern of storytelling.

Although generalization has its dangers, a number of observations about contemporary narrative style set von Trotta's work in context in another way. There is little question that filmmaking is a male-dominated art form and industry, and there is little question that film narratives unfold in a pattern that implies cause and effect. The result is an editing pattern that tries to clarify narrative causation and create emotion from characters' efforts to resolve their problems.

What of the filmmaker who is not interested in the cause and effect of a linear narrative? What of the filmmaker who adopts a more tentative position and wishes to understand a political event or a personal relationship? What of the filmmaker who doesn't believe in closure in the classic narrative sense?

This is how we have to consider the work of Margarethe von Trotta. It's not so much that she reacted against the classic narrative conventions. Instead, she tried to reach her audience using an approach suitable to her goals, and these goals seem to be very different from those of male-dominated narrative conventions.

It may be useful to try to construct a feminist narrative model that does not conform to classic conventions, but rather has different goals and adopts different means. That model could be developed using recent feminist writing. Particularly useful is the book, *Women's Way of Knowing: The Development of Self, Voice and Mind*.[2] Mary Field Belenky and her co-authors suggest that women "that are less inclined to see themselves as separate from the 'theys' than are men, may also be accounted for by women's rootedness in a sense of connection and men's emphasis on separation and autonomy."[3] In comparing the development of an inner voice in women to that of men, the authors suggest the following: "These women reveal that their epistemology has shifted away from an earlier assumption of 'truth from above' to a belief in multiple personal truths. The form that multiplicity (subjectivism) takes in these women, however, is not at all the masculine assertion that 'I have the right to my opinion;' rather, it is the modest inoffensive statement, 'it's just my opinion.' Their intent is to communicate to others the limits, not the power, of their own opinions, perhaps because they want to preserve their attachments to others, not dislodge them."[4] The search for connectedness and the articulation of the limits of individual efforts and opinions can be worked into an interpretation of *Marianne and Julianne.*

Marianne and Julianne are sisters. The older sister, Julianne, is a feminist writer who has devoted her life to living by her principles. Even her decision not to have a child is a political decision. Marianne has taken political action to another kind of logical conclusion: She has become a terrorist. In the film, Von Trotta was primarily concerned by the nature of their relationship. She used a narrative approach that collapses real time. The film moves back and forth between their current lives and particular points in their childhoods. Ironically, Julianne was the rebellious teenager, and Marianne, the future terrorist, was compliant and coquettish.

The contemporary scenes revolve around a series of encounters between the sisters; Marianne's son and Julianne's lover take secondary positions to this central relationship. Indeed, the nature of the relationship seems to be the subject of the film. Not even Marianne's suicide in jail slows down Julianne's effort to confirm the central importance of their relationship in her life.

Generally, the narrative unfolds in terms of the progression of the relationship from one point in time to another. Although von Trotta's story begins in the present, we are not certain how much time has elapsed by the end. Nor does the story end in a climactic sense with the death of Marianne.

Instead, von Trotta constructed the film as a series of concentric circles with the relationship at the center. Each scene, as it unfolds, confirms the importance of the relationship but does not necessarily yield insight into it. Instead, a complex web of emotion, past traumas, and victories is constructed, blending with moments of current exchange of feelings between the sisters. Intense anger and love blend to leave us with the sense of the emotional complexity of the relationship and to allude to the sisters' choice to cut themselves off emotionally from their parents and, implicitly, from all significant others.

As the circles unfold, the emotion grows, as does the connection between the sisters. However, limits are always present in the lives of the sisters: the limits of social and political responsibility, the limits of emotional capacity to save each other or anyone else from their fate. When the film ends with the image of Julianne trying to care for Marianne's son, there is no resolution, only the will to carry on.

The film does not yield the sense of satisfaction that is generally present in classic narrative. Instead, we are left with anxiety for Julianne's fate and sorrow for the many losses she has endured. We are also left with a powerful feeling for her relationship with Marianne.

Whether von Trotta's work is genuinely a feminist narrative form is an issue that scholars might take up. Certainly, the work of other female directors in the 1980s suggests that many in the past 10 years have gravitated toward an alternative narrative style that requires a different attitude to the traditions of classical editing.

□ FEMINISM AND ANTINARRATIVE EDITING

Although some female directors have chosen subject matter and an editing style similar to those of male directors,[5] there are a number who, like von Trotta, have consciously differentiated themselves from the male conventions in the genres in which they choose to work.

For example, Amy Heckerling has directed a teenage comedy from a girl's perspective. *Fast Times at Ridgemont High* (1982) breaks many of the stereotypes of the genre, particularly the attitudes about sex roles and sexuality.

Another film that challenges the conventional view of sex roles and sexuality is Susan Seidelman's *Desperately Seeking Susan* (1985). The narrative editing style of this film emulates the confusion of the main character (Rosanna Arquette). Seidelman was more successful in using a nonlinear editing pattern than was Heckerling, and the result is an originality unusual in mainstream American filmmaking.

Outside of the mainstream, Lizzie Borden created an antinarrative in *Working Girls* (1973), her film about a day in the life of a prostitute. Although the subject matter lends itself to emotional exploitation, as illustrated by Ken Russell's version of the same story in *Whore* (1991), Borden decided to work against conventional expectations.

She focused on the banality of working in a bordello, the mundane conversation, the contrast of the owner's concerns and the employees' goals, and the artifice of selling the commodity of sex. Borden edited the film slowly, contrary to our expectations. She avoided close-ups, preferring to present the film in mid- to long shots, and she avoided camera motion whenever possible. As a result, the film works against our expectation, focusing on the ironic title and downplaying the means of their livelihood. Borden concentrated on the similarities of her characters' lives to those of other working women.

Another antinarrative approach adopted by women directors is to undermine the notion of a single voice, that of the main character in the narrative. Traditionally, the main character is the dramatic vehicle for the point of view, the point of empathy and the point of identification. By sidestepping a single point of view, the traditional arc of the narrative is undermined. Two specific examples will illustrate.

Agnieszka Holland was already established as a director who explored new narrative approaches (she uses a mixed genre approach in her film *Europa, Europa* [1991]; see next section on mixing genres) when she made *Olivier, Olivier* (1992).

Olivier, Olivier is a story about a family tragedy. In rural France, a middle-class family has two children, an older daughter and a young son. The boy is clearly the focal point of the family for the mother. The older sibling is ignored. She is also the family member who doesn't quite fit in, a role that often evolves into the scapegoat in family dynamics. One day, the young boy is sent off to deliver lunch to his father's mother. He never returns. In spite of extensive investigation, there is no trace of the boy. The family disintegrates. The local detective is transferred to Paris, determined not to give up on the case. Six years later, he finds a street kid, aged 15, who looks like the disappeared Olivier. He is certain he has found the boy. So is the mother. Only the sister is suspicious. The father, who had left the family to work in Africa, returns. Just as Olivier returns, the family seems to heal, to be whole again. The mother, who had all but fallen apart and blamed the father for Olivier's disappearance, for the first time in years is happy.

The new Olivier seems happy, eccentric, but not poorly adjusted given his trauma. He wants to be part of this family. But one day he discovers the neighbor molesting a young boy and when the police are called, Olivier confesses that he is not the original Olivier and the killer admits to killing the original Olivier. What is to happen to this family who have already endured so much tragedy? Will they relive the original tragedy with all its profound loss? Or will the mother deny again the loss and try for a new life with the new Olivier?

What is interesting about Holland's narrative approach is that she does not privilege any one character over any other. The story presents the point of view of the mother, the father, the sister, Olivier, the new Olivier.

If Holland had chosen a single point of view, a sense of resolution might have resulted in the discovery of the fate of Olivier. Without a single point of view, we have far less certainty. Indeed we are left totally stranded in this family tragedy. And the consequence is a profound shock at the end of *Olivier, Olivier*. This is the direct result of the multiple perspectives Holland has chosen.

Julie Dash follows a singular narrative path in her film *Daughters of the Dust* (1991). However her purpose is quite different from Agnieszka Holland. Whereas Holland is looking to destabilize our identification with the multiple points of view in *Olivier, Olivier*, Julie Dash wants to stabilize and generalize the point of view: the multiple perspectives together represent the African-American diaspora experience in the most positive light.

Daughters in the Dust takes place in a single summer day in 1902, in the Sea Islands of the South. Those Sea Islands are off the coast of South Carolina and Georgia. On the islands, life has become a hybrid, not African and not American. The elderly matriarch of the family will stay behind, but she has encouraged her children to go north to the mainland to make a life. She has also told them not to forget who they are. She will remain to die in her home at Ibo Landing.

Julie Dash deals with the feelings that surround this leavetaking with the points of view of the matriarch, her daughters, a niece from the mainland (called Yellow Mary), and an unborn granddaughter who narrates the beginning and end of the story. No single voice is privileged over any other.

The conflicts around behavior—a granddaughter has been impregnated via a rape, Yellow Mary may have made her way on the mainland through prostitution, a granddaughter has an Indian-American lover with whom she may want to remain on the island—all dim next to the conflictual future these migrants may face when they move north.

In order to create a sense of tolerance and power in the women, Dash presents the men as the weaker, more emotional sex. She also empowers a matriarch as the focal center of the life of the entire family. By doing so, she diminishes the sense of tension and conflict among the women and emphasizes their collective power and stability. Together they are the family and the purveyors of continuity for the family. And by giving one of the voices—the unborn child—the privileged position of early and closing narrator, Dash frames a voice for the future. But even that voice depends for life on the continuity of family.

Consequently in *Daughters in the Dust*, Julie Dash uses multiple points of view to sidestep linearity and to instead emphasize the circularity of the life cycle. It is strong, stable, and ongoing.

Although these directors did not proceed to a pattern of circular narrative as von Trotta did, there is no question that each is working against the conventions of the narrative tradition.

□ MIXING GENRES

Since the 1980s, writers and directors have been experimenting with mixing genres. Each genre represents particular conventions for editing. For example, the horror genre relies on a high degree of stylization, using subjective camera placement and motion. Because of the nature of the subject matter, pace is important. Although film noir also highlights the world of the nightmare, it tends to rely less on movement and pace. Indeed, film noir tends to be even more stylized and more abstract than the horror genre. Each genre relies on visual composition and pace in different ways. As a result, audiences have particular emotional expectations when viewing a film from a particular genre.

When two genres are mixed in one film, each genre brings along its conventions. This can sometimes make an old story seem fresh. However, the results for editing of these two sets of conventions can be surprising. At times, the films are more effective, but at other times, they simply confuse the audience. Because the mixed-genre film has become an important new narrative convention, its implications for editing must be considered.

There were numerous important mixed-genre films in the 1980s, including Jean-Jacques Beineix's *Diva* (1982) and Joel Coen's *Raising Arizona* (1987), but the focus here is on three: Jonathan Demme's *Something Wild* (1986), David Lynch's *Blue Velvet*, and Errol Morris's *The Thin Blue Line* (1988).

Something Wild is a mix of screwball comedy and film noir. The film, about a stockbroker who is picked up by an attractive woman, is the shifting story of the urban dream (love) and the urban nightmare (death).

Screwball comedies tend to be rapidly paced, kinetic expressions of confusion. Film noir, on the other hand, is slower, more deliberate, and more stylized. Both genres focus sometimes on love relationships.

The pace of the first part of *Something Wild* raises our expectations for the experience of the film. The energy of the screwball comedy, however, gives way to a slower-paced dance of death in the second half of the film. Despite the subject matter, the second half seems anticlimactic. The mixed genres work against one another, and the result is less than the sum of the parts.

David Lynch mixed film noir with the horror film in *Blue Velvet*. He relied on camera placement for the identification that is central to the horror film, and he relied on sound to articulate the emotional continuity of the movie. In fact, he used sound effects the way most filmmakers use music, to help the audience understand the emotional state of the character and, consequently, their own emotional states.

Lynch allowed the sound and the subjectivity that is crucial in the horror genre to dominate the stylization and pacing of the film. As a result, *Blue Velvet* is less stylized and less cerebral than the typical film noir work. Lynch's experiment in mixed genre is very effective. The story seems new and different, but its impact is similar to such conventional horror films as William Friedkin's *The Exorcist* (1973) or David Cronenberg's *Dead Ringers* (1988).

Errol Morris mixed the documentary and the police story (the gangster film or thriller) in *The Thin Blue Line*, which tells the story of a man wrongly accused of murder in Texas. The documentary was edited for narrative clarity in building a credible case. With clarity and credibility as the goals of the editing, the details of the case had to be presented in careful sequence so that the audience would be convinced of the character's innocence. It is not necessary to like or identify with him. The credible evidence persuades us of the merits of his cause. The result can be dynamic, exciting, and always emotional.

Morris dramatized the murder of the policeman, the crime that has landed the accused in jail. The killing is presented in a dynamic, detailed way. It is both a shock and an exciting event. In contrast to the documentary film style, many close-ups are used. This sequence, which was repeated in the film, was cut to Phillip Glass's musical score, making the scene evocative and powerful. It is so different from the rest of the film that it seems out of place. Nevertheless, Morris used it to remind us forcefully that this is a documentary about murder and about the manipulation of the accused man.

The Thin Blue Line works as a mixed-genre film because of Glass's musical score and because Morris made clear the goal of the film: to prove that the accused is innocent.

Mixing genres is a relatively new phenomenon, but it does offer filmmakers alternatives to narrative conventions. However, it is critical to understand which editing styles, when put together, are greater than the sum of their parts and which, when put together, are not.

□ NOTES/REFERENCES

1. Our expectation for an adventure film of this period was probably established by Tony Richardson's *Tom Jones* (1963) and Richard Lester's *The Three Musketeers* (1974). In both films, the sense of adventure dictated a rapid and lively pace, the opposite of Kubrick's *Barry Lyndon*.
2. Mary Field Belenky, Blythe McVicker Cliachy, Nancy Rule Goidherger, and Jill Mattuek Torule, *Women's Way of Knowing: The Development of Self, Voice and Mind* (New York: Basic Books, 1986).
3. Ibid., 44–45.
4. Ibid., 66.
5. Kathryn Bigelow, for example, directed *Blue Steel* (1989) and *Point Break* (1991), both of which were edited in the action style we expect from the well-known male directors who specialize in this genre.

11

The MTV Influence on Editing I

■

What I have called the MTV influence on editing is principally associated with that phenomenon of the past 20 years, the music video. Initially viewed as a vehicle to sell records, those 3–30 minute videos have captured a young audience looking for quick, evocative visual stimuli presented as a background for the aural presentation of a single song or series of songs.

Although this style of film was further popularized by films such as *Flashdance* (1983), the form has its roots in more experimental filmmaking and certainly in the success of the short form, the television commercial. The MTV style is today principally associated with television although its influence has superseded television. By sidestepping the traditional set of narrative goals which include a linear narrative and a focus on plot and character, the MTV style has instead replaced it with a multilayered approach. There may be a story. There may be a single character. But the likelihood is that place, feeling, or mood will be the primary layer of the music video. It is also likely that the traditional sense of time and place with the conventions that are used to reference film time to real time will be replaced by a far less direct correlation. In fact, many music videos attempt to establish their own reference points between reality and film time. This may mean great leaps in time and place and it is the vividness of the resulting imagery that provides the new correlation. In the world of the music video, real place is far less important. In fact, they are not as important as references to other media and other forms, to the landscapes of science fiction, and to the horror film. And with regards to time, time in the music video is any time. With time and place obliterated, the film and video makers are free to roam in the world of their imagined media meditation. And their audience, young and rebellious, is free to feel the simulation of their freedom and to celebrate their rejection of tradition, from our perspective, the rejection of the tradition of narrative.

Because the MTV style sidesteps traditional narrative, it is of interest to us. How does the form coalesce to capture its audience? By focussing on the most aggressive stylist of our day, Oliver Stone, we will try to understand how the MTV style can be used and why it has such a powerful grip on the public imagination.

□ ORIGINS

Although Luis Buñuel's early antinarrative experiments in *Un Chien d'Andalou* (1929) and *L'Age d'Or* (1930) bear certain similarities to the contemporary music video, the more critical shaping device is music that has a narrative as well as emotional character. This means that we have to look to the two early Beatles' films, *A Hard Day's Night* (1964) and *Help!* (1965) for a starting point in the mid-60s. Very quickly, the Lester films were joined by John Boorman's film with The Dave Clark Five, *Having a Wild Weekend* (1965). Later, Lester's *A Funny Thing Happened on the Way to the Forum* (1966) and the non-musical series of Monty Python films that followed in the 70s (*And Now for Something Completely Different,* [1972], *Monty Python and the Holy Grail*, [1975], and *Life of Brian*, [1979]) added stylistic elements to the new genre.

How these films differed from traditional narratives and musicals needs to be articulated. Traditional musicals generally presented a narrative together with interspersed musical or dance numbers. Films such as *The Pirate* (1948), *An American in Paris* (1951), and *Invitation to the Dance* (1957) were exceptions. The best of the musicals, such as *Singin' in the Rain* (1952), *Funny Face* (1957), and *West Side Story* (1961) found a visual style to match the energy and emotion of the narratives.

Turning to the Lester films, *A Hard Day's Night* and *Help!*, on one level they are musicals for the main characters are performers. The music is integral to our understanding of the film narratives. But whereas there is a narrative that is elaborate and character-driven in the traditional musical, we must accept the fact that the narratives in *A Hard Day's Night* and *Help!* have far more modest goals. In fact, we are hard-pressed to find common sense as well as feeling arising out of the narratives of these films. In essence the narratives were an excuse for the musical numbers, which themselves were used to highlight what the Beatles represented—inventiveness, anarchy, energy. These feeling states were far more important to Richard Lester the director than a narrative about a concert or about the disappearance of a ritual ring from India and the efforts by a cult to retrieve it.

Here there are the first stylistic elements of the music video. The shaping device is the music. Narrative is less important; a feeling state is more important. From an editing standpoint, this translates as making the jump cut more important than the match cut. It also implies a centrality for pace. Given the low involvement quotient of the narrative, it is to pace that the role of interpretation falls. Consequently, pace becomes the source of energy and new juxtapositions that suggest anarchy and inventiveness.

When we move to the Monty Python films, we add a literary base for reference and a self-reflexing acknowledgement that the characters can step in and out of character and speak to the audience directly. This process results in the acknowledgement of media, of manipulation, and the more subtle notion that in spite of self-reflexivity, the form can be even more manipulative as you let your audience in on it—it's a joke, it's funny, and you, the audience, have been let in on the construction of the joke. Which in turn privileges the viewer and involves the viewer in a more conscious manner. These elements, the literary metaphor and the self-reflexive, fill out the repertoire of the music video. But over time the referent points move beyond literature and film to other media: television, journalism, the world of comic books, and now the world of computer games.

□ THE SHORT FILM

The short film and its relationship to the short story, as well as to the world of the visual arts, has yielded many explorations of form, the creations of particular styles. The work of Luis Buñuel, Maya Daren, and the more recent work of Stan Brakhage and Andy Warhol are marked by a number of characteristics we now find in the MTV style. So too video art. The antinarrative position of Buñuel, and the stream of consciousness visual style of Maya Daren have far more in common with the MTV style than they do with mainstream filmmaking. Filmmakers such as Stan Brakhage are interested in layering images—not to create a special effect but rather in a self-reflexive way to suggest this media experience, his film, is both a manipulation and reflection upon the tolls of that manipulation. And few filmmakers take a stylistic position as minimalist as Andy Warhol. Indeed, the position is so clearly about style as opposed to content, that the experience of his films becomes a comment on the medium more than any other interpretation (i.e., society, the art world).

All of these filmmakers also create a distinctive style and once their audience is in tune with their intentions, they create as powerful an identification of the audience with their work as did Richard Lester in his Beatles films. The only difference between these filmmakers and the MTV style is the role of sound, particularly music, as a shaping device. From a visual point, however, the MTV style has a great deal in common with the short film, particularly the experimental film.

□ WHERE WE ARE NOW—THE STATE
OF THE MTV STYLE

Because of the volume of music videos produced to promote records and because TV stations and international networks welcome programming that appeals to the 15- 25-year-old audience, MTV is not only here to stay, it is a powerful force in broadcasting. Its interrelationship with advertising underpins its influence.

Consequently, we must view the MTV style as a new form of visual storytelling. Part narrative, part atmosphere, sound intensive, and image rich, the form has a remarkable appeal to the new generation of film and video makers whose media viewing experience is preponderantly television.

Although the MTV style has not made a broad entry into the feature film, it has characterized much of the style of those directors who began in commercials—Adrian Lyne (*Flashdance*, 1983), Tony Scott (*Top Gun*, 1986), and Ridley Scott (*Thelma & Louise*, 1991). It has also accounted for the success of at least one new director, Ben Stiller, in his debut film, *Reality Bites* (1994). New directors such as Richard Linklater (*Dazed and Confused*, 1993), and older directors such as Luc Besson (*La Femme Nikita*, 1990) are attracted to the ideology and style of MTV. But few filmmakers have leaped as headlong into the MTV style as Oliver Stone in his film *Natural Born Killers* (1994). We will look at *Natural Born Killers* in some detail later in the chapter, but before we do, it's necessary to highlight the key characteristics of the MTV style.

□ THE IMPORTANCE OF FEELING STATES

One of the central features of the MTV style is the importance of creating a definite feeling state. This is not an issue of the need to challenge the primacy of plot. Rather it begins with the close relationship of the MTV style with music.

Music—particularly without lyrics—synthesizes human emotion. The brain processes sound. It was Bergman who faster than images stated the goal of the film experience—it should be like music. This equation of music with heightened emotional experience was applied by Bergman to the overall experience of film. The sound of music in this sense is even more concentrated than the film experience itself. And the music of a single short song can be viewed as an even greater concentration of emotion.

When we add the lyrics of a song, which tend to the poetic, we are given a direction for the emotion of the music. If there is a sense of narrative, it yields from those poetic lyrics. But to repeat, the purpose of music and lyrics is to give a defined emotional state to the feeling state that is created.

A feeling state can be sharp and deep or it can be developmental and dreamlike. In either case, the state creates a disjunctive, disconnected sense to a narrative. Because of the depth of feeling of a single sequence associated with a single piece of music, it is difficult to create a continuum of narrative. Rather we have in the longer MTV-style film a series of disjunctive sequences, memorable in and of themselves, but hardly organized on an effectively rising arc of action characteristic of the narrative film. This is why there are moments one remembers in films like *Flashdance* or *Top Gun*, but one is left without a powerful sense of the characters or the story. This does not diminish the overall film but it does make it a different kind of experience than the conventional film.

Feeling states can also appeal as dream fragments—pleasurable, but not entirely real, in the way the experience of a traditional narrative tends to be. Clearly a film that concentrates on feeling states will only appeal to an audience accustomed to it—that young audience that views and enjoys a series of visualized music videos one after the other, with no narrative connection but where each provides a distinct sensation or feeling. This audience does not mind the fragmentation nor the pace nor the brevity of the experience. For this audience, the feeling state is a desirable visual-audio experience.

□ THE DOWNGRADING OF THE PLOT

It's not that this new audience is disinterested in plot. The success of films such as Amy Heckerling's *Clueless* (1995) and Ang Lee's *Sense and Sensibility* (1995) with a young audience is proof that the narrative drive and energy in both of these love stories appeals to that audience. Ironically, both are based upon the novels of Jane Austen. But these films, although popular, are not "icons" to this young audience. Those filmic icons are *Reality Bites*, *Natural Born Killers*, and *Slacker* (1991). These icons are notable for their put-down of plot, of the elevation of adolescent rage and anarchy over the continuum of the happy ending in *Clueless* and *Sense and Sensibility*.

When plot is less important, incident, or scene, takes on a different meaning, and character becomes everything. When the logic of plot progression is less pressing, set-pieces can stand more readily. Mood, alternating shifts of mood, fantasy, play, nightmare, all can be juxtaposed more readily because their contribution to the plot progression is unnecessary.

Add to that a character who stands against the prevailing values of the society, and for the destruction of those values, and you have the hero/main character of the MTV-style film: Ethan Hawke in *Reality Bites*, Woody Harrelson in *Natural Born Killers*, Anne Parillaud in *La Femme Nikita*. It's as if the Brando character in *The Wild One* (1954) has returned and again answered the 50s question, "What are you rebelling against?" The answer: "What have you got?!"

In a standard plotted narrative, such a main character would seem reactive and immature, rootless and without a goal. In the fragmented narrative of the MTV-style film, the character is a hero in a fragmented world, a hero who can recite poetry and kill in the same breath, a hero who can't be held accountable It's his world that has made him so.

Having degraded (or downgraded) plot simulates the world of these heroes. Their audience recognizes that world with ease. It's the world they live in, the TV world, the video game world. They see it as a game to cope with the incomprehensibility of that world. For them, the MTV style is a tool, a stimuli, and a philosophy. Less plot facilitates the audience entry into the MTV world view.

□ DISJUNCTIVE EDITING—THE OBLITERATION OF TIME AND SPACE

In order to create feeling states and to downgrade plot and its importance, the filmmaker must also undermine the gestalt impulse—to make sense of what we see. To put in another way, the viewer will organize a pattern of sounds and images into a progression of thought, an applied linearity, even if one is not available on the surface.

To counteract the impulse to organize those images and sounds into the narrative that may not be present, the filmmaker must challenge the impulse more deeply. She must undermine the sense of time and space in the MTV-style film or video.

To understand how this is done, we must back up to some issues raised in Chapters 8, 9, and 10. In the work of Kurosawa, we saw him visually play with the idea that the truth was relative, that it was influenced by whoever was telling the story (*Rashomon*, 1951). In Resnais's work memory, the past and its intervention posed the question about time and its continuum. If a character is gripped by events of the past, what does this mean for their current conduct and perception (*Hiroshima, Mon Amour*, 1960)? Fellini went even further to suggest not simply the past, but the character's fantasy/fantasies about the past overshadowed the present (*8½*, 1963). In the case of Antonioni, place and the environment overwhelms character and perception. Place obliterates the time gestalt of thinking and replaces it with the objective power of place. *Will*, an expression of character's goals, is replaced by *will not, cannot*; place replacing time in importance (*L'Eclisse*, 1962).

Peter Brook poses questions about reality through his exploration of performance, and his understanding of history (*Marat/Sade*, 1966). Again, time and place are reconfigured. They become relative and less important. Herzog and Wenders both challenge the notions of personal history and objective reality (*The Enigma of Kaspar Hauser*, 1974; *Paris, Texas*, 1984).

Together these filmmakers and numerous others have challenged conventional notions of time and place in their work. Their artistic advances in turn opened up options for those working with the MTV style. Central to that style is the obliteration of a conventional sense of time and place. Even though Tony Scott's *Top Gun* has a location for the story (the Southwest) and a time (the 80s, the last phase of the Cold War), its actual dream state— the marine pilot as invincible hero and lover—actually bears little resemblance to training, to the history of the 80s; rather it resembles a cartoon, a piece of advertising. To succeed, Scott has to pay lip service to time and place but little more.

By focusing on the feeling state, by mixing dream and fear, by obliterating history, and replacing it with a new mythology, Scott uses style to move us into a less narrative experience, a more sensation experience. And he succeeds because of the work of Fellini, Antonioni, Kurosawa, and Brook in their challenges to our sense of time and place.

What we haven't focussed on yet, but now turn to, is the mechanical editing choices that help the filmmaker obliterate time and place. The first choice is to use many more close-ups than long shots. This choice withdraws the context that, when present, lends credibility to the sequence. The second choice is to emphasize foreground over background in the frame. Whether this is done by using telephoto shots rather than side angle or through the crowding of the character into the front of the frame, which can, with a wide-angle shot, distort the character, both choices yield the same result—withdrawal of visual context. Add the art direction—lighting choices that move away from realism—the sepia of *Top Gun*, the gauzed images of *Flashdance*, the hot reds alternating with the cool blues in Tony Scott's *Crimson Tide* (1995), all when combined with the oversize of the close-up and of the foreground image, undermine context. Add the use where possible of the jump cut and the overuse of pace and we have the mechanical editing repertoire of the obliteration of time and place.

□ THE SELF-REFLEXIVE DREAM STATE

To create a dream state is to imply that the viewer temporarily loses oneself in that state. The self-reflexive dream state suggests that on another level, viewers watch or reflect upon themselves dreaming, or to put it another way, to be simultaneously very involved and not involved at all.

Turning back to the Monty Python films, as well as the Beatles films, there is in both the acknowledgement by the characters that they are performing as well as participating. Almost ironic in tone, these performances veer wildly from viewing the characters as innocents and then as having enough mastery over the situation, that they step out of the role and address us, the audience, directly.

Whether the technique is Brechtian or closer to Beckett, the device allows for a range of genres—adventure to satire—that helps the MTV-style film transcend what could easily become marginalized to pictures for the music. It reinforces an attitude in its audience—the will to reconfigure their world via their dreams, all the while acknowledging, "Just playing, folks!"

But the self-reflexivity plays another, more serious, role in the MTV style. Because self-reflexivity acknowledges that it is a film being watched (as opposed to reality), this creates a tolerance for ranging more widely. It pulls the film closer to theatre, where the suspension of belief is far higher than in film (which looks real). This freedom allows for shifts in feeling, narrative, fantasy, etc., without needing to make those shifts plausible. It is after all only a film you are watching. "Go with it," is the message to its audience, and knowing that it is a media event (unlike a real dream), the audience is tolerant of those shifts in tone, time, place, etc., that are undertaken.

□ THE MEDIA LOOKS AT ITSELF

Just as the character stands apart and comments on himself within the film, so too does the media. The MTV style embraces a self-reflexivity of the particular form, film or video, upon itself, its power, and its manipulative techniques. The MTV style also embraces a referential base to comment upon as well as to include other media.

Top Gun deploys and celebrates the techniques of the TV commercial; the recent music videos of Madonna reference the paintings of Frida Kahlo; and Michael Jackson's music video, *Thriller*, is a mix of *West Side Story* meets *The Wiz* (1978), which in turn is based on *The Wizard of Oz* (1939). *Flashdance* is itself a long series of music videos.

One can imagine music videos referencing key journalistic events (an election, a revolution), famous TV situation comedies, and various other media renderings of historical events: the deaths of Abraham Lincoln, John F. Kennedy, and Mahatma Gandhi, for example, as well as media interpretations of serious social issues (AIDS, racism, spousal abuse). The MTV style will mimic and comment upon the other media's presentation of such a key events or issues.

By doing so, a reductive view can be confirmed and transcended. It says to its audience, "Everything can be criticized and by using this style, even the critics can be criticized." Rather than providing the audience with the restorative power of the classic narrative, the MTV style plays to paranoia and to narcissism. By criticizing the media itself, the MTV style criticizes the power of the media and confirms in its audience the suspicion that there is no trust out there and the last element of the society that is trustworthy is the media itself.

Having looked at the elements of the MTV style, we're ready to turn our attention to a detailed look at Oliver Stone, who represents the most artistic use of the style to date.

□ OLIVER STONE'S CAREER

After leaving the film program at New York University, Oliver Stone made his way as a screenwriter. His credits include *Midnight Express* (1978), *Scarface* (1983), and *Year of the Dragon* (1985).

As a writer-director, Stone is responsible for *Salvador* (1986), Platoon (1986), *Wall Street* (1987), *Born on the Fourth of July* (1989), *JFK* (1991), *Natural Born Killers* (1994), and *Nixon* (1995).

He has made at least three films about the Vietnam war (including *Heaven and Earth*, 1993), two films about American presidents and at least two other films about the media and violence (*Salvador* and *Natural Born Killers*). Aside from the seriousness of the subject matter and a good deal of narrative bravado, Stone has a very distinctive style—lots of camera motion and pace. He has often been criticized for manipulating—whether it is in *JFK* or *Nixon*, he is quite willing to use editing, juxtaposition, and pace to make whatever point he wishes. Although powerfully fascinated by the forceful nature of the medium, Stone is not beyond criticizing those forceful tools he himself uses. This is the source of the great controversy in *JFK*. He uses simulated footage of real life events, re-photographs them and then proceeds to declare that he is using those same tools to reveal "the truth." In this sense, he is the ideal self-reflexive filmmaker.

But to be fair to Stone, he is also part of a tradition from Eisenstein to Peckinpah of directors who see editing as the real art of directing. In *Natural Born Killers*, Stone uses this self-reflexivity to create a multilayered film experience. Using the MTV style, Stone creates an explosive, creative commentary on family, violence, and the media in America.

□ *NATURAL BORN KILLERS*

Natural Born Killers, from a story by Quentin Tarantino, tells the story of two mass murderers, Mickey and Mallory Knox (Woody Harrelson and Juliette Lewis). The film begins with a killing spree, moves back to their meeting and their three-week sweep through the Southwest. In those three weeks, they kill 52 people. They are captured, after being snakebitten, while looking for snakebite serum in a drugstore. Their captor, Detective Jack Scagnetti, seems as pathological as the two young killers. The story flashes forward a year to the maximum-security prison where they are held.

It seems that a television journalist, Wayne Gale (Robert Downey, Jr.) has a television show, "American Maniacs," where he profiles serial killers. The public is quite fascinated by Mickey and Mallory, and Wayne has fed the fascination. He proposes to Mickey and to the warden (Tommy Lee Jones) that he, Wayne, interview Mickey live on Super Bowl Sunday. Both parties are agreeable but the warden wants Mickey and Mallory put away for good. They have incited trouble in the prison; the other prisoners idealize them. He invites Jack Scagnetti to take both out of prison and dispose of them right after the interview.

This doesn't happen because the interview is so inflammatory. Mickey celebrates that he does what he does so well because he was born to it—he's a natural born killer. Upon hearing this, the prison erupts, the convicts go on a rampage. In the confusion, Mickey disarms a guard and begins to kill again. He takes hostages, including Wayne Gale, and they free Mallory and kill Jack Scagnetti; while the majority of hostages are killed by police fire. Using a guard and Wayne Gale as human shields, while Gales' TV camera records it all, Mickey and Mallory make good their escape.

In the woods, on live TV, they kill Wayne Gale, who they claim is worse than a killer, a parasite, and they go on, it seems, to live happily ever after. Mallory speaks of it being time to have a family.

This narrative description can't give more than an outline of *Natural Born Killers*. The film is actually organized in a series of set-pieces—the pre-credit introduction to Mickey and Mallory in a roadside diner; they kill all but one of the customers. A television situation comedy show follows. It introduces Mickey and Mallory, her abusive father, the impotent mother, and the young brother. This show is complete with laugh track. The show is called "I Love Mallory." The next sequence introduces Australian-American reporter Wayne Gale and his television show, "American Maniacs." On the show, they do a dramatic reenactment of two Mickey and Mallory killings. London, Tokyo—the media spreads the fame of these killers around the world.

A set-piece of Mickey and Mallory in a motel room follows. They have a spat and he amuses himself with a female hostage; she amuses herself with a gas station attendant. When he recognizes her, she kills him. A sequence with an Indian who handles rattlesnakes follows. The Indian seems to be the first person Mickey respects. Accidentally, Mickey kills the Indian. As the lovers run away, both are snakebitten. A set-piece in a drug mart follows. Both are ill. In this sequence the lovers are captured by the police. A year later in jail, Wayne Gale requests an interview with Mickey. Mickey agrees. In this sequence the hero worship of Mickey and Mallory by young people is highlighted. The interview is the next set-piece. Jack Scagnetti's parallel encounter with Mallory is the next. The strong sexual current of this sequence is juxtaposed with the romantic dimension of the first part of the live interview with Mickey—the theme is love can tame the demon. The prison riot is the next set-piece, followed by Mickey's escape. Shortly thereafter follows a final sequence in Mallory's cell. The next sequence captures their escape from prison. In the woods, the last taping of Wayne Gale's show ends with his murder on camera. The title sequence that follows is a merging of past and future images. They imply that Mickey and Mallory survive and have a family.

Looking at the sequences in a general way, one notices how much each resembles a music video. Music is the overall shaping device. The first sequence begins with Leonard Cohen's "Waiting for a Miracle." The last sequence is shaped by Cohen's "The Future." Thirty songs are used in between.

Each sequence has within itself remarkable latitude to use images of the characters, images of animals, theatrical images of monsters, dragons, headless bodies, presented in a highly stylized manner: black and white, natural color, filtered color (usually blood red), TV images of the Menendez brothers and O. J. Simpson trials, TV images from the 50s, filmic images from *The Wild Bunch*, for example, and animated cartoon-like drawings. Add to this distortions from morphing, highlight shifting to low light, and you have a range of images that runs the gamut from natural to non-natural. Often these images will be thrown together in the same sequence.

The capacity to reflect on the media itself is ever-present. Beyond the references to other films, much is made in the film of the role of television in American life. The introduction of Mickey and Mallory's meeting is presented in the form of a situation comedy. Three of their clashes with the law are presented in the form of a Saturday morning cartoon. And the actuality television style of Wayne Gale's television show, "American Maniacs," to sketch their career and to demonstrate its power on the young as well as the convicts in prison, is a frightening condemnation of the role of television in the promotion of violence.

Finally each sequence uses black-and-white and color images intertwined to pose the question: Which is imagined and which is real? The crossover doesn't make the answer any clearer. Sometimes the black-and-white images seem to be remembrances of Mickey's childhood. At other times they reference in a journalistic way the faces and feelings of the other convicts in maximum-security prison. In terms of color, it ranges from the unreal use of green as a motif in the diner sequence that opens the film. The green is the key lime pie Mickey eats, and it is the cartoon color of the diner. That green can alternate with black-and-white or with blood red. In each case the sharp shifts in color create a sense of stylization that affirms this is a media event and manipulation you are watching. Enjoy! The newsreel black-and-white interspliced goes with the confusion between reality and dream this film plays with.

These are the general elements of the MTV style in *Natural Born Killers*. More specifically, we can look at any sequence and see how Oliver Stone pushes the feeling state over the narrative linearity of plot. In the opening sequence, for example, one is aware of the extreme close-ups intercut with long shots. It is the dead eye of a deer in close-up cutting to a distorted wide-angle shot of the truck in front of the diner, complete with dead deer on its roof. Mickey is eating his pie in color and remembering his past in black and white. The camera studies him in close. The back of his head crowds the front of the camera. Mallory on the other hand is presented in long shot dancing alone initially to the music of the juke box. The camera undulates side to side, unstable as she is unstable. When she is joined by one of the men from the truck, she is seductive and suggestive and soon lethal. Here Stone jump cuts her attack on the male, details its and makes it more violent through the use of the jump cuts.

The pace increases as the killing begins, only to be slowed down when Mickey throws a knife at the man outside. The camera tracks the trajectory of the knife, emphasizing the unreality of the killing. Only the man's death brings back the sense of realism via sound. The next death, the stylized death of the waitress, is presented in almost farcical terms. The camera sways with the choosing of the last victim between the waitress and the last male. When the choice is made, Mickey shoots her but his bullet hits the pan she is holding. The impact of the pan kills her. It seems a comic moment in its presentation. She is the fourth victim of Mickey and Mallory in the diner.

The movement of the camera, the extreme close-ups, the foreground crowding of character in the frame alternating with extreme wide angle shots of action and character in the background, gives the sequence a tension that Stone uses to make the sequence function on a stylized as well as narrative level. The color shifts increase the stylization. And the occasional images of nature—tarantulas, rabbits—contextualize the events with the natural world. Whether Stone is implying the similarities or differences becomes clearer later in the Indian sequence when he uses both perspectives in nature and man's behavior. Mickey also refers to the natural order of things in his live interview with Wayne Gale.

This pattern of viewing each sequence as a music video unto itself yields when put together on a two-hour narrative frame the sense that Stone has put together a narrative that is a music video and that comments on the ethics of the music video. His style as well as the unappealing actions and goals of the main characters, gives us little choice but to consider *Natural Born Killers* as Oliver Stone's meditation on violence, and the media, in American society.

Stone has always been a vigorous filmmaker interested in ideas, society, history, but nothing before has prepared us for the artfulness of the challenge he meets and transcends in *Natural Born Killers*. As much as we don't like to acknowledge it, Stone has created in *Natural Born Killers* a meditation on what he does—manipulate, and he both celebrates and condemns the power of the media. The MTV style, its qualities and its goals, have never been used in so creative a way.

12

The MTV Influence on Editing II

■

In the last chapter we explored the characteristics of the MTV style in editing. Whereas linear narratives proceed by focusing a viewer's identification with a main character, the MTV approach proceeds using a less specific focus. Consequently, pace, subjectivity, and the close-up are not used to build an identification with the main character. In the MTV style, they are used to generate a less specific intensity. Pace and subjectivity in general are not used to move us up a dramatic arc; instead, they are used to intensify in effect a set piece that may or may not contribute to a dramatic arc. The MTV style is more clearly understood if the developmental narrative structure of the linear narrative is set aside, and if instead the narrative is seen as a series of set pieces that each embody a dramatic arc of their own. You might even consider the set pieces to be the equivalent of short films strung together by a loose shaping device. The most important point is that the editing implications of the MTV style shifts the focus from character and the structure of the narrative as a whole to the set piece itself. In a sense, the MTV style subverts the linear experience and elevates the scene over a sequence, an Act, or indeed the whole film.

Within the scene itself the MTV style focuses on feeling over the progress of the narrative. In the last chapter we looked at a single example, Oliver Stone's *Natural Born Killers* (1994). In this chapter, we expand this exploration to look at different narrative conventions that have emerged from the influence of MTV style. In the case of Wong Kar-wai's *In the Mood for Love* (2000), the filmmaker has taken a classic melodrama, a doomed love story, and by adopting an MTV approach, he alters the specificity of the narrative to become an existential meditation on yearning and loneliness. Similarly, Ang Lee's MTV editing of the fight sequences in *Crouching Tiger, Hidden Dragon* (2000) transforms a Kung Fu action film into a feminist melodrama about the clash of the "traditional" with the "modern." Very often the MTV style self-reflexively uses the media itself as a character in the narrative. Juzo Itami in his film *Tampopo* (1987) uses this characteristic both to frame his narrative as well as to interrupt the main story line. By doing so he uses the MTV style to interject his own voice into the story line, thereby giving a layered, more complex experience to what is otherwise a simple story. In the case of *Life Is Beautiful* (1998), Roberto Benigni uses his own character in the narrative as the focus for the set pieces that together propose a philosophy at odds with the plot. Here the MTV style transgresses plot to yield a powerful but very different interpretation of the narrative.

In Chapter 31, *Nonlinear Editing and Digital Technology II*, we will look at the use of the set piece in the nonlinear film. In both Terence Malick's *The Thin Red Line* (1998) and P. T. Anderson's *Magnolia* (1998), the filmmakers create powerful and intense set pieces. Although there are similarities between these two films and those discussed in this chapter on the MTV editing approach to the set piece, they also differ from the films discussed here in two areas. First, each of these two films uses a single character as opposed to multiple characters as a vehicle for the narrative. Second, these MTV-influenced films move to resolution whereas the nonlinear film more often has an open ending.

To begin our deliberation of the influence of MTV style we turn first to the D-Day set piece that occurs early in Steven Spielberg's *Saving Private Ryan* (1997).

□ THE CASE OF *SAVING PRIVATE RYAN*

Steven Spielberg's *Saving Private Ryan* is a traditional war film framed by a modern prologue. The former Private Ryan, with his wife, children, and grandchildren, visit the American cemetery where so many who died on D-Day and in its immediate aftermath are buried. He is there to visit the grave of Captain John Miller who died on the rescue mission that saved his life. The body of the narrative focuses on D-Day and the mission to save Ryan, after the War Department receives word that his three brothers have all been killed in action. Army Chief of Staff George Marshall issues the command: save the one remaining Ryan so that his mother will not have lost all 4 sons fighting for their country. Captain Miller and his men are given the tough assignment, and 6 of the 8 will die in carrying out the mission, including Miller himself. While he is dying, Captain Miller exhorts Ryan to live a worthy life or, put another way, to "make my sacrifice worthwhile." In the epilogue, Ryan in deepest sorrow tells us he has lived up to Miller's invocation.

This brief description can't capture the powerful emotions created by the experience of the film. *Saving Private Ryan* is a classic war film, and the goal for Miller, the main character, is to try to survive. His conscious self-sacrifice to save Ryan elevates the premise of the narrative to a meditation on the question of what is worth dying for, and the film implies that there are issues and events in life that are worth dying for. Whether this notion is romantic or realistic is not the point we're concerned with here. What is our concern is how Spielberg elevates the narrative beyond a conventional war story. An important if not vital contributor to this shift is the MTV style Spielberg employs in the D-Day landing sequence. This 24-minute sequence is the subject to which we now turn. The place is Omaha Beach, Dog Green Sector.

The sequence proceeds under the following subheadings. Lengths (rounded off) are noted:

1.	In the landing craft	2 minutes
2.	In the water	2 minutes
3.	At the edge of the beach—What do we do	2 minutes
4.	Movement off the beach	3 minutes
5.	Up to the perimeter (barbed wire)	3 minutes
6.	Gather weapons	3 minutes
7.	Advance on the pill box—Take machine gun emplacement	3 minutes
8.	Take the pill box and the surrounding environment	3 minutes
9.	The Beach is taken—Stop shooting	3 minutes

Before we turn to the individual sequences, here are a number of general observations that drive the overall sequence. The first observation is that although mastery of a sort is achieved by the characters by the end of the sequence, the emphasis is on the casualties, their extensive number, the pervasiveness of death on the beach, the chaos of trying to survive on the beach, and the horror of how mutilating death can be when it occurs in war. Second, Spielberg has adopted a cinema verité style involving handheld shots, a lot of telephoto images where context is flattened to emphasize crowding, and the creation of the effect that there is nowhere to hide from the steady machine gun and mortar fire. Spielberg also uses close-ups to a far higher proportion than he usually does when presenting an action sequence. Finally, as expected, pace plays a very important part in the experience of the sequence as a whole.

Now we turn to the individual sequences.

1. In the Landing Craft

The emphasis in this sequence is on intensity. We begin in a close-up of Captain Miller's shaking hands as he takes some water from his canteen. Whether it is fear of dying or just fear, the camera pulls back to other expressions of fear. A man vomits; another kisses his crucifix. Miller and his sergeant bark short, clear orders. They are in command and they have the experience few men on the landing craft have. Point of view and close-ups build the intensity. As the landing craft opens its front to allow the men to move onto the beach, those upfront are greeted with instant death. They are cut down by enemy machine-gun fire. A cutaway to the German pill box atop the beach positions the killers' point of view. To save his men Miller orders them over the side, into the water. It's the only way to survive the enemy fire. Pace, movement, and the telephoto cutaway together create the claustrophobia of imminent death in this sequence. The feeling is one of intensity and fear.

2. In the Water

Men are pushed or jump over the side. As they enter the water and sink under the surface, the sounds of combat are lost and everything slows down. Men grapple to shed the equipment that weighs them down. A rifle falls to the sea floor. Bullet tracers reach their mark and kill two soldiers as they struggle with their gear. There is a macabre beauty to their deaths. Another soldier simply drowns. Survivors emerge from the water and head for the beach. The sounds of combat return only to be muted again as underwater shots of the footsteps of soldiers are intercut with the struggle above water. Miller makes his way out of the water. He helps a soldier but to no avail. The soldier catches a bullet in his chest and his struggle not to drown is over. The feeling in this sequence is surprise—surprise that death can't be evaded. There are fewer close-ups and less pace used in this sequence.

3. At the Edge of the Beach

Here the pace and camera position change. The pace quickens and close-ups return. The cutaway to the German pill box position presents the source of the killing in a dominant (foreground) position. The throughline for this sequence is the chaos on the beach. Miller loses his hearing from a shrapnel hit close by. He looks about on the beach. A soldier with a flamethrower blows up. Another soldier loses his arm. The soldier searches out his arm and carries it looking for someone to help him. A landing craft is on fire. The soldiers on it exit ablaze. Miller empties his helmet of blood. His face is splattered with blood. The overall feeling of this sequence is beauty, stillness; there shouldn't be so much blood and death, but there is. But it's a stylized death, almost abstract. The feeling in this sequence is surprise that death can't be evaded and, as a consequence, a feeling of helplessness, of victimization. Close-ups and less pace are used in this sequence.

4. Movement off the Beach

Now the sequences increase in length. Until now there have been modest narrative goals in each of the sequences; in essence they have been more about creating a feeling than about narrative complexity. This sequence begins as a soldier in close-up tries to speak to Miller. Miller's hearing returns and his message is simple—get off this beach or die. Here the camera sits low and the telephoto lens compresses and cramps the men. The cutaway to the German machine gun creates a sense of proximity—they can't miss the Americans on the beach. The wounded scream. The shot of a gut-shot soldier is lengthy, almost endlessly painful. Miller attempts to drag a wounded man up to medical attention on the beach. By the time he reaches his goal, the wounded man is hit by shrapnel and all that is left is a body part. The feeling state is one of overwhelming chaos, violent death, and growing helplessness. So far the landing is an unmitigated disaster.

5. Up to the Perimeter

If the earlier sequences were characterized by victimization, chaos, and death, this next sequence begins specifically to move the audience away from the sense of victimization and helplessness that has prevailed until now. The focus is on Captain Miller and on movement. Handheld movement from Miller's point of view, complete with his breathlessness, creates the feeling level of this sequence. Miller reaches the barbed wire at the hill embankment where he attempts to assess the situation. He establishes radio contact with Command and lets them know that Dog One of Dog Green Sector is not open. His men, those who have survived, are pinned down. He takes a count of those alive and at the embankment. Sergeant Horvath confirms the situation. There is enormous frustration—the radio man is killed. Medics attending to the wounded on the beach are frustrated and angry as the wounded are killed where they lie as the medics try to stabilize them. This sequence is a transitional sequence; it is the first where there is a feeling of power rather than powerlessness, which is emphasized by the handheld movement up to the embankment. On the other hand, the slaughter of Americans continues.

6. Gather Weapons

The call to action in this scene is marked by quick cuts. The call creates a dynamic sense. Bangalore explosives are rushed to the scene. They are maneuvered into position; again, the handheld shot yields a powerful sense of assertion. The explosives are effectively detonated, creating a path to move up toward the pill box. Meanwhile, men continue to die. A young soldier takes a bullet in his helmet. Shocked and grateful to be alive, he removes the helmet to admire where the bullet hit. He is shot in the head and dies. Nevertheless there is a dynamic sense in this sequence, a feeling that there have been survivors in Miller's company and that they are beginning to take action against the German enemy. The prevailing feeling of the sequence is dynamic and forceful. The feeling of victimization lessens.

7. Advance on the Pill Box

The throughline in this sequence is attack. In a strategic assessment of the situation, Miller organizes his men and coordinates the attack. In this sequence his men successfully take the machine gun emplacement to the right of the pill box. The individual members of Miller's company (later patrol members) are also characterized in this sequence. Jackson the sharpshooter is a religious man; he kisses his crucifix prior to moving up. Fish the Jew provides the captain with gum so that he can create a makeshift periscope using a piece of glass gummed to his bayonet. The action in this sequence is highly fragmented. Spielberg uses many close-ups to identify the individual soldiers and to create the elements that will underscore the attack, particularly the view of the pill box through the makeshift periscope. Quick images of the pill box itself suggest its daunting quality from the point of view of these soldiers. Miller is also characterized as experienced and professional in this work. The feeling state in this sequence is mastery. Miller, his sergeant, and those he's working with closely, at least, are professional soldiers. There is a feeling of hope for the first time within the larger 24-minute sequence.

8. Take the Pill Box

   The sense of action escalates. The members of Miller's company advance their attack on the pill box. Sharpshooter Jackson eliminates a number of the machine-gunners. He also fires a grenade at the bunker. Closer to the pill box grenades are thrown into it. As soldiers exit they are shot. A torch-thrower advances and burns out the bunker. Burning German soldiers fall from the front of the bunker that had been the platform for firing down on the Americans. As we move through this sequence the number of telephoto shots that compress context begin to give way to more long shots with visual context. We no longer have the sense that the camera is crowding us. That greater sense of freedom begins to imply that the chaos and killing that have marked the sequences so far is coming to an end.

9. The Beach Is Taken

   Although sporadic shooting continues, this sequence focuses on the men who have survived. Again in close-up, Captain Miller's hands shake as he opens his canteen and drinks from it. Sergeant Horvath packs earth into a tin container marked *France*. He puts it into his knapsack where we see similar cans marked *Italy* and *Africa*. Private Fish simply cries, finally allowing his fear to emerge. The beach, littered with the dead, now becomes the focus of the sequence. There are so many. A long crane shot moves slowly in on one body whose knapsack reads his name, S. Ryan. This sequence is marked by lingering close-ups. The pace is very deliberate, even slow, to bring us to the end of Spielberg's 24-minute mini-film about the D-Day landing.

To sum up, the 24-minute sequence uses the MTV style to create a feeling: What it was like to be on Omaha Beach as an American combatant. The experience is quite unlike any created by a previous war film. This is due to the power of the MTV style.

☐ THE CASE OF ANG LEE'S *CROUCHING TIGER, HIDDEN DRAGON*

The set piece as a challenge for filmmakers is as old as Griffith's *Intolerance* (1916). The set piece has ranged from sensational to more purposeful intentions. The attack on the train in Lean's *Lawrence of Arabia* (1962) is spectacle attuned to mythmaking. The cornfield sequence in Hitchcock's *North by Northwest* (1959), on the other hand, is almost academic in its confident approach to the chase. Ranging in between we have the final shootout in Peckinpah's *The Wild Bunch* (1969) and the car chase in Friedkin's *The French Connection* (1971). Filmmakers have even begun to parody those set pieces. Witness the Spaghetti Westerns of Sergio Leone and the homages of Brian de Palma. The kung fu films of Hong Kong have used such set pieces to make a superhero of its main character.

Ang Lee has overtly made a kung fu film in *Crouching Tiger, Hidden Dragon* (2000), but his primary intent is not to create superheroes. He is far more ambitious in his intentions for the set piece. To explore those intentions, we now turn to *Crouching Tiger, Hidden Dragon*.

Ostensibly the plot revolves around the theft of a famous sword called Green Destiny. Its owner, the great warrior Li Mu Bai, has grown weary of battle; as if in a mood of existential doubt, he decides to give the sword to Sir Te, a trustworthy custodian. He asks Shu Lein, a woman he has long admired, to take the sword to Sir Te. Although Li Mu Bai is trained at Wudan Mountain, a center known for creating the greatest fighters, Shu Lein is also a very capable warrior. From their conversation, we understand that only one who is worthy of carrying it can possess the Green Destiny sword. Two more narrative notations are made in this sequence—that Shu Lein and Li Mu Bai yearn to be together, but something holds them back. The second point is that Li Mu Bai has one adversary, Jade Fox, a woman who killed his master.

The sword is delivered to Peking, and its custodian shows it to Governor Yu, but in short order the sword is stolen. Shu Lein suspects the thief is the Governor's daughter Jen. Jen, who is much younger and very willful, indeed is the thief, but much to our surprise her housekeeper is Jade Fox. Jen is unhappily scheduled to marry, a politically opportune marriage. She is disinterested, as we discover, because she loves the bandit Lo, known as Dark Cloud. In a flashback into the past, Dark Cloud stole Jen's comb, she pursued him into his home territory. There on the desert steppes of China they fought and fell in love.

The story line then follows the Green Destiny sword. First it is recovered by Li Mu Bai, who attempts to encourage Jen to become his student. (He admires her skills.) Jen in turn steals the sword again after Dark Cloud breaks up her wedding party. She runs off but soon encounters Shu Lein and then Li Mu Bai. She is captured by Jade Fox, drugged, and has to be rescued by

Li Mu Bai. There Jade Fox is finally killed but not before she has poisoned Li Mu Bai with a poison dart. Jen attempts to make the antidote for the poison but returns too late. Shu Lein sends her to her love, Dark Cloud, who waits for her on Wudan mountain. The young lovers are reunited, and Jen, asking Lo to make a wish, leaps into the air, to descend to the desert where they can once again be alone and together. The older would-be lovers, Li Mu Bai and Shu Lein, have earlier sworn loyalty and love to one another and express the wish to be reunited together in heaven.

Crouching Tiger, Hidden Dragon, ostensibly an action-adventure film, is actually also a melodrama about two capable women, Shu Lein and Jen. They struggle with traditional values and modern values, the society and the individual. Jen represents modern values, and she alone achieves a union with her lover Lo (Dark Cloud). Shu Lein, on the other hand, represents the forces of tradition; because years before her fiancé died before they married, she could not accept Li Mu Bai's attentions, nor could he offer them as he wished. Both were bound by tradition, and consequently their love was always platonic rather than physically manifest. Together, these two women represent the deep struggle for so many women in the world today: should I make my own way above all, or should the family and tradition take precedence? This is the context for the set pieces in Crouching Tiger, Hidden Dragon.

THE SET PIECES

The set pieces are approached with an MTV style. They are, in effect, self-contained, stand-alone experiences. They may or may not add to the progress of the narrative. They may or may not help the narrative build. It's my contention that the set pieces in Crouching Tiger, Hidden Dragon bend the narration away from the traditional exciting impact of a superhero saving society from a supervillain. To understand where Ang Lee takes us instead, we need to begin by examining the set pieces in a more general manner. First, of the 6 set pieces in Crouching Tiger, a woman participates in each of them. In 2 of the 6, the combatants are both women. A second observation is that a clear death occurs in only one of the set pieces. This is important because kung fu set pieces are conventionally marked by multiple deaths in every set piece. A third observation is that 3 of the set pieces take place at night, and of the 3 that take place in daylight, the environment is unusual and open: one of these takes place in the desert, the other up in the trees.

A final observation is that at least 3 of the participants—Li Mu Bai, Shu Lein, and Jen—are trained in Wudan; they can move up buildings, fly, and stop, by hand, a poison dart so small it's barely visible to the human eye. Their skills, in other words, go far beyond weaponry and introduce a kinesis not generally associated with skilled warriors. Whether this is supernatural or mind over body, it allows a woman to be strong beyond the weight and muscle of her male opponent, and it also narrows the field of worthy opposition. Only the best, only the most worthy, can fight as these 3 can.

If the set pieces are not about primacy through killing, then, what are they about? If I had to articulate the purpose of the set pieces in *Crouching Tiger, Hidden Dragon,* I would say they have much to do with the four characters who dominate the narrative: the two main characters, Shu Lein and Jen, and their two love choices, Li Mu Bai and Lo. All four are skilled in matters of war, whether from the point of view of self-defense or of attack. But Li Mu Bai in particular is looking for much more. In his restless search he has chosen to understand and experience the meaning of life first through the sword and later to move beyond the sword. If Li Mu Bai looks for meaning in the sword, Lo sees the sword or combat as a means to an end—to get what you want, whether it is material gain or social status, and be associated with freedom, ferocity, and banditry. Jen seems to want to prove that she is as good as any man. And Shu Lein seems to accept the responsibility and limits of combat—she seems to be the most mature in her articulation of what combat can and does mean.

Each of these characters exhibits skill beyond the ordinary. Their identity issues, confusions, and aspirations imbue the set pieces with an emotion that the fighting in and of itself cannot yield. The dignity each deports in the fight implies grace, and it is this sense of grace that resonates from the majority of set pieces. Only the fight at the Inn between Jen and a multitude of men does not display such grace; it's the only set piece that is almost comical in a slight woman's primacy over many large, heavily armed men. Thus grace is Ang Lee's goal in the remaining set pieces.

In a practical sense, that sense of grace is achieved through a series of visual strategies. The range of shots moves between medium shots and extreme long shots. Movement is a distinct feature of the shots—movement of the camera as well as movement within the frame. Cutting on movement makes the movement seem more dynamic. Rather than focusing on the immediate danger, Lee is anxious to see the mechanics of the fight-thrust and counter-thrust. More distance allows that skill to be foregrounded as opposed to an anxiety as to who will survive. Overall there is a formal quality to the set pieces, a quality that makes them ethereal, as if we were watching the combat of two gods rather than a thief and a protector of private property. To get a more detailed sense of this I turn to the first set piece—the robbery of the Green Destiny sword.

THE FIRST SET PIECE

This set piece, detailing the robbery of the Green Destiny sword and the consequent escape of its thief, is 6 minutes long. The theft itself is quick, and the thief quickly overcomes the guard. Once the thief escapes, Shu Lein is alerted and she becomes the primary pursuer. The guard at Sir Te's house also continues the pursuit and is puzzled by the fact that he is led to the house of Governor Yu. The thief will eventually get away when Jade Fox fires a poison dart at Shu Lein. Although she catches the dart, the shift of focus allows the thief to evade capture or harm. Additionally, although we have not been shown the identity of the thief, we note that the thief is slight, that Jen was shown the Green Destiny sword, as was her father. We also note that Jen's governess is dismissive of people like Shu Lein, although this is not the case for Jen. Consequently we believe the thief to be Jen. The only surprise is the level of her skill, which is considerable.

The major portion of the set piece is Shu Lein's pursuit of the thief. They seem equally skilled and inventive in the combat. They also alone have the capacity to climb buildings and to leap or fly in pursuit. The height of the buildings, or their number, don't seem to be a barrier. Both master space in a fashion unavailable to any of the other pursuers. In this sense, until Jade Fox tries to kill Shu Lein, they are in effect alone. Hands, feet, movement, artifacts, all become weapons in the combat. Jen even uses her whole body against Shu Lein.

The feeling that the set piece creates is that these two women are special warriors; they have a knowledge and skills available to few. Shu Lein also does not kill. She only wants the return of the stolen sword. This implies her values. She doesn't exploit her powers to show her power. She uses her power in service of something worthwhile, the retrieval of the sword. Jen, on the other hand, is less mature. She wants to get away with the theft. Since the subtext of the story is teaching Jen higher values that are in accord with her talent, this exchange with Shu Lein will be her first lesson.

Whereas the narrative has proceeded in a kind of stillness and serenity until now, the tone shifts in the set piece. First, the theft is exciting. Camera movement and cutting on movement makes the scene dynamic. The flight, particularly of Shu Lein pursuing Jen across rooftops and up the sides of buildings, is utterly graceful. The values of power or violence are nowhere to be seen in the set piece. The camera moves a good deal; it is often close to the action or, when an extreme long shot is used, the action moves away from the camera position. Again, there is a formal beauty to what we are watching. Once the fighting gets in close, Lee resorts to medium close-ups rather than extreme close-ups. This is not a fight to the death as in the combat between El Cid and his would-be father-in-law, the King's Champion, in Anthony Mann's *El Cid* (1961), a scene in which extreme close-ups were integral to the scene. Movement, pattern, move, and counter-move are more important in Lee's combat than the exercise of power. What more powerful notion can he apply to these two women? Who will be his two main characters? The fight scene is not about primacy, it's about character. This is the subtext to this set piece as well as to the final one—between Jen and Shu Lein and then Jen and Li Mu Bai.

The 6 minutes of this set piece create the feeling that will become the real theme of *Crouching Tiger, Hidden Dragon*. In a world of violence, deceit, and power, grace and inner beauty are offsetting critical values that must prevail, as they certainly do in this narrative.

☐ THE CASE OF *IN THE MOOD FOR LOVE*

Wong Kar-wai's *In the Mood for Love* is ostensibly a very simple love story set in 1962 Hong Kong. Overcrowding leads 2 young couples to rent rooms with other families. The man, Chow Mo Wan, works in a newspaper office. The woman, Su Li Zhen, works as a secretary for the head of a business. We never see his wife or her husband, but eventually we understand that his wife and her husband have been carrying on an affair. The marriages dissolve, and Chow Mo Wan and Su Li Zhen begin their own affair. The body of the film follows the course of their relationship. The relationship ends when he goes to Singapore. A few years later he returns and revisits the apartment where she used to live. He discovers that she had a son, and it is implied that the son is his. The film ends with his trip to Cambodia, where he deposits a note in a prayer box.

What is important to say about this film is that Wong Kar-wai is an unusual filmmaker who prefers to work in the experimental narrative form. Like Tom Tykwer in *Run Lola Run* (1999) and Peter Greenaway in *The Draughtsman's Contract* (1982), style is more important than the actual content. The struggle between style and content creates a powerful forum for the voice of the director. The experimental narrative is thus very much about voice. So what is it that Wong Kar-wai wants to say in this simple romantic melodrama? Before we examine how the MTV style helps create his voice, a number of observations need to be put forward.

The first observation is that a story of a romantic relationship between a man and a woman conventionally has a particular progression. They meet, he or she pursues the other, they reach a hurdle, somehow that hurdle is overcome, another crisis develops, and finally the relationship is a success or not. The story is structured with a beginning, middle, and end, and it is approached through character. Status, background, shared goals, and other elements all factor in to the success or failure of the romance, with all versions of *Romeo and Juliet* at the tragic end of the spectrum, and Nora Ephron's *Sleepless in Seattle* (1993) at the successful end of the spectrum. Wong Kar-wai's narrative follows the expected progression, but he constructs his key scenes out of minute details without actually showing the expected scenes. Consequently, the relationship is alluded to in its progression rather than treated conventionally.

A second observation is that the place, Hong Kong in 1962, is implied rather than actually seen. No cinema verité here. Hong Kong is represented by a dark street, a crowded hallway, a restaurant table, 2 workstations. There is no sense of crowding beyond the fact that the two couples are renting rooms in the apartments of others. The time, 1962, is implied through the cut of clothing, the hairstyles, and the look of a clock or a restaurant. Time and place are implied rather than pronounced, as was the case with the narrative progression.

A third is that the visual focus is on Chow Mo Wan and Su Li Zhen. His wife and her husband are never seen, and aside from his landlady, his colleague at work, and her boss, there are few other characters on view. This is a Hong Kong that is implied without its mass of people. Perhaps Wong Kar-wai means for it to be a dreamt Hong Kong.

Which brings us to the director's intention. The narrative is austere, the dialogue is austere, and the pace and camera movement are an austere equivalent. But the color, the lingering close-ups of the 2 characters, and the stylized movements are not austere; they are rich and create the mood appropriate for passion. So too is the music. Wong Kar-wai, through the dissonance between style and content, is trying to create the mood of a doomed love story. Whether he is trying to say loneliness is the human condition or whether his Hong Kong is a unique barrier to "being together," is for you to decide. What can be said is that Wong Kar-wai employs an MTV style to show how passion can only be sustained for a short time in a relationship.

THE MTV STYLE OF *IN THE MOOD FOR LOVE*

Wong Kar-wai uses two pieces of music a number of times in *In the Mood for Love*. One is a Spanish number sung by Nat King Cole, the other a romantic lament without lyrics. These pieces of music provide the shape for the set pieces. Within the set piece the music creates an aura of tremendous anticipation and romanticism. Visually, Wong Kar-wai presents movement. Chow Mo Wan smokes a cigarette under a street light. The smoke focuses our attention on his sense of anticipation. Su Li Zhen walks by. The visuals focus on the rhythm of her movement. It's as if she glides. She is swinging a pot of soup, and it too has a rhythm that Wong Kar-wai notes. His stillness, the movement of the smoke, her movement, the soup pot—all project an erotic possibility of their meeting. The movement is slowed down, the smoke is slowed down, and both together with the music builds a sense of anticipation. What the sequence leaves us with is a mood, a feeling of desire, of his desire for her.

Wong Kar-wai puts forward similar sequences as Chow Mo Wan and Su Li Zhen joust early in their relationship, bicker later in the relationship, as one feels disappointed in the other. All the while Wong Kar-wai shows us duplicity in other male-female relationships. Nevertheless, the prevailing focus is the moods that mark the phases of the main characters' relationship. The short movements, the extreme close-ups, the clarity of composition, together with the romantic lighting, all support the overall romantic feeling, the longing that pervades the set pieces. This longing in turn becomes the overall feeling accentuated by the dominance of style over content in *In the Mood for Love*.

☐ THE CASE OF *LIFE IS BEAUTIFUL*

Roberto Benigni's *Life Is Beautiful* (1997) is unusual in that its set pieces are concept-driven and their pace has almost no role in their effectiveness. They are, nevertheless, an example of the MTV style. Rather than looking to the historical examples mentioned earlier in this chapter, it's more meaningful to look at Charlie Chaplin's *Modern Times* (1936) and Woody Allen's *Sleeper* (1975).

Like those comedies, which were built up around the persona of the actor-director, *Life Is Beautiful* is a fable whose moral is that love can sustain us through terrible life experiences. Guido Orefice is a young man who comes to the city of Arezzo to follow his dream: to set up a bookstore. But the time is 1939 and Guido, as we discover 40 minutes into the story, is a Jew. The narrative is organized in two distinct sections. The first half is 1939 Arezzo, and the focus is Guido's pursuit of his dreams, particularly to catch his princess, Dora. He achieves his goal, snatching Dora from the arms of a local bureaucrat, the very evening of her engagement party. This part of the narrative focuses on the barriers to Guido's dreams: he needs a permit to open a bookstore—a permit that has to be signed by the very same bureaucrat who is to marry Dora; he is a Jew, an already persecuted minority; and he takes work of low status when he becomes a waiter. Nevertheless, his persistence and his inventiveness win over his princess, who is not a Jew.

The second half of the film takes place in 1944. He is now married to Dora, and they have a young son, Joshua. He also has a bookstore, albeit not commercially successful. But he does have a wonderful, playful relationship with his son. In short order he and his son are picked up and shipped off to a concentration camp in Northern Italy. Dora chooses to go as well. At the camp the issue is survival, since the old and the young are quickly gassed and their bodies burned. Guido makes up a game to help his son: if you earn 1000 points you will win a real tank. But to do so Joshua must listen, pretend he doesn't want snacks with jam, and generally follow his father's enthusiastic lead. Guido also finds various ways to communicate with the women's barracks that he and Joshua are alive. In this sense, he keeps both his wife and his son alive. The game continues to the last night in the concentration camp when the Germans kill all the prisoners they can before they abandon the camp due to the arrival of the Americans. Guido dies, but not before he has saved his son. Even at this last stage he has made a game of survival.

Before we look at the 3 set pieces composing the body of the narrative, let me make a few points. First, the tone, as one would expect in a fable, is not realistic. It is formal and rather fantastic, as one finds in hyperdramas[1] such as Volker Schlöndorff's *The Tin Drum* (1979) and Robert Zemeckis' *Forrest Gump* (1994).

Second, the concept that shapes the set pieces arises out of the fable's moral. The narrative as a whole, as well as the set pieces, follows the same progression: a character is hopeful, even enthusiastic; a misfortune befalls him and then, arising out of the misfortune, he finds good fortune. In other words, goodness and love prevail in spite of personal loss of economic status, freedom, even life itself. It's as if the Holocaust itself cannot dim the will of a father that his child be a child, that games, playfulness, and creativity can actually crowd out deprivation, pain, loss, and tragedy. To understand how Benigni conveys the moral we turn to three set pieces in different phases of the narrative.

THE SET PIECE IN *LIFE IS BEAUTIFUL*

The first set piece we examine occurs in the early part of the film. Guido has come to the city office where he will apply for a permit to establish a bookstore. He has only recently arrived in the city. The first phase of the set piece is Guido's enthusiasm to get on with his dream. He is told that it's lunchtime and the person who needs to sign will now go for lunch. When he complains, he is told that the next person who can sign will arrive in one hour. Guido quickly gets into an argument with the bureaucrat who now leaves. Upset, Guido looks out the window, accidentally pushing a flower-pot off the window ledge. The pot shatters on the head of the bureaucrat. Guido rushes out to apologize. He places his hat, which has raw eggs in it, on an adjacent car. The bureaucrat tells Guido he will never get the needed signature, mistakenly picks up the hat with the eggs, and puts it on his head. The eggs crack and the bureaucrat, humiliated again, is infuriated. He begins to pursue Guido, who borrows a bicycle. As he flees he crashes into the woman of his dreams, Dora, whom he refers to as princess. This is their second accidental meeting. The misfortune of losing the chance to apply for the bookstore and of being pursued by an angry bureaucrat turns into the good fortune of finding Dora again. Throughout the set piece Guido has maintained a high level of energy, first as enthusiasm, then as indignation, and finally as passion. The feeling created by the set piece is that his career will persevere in spite of setbacks.

The next set piece I will refer to as the engagement party. The set piece occurs in the restaurant where Guido works as a waiter. Tonight the bureaucrat will announce his engagement to the reluctant Dora. She is clearly being prompted by her mother to be enthusiastic about this relationship. The set piece begins with the reluctant Dora hiding in her dress under her bed covers, and ends with her riding off on a horse with Guido. The scene is filled with signs of misfortune for Guido: his uncle's white horse has been painted green to designate it as a Jewish horse. A stuffed ostrich sits atop the celebratory "Ethiopian" engagement cake (a reference to Italy's territorial ambitions), and a live poodle ends up decorating Guido's serving tray. The scene has a serious intention but absurdity abounds. Finally, to get away from the absurdity, Dora sees Guido hiding under her table and decides to join him in order to declare her love. He is clearly her type of man. He takes her home and, within the same shot, 5 years have passed. We understand because a child emerges from the door Guido and Dora just entered. The feeling created in this set piece is that society is becoming absurd and that Guido's imaginative nonconformity seems sane in comparison.

The third set piece takes place late in the film. I will call it "A good lunch in the concentration camp." Guido now works as a waiter in the mess hall. A German doctor he knew in Arezzo is now the camp doctor. That day a group of officer's children are brought to the camp. They play on the grounds and Guido encourages Joshua to play as well. When the children are called to lunch, a matron mistakes Joshua for a German child. Guido tells him to be silent, for any speech would give away that he is Italian. And so Joshua goes to lunch where his father will be one of the waiters, but he is playing the "be quiet game" according to his father. As he is offered food and being polite, he says "grazzi" to the German waiter. The waiter rushes for the matron—an Italian boy is among the Aryan youngsters. Guido hastily organizes a game among the German children. By the time the matron and waiter appear all the children are saying "grazzi." Playing a children's game has saved Joshua. Satiated with food the boy goes to sleep at the table. Guido then puts Offenbach on the gramophone and points it out of the windows. His wife hears and goes to the window. Guido is saving her as well, in this case by keeping her spirits up—he and their son are alive, and seemingly well. Once again Guido's attitude and his active imagination have saved his family. The feeling in this set piece is that play, in essence, children's games, are curative.

None of these set pieces are fast-paced, in fact, each is very deliberate, even slow. But each has a concept at its core, and each confirms the moral of the fable—love can help you overcome any adversity.

☐ THE CASE OF *TAMPOPO*

The MTV style was used to create a chaotic context for the main character in *Saving Private Ryan*. The result is to pose the question—How will he survive?—rather than the traditional question about the main character in a war film—*Will* he survive? In *Crouching Tiger, Hidden Dragon*, the MTV style realigns our expectations of the kung fu adventure film. And in *Life Is Beautiful*, the MTV style reiterates the central theme of the narrative. In each case, the MTV style has had a relation to the narrative, either deepening or altering that narrative. The MTV style is deployed for an altogether different purpose in Juzo Itami's *Tampopo* (1987). In *Tampopo*, the MTV style is altogether distinct from the narrative. What it does add is the powerful statement of mood; a mood that acts against the narrative content. The ironic tone created is the vehicle for Itami's voice.

The main narrative follows how a stranger helps a young widow transform her ordinary noodle shop into the "best noodle shop in Tokyo." This seems like a modest enough tale, but Itami approaches the story by borrowing heavily from Kurosawa and his epic "Western" *Seven Samurai* (1954), which was later remade by John Sturges as *The Magnificent Seven* (1960). This epic treatment means that the mentor character, here called Goro, has to assemble a group that can help Tampopo "save" her shop. They include an impudent young man, a "fallen" older doctor, a rich man's valet, and a rough and tumble builder. Tampopo's young son is also a member of these unlikely helpers. Goro, by the way, always appears in the film wearing a cowboy hat. The opposition to Tampopo is composed of other noodle shop owners, and, appropriately, each acts as if he is a cattle baron whose wealth is under threat from the suspicious Goro and the modest Tampopo. Soup preparation, noodle composition, pork fat—each is treated like the weaponry in a Western.

The tone Itami uses is ironic and filled with allusion to the Western genre. Occasionally Itami will also reference the gangster film. Itami effectively establishes the tone by framing the narrative, first as a film and then as a pulp novel. In the opening, a gangster, dressed like a dandy, enters a cinema with his retinue. He sets up in the first row, complete with champagne. He acknowledges that a film will be seen, then he issues a warning to a viewer: no loud eating during the film; it's rude and will lead to the viewer's violent end at the gangster's hand. Then he allows the film to proceed. In the next scene, a young man is instructed on how to eat good noodle soup. This extended introduction to soup is then acknowledged as the visualization of a book being read by a truck driver. The truck drivers are hungry and decide to stop at a noodle shop. One of them is Goro, and what follows is his introduction to Tampopo. Later in the narrative, whenever Itami feels the need (there is no logic to these set pieces), he wanders away from the narrative into an MTV set piece. Each set piece has something to do with eating. A number of set pieces have to do with the gangster from the opening. Others simply stand alone.

Before we proceed to look at two of these set pieces it would be useful to summarize their context:

1. A narrative that is essentially a melodrama is treated as a Western.
2. The Itami voice is highlighted by a sense of irony about Japanese social conventions as well as filmic narrative conventions.
3. Food, its importance and its elevation to a status beyond simple eating, unites the narrative as well as the set pieces.
4. The tone is extreme, running from playful to absurd; or, to put it another way, the tone is widely variable.

THE SET PIECE IN *TAMPOPO*

The first set piece, which occurs in the first third of the film, focuses on dining. A group of Japanese businessmen eats in the exclusive dining room of a high-class hotel. The cuisine is French. The group is principally elderly with the exception of one young man. As the waiter requests everyone's order one of the elderly gentlemen places his—a simple fish dish, beer and soup, and no salad. As the waiter moves around the table, others replicate the order of the "leader" of the group. As the waiter comes to the young man clearly the pressure is on—conform. But he doesn't. He recognizes the menu as a replication of the number one restaurant in Paris. He then proceeds to order snails and a special champagne, much to the consternation of his colleagues. Clearly he is an individual among corporate conformists.

The scene shifts to another dining room in the hotel. A "group leader" is teaching young Japanese women the etiquette of eating spaghetti. The procedure is formal, slow, and silent. The young women are very attentive. Close by, an American is served spaghetti. He proceeds to eat it vigorously and messily. The young women are taken with his zeal, and they proceed to noisily eat their spaghetti. Finally the group leader succumbs. She too begins to eat her spaghetti noisily.

This set piece is all about conformity among the upper class. What Itami is saying is enjoy yourself, conventions be damned. What is important is to be yourself and to enjoy yourself. The set piece is ironic and humorous. It's difficult to remember but he reminds us—it's only lunch.

The second set piece takes place early in the second half of the film. All efforts to learn the secret of making exceptional broth for the noodle soup have failed, and so Goro takes Tampopo to see "the doctor." He is an old man and a homeless person, living among other vagrants—in effect a community of the homeless. The "doctor" left his practice and family for this new life. Goro enlists the doctor in Tampopo's cause. As Tampopo's son is hungry, one of the doctor's colleagues, a "chef," takes the boy to the local hotel. There he breaks into the kitchen and proceeds to make him a rice omelet. The cooking is precise, and the effort yields perfection. They steal away as the hotel security guard inspects the kitchen where a light suggests mischief. They get away and the boy has a great meal.

The notion that cooking genius resides in a group of homeless people offers the opposite end of the social spectrum from the first set piece. Indeed, the sense of togetherness, respect, and aesthetic cooking sensibility, all suggest the opposite of the earlier scene where conformity and class were the order in approaching the what and how of eating.

Again, irony abounds in this set piece, but what is also critical at its core is the sense of an aesthetic about food, its creation, and its consumption. As in the first set piece, there is considerable surprise here—surprise at individual behavior and surprise about individual values. Finally, as in the first set piece, there is enormous humor. The creation of an omelet is treated with a reverence deserving of the creation of something far greater. Or perhaps Itami is saying that it all stops here, at the eye, the mouth, and the stomach. In the end, we are what we eat and how we eat it. The feeling state Itami is working with is to elevate originality in all its aspects.

□ CONCLUSION

Whether the purpose of the set piece is to highlight the voice of the author, as in the case of Itami, or to subvert the genre expectation, as in Ang Lee's *Crouching Tiger, Hidden Dragon,* the MTV set piece is a powerful tool in the filmmaker's tool box. Its use often alters conventional narrative. Used strategically that alteration can add meaning to the narrative, as in Spielberg's *Saving Private Ryan,* or it can tilt our experience toward feeling and mood rather than narrative, as in Wong Kar-wai's *In The Mood for Love.* In either case, the MTV style has a powerful impact

□ NOTE/REFERENCE

1. See discussion of hyperdrama in Ken Dancyger, "The Centrality of Metagenre" in *Global Scriptwriting* (Boston: Focal Press, 2001), 197–208. Hyperdrama is a genre structured as a moral fable for adults. It is plot driven, varying in tone, and is usually far from realism. It is characterized by the distinctive voice of its author.

13

Changes in Pace

■

Pace has been a critical editing tool since D.W. Griffith perfected the chase sequence. Although an existing dramatic climax was Griffith's goal, the purpose of pace has proved far more diverse over time. The context of this diversity begins with Sergei Eisenstein. While German expressionists such as F.W. Murnau moved the camera to avoid editing, Eisenstein built upon Griffith's ideas about pace and brought more rapid editing into filmmaking with a political rather than an entertainment agenda. In films memorializing the revolutionary spirit [*Stachka* (*Strike*), *Bronenosets Potyomkin* (*Potemkin*)] and collectivization [*Staroye i novoye* (*The General Line*)], Eisenstein worked out his theory of montage: pace, or metric montage, was one of its central traits.

The core issue for Eisenstein was conflictual—the ordinary sailor against his officers, the oppressed workers against their rulers, the people against the Czar. Pace was used to juxtapose oppression and political action in the most powerful fashion. Eisenstein was not afraid to exploit the emotionalism inherent in the audience's relationship with the film medium. Pace promoted that emotionalism and its exploitation.

□ EVOLUTION OF PACE IN FILMMAKING

Eisenstein opened the door on the issue of pace and a wide variety of filmmakers walked through that door. King Vidor effectively used pace to build an aesthetic tension in the march through the woods sequence in *The Big Parade*. Walter Ruttmann used pace to capture the energy of the city in *Berlin: Symphony of a Great City*. And Frank Capra used pace to energize his dialogue-heavy narrative in *You Can't Take it With You*. The great leaps forward, however, would await the 1950s. In that decade, with Akira Kurosawa's dynamic use of pace in *Rashômon*—together with Alfred Hitchcock's set pieces in *The Man Who Knew Too Much* and, in 1960, *Psycho*—new pathways emerged, suggesting that pace could be used for more diverse purposes.

In *Rashômon*, Kurosawa presents four versions of the same story, each from a different person's point of view. The interpretations vary widely. Kurosawa's main editing device to underscore the differences in view is variation in the pace of each of the four stories. In the case of Hitchcock, the shower scene in *Psycho* has become the second most famous set piece in the history of film, and at its editing core it is the changes in pace that move the sequence from anticipation, to the violence of the killing, to the stillness of death.

The next significant development in the use of pace was seen in the work of Richard Lester in the Beatles films *A Hard Days Night* and *Help!*. Their dynamic mixture of movement, jump cutting, and variations in point of view (performers, audience, and the media) created a filmic persona of youthful energy and joyful anarchy. There is little question that the effective use of pace in these films accelerated—dare we say it—the *pace* of pace in film. After *A Hard Days Night*, commercials and feature films were cut faster.

The next step in the use of pace seemed on one level a reversion to the ideas of Eisenstein. Sam Peckinpah's *The Wild Bunch*, particularly in its opening and climactic set-pieces, a robbery and a massacre, relies on modulation of pace to create a sense of the chaos of violence. Building out from the death scene in Arthur Penn's *Bonnie and Clyde*, the massacre that ends in the death of the final four members of *The Wild Bunch* seems the ultimate use of pace to mesmerize and simultaneously horrify its audience. At this point, pace seems to affiliate with particular genres—the police story in *The French Connection*, the gangster film in *Scarface*, the thriller in *Jaws*, and the war film in *Apocalypse Now*. In each genre and film, a different purpose might be served, but, in general, the mix of excitement and insight into the fragmented psychology of the main character captures the intent.

Perhaps no filmmaker best encapsulated both of these agendas—excitement and insight—as did Oliver Stone in his 20 years of work as a director, from *Salvador* through *Natural Born Killers*. Stone, in his use of pace, seems to be the direct descendant of Sergei Eisenstein by way of Sam Peckinpah. For each of these filmmakers, pace was the primary editing strategy for their storytelling agenda. Each wanted to move their audience by marrying an aggressive editing style to highly political, or at least politicized, content.

Although pace has been more recently affiliated with action directors such as McG (*Charlie's Angels*), and Tony Scott (*Man on Fire*), the most aggressive use of pace has been demonstrated by John Woo in his action-adventure renditions of police and gangster films (*The Replacement Killers*). The most consistent exploration of pace and its possibilities can be found in the work of Steven Spielberg, from *Saving Private Ryan* (1998) to *War of the Worlds* (2005). In order to clarify the changes in the use of pace, we now turn to its use in four different genres, starting with the docudrama.

PACE IN THE DOCUDRAMA

Jean-Pierre and Luc Dardenne made *Rosetta* in 1999. Since then, they have continued to refine their approach in *Le Fils* (*The Son*) (2003) and *L'Enfant* (*The Child*) (2005). The style is essentially a cinéma vérité approach—hand-held camera and the absence of lights and music.

Rosetta is the story of a 17-year-old girl. The film begins with her being forced from a factory job, and essentially the film follows her efforts to secure a full-time job in order to stabilize a life marked by a trailer-park existence caring for an alcoholic mother. A young man (Riquet) who works at a local waffle stand is interested in Rosetta. He confides in her, shelters her. In the end, she betrays him to his boss to secure his job. Riquet has been making waffles at home and selling them at the stand—in effect, stealing from his boss. Rosetta reports him and gets his job, but life is too challenging. She gives up the job and the film ends with Rosetta unsure about the future—not knowing whether she should take up with the young man or continue her hand-to-mouth existence.

The locations for *Rosetta* are the workplace, the waffle stand, the young man's apartment, and the trailer park. The trailer park particularly seems rural and cut off from the city. A muddy-bottom river that passes through the trailer park represents a constant threat to it; there is no pastoral sense in this film.

The Dardenne brothers rely on a hand-held camera positioned close to the characters, particularly Rosetta. They stay close, yielding few long or locating shots. Their preferences are close-ups, but they occasionally include mid-shots to allow for two characters in the frame. Pace is accelerated by a reliance on jump cutting, both in simple locations and between locations. In *Rosetta*, the Dardenne brothers are using pace principally to capture Rosetta's fierceness, her means to have what she calls "a job in order to have a normal life." This fierceness is illustrated in the opening. Rosetta is fired from her factory job. Her resistance is powerful as she tries to stay, in the end requiring security to escort her out when the efforts of the boss prove insufficient. The moving camera, the jump cutting, and the pace of this sequence palpably demonstrate Rosetta's fierceness. This quality seems to be the primary purpose of pace in the film.

A secondary purpose of the pace is to capture the instability of Rosetta's life. Her mother's condition leads the mother to be promiscuous with the caretaker of the trailer park. The caretaker plies the mother with liquor, while Rosetta attempts to moderate her drinking. Rosetta is, at different points in the narrative, facing a dire financial situation. At one point, she sells her clothes to raise cash. Her attempt to do so takes her to various second-hand outlets. Then there is a point in the film when Rosetta secures a job assisting the baker who owns the waffle outlet. The job ends after a few days, when the baker chooses to employ his ne'er-do-well son instead. Rosetta's desperation and her refusal to accept the situation are desperate moments for her character, who wants nothing more than a normal life. At each of these points in the film, the Dardenne brothers use pace to capture the instability of Rosetta's situation. Her reactions, together with the pace, serve to demonstrate the depth of her desire and desperation. Pace has rarely so powerfully evoked the inner life of a character.

PACE IN THE THRILLER

The docudrama as a genre tends to emphasize the voice of the filmmakers. How we feel about the conflict between Rosetta's fierce desire for a normal life and the very instability of her life is the space the Dardennes want their audience to occupy. How do we feel about the space they have trapped us in? The thriller as a genre has quite a different goal. Above all it's a more entertainment-oriented goal and, consequently, pace takes on differing purposes in the thriller.

For the most part, the thriller is the story of an ordinary person caught in extraordinary circumstances. If he doesn't figure out by who is and why he is being pursued, he will, in short order, be dead. If he prevails, he will be a hero. In Paul Greengrass' *The Bourne Supremacy*, the main character, Bourne, isn't ordinary. He's a CIA-trained killer. But neither are his adversaries the usual run-of-the-mill killers. Here, Bourne is being pursued by the CIA and a Russian supercriminal. Before this thriller begins to sound like the ultimate action-adventure film, a number of character and story details will serve to humanize the main character.

Jason Bourne has amnesia, and Marie, the woman he lives with, tries to help piece together his past. He knows he has killed others. He also knows he has instincts that help protect life, but he can't save Marie. In the first 10 minutes of the film, he is blamed for killing two CIA operatives in Berlin. The real killer has planted Bourne's fingerprint at the scene. And he tracks Bourne down in Goa, India. There, in his attempt to kill Bourne, he kills Marie instead. In the balance of the film, Bourne will attempt to stop the CIA, who he believes is trying to kill him. He will also recover the memory of his last time in Berlin. There, his first assignment was to kill a Russian dissident politician. Finding the politician's wife in the room, Bourne killed her as well. Realizing his past deeds, he goes to Moscow to seek out the daughter of his two victims. He tells her how her parents died, in the hope that the truth (she was led to believe at the time of her parents' deaths that the two were a murder–suicide) will help the teenager. In Moscow, Bourne is pursued, in a high-speed chase, by Marie's killer. During that chase, the killer is killed.

What is also useful to the sense of the story is that the women in the film (Marie; Pamela Landy and Nicky, both with the CIA; and the Russian victims' daughter), each in their way, are helpful to Bourne. All of the men (Russian, American, and German) are against him. Paul Greengrass, the director, also made the docudramas *Bloody Sunday* and *United 93*, and his approach to *The Bourne Supremacy* is to treat events and people as realistically as possible. Pace plays a very important role in the creation of that sense of realism.

Let's look at the way Greengrass characterizes Bourne's struggle against his loss of memory. The film opens with a series of quick images—city lights, a hotel room, a body. The images pass by quickly. They are presented as recaptured fragments of Bourne's memory. They are fleeting and they are frustrating. Together, they yield a logical explanation. As we move farther into the narrative and to Bourne's return to the city where the crime took place, and to the room where he killed the diplomat and his wife, the pace slows down and we're given fuller information. But the movement—from the fragmentary opening to the gains in memory Bourne makes—illustrates how Greengrass opts to use pace. He's using it to give us insight into the personal problem, which is the memory loss, and into the means by which the character recovers his memory. Pace is the key to the pictorialization of the problem and to its solution.

Another purpose for the use of pace is to illustrate Bourne's instinctual survivalist skills. On one level, his are lethal skills. But on the level of characterization, they illustrate a level of training that has made him anticipate and react instantly to that threat. There is a point in the film at which Bourne has been apprehended by customs officials in Naples. He is traveling under his own name rather than under the assumed identity he so often uses. A CIA operative has entered the room to interrogate Bourne. Bourne is nonresponsive. A call comes in telling the agent that Bourne is dangerous. As soon as the agent begins to reach for his gun, a rapid-fire Bourne disarms and disables him as well as the two Italian Customs police.

The characteristic instinct is even more rapid when Bourne visits another CIA "killer" in Munich. They are the only two of their kind still alive. Yet each is wary of the other. Bourne has the man secure his own hands. Nevertheless, a fight to the death ensues. This proceeds so speedily and with such a clear goal—each striving to ensure the death of the other—that the pace is breathtaking, all in the service of conveying just how dangerous and capable these men are. This editing approach is used at least a half-dozen times and each time it's exhilarating and convincing that Jason Bourne is not a man to go quietly into the night.

A third and perhaps most dramatic use of pace in this thriller is in the narrative, particularly in the plot. The scene in which Marie is killed is a pursuit, a car chase through Goa's streets, back alleys, and bridges. Greengrass must keep the narrative clear and yet capture Bourne's determination to escape as well as the killer's goal, the killing of Bourne. Greengrass focuses on the details such as Bourne switching out of the driver's seat in order to be able to return fire. The killer fires at the driver and kills Marie. The pace of this scene focuses on chaos and credibility, all the while including those critical shots needed to clarify the narrative progression of the scene. The pace is appropriate and effective to the narrative goals of the characters.

This editing idea is even more dynamically present in the climactic confrontation between Bourne and the killer on the streets of Moscow. The information that the killer is Secret Service, that he has telephone communication about Bourne's whereabouts, and that he all but owns the streets of

Moscow contrast with a wounded Bourne (shot by the killer) commandeering a cab and fleeing for his life through the streets of the city. Add to this a high-speed chase that ends in an underground tunnel in a shootout between Bourne and the killer. When Bourne shoots out the killer's tires, the killer's car smashes into a concrete pillar.

The pace of this chase differs from the car chase in *The French Connection*, in which the goal was to emphasize the crazy determination of a policeman in pursuit of a French gangster who tried to kill him. It also differs from the chase in *Bullitt*, which is all about the excitement, the thrills of a pursuit through the hilly streets of San Francisco. In *The Bourne Supremacy*, the pace is deployed to make the chase realistic, and to keep the chaotic narrative utterly clear. Greengrass succeeds in these goals. As in the other uses of pace in the film, Greengrass never forgets that editing is in service of a larger directorial idea, in this case making that narrative seem utterly realistic.

PACE IN THE ACTION-ADVENTURE

Another genre that has used pace as an important feature is the action-adventure film. Pace has long been an exciting feature of the action-adventure films, some of the best examples being found in the opening and the horse-truck chase in *Raiders of the Lost Ark*. Here the thrill of the chase is vitalized by the use of pace. Pace has been used to heighten the tension and amplify the stakes in Michael Bay's *Armageddon* and Roland Emmerich's *Independence Day*. And pace has been used to amplify the status of the main character, in essence, to verify that he and his colleagues are superheroes, as in Antoine Fuqua's *King Arthur*. But Zhang Yimou uses pace in a more subtle and surprising way in his film *Ying xiong* (*Hero*).

Hero uses stillness and pace juxtaposed to create a more formal quality to the narrative. *Hero* is the story of a nameless assassin (played by Jet Li). His ostensible role is to be rewarded by the Emperor for destroying the Emperor's most powerful enemies, Sky, Flying Snow, and Broken Sword. By giving the broken silver spear of Sky to the Emperor, the assassin gains access and proximity to the Emperor. Although he has been thoroughly searched, the assassin's proximity will allow him to quickly capture the Emperor's own sword and kill him with it. The film unfolds in the recounting of the assassin's heroic actions in defeating the above-mentioned powerful adversaries of the Emperor. Each story moves the assassin from the initial 100 paces away from the Emperor, finally to within 10 paces from the Emperor. When he has finally reached his goal of 10 paces, the assassin finds he cannot kill a man who has proved to have intelligence and vision as leader. In the end, the assassin leaves the palace and is killed by the Emperor's archers. It is as heroic a death as his three accomplices had achieved. The film ends alluding to the greatness of the Emperor, who during his reign united all of China.

Zhang Yimou stages his film as a meditation on what a hero truly is. Although his focus is upon four assassins and an Emperor, and a plot by the four to kill the Emperor, he is more interested in the inner life of each person, rather than the outcome. In short, this action-adventure film is all about character. Inner life is about passion, whether it is love of another or love of one's country. Each of these characters, including the Emperor, has passion to burn. Consequently, outer life—who wins material goods or honors or competitions—is less valued than is the fire that burns within.

Zhang Yimou uses a strategy about pace in order to pictorialize the inner life and the outer life. Since the outer life is less subtle, we turn to pace and life in the world first. The aspects of outer life—essentially the battle of the Emperor's army of invasion, the palace guard protecting the Emperor, and the battle of the assassin with Sky and later with Flying Snow—are dynamic and staged with a static camera and much cutting between extreme long shots and close-ups. The juxtaposition is dynamic but the stillness of the camera position modifies the pace. It is dynamic but formal, far from the chaos that pace creates in *The Wild Bunch*. Here the pace almost stylizes the battles. Clearly, personal power and military power are at stake, but the formal pace does not exploit the clash of powerful people or armies. Rather, the pace juxtaposes those sources of power, creating wonderment rather than conflict, beauty rather than strength.

Zhang Yimou's use of pace to create the inner sense of the character is far more subtle. Here he jump cuts in on the character's faces, almost seeking revelation or true emotion or intention. The fight between Sky and the assassin is revealing: Zhang Yimou jump cuts into the eyes or face at oblique angles, so that we don't see the whole face. Something is revealed, but, visually, part of the face is also withheld. Or the focus is on the clash of the weapons—sword and spear. The weapons become part of each combatant's body, providing an insight into how each man views his weapon. It is not a killing instrument, it is part of him. Again, pace reveals the inner life of Sky. Zhang Yimou uses the same approach to Broken Sword's calligraphy. The intent is to move away from the man as assassin and to reveal what is most meaningful to him. The use of pace in the attack on the calligraphy school, and Broken Sword's response to being under attack from a barrage of arrows from the Emperor's army, tells us much about Broken Sword. Pace is used to reveal not his tension, but rather his inner tranquility.

PACE IN THE MUSICAL

We turn now to the musical, a genre that is essentially a wish-fulfillment narrative focusing on "putting on the show" and a main character that is a performer who is unseasoned or overseasoned. The show will launch or relaunch the main character's career and secure a relationship with the leading lady. On both the plot and the character relationship levels, the character gets what he wants.

Most classic musicals, including George Stevens' *Swing Time* and Stanley Donen's *Singin' in the Rain*, follow the Busby Berkeley lead and take a mise-en-scène approach to the edit, essentially avoiding editing to capture the choreography of performance, rather than fragmenting the performance using the edit. In this sense, editing is seen as an intervention into the performance. Moving the camera was the preferred choice. Everything changed when Bob Fosse made *Cabaret*, and later *All that Jazz* (not quite a musical). In these films, pace became a dynamic option that Fosse integrated into the choreography of a performed song. Alan Parker followed with *Fame*, Adrian Lyne followed with *Flashdance*, and a kind of MTV approach became an important framework for actively using pace in the musical.

When Baz Luhrmann made *Moulin Rouge!* (2001), the use of pace in the musical changed again. Luhrmann's agenda was to use pace to not only play with his love of the musical, it was also to use pace to articulate the joy of love, the pain of love, and the depth of desire. Of course, he also wanted to articulate the love of performance as well as love for people.

Moulin Rouge tells the story of Christian, a writer who comes to Paris to write about love. But he doesn't know anything about love. In Montmartre, he falls in with a group of Bohemian housemates—performers, writers, musicians. When the group's writer is overtaken by his condition, narcolepsy, they turn to Christian to write their musical "Spectacular, Spectacular." And they want the famous courtesan-actress, Satine, to play the lead.

That night at the theater, the leader of the Bohemian team, Toulouse-Lautrec, introduces Christian to Satine. At the same time, Harold Zidler, impresario-master of ceremonies, wants Satine to meet The Duke, a rich financier, who has the means to save Zidler's theatrical ambitions. Satine mistakenly believes Christian is The Duke. She finds out soon enough that The Duke is the real Duke, but not before Christian has fallen in love. In short order, Satine falls in love with Christian. The Duke falls in love with Satine, and is an insanely jealous rich man. He finances the play to buy Satine, but, as they say, you can't buy love. The lovers defy The Duke, the show goes on, and Satine, incurably ill, dies, and Christian has learned enough about love to feel that he is now a writer.

Before we plunge into pace and love and jealousy, it is important to acknowledge that whether love and jealousy are about a performance or about a person, each translates into energy. Desire, competition, and hatred also translate into energy, and here is where pace becomes important. Pace, by its nature, creates energy or tension when it accelerates and creates calm when it goes from fast to slower. Luhrmann first establishes energy when Christian arrives by train in Paris. Christian is excited. And whether he keeps hearing his father critique his decision to come to Paris or seeks out an apartment in Montmartre, Luhrmann's use of pace articulates Christian's feeling of excitement.

When Christian meets the eccentric Bohemians who will become colleagues and friends, again pace is used. Here it's not so much Christian's excitement, but rather his disbelief that such people exist. Disbelief turns to fascination and again pace, together with art direction, including hair and makeup, both individuates and makes these characters passionate artists, ready to march forward into their culture war, a musical production.

Finally, Christian is taken to the theater to meet Satine. A performance is underway. Here the pace quickens to the point of frenzy. Movement, dance, singing, performance, passion—all mix as we get a pastiche of the joyful aspects of being a performer. Pace makes this sequence one of the most dynamic in the film. We in the audience, who may never have dreamed of dancing and singing professionally for the length of this introduction, entertain all possibilities. The scene is nothing less than a seduction of the senses. Christian is hooked and so are we.

The pace is no less powerfully deployed later in the film in the Roxanne number. Here the purpose is to illustrate the pain of passion. Jealousy is rife as both the narcoleptic Bohemian and Christian experience a deep bout of jealousy. By cross-cutting between Christian and the narcoleptic, between the lovers of each man, and by images of their rivals or imagined rivals, Luhrmann uses an accelerating pace to capture the cascading feeling of being overwhelmed with desire and jealousy. The pain in the scene is palpable and Luhrmann uses pace to measure the characters' descent into the depths of their pain. Again Luhrmann is using pace operatically to calibrate feeling— in this case, pain; in the earlier case, pleasure and desire. In all cases, pace is playing the key editing role in modulating the characters' feelings.

□ Conclusion

In this chapter we have communicated an array of uses of pace. When linked to a genre, pace deepens the audience's sense experience of the doc-udrama, the thriller, the action-adventure film, and the musical. The repertory for pace has broadened; its use now is sophisticated rather than coarse. Although much has happened since those initial forays into pace by D.W. Griffith, we must not forget the key contributions of those early pioneers, Griffith and Eisenstein.

14

The Appropriation of Style I:
Imitation and Innovation

■

In this chapter, we explore a new phenomenon, the movie whose style is created from the context of movie life rather than real life. The consequence is twofold—the presumption of deep knowledge on the part of the audience of those forms such as the gangster films or Westerns, horror films or adventure films. And that the parody or alteration of that film creates a new form, a different experience for the audience. This imitative and innovative style is a style associated with the brief but influential directing career of Quentin Tarantino (*Reservoir Dogs*, 1992; *Pulp Fiction*, 1994). In order to suggest the limits of imitation and a more startling kind of innovation, we look at Milcho Manchevski's film, *Before the Rain* (1994). Like *Pulp Fiction*, it is three stories in a single film.

In order to contextualize the theme of style, imitation, and innovation, we turn to earlier examples of filmmakers whose style was pronounced.

□ NARRATIVE AND STYLE

Style in and of itself can contribute to the narrative or it can undermine the narrative if it is not clearly dramatically purposeful. The elements of style most obvious to the viewer, are compositional elements—camera placement, movement, the juxtaposition of foreground and background people or things, the light, the sound, and, of course, the editing. Whether the filmmaker relies on the editing, the pace, to explain the narrative, or she avoids editing, moving the camera, using the planes within the frame to explain the narrative. More often style is associated with composition—naturalistic or stylized; however, editing, as I hope we've illustrated in this book, has its own style—ranging from directly expository to elliptical and metaphorical.

Two filmmakers who use a distinct style that serves the narrative well are Max Ophuls and George Stevens. In *Caught* (1949), Ophuls uses camera composition to create a style that beautifully fleshes out the narrative. A young woman, Leonora (Barbara Bel Geddes), wants to marry rich and she does. She marries Smith Ohlrig (Robert Ryan). He proves to be sadistic and cruel. She runs off and works for a Dr. Quinada (James Mason), in a poor, urban district of New York. They fall in love and the triangle is set. Will she find happiness or be destroyed for her original goal, material wealth? Ophuls uses the composition of Leonora and Smith at the outset to show his power over her. Whenever they are together the composition suggest control rather than love. Early in the film, Ophuls uses a similar composition where Smith is seeing his psychoanalyst. But here the power position in the composition belongs to the analyst. In the scene, Smith is so upset by an allegation that he wouldn't marry the girl, that he in fact calls and arranges the marriage. He will leave analysis and enter marriage to show the analyst that he himself is in control, not the analyst. The composition affirms the contrary.

Later in the film when Leonora leaves her husband, she works for Dr. Quinada. One evening, he takes her out for dinner. They dance and he proposes marriage. She tells him she loves him but that she has to clarify issues in her life (Ohlrig and the pregnancy she has just discovered). The commitment to and a visual rendering of the quality of the relationship is recorded in a single shot. Ophuls moves the camera as the lovers, in close-up, dance on the crowded dance floor. This gentle, elegant shot communicates everything about the future of this relationship.

The following shot uses three planes. In the foreground, Leonora's desk, as we pan to the left from the desk we see one partner, the obstetrician in the office, panning to the other side, Dr. Quinada. The two men talk about Leonora's disappearance and about Quinada's proposal. The obstetrician, knowing she is pregnant, suggests Quinada forget about her. The camera pans one direction or the other at least twice, but all the while Leonora's desk is in the close-up or middle-ground of the frame. Consequently, whatever the dialogue, we never forget what is being spoken about—Leonora. These two shots use movement, placement, and composition to create a sense of an entire relationship. This is style in brilliant service of the narrative purpose.

In George Stevens's *A Place in the Sun* (1951), the agenda is more complex. George Eastman (Montgomery Clift) comes east to take a job with his rich uncle. His own parents were religious and poor. He comes from a different class in spite of sharing the name Eastman. Early in the film, George is invited to the Eastman home. Having just arrived in town, he buys a suit. He then goes to see his mentor-to-be and his family. The wife and the two grown children are totally snobbish about their poor cousin. In order to create the sense of status or lack thereof, Stevens has George Eastman enter what seems to be a cavernous room. In the foreground, the wealthy Eastmans are seated. The patriarch is the only one to offer him a hand. In a series of carefully staged images, Stevens portrays the separateness of George Eastman from his relations. Stevens uses camera placement and a deep focus image. George Eastman is at the back of the frame. They also occupy the center while George is often placed to the side. When another guest arrives, she, Angela Vickers (Elizabeth Taylor) sweeps into the room not even seeing George Eastman. By the staging, and using the planes of the composition,

Stevens suggests George Eastman is the forgotten man. He simply does not have the status to be a "real" Eastman. Again, the compositonal style underscores the theme of the narrative.

□ STYLE FOR ITS OWN SAKE

It is not always the case that style supports the narrative. Often style is presented as a substitute for a weak narrative or is, in the view of the director, a necessary overmodulation simulating the thematic extremes of the narrative. To be specific about style, we need only look to films such as *Fellini Satyricon* (1970) or Cornel Wilde's *Beach Red* (1967) to see style overwhelming the content. On the other hand, in each case, the style spoke to the director's view of ancient Rome or about war. In both cases, excess was too mild a term to describe the director's view. There are times when this can work, as in *Fellini Satyricon*, but there are other instances, such as Richard Lester's *Petulia* (1968), when the style totally overwhelms the content of the film.

A good example of a film with a feeble narrative, but a remarkable style, is Orson Welles's *Touch of Evil* (1958), one of Welles's great works. The story of a murder and its investigation in a Texas border town is simply too trite for description. But beginning the film with a three-minute tracking shot of a bomb being planted in a car on the Mexican side of the border and ending with its explosion on the American side, the shot is simply a tour de force. In the course of the shot, Welles also introduces the main character, the Mexican investigator, Vargas (Charlton Heston). The murder of a Mexican drug lord (Akim Tamiroff) by the sheriff (Welles), the assault on Vargas's wife, the final recording of the guilty sheriff and his death, each of these sequences is a remarkable exercises in style. Using excessively the wide-angle lens, low camera placements, and a crowding of the foreground of the frame, Welles has created a style more appropriate to film noir than to a police story. It is a style that is garish, even corrupt. In its power it conveys something the narrative lacks—conviction.

An example of eclectic but extreme style is Stanley Kubrick's *A Clockwork Orange* (1971). The story of a futuristic England beset by violent youth and a mind-controling government, Kubrick's version of the Anthony Burgess novel is to use style as a counterpoint to the action. The camera pans gradually over an ongoing rape. Extreme close-ups of the assault on the man character's eyes forces sympathy as the victimizer becomes the victim. Kubrick tracks and zooms with an equanimity totally absent in the narrative. Eventually we are worn out by the violence and by the ironic style, left to consider our own world and its future.

A third example of style overwhelming the subject is the apocalyptic tale, *Twelve Monkeys* (1995). Terry Gilliam, better known for *Brazil* (1985), another highly stylized tale of the future, portrays the future and the present with a fish-eye lens view. Distortion is everywhere and a key to Gilliam's treatment of Chris Marker's *La Jetee* (1962). Can one prevent the future from happening? Are we all destined to be the future's victims? These are the central issues of *Twelve Monkeys*. Biological research, wealth, psychiatry, all form the nexus of man-made madness that pre-ordains the fate of the world—destruction. Few, if any, filmmakers, with the exception of John Frankenheimer in *Seconds* (1966), have relied so heavily on a distorting lens to filter their narrative. The result of using a lens that makes the world less natural, more distorted, is to distance us form the narrative and to position us for a strongly visual, highly unnaturalistic experience. The result is that we become less involved and possibly lose the apocalyptic message of *Twelve Monkeys*. This is the upshot of a surplus of style.

☐ BREAKING EXPECTATIONS

Perhaps no filmmakers represent as great a break from expectations as a trio of filmmakers with the independent filmmaking spirit—Martin Scorsese, Spike Lee, and Oliver Stone.

In his work in *Raging Bull* (1980), Martin Scorsese uses a metaphor to create a style. This tale is of a man whose aggression was so great that prize-fighting was simply an extension of his life. The metaphor Scorsese borrows is from opera. Many nineteenth-century operas included a ballet within the opera. Using the music from Verdi's *La Forza del destino*, Scorsese opens the film with LaMotta (Robert De Niro) prepping for a fight. There in slow motion the beauty of the physical movements of arms, legs, and body become ballet-like. The emphasis in this section of the "ballet" is on beauty. Later, as LaMotta actually fights, the shift is to physical clash and brutality, but the way in which the action in the ring is filmed, makes it another phase of the ballet—the combat phase.

Scorsese's metaphor set to Verdi's music creates a layer of meaning to LaMotta's life that pushes the story beyond the biography of Jake LaMotta, champion middleweight, to the battle of the titans, the gods, the kings so often invoked as the central subject of opera. Here Scorsese's stylistic choices break the expectations that *Raging Bull* will be a boxing film about a famous boxer, albeit flawed as a human being. By breaking our expectations, Scorsese creates a modern opera, the equivalent of Verdi's *La Forza del destino*.

Spike Lee also challenges expectations in much of his work. In *Jungle Fever* (1991), a film with a distinct style, Lee portrays the world of two families—an African-American family and an Italian-American family. The catalytic event is an interracial love affair between an African-American man and an Italian-American woman. The style of the film is far from documentary. When two men speak to one another, Lee photographs them from a heroic camera placement, midshot. Only the background moves.

This stylized shot forces us to think about what they are saying rather than engaging us by what we see. Later, the main character's visit to a crack house in search of his brother is akin to a series of Hieronymus Bosch paintings. Again unreality, but the power comes from the sense of how far from reality the house's occupants want to be. What we expect from Spike Lee in *Jungle Fever* is a sexual exploration of stereotypes of black men and white women; instead what we get is a meditation on racism, on family, on love, and on responsibility. By using a highly stylized approach, Lee undermines our expectations and provides us with a much greater experience.

Oliver Stone has always relied on a powerful style. Using pace, a roving camera, and an excess of close-ups, he has clearly used style to press his editorial view—war, politics, and controversial issues in American history. He is not a director who layers the case, as does Fred Wiseman in his documentaries. Instead, Stone uses style to promote his view of the case. His style is so effective that the only question the viewer can ask is why every advertiser in the country doesn't line up to hire Stone to direct their commercials!

We expect Oliver Stone to carry on this tradition of staking out an editorial position of force. In *Natural Born Killers* (1994), however, he so broadens the definition of stylistic choices that we no longer know what to expect from Oliver Stone. How can a filmmaker known for excessive style find a style even more excessive? Given the subject matter—young killers on a killing spree, followed and exploited by the media and, in turn exploiting the media—Stone anticipates the tough question of identification by using an MT style, cartoons, sitcom format, as well as mixing a black and white newsreel look with an overly decorous color. *Natural Born Killers* is awash in style. And yet we are both offended and moved by this post-modern visitation to medialand's today in the USA. Using the story thread of the rise and fall of two young lover-killers, Stone uses style to create a satire on the American relationship with guns and violence. Few films have more effectively used a surplus of style to create a new interpretation on the American dream and the American nightmare. By moving beyond our expectations of excessive style, Stone outdoes himself. He finds a style suited to his view of the subject.

□ IMITATION VERSUS INNOVATION

There is a definite demarcation point between imitation and innovation. Imitation is simply referential; we have seen it before, and the implication is we've seen it too often. It's become somewhat of a cliché. The gunfight in George Stevens' *Shane* (1953) is a good example. The gunfight between Shane (Alan Ladd) and his antagonist (Jack Palance) is staged in a careful manner. It is referential to many other gunfights we have seen. The result is predictable, imitative. That is not to say that *Shane*, as a film, is an uncreative film. On the contrary: Stevens has respected the Western myth and affirmed in this tale that primitivism will have no place next to civilization. But the gunfight itself is imitative of other gunfights in other Western films.

More novel is the gunfight at the O.K. Corral in John Ford's *My Darling Clementine* (1946) or the gunfight at the end of Howard Hawks's *Rio Bravo* (1959). Some Westerns prefer to reference earlier films—the killing of a miner in town in Clint Eastwood's *Pale Rider* (1985) references the murder of a homesteader in Stevens's *Shane*. Others choose to parody earlier films. The train sequence at the beginning of Sergio Leone's *Once Upon a Time in America* (1984) references the opening of Fred Zinnemann's *High Noon* (1952). The point here is that in order to create a new insight to a point of view, straight imitation does not do the trick; it's necessary to alter the narrative or visual style of the scene to make it seem new. The very length of the train sequence in the Leone film creates a tension about the anticipated arrival as powerful as the arrival of the train in *High Noon*. The length and the exaggerated interplay of extreme close-ups and extreme long shots in Leone's film make the train sequence and the shoot-out that follows it a fitting prologue to the epic that will follow. Leone makes something new by imitating a famous sequence from the earlier Western film.

My point here is that there is a relationship between imitation and innovation. But the filmmaker has to recognize that our engagement with the imitation will depend upon his making it seem novel and innovative.

☐ IMITATION AND INNOVATION

The heart of this chapter lies in the great and novel success of a film like Quentin Tarantino's *Pulp Fiction*. In terms of classical story forms, *Pulp Fiction* is a classic gangster film in its generic origin, but this is where the comparison ends. Tarantino also feels free to relate *Pulp Fiction* to the ebb and flow of movies and television on that popular culture. A character refers to himself as "I'm *The Guns of Navarone*." Another character portraying a Vietnam veteran recently released from a prisoner-of-war camp, who is portrayed by Christopher Walken, tells a powerful story about preserving a gold watch while a prisoner-of-war. The reference here is to the film that made Walken's career, Michael Cimino's *The Deer Hunter* (1978), where he portrayed an American fighting in Vietnam, imprisoned by the Vietnamese.

Elsewhere in the film, a restaurant is hosted by an Ed Sullivan imitator. A waiter is Buddy Holly, a waitress is Marilyn Monroe, a performer imitates Ricky Nelson. Just as the gangster film is one point of reference for *Pulp Fiction*, popular culture since 1950 is the other key referent point.

If these were its only narrative virtues, there would be little to write about. *Pulp Fiction* is also organized around three stories, a prologue and an epilogue. The prologue is continued in terms of time in the epilogue. The time frame then for *Pulp Fiction* resembles the circle rather than the straight line.

Tarantino uses this frame to break our expectations of a linear treatment of the gangster genre. If the film were linear, the story would follow a rise and fall story line. Given the circularity of the story line, Tarantino can meditate on the pursuit of work and pleasure in the world of the gangster. Both are fraught with a fatalism that underscores the fragility of life and, in the case of one of the characters, Jules (Samuel Jackson), causes him to give up the life for a pursuit that will be more spiritual.

The actual story line is, in reality, three story lines—Vincent Vega and Marsellus Wallace's wife, The Gold Watch, and The Bonnie Situation. Characters from each story line appear in the other stories. The first story is the story of Vincent Vega (John Travolta), who, with his partner, Jules, proceeds to kill some young dealers who have betrayed their employer, Marsellus. The second part of this story is the "date" Vincent has with Mia (Uma Thurman), Marsellus's wife. This drug-induced date sees Mia overdose and Vincent rescue her with the help of his drug dealer (Eric Stoltz). The overall tone of this first story is a drug-like trance. The killers, Vincent and Jules, approach their work like ministers meditating on life values and loyalty. The second phase is a cocaine-hazed seduction without sex. But playing with fire, whether it's sex or drugs, has consequences. Vincent is always aware of doing the right thing, not crossing over the line. Self-preservation is his philosophy in a profession where the long view is the short run.

The second story is the story of Butch (Bruce Willis). His gold watch has been passed down for generations of heroic but dead soldiers in Butch's family. For him the watch represents the father, and grandfather, he never knew. Butch is a boxer who has agreed to throw a fight for Marsellus, the local L.A. crime boss. Instead, he wins the fight and the money he bet on it. But now Marsellus wants to kill him. His escape is well-planned except that his girlfriend left his gold watch in his apartment. Fate pulls him back in the direction of Marsellus. Back at the apartment to retrieve the watch, he finds Vincent in the washroom, his gun in the kitchen. Butch kills Vincent, but as he escapes, he literally runs into Marsellus on the street. They try to kill one another. Absurdly they are taken into captivity by a pawn shop owner who proceeds, with the help of a friend, to rape Marsellus. Rescued by Butch, Marsellus forgives him but Butch must leave town.

The third story returns to the killing of the first story. It seems there was a hidden gunman in the backroom. He is killed by Vincent and Jules but not before he has fired five shots, all missing their target. Jules is certain divine intervention has saved his life. He will give up the life of crime. With a young black man taken from the apartment, they leave. En route, Vincent accidentally kills the young man, splaying blood and matter all over the car and themselves. Now endangered, they proceed to the home of a friend (Quentin Tarantino). The friend tells them they must leave quickly before his wife returns. They call on Marsellus for help. He dispatches Mr. Wolf (Harvey Keitel) to help set up the situation. He does so, cleaning them and the car for re-entry into the world.

Hungry, they go out for breakfast where the robbery that has begun in the prologue is now played out as an epilogue. Jules has said that he will no longer kill and he advises the robbers how to leave with their booty and their lives. The film ends at this point, although, in terms of chronology, the gold watch story is to take place at a future point.

To understand the imitative dimensions of *Pulp Fiction*, we look at the references to the popular culture, particularly television. It is not only the references to particular characters, it is also the attitudes expressed. Butch is a product of a "Leave it to Beaver" family and he becomes a boxer, the result of "Beaver" being orphaned. He is the analogue to the persona who grows up without a father; Jimmie (Quentin Tarantino) is a house-husband, a "Mr. Brady" without the Bunch, Marsellus is Othello to Mia's Desdemona, and Vincent is Iago's younger brother—all three are contemporary visions of a 50s Playhouse 90 re-visited in the 90s. Wolf is a George C. Scott character out of *The Hustler* (1961) and Jules is a character who has walked right out of a Sinclair Lewis novel made for television. The imitative dimensions of *Pulp Fiction*, although presented with great wit, would not be enough to suggest innovation.

The innovative storytelling dimension of *Pulp Fiction* has more to do with genre violation. Not only does Tarantino use black humor as the tone for *Pulp Fiction*, he actually satirizes the form's violence and its fastidious devotion to testosterone. Both Vincent and Jules, although killers, are sensitive to one another and, in Vincent's case, remarkably sensitive to Mia, Marsellus's wife. Their devotion to language, its nuances and its elegance, makes them the most unusual of hitmen. In a story form known for action and a devotion to quick solutions, this obsession with language can only be interpreted as a satire on the male propensity for action. By substituting language for action, Tarantino is also substituting one for the other, thereby undermining a key motif of the genre. Consequently, the shape of the dramatic action becomes less cause and effect and more meditation, even a search for goals.

The result, given the circularity of the narrative and the substitution of dialogue for action, is to shift the narrative heart of *Pulp Fiction* from material goals to spiritual goals for each of the main characters. First, Vincent simply wants to eschew sexuality for survival; Butch wants a piece of his family, perhaps all of his family, as represented by his father's gold watch, instead of money; and finally, Jules wants to leave the life he leads for a better one; the Lord has shown him the way to save himself—divine intervention, he calls it. Whether any of these characters will indeed find happiness we will never know (although we do witness Vincent's fate: he has a right to be cautious). The key result of the innovations Tarantino introduces is to shift us from a focus on cause and effect, or linear narrative, to a different kind of narrative, a circular narrative. The focus, consequently, shifts to character over action, and to spiritual values over material values. All of this is presented in a tone that allows Tarantino to find humor in a form not known for humor and to step outside the dramatic limitations of the form into a new kind of experience, where a self-reflexive meditation on the medium occurs as well as the narrative.

The layered experience of *Pulp Fiction* consequently allows us to be inside the film, and outside the film. The result is that Tarantino has moved far beyond imitation to a work that is remarkable for its innovation.

To give some sense of perspective on how creative *Pulp Fiction* is, we turn to another tri-partite story, Milcho Manchevski's *Before the Rain*. Set in Macedonia in 1993, *Before the Rain* is essentially three love stories, two set in rural Macedonia and one in London. Each focuses on a love that is forbidden by the surrounding society and each ends tragically as religious bigotry leads to murder. The combatants in each case are Macedonian and Albanian, Christian and Muslin.

The first story, Words, focuses on a priest, Father Kiril, who has taken a vow of silence. He finds a young Albanian woman in his room. Her hair has been shorn. She looks young, not more than eighteen. She is being pursued by Macedonians who accuse her of murder. The priest hides her, against the wishes of his superiors. The Macedonians search the grounds but do not find her. When she's found out, the priest is thrown out with her. They cannot communicate because each speaks a different language. But a bond has formed. They are discovered by the girl's grandfather and his men. The priest is sent away while the girl is beaten and accused of being a slut. She professes love and runs after him. The girl is killed by her own brother.

The second story, Faces, takes place in London. A British woman, Anne, an executive in a photography agency, has a lover, a Pulitzer Prize–winning photographer. Alexander, the photographer, is Macedonian. He wants her to return to Macedonia with him, but she refuses. She is pregnant by the husband she has left for the photographer. He leaves, and she meets her husband at a restaurant. She tells him she's pregnant by him but stills wants a divorce. In the background, an argument grows in intensity. It is between an ethnic waiter and an ethnic customer. The argument mushrooms. The implication is a re-play of the Macedonian-Albanian enmity in London. Both are thrown out. The angry customer returns and shoots indiscriminately, killing the waiter as well as Anne's husband.

Pictures, the third story, is Alexander's story. He returns after sixteen years to his home in Macedonia. He is greeted by his relatives. Only when they recognize him do they drop their enmity. Everyone seems to carry guns.

Alexander visits Hana, a school friend, a woman he clearly loves. She is Albanian. He is greeted with great hostility but clearly she was the love of his life and he has returned to see if his love is returned by her. Her father is respectful but her son threatens to kill him. He leaves.

Alexander's cousin is killed and Hana's daughter is accused. She asks if he can find her daughter. He finds and releases her, but in doing so, he is killed by his own cousin. The young woman runs off to a monastery, the very monastery of the first story.

The three stories of *Before the Rain* form a circle of time, another circle of religious hatred, and a circle of love. Each story has the same theme, and in each, the hatred destroys the love. Only time continues, but in Manchevski's world, it comes full circle, in order to repeat itself with another circle of opportunity, love, and religious hatred.

In each story, the characters of the other appear. And in each story the meditation of the main character fails to puncture the circles.

Like Tarantino in *Pulp Fiction*, Manchevski has chosen a nonlinear frame in order to layer his story. Where Tarantino used the structure to comment on the form—the gangster film—Manchevski uses the nonlinear frame to create a fable about issues larger than Macedonia or the former Yugoslavia. His goal is to say something about the struggle between the life instinct and the death instinct and to warn us that, in Macedonia, this archetypal struggle is moving towards a victory for death. Manchevski doesn't portray religion or social structures as the enemy. He shows both sides victimized and caught in a circle of self-destruction. In this film, the nonlinear structure and style help Manchevski distance himself from the particular and to suggest the general. He uses the structure to create a modern parable. Manchevski's film is innovative in every way. There is little imitation of story form. He strikes a fresh chord. Although this struggle has been told before, specifically in Elia Kazan's *America, America* (1963), it has never been told in such a novel fashion. Manchevski's style in *Before the Rain* presents an ideal example of how a style can be so innovative as to seem uniquely original.

Both these films—*Pulp Fiction* and *Before the Rain*—rely on a nonlinear structure to move them beyond imitation and to suggest a new innovative style for film narrative. It is not the case that every story is well-served by this approach. However, as these two films illustrate, the options for film narrative have been expanded by Tarantino and Manchevski.

15

The Appropriation of
Style II: Limitation and
Innovation

■

This chapter continues the exploration begun in the last chapter, which looked at the tension between style and content and how that tension generates first a distinct voice for the narrative. This voice is first articulated in the compositional choices and consequently in the organization and orchestration of those images. Style may refer to genre or it may reconsider the organization of shots into a different narrative frame, such as the non-linear frame Quentin Tarantino uses in *Pulp Fiction* (1994). In this chapter we examine 4 stylistic interventions that on one level appear to be a return to former forms, in a sense a creative reaction to the radical experience of the nonlinear story. On another level, however, these interventions represent a deepening of long evolving tendencies in film narrative. In this sense they work with the limitations of those tendencies, not so much imitating them as trying to stretch the boundaries those tendencies may have. We begin with the most conservative of these tendencies, the elevation of cinema verité.

□ THE ELEVATION OF CINEMA VERITÉ

Cinema verité, beginning with its ideological underpinnings in the work of Dziga Vertov (see Chapter 1), has been principally viewed as affiliated with the documentary. Indeed, together with the personal documentary and the educational-political documentary, cinema verité is one of the 3 principal ideologies of the documentary. Its affiliation with the dramatic film dates from the 1960s: the British kitchen sink dramas, the New Wave films of Jean-Luc Godard, and the docudramas of Peter Watkins and Ken Loach.[1] More recently there has been a resurgence of interest and activity in the use of the cinema verité style. The results of that interest have led to the most profitable film of all time (in terms of percentage of revenue to cost), *The Blair Witch Project* (1999), and to the most talked-about school of filmmaking of the 1990s, Dogme 95. Cinema verité has also had a pronounced impact on the lively Belgian school, the films of Luc and Jean-Pierre Dardenne (*Rosetta*, 1999) and Frederick Fonteyne (*An Affair of Love*, 2000), and the move to hyperrealism in the work of Erick Zonca (*The Dreamlife of Angels*, 1998) in France. The earlier work of Remy Belvaux (*Man Bites Dog*, 1992) is formative in the Belgian embrace of cinema verité. Turning to the Dogme films, a background note will contextualize the movement.

The Dogme filmmakers are led by the Danish filmmaker Lars Von Trier. Their "dogma" echoes the ethos of the New Wave declaration that their films would be a creative reaction to the dominant studio films of the day and that the style of their films would be free of those conventions. In the case of Dogme 95 that means a return to cinema verité. Von Trier together with Thomas Vinterberg, Søren Kragh-Jacobsen, and Kristian Levring have committed themselves to making films without artifice. That means no tripods, artificial light, or music. As much as possible naturalism must prevail. There is a script and there are actors, but all else looks and feels like cinema verité. The style is critical to the experience. Making it feel real, albeit a stylistic posture, is the central tenet of Dogme 95. The subject matter of the films, the fact that they are scripted, and the fact that actors are portraying the characters makes the content classic melodrama. The style, however, is the style of cinema verité. Since the declaration and the release of a number of Dogme films at least one major filmmaker has embraced the Dogme style. Mike Figgis has produced *Time Code* (2000), and there are certainly independent filmmakers such as Kevin Smith (*Clerks*, 1994) who echo the principles of Dogme.

To understand the conflict of style and content we turn to Thomas Vinterberg's film *The Celebration* (released in Europe as *Festen*, 1998). The film covers a crucial 24 hours in the life of one Danish family. The patriarch, a successful businessman named Helge, is turning 60 and the celebration of the title brings together all the extended intergenerational members of his family. Such an event is a mark of success, but the title is essentially used ironically. For Helge's 3 surviving children (there was a recent suicide by the only adult child still living at home), Christian, Helene, and Michael, the issue is whether to celebrate silently and continue living depressed and disparate lives, or whether tonight is the time to expose the family's ugly secret. The suicide was Christian's twin sister, and Christian decides to challenge the status quo. At the party, as he toasts his father, he congratulates him for being the man who continually raped him and his sister when they were children. This statement initiates a chain reaction that results in all the children turning against their father. At the very end the mother joins them, banishing Helge from the celebratory breakfast. It has been the night that changed the power structure in this family. The children at last can assume a different position, hopefully a more successful position in their emotional lives.

The Celebration is about secrets, it is about anxiety, it is about guilt within a family. How does the cinema verité style contribute to the veracity of the emotional states? How do the camera placements, the shot selections, and the organization of the shots create the feeling states that underline the narrative?

The cinema verité approach creates a general sense of veracity. It seems to capture the edgy personalities of character unmasked—the insecurity and rage of Michael, the depression and special position in the family of Christian, the power and confidence of Helge, the provocative rebelliousness of Helene, the superficiality and extroversion of the mother. But the style goes further; it also seems to catch the sense of minor characters, such as the manager of the hotel who knows his place and is the voice of the owner and no more. The chef is outspoken and ironic; he doesn't accept his place. The waitress, with her openness and charming sexuality, is in contrast to the closed Christian, whom she has always adored. The cinema verité style captures character and makes each of them seem more credible than they might if the style didn't promote a sense of actuality.

Perhaps even more striking is that the camera becomes an active participant in creating the sense of the emotional core of the characters. When Helge is photographed, it's in mid-shot. He's always in the center of the frame, and there is a stillness to the shot. Vinterberg also holds the shot longer than he does with other characters. The result is that we feel Helge's power, his control over others. In the case of Michael, the images are quite the opposite. Michael is more than insecure; he is filled with rage, and his anger, although inappropriate to the moment, is explosive. Here Vinterberg uses a camera in close to Michael, looking down and at him—almost glaring at him. The camera also moves in jerking movements toward the object of his rage, usually his wife and often other women. The camera motion is kinetic, just as are his emotions. Vinterberg also uses quick cuts, whether they are jump cuts or cutaways, to simulate Michael's emotional state.

Although Christian and the children are ultimately victorious, Vinterberg never exploits the emotional power shift via image or editing. There are no quick emotional fixes here. Toward the end the camera placement and cutting vis-à-vis Michael slows down and becomes more calm, just as Michael calms down and actually assumes a leadership role in his new position in relation to his father. The result is that we experience the new Michael as more solid, more stable, and more a man with a sense of dignity than the man who was controlled by fear and anger earlier in the narrative. This transition is particularly critical because Michael seemed the most damaged of the 3 surviving children. Different camera placement and a pace that lacks the staccato cutting surrounding Michael in Act I, indicate how far the grown children have come in these 24 hours.

One more observation about the editing style of *The Celebration* is important. *The Celebration* is not an action film nor is it a plot-driven film. Consequently, it would be expected that the editing style would be relatively slow. It's not. Because *The Celebration* is about the emotional turmoil that surrounds a key family event, and because it focuses on a 24-hour period,

Vinterberg cuts the film as if it's a thriller. In Act I all that happens prior to Christian's inflammatory toast to his father, is that we are introduced to the situation and to the characters. To make these 30 minutes dynamic, Vinterberg rapidly cuts between the arrival of the 3 children, then the guests and the preparations of each of the adult children for the party. By rapidly cutting between them, Vinterberg adds pace to the narrative purpose. He individuates the 3 children, giving each their own pace that is driven by their character. Christian is depressed, so the pace is slow, the camera distant, and the deep focus of the shots makes him seem very far away. Michael, as mentioned, is nervous, almost undone by having to prepare for the party. He berates his wife for leaving his black shoes behind, but minutes later needs to have sex with her (to lie down for five minutes) to calm down. He trips in the shower, and he trips while running to meet his father. He is a man on the verge of a nervous breakdown. Helene, on the other hand, is in a room, the room where her sister recently committed suicide. The manager of the hotel is with her. She begins to search for her sister and eventually finds the suicide note left by her. This sequence is one of distance and observation in Helene's search for her sister. The shots are longer and the movement subjectively echoes Helene's point of view. The pace is faster than the Christian sequence but not as hectic as the shots relating to Michael. Overall, the pace here creates a sense of dynamism but also emotional tension. The restlessness of the camera echoes the emotional out-of-breath quality of Helge's children. We don't yet know the why, but by the end of Act I we are emotionally exhausted and the party is just about to really begin. This is the power of the editing style Vinterberg employs. He uses cinema verité to add a layer of veracity to the narrative.

This impulse is magnified fivefold in Erick Zonca's *The Dreamlife of Angels* (1998). Isa and Marie are twentysomething young women. The narrative takes place in Lille, France, today. Isa is from the South. Both are marginal in the sense that they are uneducated, unskilled young women. Although Isa is more the drifter, she has a more optimistic personality. Marie is negative and angry. In *The Dreamlife of Angels*, Zonca frames the narrative with the friendship of these two women, and like any relationship, this one has the arc of meeting, growing closer, growing apart, and ending the relationship. Within this metastructure, Zonca explores two relationships, Isa's relationship with a young girl in a coma, and Marie's with a rich young man. The apartment in which the women live is owned by the young girl's mother, who died as a consequence of the car accident that left the young girl in a coma. The relationship between Isa and the girl in a coma would appear to be an impossible one but it isn't. In the case of Marie, Zonca follows her relationship with a rich young man who is clearly a womanizer. He is a poor choice for Marie, and when he abandons her leaving Isa to give Marie the news, Marie at first blames Isa, pushes Isa away, and then finally commits suicide.

The style Zonca has chosen reflects in a general way cinema verité—a handheld camera, tight two-shots (in cramped spaces), lots of close-ups of functional activity such as writing in a journal. The footage has a captured quality as opposed to one that is staged, and this too is symptomatic of cinema verité. But Zonca has more in mind than to observe two marginalized young women. He wants the level of observation to promote a love for his characters rather than an assessment of them. To promote this level of involvement with his two main characters, Zonca needs to adopt what I call hyper-realism, a much more intense experience than the veracity yielded from cinema verité. As a consequence, Zonca first truncates scenes. He doesn't move from an establishing shot into mid-shots of interactions between characters to a cutaway for a new idea to a close-up for dramatic emphasis to mid-shot to long-shot as he concludes the scene. Rather he is very selective. Scenes are constructed of fewer shots, and the shots that are employed are used to emotionally heat up the experience of the scene. This means that scenes are mostly presented in mid-shots and close-ups. It also means that the camera placement crowds the action. There is very little space between us and the characters.

In one scene, for example, Isa is offering breakfast coffee to Marie. They are recent acquaintances. Marie, at Isa's request, has allowed Isa to sleep in the apartment. Call this a breakthrough-in-the-relationship scene—the two will be friends. There is no detail of the bedroom's geography in the scene, only the two young women. It's as if Zonca wants to push us toward them, the last two human beings on earth. In this scene Zonca creates a sense of togetherness as well as isolation from geography, the apartment, and other people. Most of his scenes proceed with this level of intimacy vis-à-vis the young women and this level of isolation from society at large. When we do see the young women with others, Marie with an early corpulent lover or Isa with the young girl in a coma, Zonca approaches the scenes with the same sense of inclusion and exclusion. The result is intense, emotional, and involving—the hyper-realism that goes beyond cinema verité.

□ THE RETURN OF MISE-EN-SCÈNE

As a style, mise-en-scène is associated with Orson Welles in *Citizen Kane* (1941) and *Touch of Evil* (1958), with Max Ophüls in *Letter from an Unknown Woman* (1948) and *Lola Montès* (1955). These filmmakers, building upon the work of F. W. Murnau in the 1920s (*The Last Laugh*, 1924), essentially moved the camera to avoid editing. The elegance of their camera movement recorded performance and added a more subtle editorial direction. In Welles' case, a sense of aesthetic virtuosity was created; in the case of Ophüls, a sense of romantic longing and energy. The former impulse, that of technical virtuosity and the filmic aesthetic, infuse the early camera movement in the career of Stanley Kubrick (*Paths of Glory*, 1957). Only later would Kubrick use the camera movement to slow down the pace of the film in order to recreate the seventeenth-century sense of time and place in *Barry Lyndon* (1975) or the accelerated sense of the future in *2001: A Space Odyssey* (1968). The latter impulse, the moody romanticism of Ophüls, resonates in the mise-en-scène work of Roberto Rossellini and Luchino Visconti. But none of these filmmakers was as effective at using the moving camera to conjure the inner emotional state of the main character as was F. W. Murnau. Hitchcock tried to capture the feeling but was more effective when he resorted to a cutaway or subjective sound.

What about mise-en-scène today, in the era of rapid pace and authorial intervention? Today the work of Luc Besson, Oliver Stone, and John Frankenheimer reflects the influence of Eisenstein rather than Murnau. But in spite of the preference for the fast cut, there is a renewed interest in mise-en-scène, particularly in the work of Stanley Kubrick and Martin Scorsese, and it is to this work that we now turn.

Stanley Kubrick's last film *Eyes Wide Shut* (1999) differs substantially from his previous work. Kubrick has principally gravitated to genre work, which gave him an opportunity to explore aesthetic challenge and moral failure. This dialectic operates in his war films, *Paths of Glory* and *Full Metal Jacket* (1987); his satires, *Lolita* (1962) and *Dr. Strangelove* (1963); his horror film, *The Shining* (1979); his science fiction film, *2001: A Space Odyssey*; his gangster film, *The Killing* (1969); and his epics, *Spartacus* (1960) and *Barry Lyndon*. As mentioned earlier, Kubrick enjoyed the challenge of mise-en-scène and he employs it with a panache rare among filmmakers. For the most part, however, the movement of the camera seemed to be a creative challenge Kubrick warmed to. How else does one understand the lengthy tracking shot that follows the Master Sergeant about the barracks, introducing his ethos to the young recruits, in *Full Metal Jacket*? Movement does energize the scene, but it is the aesthetic virtuosity of the lengthy shot that stays with the viewer. Here the style of the scene seems to be far more important than its content. This approach to mise-en-scène is echoed in the long tracking shots in *The Shining* and in the trenches and in the chateaux in *Paths of Glory*. As I mentioned earlier, there is a deeper purposefulness to the deployment of mise-en-scène in *2001: A Space Odyssey* and in *Barry Lyndon*.

Turning to *Eyes Wide Shut*, we first note that it is neither a classic genre film nor a classic satire. Instead Kubrick has turned to a moral fable for adults. The Harfords are a materially successful New York professional couple. Bill Harford is a caring physician; she is a caring mother. But each is more in love with their own self-image than they are with one another. Consequently, to feed the personal excitement of her narcissism, Alice, the wife, plants a seed of doubt in her husband's mind: there was and may be another man in her life. The notion excites her but fills him with doubt and jealousy, and he begins a search, a desperate search, for excitement and illicit thrills. But his journey becomes a nightmare. Outrageous behavior, even murder, are the results of the narcissism he encounters in others, and in the end he is rather undone while his wife is reconciled to a relationship without ecstasy, the desired goal of self-love.

The New York the Harfords inhabit is as much a spiritual wasteland as are the chateaux of France in *Paths of Glory*. Material abundance implies that spirituality is flesh-bound, but this is not what Kubrick implies in *Eyes Wide Shut*. On the contrary, what the Harfords encounter is emptiness and here lies the moral of Kubrick's tale. The culture of narcissism leads away from spiritual fulfillment, not towards it. The question for us is how Kubrick uses a particular style that may or may not conflict with the content, to create the sense of narcissism, ennui, and the illusion that sexual adventure can satisfy the longings of self-love. These are complex and interior feelings. How does this plot-oriented director create these interior states of mind?

The options here are performance, art direction, and/or camera movement. Kubrick, of course, uses all of the above. Our interest, however, is on his use of camera movement. Here he doesn't disappoint. Kubrick's camera moves in a restless, probing, searching movement.

Two examples will illustrate how Kubrick has gone further with mise-en-scène than did the work of F. W. Murnau. To contextualize these two examples from *Eyes Wide Shut*, it's useful to look at Murnau's use of mise-en-scène in *The Last Laugh*. In 1924 Murnau made this film about an older gentleman who gained great status from his position as the doorman at a major urban hotel. But in the first Act, we see his pride, the sense of power he derives from his position. A turn of events sees him removed from his position; he lies to his neighbors and to his daughter—he is still a doorman. To be convincing he needs a uniform, and so he steals it and begins his pretense—the precursor to his tragic downfall. When he enters the hotel the camera is with him, but as he proceeds to steal the coat, the camera moves ahead of him, stopping at the coat, the object of his desire. Murnau has used mise-en-scène to pictorialize both the psychology of the old man, desperation, and his desire to do anything to regain his status. The camera movement, which is subjective and labored, then filled with a desire that outsteps the old man, provides a full sense of his inner life. This is what Kubrick achieves in the following early sequence in *Eyes Wide Shut*.

The scene is a party given by a wealthy client-friend of Bill. The first camera movement is the arrival of the Harfords. The movement, directly in front of the Harfords, is a glide fairly close to them. Both sides of the frame capture the mirrors that line the entry, and beautiful people are seen close to the periphery. The track captures the Harfords in mid-shot. They are looking at the guests and the mirrors to the sides. They are looking at themselves in the mirrors and beautiful people are looking at them. Are they comparing themselves to the other guests? It doesn't appear so. What they note is that others are looking at them, rather than each of them taking an interest in others. The effect of the tracking shot is excessive but very much directed at the subjects mid-frame, the Harfords. What we are left with is a powerful sense of their self-absorption, their unbridled, unfiltered narcissism that feeds on the image of themselves watching themselves and being watched. It's as if the main characters are becoming, in this single shot, their own objects of desire.

Our second example is also found in the same party scene. Bill has been called upstairs. The host's mistress has overdosed upstairs while his wife ministers to the guests downstairs. He calls upon Bill, his medical friend, to save the situation by saving the girl's life. Bill obliges and does so. Alice, meanwhile, is gently accosted by an older man with a distinctly elegant, illicit aura. He is not only trying to meet her, he is also trying to talk her into having an affair with him. Here the mis-en-scène is a tracking shot that follows Alice dancing with the Lothario. What is critical is that this movement also proceeds in mid-shot and the camera is placed even closer to Alice and her would-be lover. This crowding accomplishes two things. First, it gives the shot a sense of intimacy, the movement of seduction. Second, the camera, by staying close, excludes all the others. She is the only woman in this world, and he is the only man. The consequence in this case is to withdraw context. It's no longer a party in a very wealthy man's home; it's an erotic encounter. The exclusion of context heightens the intensity and narcissism of both characters. In the first tracking shot, discussed above, the narcissism was a barrier; here it is shared. In the first track there was no erotic quality, only self-absorption; in the second track, it's all erotic, directed at stimulating Alice in a way she wasn't with her "familiar" husband. In essence, Kubrick has created a sexualized dream state by using camera movement with the same intense purposefulness used by F. W. Murnau. But the focus in *Eyes Wide Shut* is the self as the subject and object of desire.

Martin Scorsese sets himself quite a different task in *Kundun* (1997). In essence, Scorsese uses mis-en-scène to create a spiritual dream state appropriate to a biography of the Dalai Lama. Scorsese has used camera movement to energize the bar scene in *Mean Streets* (1973) and to establish a sense of power (albeit posturing) for the main character's entry and movement about a restaurant in *Goodfellas* (1990). But in *Kundun* the goal of the movement is far more interior and complex.

Kundun follows the life of the current Dalai Lama from his discovery as the next Dalai Lama at age 3 to his leaving Tibet, now invaded and occupied by China, 30 years later. The historical conflicts among his advisors, the Chinese invasion, his meeting with Mao, the decision to accept exile in India, all this is covered in the narrative. But that is plot and not of central interest to Scorsese. These events are events of the secular world, the political world. Scorsese is more interested in the spiritual world, the inner life of the Dalai Lama. The challenge is to concretize this spiritual sensibility.

Robert Bresson and Carl Dreyer both took up this challenge in their work, and both used a mise-en-scène approach to create the conflict between the outer world conflict and the inner strength and belief of their characters. Bresson's *Diary of a Country Priest* (1945) and Dreyer's *The Passion of Joan of Arc* (1929) exemplify their methodology.

The first notable quality of the camera movement is that it simulates the eye line and point of view of the Dalai Lama. When we first encounter the boy he is lying down, and we see the adult world upside down. As he rises the camera rights itself and begins to move at the pace of the young boy's movement. Since he is always running, the camera moves at a fast pace. The young boy is curious, and the camera movement is not only subjective but also takes in objects and people. In every sense, the camera movement identifies the point of view with the attitudes and interests of the 3-year-old boy.

It is important that Scorsese moves the camera along this subjective arc. When he uses cutaways, they are clearly from the boy's point of view. By doing so excessively in the first scenes, Scorsese is establishing ownership by the character of Dalai Lama but also subjectivity in the most inclusive sense. The shot selection in these scenes represents the sense memory of the little boy, which creates the context for what will follow. The progression of shots doesn't follow logic but rather the feelings and interior "monologue" of a young boy with himself. What sense does he make of adults, parents, the tests the priests put to him to prove or disprove he is the chosen one, or Kundun? This is the aesthetic and psychological rationale for the shots chosen. It is also the driving notion for how and when camera movement is used to avoid editing.

To complement this subjective camera movement Scorsese uses a variety of images of the natural world. Usually he incorporates them into a sequence of travel, as when the young boy is transported to Lhasa or when his father dies and his body is disassembled for burial, which consists of feeding him to the scavengers of nature, the vultures. In these cutaways, in effect, Scorsese is always concerned with the scale of man in nature. And so the image may be the boy's caravan as a speck in the frame, with the rest of the image filled with the sun and the desert. Or the image will be of snow-capped mountains that reach to the sky. Or birds in flight from valley to mountain. Or a river that is endless until it reaches the sky at the horizon. The images are always contextual: human beings are not the masters of nature, only one of many who inhabit nature. These natural cutaways are the practical context for the actions and deliberations of men. Kundun or the Chosen One is one of many ongoing elements of natural life. The contrast of these images clashing with the subjective camera movements of a young boy provide a dialectic of the inner and the outer worlds that carries us into the notion that both exist in an ongoing and harmonious balance.

Beyond the subjective camera movement juxtaposed with the cutaways of nature, Scorsese must create a sense of a dream state, in this case a spiritual one. Here it is pattern that is important. Acknowledging the repetition of various aural patterns in the score by Phillip Glass, Scorsese harmonizes the camera movements with the score. They too tend to follow a pattern, a rhythmic repetition. The crowning of the young Dalai Lama provides a good example. A young boy arrives in Lhasa. Crowds are present, in awe of their new spiritual leader. The boy's parents are present. His advisors are present. The movement first enters the frame, then cuts away to side-to-side movements of his family, for example, and then cuts to the camera moving again into frame with the seated boy stationery. These rhythmic movements set up and follow a pattern, and they instill a formal discovery, that this young boy is making the transition from being a citizen to being Kundun, from the human to the spiritual. It is this pattern, this rhythm of the movements, that creates a special sense, a spiritual sense of the occasion of the crowning of the country's spiritual leader. What is critical here is that real time and naturalism are subverted and replaced with a feeling that is not practical or easy to articulate. It is spiritual.

Before we leave this section on mise-en-scène it is worth mentioning other notable work that tries to use the moving camera in a manner not associated with a Hitchcock, a Polanski, or a Spielberg—the thriller or action directors, in other words—nor for identification or the tension inherent in the use of the moving camera in an action sequence. (See Chapter 17.) Two of the most interesting directors are Andrei Tarkovsky (*Andrei Rublev*, 1969, and *The Sacrifice*, 1986) and Miklós Jancsó (*The Round-Up*, 1965, and *The Red and the White*, 1967). In both cases the filmmaker moves the camera to avoid editing. The lengthy takes in *The Red and the White* and *The Sacrifice* become as much an aesthetic challenge as a source of insight into the narrative. The voice of the filmmaker is as important here as the narrative elements. An example will illustrate the point, *The Red and the White*, a story of the civil war that followed the 1918 Bolshevik revolution in Russia as it spills over into middle-Europe. Jansco's camera moves from one side of the battlefield to the other and back. Geography doesn't mean a lot, nor does rank. Nothing protects the combatants from the inevitability of mutual extinction. This is the voice of Jansco: neither side is better than the other. This idea is achieved through his use of the moving camera.

Working at about the same time, Mike Nichols explores ideas about manmade machines, airplanes, killing machines, and the environment. Are they natural or unnatural? They look like birds in the sky, but they kill not for food but for more human reasons. These are the ironic notions Mike Nichols is working with as he uses zooms and camera movement to follow these manmade "birds" in *Catch 22* (1970). Nichols takes a similar ironic approach to relationships in *Carnal Knowledge* (1971). Again, the camera movement both follows the action and distances us from the characters so that we consider the nature of those male-female and male-male relationships.

More recently, Quentin Tarantino has taken up camera movement in *Pulp Fiction* (1994). In keeping with the genre subversion he is seeking, the moving camera maintains an even flow of energy as opposed to the upward arc of action and violence so central to the gangster film. Tarantino's first subversion is to replace action with dialogue. His second is to move the camera rather than to build up a sequence through pace and close-ups. In this sense, his use of camera movement is supportive of his voice (as in the case of Jansco) rather than in support of the dramatic arc of the narrative.

□ THE CLOSE-UP AND THE LONG SHOT

D. W. Griffith created a pattern of fragmentation of shots that differentiated long shots, or shots that established location and context, and close-shots, or shots that were emphatic, emotional, and intense. Eisenstein built on Griffith's innovations by using the juxtaposition of images to create conflict. In effect this meant a polarization of the kind of shots used, with Eisenstein using more close-ups than had been the practice. Those directors who sidestepped mise-en-scène and chose to be more directive about audience emotions gravitated to a disproportionate use of close-ups. Sam Peckinpah, Oliver Stone, and feature directors coming from the world of TV commercials such as Michael Bay (*Armageddon*, 1997) favored the close-up. In fact, all of the above-mentioned directors also embraced extreme close-up shots in which there is no context, shots that only make sense in juxtaposition to the other shots in the scene. Needless to say, these directors also embraced pace with vigor. Which brings us to the issue of this section: What are filmmakers today doing with the juxtaposition of the long shot and the close-up? Since I will focus on the work of Shekhar Kapur, particularly *Elizabeth* (1998) and *Bandit Queen* (1994), we need first to look at other epic filmmakers to understand how they dealt with the issue of juxtaposition.

All filmmakers have a logic for their shot selection. Otto Preminger in *Exodus* (1960), for example, uses wide-angle shots with his main character in the foreground and the ship, the *Exodus*, or the attack on Acre prison ongoing in the background. He doesn't use close-ups as much as the deep-focus cinemascope frame as a whole to advance his narrative. He is not all that interested in the juxtaposition of the long shot and the close-up. In this sense his is a mise-en-scène approach to the issue.

Anthony Mann, on the other hand, is interested in juxtaposition. Whether it's *El Cid* (1961) or *The Heroes of Telmark* (1965), he will very often move from an intense close-up to an extreme long shot. Indeed, the angles he chooses for the long shot give them scale, a heroic proportion. In a sense, the shots aren't so much dramatic (although they are) as they are scaled to create an epic or heroic sense about character or action or both.

Turning to David Lean, whether it is the burial scene in *Doctor Zhivago* (1965) or the attack on the train in *Lawrence of Arabia* (1962) or, for that matter, *The Bridge on the River Kwai* (1957), one notices how sparingly Lean uses close-ups. But when he does we are emotionally overwhelmed by them. Think of the trees swaying at the funeral in *Doctor Zhivago* or the hands pushing the detonator in *Lawrence of Arabia* or the cross driven into the ground in *Bridge on the River Kwai*. The shots are dramatically very important to the evolution of the scene that is to follow. If there is an observation to be made about Lean's close-ups it's that he uses them to plunge us into a scene, as opposed to the punctuation for the middle of a scene. In terms of his long shots, very few filmmakers have used the long shot as effectively, whether it is the winter wonderland of *Doctor Zhivago* or the scale of man as he crosses the magnificent fierce desert in *Lawrence of Arabia*. Unlike Anthony Mann, whose images grip us, impress us, and give us a sense of the hero, Lean uses the long shot as he does the close shot—for dramatic impact.

Another way to look at this issue is to contrast this work to that of Carl Dreyer, whose *The Passion of Joan of Arc* (1929) proceeds almost entirely in close shots. What we experience is first the disorientation of a loss of context, then the intensity of the close shots. Placed next to Carl Dreyer, John Ford's *The Searchers* (1956) is principally composed of long shots and mid-shots. We are left with the epic sense of the search for young family members who survived an Indian massacre. The long shots give the film a poetic, formal quality, quite different from the Dreyer experience. Perhaps the best balance of long shot and close shot is George Stevens' *A Place in the Sun* (1951). This intensely romantic tragedy modulates feeling through the use of the long shot and the close shot. Here the close shots provide point of view and dramatic emphasis. In the close shots we see Angela, the object of George Eastman's desire; in the long shots we have the perspective of class and social position and see where George fits in. Initially he is at the bottom of the social ladder. Stevens uses the shots, both close and long, to articulate the layers of the narrative. He subsumes his voice deeply in the narrative (the antithesis of Anthony Mann).

The recent filmmaker who uses long shots and close shots in a manner closest to Stevens is Steven Spielberg. Throughout *Saving Private Ryan* (1998) we are led to narrative clarity and emotional pitch through shot selection and balance. The recent filmmaker who uses long shots and close shots akin to the Anthony Mann style is Ridley Scott. Ironically, Scott's *Gladiator* (2000) is a retelling of Anthony Mann's *The Fall of the Roman Empire* (1964), with a shift in emphasis from plot to character. These, then, are the models facing Shekhar Kapur: to stick with the narrative, as do Stevens and Spielberg, or, at the other extreme, to create a heroic epic with a distinct authorial voice that pushes the narrative to an aesthetic that may look intriguing, but that may be out of scale with the content of the narrative or at the very least push a less apparent interpretation of the narrative.

Kapur lies somewhere in between, but at times he expresses one or the other of the extremes. Just as Mann will occasionally use an extremely stylized long shot, so too Kapur. *Elizabeth* is rife with extreme long shots from a point of view high above the characters. Does this represent Kapur's artistic perspective or an authorial comment? Whichever it is, the extreme long shots draw considerable attention to themselves. To coax out the meaning of this and other options, we must first turn to his film *The Bandit Queen* (1994).

The film, which is based on a real character, begins with Phoolan, at the age of 11, being promised by her father to an adult in a marriage of low caste. The family needs the money it will gain from the marriage. Phoolan, a spirited young girl, accompanies her husband. Even at this age she smarts at the injustice of boys and men who verbally and otherwise abuse her because of her low social status. When the husband insists on sexual relations (she has not yet entered puberty) she rebels and runs backs to her parents. There shame follows her through adolescence. As a young woman, now living with her parents, the head villager's son tries to rape her in a field. She fights him off, but he accuses her of seducing him. The consequence, in a hearing of the village elders, is that Phoolan is banished from the village. Again men have been unjust and only she has paid the consequences.

Phoolan joins a band of low-caste bandits and becomes the lover of its leader. In this relationship she experiences for the first time a relationship of equals. It doesn't last because he is killed and she is raped by one of his criminal patrons. The experience is so humiliating that she is consumed with a need for revenge. Her criminal career grows as does her notoriety when she returns to the village where she was raped and kills ten of its men. The perpetrator, however, eludes her revenge. Eventually she is hunted down and imprisoned, but her fame is such that she is pardoned by the government and freed at last. Phoolan's story is the biography of a low-caste woman.

In fact, Kapur makes the film much more. It's an incitement to change women and the caste system. All must change. There is too much injustice. This is the theme of Kapur's film.

How does the deployment of long shots and close-ups, their use in a pattern of juxtaposition, help articulate the narrative? And how does Kapur present a layered view of Phoolan rather than a simplistic hero-villain approach?

The first challenge for Kapur is to lead the viewer to identify with Phoolan. Initially, he uses close-ups to show us her emotive quality. All the other characters are relatively impassive or guarded, but Phoolan is open and expressive, particularly in her reaction to personal injustice. Here the close-up is deployed to differentiate Phoolan from the other characters. Kapur does not make of her a romanticized heroine or a pathetic victim; he focuses on her spirit, and he treats her character in a realistic manner.

Nor does Kapur make a case that Phoolan shares a bond with other women, that her story is their story. He is far more specific. This is Phoolan's story. She is rebellious and she is unusual. The other women seem more resigned to their status in the family and in their communities. Her mother-in-law, for example, is assertive, cold, and cruel to this 11-year-old bride. She is the privileged one in Phoolan's new home; even her son, the husband, conforms to her view of Phoolan as lazy and uncooperative. In this sense, Kapur's portrait is very specific. Phoolan is the exception rather than a symbol. He creates a believable, understandable, admirable character. She doesn't want to be anyone's victim.

To give the narrative an epic feeling, Kapur resorts to extreme long shots—Phoolan crossing a bridge with her new husband, or Phoolan in the hilly badlands that house the bandits. These images add a formal sense of the context for Phoolan's life; that context is the southern Indian subcontinent, a vast space where people can lose themselves. This aspect of Kapur's approach is very different from the cinema verité approach where the characters' environment is less the focus than the characters' relationships. By alternating between the emotional close shots of Phoolan with the formal impassivity of the long shots, one gets the sense that there will be no help for Phoolan. There is no romantic Fordian vision of the land to be had here.

The next dimension of the use of close shots and long shots is the variety of viewpoints of Phoolan that Kapur seek. I would suggest that Kapur wants to give us as diverse a portrait of Phoolan as he can. By doing so he begins to make the more general case that, on one level, Phoolan's story is every woman's story. This means that he needs to establish the powerful Phoolan as well as the powerless Phoolan. He needs to show her as woman, daughter, lover, and leader. He needs to show every aspect of Phoolan in order that the general case of women be made. He thus has to be both specific for the Phoolan's identification and layered for Phoolan to become everywoman.

I have already illustrated Phoolan as the defiant daughter and the naive young Phoolan who believes that if you tell the truth, justice should prevail. In spite of being truthful about the assault by the village elder's son, she is still banished from her home. When Kapur shows us Phoolan the lover, with her lover the bandit leader, the shots he chooses emphasize the equivalence of man and woman. They are first related to each other in the same frame (foreground and background), and as they grow intimate they are presented on the same plane. Kapur uses close shots to punctuate the passion in the relationship. Phoolan the lover is presented emotionally in the use of the close shot. The camera placement is also intimate.

Later, when Phoolan is raped by the local crime boss, the camera placement is more distant. And when she is humiliated, walking naked through the village, the placement is high and the camera is far from her. The long shot records her humiliation. Here Phoolan is the victim of unbridled, cruel male power.

When Phoolan does exact revenge on the men of her village and she has 10 of them executed by her own men, the camera is in close to Phoolan. It's as if we have to feel her power as a woman seeking revenge on the men who contributed to her past humiliation.

By moving to different visual perspectives on Phoolan using close shots and extreme long shots, and by varying the placement of the camera from looking down on her after the rape (victim) to looking close at her as an executioner, Kapur gives us multiple perspectives on Phoolan. By doing so he individuates her as a strong personality. He also creates a portrait of the various roles of women in a man's world: victim, lover, daughter, mother, powerless castaway, powerful leader.

Kapur takes up another story of a woman in *Elizabeth*, but in this case she is the sixteenth-century Queen of England rather than a woman from the lowest caste in India. But there are similarities between the two films, both dramatically and in terms of shot selection. First, a summary of the narrative.

Elizabeth begins with Elizabeth's half-sister, Mary, on the throne. Mary is a Catholic and Elizabeth is a Protestant. Religious differences and alliances pit sister against sister, and in the first Act of the film Elizabeth's life is under threat. At the end of Act I, Mary dies and the Protestant Elizabeth assumes the throne. But as a woman and as a Protestant, she is surrounded by enemies. The highest nobleman, Norfolk, is Catholic, and he wants to be king. Elizabeth's advisors suggest an alliance—marry the King of Spain or a Prince of France, both Catholic monarchies. Even Elizabeth's lover counsels an alliance. In the end she trusts one Protestant advisor, Walsingham who, as a Protestant cleric and nobleman, is interested in her survival as a Protestant Queen. The thread through the narrative is that all men (but Walsingham) treat her as a woman rather than as a monarch. In the end she realizes she must choose to be a woman or a monarch. She can't be both. She renounces her feminine (read weak) side and assumes the role of an asexual but successful monarch.

The prologue sets the directorial pattern as it applies to the conflict of Catholic versus Protestant. In an intense close-up, a woman's head is being shaved. In a close-up of her accuser, a Catholic bishop condemns her as a heretic to be burned at the stake. Quickly the scene moves to 3 heretics tied to a stake and observed by a crowd. Wood is heaped and a fire is set. The heretics complain that they burn too slowly. More wood is thrown on the fire and they perish. The scene is presented principally in intense close-up, with close-shot cutaways to the crowd and to the Catholic officials. Interspersed are a few establishing shots. Kapur cuts away to a point of view shot from above—is this his point of view, or God's point of view? Whatever it represents, it interjects a "watching" perspective. The conflict between Catholic and Protestant is being observed. The scene is very intense and unforgettably establishes the stakes in this conflict. It also sets the directorial pattern: a preponderance of close-shots with a few long shots for context, and the introduction of a third person perspective from above the action.

When we meet Elizabeth in the next scene, it is in a close-up. She is dancing with her ladies-in-waiting—in a field, awaiting the return of her lover, Sir Robert. The image of Elizabeth is soft and feminine, in sharp contrast to the presentation of Elizabeth at the end of the film, where the shots are three-quarter shots to long shots, and the distant camera placement is hard-edged and powerful but not sexual, as is the presentation when we first see her. In these opening shots Kapur uses a telephoto lens to blur the context, giving Elizabeth not only a softness, but also an openness of expression that seems so opposite to the cruelty of the preceding scene. In this scene, Elizabeth is arrested and taken to the Tower of London. For the most part we see Elizabeth in close, either via camera placement or as she approaches the camera, or the shot is a close-up. The images of the court, particularly in the Queen's chambers, are distant and more long shots prevail. When Norfolk moves through the Queen's castle toward her chamber, the point-of-view is again from high above. He and his retinue look very small indeed. The extreme long shots from a third person or from a distant on-high perspective creates an epic perspective: the struggle is not just men struggling for power; there is something bigger at stake. The implication is that an epic struggle is being observed by the gods. This alternation of very intense close-ups for emotion (the death of the Protestant heretics) or identification (Elizabeth) is alternated with extreme long shots to give the sense of a struggle that is epic.

In the scene that follows, Elizabeth is called to the Queen's chamber from her jail cell. There in the chamber, Mary weighs Elizabeth's fate. They are half-sisters, but of different religions. Mary acknowledges that Elizabeth will be Queen when she dies (she is now ill), but only if Mary doesn't sign Elizabeth's death warrant. Here both power and emotion are played out. There are long shots of the chamber that remind us that Mary as Queen has absolute power. And there are close-ups of Elizabeth and Mary where Elizabeth appeals to her as a sister not to condemn her to death. The shift from long shot to close-up, from power to emotion, captures the layers of this narrative extremely well. It is both the emotional story of a woman concerned about love, about relationships, about dignity, and it is a story about power, its scale and its absolutism. Relationships, love, and dignity have no place beside power, and in the narrative Elizabeth will eventually have to choose.

Kapur uses close-ups for the emotion, for the femininity, for the sexuality of Elizabeth (and others), and he uses the long shot to articulate power issues, whether they are about Protestant versus Catholic, or monarchy versus Church, or England versus France or Spain. He also uses the extreme long shot from a third person or on-high point of view to lend an epic scale to all the struggles listed.

□ CAMERA PLACEMENT AND PACE: THE INTERVENTION OF SUBJECTIVE STATES

Numerous filmmakers have used a subjective camera placement and/or shifts in pace to alert us that the narrative has shifted into a subjective or dream or unreal state as opposed to the in-the-world, real state that has preceded it. Beginning with Georges Méliès, best known for his film *A Trip to the Moon* (1902), subjective states have been a narrative concern and creative challenge. Luis Buñuel simply ignored the distinction between the objective and subjective from his first film, *Un Chien Anadalou* (1929), in which he simply cut directly into an altered state. Other filmmakers were more aesthetically elegant. Rouben Mamoulian used the subjective camera to establish point of view in *Dr. Jekyll and Mr. Hyde* (1932). Alfred Hitchcock used sound and the close-up in *Blackmail* (1929). Federico Fellini used sound, or its absence, and the subjective point of view, together with shifts in art direction and, of course, a narrative absurdity to assure that we would understand the difference between the objective and the subjective. Filmmakers such as Alain Resnais, on the other hand, blurred the line between them in their work. Others used black and white and color to differentiate one from the other. To examine this issue we begin with Elem Klimov's *Come and See* (1985) and then look at Darren Aronofsky's *Requiem for a Dream* (2000).

Elem Klimov's *Come and See* is a war film set in German-occupied Byelorussia. The time is 1943. The main character, Florya, is a young adolescent who volunteers to fight for the partisans. The narrative is experienced and envisioned through his eyes. The story begins with Florya finding a gun, the prerequisite for joining the partisans (to provide your own weapon). He leaves home and joins. The story ends, perhaps days or weeks later, after his initial experiences of war; he is shooting his gun for the first time and moving off into the woods with the partisans. In between he experiences the horrors of war and wartime occupation. He is left on guard duty in the woods with a young woman only a few years older than himself. The partisans move off to fight the Germans, then he and the young woman experience a German aerial bombardment resulting in his temporary deafness. The two flee to his home, but his mother and sisters have disappeared. He doesn't know it, but they have been killed by the Germans in an exercise in ethnic cleansing. He and the young woman go to an island where he is certain he will find his mother and sisters; there are many survivors but none of his family. He then goes off with a soldier to find food for the people on the island. They steal a cow, but both the soldier and the cow are killed by artillery fire. A peasant farmer hides him, but soon the Germans take him. They round up everyone in the village, including Florya, and herd them into a barn. He is allowed to leave the barn and then the Germans burn the barn with its hundreds of occupants. He is threatened with death but, it is only for the photograph a German is taking—as a souvenir. The Germans leave, and he has survived. Soon the same Germans who burnt the barn are captured. We learn that half of them are in fact fellow Russians. Sentiment among the partisans is to burn them, but they are all shot instead. Florya now fires his rifle at a portrait of Hitler. This is intercut with historical footage of the rise of Hitler. As we move through this sequence, and as the shooting proceeds, we realize that chronologically the historical footage is moving backwards in time and backwards in presentation, as if it is being eliminated. The narrative ends with a statement that more than 600 villages were burned by the Nazis as they moved through Byelorussia.

This narrative summary is a chronology of the events of the film. What is more important, however, is how Klimov creates the subjective state of Florya, the young main character. How does he feel about war, about this war, about himself, about what is happening to him and his family? Klimov is more interested in giving us the feelings of the boy. Camera placement, shot selection, and sound combine to create the internal state of Florya. The consequence is a film experience that is constantly on the verge of the unbearable, and of the unbelievable. The question for us is how does Klimov create the subjective state of the main character? Whether it is real or imagined, an expression of his fear or of his hopes, is beside the point. Klimov's task is to transport us into the inner life of an adolescent as it is shaped by external events—the losses, the possibility of imminent death, the manner of observed violence. How does he process all of these events, and how does Klimov take us into the feeling state that the boy experiences?

First Klimov begins from afar, observing Florya. He is guided by another boy in his search for a gun. This search seems almost absurd, a war game played by boys. It only becomes real when Florya digs up a gun. All we see is that the gun is attached to a hand and rigor mortis has made pulling the gun from its dead possessor a very difficult task. This absurd narrative piece sets up the paradox—a real task, getting a gun, is born out of absurd, surreal circumstance. The fun is buried, together with its previous owner, on a beach that seems an ideal setting for two kids to be playing out a war game. It's play, it's real, and it's surreal.

Shortly a glider floats by. This cutaway, also surreal, will be repeated throughout the film as a prologue to the intrusion of the real war, a German attack, which will follow. At this point the glider seems a tranquil, childlike part of the war game. We will learn its true meaning after a few more repetitions of the shot.

The narrative proceeds with the induction of the boy into the partisans. His mother pleads with him that he doesn't need to and shouldn't go. A partisan officer says that they need men with guns; he has fulfilled the recruitment requirement, and he must go. Cutaways of food being prepared and the boy's twin sister flesh out a realistic sequence. He is excited. Like all all young people, the act of going to war makes him feel older, and proud of it. He leaves. In the forest, Klimov's subjective strategy begins. The bombardment catches Florya and the young girl in a playful mood, but the mood changes quickly. Klimov uses the sound of the descending bombs to set the tone. The pitch is high and loud, and the images are in themselves descriptive of a bombing. But as the bombing proceeds he cuts to very long takes of the main character. As his eardrums are damaged, the close-up of his face focuses on his pain. The sound of the bombs then becomes louder and more distorted. The focus on Florya, on his pain, on the intensity and distortion of the sound, and on the growing distortion of constant noise, suddenly gives us the subjective aural experience of the character. Later the girl will explain that he has become crazy because he can't hear. In a sense this is what we begin to experience—his inner sense of pain and isolation from the world.

Klimov now alternates scenes of the real and the subjective. The next scene is Florya taking the young woman to his home for protection, but no one is home. There is still warm soup on the table. Florya eats and tells the girl that his mother makes good soup. This very naturalistic scene ends with Florya's notion that his mother and sisters have escaped to the island not far away. They run off, but as they do the young woman looks over her shoulder and sees naked bodies piled up behind a barn. This glimpse reveals to us that the mother and sisters have been killed. This scene proceeds naturalistically, but it is followed by the almost surreal journey to the island. The water surrounding the island is thick with oil tar that retards the progress of the characters' flight. They wade through water. The tar coats their bodies and faces. The pace slows way down, and it seems the oil tar will sink them. When they finally emerge they look inhuman.

They soon find other villagers who tell Florya that his mother is dead. They are covered with oil and tar, and a close-up registers his attempt to scream. Does he scream? Is it inner or outer reality? Florya seems demented, and the girl says he is crazy from the damage to his ears. This scene seems entirely subjective and non-naturalistic. This pattern will be repeated with each scene: the search for food, his capture by the Germans, the barn burning, the execution of the Germans. By moving back and forth Klimov creates a tension between the outer reality and the inner feeling state of the boy.

The concluding sequence continues to heighten the tension between outer and inner reality. When the boy fires his gun at the portrait of Hitler, he is trying to exorcise his anger and the source of his pain—Adolph Hitler. By cutting between the boy firing and the history of the Third Reich, Klimov is giving him a target. By running the footage of the Third Reich in reverse, he is implying that the boy's firing is turning back and erasing history. Whether this is a catharsis or a wish, the sequence is very much a subjective adolescent notion—that the boy can, by firing his gun, turn back the destruction done to his family and to his country. This subjective idea and state is then offset by the return to reality. The boy moves off to join the partisans and we are told with a title how many villages in Byelorussia were destroyed by fire by the advancing German army.

Sound, camera placement, and shot selection—particularly close-up shots where the camera is very close to the subject—create the subjective state of this young person in war. Pace plays a secondary role in particular sequences such as crossing to the island and the artillery attack that kills the soldier and the cow intended to feed the people on the island.

Darren Aronofsky's *Requiem for a Dream* (2000) is also concerned with subjective states—states that are induced by drugs. The narrative focuses on

4 characters: Harry, his mother Sara Goldfarb, his girlfriend Marion, and his friend and business partner, Tyrone. Harry and Tyrone are, as Harry calls it, in the distribution business, the distribution of drugs. Marion becomes addicted to heroin and Harry's mother, Sara Goldfarb, becomes addicted to diet pills. Initially, every character has some degree of control over their lives, but by the end, each loses control and each does what they have to to survive. Aronofsky gives each character a well-defined character arc. For Harry, it's being a guilty caretaker, torn between self-interest and responsibility to others. For Sara Goldfarb, it's loneliness or a search for acknowledgment by others (her friends, her son, the community at large, as represented by her quest for public recognition through a television appearance). For Marion, it's rebellion, first against her parents and later by blaming whomever she depends upon for money to buy drugs. For Tyrone, it's being a man torn by the need for praise and yet impulsive to a degree that undermines any achievement. In the course of their drug dependency the characters will lose everything physically and mentally, and they will be left with very little dignity.

The creative issue for Aronofsky is how to portray the shift from living in a community to living in your head. To manage the transition, Aronofsky uses a full range of devices—sound, pace, camera placement, the distortion of a fisheye, wide-angle images, pixilation, and lots of camera movement. The issue for us is first to see an outer/inner visual dialectic, and then to differentiate how Aronofsky illustrates the transition for each of the characters so that he creates a subjective state that is distinct for each.

First we'll look at the outer/inner dynamic that contextualizes and prepares us for the shift to a subjective state. Aronofsky uses two devices: the alternation between extreme close-up and extreme distance from the action, and the narrative device of intercutting reality with a fantasy.

When we first meet Harry and his mother, he is taking her television with the help of Tyrone. He pawns it to buy drugs—as he calls it "a stake"—to get his business going again. When we see Harry and Sara Goldfarb, both are in intense close-up. Aronofsky uses a split screen so they are together within the big frame but separated by the split. When Harry and Tyrone are moving the TV through the streets, the camera moves with them but is located at a distance. The use of a fisheye lens makes them seem even farther away. Aronofsky often cuts between these two extremes so that we feel very close and then very distant from the characters. He repeats this pattern when Harry and Tyrone take drugs. The drugs are shot in 3 quick close-up shots: of heroin dissolving under a flame, of the pump of heroin moving through an injection device, and then of a breakdown of the drug, whether it's in a vein in the body or externally we are uncertain. Aronofsky then cuts to Harry and Tyrone in a wide-angle shot that is initially in slow motion, then in accelerating motion. The use of an extremely wide-angle lens gives some distortion to the shot. Aronofsky repeats this sequence of shots when Harry, Tyrone, and Marion get high. Here the additional use of pixilation makes the sense of drug-induced motion powerful and unnaturally fast.

Aronofsky also uses the narrative device of a fantasy insert to create a sense of the dissonance between the outer and inner world. Sara Goldfarb will often see herself as a character in the TV game show she watches religiously. Harry dreams of stealing a policeman's gun. Tyrone dreams of his childhood, of its perfection and his idealized relationship with his mother. When Marion is having dinner with her therapist (he is clearly interested in her sexually), she dreams of driving a fork through his hand as it reaches out to her. These inserts clarify the thoughts of the characters, but principally they articulate the desire to be or to do what they cannot be or do in real life.

To create distinctive subjective states for each of these characters, Aronofsky initially uses pace to illustrate their individual goals. They all energetically want something: Sara Goldfarb wants to be thin; Harry wants to be helpful; Tyrone wants to be successful; and Marion, principally, wants thrills, including the thrill of being high. Having established their goals, Aronofsky will explore what thwarts their goals. This involves close-ups. For Sara, it's a close-up of chocolates. Following the shot of the chocolates, Sara gets a phone call that she has been chosen to be on television. It is clearly a sales come-on for something, but to her it's the beginning of a new opportunity. Immediately she gets her hair colored so she will look younger and tries to get into her red dress, but she can't. This introduces the issue of diet. When she visits a doctor he puts her on medication—amphetamines to lose weight, and sleeping pills to sleep—and her journey into a distorted world begins. Now Aronofsky uses a visual shorthand: the mailbox close-up registers her anticipation of the TV invitation or the application to appear. The fridge far away represents the objects of desire, food. The pills in close-up represent the means to the end—her appearance in the red dress. But her hallucinations become more frequent; she sees and hears fragments. When she visits the doctor late in her experience, her pills are working less well. She sees him far away, his movements are pixilated, and his voice is distant and distorted. We now have a representation of an extremely dissociative state. The establishment of this state precedes her final act of desperation: her appearance at the TV station, disheveled and demanding to appear on TV. This act develops along the path of disconnectedness, and Sara is taken off to Bellevue for involuntary confinement and shock treatment. She has lost touch with reality; she is totally within her own subjective state.

Aronofsky parallel cuts between the descent of Harry, Tyrone, and Marion together with Sara. Their arcs proceed downward into loss and humiliation. By using the alternation of very close and extremely long shots (with a fisheye lens to make us seem even further), and by using sound and image and changes in pace, Aronofsky brings us into the inner world and the descent into the self that characterizes the effect of drugs on these 4 characters. The style is critical in creating our feeling for each of these characters from the most internal subjective perspective.

A final comment: there is a great deal of energy in this film. Pace and movement energize these characters even though they are caught in an inertia brought on by drugs. Each of them acts, but the inappropriateness of their actions harms rather than helps them. These are characters who can't save themselves or each other in spite of their desire to help the others.

□ NOTE/REFERENCE

1. The American experience with cinema verité techniques in dramatic films is strongly identified with the work of John Cassavetes in films such as *Shadows* (1959) and *Faces* (1968). Haskell Wexler in his film *Medium Cool* (1969) and later Michael Ritchie in his films *Downhill Racer* (1969) and *The Candidate* (1972) also experimented with the form.

16

The Appropriation of Style III: Digital Reality

■

From the earliest days, film has struggled with two opposite impulses—to make its narratives as realistic as possible and to create the fantastic, the reimagined reality. These two impulses were represented in the late 1890s and early 1900s by Louis Lumière and his brother, and by George Méliès. Now, over 100 years later, digitization of the image, including special effects and post-production, has fused the two opposite worlds. Now images can look real and yet can originate out of an imagined reality rather than out of a captured (filmed) reality. In this chapter our goal is to examine how artifice has become real and how realism of the old-fashioned sort has taken on a new meaning in the film experience.

What needs to be said at the outset is that editing has always actively supported both impulses. The extreme long shot and the long shot were the primary means editors and directors first used to articulate imagined reality and the fantastic. The long shot, the close-up, and the cutaway were used to convey both physical and emotional reality. In terms of editing styles, the jump cut and pace have been used to create imagined reality, while seamless continuity cutting—parallel action, match cutting—follow the principles of screen direction and have supported a sense of physical and emotional realism.

Immediately the contributions of digital reality have challenged both sides. The consequence has been an increased effort to create and exploit imagined reality and physical reality. As editors and directors appropriate new stylistic choices to gain advantage in one direction or the other, audiences are left in a state of suspended belief. For them, the questions become: "What is real?" or "I can't believe anything!" or "I surrender to the film, knowing it's not real." This begins to sound cynical, but it is not meant to be. Editors and directors are taking more extreme stylistic positions and the result is a kind of transparency about pushing artifice or pushing realism. Peter Jackson (*King Kong*) is having lots of fun on that island as a giant gorilla, numerous dinosaurs and innumerable giant insects all pursue the humans. And so are we having fun. But we know it is digitized reality.

□ ARTIFICIAL REALITY

To understand this "imagined reality" more deeply, its best to consider the operational choices different filmmakers have used to achieve an imagined reality by pushing artifice. Consider five options as pathways to what I will call *artificial reality*. These pathways are the use of video rather than film, the use of constructed artifice, the use of the imagined over the observational, the use of spectacle, and the use of special effects. Each of these options is clearly artificial. At times, the director's goal is playful, as it was in the case of Peter Jackson in *King Kong*. More often, the director has a greater purpose in mind, ranging from a Brechtian intervention in Lars von Trier's *Manderlay* and *Dogville* to rescale the story, to making it larger, as Ridley Scott does in *Gladiator*. I turn now to these options.

VIDEO OVER FILM

The first pathway is the choice of *video over film*. Film, in its finer grain, has a depth and sharpness that projects realism. Video, on the other hand has a flatness and a tendency to desaturate color, resulting in a pastel quality that projects artifice. Filmmakers sometimes opt for video as a cheaper option to film. In the case of Michael Mann in *Collateral* and of Coline Serreau in *Chaos*, the choice was aesthetic—the choice was to use artifice in their conceptualization of the narrative.

Coline Serreau's *Chaos* (2001), a fable of contemporary life in France, focuses on two women, the Caucasian Hélène and the Algerian Malika. Both are in trouble because they are women. The film opens when Hélène and her husband witness the severe beating of the young prostitute, Malika. The husband insists they do nothing and Hélène complies. But she feels so guilty and outraged that she seeks out the critically ill Malika and stays by her side until she is almost recovered. Hélène has to contend with an indifferent, selfish husband and son. Malika has to contend with the criminal ring that has exploited her and the father who wanted to sell her into marriage with an older man. The two women, with the help of Hélène's mother-in-law, claim justice and revenge against all of the men who have so callously controlled and depreciated their lives.

Serreau's concept is to present the women differently. Hélène has the typical hurried life of the upper middle class. All of the men in her life view her as "serving" them. Husband, son, boss—all see Hélène as in service to them, to be tolerated, rather than as a partner and an equal. Serreau plays on this characterization of Hélène until late in the film, when, as a lawyer, she is helpful to Malika. Until that point, she is presented as the men see her—subservient. Serreau's approach is light and comic, as if Hélène's life is a soap opera, a *comedic* soap opera. Using video and fast cutting emphasizes the plastic, unreal quality of her life and her life as a wife, mother, and employee. She is clearly capable and living an upper middle-class life. The use of video here trivializes that life, focusing on its hurried and harried qualities. The use of video contributes to the notion of trivialization and also makes light, rather than tragic, her role in the family.

In the case of Malika, her life is anything but light; indeed, it verges on the tragic. When we learn about her life, it begins with the suicide of her mother in Algeria. In France, she is shunned by her father's new wife and in short order is sold into marriage with an elderly Algerian. When she escapes, she is without a passport or resources. She is forced into prostitution by a man who buys her food. As she moves up the prostitution ladder, her intelligence and her ability to exploit her skills bring her into conflict with her "owners." An elderly client wills her his fortune and the mob claims ownership. Malika's refusal to accept this leads to the beating and to their relentless pursuit of her. Hélène saves Malika from the mob's clutches, and Malika and Hélène plan revenge. They also plan to save Malika's younger sister from the fate of loveless marriage and from the same exploitation planned for her as it had been for Malika.

The use of video does not lighten the Malika story. But it does help the audience experience her story as a fable. Serreau uses the story form to present her ideas about contemporary women as a cautionary tale. Malika, as in the case of Hélène, is a modern French woman, albeit from a more traditional culture. Serreau is saying that women from whichever culture they come from must act to save each other. They cannot rely on men. Mothers, wives, and sisters: all women must stand together in a modern war against tradition and a male power structure that will only use them. By using video, Serreau enhances the artifice of the story and emotionally distances us from Hélène and Malika. They become symbols in the battle of women and men. Video helps Serreau move the fable into a representation about modern life, rather than being only a slice of modern life. Artifice and certain story forms, such as the fable, enhance one another. In this sense, video, by making Malika's story as unreal as Hélène's is, moves the film into a stylistic choice that strengthens its message.

CONSTRUCTED ARTIFICE

A second pathway to imagined reality is what I will call *constructed artifice*. Lars von Trier's *Dogville* and *Manderlay* provide useful examples of constructed artifice. *Dogville* is set in an imaginary Appalachian town in the 1930s. Thematically, a city woman, an outsider, comes to town. She is running away from her life and her family. The town is very suspicious of strangers: even a man attracted to the outsider will, in the end, side with his fellow citizens against her. Small-town thinking and its purveyors, the citizens, punish her. Only when her father, a mob boss, arrives to reclaim her, will she act as he would and punish her persecutors. "Like father, like daughter" proves to be the revealing cliché that ends *Dogville*.

The constructed artifice is created as follows: The film is made on a large set. Houses are demarked by masking tape. Lighting is anti-dramatic. Long takes give the film the appearance of a play being workshopped prior to sets being built for the production. Everything about the film oozes artifice, as opposed to any sort of realism. The result tests our capacity for imagined reality, but eventually we get past the non-houses and enter the lives of the characters. One can see *Dogville* as another mischievous film from Lars von Trier, or one can see it as an upshot of digital reality, a reaction to it, a film that openly and stylistically states, "it's not real." Constructed artifice is the second pathway to an imagined reality. What I will call *the imagined as the observational* is the third pathway.

THE IMAGINED AS THE OBSERVATIONAL

Steven Spielberg's *War of the Worlds* (2005) provides an excellent example of the imagined as the observational. The story is a straightforward tale of survival. A father who has been a so-so parent (Tom Cruise) has his two children for the weekend. The children's tolerance of their father verges on contempt. In short order, Earth is invaded by hostile and otherworldly beings. The focus is Bayonne, New Jersey, but reports allude to a widespread invasion. The fate of father and children is challenged and in the course of their flight, the father will be heroic and restored as a good father.

The artifice of *War of the Worlds* is to make the invasion and the first attack essentially an observable, credible reality, although in fact it's imagined. No constructed artifice here. Rather, Spielberg attempts to make this invasion as credible as the Normandy landing in *Saving Private Ryan*. Moving from a lightening storm in the sky, to wind coming in from the Atlantic, the invasion proceeds with rumbling sounds coming from beneath the surface, the appearance of a sink hole, the slow emergence of what appears to be a giant spaceship, and the laser-like attack and the consequent vaporization of humans and the destruction of property. Eventually, the scale of the attack intensifies, and cars, buildings, and even the Bayonne skyway give way under the attack. Each stage threatens the main character and he and his children provide the human guide focus for the action. Each of these actions is presented in a developmental credible fashion, although each is imagined. The slow, incremental development of the threat and the attack makes it more observational. Later in the film, when the creatures from outer space are introduced as giant, worm-like beings, we are in imagined artifice, and the credible observational sense of the first attack is lost. In the first attack, however, we have an excellent example of the imagined and the observational merging to form a very credible sense of the threat to the world.

USE OF SPECTACLE

A fourth pathway to pushing artifice is to sidestep the observational and to embrace the imagined reality for purposes of creating *spectacle*. Useful examples here include Ridley Scott's *Kingdom of Heaven* (2005) and his *Gladiator* (2000). Both are epic struggles, the first the Christian–Muslim war for control of Jerusalem, the second the struggle between the Roman General Maximus and the Roman Emperor Commodus. In *Gladiator*, a dying

Emperor Marcus Aurelius names Maximus to succeed him; Marcus Aurelius' disappointed son, Commodus, kills his father, and orders Maximus killed. Maximus, enslaved, becomes a gladiator, eventually to great fame. When he is invited to fight at the Colosseum in Rome, he confronts the Emperor Commodus. Only one man will triumph. In the end, Maximus, although seriously injured, kills Commodus. He has achieved his goal, vengeance, but dies from his wounds.

In *Gladiator*, Ridley Scott uses imagined reality to increase the epic scale of the personal struggle. It's not important to Scott that the settings be believable. The battle against the German barbarians, the arena in the desert, and the Roman Colosseum are each presented in a highly designed artificial visualization. Each is intended to give scale to the personal struggle of Commodus and Maximus and, in an imagined way, each does precisely that. Scott isn't seeking believability. Rather, his goal is larger than life, epic. By relying on a highly stylized set of extreme long shots of the battle, of the Colosseum, and of the arena in the desert, Scott is allowing imagined reality to contextualize the personal story, making the imagined reality of the battle for Jerusalem more schematic than, and not as effective as, is the use of imagined reality and personal conflict in *Gladiator*. This illustrates the importance of the linkage of pushing artifice to effective narrative goals. Without the linkage, the artifice proves to be empty rather than effective.

USE OF SPECIAL EFFECTS

The last pathway we discuss to push artifice is the use of *special effects* to animate the narrative. Here *The Lord of the Rings: The Return of The King* provides a useful example. Peter Jackson uses a large palate to pictorialize Tolkien's classic tale. The three films of the Tolkien trilogy tell the story of good vs. evil in a mythical land, Middle Earth. At the wizard level, Gandalf represents good and Sauron represents the forces of darkness. Kings and kingdoms and noblemen focus on the kingdoms of Gondor and Rohan. The commoners are represented by the little people, specifically the hobbits. The humans, kings, and hobbits struggle against the non-human Orcs and their giant vultures and elephants. Serpents abound between human lands. The plot will follow the effort to transport a ring, which has a power that corrupts the men who possess it. The hobbit Frodo, the epitome of good will, is sent on this mission. His friend Sam goes along with Frodo to aid him. En route, they meet Smeagol, a Gollum, formerly a man corrupted by the possession of the ring. Gollum is a now half-man, half-creature, torn between corrupt action and moral action. A group of knights accompany the warrior Aragorn to protect the passage of Frodo. Frodo and Aragorn are separated and only reunite at the end of the journey. Aragorn returns to the kingship of Gondor, and Frodo succeeds in the destruction of the ring. Each man is changed by the journey, but in the end human and humane values overcome the forces of evil and destruction, and Middle Earth survives.

In order to pictorialize such an epic tale of an imagined world, Peter Jackson has used special effects in order to create the imagined reality of Middle Earth. The city Minas Tirith, capitol of Gondor, and Mordor, the dead city, are pictorialized as the center for good and for evil. The armies of Mordor and the armies that fight to save Minas Tirith are presented via special effects and their presentations animate metaphorical visions of good and evil. The giant vultures, the elephants, and the Orcs ooze repellent qualities, while the king of Rohan and the to-be king of Gondor, Aragorn, ooze nobility, the best of human qualities. As for Frodo and the hobbits, they begin as innocents, but increasingly gain a more complex view of the world; short people and ugly monsters—all are pictorialized using special effects technology. What I'm trying to say is that much of the film is artifice.

As in the case of *Gladiator*, the artifice works because it is linked to personalized dramatic tensions—for example, the relationships of Frodo, Sam, and Smeagol are conflictual and complex. Without the emotions arising out of these relationships, the scale of the special effects would have far less meaning. When linked to effect emotionalized narrative, however, the special effects amplify the characters' struggles. In this case, artifice contributes powerfully to the audience experience.

□ Realism

The other stylistic choice filmmakers have taken up is pushing realism. In their way, they have pursued realism as aggressively as Ridley Scott and Peter Jackson have pursued an imagined realism that openly embraced artifice. The most useful start point for this impulse is to reiterate that cinéma vérité staked a position in narrative film starting in the 1940s, in location shoots such as those of Elia Kazan's *Boomerang!* and *Panic in the Streets*, through the late 1950s, as captured in the reality filmmaking of Karel Reisz in *Saturday Night and Sunday Morning* and John Cassavetes' *Shadows.* In the 1960s, Arthur Penn (*Mickey One*), John Frankenheimer (*Seconds*), and Sydney Lumet (*The Pawnbroker*) favored a cinéma vérité approach to their subjects, and in the 1970s, Michael Ritchie took up the style (*Downhill Racer*). By the 1990s, appearance of the Danish Dogme films (Docudrama in the U.K.; Ken Loach's *Land and Freedom*) and the work of Mike Leigh had made cinéma vérité an accepted stylistic tool for dramatic material.

Thomas Vinterberg's *Festen* (*The Celebration*) launched the Dogme films, exemplified by no artificial lights, no artificial sound, no tripod. Lone Scherfig's *Italiensk for begyndere* (*Italian for Beginners*) and Kristian Levring's *The King Is Alive* consolidated the reputation of cinéma vérité at the turn of the century. At the same time, Belgian filmmakers began to use the docudrama style for a wide variety of story forms, from gangster (*Man Bites Dog: It Happened in Your Neighborhood*) to melodrama (*Rosetta*). Cinéma vérité as a style became mainstream when Woody Allen used it in

Husbands and Wives and Steven Spielberg used it in *Schindler's List* and *Saving Private Ryan*.

If spectacle—the epic—underscores imagined realism, it is the human scale, both in inner life and outer life, that is the goal of those styles undertaken to push realism. In Vinterberg's *Festen* (*The Celebration*), the jump cutting is used to create the chaotic lives of two of three living siblings. The stillness of the camera and the longer takes illustrate the cold-bloodedness of a patriarch who continually raped his twins when they were children. If the Dogme films have once again popularized realism, particular filmmakers have worked with variants of style to seek out levels of realism. The most orthodox in their goals are the Dardenne brothers, who in a series of films, *La Promesse*, *Rosetta*, *Le Fils* (*The Son*), and *L'Enfant* (*The Child*), have made an art of the observational. Their focus is the smallest of behaviors, actions, and goals.

In each of the Dardenne films, the world is made up of children and adults. In *Rosetta*, a mother is nothing but an alcoholic barrier to the teenage daughter, Rosetta. In *Le Fils* (*The Son*), an adult who works with troubled teenage boys is the main character. Goals and relationships are grounded in small actions—working, preparing a meal, moving from work to home or from home to work. Nothing extreme occurs and yet there is an intensity to these films quite unlike a film grounded in one catastrophe after another—*The Poseidon Adventure*, for example. The hand-held camera movement, the proximity to the character, the movement, and the jump cutting together produce a heightened sense of each action, each behavior, and each interaction. The cumulative effect of a Dardenne brothers' film is an excruciating level of pain and pathos. We feel we have lived through a human war and are drained by the experience. Here the active observance of character makes the experience participatory for us.

The next level of the observational principle is to strip away the empathic style of the Dardenne brothers and to replace it with an alternative action style that is active without empathy. This approach is best captured by Philippe Grandrieux in his film *Sombre* (1998). *Sombre* tells the story of a serial killer in rural France. He kills throughout the film, and neither remorse nor psychological explanation is offered. Instead Grandrieux presents the killings using a hand-held camera. Jump cuts alternately voyeuristically show the action and avoid showing the action, creating the feeling that what is in fact shown is accidental. The result is disturbing.

In between the killings, Grandrieux has long tracking shots from the point of view of the killer. Traveling through the mountains, the rural population selling, working in their recreation, is captured but not understood. No empathy for the population, or for the killer, is evoked: only the sadness of not being connected. The pace, when it changes, implies that the killer needs the excitement of contact, and then of empowerment, and then of domination and destruction. The shot selection and the edit pattern create the feeling of desire and alienation and disturbance of the murderer. Nothing is explained. Psychology is sidestepped. Only the actions are presented, and those actions, habitual desire and destruction, are disturbingly captured by the moving camera by the proximity of its placement, its point of view, and the jump cuts. Here style suggests or implies psychology: I can't help myself. I love it. And I hate it. This is the upshot of the observational aggressive realism of that style. *Sombre* is well-titled. Pushing realism here is powerful, troubling. The human scale, although not understood, is experienced by the audience. *Sombre* and action direction represent the second pathway to pushing realism as a style.

The third pathway is to explore the option of heightened realism. By heightened realism I have in mind a sense of inner realism. What if Philippe Grandrieux took us into the mind of the serial killer in *Sombre*? The recent explosion of biographical films centering on personalities—Howard Hughes (*The Aviator*, 2003), Ray Charles (*Ray*, 2004), Johnny Cash (*Walk the Line*, 2005), and Truman Capote (*Capote*, 2005)—provides the insight here. In each case, the plot is about a career or a critical phase of a career, the writing of *In Cold Blood* in *Capote*, for example. But the sense of heightened realism comes from the inner life of the character: What motivates their behavior, their achievement? For Howard Hughes it's a pathological fear of the hygienic danger of the other. For Ray Charles it's the question of whether blindness is a barrier in life or a motivation. For Johnny Cash it's the guilt and anger he feels about the death of his father's favored son. And in the case of Truman Capote it's a malignant ambition that drives the author to creative heights and to personal depths.

In order for the sense of heightened realism to be credible, the complexity of two relationships needs to be explored. In *Capote*, those relationships are between Truman and one of the killers, Perry, and between Truman and Harper Lee, his old friend. In the case of Harper Lee, she accepts Truman, his strengths and his weaknesses. She represents, in her acceptance, the option of Capote's creative potential. Perry, the killer who Capote befriends in order to exploit for career purposes, represents the personal depth Capote reaches in order to further his ambition. Both relationships help create an inner complexity to an outwardly clever, vain writer. It is the inner complexity that gives *Capote* a heightened realism.

The other biographies are equally adept at providing the relationships to explore the inner life of their creative, driven subjects. Without this sense of an inner life, these films wouldn't resonate as emotionally with their audiences. Heightened realism is the critical pathway to creating output of each of these accomplished characters.

Another pathway to pushing realism is to opt for the docudrama as the story form. Here Steven Spielberg's *Munich* provides a good example. The template for the film is the terrorist massacre of Israeli athletes at the 1972 Olympics. The attack on the athletic residence and the consequent murders are presented in a fragmented sequential series of scenes, with the massacre itself in the final sequence of the film. The more contemporary plot is the commissioning of a team of Israeli assassins to hunt down and kill the perpetrators. The leader of the team is Avner (Eric Bana), and his Mossad handler is Ephraim (Geoffrey Rush). From the commissioning of the killings by Prime Minister Golda Meir, together with the Army and Intelligence chiefs, through the creation of the team, the film unfolds through a series of killings until Avner, having lost half-his team, loses his will to kill and begins to question the eye-for-an-eye philosophy that initiated the revenge killings. In the last scene of the film, a paranoid Avner has joined his family in Brooklyn. Against a New York skyline that includes the Twin Towers (which we, the audience, know will be destroyed in the future, on September 11, 2001), Ephraim tries to convince Avner to return to Israel. Avner refuses and the film ends inconclusively: among those Palestinians responsible for the Munich attacks, a number have survived; among the Israelis, a number of the assassins have died.

In *Munich* Spielberg is exploring the case for an eye for an eye and is suggesting that an eye for an eye is not the answer. Implicitly, he is making the case for political rather than quasi-military action as the only path to peace. In the film, Spielberg pushes a sense of realism that is credible and complex. Avner may be a killer but he's also a family man who cares deeply about his wife and baby daughter. He also cares about the daughter of a Palestinian he plans to kill. Avner is also presented in a number of scenes with his mother. Those scenes imply the difficulty of growing up as the son of a military hero. His complexity as a character is attuned to the complexity of his victims as well as of his accomplices, inside and outside Mossad. Being a son, being a father, being a husband, and being a man, each layer of Avner contributes to the complexity of our response to the film.

In *War of the Worlds*, Spielberg made imagined reality and artifice observational, credible. In *Munich*, he's trying to make real events and real people credible. I've already mentioned the complexity of character. Killing is also complex. Spielberg's made every effort to portray the killing of the athletes in Munich realistic. Because it was a real turning point in global terrorism, he spreads the murders out through the entire film. By doing so he makes the event inevitable and iconic, more important than it would have seemed if the killings had simply opened the film. In the same sense, by presenting the conclusion of the film against the backdrop of the Twin Towers, again Spielberg is making the conversation more important and iconic. It's a reminder to current audiences that the Munich killings and the attack on the Twin Towers are a continuum. We all are linked, Israelis, Americans, and citizens of the world, by these attacks. Whether they occur in Munich or in New York, they form phases in a struggle that has been ongoing for more than 40 years. Spielberg wants us to consider that continuum and to reflect upon the eye-for-an-eye response: it hasn't worked all these years—time for a different response. This is the upshot of the use of the docudrama in *Munich*. Its pushes realism and it strengthens the voice of the writers and of its director.

II

EDITING FOR
THE GENRE

■

■

■

■

17

Action

■

Because film is a visual medium, movement, which was originally the novelty of the medium, has naturally become its showpiece. Nothing better illustrates the power of movement in film than the action sequence. Action sequences are a key reason for the success of the Western and gangster genres. Whether it features a chase, a showdown, or a battle, the action sequence has a visceral appeal for audiences. This type of sequence is not confined to the genres where action seems natural, however. From the horror movie to the comedy, filmmakers have found action sequences to be a valuable device. Blake Edwards used action sequences in many of his comedies, most notably the *Pink Panther* series (1964–1978) and *The Great Race* (1965). Charles Crichton used the action sequence often in *A Fish Called Wanda* (1988). One of the best action sequences can be found in Peter Bogdanovich's *What's Up, Doc?* (1972).

To set the context for the following analysis, it is important to understand the dramatic and psychological characteristics of the action sequence. The editing principles rise out of those characteristics.

An action sequence is an accelerated version of the traditional film scene. The characters in a typical scene have different goals. In the course of the scene, each character attempts to achieve his or her goal. Because the goals tend to be opposed to one another, the scene could be characterized as a clash. The scene ends when one character has achieved his or her goal. This is the dramatic character of a scene. In an action sequence, there is an accelerated movement; the urgency of each character heightens their actions and also, therefore, their opposition to the goals of the other characters. The subtleties of the typical scene are set aside for an urgent expression of those various and opposing goals. The scene plays faster, and the nature of the clash of goals is more overt. In this sense, action sequences are more dynamic than typical scenes. They are often turning points or climactic scenes in a film.

From a psychological point of view, action sequences are scenes at the edge of emotional and physical survival The achievement of one character's goals may well mean the end of another character. This is why the action sequence so often plays itself out as a matter of life or death. It is critical that the audience not only understand the goals of each character in such a scene, but also that the audience choose sides. Identification with the goals of one of the characters is key to the success of the action sequence. Without that identification, the scene would lose its meaning. The audience must be at the edge of physical survival with the character; if it is not, the action sequence fails in its strength: excitation, deep involvement, catharsis. To identify, we must go beyond understanding the goals of the characters. We must become emotionally involved with the character.

Because the moment of survival is central to the action sequence, many action sequences are fights to the death, car chases, assassination attempts, or critical life-and-death moments for one of the characters.

The editing of action sequences can be demonstrated around particular issues: identification, excitation, conflict, and intensification.

To encourage identification, particular types of shots are useful, including close-ups and point-of-view shots. Some directors, such as Otto Preminger, like to crowd the actors by placing the camera very close to them. Another factor affecting point-of-view shots is whether the camera is at the actor's eye level or is higher or lower. A camera that looks down on an actor portrays the character as a victim; a camera that looks up at an actor portrays the character as a dominant or ominous presence. A contemporary director who is particularly good at encouraging identification is Roman Polanski. His point-of-view shot is eye-level, with the camera positioned at the actor's shoulder. The camera hovers there, seeing what the character sees. Both close-ups and point-of-view shots encourage identification. A close-up can be created from an objective camera placement, for example, from the side. The close-up itself encourages emotional involvement and identification, as does subjective camera placement.

Excitation is accomplished through movement within shots, movement of shots, and variation in the length of shots. Pans, tilts, and zooms are used to follow characters moving within shots. Trucking, tracking, dollying, handheld, and Stedicam shots follow the motion; the camera itself moves to record these shots. Moving shots are more exciting when the point of view is subjective; these shots also encourage identification. Finally, using pace and making shots shorter will increase the excitement of a sequence.

Conflict is developed in an action sequence by crosscutting. For example, in a two-character scene, each character attempts to achieve a goal. As this effort is being made, the conflict is presented by crosscutting between the efforts of each character. Crosscutting is a central feature of the action sequence.

Intensification is particularly important as we move toward the conclusion of the scene, the point at which one character achieves his or her goal and the other character fails. Intensification is achieved by varying the length of the shots. Conventionally, it means shortening the shots as the sequence approaches the climax. However, variation—for example, switching between a series of shorter shots and the pattern set earlier—also produces some intensification. Most action sequences use variation. The behavior of the characters is another source of intensification.

Thus, action sequences are characterized by their use of pace, movement, and subjective camera placement and movement. Where necessary, long shots are used to follow the action, but the critical impact in the action sequence is achieved through the use of close-ups and subjective shots that are paced for intensity.

The ride of the Ku Klux Klan in D.W. Griffith's *The Birth of a Nation* (1915) began a tradition of filmmakers creating action set-pieces. Eisenstein followed with the Odessa Steps sequence in *Potemkin* (1925) and later with the baffle on the ice in *Alexander Nevsky* (1938). In the same formal vein, King Vidor created a great action sequence in the mobilization to stop the advance of the railway in *Duel in the Sun* (1946). One of the greatest action sequences of all is the samurai defense of the peasant village in Akira Kurosawa's *The Seven Samurai* (1954).

Particular directors excelled at large-scale action sequences. Cecil B. DeMille made an extravaganza of his action sequences. Notable are his films *The Plainsman* (1936), *Northwest Mounted Police* (1940), and *Unconquered* (1947), although DeMille is most famous for his Biblical films, such as *The Ten Commandments* (1923 and 1956).

Other directors were known for the entertainment quality of their action sequences. Few sequences are more entertaining than the thuggee attack on the village in George Stevens's *Gunga Din* (1939) or as exciting as the robbery in Jules Dassin's *Rififi* (1954).

Although not as critically acclaimed as the aforementioned, there were several other great directors of action films. Henry Hathaway, for example, directed a number of great action sequences in numerous genres, including adventure films (*The Lives of a Bengal Lancer*, 1935), gangster films (*Kiss of Death*, 1947), war films (*The Desert Fox*, 1951), and Western films (*Nevada Smith*, 1966). Another American action director of note is Don Siegel. As Andrew Sarris says about Siegel, "The final car chase in *The Lineup* (1958) and the final shoot-up in *Madigan* (1968) are among the most stunning displays of action montage in the history of American cinema."[1] Since that was written, Siegel has been prolific; the money drop in *Dirty Harry* (1971) should also be added to Sarris's list.

Other directors who have received a good deal of critical attention for their nonaction films have managed to produce some of the most creative action sequences, which have remained in the public memory. The final shoot-out in Fred Zinnemann's *High Noon* (1952),[2] the chariot race in William Wyler's *Ben Hur* (1959), the assassination in the woods in Bernardo Bertolucci's *The Conformist* (1971), and the attack on the train in David Lean's *Lawrence of Arabia* (1962) are among the most notable sequences. Even more surprising are the visual set-pieces by directors such as Joseph L. Mankiewicz, who is best known for his sophisticated melodramas. Consider, for example, the sequence in *Five Fingers* (1952) that shows the attempt to capture a spy,

Aiello (James Mason), who has been discovered stealing information about the Allied invasion of Europe. Equally surprising is Orson Welles's finale to *Touch of Evil* (1958), a film that begins with a 3-minute uncut tracking shot. In the final sequence, Varguez (Charlton Heston) records the sheriff confessing his crime to a colleague. The action takes place on and below a bridge, and it is cut in a remarkably dynamic fashion.

☐ THE CONTEMPORARY CONTEXT

Action has exploded recently in the U.S. film industry. It seems that the more action a film has, the more successful it is. Advances in technology and special effects have played a role here; however, the renewed popularity of action movies has meant the development of a cadre of directors who are the Siegels and Hathaways of their day. Action sequences have become far more important and expensive than they were in the time of Siegel or Hathaway. These directors have become the most successful and the most sought-after in the world, and they come from around the world. From England we have Peter Yates (*Bullitt*, 1968), John Boorman (*Point Blank*, 1967), John Mackenzie (*The Long Good Friday*, 1980), and John Irvin (*The Dogs of War*, 1980). From New Zealand comes Roger Donaldson (*No Way Out*, 1987); from Australia, George Miller (*Mad Max 2*, 1981), Bruce Beresford (*Black Robe*, 1991), Carl Schultz (*The Seventh Sign*, 1988), Phillip Noyce (*Dead Calm*, 1988), and Fred Schepsi (*The Chant of Jimmy Blacksmith*, 1978); from Canada, James Cameron (*Aliens*, 1986) and David Cronenberg (*The Fly*, 1986); and from Holland, Paul Verhoeven (*Robocop*, 1987). These filmmakers, together with John McTiernan (*Die Hard*, 1988) and Steven Spielberg (*Jaws*, 1975), are responsible for the majority of commercial successes in the past two decades. The action sequence and its direction have become the most commerically viable subspecialty in film.

To understand what these filmmakers are doing differently, it's important to state that they are meeting the growing public appetite for action films with all of the technology and editing styles available to them. Some filmmakers move in a realistic direction. For example, John Frankenheimer's extensive use of hand-held camera shots in the Israeli attack on the Beirut terrorist headquarters near the opening of *Black Sunday* (1977) creates a sense of journalistic veracity. The scene could have been shot for the evening news. James Cameron, on the other hand, was not interested at all in credibility in *The Terminator* (1984). The first encounter of the Terminator with Sara Connor and Reese, the man sent from the future to save her, is set in "The Tech Noir Bar." Many are killed by the Terminator (Arnold Schwarzenegger) in his effort to kill Sara (Linda Hamilton). The cartoonish quality of the sequence continues as the Terminator steals a police car to carry on his chase. This action sequence is quite exciting, but its goals are different than Frankenheimer's in *Black Sunday*.

The same polarity is found in two of the greatest car chases ever filmed. In Peter Yates's *Bullitt*, a 12-minute car chase looks real, but the emphasis is on the thrill of the chase. *Bullitt* (Steve McQueen) is followed by two criminals but ends up chasing them. As the chase becomes more dangerous through the streets and highways of San Francisco, the bullets fly and the car crashes add up, leading to a fiery crash. The crispness of the cinematography provides a depth of field that beautifies this sequence, rendering it less real. It reminds us that we are watching a film produced carefully with talented stunt men. It's the choreography of the chase rather than the implications of its outcome (that two men will die) that captivates our attention.

Contrast this with the car chase sequence from William Friedkin's *The French Connection* (1971). A French killer attempts to kill Popeye Doyle (Gene Hackman) in front of his apartment building but instead shoots a woman who walks in front of Doyle at that fateful moment. Doyle runs after the man. When the man eludes him and gets on the subway, Doyle commandeers a civilian's car and follows him below the train track. The killer shoots a security man on the train and forces the train to continue. Doyle follows in the car. The driver of the train has a heart attack. There is another killing, and the train becomes a runaway. It doesn't stop until it crashes into another train. Doyle has followed, crashing, avoiding crashes, but remaining steadfast in pursuit. He stops where the subway train has crashed. He sees the killer and orders him to stop. The man turns to run away, and Doyle shoots and kills him.

This sequence, which runs more than 10 minutes, was filmed in the streets of New York. Just as Frankenheimer chose to use cinema verité techniques, so too did Friedkin. The camera work throughout this sequence is rough and handheld; the cutting is on handheld movement. Together with the violence of the pursuit and the overmodulated sound effects (to simulate unrefined sound, as in cinema verité), the effect of these techniques is violent and realistic. The roughness of the whole sequence contributes to an authenticity that is absent in the *Bullitt* sequence. Again, the goals are different. Both sequences are exciting, but the editing elements that come into play move in two different directions: one toward a technological choreography, the other toward a believable human struggle in which technology is a means rather than an end.

Another issue to be considered is directorial style. Paul Verhoeven has a very aggressive directorial style. He combines the power of technology—the cars, the machines—with a mobile camera that always moves toward the action. As the camera moves, the cutting adds to the dynamism of the scene. The final scene in *Robocop*, the gunfight in the steelworks, features many of the strengths of the chase sequence of *Bullitt*—the crispness and choreography of the action sequence—but added to it is the aggressive camera in search of the visceral elements of the sequence, and Verhoeven managed to find them.

In the final attack in *Mad Max 2*, George Miller also is interested in the technology—the bikes, the trucks, the weapons—but he lingers over the instances of human loss that occur in the sequence. Like Verhoeven, Miller has a roving camera, but where Verhoeven moves in on the action, Miller is more detached. Miller follows action to explain the narrative; Verhoeven uses camera movement to overstate the narrative. Despite a high level of action in the Road Warrior sequence of *Mad Max 2*, the result of Miller's technique is the opportunity to detach and reflect; this opportunity is not available in *Robocop*. Miller loves the technology, but he also seems to be able to generate more empathy for the fate of his characters. Both are exciting sequences, but the personalities of the directors lead us to different emotional responses to their two action sequences.

Another directorial approach is taken by Steven Spielberg. Like Alfred Hitchcock, Spielberg seems to be interested in the filmic possibilities of the action sequence. His 12-minute prologue to *Indiana Jones and the Last Crusade* (1989) is a model of the entertainment possibilities of a chase. The young Indiana Jones has stolen the Cross of Coronada from a group of archeological poachers. They chase him on horseback, by car, and on foot on a moving train. Throughout the sequence until the boy is confronted by the sheriff about the theft, the emphasis is on the chase and the will of Jones to stand up for his belief that artifacts belong in museums, not in the hands of fortune hunters. Spielberg used a moving camera and a genteel cutting style to emphasize the fun in the sequence. The result is an enjoyable sequence that has humor and excitement. This, however, is not always Spielberg's filmic goal.

Spielberg had quite a different goal for the beach-kill sequence early in *Jaws*. Spielberg focused on the anxiety of the sheriff, who sits on the beach fearing that the shark will strike again. His anxiety is not shared, however. Children and adults frolic on the beach. Spielberg crosscut between point-of-view shots of the sheriff and shots of various red herrings: a swim cap in the water, a young woman screaming as a young man lifts her high in the water. When the kill finally comes (the victim is a young boy from the first shot of the sequence), the shock is numbing. The quick cutting and the randomness of the opposite emotions of the beach-goers and the sheriff create a tension that is overwhelming. Point of view and crosscutting create a purely filmic action sequence that is extremely powerful. Spielberg's filmic goal was not the joy of filmmaking, but the power of editing. It's not what he shows, but rather the ordering of the shots—an editing solution (similar to Hitchcock). In a story about primal fear and raw power, Spielberg found a successful filmic solution. That solution is manipulative, but that's what the story required. Similarly, Indiana Jones's story called for excitement and pleasure, emotions that are central to the success of the adventure genre.

We turn now to a detailed analysis that compares the style of action editing in a film made 75 years ago to an action sequence from a film produced 21 years ago.

□ *THE GENERAL*: AN EARLY ACTION SEQUENCE

Buster Keaton's *The General* (1927) is set during the Civil War (Figure 17.1). Johnny Gray (Keaton) is a railroad engineer who attempts to enlist when the war begins. He is refused. His girlfriend, Annabelle (Marion Beck), views the rejection as a result of his cowardice. Most of the story relates to a Union plot to steal Gray's train, which is called "the General," and take it north. Johnny Gray is outraged when the train is stolen. He pursues the Union men to recapture the train. Unbeknownst to Johnny, Annabelle was in one of the cars and has been taken along with the train.

   The action sequence that is described here is the taking of the train and Johnny's pursuit of it into Union territory. This sequence is very lengthy by current standards for an action sequence. At 18 minutes, it is one of the longest action sequences ever produced (Figures 17.2 and 17.3).

Figure 17.1   *The General*, 1927. Still provided by Moving Image and Sound Archives.

Figure 17.2   *The General*, 1927. Still provided by Moving Image and Sound Archives.

The sequence can be brokens down as follows:

1. The Union men steal the train.   1.5 minutes   15 shots

2. Johnny chases the train on foot,   2.0 minutes   22 shots
   using a transom (a hand-cranked
   vehicle that rides along train
   trestles) and a bike.

3. Johnny finds a train to use.   1.0 minute   12 shots
   He thinks it is a troop train, but
   the troop trains are not attached
   to the engine.

4. Johnny finds a wheeled cannon.   4.5 minutes   33 shots
   He uses it against the enemy.

5. The Union men try to stop   3.0 minutes   22 shots
   Johnny's pursuit. They detach a
   caboose, drop firewood, and
   fire up another car.

Figure 17.3   *The General*, 1927. Still provided by Moving Image and Sound Archives.

6. Johnny is desperate to keep his locomotive in pursuit.	3.0 minutes	22 shots
7. Johnny passes into enemy territory. He must abandon the chase.	3.0 minutes	34 shots

What is notable about this sequence is that the shots are set up to clarify the narrative and to detail narrative twists, for example, the shot where the cannon, loaded and detached from Johnny's engine, begins to tip downward and threaten Johnny rather than the enemy. Such narrative twists, which are the source of humor in the scene, require setup time and detailing to make sense. For an action sequence, the shots seem quite careful and long. This pattern is typical of all of the shots in this sequence.

Another characteristic of the sequence is that it proceeds at a leisurely pace by modern standards. This is not entirely due to the age of the film: In Russia, Eisenstein was cutting *Potemkin* at a pace that, by comparison, is rapid by recent editing standards. Pace, although not an active characteristic in Keaton's chase sequence, does pick up in the very last scene of the sequence, which has some crosscutting.

The sequence has many moving shots. In fact, the majority of the shots are moving shots. There is very little that is static in the sequence. There is some use of subjective camera placement, but the majority of moving shots are used to clarify the narrative. The camera is placed so that we see what Keaton felt we need to see to understand the narrative. In this sense, Keaton did not use movement to encourage identification with the protagonist or his goal. The audience's understanding of the goal seems to have been enough.

Finally, the entire sequence proceeds without a single close-up. There are midshots of Johnny's reaction to or his surprise at a turn of events, but there are no intense close-ups to encourage our identification with Johnny or his cause. Emotionalism plays no part in this action sequence.

This 18-minute action sequence proceeds in an exciting exposition of the chase. The articulation of the twists and turns of that chase and of the comic possibilities of the scene seems to override the need to manipulate the audience with pace and intensity. Character (Johnny) and technology (the trains) are the center of the action sequence, and as in the *Bullitt* car chase, we admire it from outside as spectators rather than relate to it from the inside as participants.

□ *RAIDERS OF THE LOST ARK*: A CONTEMPORARY ACTION SEQUENCE

Steven Spielberg and George Lucas directed and produced *Raiders of the Lost Ark* (1981) together. The film exemplifies many remarkable action sequences. The focus here is on the sequence in which Indiana Jones chases and captures the trunk containing the Lost Ark of Canaan.

The film tells the story of adventurous archeologist Indiana Jones and his pursuit of the Ark. He is competing with a French archeologist and his financiers, the pre-war Nazis, who believe that the Ark has supernatural power. Only Indiana Jones and his associates can prevent the Ark from falling into unfriendly hands. The chase occurs in the latter third of the film after the Ark has been excavated from an ancient Egyptian city. The Nazis have the Ark, and Indiana Jones wants to retake it. As the scene opens, he is on foot, and the Ark is on a truck. When asked what he will do to retake it, he responds that he doesn't know and he's making it up as he goes along. This devil-may-care flippancy is key because it alerts the audience that, in keeping with the rest of the film, Jones will find himself in danger but will be inventive in eluding destruction. The fun comes in watching him do so. This is the spirit of the chase sequence (Figure 17.4).

The 7½-minute sequence can be broken down as follows:

1. Mounted on a horse, Indiana   1 minute, 15 seconds   21 shots
   chases the truck.

Figure 17.4   *Raiders of the Lost Ark*, 1981. Courtesy Lucasfilm Ltd.™ and ©
Lucasfilm Ltd. (LFL) 1981. All rights reserved.

2. He captures the truck.	0.45 seconds	31 shots
3. He duels with men on a half-truck and a motorbike.	1 minute, 20 seconds	48 shots
4. The soldiers in the back of the truck attempt to recapture the truck.	1 minute, 5 seconds	38 shots
5. The Nazi commander in the back of the truck attempts to recapture it.	2 minutes	57 shots
6. Indiana escapes from the Nazi command car.	1 minute, 5 seconds	15 shots

Spielberg used long shots to make sure that we understand what is happening in the sequence. For example, in one shot we see Jones catch up to the truck. When Spielberg wanted these shots to provide information, he used both the foreground and background. He positioned the camera in these shots to film both in focus. When he wanted to use a long shot more dynamically, however, he adjusted the depth of field to lose the foreground and the background. An example of such a shot occurs in the opening scene of the chase when Jones is mounted on a horse. The loss of foreground combined with the jump-cutting makes his pursuit on horseback seem faster and more dynamic. For the most part, however, individual scenes are constructed from midshots and close-ups, including cutaways that make a point in the narrative, for example, the German commander giving the truck more gas to go faster in the hopes of crushing Jones between the truck and the command car. Close shots are very important in the creation of this sequence. They are used to enhance narrative clarity but also to intensify the narrative.

Besides the close-ups, the camera position often puts us in the position of Indiana Jones. Not only do we see his reactions to events, but we also see the events unfolding as he sees them. This subjectivity of camera placement gives us no choice but to identify with the character.

Another important element in the sequence is the pace. Shots often last no longer than a few seconds. In general, the pace quickens as we move through the sequence. In the first scene, the average shot is just under 4 seconds. In the last scene, the average shot is just under 5 seconds. In between, however, the pace varies between just under 2 seconds to just over 1 second. In the second scene, when Jones has reached the truck and is struggling to capture it, the scene has 31 shots in 45 seconds. In the next scene, his struggle with the half-truck and the motorbike, the pace is maintained with 48 shots in 80 seconds. This pace eases only slightly as the soldiers who have been guarding the Ark try to take the truck from Jones. Here, there are 38 shots in 65 seconds. The greatest personal threat to Jones occurs when he is literally thrown out of the truck by the German commander. This more personal combat takes longer and is more complex. The scene has 57 shots in 2 minutes, and it is the climax of the sequence. Once Jones's personal safety is no longer at risk, the pace shifts into a more relaxed final scene. Pace plays a very critical role in the effectiveness of this action sequence.

In the entire sequence, Spielberg used 210 shots in $7\frac{1}{2}$ minutes. He included all of the elements necessary to get us to identify with Indiana Jones, to understand his conflict, and to struggle with him for the resolution of that conflict. Spielberg succeeded with this sequence in terms of entertainment and identification. It represents the exciting possibilities of the action sequence.

What can be learned from comparing the Keaton sequence and the Spielberg sequence? At every point of both action sequences, the filmmaker's goal is narrative clarity. The audience must know where they are in the story. Confusion does not complement excitement. Good directors know how the action sequence helps the story and positions the audience. Is the sequence intended for entertainment, as both of these sequences are, or is it meant solely for identification, like Frankenheimer's action sequences in *Black Sunday* and the assassination sequence that ends *The Manchurian Candidate*? The filmmaker's goal is critical.

Another element that seems similar in both sequences is the role of moving vehicles. Both filmmakers were fascinated with these symbols of technology and how they act as both barriers and facilitators for humans. Both filmmakers demonstrated a positive attitude about technology—unlike

Stanley Kubrick in *Dr. Strangelove* (1964) and *2001: A Space Odyssey* (1968)—and their approach to the trains and trucks is rather joyful. This attitude infuses both sequences.

Perhaps the greatest differences between the two approaches are in how manipulative the filmmaker wanted to be in making the action sequence more exciting and the identification more important. Spielberg clearly valued pace, the close-up, and the importance of subjective camera placement to a far greater degree than did Keaton. This is the recent pattern for action sequences: to use all of the elements of film to make them as exciting as possible. The interesting question is not so much why Spielberg needed to resort to these manipulative techniques, but rather why Keaton didn't feel the same way.

Both sequences are very exciting despite the 50 or so years between the two productions, but their approaches differ considerably. It is here that the artistic personality of the director comes into play. It also suggests that the modern conventions of the action sequence, albeit strongly skewed in the direction of Spielberg's approach, may be wider than we thought.

□ NOTES/REFERENCES

1. Andrew Sarris, *The American Cinema* (Chicago: University of Chicago Press, 1968), 137.
2. Conjecture and reputation have credited the success of that film to editor Elmo Williams, although the assassination attempt on Charles De Gaulle in Zinnemana's *The Day of the Jackal* (1973) is as great a sequence.

18

Dialogue

■

The dialogue sequence is one of the least imaginatively treated types of sequences, although this has started to change. The editor must understand what is most important in a dialogue sequence. Generally, a director can opt to film a dialogue sequence in a two-shot or in a series of midshots from over the shoulder of each of the participants. Most dialogues proceed as two-character dialogues; occasionally, more than two characters interact in a dialogue sequence. Margo's party for Biull in *All About Eve* (1950) is a good example of the latter type of dialogue sequence.

The choices, then, are not many. The director might include an establishing shot to set up the sequence or might provide close-ups of the key lines of dialogue for emphasis. Many directors do not include close-ups because if the script is well written, the lines and performances can carry themselves. It's quite another matter if the dialogue is poor. In this case, the sequence will need all the help the director and the editor can provide.

Additional issues for the editor include whether to use more close shots than medium shots and whether to use an objective shot watching a conversation rather than a subjective shot, that is, an over-the-shoulder shot watching the speaker. Should the editor use the reverse shot of the listener? Is variety between listener and speaker possible and advisable? Is a crossover from speaker to listener and then back possible and advisable? These are the types of questions that the editor faces when cutting a dialogue sequence.

The meaning of the dialogue to the story as a whole helps the editor make those decisions. A piece of dialogue that is important for advancing the plot requires a close-up or some shift in the pattern of shots to alert us that what we are hearing is more important than what we've heard earlier in the sequence.

A piece of dialogue that reveals key information about a character calls for a similar strategy. The editor must decide whether the piece of character information or plot information could be conveyed visually. If the point of the dialogue cannot be conveyed visually, editing strategies are critical. If the dialogue can be reinforced visually, editing strategies become unnecessary.

If the dialogue is used to provide comic relief or to mask character intentions, other editing strategies are required. In this case, the reaction of the listener may be more important than watching what is being said.

The editor and the director must always be in accord about the meaning of the sequence, the subtext, or any other interpretation of the dialogue, and they must be able to break down the dialogue sequence in the filming and reconstitute it in the editing to achieve that meaning. Dialogue is not always used in the most obvious manner. The relationship between dialogue and the visualization of the dialogue has broadened and become more interesting.

□ DIALOGUE AND PLOT

The direction of a dialogue sequence is influenced by the genre, and certain genres (the melodrama, for example) tend to be more sedentary and dependent on dialogue than others. The action-adventure genre, which is less reliant on dialogue, offers an example of more fluid editing.

In *The Terminator* (1984), James Cameron used an interesting dialogue sequence to advance the plot. Reese and Sara Connor are being chased by the Terminator. Their car weaves and crashes throughout this sequence. They are under constant threat. Cameron intercut between the excitement of the car chase and Reese and Sara talking to one another. This dialogue fills in a great deal of the plot. Reese told Sara earlier that he and the Terminator are from the future. During this sequence, he describes John Connor, who is leading the fight against the robots and technocrats who dominate the future. Sara discovers that she will become John Connor's mother and that the Terminator was sent back in time to kill her before she could have the child. If she dies, the future will change, Reese explains. This is why it's critical that he protect her.

The dialogue itself is presented as we would expect, with over-the-shoulder shots mostly of Sara as she listens and reacts, but also of Reese, who will be John Connor's father. Because the shots are in the car, they are in the midshot to close-up range. Subjective camera placement is the pattern.

The dialogue here is important, and there is a lot of it. By intercutting with the chase, Cameron masked the amount of dialogue and conformed to the conventions of the genre: Don't slow down the action with conversation.[1] The dialogue is presented in a classic manner, but because it's crosscut with its context, the chase helps mask it.

A more direct approach to the dialogue sequence is exemplified by Woody Allen in the climactic scene toward the end of *Manhattan* (1979). In this contemporary story of New York relationships, the main character, Ike (Allen), has committed to a relationship with Mary (Diane Keaton), a writer close to his age. He has put behind him relationships with 17-year-old Tracy (Mariel Hemingway) and his two ex-wives. Mary, who was formerly the mistress of Ike's closest friend, Yale (Michael Murphy), has decided at Yale's prompting to take up with him again. His 12-year marriage does not seem to be an impediment. In this dialogue sequence, Ike confronts Yale and accuses him of immaturity and self-indulgence: "But you—but you're too easy on yourself, don't you see that? You know-.-.-.-that's your problem, that's your whole problem. You rationalize everything. You're not honest with yourself. You talk about-.-.-.-you wanna write a book, but, in the end, you'd rather buy the Porsche, you know, or you cheat a little bit on Emily, and you play around with the truth a little with me, and the next thing you know, you're in front of a Senate committee and you're naming names! You're informing on your friends!"

This dialogue sequence is in many ways the climax of the film because the main character has finally come to realize that relationships that proceed without a sense of morality and mutual respect are doomed and transitory and that the maturity that leads to healthy relationships is not related to age.

The dialogue sequence begins with three camera setups and a long establishing shot of the location where the conversation takes place. The two characters approach a blackboard, which has two skeletons hanging in front of it. The long establishing shot (after the two enter the classroom) sets up the sequence. After the establishing shot, the film moves into two tight midshots, one of Yale, the other of Ike. The frame with Ike includes the head of one of the skeletons so that the shot presents as a two-shot with Ike and the skeleton. For the balance of the dialogue sequence, the two midshots of Yale and Ike are intercut. The sequence ends with Ike leaving the frame so that all we see is the skeleton. Ike's last line refers to the skeleton; he says that when he looks like the skeleton, when he thins out, he wants to be sure "I'm well thought of."

This sequence, like the dialogue sequence in *The Terminator*, advances the plot, but its presentation is much more direct. It is not presented in an overly emotional manner. The direction makes it clear that we must listen to the dialogue and consider what is being said. The presence of the skeleton adds a visual dimension that adds irony to the dialogue. This dialogue sequence exemplifies the simplicity that allows the dialogue to be heard without distraction.

□ DIALOGUE AND CHARACTER

Black Sunday (1977), directed by John Frankenheimer, is the story of a terrorist plot to explode a bomb over the Super Bowl. The plot is uncovered by an Israeli raid in Beirut, and the story that unfolds contrasts the terrorists' attempts to carry out the attack and the FBI's efforts to prevent it. For the authorities, this means finding out how the attack will be conducted and who will carry it out. Dalia (Marthe Keller) and Michael (Bruce Dern) are the primary terrorists. She is a Palestinian, and he is an American, a pilot of the Goodyear blimp used at the Super Bowl. Michael is very unstable, a characteristic illustrated through a dialogue sequence.

Dalia has returned to Los Angeles from abroad. She has arranged for the explosives necessary for the attack. Michael is very distressed because she is 3 days late. He worries that something is wrong. He is very angry and threatens her with a rifle. She tries to pacify him and manages to calm him down.

This scene is filmed in mid- to close shots. The shots are primarily hand-held, and the camera always has some degree of movement, even in still shots. There are moving shots as well.

Within this highly fragmented sequence, Dalia enters a dark room. When she turns on the light, she is confronted by Michael, who is aiming a rifle at her. The rapid series of handheld shots underscores the nervousness of the scene and principally Michael's instability. She moves, he moves, the camera moves. They do things: Dalia unpacks a small statue that holds explosives, Michael examines the statue, she undresses, he puts down the rifle. Throughout the scene, they are speaking, he belligerently and she in a soothing way to assure him that all is well.

The sequence, which is highly fragmented with lots of movement, seems realistic with its heightened sense of danger. The movement supports the goal of establishing Michael's instability, which is a prime quality in his role as terrorist. The goal of the sequence comes across clearly, as does a sense of urgency and realism.

A very different type of sequence establishes character but does not provide as clear a sense of the dialogue's role in its establishment. In Robert Altman's *McCabe and Mrs. Miller* (1971), we are introduced to gambler John McCabe (Warren Beatty) as he enters the small mining town of Presbyterian Church. He takes off his coat and searches for the bar. He is dressed differently than the others in the bar. In the first scene in the bar, there is a dialogue exchange. The dialogue is neither textured nor localized; it's about the price of liquor and the price of playing a card game. The goal of the scene is to position McCabe among the town's occupants as a negotiator and as something of an entrepreneur. The scene establishes this.

The scene proceeds in a highly fragmented fashion, with only a short establishing shot. Many close-ups feature McCabe and the miners; McCabe is seen as something of a dandy, and the miners appear dirty, wild-eyed, and something less than civilized. The scene does establish McCabe's importance with a number of close-ups, but the dialogue itself is not direct enough to characterize him. The intensity of the scene comes from the visual elaboration of his appearance among the miners of Presbyterian Church.

Another element that pushes us to the visual in this scene is the use of overlapping dialogue. Many characters speak simultaneously, and we are aware of the discreteness of their conversations, but as their comments bleed into those of others, the effect is to undermine the dialogue. The scene moves dialogue from the informational status it usually occupies to the category of noise. Language becomes a sound effect. When we do hear the dialogue, it is the speaker who is important rather than what is being said.

Like the dialogue sequence in *Black Sunday*, we come away from this sequence with a definite sense of McCabe's character. However, unlike the scene in *Black Sunday*, the meaning of the dialogue becomes trivialized and expendable.

□ MULTIPURPOSE DIALOGUE

Mike Nichols was very creative about the editing of his dialogue sequences in *The Graduate* (1967). In the first dialogue sequence, Benjamin (Dustin Hoffman) confesses to his father that he is worried about his future. The entire scene is presented in a single midshot of Benjamin. When the father joins the conversation, he enters the frame and sits out of focus in the foreground.

More typical is the famous seduction scene in which Mrs. Robinson (Anne Bancroft) proposes an affair to Benjamin. This scene fits into the overall story about Benjamin Braddock, a college graduate who is trying to develop a set of values that make sense to him. He rejects the materialistic values of his family and their peers, but he doesn't know what should replace them. In his confusion, he becomes involved in an affair with the wife of his father's partner. He later develops a relationship with her daughter. His behavior suggests his confusion and his groping toward the future. His affair with Mrs. Robinson is the first relationship in the film that suggests his state of confusion.

The seduction scene can be broken down into three parts, all of which depend on dialogue. In the first, Mrs. Robinson invites Benjamin, who has driven her home, inside for a drink. She offers him a drink, plays some music, and sits with her legs apart in a provocative position. Benjamin asks if she is trying to seduce him, but she denies it.

In the second part, Mrs. Robinson asks him up to her daughter's bedroom, offering to show him a portrait of her. She begins to undress and throws her watch and earrings on the bed. She asks him to unzip her dress, and her intentions are unmistakable. He unzips her dress but then leaves the room and goes downstairs.

In the third part of the sequence, Mrs. Robinson speaks to him from the bathroom upstairs. She asks that he bring her purse. He does, but he refuses to take it into the bathroom. She asks that he take her purse into Elaine's bedroom, where she joins him, naked. He is shocked and wants to leave. She tells him that she will be available to him whenever he wishes. Only the arrival of her husband ends the sequence with Benjamin's virtue unsullied.

Dialogue can be used to advance the plot, to reveal a character's nature, or to provide comic relief. In this sequence, dialogue is used for each of these purposes. The advancement of the plot is related to Mrs. Robinson's proposal of an illicit affair, which will take Benjamin further down a particular path. In terms of characterization, the sequence illustrates how manipulative Mrs. Robinson is and how naive Benjamin can be. His youth and inexperience are such that he can be manipulated by others. As to the humor, the sequence abounds in surprises. When Mrs. Robinson confesses that she is neurotic, Benjamin responds, "Oh, my God!" as though she had confessed to a capital crime. Mrs. Robinson's lying—the dissonance between what she says and does—is also a continuing source of humor.

The sequence, then, has many purposes. How was it edited? Nichols and his editor, Sam O'Steen, cut the film subjectively. The foreground–background relationship was used to highlight power relationships as well as Benjamin's subjective perspective. Benjamin appears in the foreground when Mrs. Robinson speaks from the background, or he is in the background speaking when she is in the foreground. The famous image of Mrs. Robinson's uplifted leg in the foreground with Benjamin in the background provides a good example of how the dialogue is presented. This foreground–background relationship is maintained throughout the different phases of this sequence. It is most clearly manifested in the final sequence in which the naked Mrs. Robinson appears in the foreground and there is an intense close-up of Benjamin in the background. In this scene, the focus is on Benjamin throughout, with quick intercutting of her breasts or belly almost presented as flash frames. This quick cutting, which implies the wish to see and the wish to look away, is only part of the sequence in which pace plays an important role. In the balance of the sequence, the rule is subjectivity and the foreground–background interplay of reverse angle shots to highlight the dialogue and the speaker.

The sequence exhibits complex goals for the dialogue and yet manages to have sufficient visual variety to be stimulating. Nichols did use distinct close-ups of Mrs. Robinson and Benjamin at one point, but the dialogue itself doesn't warrant them. The close-ups seem to be offered as variety in a lengthy sequence that relies on subjective foreground–background shots.

□ *TROUBLE IN PARADISE*: AN EARLY DIALOGUE SEQUENCE

As stated earlier, the very first dialogue sequences were visually structured to facilitate the actual recording of the sound. Consequently, the mid- to long shot was used to record entire dialogue sequences.

As the technology developed, more options complemented the midshot approach to the dialogue sequence. But as important as the technology proved to be, the creative options developed by directors were equally effective in broadening the editing repertoire of the dialogue sequence.

By examining the creative style of an early dialogue sequence and following it with the examination of a contemporary dialogue sequence, the reader gains perspective on the developmental nature of editing styles. The reader can also appreciate how much those changes have contributed to the spectrum of current editing styles.

Trouble in Paradise (1932) was written by Samson Raphaelson and Grover Jones and directed by Ernst Lubitsch. Lubitsch's direction of the dialogue sequences in *Trouble in Paradise* represents an economy of shots unprecedented in film with the possible exception of Luis Buñuel's work (Figure 18.1).

When he wished, Lubitsch could be very dynamic in his editing of a dialogue scene. For example, toward the end of the film, two of the three main characters are committing themselves to one another. Madame Colette (Kay Francis) speaks. She has been trying to seduce her secretary, Gaston (Herbert Marshall), and this is her moment of triumph. She doesn't realize that he is a thief whose interest, thus far, has been her money. The two embrace, and she says they will have weeks, months, and years to be together. Each word—weeks, months, years—has a different accompanying visual. The first is of the two embracing, as seen in a mirror in the bedroom. The second shows the two of them in midshot embracing. The third shot is of their shadows cast across her bed as they embrace. Not only is the sequence dynamic visually, it is also suggestive of what is to come.

Figure 18.1 *Trouble in Paradise*, 1932. Copyright © by Universal Studios, Inc. Courtesy of MCA Publishing Rights, a Division of MCA Inc. Still provided by British Film Institute.

Lubitsch usually did not take quite as dynamic an approach. He tended to be more indirect, always highlighting through the editing the secondary meaning or subtext of the dialogue. An excellent example is the second scene in the film, which follows a robbery. It opens on Gaston, posing as a baron, instructing a waiter about the food and the champagne and about how little he wants to see the waiter. The anticipation is crosscut with a scene that reveals that a robbery has taken place. The baron's guest, Lili (Miriam Hopkins), arrives. She seems to be a very rich countess who is spending time in Venice, but she is not what she appears to be. We realize this when she receives a call and pretends that it's an invitation to a party, but the cutaway shows that it is her poor roommate.

During this sequence, which appears to be a romantic interlude between the baron and Lili, there is a lengthy cutaway to the victim of the robbery (Edward Everett Horton) as he is being interviewed by the police. He provides some detail about the thief, a charming man who pretended to be a doctor.

When the film cuts back to the baron's suite, the relationship has progressed. The two are eating dinner, and the talk seems to be less about gossip and more reflective of the baron's unfolding romantic agenda for the evening. The dialogue sequence is presented as a mid-two-shot with both parties seated. During the meal, Lili tells the baron that she knows he is not who he appears to be: He is a thief who stole from the guests in suites 203, 205, 207, and 209. The baron is calm and notes that he knows that she knows because she stole the wallet he had stolen from the guest.

A short sequence of shots follows as the baron locks the door, closes the curtains, and approaches Lili in a menacing fashion. He raises her from her seat and shakes her. A close-up of the floor shows the wallet that falls from her dress.

Seated again in midshot, but now in a different tone, they profess their affection for one another and describe other items they have stolen from one another: a brooch, a watch, a garter belt. He introduces himself as Gaston, revealing his true identity, and now they really do seem to be in love. They have shed their facades and discovered two like-minded thieves. A series of silent shots follow that suggests the consummation of the relationship and the consolidation of a partnership.

This sequence used crosscutting to suggest another meaning to what was said through the dialogue. Where possible, Lubitsch also used short visual sequences to build up dramatic tension in the scene, but for the most part, he relied on the midshot to cover the sequence. In the entire 15-minute sequence, there are no more than four or five close-ups.

Later in the film, Lubitsch shed his reliance on crosscutting to suggest the subtext of a dialogue sequence. It's useful to illustrate how he undermined the dialogue in this sequence to get to the subtext.

Gaston and Lili are now a team. They have stolen a diamond-studded handbag from a rich widow, Mme. Colette. When they read in the paper that she is offering a reward of 20,000 francs for the bag, Gaston decides to return it. Madame Colette is a young romantic widow who is pursued by older, more serious suitors who are not to her taste. When she meets Gaston as he comes to return the bag, she is clearly charmed by him.

In the scene that follows, Lubitsch allowed the performances and the consistent use of a two-shot of the characters to communicate all of the nuances of meaning. In the scene, Mme. Colette is taken with Gaston, but he must convince her (1) that he is a member of her class and (2) that his intentions are honorable. The two talk about the contents of her purse; Gaston criticizes one of her suitors as well as her make-up. She seems to appreciate his interest, and when she is embarrassed about giving him the reward, he assures her that she needn't be: As a member of the nouveau poor, he needs the money.

He follows her up the stairs, where she looks for her checkbook. In this scene, she demonstrates her reliance on others. She can't find her check-book, and she alludes to the ineptitude of the secretary she had to fire. While she looks for the checkbook, Gaston looks for the safe. It is in the secretary desk in the bedroom. Although he speaks of period furniture, he is obviously scouting a new location for robbery.

As she opens the safe, Lubitsch cuts to a close-up of Gaston's fingers as they mimic the turns of the dial on the safe. Once she gets the safe open, he scolds her for keeping only 100,000 francs in the safe. She is indifferent to his criticism, and the following dialogue closes the scene. The two charac-ters are seated on a chair. The midshot is tight on the two of them.

GASTON (sternly, an uncle): Madame Colette, I think you deserve a scolding. First you lose your bag—
COLETTE (gaily): Then I mislay my checkbook—
GASTON: Then you use the wrong lipstick—
COLETTE (almost laughing): And how I handle my money!
GASTON: It's disgraceful!
COLETTE (with a flirtatious look): Tell me, M. Laval, what else is wrong?
GASTON Everything! Madame Colette, if I were your father—(with a smile) which, fortunately, I am not—
COLETTE (coquettish): Yes?
GASTON: And you made any attempt to handle your own business affairs, I would give you a good spanking—in a good business way, of course.
COLETTE (complete change of expression; businesslike): What would you do if you were my secretary?
GASTON: The same thing.
COLETTE: You're hired!
FADE OUT

This elaborate scene, which reveals the character of Mme. Colette and Gaston as well as advances the plot, has a very specific subtext: the verbal seduction of Gaston by Mme. Colette and of Mme. Colette by Gaston. The dialogue contributes to the progress of this new relationship. Consequently, by focusing on a midshot of the two characters together, first standing and then sitting, Lubitsch directed for subtext regardless of the actual lines of dialogue. Because of his direction of the actors in this sequence, he relied less on editing than he had to in the Gaston–Lili seduction sequence.

Both approaches are options for the editor. The earlier sequence relied more on editing; the second sequence relied more on performance and direction.

□ *CHINATOWN*: A CONTEMPORARY DIALOGUE SEQUENCE

The dialogue sequences in *Chinatown* (1974) differ considerably from those in *Trouble in Paradise*. Although the sequences described here are also about seduction, the approach that director Roman Polanski took in the dialogue scenes is more aggressive than that of Ernst Lubitsch. Although the differences are, in part, related to the different genres or to preferences of the directors, contemporary conventions about the dialogue sequence also suggest a more assertive, less subtle approach to its editing.

Robert Towne's script for *Chinatown* is film noir, with all of its highly stylized implications, whereas the Raphaelson/Jones script for *Trouble in Paradise* is a romantic comedy closely aligned with a theatrical comedy of manners. Lubitsch's direction was subtle and slightly distant, but Polanski's direction verged on the claustrophobic. To be more specific, Lubitsch set up shots so that the action takes place in front of the camera, an objective position. He rarely resorted to subjective camera placement. Lubitsch also relied on the midshot to long shot for his sequences. Polanski, on the other hand, favored subjective camera placement. When Gittes (Jack Nicholson) speaks, the camera sees what he sees. Polanski crowded the camera up against Gittes shoulder at his eye level, so that there would be no mistake about the point of view. Polanski used the foreground–background relationship to set the dialogue sequence in context. He also favored the close-up over the midshot. The result is a dialogue sequence of intense emotion and pointed perspective.

The following sequence occurs about an hour into the film. Evelyn Mullwray (Faye Dunaway) has arrived at the office of private investigator Jake Gittes. She wants to hire him. Earlier in the film, another woman claiming to be Evelyn Mullwray had hired Gittes to watch her husband, whom she suspected of infidelity. The husband was then killed.

The first part of the scene presents Gittes pouring himself a drink with his back to Evelyn or reading his phone messages while speaking to her. She, on the other hand, is presented entirely in close-up. She wants to hire Gittes to find out why her husband was killed. He suggests that it was for money; when he says this, we see him in midshot reading his phone messages.

When she offers him a substantial sum of money, he looks up and begins to talk about her background, about her marriage to Hollis Mullwray, who was considerably older, and about the fact that Mullwray was her father's former partner. When Gittes mentions her father's name, Noah Cross (John Huston), the shot shifts to a close-up of her reaction. The camera holds on her while Gittes mentions her father's name, then the film cuts to a close-up as she fumbles with her handbag to remove a cigarette holder and lighter. There is a close-up of Gittes as he says, "Then you married your father's business partner." A quick series of close-ups follows. Gittes refers to Evelyn's smoking two cigarettes simultaneously, and this part of the sequence suggests how nervous she is about the topic of her father. The visual holds on a close-up of Evelyn while Gittes asks her about the falling out between her husband and her father. The secretary enters with a service contract for Evelyn to sign. The conversation continues over a midshot of Gittes looking over and signing the contract. When he offers Evelyn the contract, she enters the foreground of the shot while Gittes remains in midshot in the background.

By relying on close-ups of Evelyn as often as he did, Polanski suggested the importance of her truthfulness in the scene. She is closely scrutinized by the camera for clues as to whether she is telling the truth or not. Polanski also supported this search for clues by focusing on Evelyn while Gittes speaks. At the end of the scene, the camera is focused on Gittes and the legal dimension of their relationship: the service contract. By editing this sequence as he did, Polanksi gave the meeting a subjective character and intensity that the dialogue itself does not have. Like Lubitsch, he has tried to reveal the subtext through the editing of the sequence.

Later in the film, when the relationship between Gittes and Evelyn has taken a more personal turn, Polanski uses a different approach. In one scene, Gittes is under the impression that Evelyn is holding against her will a young woman whom he believes was Hollis Mullwray's mistress. In fact, the young woman is Evelyn's daughter. The scene is one of confrontation between Evelyn and Gittes (Figure 18.2).

Polanski used a moving camera here. The camera follows Gittes as he enters the house. It follows him as he telephones the police about the whereabouts of the girl. The camera continues to move until Gittes sits down. In this first phase of the scene, we see Evelyn in tight midshot in the background with Gittes crowded into the foreground. Their relationship is visually reinforced. They speak strictly about the whereabouts of the girl. Once Gittes calls the police and takes a seat, the conversation shifts to the identity of the killer.

This portion of the dialogue sequence begins with Gittes seated in the background and Evelyn in the foreground. Once he makes his accusation, he stands, and close-ups of Gittes and Evelyn are intercut. He accuses her of accidentally killing her husband. She denies it. The dramatic intensity is

Figure 18.2 *Chinatown*, 1974. Courtesy of Paramount Pictures. Copyright © 1974 by Paramount Pictures. All Rights Reserved.

matched by the cutting of close-up to close-up. Gittes shakes her, and she denies the charges.

Gittes now shifts the conversation to the identity of the girl she claimed was her sister. The close-ups continue. Evelyn states that the girl is her daughter. Gittes slaps her. The film cuts to a tight two-shot with Gittes in the foreground and Evelyn in the background. Now, in a single shot within this frame, she claims that the girl is her sister and her daughter. She makes this statement again, and again Gittes slaps her. The camera moves as Gittes pushes her down. The entrance of her servant works as a cutaway to break the tension. She sends him away, and the film cuts to a close-up of Evelyn, who explains that her father was the father of her daughter, Catherine. A reaction close-up of Gittes allows the audience to see his emotional shift from anger to pity for Evelyn. Now, the close-ups are principally of Evelyn while she explains about her marriage and Catherine's birth.

Gittes agrees to let Evelyn go. She will go to her servant's home. As she begins to walk around, she tells Gittes that the glasses he found were not her husband's. She couldn't have been the killer. The sequence shifts to a close-up of Gittes and then of the glasses. She returns with Catherine, introduces her, and gives Gittes her servant's address. She asks if he knows where it is. The camera moves in on Gittes as he says it is located in Chinatown.

The sequence ends with Gittes in the foreground dropping the window blind with Evelyn and Catherine in the background as they prepare to drive off.

This sequence is presented in a much more intense manner than the first sequence described. The subjectivity, the moving camera, and the abundance of close-ups and cutting all support the notion of a scene of great dramatic importance. The editing is very dynamic, and yet everything we learn is revealed through the dialogue. The scene exemplifies the dynamic possibilities where plot is revealed. It is, however, a scene that has tremendous emotional impact, principally because of the editing of the sequence. It offers a very different editing model from the seduction scene between Mme. Colette and Gaston in *Trouble in Paradise*. The direction is far more aggressive and the editing is less subtle. It also illustrates the more aggressive approach currently being taken to the dialogue sequence.

□ NOTE/REFERENCE

1. I am indebted to my colleague, Paul Lucey from the University of Southern California, for drawing this example to my attention. He calls this "torquing the dialogue," an apt mechanical image appropriate to the location of the dialogue and to what the chase does to it as the intercutting proceeds.

19

Comedy

■

When examining the editing of a comedy sequence, it is critical to distinguish the role of the editor from the roles of the writer and the director. The burden of creative responsibility for the success of verbal humor, whether a joke, a punch line, or an extended witty repartee, lies with the writer for the comic inventiveness of the lines and the director and actor for eliciting the comic potential from those lines. The editor may cut to a close shot for the punch line, but the editor's role in verbal humor is somewhat limited.

With regard to visual humor, the editor certainly has more scope.[1] Indeed, together with the writer, director, and actors, the editor plays a critical role.

It is important to understand that humor is a broad term. Unless we look at the various types of comedy, we may fall into the trap of overgeneralization.

□ CHARACTER COMEDY

Character comedy is the type of comedy associated with Chaplin, Keaton, Lloyd, and Langdon in the silent period, and with the Marx Brothers, W. C. Fields, Mae West, Martin and Lewis, Laurel and Hardy, Abbott and Costello, and Woody Allen in the sound period. Abroad, these ranks are joined by the great comedians Jacques Tati, Pierre Etaix, Peter Sellers, and John Cleese.

The roles of these character comics were associated with the particular personae that they cultivated, which often did not change throughout their career. A character role is somewhat different from a great comic performance by a dramatic performer—for example, Michael Caine in *Alfie* (1966)—in the sense that this screen persona provides a different relationship with the audience. It allows Woody Allen to address and to confess to the screen audience in *Annie Hall* (1977); it allows Chaplin's Tramp to be abused by a lunch machine in *Modern Times* (1936); it allows Groucho Marx to indulge in non sequiturs and puns that have nothing to do with the screen story in *Duck Soup* (1934). The audience has certain expectations from a comic character, and it is the job of the editor to make sure that the audience isn't disappointed.

□ SITUATION COMEDY

The most common (on television and in film) is the situation comedy. This type of comedy tends to be realistic and depends on the characters. As a result, it is generally verbal with a minimum of pratfalls. The editing centers on timing to accentuate performance; the editor's role with situation comedy is more limited than with other types of comedy sequences.

□ SATIRE

A third category of comedy is satire. Here, because anything goes, the scope of the editor is considerable. Whether we refer to the dynamic opening of Paddy Chayefsky's *The Hospital* (1971) or Terry Southern and Stanley Kubrick's *Dr. Strongelove* (1964), which ranged from absurdist fantasy to cinema verité, the range for the editor of satirical sequences is challenging and creative.

□ FARCE

The editor is also very important in farce, such as Blake Edwards's *The Pink Panther* (1964), and in parody, such as Sergio Leone's *The Good, the Bad, and the Ugly* (1967). In *The Pink Panther*, for example, the quick cut to Robert Wagner sneaking out of Inspector Clouseau's bedroom, having hidden in the shower, is instructive. Earlier, Clouseau had turned on the shower without noticing its occupant. When the wet Wagner sneaks from the room, his ski sweater, which, of course, is now wet, has stretched to his toes. Logically, such an outcome is impossible, but in farce, such absurdity is expected.

□ EDITING CONCERNS

Beyond understanding the characteristics of the genre he is working with, the editor must focus on the target of the humor. Is it aimed by a character at him- or herself, or does the humor occur at the expense of another? Screen comedy has a long tradition of comic characters who are the target of the humor. Beyond these performers, the target of the humor must be highlighted by the editor.

If the target is the comic performer, what aspect of the character is the source of the comedy? It was the broad issue of the character's sexual identity in Howard Hawks's *Bringing Up Baby* (1938). The scene in which Cary Grant throws a tantrum wearing a woman's housecoat is comic. What the editor had to highlight in the scene was not the character's tantrum, but rather his costume. In Sydney Pollack's *Tootsie* (1982), the source of the humor is the confusion over the sexual identity of Michael (Dustin Hoffman). We know that he is a man pretending to be a woman, but others assume that he is a woman. The issue of mistaken identity blurs for Michael when he begins to act like a woman rather than a man. Here, the editor had to keep the narrative intention in mind and cut to surprise the audience just as Michael surprises himself.

Comedy comes from surprise, but the degree of comedy comes from the depth of the target of the humor. If the target is as shallow as a humorous name—for example, in Richard Lester's *A Funny Thing Happened on the Way to the Forum* (1966), two characters are named Erronius and Hysterium—the film may elicit a smile of amusement. To develop a more powerful comic response, however, the very nature of the character must be the source of the humor. Jack Benny's vanity in Lubitsch's *To Be or Not to Be* (1942), Nicolas Cage's sibling rivalry and the anger it engenders in Norman Jewison's *Moonstruck* (1987), and Tom Hank's immaturity and anger in David Seltzer's *Punchline* (1989) are all deep and continuous sources of comedy arising from the character.

When comedy occurs at the expense of others, the degree of humor bears a relationship to the degree of cruelty, but only to an extent. If the character dies from slipping on a banana peel, the humor is lost. The degree of humiliation and pain is the variable. Too much or too little will not help the comic situation. This is why so many directors and editors speak about the difficulty of comedy. Many claim that it is the most difficult type of film to direct and to edit.

Examples of this type of humor range from the physical abuse of the Three Stooges by one another to the accidental killing of three little dogs in *A Fish Called Wanda* (1988). This type of humor can be present in a very extreme fashion, such as in the necessity of Giancarlo Giannini's character in *Seven Beauties* (1976) to perform sexually with the German camp commandant. Failure will mean death. This painful moment is excruciatingly funny, and the director and editor have wisely focused on the inequity, physical and political, in the relationship of the momentary lovers. The reversal of the conventions of gender roles is continually reinforced by images of her large form and his miniature one. The editing supports this perception of the power relationship and exploits his victimization.

Equally painful and humorous is the situation of the two principal characters in Ethan and Joel Coen's *Raising Arizona* (1987). The husband and wife are childless, and to solve their dilemma, they become kidnappers and target a millionaire with quintuplets. The abduction of one of the children is a comic scene in which the editor and director reverse the audience's perception of who the victim is. The kidnapper is presented as the victim, and the child is presented as the aggressor. He moves about freely, eluding the kidnapper, and the implication is that his movement will alert his parents.

Whether the source of the comedy is role reversal, mistaken identity, or the struggle of human and machine, the issue of pace is critical. When Albert

Brooks begins to sweat as he reads the news in *Broadcast News* (1987), the only way to communicate the degree of his anxiety is to keep cutting back to how much he is sweating. The logical conclusion is that his clothes will become wringing wet, and of course, this is exactly what happens. Pace alerts us to the build in the comedy sequence. What is interesting about comedy is that the twists and turns require build or else the comedy is lost. Exaggeration plays a role, but it is pace that is critical to the sequence.

Consider the classic scene in *Modern Times* in which Chaplin's character is being driven mad by the pace of the assembly line. His job is to tighten two bolts. Once he has gone over the edge, he begins chasing anything with two buttons, particularly women. The sequence builds to a fever pitch, reflecting the character's frenzied state.

Pace is so important in comedy that the masterful director of comedy, Frank Capra, used a metronome on the set and paced it faster than normal for the comedy sequences so that his actors would read the dialogue faster than normal.[2] He believed that this fast tempo was critical to comedy. Attention to pace within shots is as important to the editing of comic sequences as is pace between shots.

If we were to deconstruct what the editor needs to edit a comedy sequence, we would have to begin with the editor's knowledge. The editor must understand the material: its narrative intention, its sources of humor, whether they be character-based or situation-based, the target of the humor, and whether there is a visual dimension to the humor.

The director should provide the editor with shots that will facilitate the character actor's persona coming to the forefront. If the source of the humor is a punch line, has the director provided any shots that punctuate the punch line? If the joke is visual, has the director provided material that sets up the joke and that executes it? Unlike other types of sequences, a key ingredient of humor is surprise. Is there a reaction shot or a cutaway that will help create that surprise? The scene must build to that surprise. Without the build, the comedy might well be lost.

Another detail is important for the editor: Has the director provided for juxtaposition within shots? The juxtaposition of foreground and background can provide the surprise or contradiction that is so critical to comedy. Blake Edwards is particularly adept at using juxtaposition to set up the comic elements in a scene. The availability of two fields of action, the foreground and background, are the ingredients that help the editor coax out the comic elements in a scene. For example, if the waiter pours the wine in the right foreground part of the frame, the character begins to drink from the wine glass in the middle background of the frame. The character drinks and the waiter continues to pour. This logical and yet absurd situation is presented in *Victor/Victoria* (1982). Edwards often resorts to this type of visual comedy within a shot. These elements, combined with understanding how to pace the editing for comic effect, are crucial for editing a comedy sequence.

□ THE COMEDY DIRECTOR

Comedy may be a difficult genre to direct, but there are some directors who have been superlative. Aside from the great character comics who became directors—Chaplin, Keaton, and, in our time, Woody Allen—a relatively small number of directors have been responsible for most of the great screen comedies. Ernst Lubitsch was the best at coaxing more than one meaning from a witty piece of dialogue. His films, including Noel Coward's *Design for Living* (1933), Samson Raphaelson's *Trouble in Paradise* (1932), and Billy Wilder's *Ninotchka* (1939), are a tribute to wit and civility. Howard Hawks, particularly in his Ben Hecht films (*His Girl Friday*, 1940; *Twentieth Century*, 1934) and his screwball comedies (*Bringing Up Baby*, 1938; *I Was a Male War Bride*, 1949; *Monkey Business*, 1952), seemed to be able to balance contradictions of character and the visual dimension of his scenes in such a way that there is a comic build in his films that is quite unlike anyone else's. The comedy begins as absurdity and rises to hysteria. He managed to present this comedic build with a nonchalance that made the overt pacing of the sequences unnecessary. His performers simply accelerated their pace as the action evolved.

In his films (*Mr. Smith Goes to Washington*, 1939; *Mr. Deeds Goes to Town*, 1936), Frank Capra was capable of relying on lively dialogue and surprising behavior by his characters to generate the energy in his comedy sequences. Capra, however, was more likely than other directors to use jump-cutting within a scene to increase its energy. Preston Sturges was similar to Capra in that he resorted to editing when necessary (*The Great McGinty*, 1940; *Sullivan's Travels*, 1941), but he usually relied on language and performance to develop the comedy. He differed from the aforementioned directors in the satiric energy of his comedy. Whether it was heroism (*Hail the Conquering Hero*, 1944) or rural morality (*The Miracle of Morgan's Creek*, 1944), Sturges was always satirizing societal values, just as Capra was always advocating them. Satire is always a better source of comedy than advocacy, and consequently, Sturges's films have a savage bite rare among comedy directors.

Billy Wilder was perhaps most willing to resort to editing juxtapositions to generate comedy. That is not to say that his films don't have other qualities. Indeed, Wilder's work ranges from the wit of Lubitsch (*The Apartment*, 1960) to the absurdism of Hawks (*Some Like It Hot*, 1959) to the satiric energy of Sturges (*Kiss Me, Stupid*, 1964). Like Hawks, Wilder also made films in other genres. Consequently, the editing of his films is more elaborate than that of the directors mentioned above.

Contemporary directors who are exceptional at comedy include Blake Edwards (the *Pink Panther* series) and Woody Allen. Edwards is certainly the more visual of the two. We will look at an example from his body of work later in this chapter. Woody Allen, on the other hand, is interested in performance and language in his films. Consequently, the editing supports the story and highlights the performance of his actors. His work is most reminiscent of Ernst Lubitsch in its sense of economy. Although there are marvelous sequences that rely on editing in *The Purple Rose of Cairo* (1985) and *Radio Days* (1987), editing rarely plays a prominent role in the creation of comedy in his films.

Another director that should be mentioned here is Richard Lester (*A Hard Day's Night*, 1964; *Help!*, 1965). Of all of the directors mentioned, Lester most relies on editing to achieve juxtaposition and surprise. It would be an exaggeration to say that this makes him the most filmic of the comic directors, but his use of editing does make him particularly interesting.

The aforementioned are the great American directors of comedy. There are exceptional foreign directors as well, particularly the French actor-director Jacques Tati, whose films (*Mr. Hulot's Holiday*, 1953; *Mon Oncle*, 1958) are classics of screen pantomime. Also important to mention are some individual directors who are not known for comedy but have directed exceptional film comedies. They range from George Stevens (*The More the Merrier*, 1943) to Lewis Gilbert (*A Fish Called Wanda*). Joan Micklin Silver directed the comedy-drama *Crossing Delancey* (1988), and George Roy Hill directed the broad, outrageous *Slap Shot* (1977). The best comedy on screen recently has been directed by comedy performers who became directors: Woody Allen, Steve Martin, Rob Reiner, and Danny De Vito. Although there has been good comic writing by James Brooks, John Hughes, and John Patrick Shanley, comedy in the 1980s and 90s has not had the resurgence of the action film. Comedies are being produced, but with the exception of Woody Allen and John Cleese, great screen comedy is still elusive. There are new comic characters—Bill Murray, Robin Williams, Jim Carrey, Mike Myers—but their screen personae have not been as powerful as those of their predecessors.

□ THE PAST: *THE LADY EVE—* THE EARLY COMEDY OF ROLE REVERSAL

The Lady Eve (1941), by writer-director Preston Sturges, tells the story of a smart young woman (Barbara Stanwyck) who is a professional gambler. She meets a rich young man (Henry Fonda) aboard an ocean liner. She determines their fate; they fall in love. When he learns that she is a gambler, he breaks off the relationship. Ashore, filled with the desire for revenge, she dons a British accent and visits his home. She convinces him that, because she looks so much like the first woman, she must be someone else. He falls in love with her again. On their honeymoon, she confesses to a string of lovers, and he leaves her. He sues for divorce, but she refuses his settlement. He goes away. They meet again aboard a ship. Believing that she is his first love, he falls for her again. As they confess to one another that they are married, the door closes and the film ends.

Although the film relies strongly on verbal comedy, Sturges also exploited the dissonance between the verbal and the visual. When Pike (Fonda) takes his first meal on the ocean liner, every woman in the dining room tries to capture his attention. In an elaborate sequence, Eve (Stanwyck) watches in her make-up mirror as Pike avoids the attention of various women. She seems dispassionate until the film cuts to a midshot that reveals her indignation at the situation. This is followed by a close-up of her foot, which she has extended to trip Pike. In the next shot, he is flat on his face, having smashed into a waiter bearing someone's meal (Figure 19.1). The contrast between her dispassionate appearance and her behavior provides the surprise from which comedy springs. The indignation he expresses after his fall turns into an apology as she accuses him of breaking the heel of her shoe. He introduces himself, but she dismisses it, saying that everyone knows who he is. The verbal twists and turns in this sequence are typical of the surprise that characterizes the film. The wittiness of the dialogue, the visual pratfalls, the verbal twists, and the superb performances are the major sources of humor in the film.

Aside from the exceptional quality of the script, Sturges's approach to the editing of the film is not unusual. Later in the film, however, there is a sequence that relies totally on the editing to create comedy. Pike is

Figure 19.1 *The Lady Eve*, 1941. Copyright © by Universal City Studios, Inc. Courtesy of MCA Publishing Rights, a Division of MCA Inc. Still provided by British Film Institute.

now married to Eve, who is posing as Lady Sedgewicke. They are on their honeymoon. To avenge herself for the first round of their relationship in which he left her because she was a gambler, Eve has decided to confess to a string of lovers. She begins slowly and tells him about eloping with a stable boy at the age of 16. Instead of cutting directly to a shot that reveals Pike's disappointment, Sturges cut to a shot of the train rushing through the night. This first confession is paced slowly, but as the confessions come faster, Sturges cut to the train rushing through a tunnel. The pace of editing quickens between her confession, his response, and the train. It leads us to the aching disillusionment of the new husband.

The entire sequence concludes with the train stopping and Pike leaving the train and the marriage. After the first story of the elopement with the stable boy, the cutting takes over, illustrating Pike's rising temper and her candor. The motion of the train underscores the emotion of the situation. It also provides a visual dimension beyond the verbal interchange. The rushing train implies the termination of the relationship rather than the consummation of the marriage. The result is comedy.

The approach that Sturges took, with its reliance on verbal humor and the occasional use of visual humor, is typical of the comedy sequences of his time.

□ THE PRESENT: *VICTOR/VICTORIA*— A CONTEMPORARY COMEDY OF ROLE REVERSAL

In 1982, Blake Edwards wrote and directed *Victor/Victoria*. In the 40 years between *The Lady Eve* and *Victor/Victoria*, the balance between the verbal and visual elements of comedy shifted. Today's films have a much greater variety of visual humor.

Victor/Victoria is the story of a young performer, Victoria (Julie Andrews) who is not very successful in 1930s Paris until she meets a gay performer, Toddy (Robert Preston), who suggests that she would improve her career if she pretended to be a man who pretended to be a female performer. She follows his advice, pretends to be a Polish count, and under Toddy's tutelage, she is an instant success. An American nightclub entrepreneur, King Marchand (James Garner), sees her perform and is very taken by her performance and by her female stage persona until he discovers that she is "Victor." He doesn't believe that she is a man and tries to prove that she really is a woman.

This story about mistaken identity and sexual attitudes has a happy conclusion. The humor, both verbal and visual, usually generates from the confusion about sexuality. For example, one of the best visual jokes in the film is a close-up of King and "Victor" dancing cheek-to-cheek (Figure 19.2). They are clearly romantically involved with one another. In a preceding

Figure 19.2 *Victor/Victoria*, 1982. © 1982 Turner Entertainment Company. Still provided by British Film Institute.

scene, she had acknowledged that she is a woman, and they initiated their relationship. The dancing shot begins in a close-up of the two lovers, and when the camera pulls back, we see that they are dancing cheek-to-cheek in a gay bar. All of the other loving couples are male.

A more typical comedy sequence occurs early in the film. Victoria and Toddy are eating a meal that they can't afford in a French café. The sequence illustrates their hunger and the instrument of their escape: a cockroach that Victoria intends to put onto her salad. She tries to dump the cockroach from her purse onto the salad, but a close-up shows that she has failed. When the suspicious waiter asks her how her salad is, she is jumpy. Toddy asks for another bottle of wine to distract the waiter, who notices they haven't finished the first bottle yet. In a close-up, the cockroach moves from the purse to the salad. Victoria sees the cockroach and screams. The suspicious waiter collides with another waiter, and the cockroach is flung onto another table. Attracted by the commotion, the manager comes to the table. In midshot, he attempts to calm the situation, but he, too, is suspicious. The following shots of Toddy defending Victoria and of the manager handling the accusation create the sense that either Toddy or Victoria will be held responsible for the bill. Just as the situation seems to be lost, the film cuts to a close-up of the cockroach on a patron's leg. The dialogue of Toddy and the manager continues on the sound track, but the visuals shift to the cockroach. The film cuts to a close-up of the patron as she screams and then quickly cuts to an exterior shot of the restaurant, where we see the growing pandemonium from afar.

The twists and turns of this sequence provide the context for the humor. The waiter's behavior and the cockroach constitute the surprises that give rise to the comedy. Edwards clearly understood the role of conflict and contrast in the creation of comedy. The editing follows the development of the conflict and at strategic points introduces the necessary elements of surprise. The comedy in this sequence is primarily visual, although there is some verbal humor, particularly from the waiter.

Edwards's use of visual humor to by-pass the obligatory but uninteresting parts of the narrative demonstrates how useful the comedy sequence can be. The obligatory part of the narrative is the introduction of "Victor" to a music impressario who can help her career. Toddy takes her to the impresario's office where the secretary tells them that her boss is unavailable. The scene has been played many times before: The characters lie to or charm the secretary, the would-be performer wows the impresario, and a career is launched. To avoid this trite approach, Edwards introduced a new element. While Toddy and "Victor" wait to see the great man, another would-be star enters: a tuxedo-clad gentleman with a bottle of champagne who claims to be the greatest acrobat in the world. The secretary refuses him entry as well.

The man opens the bottle of champagne, offers the secretary a glass, and proceeds to do a handstand, cane placed in the champagne bottle, his other hand on the secretary's head. This distraction has allowed Toddy and "Victor" to join the impresario in his office. On the sound track we hear Toddy's pitch and the impresario's skepticism. As "Victor" sings, the acrobat is a tremendous success; he has let go of the secretary and is supporting himself with only the cane in the champagne bottle. As Victor hits a high note, a close-up of the champagne bottle shows it shattering, and a long shot shows the acrobat falling. His fall brings everyone out of the inner office, and the scene ends. "Victor" is a success. The humor of this scene masks its obligatory narrative role.

Later, when King Marchand is attempting to prove Victoria's real identity, his ruse to get into her apartment is presented visually. In the hallway, King and his bodyguard attempt to follow a housecleaner into the apartment. Victoria's neighbor, who is interested only in putting his shoes out in the hallway for cleaning, is a reappearing character. Whenever either King or the bodyguard is in the hallway entering or exiting Victoria's apartment, the film cuts to the neighbor and his shoes. Straight cutaways show his evolving fears, which range from concern about his shoes to fear about the type of friends his neighbors have. Inside the apartment, the potential consequences of Victoria and Toddy's discovery of King develop the tension that is the source of the humor.

All of the comedy in this lengthy sequence is visual, and thus the editing is crucial. Cutting away from the action to provide necessary plot information keeps the sequence moving. The twists and turns of the plot are highlighted by ample close shots and visual juxtapositions that give the sequence a visual variety that differentiates it from Chaplin's style of filmed pantomime performance. In this sequence, performance is important, but the staging and editing are the sources of the humor. Repetition of characters and situations—for example, the neighbor and his shoes—helps to flesh out the sequence and add humor. The neighbor is not necessary to the narrative story; his only purpose is comic. Both narrative and comedy fuse in this sequence. We discover that King knows "Victor" is really a woman (the narrative point of the scene), and we've had an amusing sequence that entertains while informing.

□ CONCLUSION

A comparison of *The Lady Eve* and *Victor/Victoria* reveals the decline in the importance of the spoken word. Dialogue, whether comedic or not, is no longer written as Sturges, Wilder, and Raphaelson wrote dialogue. Although also true of television programming, television commercials, and media presentations, films in particular now rely more on the visual for humor than they did in the past. This shift away from the verbal is evident in *Victor/Victoria*. Visual comedy implies a greater role for the editor than verbal comedy does.

The pace of the cutting for comic effect in *The Lady Eve* is not very different from the pace in *Victor/Victoria*. In addition, both films emphasize cutting that highlights character-related sources of humor. In a sense, both films are about gender politics, and just as Sturges was quick to emphasize the primacy of Jean/Eve over Pike, so too was Edwards quick to cut to King Marchand's unease and insecurity when he thinks he is falling in love with a man.

Editing to highlight the source of the tension and therefore of the comedy was a primary concern for both Sturges and Edwards. Surprise and exaggeration are critical dimensions in the creation of their comedy. The editor does not play as important a role in the comedy sequence as in other types of sequences. However, as the work of both Sturges and Edwards illustrates, the editor can make a creative contribution to the efficacy of comedy.

□ NOTES/REFERENCES

1. Ralph Rosenblum's discussion of working with directors William Friedkin and Woody Allen in his book *When the Shooting Stops-.-.-.-*(New York: Da Capo Press, 1986) illustrates how critical the editor can be in transforming the same material from not funny to funny.
2. Frank Capra, *The Name Above the Title* (New York: Macmillan, 1971), 35–56, 244–252.

20

Documentary

■

The documentary sequence has very different criteria for success than those of the dramatic sequence. Both must follow certain rules of editing to communicate with the audience, but beyond simple continuity, the differences far outweigh the similarities. As Karel Reisz suggested, "A story-film—and this will serve as a working distinction between documentary and story-films—is concerned with the development of a plot; the documentary is concerned with the exposition of a theme. It is out of this fundamental difference of aims that the different production methods arise."[1]

The production of the dramatic film is usually much more controlled than that of the documentary. The story is broken down into deliberate shots that articulate part of the plot. Performance, camera placement, camera movement, light, color, setting, and juxtaposition of people within the shot all help advance the plot. The editor pieces together the shots, orders them, and paces them to tell the story in the most effective way.

The documentary generally proceeds in the opposite manner. There are no performers, just subjects that the filmmaker follows. Camera positioning tends to be a matter of convenience rather than intention, and lighting is designed to be as inobtrusive as possible. Documentary filmmakers tend to adhere to their definition of a documentary: a film of real people in real situations doing what they usually do. Consequently, the role of the director is less that of the orchestra conductor than that of the soloist. He tries to capture the essence of the film by working with others—the cinematographer, the sound recordist, and the editor. The documentary film is found and shaped in the editing.[2]

There are exceptions. Some documentaries are staged—Robert Flaherty's *Man of Aran* (1934), for example—and some dramatic films proceed in an extemporaneous fashion—John Cassavetes's *Faces* (1968), for example. Whether the staging of Flaherty's work made it less reliant on the editor is questionable.[3] These crossovers have become increasingly notable with the docudrama work of Peter Watkins, Ken Loach, and Don Owen. The editor played an important part in those films.

In the documentary sequence, then, the editor has a crucial and creative function. Given the goals of the documentary, that function gives the editor more freedom than the editing of a dramatic film. With freedom comes responsibility, however.

□ QUESTIONS OF ETHICS, POLITICS, AND AESTHETICS

Documentary filmmakers go out and film events that affect the lives of particular people. They film in the place that the event occurs with the people who are involved. They then edit the film. Questions immediately arise. Would the truest representation of the facts be obtained by simply stringing all of the footage together, or is some shaping necessary?

As soon as the shaping process begins, ethical questions arise. Is the event honestly presented? Does it accurately reflect the perceptions of the participants? How much ordering of the footage is necessary to make the event interesting to an audience? Do the filmmaker and editor betray the event and the participants when they impose dramatic time on the footage?

The editing of documentary footage often leads to a distortion of the event. The filmmaker's editorial purpose often supersedes the raw material. From Leni Riefenstahi in *Triumph of the Will* (1935) to Michael Moore in *Roger and Me* (1989), filmmakers have edited documentaries to present their particular vision. For them, the ethical issue is superseded by the need to present a particular point of view.

The documentary is sometimes referred to as a sponsored film. Whether it is a public affairs documentary or a documentary underwritten by a local church, the sponsor has a particular goal. That goal may be journalistic, humanistic, or mercenary, but it always has on impact on the film that the director and editor make.

Unlike the dramatic film, the goals of the documentary are not entertainment and, ultimately, economic success. Nevertheless, those goals must be met, or the sponsor may claim the footage from the director, just as Sinclair Lewis took Eisenstein's Mexican footage. This is one of the reasons why some filmmakers finance their own documentaries. Financial independence may mean low-budget filmmaking, but it also gives rise to a personal filmmaking style that only independence can provide. Most documentary films are sponsored, however, and the sponsor usually has an impact on the type of film that is created.

One of the most interesting dimensions of the documentary is the aesthetic freedom that is available even within the ethical and political bounds. Filmmakers are basically free to experiment with any mixture of sound and visuals that captures an insight they find useful. Their choices may be incidental to the overall shape of the film. When Leni Riefenstahl decided that the beauty of the human form was more important than the Olympic competition and its outcome in *Olympia* (1938), she made an aesthetic decision that influenced both the shape of the overall film and the content of the individual sequences.

When Humphrey Jennings decided to use music as the predominant sound in his wartime propaganda film *Listen to Britain* (1942), he opted to omit the interviews and footage of political leaders and instead selected a freer presentation of the images and the message of the film. This aesthetic choice influenced everything else in the film.

The range of aesthetic choices in the documentary is far wider than is available in the dramatic film. Consequently, in the documentary, the editor can stretch his or her editing experience. It is in this type of film that creative editing is most encouraged and learned.

☐ ANALYSIS OF DOCUMENTARY SEQUENCES—*MEMORANDUM* (1966)

This chapter uses a single film, *Memorandum* (1966), to examine the documentary. *Memorandum* was produced at the National Film Board of Canada. Donald Brittain and John Spotton directed it, and Spotton also photographed and edited the film. The documentary examines the Holocaust from a retrospective point of view. The film centers around the visit of a concentration camp survivor, Bernard Lauffer, to Bergen-Belsen, the camp from which he had been liberated 20 years earlier. In April 1965, Lauffer traveled to Germany with his son and other survivors.

The filmmakers built on his visit to present modern Germany at a time when Israel was opening its embassy for the first time and war criminals from Auschwitz were on trial. Interviews with Germans who served in the war intermingle with newsreel footage of Hitler and the concentration camps. Old and new footage are unified by the narrator. Always, the question is asked: How could the Holocaust happen in a land as cultured as Germany? The role of the doctors and the churches is also explored.

In a film of less than an hour, the filmmakers presented an examination of the Holocaust. They used the film to remind the audience that once such an event enters the public consciousness, it becomes part of that consciousness. The film warns that those who were responsible for the Holocaust were ordinary men who loved their wives and children, men who killed by memorandum rather than pull the trigger themselves.

The commemoration of the 20th anniversary of the liberation of Bergen-Belsen ties the film together. *Memorandum* does not pretend to be a cinema verité treatment of the life of a concentration camp survivor. That would be another film.

SIMPLE CONTINUITY AND THE INFLUENCE OF THE NARRATOR

In the prologue to *Memorandum*, we watch a waitress washing beer mugs and preparing service for the beer garden. We see close-ups of what she is doing, and then a series of shots follows her as she goes about her duties. This simple continuity presents a young woman performing one aspect of her job. The size of the beer mugs and her uniform tell us that the setting is Germany (Figure 20.1).

On the sound track, the narrator introduces the place and time: Munich, summer of 1965. The young woman is Fräulein Bellich. The narrator says, "She was born in 1941, the year Hitler decided she should never see a Jew. But that's finished now."

Without the narration, the footage of Bellich might have opened a film about Munich, beer gardens, or German youth. However, when the narrator Donald Brittain mentions Hitler, he adds direction to the visuals. When Brittain says of the Holocaust, "But that's finished now," he adds irony to the narration because the film is dedicated to the proposition that it isn't finished. As this sequence shows, even simple visual continuity can be directed and shaped by sound.

A sequence that follows the prologue illustrates how simple continuity can be supported by the narration. The sequence, which features a Jewish funeral in Hanover, begins with a shot of the Hebrew markings on gravestones in the Jewish cemetery. This provides visual continuity with the prior scene, which ended on the Hebrew lettering of the Israeli embassy sign in Cologne. All of the participants of the funeral seem to be elderly. The shots detail the funeral procession, which is led by a rabbi. We see the German police on guard, and we seen the mourners, primarily the widow. The sequence ends with the widow grieving, dropping a shovelful of dirt on the lowered casket.

The visuals are primarily close-ups except for the long shot of the procession as it nears the grave site. The close-ups give the sequence an

Figure 20.1 *Memorandum*, 1966. Courtesy National Film Board of Canada.

intensity that underscores the feelings of the participants of the funeral. The narrator introduces the funeral and speaks about the right to hold a Jewish funeral in modern Germany, a right that was denied to all who died in the concentration camps. He also talks about the number of people who died. The German Jewish community of 500,000 before the war became a community of 30,000 in 1965, and most of the survivors are elderly. With a tone of irony, the narrator implies that it is a special privilege for a Jew to be buried in Germany.

These two sequences illustrate how the narration can support the visual or direct it to another meaning. They also illustrate the importance of sound in the documentary.

THE TRANSITIONAL SEQUENCE

To move from the present into the past, Spotton and Brittain adopted a gradual approach that embraces new footage and slowly moves into archival footage. The narration plays a key role in identifying the time period, but in this sequence, the visuals play a stronger role. One sequence begins with close-ups of the telephone operators of a German hotel. The camera passes through the doors of a fancy hotel where elegance and propriety are clearly elements of modern German life. The narrator introduces Lauffer, who is dining with his colleagues in the hotel. The narrator describes how Lauffer was unwelcome in Germany 24 years earlier and how his treatment and the treatment of other Jews "has drained the German landscape of its humanity." This sound cue leads to a German announcement from the war that Communists, partisans, and Jews are to be arrested and confined in concentration camps.

We see a radio, a military cap, and symbols of the authority that the Germans exercised over the Jews. The film then cuts to visuals of artifacts and monuments to the victims of the Holocaust: a towering statue in Austria, a torture instrument in Warsaw. The narrator tells us that torture was too dignified a fate for the Jews and that there were other places than torture chambers for the Jews.

The next scene is of the museum at Dachau, where visitors walk past enlarged pictures of the inmates. Visuals of medical experiments are explained by the narrator. Shots of the museum visitors are interspersed with images of "medical experiments." Images of an experiment where the human subject dies conclude this scene. The narrator's explanation underscores the inhumanity of the closely shot images (Figure 20.2).

From the still image of death, Brittain and Spotton cut to the moving image of Hitler opening the Dachau camp in 1933. The footage was shot on a large scale and seems rather operatic. The narrator takes us from the opening of the camp to a newsreel celebrating Hitler's accomplishments, particularly the opening of the autobahn in 1936 (Figure 20.3).

This scene is followed by archival shots of the large-scale destruction of Jewish property in 1938: Krystallnacht. This event is downplayed by Joseph

(A)

(B)

Figure 20.2A and B *Memorandum*, 1966. Courtesy National Film Board of Canada.

Goebbels in archival footage. The visuals are calm and rather benign, but the narration is ominous. Brittain describes Hitler's comment that war will bring the annihilation of Europe's Jews and discusses how this remark was interpreted as a figure of speech. The final shot is of a crowd cheering Hitler. The next sequence begins with a shot of a modern crowd.

(A)

(B)

Figure 20.3A and B *Memorandum*, 1966. Courtesy National Film Board of Canada.

The narrator takes the lead in this sequence to move us between periods: from Lauffer to the artifacts of the camps, from the artifacts to the modern tour of Dachau, from Dachau to the newsreel footage of Germany in the 1930s. Within each scene is a visual variety that punctuates a world of contrasts. The first contrast is of modern, affluent Jews and older, apprehensive

(C)

Figure 20.3C *Memorandum*, 1966. Courtesy National Film Board of Canada.

concentration camp survivors; the second is of the symbols of torture in the past and of the victims. The third contrast is of the museum, where healthy visitors look at photographs of the most grotesque medical experiments ever undertaken on humans, and the final contrast is the footage of Hitler and Germany in the 1930s and the progress of modern Germany. The narration provides the contrast between what we see and what we know will happen.

Throughout this sequence, the issue of conflict and contrast in each scene carries us toward the fuller introduction of the past. This sequence visually introduces the history of the Holocaust, and it marks the beginning of the shift toward a greater emphasis on the past than on the present. The narrator is important in this sequence, but not as important as the visuals in preparing the transition to the past.

THE ARCHIVAL SEQUENCE

When archival footage is used, the narrator becomes critical. In the sequence where the narrator begins to tell us Lauffer's story, the film focuses on Lauffer's hands and the documents he holds. The narrator tells about the Germans' offer to sell Lauffer's brother's ashes to the family for 24 marks. The Warsaw ghetto was the first of 11 places where Lauffer was confined during the war. The film cuts to archival footage of a close-up of a Jew holding his documents. The cut from an image of documents in 1965 to a similar image of documents in 1942 provides a visual continuity for the transition into the past.

The narrator and Lauffer both speak of life in the ghetto. We see a Jewish committee meeting with German officials as Lauffer describes that the committee was composed of good people. The narrator suggests that centuries of oppression have trained the Jews to wait for a bad situation to improve. The narrator editorializes about the deterioration of life in the ghetto and how it was the children who suffered the most. The images support the narration. When Brittain speaks of dehumanization in the ghetto, the footage illustrates that dehumanization.

Archival footage shows Hitler at Berchtesgaden greeting a young child. Over this footage, the narrator tells us that Hitler decided in 1941 that all of the Jews of Europe were to be systematically exterminated. He details Lauffer's losses: his four brothers, four sisters, and parents were killed. In this sequence, the juxtaposition of the visuals and their tranquility contrast with the narration. The sequence ends with visuals of children playing. The narrator tells us that they were photographed for propaganda purposes and then led into the gas chambers. The narration thus goes beyond the visuals to rectify misinformation that the visuals present (Figure 20.4).

The archival sequence is presented carefully. It begins with a direct correlation between visuals and narration and gradually begins to use the images as a counterpoint to the narration. The film returns to an almost direct correlation between narration and visuals as the sequence ends. The sound track is thus the critical shaping device in this archival sequence.

Figure 20.4   *Memorandum*, 1966. Courtesy National Film Board of Canada.

A SEQUENCE WITH LITTLE NARRATION

One sequence in *Memorandum* documents a visit to Auschwitz. Lauffer had grown up 9 miles from Auschwitz, he had helped build it, and his parents had died there. This narration serves as the transition into the visual sequence at Auschwitz. The narrator's few comments primarily prepare the audience for the sequences to come; he mentions two of the featured topics: Papa Kadusz's chapel and Wilhelm Bolge's cruelty to inmates. Both men went on trial in Hamburg. The trial itself is featured in a later sequence. The narrator also explains about the location where Rudolf Hess was hanged by the Poles; he speaks about Hess as a family man. This commentary takes us into the next sequence, which is archival and concentrates on Heinrich Himmier's paternal attitude toward the S.S. men who carried out the killings of Jews. The narration leads to an articulation of the methodology of death. The principal goal of the narration in the Auschwitz sequence is to provide a transition or foreshadowing for later sequences (Figures 20.5 and 20.6).

The visuals in the Auschwitz sequence, which is organized as a tour of the camp, are presented very differently than in every other sequence. The sequence follows visitors and their Polish guides through the different areas of the camp to see the locations where Jews entered the camp and where they were killed. Because they were filmed primarily as long shots, the human images seem distant and dispassionate. There is little camera mobility compared to earlier sections, and as a result, the sequence proceeds visually at an unhurried pace.

Figure 20.5 *Memorandum*, 1966. Courtesy National Film Board of Canada.

Figure 20.6 *Memorandum*, 1966. Courtesy National Film Board of Canada.

When children's artifacts are shown, the shot is a slow, handheld shot that lingers. The camera moves to animate the statue of a child, but for the most part, movement follows action. Natural sound allows us to listen to the guides explain about the concentration camp. It is only when the narrator speaks of the torture that Bolge inflicted on the Jews in the camp that we see the first close-ups of the visitors. Two or three shots of the faces of the visitors are the closest that Brittain and Spotton come to using any visual intensity in the sequence. These shots stand out in contrast to the predominance of long shots in the sequence.

The Auschwitz sequence was designed to be as similar to cinema verité as possible. It is one of the most journalisticlike sequences in the film.

THE REPORTAGE SEQUENCE

Toward the end of *Memorandum*, the sequence about Lauffer's visit to Bergen-Belsen is presented as straight reporting (Figures 20.7 to 20.12). The narrator relinquishes his editorial role and simply introduces people and places. Although he fills in the details of Lauffer's survival in Bergen-Belsen before liberation, the narrator's role is principally to support the visuals and synchronous sound of the participants as they speak or are interviewed.

The sequence begins with a cocktail party held the night before the visit. The organizers and participants greet one another, and we are introduced to Brigadier Glynn Hughes, who led the British forces that liberated Bergen-Belsen in April 1945. We are also introduced to two former inmates,

Figure 20.7 *Memorandum*, 1966. Courtesy National Film Board of Canada.

Figure 20.8 *Memorandum*, 1966. Courtesy National Film Board of Canada.

Figure 20.9   *Memorandum*, 1966. Courtesy National Film Board of Canada.

Figure 20.10   *Memorandum*, 1966. Courtesy National Film Board of Canada.

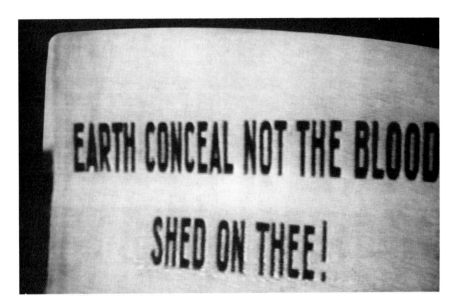

Figure 20.11   *Memorandum*, 1966. Courtesy National Film Board of Canada.

Figure 20.12   *Memorandum*, 1966. Courtesy National Film Board of Canada.

Clare Silvernick and Joseph Rosenzafft, who led the inmates who were liberated from the concentration camp. The interaction among the participants is warm and friendly, and the scene ends with Rosenzafft's resolve to survive.

The film cuts to Bergen-Belsen on the day of liberation. The archival footage used here is the most difficult in the film to watch. At the time of liberation, death and disease were omnipresent. The narrator tells us that Lauffer weighed 70 pounds, and Lauffer himself tells about receiving a cigarette from one of the liberators, taking two puffs, and collapsing. The archival footage continues with the British liberators and Kramer, the camp commandant, who was captured. In this scene Lauffer seems to enter a dialogue with the narrator about Josef Kramer's execution and how easy a death Kramer experienced compared to the deaths of the camp's inmates. The sequence ends with the delousing of inmates who are so emaciated that it's difficult to believe that they will survive.

The next scene is of the town of Belsen in 1965. The visuals show its citizens pouring out of a church after Sunday Mass. The majority appear to be older people. The narrator talks of their not knowing of the camp during the Holocaust, although there was too much evidence toward the end of the war to deny. Brittain also editorializes about the appeal of Nazism in this rural region.

On the bus ride to Belsen, Lauffer speaks of his views about Germany, how it appears, and how he feels. The rain continues as the group leaves the buses.

On the site, Brigadier Hughes is interviewed about the day of liberation. He is jovial and jokes about still having Commandant Kramer's desk. The interviewer asks him whether this makes him feel strange. Hughes replies, "Not at all. It's a very good, heavy desk." Lauffer and Silvernick watch with pained expressions.

In the next scene, Lauffer and his son visit the grave of an uncle who died 3 days after liberation. A young Christian penance group is introduced. The members are helping to build an information center at Belsen. They are disillusioned with the values of their parents. They are young, and yet they seem to be tentative about being photographed at the Bergen-Belsen camp.

The site visit officially begins. The survivors walk past mounds of buried dead. In one of these mounds, Anne Frank is buried, the narrator tells us. Handheld shots follow Lauffer and his son. The survivors take on a somber tone as they approach the monument to the dead. The group approaches the site, lays down a wreath, and says a prayer for the dead. The camera films the scene as a long shot, and a series of close shots includes Hughes and Rosenzafft. A moving shot catches the survivors consoling one another.

The synchronized sound scene gives way to another. A frustrated Lauffer speaks of the mounds of buried dead as the group walks back to the bus. He can't find the proper words, but his son helps him. "Here lie five hundred," he says. "Next year, it will be four hundred. They want to minimize what happened here." Lauffer suggests that the Germans should not have beautified the site; they should have left it as they found it in 1945. The film cuts to the hotel in Hanover, and the sequence is over.

Perhaps more than any other part of the film, this sequence featuring the commemorative visit to Bergen-Belsen proceeds as straight reporting of the events. The archival footage of the camp at the time of liberation and the shots of the town in 1965 flesh out the sequence, providing context for the visit. In a sense, the entire film leads up to this sequence. In it, Brittain and Spotton let the footage speak for itself. There is a minimum of editorializing in the narration and minimal use of the kind of juxtaposition of sound and picture used extensively earlier in the film.

This sequence, however, does conform thematically with the other sequences described in this chapter. They all examine the Holocaust from two perspectives—past and present—and they all remind the viewers of the character of the Holocaust as well as of the deep feeling of its survivors, like Bernard Lauffer, and their commitment not to forget.

☐ NOTES/REFERENCES

1. Karel Reisz and Gavin Millar, *The Technique of Film Editing* (Boston: Focal Press, 1968), 124.
2. Reisz's suggestion in *The Technique of Film Editing* has not been challenged by time. The documentary remains an editor'smedium.
3. Helen Van Dongen, Flaherty's editor on *Louisiana Story* (1948), is credited with having made key contributions to the effectiveness of that film.

21

Imaginative Documentary

■

As discussed in Chapters 7 and 25, realism is the basis of the documentary. When a documentary is edited, the footage of an event is made to conform 10 an interpretation of the event that, within the parameters of sponsorship, is truthful. The greatest expression of this characteristic of the documentary is found in cinema verité works.

What if the filmmaker's goal is to reveal an insight or an interpretation that wouldn't be available from a straightforward editing of the footage? What if the filmmaker wishes to deconstruct a wrestling match so it can be viewed as a struggle of good against evil? This isn't quite the interpretation we would derive from straight documentary footage of a wrestling match, but with the addition of a sound track and with a ritualized pattern of editing, this is precisely the interpretation we derive from *Wrestling* (1960).

☐ ALTERING MEANING AWAY FROM THE LITERAL

The imaginative documentary uses the tools of editing to fashion a unique interpretation from documentary footage. That this can be done is a tribute to the power of editing and to the imagination of such filmmakers as Robert Flaherty, Humphrey Jennings, and Lindsay Anderson.

The editor has many options for creating a new interpretation of reality. The editing style of Leni Riefenstahl in *Olympia* (1938) is an excellent example. Sound offers many options, as does the juxtaposition of sequences and the use of different types of shots. Close-up can be used effectively, and pace can be used to create a fresh interpretation.

Sound effects and music play a role in the success of Basil Wright's *Night Mail* (1936). A poem that is written and read to simulate the motion of the wheels of a train creates a mythology in that film about the delivery of mail. The playful sounds of the amusement park are modulated to underscore the fun and to emphasize mystery and danger in Lindsay Anderson's *O'Dreamland* (1953). Narration and sound are used ironically to alter the meaning of Basil Wright's *Song of Ceylon* (1934), and sound is used to undermine what is being shown in *I Was a 90-Pound Weakling* (1964). In all of these examples, sound shifts the images to another level of meaning.

The editor can also choose to crosscut sequences or shots to elicit another meaning from the visuals. In *Diary for Timothy* (1945), Humphrey Jennings crosscut between a theatrical performance of Hamlet and a dispassionate canteen discussion about the mechanics of a V1 rocket as it is launched. On one level, this sequence connects culture and everyday life, but on another level, it allows the content of each sequence to comment on the other. The gravedigger scene in *Hamlet* is black humor about loss; the canteen conversation about the destructive power of an enemy rocket connects to that scene with its anticipation of death. The explosion of the rocket during the sequence accentuates the imminence of death. By crosscutting the two scenes, Jennings linked past and future in a present that, although it might be momentary, embraces both high culture and the everyday pleasure of a canteen conversation.

Robert Flaherty's *Louisiana Story* (1948) is instructive about the power of juxtaposing individual shots. As he did in *Man of Aran* (1934), Flaherty juxtaposed a tranquil image of great beauty with an image of great danger. In *Louisiana Story*'s opening series of shots, an image of a beautiful leaf is followed by an image of an alligator slinking through the dark water. A bright shot is followed by a dark shot, and in this brief juxtaposition, which Flaherty resorted to more than once, he revealed the natural order of the bayou. Wonder and danger coexist, and neither is preeminent over the other. Because Flaherty and editor Helen Van Dongen don't pace the footage to editorialize, there is an egalitarian sense about this natural order. Tension is evident, but it is not an inordinate tension. This sense of the egalitarian is at the heart of Flaherty's work, and in his juxtaposition of shots, we see how it is suggested in microcosm.

The close-up can also help shift the meaning of documentary footage away from the most truthful interpretation. This is accomplished by using the close-up as a cutaway—a new idea—introduced into a sequence of shots with a general continuity. Flaherty's famous opening sequence of *Louisiana Story* proceeds in a gentle but mysterious way to introduce us to the bayou and its natural inhabitants: the flowers, the insects, the alligators, and the snakes. Into this milieu, Flaherty positioned the main character of the film, a Cajun boy named Alexander Napoleon Ulysses Latour. The boy's presence in the scene increases until he is as natural a part of the bayou as are the flora and fauna. Flaherty and Van Dongen then introduced two images of bubbles coming to the surface of the water. The first time, the narrator refers to the bubbles as "mermaid bubbles," but the second time, there is the sense that the bubbles signal a new presence. We don't know yet that the film is about the construction of an oil rig in the bayou and about how the discovery of oil affects Alexander and the creatures and plants of the bayou. Nor do we necessarily know that the film was sponsored by a large oil company involved in oil exploration. At this early stage of the film, the close-ups of the rising bubbles suggest that another, as yet unidentified, element will join the boy and the other inhabitants of the bayou.

Finally, pace can alter the meaning of documentary footage. The direc-tor and editor have the option of slowing down or accelerating the pace of the footage. These options will affect meaning in different ways. The slow motion shot is an alternative to slowing down the edited pace of the footage. The impact of picking up the pace is perhaps most readily understood. Consider, for example, the stop-motion sequence in Godfrey Reggia's *Koyaanisqatsi* (1983), with its accelerated speed of urban traffic, or the quick pace of the cutting in Arthur Lipsett's *Very Nice, Very Nice* (1961). Both film sequences give the impression of an urban metropolis rushing to its demise. Pace of this speed changes a film from a document of life in New York, for example, to a comment on the quality of life in New York. So great is the strength of the pacing in these films that we must draw the conclusion that speed is destructive to humans and to the human spirit.

□ THE WARTIME DOCUMENTARY: IMAGINATION AND PROPAGANDA

The remainder of this chapter provides a more detailed examination of Humphrey Jennings's *Listen to Britain* (1942). It explores how Jennings edited his film to be more than a record of everyday life in war-torn Britain (Figure 21.1).

Figure 21.1 *Listen to Britain*, 1942. Courtesy of Museum of Modern Art/Film Stills Archive.

Listen to Britain was one of many documentaries made during World War II. The most prominent documentary filmmakers in the United States were Frank Capra, John Huston, and William Wyler. These filmmakers came from Hollywood and used the techniques Hollywood knew so well. They applied what had primarily been narrative or dramatic techniques to the documentary to create propaganda films that supported the Allied cause. The *Why We Fight* series, with its reliance on newsreel footage, best exemplifies that wartime effort. The series borrowed heavily from Nazi propaganda films and consequently relied on an editing style of juxtaposition and pace. Narration for content and style was also very important.

The German propaganda film, particularly the work of Leni Riefenstahl, was highly visual and dynamically cut. German films focused on the creation of a cult of leadership around Hitler and on the supernatural power with which he was supposedly endowed. Both the German and the American propaganda films were highly effective and given to metaphor.

□ THE CASE OF *LISTEN TO BRITAIN*

The British war documentary ranged from direct, narration-driven films such as *Desert Victory* (1943) to the nonnarrative treatment of *Listen to Britain*. Jennings's treatment of a Britain under assault from the air and under threat of invasion was unhurried and indirect. As Alan Lovell and Jim Hillier write,

> It is a most unwarlike film. Its basic motivation is a balance between menace (to a culture rather than to material things) on the one hand and harmony and continuity from the past on the other. Images of menace are constantly juxtaposed with the images of the population's reactions. Almost all images gain complete meaning only when seen in context. Thus the fighter planes fly over harvesters and gunners in the fields, working side by side; the sandbags, empty frames and fire buckets at The National Gallery are intercut both with steady tracking shots of the calm faces of the audience or shots of people eating sandwiches or looking at paintings and accompanied by Mozart.[1]

Jennings was unique in his approach to the documentary. His colleagues at the Crown Film Unit, although they admired him, did not understand how he could achieve so great an impact in his films. As Pat Jackson, a colleague of Jennings, suggests, a good part of his success was achieved in the editing room: "Humphrey would interpret a situation in disconnected visuals, and he wouldn't quite know why he was shooting them, probably until he got them together. Then he created a pattern out of them. It was as though he were going out to collect all sorts of pieces, cut already, for a jigsaw puzzle, and wasn't quite certain about the picture that jigsaw puzzle was going to be until he had it in the cutting room, and here he was enormously helped by [Stewart] McCallister."[2] This view is echoed by the producer of *Listen to Britain*, Ian Dalrimple,[3] and the impact of the film abroad is discussed by filmmaker Edgar Anstey.[4]

The key to the success of *Listen to Britain* is its imaginative use of sound and image. As Paul Swann suggests, "[Jennings's] subtle cross structuring of sound and visual images instilled a uniquely poetic element in his films."[5]

Listen to Britain, a film of 21 minutes in length, does not focus on any particular character or event. It depicts wartime Britain with a focus on London, pastoral farmland, the industrial heartland, and the vulnerable coast. Jennings included shots of civilians at work and soldiers enjoying themselves in individual recreation and marching in organized columns as they pass through a small town. Many of the people included are women principally because the men were away at war. The film focuses on culture, both popular culture—a dance in Blackpool, luncheon entertainment by Flanagan and Allen—and high culture—Myra Hess performing Mozart at The National Gallery. Jennings also included sequences of individuals and groups passing the time by singing.

Throughout the film, work and leisure activities are presented in an unhurried fashion. Whether people are working on an assembly line manufacturing Lancasters or sitting in the audience listening to a lunchtime concert, there is no anxiety, only a concentrated involvement in the tasks of war and everyday life. The film gives the impression of a calm, strong, determined population, a population where the queen can sit at a lunchtime concert as one of her people rather than the cult of leadership central to the German propaganda film or, for that matter, the cult of ideology so central to the dramatic fabric of the American propaganda film. Jennings managed to transcend politics and economics to present a purely aesthetic, cultural response to the problem of war, and it's a very powerful response.

Central to the structure of *Listen to Britain* is a dialectic set of sequences. Each sequence interacts with the next through sound and juxtaposition. Pace is never relied on too heavily.

The film can be broken down into the following sequences:

1. Farming goes on in spite of the war.
2. Soldiers relax at the Blackpool dance hall.
3. The work for war goes on at night.
4. Canadian soldiers wait for an assignment.
5. The manufacture of the Lancaster bomber is ongoing.
6. Ambulance workers wait.
7. The British Broadcasting Corporation (BBC) speaks to and for Britain in the world.
8. The work of war proceeds from dawn forward.
9. Families are left behind while loved ones go to war.
10. War workers are mostly women.
11. Popular performers entertain workers at the lunch halls.

12. Guest artists perform in museums at lunch.
13. War and great culture have intermingled in the past.
14. The British people serve in the factories and in the armed forces.
15. "Rule Britannia": the determination of a nation.

Every sequence reminds us that Britain is at war. In the first sequence, the rustle of the trees and of the wheat fields is complemented by the roar of a Spitfire flying overhead. Toward the end of that sequence, a shot of spotters at their posts on the coast facing the English Channel is a reminder of Britain's vigilance against potential invaders.

Either a sound effect or a visual acts as the reminder of war: soldiers in uniform at Blackpool, the morning march of civilians carrying helmets along with their lunch bags, the sandbags piled high against a tall window in The National Gallery. In one sequence, children play in the schoolyard of a sleepy town as if there were no war, but the shot of a woman looking at a photo of her uniformed husband and the sound of a motorized column moving through the town are reminders about how close the war is.

Between each of the first three sequences, Jennings referred to the spotters and those on guard watching the skies and the sea for the enemy. These shots support the idea that although the sequences may be about recreation or rural beauty, the real theme of the film is war. The waiting and watching and civilian preparation are part of the process of being at war. So is the ambulance service and the war manufacturing.

Gradually, Jennings shifted the focus from waiting for war to preparing for war. Beginning with the sequence that shows the manufacture of the Lancaster bomber, Jennings began to concentrate on the war effort. Sequences 5, 8, 10, and 14 are about the effort at home to prepare for war. Although less obvious, sequences 6, 9, 11, and 12 are also about people involved in the war effort. However, these sequences do not show them at work, but rather at lunch or listening to a noontime concert. Jennings seems to have been saying that the British know how to prepare for war, and they are confident enough to enjoy a respite from the lathe, the iron furnace, and the assembly line. The British value culture and companionship.

Sequences 7 and 13, the sequences about the BBC and about the past—Horatio Nelson and Trafalgar, the architecture of the Empire—all suggest the power and influence that is Britain. These two sequences rely heavily on sound. In sequence 7, a series of sound dissolves suggest not only that the BBC is important within England, but also that it reaches in every direction; the last sound reference, "This is the Pacific Services," represents the BBC's influence on the land, air, and merchant navy forces in that region. In sequence 13, the soaring orchestral treatment of Mozart's Concerto Piano Forte in C Major accompanies images of Trafalgar Square; the monument to Nelson seems almost to come alive as the dynamic cutting suggests a historical continuity that is irresistible in its power. In sequences 7 and 13, the abstract idea of Great Britain is a long-standing, far-reaching, and impregnable nation. Although nothing is said verbally, the juxtaposition of these sequences acts as an apex for the ideas arising out of the film as a whole. There is something emotional about Jennings's reliance on music in sequence 13. This sequence prepares us for the anthemlike quality of the last sequence, in which the manufacturing for war is presented to the sounds of "Rule Britannia."

A notable characteristic of *Listen to Britain* is the level of feeling Jennings achieved without the use of even a single close-up. Much of the film is presented in midshots and slow-moving shots.

Through the juxtaposition of sequences and a gradual build-up caused by the pattern of filming and editing, Jennings created a sense of Britain's invincibility. To appreciate how indirect his editing is, we must look at a single sequence. Many sequences are unified by a single piece of music, for example, the Blackpool sequence, the two lunchtime concerts, the sequence in which the Canadian soldiers are waiting. Other sequences are less obviously unified, for example, the sequence featuring the manufacture of the Lancaster bomber.

The transitional image of spotters watching for German planes dissolves to the sight and sound of a train pulling out of a station. The trains move without lights. The film cuts to the manufacture of an airplane and then to a Lancaster taking off. The film pans to an ambulance station, and we are into the next sequence.

This sequence is flanked by images of civilians preparing for war. In between, the images are of the production for war. The sound throughout highlights the natural sounds of the production process and of an airplane in flight. The sounds of the preceding and following sequences are overlapped to create a smooth flow into and out of the sequence. Although the sequence has no visuals in common with the preceding and following sequences, the sound overlaps provide continuity.

As is so often the case in the documentary, the continuity of ideas flows from the sound track. Jennings may juxtapose visual sequences to one another, but the ideas are more directly ordered by sound continuity. His approach is less direct, but nevertheless not confused, because the overall pattern of the juxtapositions has a sound continuity.

□ CONCLUSION

A direct plea for help for Britain might have seemed logical for a film like *Listen to Britain*, but Jennings succeeded with a different approach. He wanted to communicate the qualities of Britain that made it worth helping: the dignity and culture of the great nation. By using an imaginative approach to this goal, Jennings fashioned a film that even today exemplifies the possibilities for sound and image. Jennings undertook in 1942 with *Listen to Britain* what Francis Ford Coppola would undertake in 1979 with

Apocalypse Now: the creation of an entire world (or at least the image of that world). In Jennings's case, it was a world worth saving; in Coppola's, it was not.

□ NOTES/REFERENCES

1. Alan Lovell and Jim Hillier, *Studies in Documentary* (London: Martin Secker and Warburg, 1972), 86.
2. Quoted in Elizabeth Sussex, *The Rise and Fall of British Documentary* (Los Angeles: University of California Press, 1975), 144.
3. Ibid.
4. Anstey felt the film was too oblique, but it was far more successful abroad than Jennings's more direct film *Fires Were Started* (1943); see ibid., 146.
5. Paul Swann, *The British Documentary Film Movement, 1926–1946* (Cambridge: Cambridge University Press, 1989), 162–163.

22

Innovations in Documentary I

■

Too often in the past two decades, the announcement has been made, "The documentary is dead." But stubbornly it has not come to pass. The reason, principally, is the documentary's flexibility. For so long associated with educational and political goals, the documentary has more recently aggressively embraced the entertainment impulse that has swept through broadcast news and reality programming. Less obvious but no less important is the documentary's hold on past generations. Its affiliation with political, social, and educational goals has given documentary a gravitas or weight that is deeply meaningful. The form consequently has not lost its audience as so many other story forms have. Whatever the reason, the announcement that the documentary is dead has been an empty one. The documentary is alive and evolving. In this chapter we will address a number of its innovations, the changes in the personal documentary, the expansion in the use of narration in a fashion differing from earlier uses, and the interface between documentary and drama. First we turn to the shifts in the personal documentary.

☐ THE PERSONAL DOCUMENTARY

The personal documentary is different from the social/political documentary or the cinema verité documentary. The cinema verité documentary, which is rooted in the philosophy of filmmaking of Dziga Vertov, suggested that the great strength of the documentary and of film was its capacity to capture real life events as they happen. For Vertov, this represented the highest aesthetic of the medium. The result is films such as *The Man with a Movie Camera* (1929), which was the inspiration for a school of documentary, principally the cinema verité school. The Free Cinema movement in England in the 1950s, the Direct Cinema in France in the late 1950s and early 1960s, and the Candid Eye series in Canada in the 1950s, all essentially owed a debt to Vertov. In the United States, the work of Richard Leacock and D. A. Pennebaker in the 1960s gave way to the work of Barbara Kopple in the 1970s and to the self-reflexive filmmaking of Ross McElwee (*Sherman's March*, 1986) in the 1980s and of Rob Moss (*The Tourist*, 1992) in the 1990s. All are fundamentally cinema verité filmmakers. Finally, the

Dogme films of Lars von Trier, Thomas Vinterberg, and Kristian Levring owe much in terms of their style to the work of Vertov. They are, however, dramatic films rather than documentaries. Cinema verité then represents one of the three "paths" of the documentary.

The second ideology of the documentary is based on the ideas of John Grierson, the British filmmaker and executive producer who first established government film units in Great Britain and later in Canada. Grierson believed that the documentary should have an educational purpose. If we broaden the term education to include social and political education we see how this ideology also embraces the propaganda film (a particular education, or one we don't necessarily believe in, we call propaganda). Whether one looks at the British sponsored documentaries of the 1930s, or the work of Leni Riefenstahl, or of Frank Capra, or the later work of Grierson at the National Film Board of Canada, we see a continuation of this philosophy of documentary. Sponsored films, educational films, corporate films, all fall under this category. Perhaps a more precise definition of this ideology of documentary would be purposeful documentary.

The third ideology or "path" of documentary is that of the personal documentary, which we associate with the work of Robert Flaherty (*Nanook of the North*, 1922). Although he filmed on location in the Arctic, Flaherty shaped *Nanook* to fit his vision of the struggle of man against nature. This noble, romantic, epic struggle is repeated in Flaherty's films about life in the South Sea Islands, the Aran Islands, and the bayous of Louisiana. Flaherty chose real subjects, but cast, filmed, and staged it to suit his sensibility, as opposed to recording what he found in those far-flung settings. This is the nature of the personal documentary: its tone is personal, based on the views of the filmmaker rather than on the anthropological actuality in the field.

This particular approach is clearly at the heart of Luis Buñuel's *Las Hurdes* (*Land without Bread*, 1932), the work of Humphrey Jennings (*Diary for Timothy*, 1945), and the docudrama work of Peter Watkins (*Culloden*, 1964) in the 1960s. Buñuel and Jennings use their subjects to convey their ideas about society and its obligation to its people, Watkins uses his subjects to convey his ideas about Scottish nationalism and British imperialism, just as Flaherty used his Louisiana story to convey his own ideas about childhood and its innocence. We now turn to the recent work in the area of the personal documentary.

A good starting point is to define particular characteristics that not so much delimit personal documentary as together distinguish this particular branch of the documentary. First, the striking visual character of the personal documentary. Most documentaries are content-driven, although the visual dimension has been critical in the propaganda documentary work of Riefenstahl and Jennings. In the personal documentary the visual aesthetic of the work is prominent. Flaherty had a poetic style suitable to his approach to his subject matter. Peter Watkins has a pseudorealistic style that supports the seriousness of intention in his work. In the case of Errol Morris, whose work we will turn to shortly, the style is distinctly oblique. In each case the visual aesthetic is so powerful that it draws great attention to itself beyond the organization of the content.

A second characteristic of the personal documentary is the mixed use of staged or performed footage with actuality footage. This finds its extreme form in Flaherty's work and in the more recent work of Peter Watkins. All of Watkins' *Edvard Munch* (1974) is staged, but it is filmed as if it is captured or cinema verité actuality footage. More often the film is a mix, as in Errol Morris' *The Thin Blue Line* (1988). How the two styles of footage blend is often masked, although Morris' staged material is so stylized (e.g., the murder scene) that it is clearly not documentary footage. The models for other extreme footage that blends easily with documentary footage are John Cassavetes' *Shadows* (1959) and Gillo Pontecorvo's *The Battle of Algiers* (1965), both films that are entirely staged.

A third characteristic of the personal documentary is the use of irony. The source for this impulse is Luis Buñuel's *Land without Bread*. More recent examples include Errol Morris and Werner Herzog, whom we will turn to shortly. Herzog was very influenced by the documentary work of the West Coast filmmaker Les Blank, who documented Herzog's own filmmaking practice in *Werner Herzog Eats His Shoe* (1980).

The most vigorous characteristic of the personal documentary is the issue of voice. Voice can be established directly through the narration, or generated out of a distinctive visual style, or through the deployment of irony generated out of the counterpoint of the narration or music with the visual, or out of a combination of any or all of the above. Clearly the singularity of the personal documentary emanates from its distinctive voice. That voice may be grounded in the political, as in the docudramas of Peter Watkins, or it may allude to the political to highlight the personal, as in the work of Michael Rubbo (*Waiting for Fidel*, 1974), or it may be entirely personal, as in Herzog's *My Best Fiend* (1999). In each case voice is so pronounced that it overwhelms the more objective or general intentions of the documentary.

We turn now to the films and their filmmakers, beginning with Herzog's film *My Best Fiend*. Herzog is best known as the dramatic filmmaker of a series of films—*Aguirre: The Wrath of God* (1973), *Nosferatu: The Vampyre* (1979), *Fitzcarraldo* (1982), and *Woyzek* (1979)—all made with the actor Klaus Kinski. Although Herzog made other dramatic films and documentaries, he is best known for these films made with Kinski. *My Best Fiend* is a personal documentary about his relationship with Kinski. As Kinski died in 1991, the film is an amalgam of clips from the films he made with Herzog: broadcast footage of a Kinski performance, amateur footage, as well as excerpts from *Burden of Dreams* (1983), the documentary by Les Blank about the making of *Fitzcarraldo*. Contemporary footage consists of interviews with two of Kinski's costars, Eva Mattes from *Woyzek* and Claudia Cardinale from *Fitzcarraldo*. Herzog also retraces the places of some of his work with Kinski, including South America for *Aguirre: The Wrath of God* and *Fitzcarraldo*, and Austria for *Woyzek*. He even visits the home where the would-be actor Kinski, as a boy of 13, rented a room.

My Best Fiend is not so much a biography or a vanity portrait of an important actor as it is an examination of a difficult, almost impossible relationship between a director and an actor. Were they friends or enemies? Did they creatively unleash a talent in the other that was more than the sum of their individual abilities? Is the film the portrait of madness as genius, or all of the above?

At no point does Herzog question his own attraction to extreme subject matter—the dictatorial impulse of a Spanish soldier 8000 miles from home in *Aguirre: The Wrath of God*; the mad act of dragging a boat over a mountain so that a town can have what the main character feels the town needs, opera, in *Fitzcarraldo*. What is clear is that Herzog himself is attracted to the madness in genius and to the genius in madness. Rarely does he approach the madness issue directly, but what lingers about Herzog's work is that there is a magical quality to those who struggle against nature, man, and their own nature to achieve their goals. What better actor could he choose to portray these complex but fascinating characters than the complex, fascinating Klaus Kinski?

This personal examination of the relationship between director and actor leads Herzog to conclude that he and Kinski were alter egos. They needed each other to make the magic they achieved in the five films they made together. As Herzog journeys back geographically to the places he made films with Kinski, we begin to understand that although Herzog is speaking about Kinski he is in fact revealing himself. *My Best Fiend* begins to look more like a portrait of a director's creative state, one fueled by an emotional war with his primary actor, Klaus Kinski. That state, however achieved, is the basis for one of international cinema's great careers. The play on words in the title, "best" and "fiend," one word implying pleasure and the other torture, begins to take on a layered meaning: is Herzog invoking contradiction and chaos or constructed creativity? Whichever is his goal, Herzog creates a paradox—the triumph of the personal demons of each man to create together great art.

Whether personal documentary is about self-revelation, self-exploration, or simply self-promotion, voice is central to its articulation. Few documentarians have as singular a voice as does Errol Morris. In many ways he uses his voice to explore eccentricity in the American character. In *Fast, Cheap and Out of Control* (1998) Morris celebrates eccentricity. In *Mr. Death* (2000) the exploration implies the tragic in eccentricity.

Mr. Death has as its subtitle, *The Rise and Fall of Fred A. Leuchter, Jr.* In the first half of the narrative Leuchter, the son of a prison worker, grows up in Massachusetts to become a leading expert in execution equipment. He explains his mission: to make execution humane, whether by electrocution or lethal injection. Leuchter alludes to a creative touch that will bring death quickly and efficiently. As a tour guide of the mishaps and messy nature of execution, Leuchter takes a me-against-them attitude. "They" are the wardens, state officials, and so-called professionals that have been cruel and unusual in their punishment of death-house convicts. His matter-of-fact description of heads blowing off and eyes popping out is intended to support his mission as a humane hero to the soon-to-be-dispatched and their families. As Leuchter describes his growing professional success, his personal success, a marriage, all of which become the final act of his ascent, Morris intercuts black and white with color footage. By doing so Morris is implying a layer of artifice, mixed in with realism. The irony is unavoidable. The execution room scenes are highly stylized through the use of backlight. Mock heroism is the tone in this section of the film.

The second phase of the narrative takes up the late 1980s request by Ernst Zundel, a Holocaust denier in Canada, for Fred Leuchter to act as his expert witness. The mission is to visit Auschwitz and Birkenau to explore whether gas executions actually took place there. The visit becomes the honeymoon for the newly married Leuchters. The location scene is filmed in handheld cinema verité style. TV footage of the infamous Zundel trial, a trial prompted by Zundel's campaign against Holocaust denial, in Toronto is intercut with a more recent interview with Ernst Zundel.

To substantiate his investigation, Leuchter takes numerous rock samples at locations claimed to be gas chambers or adjacent to gas chambers. Back in Massachusetts he tests these samples and finds no trace of Cyclon B, the gas used to kill the inmates at Auschwitz. Leuchter writes a report claiming that no gassing of inmates took place at Auschwitz or Birkenau. The Leuchter report is submitted to the trial in defense of Zundel's claim that the Holocaust never took place. Historian and Holocaust denier David Irving is interviewed to illustrate the receptivity for Leuchter's report among a certain constituency, neo-Nazis in Europe and Latin America. The Canadian Court, on the other hand, found Zundel guilty, impugning its own assessment of the Leuchter report. In short order Leuchter moves from being a useful contributor to society to a pariah. First his business suffers due to the bad publicity his expert testimony yields, and indeed, he becomes a laughingstock. His business fails, and then his marriage fails. He moves West in an effort to restore himself, but the occasional speaking engagement isn't enough, and by the end Leuchter is destroyed. He remains provocative and unapologetic about his report, and by the end of the film we leave him on a road somewhere in California, a lonely and alone figure of ridicule. Only in this last phase of the narrative does Morris return to stylization.

Morris' voice is focused on two devices—the mix of stylized or dramatized footage with cinema verité footage and the use of irony. Irony permeates the structure of the narrative. By elevating the creation of killing machines with a humane goal, Morris undermines the seriousness with which he constructs Leuchter, the hero, in the early half of the film. Morris carries on using irony as Leuchter chips away at the concrete bunkers at Auschwitz, earnest in his pursuit and tickled to be away from the United

States for the first time. Although Leuchter is on his honeymoon, we never see him with his wife. He acts like a kid in a playground. But it's not a playground, it's Auschwitz—where 3 million people were killed. The irony is lost on Leuchter, who increasingly appears to be a naïf rather than an expert on anything. Zundel and Irving both appear to be canny, knowing, and unironic. Beside them, Leuchter looks more and more like the rube who's been had.

Death and the Holocaust: weighty matters, and yet Morris has chosen Fred Leuchter as his prism. Leuchter is an eccentric, but the subject—death—makes *Mr. Death* no laughing matter. Rather it's a human tragedy.

Fast, Cheap and Out of Control is Morris' celebration of eccentricity. The film is basically a portrait of 4 men who are enthusiastic about their work. Each has a rather out-of-the-ordinary vocation, and each is a zealot about his work. Dave Hoover is a wild animal trainer; George Mendanca is a topiary gardener; Ray Mendez is a mole rat expert; and Rodney Brooks is a robot designer. Aside from their enthusiasm for their work, the animal kingdom is the linkage. The robots that Rodney designs look like large insects, and the leafy sculptures that George creates are in the image of animals, such as a dinosaur. Less apparent but no less common among the 4 men, is a sense of play. In the case of Ray and Rodney, they are almost childlike in their enthusiasm. George and Dave are more mature, more adolescent in their approach to their work.

Although the major focus of the film is the interviews with the 4 men together with visual illustration of their work, Morris intertwines 2 additional thematic threads in the story. First he cuts away to film serials, such as "King of Jungleland" and "Zombies of the Stratosphere." King of the Jungleland stars Clyde Beatty, best known as a lion trainer prior to and during his Hollywood career. In the serial, Beatty has to fight lions and many human adversaries. Morris' second intervention is circus footage, from clowns to lion acts to trapeze acts. The reaction of the audience is also a visual element. Both visual interventions are entertainments, both attract a young audience, and both are about the dangerous interface between the natural or animal world and man, and both are about adults playacting at being adults—they are really all kids at heart.

Fast, Cheap and Out of Control has a very distinctive style. Whereas Morris mixed cinema verité and a dramatic style in *Mr. Death*, in *Fast, Cheap and Out of Control* he uses mostly interviews that are presented in traditional documentary style. The balance of the material runs from the dramatic (the serial) to almost hyperstylized footage. The circus material in particular is presented using oblique camera placements and angles. Whether Morris is trying to introduce the notion of instability or danger or both, he moves far from realism in the circus footage. The same can be said for the robot laboratory footage, where Morris tries to impute point-of-view shots that "humanize" the robot. He also uses oblique angles to film the topiary garden. The use of extreme angles and wide-angle lenses "animates" the animal sculptures. It also gives them a looming, menacing presence. In the case of the actual animals, the mole rats, lions, and tigers, Morris approaches them with a naturalistic visual style that emphasizes their being captive. The consequence is to create empathy for these animal "victims" of man. Camera placements and lens selection are utilized to capture this sense of the animals. The style distinctively sets up a sense of play about representing reality; indeed, the style seems the playful equivalent of the zeal the interviewees feel for their professions. Errol Morris isn't going to be left out. He feels equally zealous about his profession: filmmaking.

The clash of dramatic footage, from the serial, with the documentary or actuality footage is not quite as great as it was in *Mr. Death*. Morris' approach to the actuality footage is so stylized that it seems more in harmony with the artifice of the serial than it does in conflict.

As in *Mr. Death*, irony is plentiful in *Fast, Cheap and Out of Control*. Each of the interviewees is a grown man, but Morris chooses to focus on only one dimension of their adult lives—their profession, and the how and the why of it. As in the case of Fred Leuchter, these men have a vocation where they don't have to interface with others. They are loners working at an unusual profession that is enormously gratifying to them. But as in the case of Leuchter, they are not adding obvious value to mankind. They are marginalized men gaining their status from their work as an act of individuality, of free will. In a sense the irony is that regardless of the vocation, Morris is looking at each of these men as a purveyor as well as a victim of his acts of free will. I don't mean to overemphasize Morris as a film moralist, but on one level that's exactly what he's doing, and it's his sense of irony about man and animal that is pointing us in this direction. Which brings us finally to the issue of voice in Morris' work.

We can say that Errol Morris wants to explore the American character, that he wants to look at men at the margin of society, that he wants to look at the eccentric in this society. I believe that Morris, as in the case of Werner Herzog, is looking at his own psychology. He sees wonderment, he sees difference, he sees play, and he sees the downside to excess. All these are themes he explores in his characters, and all these characteristics capture his approach to filmmaking. In a sense his films are probes: how excessive can I be, before I too suffer the fate of a Fred Leuchter? This is the creative path Morris walks down. He has chosen the documentary as his medium, but he has modified it to such an extent that it is barely recognizable as documentary. This is Errol Morris's contribution to the personal documentary.

□ CHANGES IN THE USE OF NARRATION

Although narration is totally absent (by definition) in cinema verité, it is a formative presence in the other genres of documentary. Narration, as one of the three layers of sound (dialogue and music are the others), is a very powerful tool. As we will see in our discussion of Clement Perron's *Day After Day* (1965) in Chapter 28, "The Sound Edit and Creative Sound," narration has the capacity to alter the meaning of the visual. The classic role of narration, "the Voice of God," was essentially interpretive. Since filmmakers have begun to range in their use of narration, it is useful to look at the possibilities for narration and then to move on to novel examples of these uses.

If we were to summarize the uses of narration we could categorize the narrator as observer, as investigator, as guide, or as provocateur. Within these larger categories the narrator can be objective or subjective, intimate or distant, harsh or ironic, young or old, professional or anecdotal. Every choice will influence our perception and experience of the film. Consequently, the filmmaker must make a decision about how he or she wants us to experience the film narrative.

THE NARRATOR AS OBSERVER

Narrators as observers presume that their mission is to allow us to accompany them on a tour of a place, a person, or an idea. The position of the narrator can be as an expert, a companion, or an innocent in the process of discovery. This latter notion was made famous by Michael Rubbo, the Australian documentarian who made films for the National Film Board of Canada for two decades. Rubbo himself becomes a character in his work; he is a participant-observer. This is his approach in Vietnam with *Sad Song of Yellow Skin* (1970), in Cuba with *Waiting for Fidel* (1974), and in Paris with *Solzhenitsyn's Children-.-.-.-Are Making a Lot of Noise in Paris* (1979). Thematically, each film has rich subject matter: the effect of the war or the quality of life issues for expatriates trying to live in Vietnam; the potential meeting of a capitalist and politician from Canada with Premier Fidel Castro; the intellectual currents of a city where ideas mean everything in *Solzhenitsyn's Children-.-.-.-Are Making a Lot of Noise in Paris.*

Rubbo is an ingenuous observer. In order to personalize complex material but also to explore that material, Rubbo sets himself up as a curious observer who hasn't quite made up his mind. We know that his experiences will shape his views, and by acting as a guide who is processing the material as he discovers it, Rubbo, at times naive, at other times skeptical, provides us with an avenue into material that otherwise would be heavy slogging for the audience. His role as observer also makes his documentaries lighter and more entertaining.

Amir Bar-Lev's *Fighter* (2000) is no less ambitious than Rubbo's work, but his approach is to use a constant on-camera observer. *Fighter* is the story of two Czech Holocaust survivors, Jan Weiner and Arnost Lustig. Bar-Lev films their contemporary return to Czechoslovakia in order to trace Weiner's escape during World War II. They travel from Czechoslovakia to Croatia and then to Italy, where Weiner was imprisoned as an undesirable alien, and finally from Italy, his escape to join the British Air Force, where he participated in the Allied bombing of Germany. Bar-Lev intercuts archival historical footage as well as family photographs of Weiner. Arnost Lustig, now a friend of Weiner's as well as a fellow Holocaust survivor, is the observer for the film.

Because Lustig is a writer, he tries to interpret Weiner's actions throughout the journey. Weiner, the fighter of the title, is a man of action rather than words. The journey stirs up deep feeling and multiple wounds—the tragic loss of his mother in a concentration camp in Czechoslovakia; the awful fact of the suicide of his father in Croatia in 1942 while Weiner is staying with him. His father commits suicide to allow the young Weiner to travel West, unburdened by an elderly, less able, parent. Lustig attempts to give words to the feelings of Weiner, but Weiner turns against his friend. Words detract and undermine Weiner's capacity to cope, to hold on, to go forward. He breaks with Lustig and, in effect, walks out on the film.

What is important about the use of Lustig as a character and observer is that the contrast between the two men allows the audience to feel the pain of a man who refuses to see himself as a victim. Jan Weiner sees himself as a fighter. We see this side of him, but thanks to the presence of Arnost Lustig as an observer, we also feel the depth of the tragedies in his life, and he becomes all the more admirable a character for that contrast.

THE NARRATOR AS INVESTIGATOR

Investigations imply a goal: to come to an understanding of an issue or person by means of the investigation. The consequence is a more purposeful documentary. Unlike the political or social issue documentary, the investigative documentary does not endeavor to make a case. Consequently, the investigative documentary is not at all a polemic.

In *The Ballad of Ramblin' Jack* (2000), Aiyana Elliott is trying to understand her father, the singer Jack Elliott. Mixing home movies, archival footage, contemporary interviews, and the equivalent of a current concert tour, Aiyana Elliott seeks to know a man she barely knows, her father. By looking at his professional and personal life, she may find the key to connecting with the most elusive significant person in her own life. Her father divorced her mother when Aiyana was a small child. Today, as a filmmaker, five years out of film school, Aiyana wants to reconnect with her father, and making a film about him is the logical vehicle for that attempt.

Jack Elliott, the son of a Jewish doctor in Brooklyn, decided he wanted to be a cowboy and eventually a cowboy balladeer. Elliott lived and performed with Woody Guthrie in the 1950s, and as his fame grew he became a powerful influence on Bob Dylan in the 1960s. But by the 1970s Elliott is a forgotten man, only to be rediscovered 20 years later by no less a fan than President Bill Clinton. Aiyana Elliott tries to understand the why of her father's career: his lack of ambition; his disorganized approach to his career; his chaotic personal life, including 4 wives. But in the end she sees that Jack

Elliott is a man who is most comfortable on stage making up the set as he goes along; he is a great performer and a poor father. Although she doesn't seem to come to a deeper understanding of their relationship, she has made a film that is a tribute to an artist who was a transitional figure in folk music: the man between Woody Guthrie and Bob Dylan.

Ray Muller also strives for understanding in his film *The Wonderful, Horrible Life of Leni Riefenstahl* (1995). Leni Riefenstahl, one of the towering figures in film history, is the subject. Muller interviews Riefenstahl, aged 90, at many of the locations of her films, and of course at an editing bench. He also interviews her at various Berlin locations. Interspersed with the interviews are clips from her films, the two most important being *Triumph of the Will* (1935) and *Olympia*, Parts I and II (1938).

The goal of Muller's investigation goes beyond a portrait of the film-maker. Muller wants to know how involved she was with the Nazi party, with Hitler, and his goals. He wants to test the idea, how much did you know, and how much responsibility should you bear for making films for the Nazis? These are issues Muller goes back to around the 2 key films but also around a supportive letter Reifenstahl wrote to Hitler in the early 1940s. He also returns to these questions when dealing with Riefenstahl's postwar hearing at the hands of the Allies (she was cleared), which resulted in the end of her filmmaking career, and her consequent efforts to restore her reputation right up until this film is made. To the end Riefenstahl claims her goals were artistic not political, that had she known about the fate of the Jews and other persecuted minorities, she would have felt differently. She never recants, but does lament the suffering she has experienced for the past 50 years.

Muller draws no conclusion, but his continual probing poses the key questions about art and morality. He leaves us, his audience, with the conclusion we ourselves wish to come to.

THE NARRATOR AS GUIDE

If the investigator is looking for understanding, the guide already has it. Through the narration the guide helps us understand. Multiple guides are used to layer that understanding, usually first on an intellectual level, then on an emotional level. Mark Jonathan Harris uses multiple guides to engage us with his films in both of his Oscar-winning documentaries, *The Long Way Home* (1997) and *Into the Arms of Strangers* (2000).

The Long Way Home is the story of the survivors of the Holocaust from the end of the war in 1945 to the birth of the State of Israel in 1948. It is the story about people who survived Hitler's death camps only to discover they could not return to their former homes. Many who did not return were killed. And so their hopes turned principally to the West and to Palestine. The British Mandate resisted Jewish immigration into Palestine, and the consequent civil disturbance eventually caused Britain to end the mandate, the precursor to a UN-supported partition of Palestine with a homeland for the Jews and a homeland for the Arabs. The film ends with the birth of the State of Israel, implying that at last the survivors of the Holocaust have a home in Israel.

This brief précis of the narrative provides the skeleton. How does the filmmaker use narration to shape and to layer the narrative?

First, to provide unity and transition for the entire narrative, Harris uses the classical, informative guide who can explain the politics of President Truman's choice to support first Jewish immigration and then the State of Israel against the advice of his Departments of State and Defense. The narrator can also detail the story of the 1946 Kelce massacre of 41 Jews who had returned to their homeland in Poland after the war. These narrative knots, where considerable visual material would be needed to capture the issue, are explained by the principal narrator. The history, if you will, is the principle responsibility of the narrator. The actor Morgan Freeman reads the narration.

The other narrators are more personal. Here memoirs, letters, diaries, and oral histories of the 1945–1948 period provide the emotional texture of the narrative. These guides—survivors of the Holocaust, and American soldiers who liberated the camps, who guarded and supervised the camps, including the initial commander, General George Patton—offer deep insights into the emotional states of survivors and liberators. Despair, loss, hope, a future, all the planes of human feeling and existence are explored by these guides. Often actors are used to render these confessional pieces of narration. These "sound close-ups" emotionalize the archival footage. There are also interviewees: survivors, including the chief rabbi of Israel; 2 American rabbis who were instrumental in helping the survivors; an American volunteer who helped Jews escape illegally from Europe to Palestine; and Clark Clifford, who worked diplomatically for President Truman.

In *The Long Way Home* it is the multiple or layered use of narrators that guides us through the complex history of the period as well as its equally complex emotional turbulence. Harris uses the same layered strategy for his narration in *Into the Arms of Strangers*. But in this film the more personal guides also appear on camera. They are the children of the Kindertransport, now adults, 50 years after the traumatic war years. The story begins in 1933 with the ascent of Hitler to power in Germany. For children, the changes under the Nazis were subtle and not always apparent. But all that changed with the pogrom in November 1938, the night of shattered glass known as Krystallnacht. Throughout Germany and Austria and the Sudentenland, the annexed portion of Czechoslovakia, Jewish businesses were looted, Jewish synagogues were burned, and Jews were harassed, beaten, and killed. Many died. It proved to be a turning point for the Jews in Germany.

Consequent to Krystallnacht, Jews tried to leave Germany, but exit visas were hard to come by and entry visas to other countries even harder. Great Britain decided that it would accept as many children from Germany as possible. The conditions were that the children had to be under 17, that 50£ had to be paid for their support, and that a British home must be willing to take them in. The program, which began in December 1938 and continued until the beginning of World War II in 1939, was known as the Kindertransport. Children from Germany, Austria, and Czechoslovakia participated in the transport.

Into the Arms of Strangers tells the story of the Kindertransport and follows 10 children who participated. Their interviews as well as archival footage, home movies, and photographs provide the visuals for the film.

As in *The Long Way Home* there is a primary narrator who explains the historical progression. That narration, read by Judi Dench, provides the general informational shape for *Into the Arms of Strangers*. With the overarching narrative as the guide track for the film, Harris proceeds to use the 10 participants as the personal guides to the story of the Kindertransport. They include 6 women and 4 men; 5 are from Germany, 3 from Austria, 1 from Czechoslovakia, and 1 from Poland who had made his way to Germany by 1939. Their stories focus on life prior to 1938, Krystallnacht; their leave-taking from their parents; the transport itself; life in England; in the case of the young man from Poland, his transport to Australia on the HSS Deruna, and his return to join the army; the reunion with parents where the parents survived, or the experience of learning of the death of the parents; and the aftermath of the Kindertransport experience. What is clear from the stories is that the Kindertransport saved thousands of children's lives, but that it was a scarring event for the children; in a sense it was the seminal event in the lives of these 10 people.

In *Into the Arms of Strangers*, the narration provides multiple points of entry into a complex historical event. By using a general narration for historical information and participants for personal information, Harris has created a tiered entry into the narrative—informational and emotional lines emanate out of the two layers of narration. Although the narrators are on-camera in *Into the Arms of Strangers*, they serve the same purpose as the off-camera readings of letters, diaries, and memoirs in *The Long Way Home*—to personalize a complex historical event and to give emotional resonance to a Holocaust event too easily overwhelmed by statistics and scale. By using multiple narrators as guides, Harris brings us to the emotional core of the issue and we begin to understand.

THE NARRATOR AS PROVOCATEUR

The provocateur has a specific goal in his documentary: to promote change. The nature of the narration may be direct or ironic, but in both cases the goal remains the same. Justine Shapiro and B. Z. Goldberg in their film, *Promises* (2001), are very direct. They want their film to contribute to the possibility of peace in the Middle East. Goldberg is the narrator, both on and off camera.

Promises was filmed in Israel and in the West Bank from 1997 to 1999. The film follows 8 children, 4 Israeli and 4 Palestinian. In Israel, the children include an ultra-orthodox child, the son of a West Bank settler, and a set of twins, grandchildren of Holocaust survivors. In this sense, the full political spectrum, from liberal to conservative, is represented. Among the Palestinian children, the spectrum is from urban (settled) to refugee (unsettled) and includes a young girl. All other participants on both sides are male. Shapiro and Goldberg are interested in the attitudes of the children toward one another. The film includes their families but only in a limited sense. The major part of the film focuses solely on the children. The film's last section brings together the Israeli twins with the 2 children (male and female) from the West Bank refugee camp. The implicit question is whether the children can get along for an afternoon. They do, but when the filmmakers return to interview them 2 years later, they have not maintained contact and their attitudes have hardened.

Shapiro and Goldberg have tried with *Promises* to illustrate the complexity and depth of opposing attitudes in the Middle East between Israelis and Palestinians. They are also attempting to say, by the nature of the film's structure, that it begins with the next generation. We have to get them together if there is to be hope for peace in that region. Their direct approach is an emotional provocation to try.

Ron Mann's *Grass* (2000) takes a very different approach. *Grass* is an exploration of American attitudes toward marijuana from the 1930s through the 1990s. Both the government's and the public's attitudes are examined. The information line is essentially to trace the history of marijuana in the United States, from its entry via Mexican migrant workers at the turn of the century to its status today—as a criminalized drug that the government spends billions of dollars to eradicate. The dramatic line of the narrative is how marijuana has been affiliated with dangers to society. Over time it has been affiliated first with the outsider (Mexicans); then with a scapegoated minority (the black community); then with murder; then with mental illness and its consequences; then with heroin use; and finally, with "never fulfilling your potential" or, to put it another way, "to be a loss to society." The government, primarily through the Commissioner of the Federal Bureau of Narcotics from 1930 onward, mounted a vigorous attack to criminalize the drug. The head of that department, Commissioner Harry J. Anslinger, made it his personal mission to eradicate marijuana from the American landscape. Although there are powerful figures, such as Mayor Fiorella LaGuardia of New York, who question and commission scientific studies to evaluate the drug, the government continues a 45-year assault on the drug and its users. The expense of this war and the number of users grow anyway. In 1977 then-President Jimmy Carter attempted to decriminalize the drug but his effort failed. Nevertheless, a number of states have since decriminalized marijuana usage. But until the end of the century marijuana use has remained a criminal activity from the point of view of the Federal Government.

Grass is a provocation to change the law and align it with scientific knowledge about the drug. The film takes an adversarial position to the law. To flesh out this position, the filmmaker Ron Mann uses as his narrator Woody Harrelson, an actor with a liberal reputation and a knack for portraying antiestablishment characters. The more extreme layer of provocation, however, comes from the visuals. Mann uses film clips from archival antimarijuana films as well as graphics, to make his case. The film opens with a clip about marijuana that poses the question: "Marijuana, Threat or Menace?" The clips increasingly become extreme, melodramatic illustrations of the madness, rapacity, and murder that follow from marijuana usage. The irony and provocation then arises principally from the visuals. But the narration also is provocative in its use of language. Mexicans are characterized as blood-curdling murderers. Commissioner Anslinger is called a "prohibitionist" and a "law-and-order evangelist." Mayor LaGuardia, on the other hand, is "skeptical about government claims" about marijuana. Commissioner Anslinger is portrayed as a villain while Mayor LaGuardia is a fair-minded hero. This kind of characterization also presents Presidents Nixon, Ford, and Reagan's opposition to marijuana and the youth movement and the movement for decriminalization as heroic. The narration, although more tempered than the visuals, advocates changing the marijuana laws in the United States. This is the provocation of the narration in *Grass*.

☐ CONCLUSION

The changes in the narration imply the richness that has kept the documentary lively and alive as a genre. It is important, however, to understand that just as there are subgenres within the documentary, innovation in techniques such as narration, as much as the movement to explore voice in the documentary, are responsible for keeping the genre alive and as critical a center for innovation as it was in the 1920s, 1930s, and 1950s.

23

Innovations in Documentary II

■

Fahrenheit 9/11 (2004), by Michael Moore, represents a watershed in documentary film history. On one level, having earned almost $200 million, including ancillary revenue, it is the most commercially successful documentary of all time. Earnings rivaled the vast majority of dramatic films made in 2003. On another level, however, the film demarks the adoption of dramatic-entertainment values as opposed to the educational-informational values more often associated with the documentary. *Fahrenheit 9/11* was certainly not the first documentary to do so; Moore's film was simply the documentary that garnered the most attention for doing so.

Other areas of the media, particularly news broadcasts on television, have softened their approach to the news. They, too, have adopted "entertainment" values. Simultaneously, TV drama and a segment of the feature film industry have adopted "information-documentary" values: witness reality TV and the rise of a documentary approach on shows such as "Law and Order" and the CSI series.

In this chapter our interest is this trend toward entertainment values in the documentary. Is it a new trend? Is it a progression or a regression? To contextualize these questions, it's important to acknowledge that the documentary has flirted with entertainment and dramatic values from the outset. If we use Dziga Vertov's *Chelovek s kino-apparatom* (*Man with a Movie Camera*) (1929) as the antithesis of dramatic values in the documentary, we note that Vertov's film has no main character in the traditional sense, that there are no antagonists, and that there doesn't seem to be a plot, only a slice-of-life approach to a day in the life of a cameraman and a day in the life of a city.

Vertov represents the classic cinéma vérité sensibility that reemerges in direct cinema in England, in the candid eye series in Canada, and in the American work of Fred Wiseman and the Maysles brothers. But other visions of documentary emanated from the work of Robert Flaherty and John Grierson, working in the same era as Vertov. In the case of Robert Flaherty, a romantic vision was applied to Eskimo life in the Arctic. In *Nanook of the North* (1922), Nanook heroically makes his way in spite of the hardships of securing food and shelter in the world's harshest environment. Grierson, too, plied his heroic humanist agenda to labor relations and to the delivery of the mail, in *Night Mail* (1936). In each of these films, dramatic ideas are used to enoble the documentary subject.

The stakes as well as the dramatic techniques employed become more evident in Leni Riefenstahl's *Triumph des Willens* (*Triumph of the Will*, 1934) and Frank Capra's *Why We Fight* series (1942–1944). In Riefenstahl's film, Adolph Hitler is the heroic main character who arrives from somewhere above the clouds to save his nation. The same Adolph Hitler is the principal antagonist in Capra's *Divide and Conquer* (1943). Capra uses Riefenstahl's own footage as well as newsreel, even Hollywood, film footage to illustrate what a duplicitous bad guy Hitler really is.

Alain Resnais used a dramatic strategy to juxtapose 1954 Auschwitz (color) with 1944 Auschwitz (black and white) in his *Nuit et brouillard* (*Night and Fog*, 1955). The raw footage itself was sufficiently shocking—the conflictual strategies hardly seemed necessary. The same can be said for Marcel Ophül's *Chagrin et la pitié* (*The Sorrow and the Pity*, 1969), in which the juxtaposition of the Vichy government's behavior toward its Jews was in stark contrast to the nationalistic resistance claims made by French politicians post-World War II.

By the late 1980s, however, particularly with the work of Errol Morris (*The Thin Blue Line, Mr. Death: The Rise and Fall of Fred A. Leuchter, Jr.*), the use of dramatic strategies in the documentary became more novel and appealing to documentary makers. Morris principally used a protagonist or antagonist model in his films. In *Mr. Death* (1999), holocaust deniers, including Mr. Death, are the antagonists. In *Fast, Cheap & Out of Control* (2001), the four main characters are nonconformists in an increasingly conformist world. In *The Fog of War: Eleven Lessons from the Life of Robert McNamara*, McNamara is a protagonist who is his own antagonist.

Similarly, in *Grizzly Man* (2005), Werner Herzog investigates the death of Timothy Treadwell, a wildlife preservationist killed by a grizzly after spending 13 summers among the bear population in Alaska. Here the conflict is man vs. animal, or man, advocate of animal life, or, to put it another way: Friend or food—what is the nature of man in nature? Herzog structures the film as an investigation into this relationship, and what he concludes is that Timothy Treadwell and the grizzly saw the relationship differently and therein lays the tragedy of Treadwell. And by using the chronology of the relationship as the plot, Herzog is able to create the conflictual tension that plot always brings to the goal of the main character.

This use of plot as a shaping device is rarely as powerfully used as it is in Andrew Jarecki's *Capturing the Friedmans*. The film relies on the protagonist–antagonist relationship as well as on a plot. The main character is definitely Jesse Friedman, a teenager when he is sentenced to go to jail as a pedophile, having been found guilty of abusing children in the basement of his home together with his father, Arnold Friedman. Ostensibly the children (boys) were there to be tutored in computer and math skills by their teacher, Arnold Friedman. The antagonist is Arnold Friedman, the main character's father. The plot is the accusation of child molestation, the investigation, the trial, and the impact of these events on the Friedman family.

Director Jarecki clearly sympathizes with Jesse and believes he is innocent, even though Jesse, along with his father, is sentenced to significant jail time. Jarecki is also interested in the impact of the events upon the Great Neck, New York community in which they took place. From the point of view of the narrative choices and editing style, Jarecki has treated *Capturing the Friedmans* as a thriller.

Another example of a documentary film structured as a thriller is Nathaniel Kahn's *My Architect*. The film begins with the director discovering, at the death of his father, the architect, Louis Kahn, that the father had two other families (two other wives and two other children). As the youngest of all of Kahn's children, Nathaniel sets out to find out who his father, was personally and professionally. In the course of his investigation, he and his audience learn a great deal about Louis Kahn. We learn he was one of the great American architects of the 20th century. We also learn that he is utterly unorthodox in how he has conducted his personal life. Aside from structuring the film as an investigation into a mystery, Nathaniel Kahn poses as the naive narrator of the investigation. By doing so he is attempting to dramatize the sense of surprise and wonder at each revelation. By assuming this pose, Kahn lightens what might have become heavy, even tragic, in the unfolding. The pose lightens the tone of this documentary, and by doing so, Kahn moves us away from realist interpretation and judgment of his father. The alternative, creative tolerance, is the upshot of Kahn's narrative choices.

Jeffrey Blitz's documentary *Spellbound* (2002) has launched two dramatic films and a Broadway musical. Rarely has a documentary spawned as much emulation. *Spellbound* follows the lives of eight diverse American teenagers as they move from the regional, to the national spelling bee competition. And so, there are eight main characters, each humanized and individualized. And there is a plot—the regional competitions and the national competition. Clearly there can be only one winner, but the pride of each of the families in their children is so strong that it outweighs the disappointment of the seven who have lost the competition. Blitz has managed to make each of these main characters a winner in their own right. *Spellbound* abounds in dramatic values. One of the students is the local genius in his small rural school. Only his size protects him from the taunts of his classmates. A Hispanic girl, the child of Spanish-speaking illegal immigrants, is proud to be the "educated" child in her family. Each of these children faces challenges in their own environment. Again, the drama doesn't emanate from the competition alone.

Each of the films discussed so far has dramatic and entertainment values unusual in a documentary film. But to capture the sense of crossover between the documentary and the drama, the rest of this chapter focuses on two films about the same subject—the Munich massacre of Israeli athletes at the 1972 Olympic Games. This tragedy is the subject of Kevin Macdonald's

1999 documentary, *One Day in September*. It is also the subject of Steven Spielberg's 2005 drama, *Munich*.

Let's look at the dramatic film first. Although *Munich* focuses on the aftermath of the massacre, the presentation of the massacre itself is the baseline for all that follows. An Israeli assassination team is organized with its goal to kill not only the assassins (three survived the day of the massacre), but also the Palestinian planners of the massacre. The revenge killings take place principally in Europe, but there is at least one attack in the Middle East. In the course of those assassinations, half of the Israeli team is killed, and, in the end, the leader of the team refuses to carry on. He joins his wife and child in Brooklyn, where the film ends inconclusively.

From the point of view of the narrative choices Spielberg makes, he is clearly opting for documentary-informational choices as opposed to dramatic-emotional choices when it comes to the main character, the antagonist, the use of plot, and the story form or genre he uses to frame the narrative. Let's begin with the main character, Avner (Eric Bana).

If we contextualize the Spielberg approach to the main character, we note the heroic nature of an ordinary main character in Sheriff Brody (Roy Scheider) in *Jaws* and in John Miller in *Saving Private Ryan*, or the heroic nature of an outsider in the young boy (Henry Thomas) in *E.T. the Extra-Terrestrial* or in Oscar Schindler (Liam Neeson) in *Schindler's List*. In every case, the main character becomes a reluctant hero. That is not the case of the Avner character in *Munich*. If anything, Avner's commitment at the outset not only softens but, over time, he also questions the mission to which he has been assigned. He is reluctant, but he is certainly not heroic by the end of this narrative.

Turning to the issue of an antagonist, we find a similar outcome. In *Saving Private Ryan* the German, who Miller's patrol spares, ends up cruelly killing the Jewish member of the American company. He is the vicious face of Naziism, just as Amon Goeth is its face in *Schindler's List*. Each of Spielberg's films has a definite antagonist, human or otherwise, with the exception of *Munich*. In a situation where we would expect a Palestinian antagonist, there is no such character. In fact, Spielberg humanizes two of the Palestinians to be killed, one with a daughter and the other with his impassioned speech about the Palestinian cause. There is tragedy in *Munich*, but no clear antagonist.

Turning to the plot, the assassination of the assassins and their planners, there is no rising arc here. Although the early assassinations have a powerful sense of revenge, this softens over time. The last visualized attempt at assassination actually fails and it is clear by the end that the mission is incomplete. There is no climactic battle (*Saving Private Ryan*) or clear resolution (*Jaws*) to the plot. Consequently, as in the case of the main character and the use of an antagonist, the use of plot in Munich has been intentionally muted. The reason is not unclear—Spielberg intends *Munich* to be a meditation on vengeance. Does an eye for an eye work for political goals? Spielberg's answer is clearly "no." Consequently, Spielberg uses the docudrama as the story form of choice in *Munich*. Rather than telling a story of vengeance and power, Spielberg seems more interested in examining that pattern of political behavior in the Middle East and in challenging its purposefulness. Using the docudrama allows Spielberg to embrace realism without relying on pulp or pop dramatic effects to make his point. Although the result may disappoint fans of earlier Spielberg films, it is clear that by embracing "documentary-educational" goals, Spielberg is trying to wean his audience from the facile answers that so often emanate from the simplification of political issues when they are framed by dramatic considerations. Clearly Spielberg is looking to change the paradigm and to present a serious, thoughtful meditation on the intractable history of the Middle East in the 20th century.

One Day in September is Kevin Macdonald's documentary treatment of the single day at the Olympics in Munich when the kidnapping and killing of the Israeli athletes occurred. Aside from the detailed treatment of the events of that day, Macdonald includes contemporary interview material with the Dutch wife of one of the victims and the Israeli daughter of another victim, plus interview material with the sole surviving Palestinian who participated in the massacre, as well as a number of the Germans who participated either as police or government officials that day in September. And also interviewed is the Israeli sent by Mossad to represent Mossad's interests at the site of the kidnapping and, later, at the airport where the Germans attempted to rescue the hostages.

Macdonald begins his documentary by introducing the site, Munich, of the 1972 Olympics. Thirty-six years after the 1936 Olympics that Hitler used to glorify the new Nazi Germany, Germany would now use the 1972 Olympics to show how the country had changed consequent to the end of World War II. Problematic was the decision to have unarmed security people at the Olympic village, rather than a trained security force. After giving the background of the fencing coach and the wrestling coach, both having been child Holocaust survivors who emigrated to Israel after the war, Macdonald contextualizes the significance for these men to return to Germany as free men, as equals to their German hosts.

Having given the victims a human face, Macdonald proceeds with the events of that fateful day. He begins by describing the Olympic village and how the Palestinian team gained access to the village (a subterfuge orchestrated by the Eastern German authorities). The narrative then proceeds with entry into the first Israeli apartment. There the injured wrestling coach is forced to take the Palestinians to another apartment, that of the wrestlers, who he feels might be able to overwhelm the Palestinians. And so, the Palestinians gain entry to two apartments, those of the coaches and of the wrestling team. In the ensuing struggle, two of the eleven Israelis are killed (not at the same time). The body of the wrestling coach is dumped off of the apartment balcony and in this way the world is informed that the kidnapping has taken place. A ransom demand (the freedom of 200 Palestinians from Israeli jails) is made.

What follow is Israel's refusal to negotiate and the efforts of the Germans to negotiate with the terrorists. Israel offers to dispatch a team to rescue the hostages, but Germany refuses. There are no trained German military personnel to deal with the circumstance that has arisen. Naivety and surprise characterize the German response throughout the day. Olympic officials decide in spite of events that the Games should continue. The hostage-taking has nothing to do with the events. Media reportage of the events of the day falls to Jim McKay, a network sports commentator. Occasional audio of Peter Jennings, reporting for ABC News, is also included.

The deadline passes three times as negotiators secure an extension. By the third time, Olympic officials, under pressure, decide to suspend the games in the face of the crisis. A deal is struck to transport the Palestinians and their prisoners out of Germany to an Arab country. The deal is a ruse to get the terrorists and prisoners out of the Olympic village and to relocate them to a place where a rescue will be attempted. The ambush site, however, is staffed by too few snipers, and the German volunteer force aboard the plane intended to overcome the terrorists votes to abandon the plane minutes before the terrorists arrive by helicopter at the airport and awaiting aircraft. Without communications equipment, without experience and knowledge of the terrorist numbers, the Germans do not effect a rescue, and although five of the terrorists are killed, it's not before all nine Israeli hostages are murdered. The rescue attempt has failed. Within 3 weeks, the German authorities make a deal to get the three surviving terrorists out of Germany. They are never put on trial. Two are consequently killed by an Israeli assassination squad. Although it's unstated, the age of global terrorism began that September, 1972, in Munich. Now, more than 30 years later, it's more global than ever, and far more lethal.

How does Kevin Macdonald rely on dramatic strategies in his editing choices of *One Day in September*? How does he deal with his main character? Macdonald chooses the two coaches, the fencing coach and the wrestling coach. Both men will die in the attack, but, although each is a victim, it is their love of life that Macdonald embraces. Each of these men was a very positive person who changed lives, especially the lives of their families. And it is the families of each man, the wives and the children, who represent the men in the film. By approaching the main characters in so personal a way, Macdonald deepens our emotional connection with the victims. It takes their deaths out of the political realm and very much makes *One Day in September* a personal story.

Turning to the antagonists of *One Day in September,* one would expect that the antagonists would be the terrorists who killed the eleven athletes. I didn't find this to be the case. Instead, Macdonald surprises us. It is the German authorities responsible for the conduct of the Games and for the safety of the athletes who are the antagonists. Not far behind is the Olympic Committee, who continually tries to wash their hands of the event of the kidnapping and massacre. By doing as he does, Macdonald points out that nations have political responsibilities for the safety of guests and of their own citizens. When the three surviving terrorists are flown out of Germany, even the Germans interviewed are embarrassed by the moral implications of their government's actions. And so MacDonald has framed events in a very personal way. The hosts have let down their guests and that has led to a tragedy that continues to resonate throughout the world. East–West, Arab–Israeli, new Germany vs. the old Germany—each is sidestepped to tell this story in the most personal, emotional manner possible.

Turning to how Macdonald has used the plot, the events of that tragic day, he treats the events as a thriller. Although we who are watching know the outcome, Macdonald's introjections of options and opportunities suggest that events did not have to turn out the way they did. And by using the overlay of indifference from athletes and Olympic officials to those events, Macdonald implies the age-old maxim of anti-Semitism. Would these events have occurred if the athletes had been another nationality rather than Israeli? His implication is unmistakable: in Munich, there is the wish that Israelis and Arabs handle their own problems—anywhere but here. And that, too, becomes part of the tragedy of the events of that day.

Macdonald uses plot as dramatically as Costa-Gavras does in *Z* and as Alan Pakula does in *All the President's Men*. The result is that Macdonald's use of dramatic strategies makes his film, in spite of its horrific events, entertaining, whereas the documentary strategies Steven Spielberg adopts in *Munich* make his dramatic film less entertaining and more "documentary-educational." These two films capture an important trend—the movement of the documentary toward the dramatic film, and, conversely, the movement of a segment of the dramatic film industry toward the documentary.

24

Ideas and Sound

■

Just as a visual juxtaposition or a cutaway can introduce a new idea or a new interpretation, so too can sound. Chapter 20 discussed how the narration altered the meaning of the opening visuals in *Memorandum* (1966). Any of the elements of sound—music, sound effects, dialogue—can accomplish this. The juxtaposition of different sounds or the introduction of a sound "cutaway" can be as effective as a visual in introducing an idea. This concept is so important that this chapter is devoted to it.

David Bordwell and Kristin Thompson provide a useful framework for the consideration of ideas and sound. Their article, "Fundamental Aesthetics of Sound in the Cinema," suggests how the characteristics of sound—loudness, pitch, timbre—affect how we receive and respond to sound as it is presented on the screen (synchronous dialogue, sound effects) and off the screen (music, narration). Their attention to rhythm, fidelity, sound space (the proximity or distance of sound in a film), and time provides a three-dimensional framework from which to consider changes in sound.[1]

☐ MUSIC

The broadest generation of ideas develops from the musical decisions of the filmmaker. The mixture of "Home on the Range" and the music of Edward William Elgar in Humphrey Jennings's *Listen to Britain* (1942) suggests that patriotism and culture are a potent mix that suggests national strength. If Jennings had selected only the music of the upper class or of the lower classes, that sense of unity and strength would not have resulted, and the purpose of the film—it was a propaganda piece for British and North American consumption—would have been compromised. Similarly, Benjamin Britten's elevated score in *Night Mail* (1936) suggests the poetic and epic importance of the railway's delivery of the mail.

In the fiction film, one of the most interesting uses of music can be found in Stanley Kubrick's *A Clockwork Orange* (1971). In this futuristic story, a society is consumed by violence perpetrated principally by the younger generation. Kubrick often used music to suggest the regimented character of the violence, but when he selected "Singin' in the Rain," the title song from one of Hollywood's greatest musicals, he chose music that most audiences associate with joy and pleasure. When first introduced in the film, the song is sung by Alex (Malcolm McDowell) as he attacks the male owner of a home he and his friends have invaded and as he rapes the man's wife. The song could hardly be used more ironically. In this scene, the music creates so much dissonance with the visual that the visual seems much more horrific.

□ SOUND EFFECTS

Sound effects can be equally powerful in their introduction of an idea into a scene. The classic example is the scream in Hitchcock's *The 39 Steps* (1935). As we hear the scream, we see a train. Not only is a transition accomplished, but the simulation of human and mechanical elements makes the human response seem louder and more terrifying. In Kurosawa's *The Seven Samurai* (1954), the attack on the village provides an excellent example of the use of sound, space, and loudness. When the attackers are riding against the village, the hooves of the horses create a noise that seems like thunder. This sound effect makes the attackers seem more threatening. As they approach, the loudness becomes almost overwhelming. Kurosawa used space in this way throughout the film to help create the sense of achievement of the seven samurai in defending the village. The sound helps create the sense that the odds against them were great.

In *Days of Heaven* (1973), Terence Malick used sound effects the way that most writers use dialogue. When it rains, he wants us to feel wet, and when we are in a steel plant, he wants us to feel overwhelmed by the sound of the machines and the pouring of the molten metal. When the main characters drift to work in Texas, the sound of the crickets and rustling wheat are as important as the spoken word.

In *Days of Heaven*, Malick gave disproportionate sound space to nature, resulting in a sense of the natural flow of events, a kind of equity of rights between the land and its inhabitants. Despite the travails of the characters, the land has great majesty. The sound effects play an important role in creating that characteristic.

□ DIALOGUE

As mentioned earlier, dialogue can also yield results beyond the literal content of the words. In Richard Lester's *A Funny Thing Happened on the Way to the Forum* (1966), when Sudellus (Zero Mostel) speaks loudly and his master's son, Hero, whispers softly in response, the shift in tone immediately tells us something about each character. The same is true of Orson Welles's *Citizen Kane* (1941). When Kane and Leland speak, the tone, pitch, and loudness variations tell us about their relationship and about the power of each. When HAL speaks in a crisp, articulated voice in Stanley Kubrick's *2001: A Space Odyssey* (1968), there is a distinct difference from the low, flat tones of the astronauts.

Changes in the tone, pitch, and timbre of one character's dialogue introduce the idea that something has changed. They can also foreshadow change for that character. Variations in dialogue between characters can be used to reveal their differences. In each case, the changes introduce a new idea into the scene.

When Robert Altman modulated the voices of many of his characters in *Nashville* (1975), he used tone, timbre, pitch, clarity, and sound space to identify the characters, indicate their current moods, signal changes in mood, and create a sense of each character at a particular moment. Because Altman often overlaps and crowds his dialogue tracks, the audience must listen carefully to his films as well as watch them. Cues about how to feel at a particular instant can come from the visual or the sound. Altman is one of the most important directors when it comes to the use of dialogue sound tracks to introduce ideas. Because he is less interested in the words themselves, the other characteristics of the dialogue—the loudness, pitch, and so on—become all the more telling.

□ FRANCIS FORD COPPOLA: EXPERIMENTATION WITH SOUND

Francis Ford Coppola's entire career seems to have been driven by a need to innovate and to find artistic solutions to narrative goals. Early in his career, he used music to suggest that *You're a Big Boy Now* (1966) was more than a story of one teenager, but rather—like George Lucas's *American Graffiti* (1973)—the story of an entire generation. In *The Conversation* (1974), he elevated the sound effect to the equivalent of dialogue. The film's lead character is a private investigator who specializes in sound recording. Listening is his vocation, understanding is his obsession, and misunderstanding is his fear. In short, he is consumed by sound. Coppola was adventurous in using sound, particularly effects and fragments of conversation, to reflect his character's shifting state of mind.

Perhaps the greatest concentration of Coppola's innovation in sound is his film *Apocalypse Now* (1979). Working with Walter Murch as sound designer and Richard Marks as editor, Coppola created a film as innovative in its use of sound as Cavalcanti's documentary work in the 1930s. We turn now to *Apocalypse Now* to explore the use of sound to introduce ideas into the narrative and to see how sounds are juxtaposed with the other elements of the film.

Apocalypse Now is the story of Captain Willard who is assigned covert operations that often include infiltrating the enemy line and assassinating the opposition's military leaders. Willard (Martin Sheen) is assigned to travel deep into the war zone, cross into Cambodia, find Colonel Kurtz (Marlon Brando), and kill him. Kurtz, who was also assigned covert operations, has gone beyond orders, killed officials of South Vietnam, and started to operate independently. Convinced that Kurtz is now a danger, the army and the CIA want him killed.

Willard is transported to his mission on a small Navy gunship with a crew of four. Their voyage is presented as a voyage into "the heart of darkness," from modern, organized life to a barbaric primitivism. Along the way, they are aided by American helicopter gunships under the control of a colonel (Robert Duvall) who is an avid surfer. He professes to "love the smell of napalm in the morning" because "it smells like victory." Later, when they meet Kurtz, an other-worldly quality is evident. Kurtz's camp looks like a wartime version of hell, and Willard releases Kurtz from his torment by killing him. The dying Kurtz whispers, "The horror, the horror.-.-.-."

A verbal description cannot capture the non-narrative character of this film. For the audience and for Coppola, it is a voyage into the American heart of darkness. The non-narrative elements of the film, the sound track particularly, help create the interior world that lies beneath the images that Coppola and cinematographer Vittorio Storaro created.[2]

The opening of the film features a visual and aural barrage that immediately implies an interior journey. An image of a forest alight as napalm bombs hit and explode is followed by a shot of a helicopter hovering. The soundtrack does not emphasize the natural sounds of these images. We do not hear the bombs explode at all, and we hear the helicopter rotors whir quietly. Instead, the soundtrack features Jim Morrison and The Doors singing "The End." A close-up of Willard in a hotel room is superimposed over the images of the helicopter and the napalm explosions. The visuals could reflect the end of the world or the plight of a man going mad. The intensity of the close shot of Willard supports the notion that Willard has lost his mind.

Eventually, the scene turns to the waking moments of Willard, who, as he tells us in the narration, is waiting in Saigon for an assignment. As he looks out at the street, the sounds of the street emerge, but as he talks about how he would prefer to be on assignment, the sounds of the jungle replace the sounds of the city and the silence of the hotel room. Coppola used sound effects in this sequence to create the interior space that Willard occupies. He would rather be in the jungle, and what we hear are the sounds of where he wants to be rather than the sounds of where he is.

As Willard begins his tai chi movements in his room, he enters yet another state, and the sitar music and its pace articulate his descent into a state of pure aggression. Only when he smashes his hand is he brought back to the physical world. The sounds keep carrying him into an internal state, however. When two army officials arrive with his orders, natural sound returns.

A second important element of Coppola's use of sound is the narration. Willard serves as the narrator as well as the lead character. This is an unusual element in a feature film. Because the nature of the feature film is to create a believable illusion, the story is usually presented through unfolding action that is edited to create continuity within the confines of dramatic time. In a feature film, narration reminds viewers that they are watching an experience through someone else's filter. Woody Allen can use narration successfully in feature films because we relate to him on two levels: as a writer-performer and as a narrative filmmaker. In the work of most other filmmakers, narration alters the relationship of the viewer to the film to the detriment of the latter.

A few filmmakers other than Woody Allen have successfully used a narrator in their films: for example, the Fred MacMurray character in Billy Wilder's *Double Indemnity* (1944) and the William Holden character in *Sunset Boulevard* (1950). In both examples, however, there was a plausible basis for the narration. In *Sunset Boulevard*, Wilder used the narration at the beginning of the film as a prologue to pique the audience's curiosity about the death of the Holden character. He used the narration later to allow the character to comment on the people who killed him: his agent, his producer, and Norma Desmond and her waxworks. In *Double Indemnity*, the MacMurray character also has been shot. Before he dies, he tells his story into a dictating machine for the insurance investigator. This confession is the basis for the narration, which again plays the role of arousing the audience's curiosity.

In *Apocalypse Now*, the role of the narration is to reinforce Willard's interior journey, which provides the subtext of the film. The narration provides continual observations, insights, and interpretations of events. Willard repeatedly shares information about Kurtz through the narration. Because Kurtz is an important character who does not appear until the last 25 minutes of the film, the narration provides the necessary background about him. At one particular point in the narration, there seems to be a fusion between Willard and Kurtz. Willard professes to be puzzled about Kurtz, but as they proceed deeper into the jungle, his puzzlement is replaced by respect. Before they meet, the narration links the two men and hints that Kurtz is the dark side of Willard's personality. When Willard kills Kurtz at the end of the film, he kills or denies part of himself.

Beyond this dimension of the narration, its tone and pitch suggest that confidential information is being shared. Whenever another character asks about his mission, Willard replies that the information is classified. Willard holds himself aloof from the others; he seems to be self-reliant and doesn't interact unless it's necessary. Through the narration, therefore, Willard shares more with us than with his fellow characters. In this way, the narration further supports Willard's interior world. His secretiveness with the others is not exclusive, but his tone in speaking the narration suggests he may soon totally withdraw from the others.

Willard's state of mind also drives the use of silence in *Apocalypse Now*. Sound in all its manifestations is omnipresent in the film. The sound track is not as crowded as in Robert Altman's *Nashville*, but nevertheless it is full. In the midst of this sound, silence is unusual. It, too, introduces an idea whenever it becomes predominant: the idea of mortal threat.

Three examples from the film demonstrate how Coppola exploited silence. First, when Willard and Chef (Frederic Forrest) are deep in a jungle thicket, the noise of the insects and animals is overwhelming, and the sound of their movement through the thicket is pronounced. Suddenly, the insects and animals become silent. As the two characters become aware of the developing silence, they slow their movements, anticipating danger. The silence becomes more obvious, and suddenly a tiger pounces out of the jungle at Chef. Willard shoots the tiger, but the terror of the silence and its aftermath are too much for Chef. He collapses, swearing he will never leave the boat again, and he doesn't.

Later, during a skirmish with Montagnard tribesmen, the sounds of machine-gun fire, the panic of the crew, and the whistle of arrows rushing through the air give way to an almost total silence at the instant that Chief Phillips is killed by a Montagnard spear. Everyone is incredulous that, in the midst of the boat's superior firepower, it is the primitive spear that is the killing instrument. The silence at this moment underscores the feeling among the crew members.

Finally, as the patrol boat enters Kurtz's camp and is greeted by boatloads of primitives, the silence suggests the danger that the three survivors now face. The silence and tranquility of the boat's movement suggest that its occupants are holding their breath. This is a moment of fear and anticipation: They have finally found Kurtz. The silence is powerful in this scene, and it foreshadows the death that will come in Kurtz's camp.

If silence anticipates death, then electronically produced sound effects play a similar role when they replace natural sounds in *Apocalypse Now*. As the patrol boat proceeds down the river in search of Kurtz, the crew becomes increasingly unnerved. Willard is the exception. As they move downriver, they become involved in various armed conflicts. After the crew experiences two losses, four of the crew members enter a continuous drugged state. One of them paints his face as camouflage.

During the panic attack on a civilian sampan, the natural sounds of life and death permeate the sequence. Afterward, though, the sound effects become increasingly synthesized and unnatural. By the time the boat has reached the last American outpost, totally synthetic sound has replaced natural sound. Only gunfire, dialogue, and rock instrumentals can be heard. The transition from natural sound to synthesized, abstract sound supports the idea that the crew members are losing their sense of reality. As they move deeper into themselves, whether out of fear or self-loathing, the loss of reality is signaled by the introduction of synthetic sound. By the time the crew reaches the last outpost, they've entered another world and they are primed for the last part of their journey into Cambodia to find Colonel Kurtz.

With Walter Murch, Coppola used sound effects and narration to create a sound space that suggests the interior worlds of Willard and, later, the crew. He used a very different approach to the deployment of sound in the external action of the story. The approach is highly stylized, as illustrated by the helicopter attack on the enemy checkpoint on the river. In this sequence, the helicopter unit's colonel becomes enthusiastic about ferrying the boat around the enemy checkpoint when he discovers that one of the crew members, Lance (Sam Bottoms), is a champion surfer. He and a few of his comrades are also California boys who love to surf. They will keep the enemy busy while Lance takes advantage of the opportunity to demonstrate his skill. They attack at dawn, and after losing a number of helicopter gunships, effect the transfer of the gunboat from one part of the river to the other. They also manage to surf. The absurdity of war mixed with recreation presents a different kind of madness from that of Kurtz or Willard, but it is nevertheless a form of madness.

The attack begins at dawn with a cavalry bugle call to charge. This sound effect has no meaning for the enemy—they are too far away to hear—but it provides a reference to the past. The cavalry charge is reminiscent of the golden days of the American West, and the colonel's cowboy hat supports this mythology (Figure 24.1).

As the helicopters approach their target, the colonel orders that music be played. His helicopter is equipped with loudspeakers, which play Richard

Figure 24.1   *Apocalypse Now*, 1979. Courtesy Zoetrope Corporation. Still provided by Moving Image and Sound Archives.

Wagner's *Die Walküre*. This powerful and majestic music stylizes the approach of the helicopters and transforms them into creatures of the gods, bearing a thunderous message. The editing of the approach emphasizes this stylization and moves the attack from realism toward mythology. Only by crosscutting the scene with shots of the Vietcong outpost and its children and civilians did Coppola bring the sequence back to reality (Figure 24.2).

Once the attack begins in earnest, the music and effects give way to the colonel's dialogue. His dialogue, which is brave, foolhardy, and commanding, is another anchor that holds the sequence to realism. When the helicopters and Marines are on the ground, the agony of death and war take over. Although the colonel does not seem vulnerable to this aspect of the war experience, his men are, and their screams of agony are presented in a very realistic, almost cinema verité, style. This contrasts with the presentation of the colonel and the attack he staged on the outpost. The deliberateness of the colonel—the cavalry charge, the opera music, the comments about napalm and victory—is presented in a stylized, nonrealistic manner. The result is an uneasy mix of the stylization and abstraction of death and the intense chaos and realism of death. With their use of sound, Coppola and Murch suggested that these two realities coexist (Figure 24.3).

Figure 24.2   *Apocalypse Now*, 1979. Courtesy Zoetrope Corporation. Still provided by British Film Institute.

Figure 24.3   *Apocalypse Now*, 1979. Courtesy Zoetrope Corporation. Still provided by Moving Image and Sound Archives.

In *Apocalypse Now*, examples abound of sound creating or suggesting a new interpretation of the visuals or introducing a new idea to supersede what the visuals suggest. Coppola and Murch were relentless in their pursuit of creative possibilities for the use of sound. In their films a decade later, David Lynch and Martin Scorsese followed in Coppola's path, exploring the notion that sound can be used to introduce new ideas and new interpretations.

□ NOTES/REFERENCES

1. David Bordwell and Kristin Thompson, "Fundamental Aesthetics of Sound in the Cinema," in E. Weiss and J. Belton, eds., *Film Sound: Theory and Practice* (New York: Columbia University Press, 1985), 181–199.
2. The John Milius–Francis Ford Coppola script for *Apocalypse Now* was based on Joseph Conrad's *Heart of Darkness*, which was set in central Africa.

III

PRINCIPLES OF EDITING

■

■

■

■

25

The Picture Edit
and Continuity

■

Much has been written suggesting that the art of film is editing,[1] and numerous filmmakers from Eisenstein to Welles to Peckinpah have tried to prove this point. However, just as much has been written suggesting that the art of film is avoidance of editing,[2] and filmmakers from Renoir to Ophuls to Kubrick have tried to prove that point. No one has managed to reconcile these theoretical opposites; this fascinating, continuing debate has led to excellent scholarship,[3] but not to a definitive resolution. Both factions, however, work with the same fundamental unit: the shot. No matter how useful a theoretical position may be, it is the practical challenge of the director and the editor to work with some number of shots to create a continuity that does not draw unnecessary attention to itself. If it does, the filmmaker and the editor have failed to present the narrative in the most effective possible manner.

The editing process can be broken down into two stages: (1) the stage of assembling the shots into a rough cut and (2) the stage in which the editor and director fine-tune or pace the rough cut, transforming it into a fine cut. In the latter stage, rhythm and accentuation are given great emphasis. The goal is an edited film that is not only continuous, but also dramatically effective. The goal of the rough cut—the development of visual and sound continuity—is the subject of this chapter; the issue of pace is the subject of Chapter 26. Both chapters attempt to present pragmatic, rather than theoretical, solutions to the editing problem because, in the end, the creativity of editing is based on pragmatic solutions.

The editing problem begins with the individual shot. Is it a still image or a moving image? Is the foreground or the background in focus? How close is the character to the frame? Is the character positioned in the center or off to one side? What about the light and color of the image and the organization of objects or people relative to the main character? A great variety of factors affect the continuity that results when two shots are juxtaposed. The second shot must have some relationship to the first shot to support the illusion of continuity.

The simplest film, the one that respects continuity and real time, is the film that is composed of a single, continuous shot. The film would be honest in its representation of time and in its rendering of the subject, but it probably wouldn't be very interesting. Griffith and those who followed were motivated by the desire to keep audiences involved in the story. Their explorations focused on how little, rather than how much, needs to be shown. They discovered that it isn't necessary to show everything. Real time can be violated and replaced with dramatic time.

The premise of not needing to show everything leads quite logically to the question of what it is necessary to show. What elements of a scene will, in a series of shots, provide the details needed to direct the audience toward what is more important as opposed to less important? This is where the choice of the type of shot—the long shot versus the midshot, the midshot versus close-up—comes into play. This is also where decisions about camera placement—objective or subjective—come into play. The problem for the editor is to choose the shot that best serves the film's dramatic purpose. Another problem follows: Having chosen the shot, how does the editor cut the shot together with the next one so that together they provide continuity? Without continuity (for example, if the editor cuts from one close-up to another that is unrelated), viewers become confused. Editing should never confuse viewers; it should always keep them informed and involved in the story.

Narrative clarity is achieved when a film does not confuse viewers. It requires matching action from shot to shot and maintaining a clear sense of direction between shots. It means providing a visual explanation if a new idea or a cutaway is introduced. To provide narrative clarity, visual cues are necessary, and here, the editor's skill is the critical factor.

□ CONSTRUCTING A LUCID CONTINUITY

Seamlessness has become a popular term to describe effective editing. A seamless, or smooth, cut is the editor's first goal. A seamless cut doesn't draw attention to itself and comes at a logical point within the shot. What is that logical point? It is not always obvious, but viewers always notice when an inappropriate edit point has been selected. For example, suppose that a character is crossing the room in one shot and is seated in the next. These two shots do not match because we haven't seen the character sit down. If we saw her sit down in the first shot and then saw her seated in the second, the two shots would be continuous. The critical factor here is using shots that match the action from one shot to the next.

□ PROVIDING ADEQUATE COVERAGE

Directors who do their work properly provide their editors with a variety of shots from which to choose. For example, if one shot features a character in repose, a close shot of the character as well as a long shot will be filmed. If need be, the props in the shot will be moved to ensure that the close shot looks like the long one. The background and the lighting must support the continuity.

Similarly, if an action occurs in a shot, a long shot will be taken of the entire action, and later a close shot will be taken of an important aspect of the action. Some directors film the entire action in long shot, midshot, and close-up so that the editor has maximum flexibility in putting the scene together. Close-ups and cutaways complete the widest possible coverage of the scene.

If the scene includes dialogue between two people, the scene will be shot entirely from one character's point of view and then repeated from the other's point of view. Close-ups of important pieces of dialogue and close-up reaction shots will also be filmed. This is the standard procedure for all but the most courageous or foolhardy directors. This approach provides the editor with all of the footage needed to create continuity.

Finally, considerations of camera angles and camera movement dictate a different series of shots to provide continuity. With camera angles, the critical issue is the placement of the camera in relation to the character's eye level. If two characters are photographed in conversation using a very high angle, as if one character is looking down on the other, the reverse-angle shot—the shot from the other character's point of view—must be taken from a low angle. Without this attention to the camera angle, the sequence of shots will not appear continuous. When a film cuts from a high-angle shot to an eye-level reaction shot, viewers get the idea that there is a third person lurking somewhere, as represented by the eye-level shot. When that third person does not appear, the film is in trouble.

□ MATCHING ACTION

To provide cut points within shots, directors often ask performers to introduce body language or vocalization within shots. The straightening of a tie and the clearing of a throat are natural points to cut from long shot to close-up when there is no physical movement within the frame to provide the cut point.

Where movement is involved, "here-to-there" is a trick directors use to avoid filming an entire action. When an actor approaches a door, he puts his hand on the doorknob; when he greets someone, he offers his hand. These actions provide natural cut points to move from long shot to close-up. A favorite here-to-there trick is raising a glass to propose a toast. Any action that offers a distinct movement or gesture provides an opportunity within a shot for a cut. The more motion that occurs within the frame, the greater the opportunity for cutting to the next shot.

It is critical that the movement in a shot be distinct enough or important enough so that the cut can be unobtrusive. If the move is too subtle or faint, the cut can backfire. A cut is a promise of more information or more dramatic insight to come. If the second shot is not important, viewers realize that the editor and director have misled them.

Match cuts, then, are based on (1) visual continuity, (2) significance, and (3) similarity in angle or direction. A sample pattern for a match cut is shown in Figure 25.1. The first cut, from the long shot to the close-up, would be

Figure 25.1   **Sample pattern for a match cut.** (A) Long shot of character 1. (B) Close-up of character 1. (C) Reaction shot of character 2; includes character 1 in profile. (D) Midshot of character 1. (E) Midshot of character 2.

continuous because character 1 continues speaking in the close-up. The next shot is a reverse-angle reaction shot of character 2 from her point of view. After the reverse-angle shot of character 2, we return to a midshot of character 1, and in the final shot, we have a midshot of character 2 speaking. The cuts in this sequence come at points when conversation begins, and the cutting then follows the conversation to show the speaker.

The camera position used to film this sequence must not cause confusion. The straightforward approach, in which character 1 is photographed at a 90-degree angle, is easiest. The reverse-angle shot of character 2 would also be a 90-degree angle (Figure 25.2). If the angle for the reverse shot is not

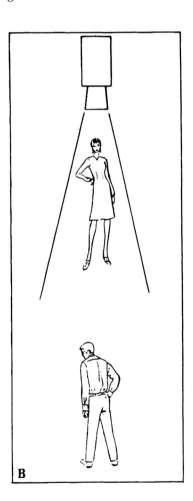

A

B

Figure 25.2   **Positioning the camera for a match cut.** To photograph character 1, the camera is placed in front of him, as shown in (A). To photograph the reverse-angle shot of character 2 so that shots 1 and 2 match, the camera is positioned behind character 1, as shown in (B).

90 degrees (head on), but rather is slightly angled, it will not appear continuous with the 90-degree shot of character 1. Strict continuity is only possible when the angle of the first shot is directly related to the angle of the next shot. Without this kind of correlation, continuity is broken.

□ PRESERVING SCREEN DIRECTION

Narrative continuity requires that the sense of direction be maintained. In most chase sequences, the heroes seem to occupy one side of the screen, and the villains occupy the other. They approach one another from opposite directions. Only when they come together in battle do they appear in the same frame.

Maintaining screen direction is critical if the film is to avoid confusion and keep the characters distinct. A strict left-to-right or right-to-left pattern must be maintained. When a character goes out to buy groceries, he may leave his house heading toward the right side of the frame. He gets into his car and begins the journey. If he exited to the right, he must travel left to right until he gets to the store. Reversing the direction will confuse viewers and suggest that the character is lost. Preserving this sense of direction is particularly important when a scene has more than one character. If one character is following another, the same directional pattern will work fine, but if they are coming from two different directions and will meet at a central location, a separate direction must be maintained for each character.

If a character is moving right to left, he exits shot 1 frame right and enters shot 2 frame left (Figure 25.3). The cut point occurs at the instant when the character exits shot 1 and enters shot 2. The match cut preserves continuity and appears to be a single, continuous shot. If there is a delay in the cut between when the character exits shot 1 and when he reappears in shot 2, discontinuity results, or the cut suggests that something has happened to the character. A sound effect or a piece of dialogue would be necessary to explain the delay.

Equally as interesting an issue for the editor is whether to show every shot in the sequence with the character moving across the frame in each shot. Editors often dissolve one shot into another to suggest that the character has covered some distance. Dissolves suggest the passage of time. Another approach, which was used by Akira Kurosawa in *The Seven Samurai* (1954) and Stanley Kubrick in *Paths of Glory* (1957), is to show the character in tight close-up with a panning, trucking, or zoom shot that follows the character. As long as the direction in this shot matches that of the full shot of the character, this approach can obviate the need to follow a character completely across the frame. Cutaways and the crosscutting of a parallel action can also be used to avoid continuous movement shots. If a character changes direction, that change must appear in the shot. Once the change is shown, the character can move in the opposite direction. The proper technique is illustrated in Figure 25.4.

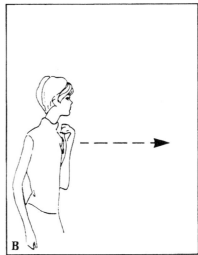

Figure 25.3   Maintaining screen direction for the match cut. If a character exits frame right (A), she must enter the next shot frame left (B).

These general rules are applicable whether the shots are filmed with the camera placed objectively or with it angled. Movement need not occur only from left to right or right to left. Diagonal movement is also possible. The character might enter at the bottom left corner of the frame and exit at the upper right corner. Here, the left-to-right motion is preserved. Filmmakers often use this camera position because it provides a variety of options. There is a natural cut point as the character begins to move away from a point very close to the camera. In this classic shot, we see the character's back full frame, and as she walks away from the camera, she comes fully into view. The shot starts as a close-up and ends as a long shot. The director can also choose to follow the character with a subjective camera, or the director can use a zoom to stay with the close-up as the character moves through the frame. In all of these cases, diagonal movement across the frame provides more screen time than left-to-right or right-to-left movement. This makes the shot economically more viable, more interesting, and, because it's subjective, more involving. The shot lasts longer on screen, thereby implying more time has passed. Also the costs of production are so great that a shot that is held on screen longer is better from a production cost point of view.

A shot with diagonal movement that starts as a long shot and ends as a close-up is also involving, and it allows the most literal rendering of the movement (Figure 25.5). An alternative would be to follow the actor's movement with the camera or zoom, maintaining a midshot or close-up throughout the shot. Any of these options will work as long as screen direction is preserved from shot to shot and continuity is maintained.

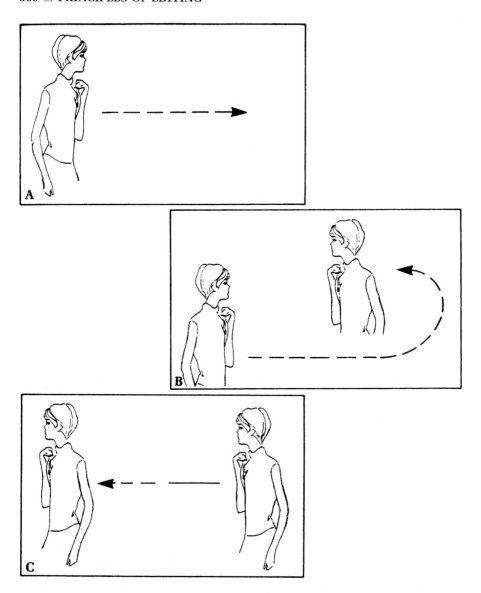

Figure 25.4   Maintaining continuity with a change in direction. (A) Character moves left to right. (B) Character is shown changing direction. (C) Character moves right to left.

□ SETTING THE SCENE

Match cutting and directional cutting help the editor preserve continuity. The establishing shot, whether it is an extreme long shot or long shot that sets the

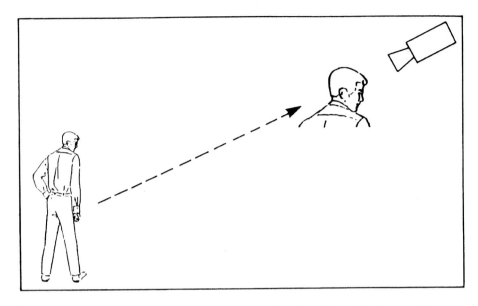

Figure 25.5 Following diagonal movement. The shot shown begins as a long shot and ends as a close shot.

scene in context, is another important tool. Karel Reisz refers to the scene in *Louisiana Story* (1948) that begins in a close-up. The setting for the sequence is not established until later.[4] What about stories that take place in New York or on Alcatraz or in a shopping mall? In each case, an establishing shot of the location sets the context for the scene and provides a point of reference for the close-ups, the follow action shots, and the visual details of the location.

Most filmmakers use an extreme long shot or a long shot to open the scene. It provides a context for the scene and allows the filmmaker to explore the details of the shot. The classic progression into and out of a scene (long shot/midshot/close-up/midshot/long shot) relies on the establishing shot. The other shots flow out of the establishing shot, and thus a clear continuity is provided. Classically, the establishing shot is the last shot in the scene as well as the first. Many filmmakers and editors have found ways to shorten the regimentation of this approach. Mike Nichols, for example, presented an entire dialogue scene in one shot. By using the zoom lens, he avoided editing. Notwithstanding novel approaches of this type, it is important that editors know how to use the establishing shot to provide continuity for the scene.

□ MATCHING TONE

Variations in light and color from shot to shot can break continuity. These elements are under the cameraperson's control, but when variations do exist between shots, they can be particularly problematic for the editor.

Laboratory techniques can solve some minor problems, but there are limits to what is possible. Newer, more forgiving film stocks have improved the latitude by overcoming poor lighting conditions and lessened the severity of the problem. The best solution, however, is consistency of lighting, cameraperson, and the sensitivity of the director to that working relationship. If all else fails, it may be necessary to reshoot the affected scenes. This requires the flexibility and understanding of the film's producers.

The editor's goal is always to match the tone between shots, but the editor's ability to find solutions to variations caused by poor lighting control is limited.

□ MATCHING FLOW OVER A CUT

What is the best way to show action without making the continuity appear to be mechanical? Every action has a visual component that can be disassembled into its various parts. Having breakfast may mean removing the food from the refrigerator, preparing the meal, laying out the dishes, eating, and cleaning up. If a scene calls for a character to eat breakfast, all of these sundry elements would add up to some rather elaborate action that is probably irrelevant to the scene's dramatic intention.

To edit the sequence, the editor will have to decide two things: (1) which visual information is dramatically interesting, and (2) which visual information is dramatically necessary. The length of the scene will be determined by the answer to these two questions, particularly the latter. Dramatic criteria must be applied to the selection of shots. If a shot does not help to tell the story, why has it been included in the film?

For example, if it is important to illustrate the fastidious nature of the character, how that character goes about preparing breakfast, eating, and cleaning up might be important. If the character is a slob and that is the important point to be made, then here too the various elements of the breakfast might be shown. However, if it is only important to show how quickly the character must leave home in the morning, the breakfast shots will get short shrift. The dramatic goals, first and foremost, dictate the selection of shots.

Once shots are selected, the mechanical problem for the editor is to make the cuts in such a way that undue time is not spent on shots that provide little information. Is there a way to show the character eating breakfast quickly? The answer, of course, is yes, but the editor does not accomplish this goal by stringing together shots of the character involved in each element of the activity. The screen time required for all of these shots would give the impression of the slowest breakfast ever eaten.

The editor has to find elegant ways to collapse the footage so that the scene requires a minimum of screen time. The shots of the breakfast, for example, can be cut down to a fraction of their previous length, and the scene can be made to flow smoothly and quickly. Consider a shot in which the character enters the kitchen, approaches the refrigerator, removes the milk and juice, and places them on the counter. It is not necessary to watch him traverse the kitchen. By cutting the long shot when he still has some distance to go, moving to a close shot of the refrigerator, holding for a second, and then showing his hand enter the frame to open the refrigerator door, we have collapsed the shot into a fragment of its original length. If the shot that follows this shows the character placing the milk and juice on the counter, we can drop the part of the previous shot where he removes the milk and juice from the fridge and carries them to the counter.

In this hypothetical example, we used a fragment of a shot to make the same point as the entire shot, using considerably less screen time as a result. By applying this approach to all of the shots in the breakfast scene, the vital information will be shown, and the screen time will suggest that the character is having a very quick breakfast. Continuity and dramatic goals are respected when the editor cuts each shot down to its essence. The flow from shot to shot is maintained without mechanically constructing the scene in the most literal sense of the shots. Literal shots do not necessarily provide dramatic solutions.

□ CHANGE IN LOCATION

This principle of cutting each shot down to its essence can be applied to show a character changing location. Rather than show the character move from point A to point B, the editor often shows her departing. If she is traveling by car, some detail about the geography of the area is appropriate. Unless there is a dramatic point to the scene other than getting the character from point A to point B, the editor then cuts to a street sign or some other indication of the new location. If the character traveled from left to right, the street sign will be positioned toward the right of the frame. Directors often use a tight close-up here. After holding a few seconds on the close-up, the character enters from frame left, and the zoom back picks up her arrival. If the shot is not a zoom, the character crosses the frame until she stops at the destination within the frame. With these few shots, the audience accepts that the character has traveled from one location to another, and little screen time was required to show that change in location.

□ CHANGE IN SCENE

To alert the audience to a change in scene, it is important to provide some visual link between the last shot of one scene and the first shot of the next. Many directors and editors now cover this transition with a shift in sound or by running the same sound over both shots. However, this inexpensive method shouldn't dissuade you from trying to find a visual solution.

If there is a similarity in movement from one shot to another, visual continuity can be achieved. This works by tracking slowly in the last shot of the first scene from left to right or from right to left. Because the movement is slow, the details are visible. The cut usually occurs when the tracking shot reaches the middle of the frame. In the next scene, the movement is picked up at about the same point in midframe, but as the motion is completed, it becomes clear that a new scene is beginning.

A change in scene can also be effected by following a particular character. If he appears in a suit in the last shot of one scene and in shorts in the first shot of the next scene, the shift occurs smoothly. Other elements help ease the transition, for example, the character might be speaking at the end of the first scene and at the beginning of the next.

Finally, a straightforward visual cue, such as a prop, can be used to make the transition. Suppose, for instance, that one scene ends with a close-up of a marvelous antique lamp. If the next scene begins with a close-up of another antique lamp and pulls back to reveal an antique store, the shift will be effective. The visual link between scenes allows a smooth transition to take place. The scenes may have very little to do with one another, but they will appear to be continuous.

□ NOTES/REFERENCES

1. Eisenstein and Pudovkin have written extensively to this point.
2. This view was put forward by André Bazin in *What Is Cinema*, Vols. I, II (Berkeley: University of California Press, 1971).
3. A fine example is Brian Henderson's "The Long Take," in *A Critique of Film Theory* (New York: E. P. Dutton, 1980).
4. Karel Reisz and Gavin Millar, *The Technique of Film Editing* (Boston: Focal Press, 1968), 225.

26

The Picture Edit and Pace

■

Once the rough assembly is satisfactory, the question of narrative clarity has, to a certain extent, been satisfied. Shots flow from one to another and suggest continuity. What is still lacking is the dramatic emphasis of one shot relative to another. This is the role of pace, which is fine-tuned in the second editing stage. The product of this stage, the fine cut, is the culmination of all of the editor's decisions. At the end of the fine cut, the choices have all been made, and the sound tracks have been aligned and prepared for the mix. The stage between rough cut and final sound mix is the subject of this chapter. The goal of this stage is to introduce dramatic impact through the editing decisions.

Pace is most obvious in action sequences, but all sequences are shaped for dramatic effect. Variation in pace guides viewers in their emotional response to the film. More rapid pacing suggests intensity; slower pacing, the reverse.

Karel Reisz explores the opposite of editing for pace in his discussion of Hitchcock's *Rope* (1948), a film that was directed to avoid editing.[1] The entire film looks like a single long take. Reisz argues that too much screen time, which could have been used more productively, is wasted moving the camera from one spot to another.

This notion may seem obvious, but when we look at the opening of Welles's *Touch of Evil* (1958), we may back away from too general a statement about using camera movement to avoid editing. This 3-minute sequence follows a car from a scene in which a bomb is planted in its trunk to a scene showing the owner returning with a guest to a scene in which they drive from Tijuana across the border into California. During the drive, we see Varguez (Chariton Heston), a Mexican policeman, cross the border with his new wife (Janet Leigh). They occupy the foreground while the doomed car moves across the border in the background. Soon after, the car passes them and explodes. The explosion leads to the first cut in the film.

Welles chose to begin his film with an elegant tracking shot through town and across the border. He could have fragmented the scene into shots that showed the bomb being planted and the owner returning and intercut the car with Varguez as each progressed across the border. If he had taken this approach, the pacing would have progressively quickened as we moved toward the explosion. The pace, rather than the contradiction between foreground and background, would have heightened the tension of the film.

In *Touch of Evil*, Welles avoided editing, avoided the pacing, and yet opened the film with a mesmerizing and powerful sequence. This example suggests that pace isn't everything. It reminds us that composition, lighting, and performance also count.

Having suggested the limits of pace, let's turn now to the possibilities of pace. Many directors specializing in political thrillers have used pace to empower their message. Costa-Gavras's exposé of Greek injustice in *Z* (1969) and Oliver Stone's exploration of political assassination in *JFK* (1991) both rely on juxtaposition and pace to drive home a particular point of view.

Another genre in which pace plays a central role is the adventure film. In both the mixed genre adventure film, such as Joel Coen's *Raising Arizona* (1987), and the straightforward adventure film, such as Steven Spielberg's *Raiders of the Lost Ark* (1981), pace helps provide the sense of energy and excitement that is at the heart of the genre's success.

Whether it is the excitement of an adventure film or the indignation of a political thriller, pace is the key. The role of pace varies in different genres, but it always comes into play to some degree.

□ TIMING

One element of pace is the timing of particular shots. Where in a sequence should a particular close-up or cutaway be positioned for maximum impact? When is a subjective shot more powerful than an objective one? What is the most effective pattern of crosscutting between shots or juxtapositions within shots? These are editing decisions that directly affect the issue of dramatic effectiveness.

The editor's understanding of the purpose of the sequence as a whole helps her make these decisions. The purpose of the sequence might be exposition or characterization. Within these broad categories, the editor must decide how much visual and aural explanation and how much punctuation are needed to make the point. Finally, she must decide whether to take a straightforward editing strategy or use its alternative: a more indirect, layered strategy. For example, in a comedy film, the strategy of editing for surprise might be most appropriate. In comedy, surprise is critical. If the edit is not properly timed, the comedy is lost. Surprise is also useful in the thriller. In most other genres, though, a more straightforward approach is generally taken.

An example of surprise used for comic purposes can be found in Joel Coen's *Raising Arizona*. A 6-minute comedy sequence is difficult to sustain, particularly if it is an action sequence, but it succeeds in *Raising Arizona*. In the film. Hi (Nicholas Cage) and Ed (Holly Hunter), a childless couple, have stolen a baby from a rich businessman whose wife has had quintuplets. Hi is a former criminal, and Ed is a former law-enforcement officer. In this sequence, Hi decides to revert to crime in his old milieu, the local convenience store. Ed is not happy about this decision. Not only would Hi be breaking the law, but if caught, his actions would deprive their new child of its "father."

The sequence begins with Hi and Ed expressing concern about the future. They stop at a convenience store to buy disposable diapers for the baby. Ed plays with the baby while Hi enters the store. The first surprise comes when Hi decides to rob the store of a box of diapers and as much cash as he can get. The clerk pushes a silent alarm.

The next surprise is Ed's response once she sees Hi robbing the store. She becomes angry and leaves, deserting him. Hi is surprised by Ed's action, but not as surprised as he is by the store clerk, who has now a Magnum .357 in his hand and is trying to kill him. Hi flees on foot, but the police sirens suggest he is in trouble. He runs after Ed, with the police cars in pursuit.

Hi escapes into a backyard, only to be accosted by a watchdog. The dog lunges, but it is chained to an anchor, which saves Hi's life. Hi continues to run, but the dog is persistent and pulls the chain's anchor from the ground. The dog joins the police and the clerk in their pursuit of Hi. At this point, Ed, who has gotten over her anger, returns to pick up Hi, but she can't find him. Hi, now desperate, stops a truck on the road. He threatens the driver, who takes him into the truck.

Other neighborhood dogs take off after Hi, who is now being chased by dogs, the police, a store clerk, and his wife. The clerk fires his gun and shatters the truck's windshield. As the driver turns to avoid the onslaught, the first dog jumps the armed clerk by mistake. To avoid the police, the truck driver changes direction, putting the truck on a collision course with a house.

The truck driver, terrified by threats approaching from all sides, puts on the brakes. The sudden stop sends Hi flying through the front of the truck. The truck driver backs up and escapes. Meanwhile, Hi has been deposited on the front steps of a house. He runs through the house, closely pursued by the police and the dogs.

He escapes into a supermarket, where he picks up another box of diapers (he lost the other package). The police and the dogs are still in pursuit, and now the supermarket manager begins firing at Hi with a shotgun. The panicking customers add to the chaos, and Hi escapes. He loses the second box of diapers, but he is picked up by Ed outside the supermarket. They escape.

In this sequence, the timing of the surprises—the clerk's gun, the dog's tenacity, the truck driver's panic—all depend on the editing of the scene. In each case, a quick cut introduces the surprise, often in an exaggerated visual. The clerk's Magnum, for example, seems like a cannon due to its proximity to the camera and the use of a wide-angle lens. The quick cut and the visual exaggeration yield the desired comic effect.

□ RHYTHM

In general, the rhythm of a film seems to be an individual and intuitive matter. We know when a film does not have a rhythm. The jerkiness of the editing draws attention to itself. When the film has an appropriate rhythm, the editing appears to be seamless, and we become totally involved with the characters and the story. Of course, intuition alone is not enough. Some practical considerations help determine an appropriate length for particular shots within a sequence.

The amount of visual information within the shot often determines the length of the shot. A long shot, which has more visual information than a close-up, will be held for a longer time to allow the audience to absorb the information. If the information is new, it is appropriate to allow the shot to run longer so that the audience can become familiar with the new milieu. Moving shots are often held on screen longer than static images to allow the audience to absorb the shifting visual information. A cutaway that is important to the plot is generally extended to establish its importance.

Conversely, a close-up with relatively little information will be held on screen for only a short time. The same is true for static shots and repeated shots. Once the shot's visual information has been viewed, it's not necessary to give equal time to a second or third viewing.

It's not possible to provide absolute guidelines about the length of shots. However, it is important that the editor develop a sense of the relative lengths of shots within a sequence. Shots should never be all the same length. If they are all long or all short, the lack of variety deadens the impact of the sequence. It will have no rhythm. In the pacing of shots, rhythm requires the variation of the length of the shots.

Rhythm is also affected by the type of transition used between sequences. A straight cut can be jarring; it leaves us confused until a sound or visual cue suggests that a change has taken place. A dissolve at the end of one sequence into the beginning of the next makes a smooth transition and provides a visual cue. The dissolve, which is often associated with the passing of time, can also imply a change of location. The rhythm between sequences is smoother when dissolves are used.

A fade-out is occasionally used at the end of a sequence. Although it is clearly indicative of the closure of one sequence and the beginning of the next, the fade is currently not as widely used as it once was. It is still more popular than the wipe or iris shot, but it is certainly less popular than the dissolve.

If the editor's goal is to make a sequence seamless, his first criterion is to understand and work to clarify the emotional character of the scene. To do so most effectively, the editor must respect the emotional structure of the performances. This means trusting that a pause between two lines of dialogue is not necessarily a lapse, but rather part of the construct of the performance. To edit out the pause may make superficial sense, but makes no sense whatsoever in terms of the performance. The editor must learn to distinguish performance from error, or dead space. It may be as simple as following action to its conclusion, or it may be more complex, involving the subtle nuances of the delivery of dialogue or nonverbal mannerisms. Cutting into the performance may break the rhythm established by the performer in the scene or sequence.

Understanding both the narrative and the subtextual goals of a scene will also allow the editor to follow and modulate the editing so that it clarifies and emphasizes rather than confuses. The editor will be able to determine how long the shots need to be held on screen and how much modulation is necessary to make the point of the scene clear. The editor will then be able to use the most dynamic tools, like crosscutting, and the most minimal, the long shot, for maximum effect.

A simplified example of rhythmic pacing can be found in the "Tomorrow Belongs to Me" sequence in Bob Fosse's *Cabaret* (1972). A young boy stands up in a rural beer garden in 1932 Germany. He is dressed in a Hitler Youth uniform, but he is young enough to have an innocent, prepubescent voice. The impression he gives is of youthful beauty and optimism. As the song progresses, the orchestration becomes more elaborate, and the young man is joined by others. By the end of the song, Germans of all ages have joined in a defiant interpretation of the lyrics. By editing rapidly, using many closeups, and cutting to Germans of all ages, Fosse produced a powerful sequence foreshadowing Nazism. The editing helps create the feelings of both innocence and aggression as the singers shift from a simple, innocent interpretation of the song to an aggressive one. The shifting emotional tone of the scene is modulated, and the result illustrates not only the power of pacing, but also how the modulation of pace enhances the power of a scene.

A more subtle and complex example is the 9-minute sequence that serves as the dramatic climax of Bernardo Bertolucci's *The Conformist* (1971). Marcello (Jean-Louis Trintignant) is an upper-middle-class follower of Mussolini in pre-World War II Italy. He wants to be accepted by the Fascists, but at his initiation, they ask him to help in assassinating an exiled dissident in Paris. The man is Marcello's former professor. On his honeymoon in Paris, Marcello reestablishes contact with Professor Quadri and gains his trust. He also falls in love with the professor's young wife, Anna (Dominique Sanda). He warns her not to accompany her husband on his trip, but at the last minute, she chooses to travel with him.

The assassination sequence that follows reveals Marcello's true nature as a coward and facism's true nature as a brutal ideology that does not tolerate dissidence. The sequence can be broken down into five sections plus a prologue: prologue (2 minutes, 45 seconds), (1) the trap (2 minutes), (2) the murder of the professor (1 minute, 25 seconds), (3) Anna's attempt to be saved (1 minute), (4) Bangangan's response (40 seconds), and (5) the murder of Anna (1 minute, 30 seconds).

Given the extreme dramatic nature of the events, Bertolucci did not rely on rapid pace. Instead, he varied the shots between subjective close-ups and objective traveling shots. Only in the last sequence, the murder of Anna, did he use subjective camera movement. Bertolucci also varied foreground and background. The long shots are wide-angle shots of the fog- and snow-shrouded road through the forest. The early morning light throws shadows that are as stately as the trees of the forest. In the close-ups, Bertolucci used a telephoto lens that collapsed and blurred the context. The close-ups are interior shots in Marcello's car or in Professor Quadri and Anna's car. By varying close-ups, long shots, and point-of-view shots, Bertolucci set up a visual tension that is every bit as powerful as if he had relied on pace alone.

In the first scene in the sequence, Marcello muses about Quadri and Anna. He wishes he were not there. His driver, Bangangan, is a Fascist to the core. He has no dreams, only memories of his induction into the ideology that organizes his interior and exterior lives. The reverie of this scene was created with very lengthy takes, including a 50-second close-up of Marcello. In this shot, Bertolucci dropped the focus and slowly panned to Bangangan, also in close-up. Bertolucci avoided editing the interior car shots to create a greater sense of unity inside the car. He alternated the interiors with wide-angle objective tracking shots of the car moving through the forest. The result is a highly emotional stylization. The scene has an emotional reality but seems almost too beautiful to be real.

The next shot shifts to the interior of Quadri's car. Anna and Quadri appear in a crowded close-up. The subjective point of view shows the road ahead as Anna looks back and tells Quadri that she thinks they are being followed. He dismisses the idea. Anna's sense of the danger ahead is offset by his assurance that he sees nothing.

The scene proceeds in a very stylized manner to show their car cut off by a feigned accident in front of them and Marcello's car stopped behind them. Close-ups of each statically present the stand-off that precedes the murder. Only Quadri's insistence on seeing to the well-being of the other driver breaks the stillness. Anna asks him not to go. He finds the driver unconscious and the car locked. Anna locks her car. The static shots stretch out the sequence, which is long at 2 minutes. This pause is emotionally tense because we see the scene through Marcello's eyes. He knows what is coming. Although the scene is more rapidly cut than the prologue, it is nevertheless slowly paced.

The murder of Quadri is cut much faster. The killers come from the woods. They are joined by the driver of the front car. The killing itself is presented as a version of the killing of Shakespeare's *Julius Caesar*. All of the killers participate. They use knives, and the death is drawn out. Because of the nature of the content, this scene is more rapidly paced than the previous scenes in this sequence.

The next scene, Anna's attempt to save herself, relies less on pace than on performance and close-ups. The pain and poignancy of Anna screaming for Marcello to save her is accentuated by their relationship and by the situation. She pulls on the door of his car, facing him, screaming for her life. His inability or unwillingness to help her represents the emotional high point of the sequence. This is Marcello's moment of truth, his opportunity for salvation, but it is not to be. Love is not great enough to overcome politics. He does not rescue her, and she runs off to her fate. The shots in this scene are held much longer than the shots of the preceding murder scene.

The next scene is short. Bangangan editorializes on his disdain for Marcello and categorizes him with every other group that the Fascists hate. This scene is not very long, but it provides an opportunity to pause between the two most powerful scenes in the sequence. It allows the audience to recover somewhat from the shock of Marcello's failure to save Anna.

The final sequence, the murder of Anna, does not rely on pace, although it is one of the most powerful scenes in the film. Instead, Bertolucci used subjective camera footage of the murderers as they chase Anna through the woods. The camera is handheld, and consequently, the action seems all the more real. The Fascists fire at her, passing the automatic pistol to one another. She is shot, falters, and then falls. The camera moves unsteadily around her bloodied body, and even after her death, it continues to circle before finally retreating from the woods with the killers. The shifts in pace in this scene have more to do with the pace of the movement itself than with the editing. That movement slows once Anna has been shot and continues at a slower pace until the end of the sequence.

This sequence uses a varied pace to carry us through a wide range of emotions. It also identifies a clear emotional role for each of the characters. In fact, Bertolucci remained very close to those roles through his use of close-ups. By varying the close-ups with objective long shots of the forest, Bertolucci added a layer of tension that supported the pace when he chose to rely on it.

This entire sequence is 9 minutes long on the screen. To the extent that we are involved in the sequence, we suspend our sense of real time. In real time, the sequence might have taken 5 minutes or 5 hours. Certain parts of the sequence are given more time than might have been expected. Anna's plea for help, for example, is as long as each murder. Realistically, it would not have taken so long given the proximity of the murderers. However, Bertolucci felt that it was important to give Marcello a chance for redemption and a chance to be incapable of it. This, as much as the loss of a woman he loves, is Marcello's tragedy. The length of Anna's plea for help is thus dramatically important. Pace is affected by the importance of the scene to the film. If the scene is sufficiently important, it may be extended to suit its dramatic importance to the story.

□ TIME AND PLACE

Pace can help establish a sense of time and place. Examples from Stanley Kubrick's *2001: A Space Odyssey* (1968) and *Barry Lyndon* (1975) were discussed in Chapter 10. Kubrick exploited pace to the same extent in the battle for Hue in *Full Metal Jacket* (1987) (Figure 26.1) as he did in his earlier

Figure 26.1 *Full Metal Jacket*, 1987. Courtesy of British Film Institute.

works. The pace of the sequences, the cinema verité camera style, the set design, and the sound create the setting of Hue, Vietnam, in 1968. The actual city was re-created on a set in England for the film. Martin Scorsese relied heavily on pace to help him create his version of New York in *Mean Streets* (1973), and George Lucas relied on music and pace to create his view of Northern California in the early 1960s in *American Graffiti* (1973).

Few filmmakers have been more effective at using pace to create a sense of time and place than Carroll Ballard was in *The Black Stallion* (1979). The first 45 minutes of the film are largely silent. The first third of the film tells the story of young Alec, who is on a ship near the coast of North Africa. The year is 1946. Alec becomes fond of a black horse on board the ship. It is an Arabian, untamed and seemingly untameable. The ship encounters bad weather, and a fire on board threatens the passengers' lives. Alec's father saves his life, and the boy saves the horse's life.

For the next 30 minutes, the scene shifts to a deserted island where the boy and the horse, seemingly the only survivors of a shipwreck, become friends and in so doing, save each other. Two primary locations are featured in this section of the film: the ship and the island. Ballard realized that he had to create both from the perspective of an inquisitive 11-year-old child. He did this with a magical realism. The images are almost other-worldly, and the editing recognizes Alec's sense of the importance of particular details about the horse, his father, and the world. He is not afraid of the world; rather, he is part of it.

Time is collapsed for all but the important events. We know that much real time has passed, and we accept the mundane details of life on the island: food, shelter, and warmth. Alec's relationship with the horse, which is carefully developed in the sequence, is detailed in almost a magical progression. The boy gains the horse's trust by offering him food and later takes him into the water where he gradually mounts the horse. The magical character of this part of the film is enhanced by shots of the boy and the horse from the perspective of the sandy ocean bottom. They appear as intruders, and somehow it unifies them in the context of the mysterious sea. Ballard alternated this sequence with traveling shots of boy and horse filmed from high above the water. The effect is to reinforce the specificity of the time and place.

□ THE POSSIBILITIES OF RANDOMNESS UPON PACE

One of the remarkable elements of editing is that the juxtaposition of any grouping of shots implies meaning. The pacing of those shots suggests the interpretation of that meaning. The consequence of this is seen in microcosm when a random shot or cutaway is edited into a scene: it introduces a new idea. This principle is elaborated where there are a number of random shots in a scene. If edited for effect, the combination of shots creates a meaning quite distinct from the sum of the individual parts. This shaping is, in effect, pure editing.

A specific example suggests the possibilities. Francesco Rosi's *Three Brothers* (1980) opens with an image of an artificial building—a parody of a building suitable to a dream—in the background and a group of large rats in the foreground. The rats approach the camera. The cut to the next shot, a close-up of a young man asleep, suggests that he is dreaming of the rats. The scene that follows shows that he lives and works in an institution for juveniles. Was he dreaming that his wards are rats or that the other members of society are? The two opening shots are set into context by the scene that follows, but the juxtaposition implies potential meanings beyond the content of either shot.

In Ingmar Bergman's *Winter Light* (1962), a disillusioned minister serves a small parish. One man has lost his faith and contemplates suicide. Others want to relate to the minister, but he is unable to relate to them. Bergman used juxtapositions to detail the minister's disillusionment. A series of exterior dissolves at the end of the sermon imply his distance from the parishioners. Later, a parishioner who wants to take care of him (the minister's wife has died) has left him a letter. He reads the letter, which explains how she feels about him. Bergman cut from his reading the letter to the woman in midshot confessing her feelings. By cutting in that second shot, Bergman moved us from the minister's dispassion and indifference to the parishioner's passion. He altered the meaning of one shot by shifting to another.

The shots don't necessarily provide continuity; the contradiction between the shots alters the meaning of the scene.

The films of Rosi and Bergman suggest how the juxtaposition and organization of shots can layer meaning. The pacing of the shots themselves deepens the effect of juxtaposing random shots.

□ NOTE/REFERENCE

1. Karel Reisz and Gavin Millar, *The Technique of Film Editing* (Boston: Focal Press, 1968), 233–236.

27

The Sound Edit and Clarity

■

In the picture edit, the rough assembly begins the process of narrative clarification. The goal at the end of the rough picture assembly is a clear narrative in which performance and story progression can be evaluated. The goal of the rough sound edit is equivalent: to achieve believability of performance and a progressive sense of the story. Issues of dramatic emphasis and metaphor are left for the fine cut for sound as well as visuals. The fine-tuning of the sound edit is discussed in the next chapter. In this chapter, the concerns are achieving a narrative exposition parallel to the picture edit, developing the necessary sense of realism, and deciding how much or how little dialogue is necessary to achieve those goals.

Because sound is more rapidly processed by the viewer than are the visuals, the problem of believability is magnified. If the sound does not seem believable, the visuals will be undermined and audience involvement will be lost. Believable sound is thus central to the experience of the film. Consequently, the most urgent task of the sound edit is to create believable sound.

This chapter suggests the practical agenda for the first phase of the sound edit. Narrative clarity and believability are the primary goals. To set the process in context, it is useful to examine an overview of the sound edit. The issues of sound are specifically discussed in Chapters 2 and 24, and sound is an important topic of other chapters.

The three general categories of sound are dialogue, sound effects, and music. In documentary and sometimes in fiction film, the fourth category of narration (or, as it is called in the United Kingdom, commentary) is added.

Sound clarity in dialogue is so important that separate tracks are used for the principal actors, and other tracks are used for important secondary characters. Separate tracks are used for sound effects, and separate tracks are used for music. This degree of separation provides maximum flexibility for the sound engineer when the sound tracks are eventually mixed together. The master mix might incorporate from 6 to 60 individual tracks. The greater the number of tracks, the greater the flexibility for the sound mixer. Sound separation, whether of effects or dialogue, allows sounds to be layered and provides the clarity that ensures that a key line of dialogue is not undermined by a sound effect or drowned out by music. The producer, director, editor, and sound mixer look for more than clarity in the mix; they also want dramatic emphasis and highlighting. They use contrast to underscore meaning. The key word here is *orchestration*. When mixed, the sound tracks yield levels of meaning that are unavailable from a single sound track.

The separation of sound effects makes possible a smoother transition from one sound to another. The mixer need only fade out one effect and fade up another. An equally useful technique is to use a continuing sound over two disparate visuals. Even if the visuals take place in different locations and relate to different dramatic purposes, the continuity of a sound, whether an effect or a piece of dialogue, implies a link between the two shots or scenes. The sound mix can thus separate or link; it can imply the passage of time or the continuity of time. How to use sound is decided in the sound mix.

The work associated with the mix itself is substantial: the creation of up to 60 tracks in a feature film. Not all of those tracks are created on location or on a set. Original sound is an important element in the creation of the sound tracks, but manufactured sound is equally important. In sound effects and dialogue tracks, sound is manufactured in the name of believability during the post-production process. Dialogue is often redubbed or looped to strengthen intonation or intention. This is done in a studio with the performer redelivering her lines as she watches a projection of the performance.

Sound effects libraries, re-created effects that sound like a slap or a cricket or a footstep, and synthesized sound effects are all available during the post-production process. Music, however, is created and re-created separately in post-production. Narration is often written at this stage to underscore or clarify the visuals.

All of these sound details are worked out in the editing phase. What the production has not provided in original sound will be created in post-production. Because of the number of tracks used, the sound edit is even more elaborate and requires many more decisions than the picture edit. Because a wrong decision can undermine the visuals so readily, the sound edit is complex and critical. Without an effective sound track, the visuals will not succeed.

☐ GENERAL GOALS OF THE SOUND EDIT

The first task that the editor faces is determining the narrative point of the scene. The narrative point must be supported or, more precisely, surrounded by sound. In a film like Gillo Pontecorvo's *The Battle of Algiers* (1965), which was a dramatic re-creation of the Algerian struggle for independence from France, authenticity is central to our involvement with the film's story. Because the film was composed entirely of re-created footage (not newsreel footage) of the war, the sound effects and the timbre of the sound had to mimic the authenticity of the news. Nothing on the sound track could suggest a film set. Consequently, the "liveness" of the effects and dialogue had to be as close to cinema verité as possible. Particular sounds unique to the Algerian location and culture had to be included to reinforce the film's sense of place and time.

William Friedkin's *Sorcerer* (1977), a remake of the French classic, *The Wages of Fear* (1952), used a similar strategy to establish credibility. Although the story is fiction, Friedkin revealed the history of each of the four lead characters in the prologue. He made those histories as realistic as possible. One of the characters, a Palestinian, is shown on a terrorist bombing mission in Jerusalem. The attack is presented exclusively in cinema verité fashion. The sounds of daytime activity in Jerusalem, the explosion, and its aftermath are presented in a loud, unadulterated fashion. Friedkin seems to have designed the sound to be as raw as the visuals. This sequence is powerful until the artifice of the musical track by Tangerine Dream reminds us that we are watching a film. The music works against the narrative tone of the scene, but the use of music is not the sound editor's decision. The editor's goal is to find and deploy sounds that in tone and intent support the narrative goal of the scene.

A scene has an emotional intention as well as a general narrative point, and this too can be culled and supported by the sound track. In his classic *Cries and Whispers* (1972), Ingmar Bergman used an opening that relies exclusively on sound effects for its impact. The film tells the story of a young woman (Harriet Andersson) who is dying of cancer. She lives on an estate where her two sisters and a housekeeper attend to her. The opening sequence has no dialogue, and is lengthy at 5 minutes. It is dawn. A series of images of the estate are followed by a series of images of clocks in the house. Finally, we see the sisters, who are all asleep. The young woman who is ill soon wakes in pain.

The sound effects are presented in a heightened tone that is far louder than the natural sounds. A bell rings loudly to announce the time. When the character wakes, her breathing is added to the ticking clock and the ringing bell. Her breathing, which is labored and occasionally broken by a sudden pain, is as loud as the delivery of a line of dialogue.

The emotional character of the scene suggests the continuity of time and life. Occasionally, a change is brought home by the nature of breathing, which can be difficult or even threatened. The contrast of the temporary nature of life in the midst of the continuity of time, which is represented here by the clock, is both the tragedy of human life (it ends) and the essence of the natural context for life (it continues with the regularity of a clock). The close-ups Bergman used to visually present the clocks and the women are magnified in their intensity by the pitch of the sound effects and by the way they are used to break the silence. The title of the film couldn't be more apt; it refers to the sounds of dying.

In the next scene, the woman writes in her diary and speaks the narration. The same pitch is used for the sound of the lifting of the inkwell and the scratch of the pen. Both have more force than the voice of the character. They prepare us emotionally for the scene that follows.

It is not necessary to rely exclusively on sound effects for emotional tone. Istvan Szabo opened *Mephisto* (1981) with the presentation of an opera. The diva is clearly enjoying her performance, as is the audience. As the performance ends, Szabo held the applause and cut to a dressing room backstage where Hernrich Hofflin (Klaus Maria Brandauer), the Mephisto of the story, is torn apart with jealous rage. He cries and beats himself as the audience applauds the diva. This linking of her fame and his envy frames the emotional core of the story. Although he compliments her in the next scene, we know his true character, which was revealed through sound.

□ SPECIFIC GOALS OF THE SOUND EDIT

Every story has a sense of time and place that must be created visually and aurally. We have already discussed the newsreel allusions in *Sorcerer* and *The Battle of Algiers*. This technique works fine, but not every film is set during the past 50 years. Many are set much further in the past or even in the future. The need of these films to establish credibility is no less than that of a contemporary story. Examples illustrate the problem and suggest possible solutions.

Jean-Jacques Annaud's *The Bear* (1989) is set in British Columbia about a hundred years ago. The film tells the story of an orphaned bear cub that is adopted by an adult male brown bear. Their experience of civilization, represented by two hunters, is the backbone of the story.

There is some dialogue in the film, but for all intents and purposes, the film relies principally on sound effects and music. Consequently, the sound effects are very important to the film. Annaud used them as most directors use dialogue. He created identifiable effects to individualize the animals. For the most part, he used a symphony of natural sounds. The only exception is the humanized sound that emanates from the bear cub. Throughout the film, the cub sounds increasingly like a human infant. Annaud's intention may have been to enhance our emotional identification with a nonhuman main character. Except for this one sound exaggeration, Annaud's use of sound was remarkably naturalistic to the point of austerity. The naturalism of the sound creates a believability about the time and place. The costumes and mode of speech only confirm that sense of time and place.

One sound moment is worth noting because it is the dramatic high point of the film. The adult bear comes upon one of the hunters who wounded him earlier. They have come back with dogs to search for him. The hunter left the camp to find some water. As he drinks, the bear approaches him. The bear does not attack, but instead roars his disapproval from about a foot away. The pitch of the roar is menacing and violent. The hunter covers his ears in pain and terror. This stand-off seems to continue for quite a long time until the bear decides that he has punished the human for harming him and leaves. The hunter runs to retrieve his rifle and prepares to kill the retreating bear. Then, however, he abandons his goal. The bear stood down his foe, the human, and by allowing him to live, invited him to change his behavior. This entire scene revolves around the single sound effect of the bear's roar. Never has the fury and the beauty of nature been more evocatively portrayed.

A second example is Edward Zwick's *Glory* (1989). We have many photographs of the Civil War, but we have no sense of the sounds of that conflict. In this film, Zwick created an emotionally powerful portrait of war's violence and its opportunity for dignity and self-sacrifice. *Glory* tells the story of the 54th Regiment, which was the first black Union regiment to fight during the Civil War.

The regiment is trained and led by Colonel Robert Shaw (Matthew Broderick), a Boston blue blood. Zwick used the sounds of war—muskets, cannons, horses' hooves, men's cries—to re-create the immediate character of war. Zwick also used music and dialogue to set in context the complex human issues of the film: the struggle to act with dignity to transcend the differences among blacks and whites, to find the common humanity that bonds these men despite their different goals. Zwick often relied on close-ups to underscore the emotional character of the scenes. However, it is the orchestration of the sound that convinces us of the time and place.

Just as sounds that create a sense of time and place are crucial, so too are sounds that are associated with various characters throughout the film. The sound motifs condition the audience emotionally for the intervention, arrival, or actions of a particular character. They can and should be introduced as early in the editing stage as possible. They can be very useful in the rough cut, where they help clarify the narrative functions of the characters and provide a sound association for those characters as we move through the story.

The Seventh Sign (1988), by Australian filmmaker Carl Schultz, illustrates the successful use of sound motifs. The film, about an anticipated cataclysm that will destroy the Earth, is a struggle between good, represented by an angel (Jurgen Prochnow), and evil, in the form of Satan's representative, Father Lucci. Although the story moves from Haiti to the Negev Desert, the microstory is about a young couple (Demi Moore and Michael Biehn) from Venice, California. They are expecting a child. The angel rents a room in their home to protect the child.

The film's characters are surrounded by the sounds of nature, which are forcefully presented. Because the cataclysm that will destroy the Earth will be a natural disaster, the foreboding presence of nature is the sound motif that foreshadows the disaster. A liturgical chorus introduces the angel's first appearance in Haiti and signals his reappearance in the film. The sounds of children are associated with the pregnant woman. When we see her in the doctor's office, at a nursery school, or on a playground, she is surrounded by the sounds of children.

The use of sound motifs can help shape a story that requires many characters and many locations. They are not as necessary for less ambitious stories that have few locations. However, as an editing device, sound motifs are often useful and may be used even in small-scale films.

Finally, sound can be scaled down to move a scene away from naturalism and believability. In *Valmont* (1989), Miles Forman decided to work against the natural drama of the climax of the film. Valmont has provoked a young rival to a duel and has arrived at the appointed place in a drunken state. This is the final step in his self-destruction.

Forman chose not to show on screen the moment of Valmont's death. He used the sound in the scene to work against the expected emotional build-up. He stylized the sound effects to make them seem less than natural. The austerity of sound in this scene does much to undermine its emotional potential. The nonspecificity of the sound and its lack of directedness conform to Forman's visual approach to Valmont's death. Forman's subtlety is instructive to the editor: Sound can be used to build up or to down play a scene.

☐ REALISM AS A GOAL

Naturalistic sound effects and believable dialogue are the basis for creating a realistic film. How far should the editor proceed to achieve this goal? The answer to this question is as important as the editor's understanding of the narrative point and emotional character of a scene.

In the rough cut, the editor must begin to catalogue a series of sounds that will support the realism of a scene. These sounds can be the underpinnings to the narrative and dramatic center of the scene, or they can be deeper background sounds that support the film's sense of realism. It's likely that the sounds captured on location during filming are not pronounced enough to be dramatically useful because they are lost in the delivery of the dialogue. These sounds will have to be recaptured or re-created for the film's sound track. The first step is to catalogue the necessary sounds.

After the sounds have been recorded, they are laid down on one of the numerous effects tracks so that they can be tested with the visual to which they are related. This process is followed for all of the sound effects so that the various effects can always be heard in relation to the scene's visuals. To build up these tracks for maximum flexibility, the sound effects are laid down in such a way that they overlap other sounds. They can thus be faded in or out as needed during the actual sound mix. However, the editor cannot match-cut one sound effect to another as he would do for visuals that flow into one another. The effects must be available to highlight the visuals and make them seem more real, but the effects must be organized for the mix in such a way that one sound does not abruptly end or seque to another sound. This would be disruptive and would draw attention to itself rather than help create the necessary sense of realism.

The same principle applies to dialogue. If the sound of the dialogue seems imperfect, the performance or the position of the microphone undermine the visual. Sometimes a scene can be post-dubbed in a sound studio; more often, though, the scene has to be reshot. The delivery of the dialogue must contribute to the film's sense of realism.

□ DIALOGUE AS SOUND

A key question related to the narrative goal of a scene is whether the dialogue plays a central role. Numerous directors use dialogue indirectly. Although this is the exception, some directors—like Robert Altman, Richard Lester, and, more recently, Jim Jarmusch and Terry Malick—have used dialogue as a sound effect rather than for the information it imparts.

This question must be asked throughout the sound edit because some dialogue is crucial, and some is not. For the editor, the distinction between the two categories is important. With the exception of Woody Allen (for whom language is central), many directors de-emphasize dialogue, which elevates the visual to greater importance and reduces language to the level of the sound effect.

This is perhaps nowhere better illustrated than in the work of David Lynch. That is not to say that Lynch is not interested in sound. In fact, his work is extremely sophisticated in its deployment of sound. Language, however, is nothing but another sound in Lynch's work. A good example is Lynch's key film of the 1980s, *Blue Velvet* (1986), the story of a kidnapping in a small town. The main character attempts to help a singer whose husband and son have been kidnapped by the town criminal (Dennis Hopper). The young man and his girlfriend are not so much civic-minded as they are bored with small-town life, and they become voyeurs.

There is much dialogue in this film, but it does not help us understand the narrative or the motivation of the characters. *Blue Velvet* is an antinarrative story, and Lynch used dialogue to contribute to the story's contradictions. Language, which is traditionally used to bring clarity to issues or situations, is deployed in this film to add to the intentional confusion.

Lynch, trying to create a sensational and sensual experience, attempted to undermine all that is cerebral or rational. The first victim is the dialogue. We can hear it, but it doesn't help us to understand the story. The sound effects are used to underscore the emotional character of a scene (note the primal asthmatic scream of Hopper's character during the rape scene), but the dialogue takes us away from explanation, its usual role, thereby leading us to even greater anxiety as we experience the film. Lynch's unusual use of language is available to the editor. This option is increasingly used by filmmakers.

□ THE SOUND EDIT AND
THE DRAMATIC CORE

Every film has a central idea that drives the story. This dramatic core may be reinforced by the film's sound. It is useful to find a powerful sound idea to support that dramatic core from the perspective of the sound.

The sounds of nature deployed by Jean-Jacques Annaud in *The Bear* were mentioned earlier. Clint Eastwood used jazz improvisation in *Bird* (1988), the story of Charlie Parker. Performance pieces punctuate the film, but beyond that, the improvisation dictates the dramatic structure and the interplay of shots within scenes. Parker was a genius and an addict; improvisation was at the core of his musical and personal lives. Improvisation is both the core idea and the basic sound motif of the film.

The core dramatic idea of Sam Peckinpah's *The Getaway* is that any mode of life is preferable to a life in prison. Sam Peckinpah used the noise of a cotton-weaving machine in the opening 5 minutes of *The Getaway* (1972). The story of Doc McCoy (Steve McQueen), a Texas bank robber, opens in prison, where McCoy cannot qualify for parole without the intercession of a crime boss who wants McCoy to work for him. The sound of the machine carries over from the factory floor to the exercise yard to the parole hearing to McCoy's cell. With its loudness and regimentation, the machine represents death to this character.

Peckinpah used this repetitious sound effect to make a point about McCoy's loss of freedom in jail. He cannot get away from the sounds of the prison factory no matter how hard he tries. The sound's constancy is a reminder of his loss of freedom. Peckinpah intercut scenes of the parole hearing with shots of McCoy in various prison locations and images of McCoy and his wife making love. All the while, the sound is constant, uninterrupted by fantasy or reality. The value of freedom is the core dramatic idea of *The Getaway*. McCoy will do anything to get free and to maintain his freedom. This core concept is highlighted by the sound of the cotton-weaving machine.

□ THE SOUND EDIT AND THE PICTURE EDIT

To understand the goals of the rough sound edit, it is critical to understand the goals of the picture edit because they must proceed in tandem. They should help to clarify the narrative, and they should support the emotional character of the scene.

The deployment of particular types of sound can help the audience maintain a sense of time and place and can clarify the movement from place to place. It is useful to use special sounds as motifs for particular characters. Sound should help create and maintain a sense of realism throughout the film. The sound should support a particular dramatic core idea, just as the images should.

Music decisions are not made during the rough sound edit, but decisions regarding the use of dialogue and sound effects are. The goal of the rough edit should be to build up the tracks as much as possible, using a flexible number of tracks so that there is adequate opportunity to balance them for maximum dramatic effect during the sound mix.

28

The Sound Edit and Creative Sound

■

Many decisions about the sound track are made during the rough cut. The first steps toward creating a sense of believability are taken then. However, that believability must be enhanced and amplified. In the final phase of sound editing, the punctuation of dramatic and narrative elements is central. Is all of the dialogue presented in the rough cut necessary? No more dialogue than is absolutely necessary should be used. The sound effects tracks are enhanced so that the appropriate atmosphere is established. Character credibility is another important concern.[1] A music track that translates the underlying emotions of the film is created and added in this last phase. This chapter looks at this final stage of sound editing and the creative opportunities it offers the editor.

When punctuation and articulation are the goals of the sound edit, the assortment of creative devices used can range from synchronous sound to asynchronous sound. As Pudovkin so clearly stated in his book, *Film Technique and Film Acting*, asynchronism offers the opportunity for enhanced depth.[2] The counterpoint of sound and visual are the perfect vehicles for asynchronism.

☐ PUNCTUATION

During the rough edit, a meaning was established, and it has been corroborated visually and aurally. The sound editor's task is to punctuate that meaning during the final stage of the editing process. The goal may be to establish without question a specific point in the scene, or it may be to emphasize the ambiguity of the scene through the addition of a particular sound. In either case, the addition of sound effects or more dialogue will help the editor accomplish that goal.

The opening sequence of Vincent Ward's *The Navigator* (1980) offers an excellent example of punctuation. A young boy wanders off. A subtitle suggests the period: the Dark Ages and the Bubonic Plague. The images of the boy are strongly affected by the sound Ward chose to accompany them.

A bell tolls, and liturgical music supports images of the sky. The sound of water drops gives way to a torch falling through the air. A man's voice seems confined to a cave. There is a powerful echo.

All of the sounds have a dreamlike quality unconnected to the visuals. The effect is to create a dream state around the boy. The pitch and timbre of the sounds and their separation from the visuals provide the dreamscape for the balance of the film. What Ward has done is to aurally convince us that the story we are about to experience is a dream. Perhaps it's a boy's fear of nature that provokes the dream; whatever the cause, the emphatic character of the sound sets a tone for the balance of the film. This is punctuation.

A very different but nevertheless effective example can be found in Nicolas Roeg's *Performance* (1970). A criminal (James Fox) carries violence too far, betraying his boss. He runs away. He rents a room from a rock performer only to find that this hiding place and its proprietor result in a blurring of his sense of self. The jagged picture edit creates an overmodulated, emotional milieu in which something must explode. In this case, it's the main character, Chas (James Fox). He is a hoodlum who does not accept his identity as a hireling.

To give the society Chas inhabits a sense of disorder, Roeg created a montage of sound. Cars, particularly cars in motion, are accompanied by loud rock and roll music. These shots are intercut with the silence of the main character during a sexual encounter. Roeg used machine sounds— computers and movie and slide projectors—to disorient us. Sound is used to emphasize the confusion of society and of the main character (this foreshadows the later blurring of his identity with the character played by Mick Jagger). Unlike the dreamlike sound in *The Navigator*, the sound in *Performance* emphasizes the confusion that is central to the character's actions and reactions in the film.

One final example of punctuation illustrates how a sound motif can be used repeatedly to create the core of an entire scene. Philip Kaufman's *The White Dawn* (1974) tells the story of the clash of the white culture and the Canadian Eskimo culture in the late nineteenth century. Three stranded sailors from a whaling boat are rescued by Eskimos. When they recover, they watch the chief of the village fight and kill a polar bear.

The scene is constructed in terms of three sources of sound: one is human and primarily verbal, and two are animal—the bear (who seems supernatural) and a dog pack. The dog pack provides the emotional base for the scene. The dogs growl and howl, alerting the village to the presence of danger. As the Eskimos prepare, the dogs become more aggressive. As the attack on the bear begins the dogs go wild. The bear's response when stabbed by a spear is anger, but the bear remains supernatural. As the thrusts continue, it becomes more bellicose, but it never attacks the Eskimo chief. As the bear dies, the dogs are wildly belligerent.

In this sequence, the supernatural gives way to the natural. The struggle between the supernatural (the bear) and the natural (the dogs) continues to be a theme throughout the film. It is established by the noise that the bear and the dogs make. The struggle between the supernatural and the natural is punctuated through the sound effects.

□ AMPLIFICATION

The process of amplification can expand the realism of the film to embrace emotional as well as physical realism, or it can alter the meaning of the visuals to suit the intended vision. The process, then, is not so much emphasis as it is expansion or alteration.

AMPLIFICATION TO EXPAND MEANING

Perhaps no task of the sound editor is more important than the decision about physical realism versus emotional realism. The opposite extremes are present in two cinema verité documentaries. Roman Kroitor and Wolf Koenig's *Lonely Boy* (1962) uses natural sound and music to reinforce the credibility of Paul Anka and his audience and to suggest that Anka is an ongoing phenomenon in the North American entertainment industry. Clement Perron's *Day After Day* (1965) features an exotic narration voiced by a character who pretends she is a flight attendant on a plane to Montevideo as well as a poet reflecting on children's nursery rhymes. The physical world that is presented visually is a Quebec paper-mill town in winter. The sound track alludes to the spiritual desperation of the citizens of the town rather than to the physical world that they inhabit and that we see. These two examples present the spectrum of options for the amplification of the sound. It is in nonsynchronous sound that asynchronism is most creatively applied.

The same sound can serve both the physical and the emotional meaning of a film. Akira Kurosawa's use of the noise of a subway train in *Dodes'Ka-Den* (1970) is one of the best examples of a sound that comes to have more than its literal meaning.

Editors and directors are usually more modest in their goals. In *The Train* (1965), for example, John Frankenheimer was content to use the sound of the train to support the action/adventure elements of his story. Set in France during the last days of World War II, the film details the efforts of a German colonel (Paul Scofield) to move the great paintings of France from Paris to Berlin. A French railman (Burt Lancaster) thwarts his efforts. Because almost all of the action occurs on or around the train, the noise of the train is one of the critical sound effects in the film. Although great emotion is expended on the attempt to stop the train, those sounds are never used for anything other than physical realism. This is appropriate in an action/adventure film.

For an example of an action/adventure film in which the sounds of the train take on another meaning, we need only look at Hitchcock's *The 39 Steps* (1935). The coupling of a visual of a woman screaming as she finds a corpse with the sharp whistle of a train as it passes through a tunnel gives the train a very human quality. Indeed, from that point on, it is difficult to experience the train purely as a mode of transportation. Other filmmakers have used trains and the noise of trains in this expansive way. David Lean with *Doctor Zhivago* (1965) and Andrei Konchalovsky with *Runaway Train* (1985) are two examples.

In the action genre, John McTiernan used sound to support the physical realism of *Die Hard* (1988). This police story, set in a modern high-rise in Los Angeles, pits a New York policeman (Bruce Willis) against a group of international terrorists. The action scenes are presented dynamically, and the sound always supports the physical character of the action. When a terrorist blasts a window with automatic-weapon fire, the sounds we hear are the gunshots and the shattering glass. We rarely (if ever) hear the breathing of the characters. The sound throughout the film confirms the most obvious physical action that takes place. The emphasis is on physical reality, and the goal of the sound is to amplify that reality.

Sam Peckinpah's *Straw Dogs* (1971) suggests a different goal for the sound. Like *Die Hard*, *Straw Dogs* is a film with a great deal of action. An American mathematician David Sumner (Dustin Hoffman) and his wife, Amy, are spending a year in her hometown in England. The townsfolk are a troubled bunch. Taunted and teased, the mathematician is finally pushed to defend his home against the attack of five men from the town. The local five ne'er-do-wells include an elder, Tom Venner; his son, Charlie; Norman Scott; and Chris Kawley. The attack on the isolated house is the long action sequence (25 minutes) that concludes the film. Earlier in the film, one of the men, Charlie Venner, raped Amy, Sumner's wife (Susan George), and now the men are on the hunt for Henry Niles, the slow-witted member of the community (David Warner) who they fear has molested Tom Venner's daughter.

Peckinpah included sounds of gunshots and shattering glass in *Straw Dogs*, but he was looking for more primal feelings than excitement about action. Two scenes are notable for their use of sound to expand the sense of realism within the scene.

Before the violent confrontation at their farm, the couple attend a church social. All of the main characters attend: the couple, the Venners, their friends, Henry Niles, the young girl whose disappearance will cause the action, the town magistrate, and other residents. For the mathematician's wife, the scene is fragmented by a cutaway to her memory of the rape, and she is so overwhelmed that she and her husband leave early in the evening. The young girl and Henry Niles do likewise.

Aside from the rapid editing of this sequence and the destabilizing camera angles that Peckinpah chose, there is also a special sound in the extended introduction to this scene. Peckinpah carried the sound of children's noise-makers through the scene. No matter what the visual is, the sound of the noisemakers pervades the scene. The shrillness of the sound gives the opening segment of the church social a relentless, disturbing quality.

If physical realism were the goal, the sound would be very different. Peckinpah was more interested in expressing the woman's emotions about being in the same room as the men who raped her. Peckinpah was also interested in using sound to foreshadow the emotional and physical violence that would follow. The pitch and tone of the noisemakers play a critical role in establishing this emotional plane.

Later, once the attack at the farm has begun in earnest, Peckinpah relied on rapid cutting less than he did in the church sequence. Instead, Peckinpah relied on a counterpoint of sound and visual action to deepen the terror of this extended sequence.

The sounds are the sounds of attack and defense: gunshots, shattering glass, the squeal of a rat thrown through the window to frighten the couple inside, and, of course, screams of terror and pain. These are the expected sounds: the sounds of the physical reality of the sequence.

During this extended scene, the main character is metamorphosed from the mathematician-coward of the first two-thirds of the film into a man who defends his home with all the guile and will he can muster. Peckinpah used the sound to announce this emotional transition. Peckinpah amplified the sequence by superimposing this emotional realism over the physical realism of the scene. Part way through the scene, the mathematician puts on a record of bagpipe music. This music plays continually over the next third of the sequence. The introduction of the orderly bagpipes into the chaos of the action signals his intentions to take control of the field of action. No longer the coward, he uses his intelligence and will to defeat a superior number of armed adversaries. The bagpipe music amplifies the emotional reality of the main character and of the scenes that follow. By playing against the tone of the visual action, the sound makes the visuals that much more powerful.

In nonaction sequences, the issue of physical realism versus emotional realism is no less compelling. In *L'Enfant Sauvage* (1970), François Truffaut recounted the true story of the Wild Child of Avignon. The child does not speak or relate to humans normally. The film describes the capture of the 10-year-old and his induction into civilized society in the late eighteenth century. As the film opens, we see the child in the woods, scavenging food from an abandoned vegetable basket. He eats and drinks by a stream and then is pursued by a hunting party and their dogs. His efforts to elude the dogs and their masters suggest that he is more animal than human. The sounds of this opening are entirely natural: the sounds of the woods and of the chase. Nothing on the sound track implies more than the physical reality of the scene.

Bertrand Tavernier's *A Sunday in the Country* (1984) illustrates the expanded use of sound. The scene is rural France before World War I. An elderly painter lives in the country where he is attended by his middle-aged housekeeper.

The scene opens with natural rural sounds, particularly of the fowl in the yard and beyond. As the camera tracks, we hear an old man, Monsieur l'Admiral. We hear him singing before we see him. He hums a tune as he opens the curtains. He continues humming and singing as he opens the shutters. He walks about and puts on his shoes. The camera tracks, observing his paintings, and his movements. When he hears a female voice, the point of view changes to the base of the stairs that he will descend. The woman's voice, we soon learn, belongs to his housekeeper, Mercedes. She sings, too, and the camera shifts to follow her movements in preparing breakfast and cleaning. They speak only when he asks where the shoe-cleaning kit is.

Before the dialogue begins, we are introduced to the place, the time, and the characters through the tone and pitch of their voices. Their voices are relaxed and steady, confident in greeting the day. They establish an emotional character beyond the physical reality of the awakening in the country. Their voices imply that all is well. The informal singing and humming set the tone for the film and establish an attitude more complex than the feeling we have for the child in the opening of Truffaut's *L'Enfant Sauvage*. A different sense of realism is established in Tavernier's film. Sound and camera movement are the key elements in guiding us to two vastly different film openings.

AMPLIFICATION TO CHALLENGE MEANING

Occasionally, the realistic sound will not do justice to the effect that the editor and director seek. When this is the case, they resort to a sound effect that challenges the implication of the visuals. By doing so, they do more than challenge the scene's sense of physical realism; they also begin to alter that sense of realism.

The alteration can be simple. In James Cameron's *Aliens* (1986), not only are the monsters visually grotesque, but they accompany their attacks with a high-pitched squeal. Whenever the aliens are present, the squeal can be heard. Late in the film, Ripley (Sigourney Weaver) rescues a young girl and fights to escape from the aliens. A deep rumble foreshadows her introduction to the mother alien. Ripley and the girl have inadvertently stumbled into the breeding area. The rumbling signals danger, but it's a vastly different danger than Ripley faced from the aliens. The shift from high-pitched squeal to deep rumble foreshadows a change and alludes to the different magnitude of the danger.

This example provides a simple illustration of how a change in sound effects can alter meaning. Another science-fiction film demonstrates how the quality of tone and pitch can alter our response to a character. At the beginning of Steven Spielberg's *E.T. the Extra-Terrestrial* (1982), E.T. is visually presented as a mysterious, even foreboding, character. The response of the human characters suggests a danger. However, the sounds that accompany the images—E.T.'s hand, for example—are childlike. Rather than a dangerous killer, E.T. sounds like an out-of-breath cartoon character. Instead of feeling threatened, we feel sorry for him. The friendly replaces the dangerous perception of the extra-terrestrial in Cameron's *Aliens*. The shift in our perception of E.T. is accomplished strictly through sound.

Another approach to using sound to give the visuals new meaning is to withdraw the realistic sound and replace it with sound that achieves the intended meaning. In John Boorman's *Excalibur* (1981), King Arthur's struggle to bring idealism and power into balance is given a screen treatment that includes physical realism, and the world of magic and superstition. In fact, the physical realism is superseded by the influence of magic and the power of superstition. Aside from using a vivid visual style, Boorman had to find ways to evoke with sound the pivotal events in the legend of King Arthur. For example, when the magical sword Excalibur is yielded to Merlin by the Lady in the Lake and when it is returned to the lake by Percival as Arthur dies, Boorman lowers the volume of the obvious sound effects: the water, a hand rising out of the lake, metal rising against the resistance of the water. These would be the obvious sound effects if the scene were intended to emphasize naturalism. However, it is the supernatural that the scene needs to create. Boorman chose to emphasize the music, in this case, Wagner's version of the Arthurian legend, "Parsifal." The music and the images transcend the physical reality of the action.

The replacement of the expected sound with a sound effect that shifts the meaning of the visuals to the opposite extreme alters the effect of the visual-sound juxtaposition. Examples mentioned earlier in this chapter include the polar bear in *The White Dawn*. It is transformed through nonrealistic sound into a supernatural force when it appears in the village. Another example is the use of a humanlike voice for HAL in *2001: A Space Odyssey* (1968). In this film, HAL becomes an excessively human computer that works with humans who are devoid of signs of their humanity. In both *The White Dawn* and *2001: A Space Odyssey*, the unexpected sound quality enhances the contrast that is sought. The principle of asynchronism, or counterpoint, strengthens the dramatic impact of the scenes described.

□ TRANSITION AND SOUND

Dialogue, sound effects, and, occasionally, music are used as bridging devices to unite scenes. Transition is necessary to imply continuity when changes in location or time are involved. A dialogue overlap between scenes or a sound effect dissolve from one scene to another will imply that transition. Editors often rely on repetition, or the echo effect, to achieve this transition. A word is repeated at the end of one scene and at the beginning of another, or a sound effect may be used. For example, in *Cries and Whispers* (1972), a ticking clock can be heard, and as we move to another room, the clock chimes as it strikes the hour. The tick of the clock is cut to the chime of the hour; both sound effects relate to time. The continuity provided by the two sounds masks the shift in location from one room to another.

□ MUSIC

The mood and emotions on which a screen story is based are translated by the music track. This track is added to the fine cut of the picture, though musical ideas are developed through the production and post-production phases.

The music can be direct in its emotional invitation like Maurice Jarre's music in *Doctor Zhivago* (1965), or it can be subtle like Christopher Komeda's music in *Rosemary's Baby* (1968). In the latter example, the music for this horror film is an extemporaneous lullaby that adds irony to the visuals. Komeda's music strengthens the impact of the film with its irony.

The process of translation amplifies the dramatic material, such as Charlie Parker's performance pieces in *Bird* (1988). This is often the practice when the subject matter is performers or performance. Mark Rydell's *For the Boys* (1991) is another example of this approach to the music track. Beyond the authenticity that this music brings to the subject, there is also an elevating impact because the music, independent of the film, has a meaning for the audience. This is the reason for the nostalgia tracks in such films as Martin Scorcese's *Mean Streets* (1973), Carl Reiner's *Stand by Me* (1986), and Lawrence Kasdan's *The Big Chill* (1983). They help place the film in an era, as much as do the characters of the film.

In most films, however, the filmmaker looks for a direct emotional interpretation through the music track. It needn't be solely romantic. It can be enigmatic, like Bernard Herrmann's music for *Vertigo* (1958), or it can be stylized, like Quincy Jones's music for *The Pawnbroker* (1965).

Another factor is the degree of orchestration. John Williams composed full orchestrations for such films as *Empire of the Sun* (1987). The results are an enveloping complex of emotions that seems to suit the scale of Steven Spielberg's work. Ry Cooder, on the other hand, provided a very simple instrumentation for *Paris, Texas* (1984). This minimalist approach does not invite the audience to become involved with the film. The orchestration decision is made to suit the material. The key is to try to create a suitable emotional context for the screen story.

The coordination of the music with the fine cut of the film is controlled down to the beats of the musical score. Once this is accomplished, the music track—whether stylized or directed, heavily orchestrated or simplified, lyric—intensive or instrumental, referential or original—invites the audience to become engaged in the film. As Eisenstein discovered with

Sergei Prokofiev and as Mike Nichols discovered with Simon and Garfunkel, when the music track works with the visuals, the sum is greater than the parts. This is the power of editing and, when it works, the art of editing.

□ NOTES/REFERENCES

1. The blind man in Jocelyn Moorehouse's *Proof* (1991) hears with great acuity. Consequently, the sound effects take on a greater importance and greater amplification in keeping with the character's emotional and physical state.
2. V. I. Pudovkin, *Film Technique and Film Acting* (London: Vision Press, 1968). Reprinted in E. Weis and J. Belten, *Film Sound* (New York: Columbia University Press, 1989), 86–91.

29

Innovations of Sound

■

In the era of digital Dolby sound, a logical question to pose is whether the technical innovations in sound, which have been considerable, have led to a new aesthetic, or at least to a number of innovations that broaden the sound repertoire. The answer is no and yes. Before we discuss those innovations, it's useful to look at how we have gotten to where we are in sound.

As mentioned earlier, the earliest use of sound in film quickly progressed from novelty to creative deployment in the work of Alfred Hitchcock (*Blackmail*), Rouben Mamoulian (*Applause, Love Me Tonight*), and Fritz Lang (*M*). Sound was used to create a sensory feeling about different environments and to provide insight into a character's state of mind. It was also used more simply to transition from place to place, or to allude to changes in time and place. Finally, sound was used to provide continuity in complex narratives—the police search in *M*, for example.

Working with narration, sound effects, music, and dialogue, Orson Welles advanced the creative use of sound mightily in *Citizen Kane* to tell the 75-year-long story of Charles Foster Kane in 120 minutes. Consequent to the creative use of radio techniques Welles used in *Citizen Kane*, the idea of the use of sound in film broadened along two general pathways—to deepen the sense of realism, and to recast the use of sound not so much to challenge realism, but rather to create a deeper pathway. This might mean the portrayal of the innermost thoughts of the character (the narration in *Apocalypse Now*), or it might mean the use of differing musical styles to suggest the inner life of two very different characters, as in Bernardo Bertolucci's *Besieged*. The key here is inner life, and the contradiction of inner, or private, life and outer, or public, life introduced a whole new palate for directors. It wasn't so much about motivation or creating conflict as it was about deepening the audience's relationship with a character. Federico Fellini (*8½*), Michelangelo Antonioni (*L'eclisse*), John Boorman (*Point Blank*), Martin Scorsese (*Raging Bull*), and Francis Ford Coppola (*The Conversation*) were interested in deepening our feeling for and understanding of their main characters. Sound effects, music, and narration became the sound pathway to that more internal sense of character. At the same time, Stanley Kubrick (*Full Metal Jacket*), Thomas Vinterberg (*Festen*; in the U.S., *The Celebration*), and the Dardenne brothers (*Rosetta*) all used sound, and its absence, to enhance the sense of realism of their films.

Worth noting is those filmmakers who were less interested in our relationship with their characters than they were in the amplification of their ideas about the narrative—in short, their voice. These filmmakers would shock us out of a relationship with their character and coax us into a relationship with their ideas. They include Neil Jordan in *The Butcher Boy*, in which the narration is charmingly creative while the visual life of a boy who kills is alarmingly depressing. Another example would be Werner Herzog's *Aguirre: The Wrath of God,* in which the destructive narrative is articulated in dialogue while effects and music are left to create a spiritual scale to contrast with the obsessive material goals of the characters.

The selection of effects, the pitch of those effects, the nature of a narrator, the words they speak, how they say those words, the deployment of differing music for each significant character (thereby "tagging those characters"), the use of music to create a sense of time and place, the use of music to set the tone for the film, and, of course, the use of sound as transitional editing device, or as continuity device, all have become part of the repertory of sound as a tool of editing. So much, in fact, has gone on in sound work that we use the balance of this chapter to cite specific examples and to suggest how these innovations have widened the range of sound choices in the edit.

Perhaps a useful way to begin our exploration is to use specific examples of a new or different use of the three primary sound options—effects, music, and dialogue—and to show how each has been used in a novel or new fashion. We begin with a simple idea, that cultures are different from one another. In *Black Hawk Down* (2001), director Ridley Scott is dealing with the 1992 invasion of Somalia. The country had fallen into anarchy in 1991 and warlords fought for control while the general population suffered the consequences of that anarchy. The American forces invaded in order to stabilize the country, but the invasion failed when 18 American soldiers were killed attempting to capture the most prominent warlord in a raid on central Mogadishu. The failure of the most powerful country in the world to execute its goal was a stark reminder that power has its limits.

Ridley Scott uses sound to create that sense of power. The American marines and Delta force are presented by representing their technological might—the whirring of Black Hawk helicopters and their steady drone in unison preview that technology. The sound of helicopters gives way to awesome firepower from an array of weaponry. The sounds of technology represent the American power. In contrast, Mogadishu and its inhabitants, including the members of the warlord's army, are represented by the Eastern music of the bazaar and the sounds of the souk (the marketplace). This contrast—of music and the sounds of commerce in the souk against the sounds of technological power—creates a culture clash, pitting against each other the primitive and the modern, the past and the future. What is interesting about the use of sound in *Black Hawk Down* is that it explores that clash of cultures and raises the question that the modern doesn't always prevail over the primitive, particularly in a native primitive environment that is removed in every way from the habitat of the modern.

Working again with this idea of two worlds clashing with one another, Catherine Hardwicke uses the adolescent/adult worlds as the contrasting fault line in her film *Thirteen*. The film chronicles the descent of a 13-year-old into the dangerous world of sex, drugs, and criminal behavior. Befriending an older, bolder, popular girl, the main character seeks out experience and acceptance that puts her in harm's way. Her mother, the narrative's adult representative, is caught up in her own difficulties and is incapable of protecting her daughter.

The adolescent world in *Thirteen* is represented by the provocative, in-your-face lyrics and music of hip-hop. Taunting and provocative, the music portrays the adolescent world as angry and active in challenging social norms in the areas of sexuality, drugs, and personal behavior. The presentation of this world is presented loudly, almost over-modulated, to represent its intensity and its overwhelming nature. It is a world that is attractive to and dangerous for Tracy, the main character. The adult world focuses on Tracy's mother, her clients, and her lover. As a single mother trying to cope with two teenagers and desperately enmeshed in a life in which she is drawn to poor choices, this adult needs as much support and guidance as her daughter does. Nevertheless, the adult world is represented by natural sound—quiet, almost despairing. None of the excitement of the music track is here. The relative quiet implies the quiet despair of the adult world, hardly a magnet for the 13-year-old Tracy. In fact, Tracy sees her mother's poor choices and is angry that her mother makes them. The adult world, then, is anxious and desperate. The sound design leads in the creation of that world. What is important here is how sound and its differences create the two worlds—the adolescent world and the adult world.

The two worlds are embodied in a single person in David Cronenberg's *Spider* (2001). In the present, Spider is released from a long stay in a mental institution. Being out in the world, Spider revisits the neighborhood in which he grew up. That world and that time (his childhood) represent Spider's past and his problem. Whether these two worlds will fuse, casting Spider back into a mental abyss, is the subject of the narrative in *Spider*. For us, the issue is how the sound is used to portray the two worlds—Spider in the present world, and Spider's internal world as he grew up.

Initially the world is presented in an idealistic melody over the credits. Howard Shore relies on piano and voice to elegize a state of childhood that never existed for Spider. Spider's contemporary world is a world of whispers, inarticulate sporadic sound, and atonal simple instrument music, unresolved, seemingly going nowhere in a dramatic sense. The past world, the world of Spider's childhood, is presented with minimalist sound, initially no music, sharp effects presented sporadically, and sharp dialogue clearly understood. As this past world begins to come together with Spider's contemporary world, his understanding of past events suggests a fusion. Music continues from present sequences into past sequences. And it becomes multi-instrumental and directional in the sense that the music becomes increasingly dramatic. As Spider begins to realize that he, not his father, is responsible for the death of his mother, this becomes even more the case. The idealistic music score is reintroduced (idealism) together with darker strains (atonal), and in this sense the music illustrates how Spider the adult and Spider the boy fuse. This also prepares us, first for the fusion of his mother as a "mother" and as a "tart" and then for the fusion of his mother and the owner of the halfway house where the adult Spider lives. As Spider's understanding shifts from seeing his father as killer to realizing that he, Spider, is the killer of his mother, the sound focuses on his dialogue as an echo of, first, his father's accusation, and, finally, of the female owner of the halfway house and her accusation. As Spider is taken back to the mental institution, the visual image shifts from adult to boy, a shift already prepared for by the music. The two worlds have become one.

In David Cronenberg's *A History of Violence* (2005), the two worlds are Tom's current life—tranquil, predictable, ordinary—and Tom's former life as Joey Cusack—violent, unpredictable, and anything but ordinary. Since this is a film about a second chance but also about the enduring nature of survivalism as an operating principle in a world that is truly a jungle, Cronenberg's sound idea is that there is a surface, but that underneath that surface, all is different, even opposite.

Two scenes will illustrate this upside-down world. The film opens with two men leaving their motel and about to begin the next phase of their travel. All seems mundane until "the leader" asks the second man to fill the water jug from the motel office cooler. When he does so, we see that the staff of the motel have been brutally killed. The scene ends when the second man shoots the lone survivor, a young girl who has woken up. Initially the sound is strictly sound effects and dialogue. The languorous camera movement sets the tone—mundane and monotonous. The effects are natural, the dialogue ordinary. Only when the second man is in the office and we see the first body does the music begin. It is the music that suggests the world is different than it appeared to be. The same pattern is used four scenes later when the men enter Tom Stall's diner. He is just closing up. The two men are in need of money. It appears that they are interested in rape, killing, and money. When Tom throws coffee into the face of "the leader," the music continues as he kills both men and saves the situation. The predictability of the robbery and violence uses natural sound while the underneath or revelation, of Tom's own capacity for violence, is cued by the use of music. In Cronenberg's *A History of Violence*, the superficial world and the jungle, or violent, world are the two worlds.

We turn now to a different sound idea—the use of a narrator to create a new perception about the visuals. Exposition may be the goal, or the goal may be to convey a private insight about character or plot, but this differs from what we are seeing. Or the narrator may layer the narrative, adding complexity to the narrative. We begin with Paul Greengrass' *The Bourne Supremacy*.

Jason Bourne is a trained CIA assassin. He has lost his memory, perhaps a form of post-traumatic stress disorder. His very first killing took place in Berlin and the plot of *The Bourne Supremacy* emanates out of that killing. His handler was corrupt and the killing of a Soviet politician and his wife eliminated an obstacle for a Russian oligarch. Money changed hands, enriching two corrupt CIA officials as well as the Russian oligarch. Bourne will discover the truth about that killing in the course of the film and will try to make amends to the surviving daughter of those he killed in Berlin. As the film begins, Bourne is struggling to recover his memory, but at this stage it's a fragmented nightmare.

Greengrass opens the film with slowed-down visuals—the lights of a city, a pistol, much unclear movement. The meaning is driven by a sound montage of fragmented words, often repeated. The words—"It's not a drill soldier," "Live project," "You're a go," "Training is over"—are repeated, initially unclear and distant, eventually clear. The voice, authoritative, is not Jason Bourne's, but in all likelihood is that of his commanding officer. The sequence ends when, with a loud gunshot, the deed is done, and Jason Bourne is as marred by it as is the family of his victims.

This sound montage is presented as a memory fragment and this is how the sound is presented. In a minute, the exposition of what is lost is established. The "why" of it we don't understand. The explanation will unfold in the narrative that follows. Here, the fragmentary sentences serve as a poetic narration, urgently presented, but not at all clear. The mock presentation, unclear to clear with each repetition, sets up the idea of a memory lost; Bourne's (and our) effort to understand that idea, from the authoritative voice-of-God narration, is often central to the broadcast documentary.

A second example of narration is its use in Wolfgang Becker's *Good Bye Lenin!* (2003). The film is a personal story with a large political overlay. The main character, Alex, is a young adult who has grown up in East Germany (German Democratic Republic). His father abandoned the family for the West when he was a boy, and since then Alex's lifeline has been his mother. She represents family and family values to Alex. But his mother is ill. She suffers a stroke, just days before the Berlin Wall comes down and East and West become one Germany. When she awakens from a coma, change is galloping in her beloved GDR, and it no longer exists. But she is not told, because the doctor says that any change or shock may prompt a second, and this time, fatal, stroke. Alex is willing to do anything to prevent such an event. He organizes a fiction:, his mother's room, the TV shows, the food—nothing has changed. This requires quite an effort, but Alex wants to save the small family he has and so the effort is worth it. A great deal of family history is revealed, and how Alex feels about that history and how he feels about the GDR and life after the GDR. What drives this character is his passion for family, including the young Russian nurse who attends his mother in the hospital. Alex is not a political character. Work life before and after is focused on getting by. Alex is not a born-again capitalist or German nationalist. In this film he's mostly a son.

Becker uses the narration to give voice to Alex's priorities. He begins his narration with the day his father left the family for the West. Consequently, Becker will use the narration to bring the focus back to the family. In spite of everything going on around him, it's the family that is the most important to Alex. Here narration is used as a personal counterpoint to the political story—the fall of the Wall, Communism vs. Capitalism, and the German layer to this struggle, idealism vs. materialism. By using the narration to remind the audience that *Good Bye Lenin!* is the story of one family, Becker holds on to the sweetness of a young man's desire to keep his family intact in spite of the tidal wave of politics. The consequence is a layered story that keeps its emotional rudder. Billy Wilder's *One, Two, Three* (1960) comes to mind. In Wilder's story, it's all about politics, and the personal story of a Coca Cola executive is as much a source of satire as are Communism and Capitalism.

A third example of the dual use of narration is Terrence Malick's *The New World* (2005). Malick previously used multiple narrators in *The Thin Red Line* to give voice to the inner thoughts of his characters; confessional and poetic, the narration personalized this war epic. His use of narration in *The New World* echoes more closely the narration in his *Days of Heaven*, in which a young girl speculates upon hard times in a young yet optimistic United States. In *Days of Heaven*, the narration elevated the characters, made them iconic, almost mythical. In *The New World*, the myth of America as "Paradise Lost" is in the foreground of Malick's treatment of the arrival of Europeans to settle Virginia. Their settlement, Jamestown, is an encroachment upon the native population. Nothing will ever be the same again.

Malick examines the fate of Pocahontas, an Indian princess who turns away from her father, the Algonquian king, in order to save and later help a white man, Captain John Smith. The relationship between Smith and Pocahontas makes up the first two-thirds of the film and serves to exemplify how Malick fashions dialogue into narration, in turn making both of these characters, Pocahontas, and John Smith, bigger, iconic, and mythical, rather than simply a white man and his Indian lover.

The narration begins when John Smith, accused of mutiny during the Atlantic crossing, has been freed from incarceration after arrival in Jamestown. The Commander of the Jamestown expedition gives Smith a second chance. As a soldier, he will be given special responsibility to contact the local Indian king. In his narration, Smith speculates about life in this New World. He expresses his hopes that the economic and sociological fetters of civilized life can be reconsidered in this new setting. He expresses his hopes for a different future for him and his kind, the men under his charge. In this sense, Smith's narration speaks of an ideal, his wish for a different and a better life.

Smith is taken captive by the Indians; it is Pocahontas who asks for his life to be spared. This begins their relationship and Pocahontas is then the subject of the narration. After praising her rare beauty and spirit, the narration shifts to the other Indians. For Smith, they represent a new ideal—they are loving and know no jealousy or envy, no guile, only authenticity. For Smith, their nature is the ideal that men like him (Europeans) should aspire to.

Smith's narrative returns to Pocahontas, but now his narration speculates about love, and how rare a gift it is. Should one not take what is offered? The narration has become reflective, even uncertain. While the visuals illustrate that John Smith is becoming increasingly involved with the life of his Indian hosts, a second narrator, Pocahontas, joins the speculative meditation on her relationship with Smith. At first she is tentative, but shortly she commits herself to love Smith above all else. Her speech is simple but poetic.

At this point, Malick is using the narration to suggest that the relationship between Smith and Pocahontas is progressing. The sound advances the exposition, while the visuals create mood—tranquility, playfulness. And it is at this point that Smith and Pocahontas represent the merging of two cultures, the old and the new. They have become an ideal, a new beginning for Europe, a new chance to be pure and authentic, to represent love in Paradise. It is the narration that has to lift the individual story of a man and a woman to the iconic, the mythical. Malick is totally successful in suggesting the possibility of progress emanating from the love of an Indian woman for a white man. The balance of the film is devoted to how this chance was lost and how Paradise was transformed into the usual hell, the perennial effect of civilization.

Anthony Minghella provides us with our last example of a novel use of narration. Working with Walter Murch on the Civil War epic, *Cold Mountain* (2003), Minghella's goal is to suggest that Ada and Inman, the two lovers of the narrative, are the only people who exist, in their world. Of course, many others play important roles in this story, but balancing the Civil War, the most traumatic event in the country's history, with a personal story is the task of Minghella and Murch.

Although the principal time frame is the last year of the war, Minghella has to link the past—Ada's arrival in Cold Mountain, which is a shift from urban to rural life for her and her minister father—and the evolution of the Ada–Inman relationship, from their meeting to the chaste leave-taking as he joins the army to support the Confederate cause. In 1864–1865, the narrative follows Inman the soldier, his sense of the futility of the War, and his desertion and to return to Cold Mountain. In the town of Cold Mountain, he takes up with Ada, impregnates her, and dies defending her against the exploitative local militia members, who have become the enemy within for the townspeople of Cold Mountain.

Minghella and Murch use Ada's letters as the source of narration, the beacon for Inman and the only worthwhile reason for living. In a sense, Minghella uses the letters as the inspiration for Inman's desertion, a positive goal in a decidedly negative world, the world of war and death. Murch also uses the narration to suggest that in their worlds, Ada and Inman are the only two people. Everyone else and all other intrusions need to be contextualized as less important. This means that the battles that open the film are downplayed from a sound perspective. Consider the pitch and sounds of battle in Antoine Fuqua's *King Arthur* as the opposite of the balance of sound in *Cold Mountain*. Although this makes for an eerie sense of the Civil War in the film, the director and editor's intentions are very clear. Here narration is used to personalize and to distance us from the intrusion of war. Ada and Inman are self-insulated and exist only in their world.

30

Nonlinear Editing and Digital Technology I

■

Today we no longer speak of the coming technological revolution or how digital technology will transform sound, special effects, film and video editing. The revolution is here. Our concerns in this chapter are the issues of technological revolution in film and video and its potential for aesthetic evolution.

☐ THE TECHNOLOGICAL REVOLUTION

Film and video, the two most technology-dependent art forms of the twentieth century, have witnessed a profound acceleration in change, the shift from analog to digital-driven technology. The implications are enormous. In pre-production, computer software is available for pre-visualization of scenes. Color and design opportunities, in essence computer animation, deepens the predictability of the potential elements of an image. During production, nonlinear editing allows for rapid assemblies that provide feedback on the questions: Am I making the intended dramatic point in the scene? Digital cameras will replace film- and electronic-based videotape as the originating source of the image. The digitization process allows any part of the image to be withdrawn, an additional element to be added if necessary. In post-production, it is possible for the editor to consolidate in his role, sound editing, picture editing, sound mixing, special effects, and printing, at least if the release form is videotape. The editor could also write and input the music track using her nonlinear editing system! The degree of consolidation that is possible is probably not wise for one person to undertake, but the critical point is that the digital revolution makes it possible.

Digital opportunities include delivery systems (films simply will be beamed digitally over fiber optic lines to theatres, thus by-passing standard projection systems) and the interface between entertainment, education, and economics (they can meet on the Internet). Movies will be available on demand (satellite or phone line) and editing will occur between client and producer on the Internet rather than in an office in Los Angeles or New York.

The means to produce quality visual stories will drop, democratizing the cost of production. Who will dominate this system, if anyone, remains to be seen. Web sites may become the Cannes Film Festival marketplaces of tomorrow. All this is possible because of the digital revolution.

□ THE LIMITS OF TECHNOLOGY

The best place to begin is to state the obvious—that a computer-driven editing machine such as an Avid or Lightworks, no matter how sophisticated, cannot make the creative decision of where to cut and why. The decisions for continuity or dramatic emphasis are creative, if you wish aesthetic, choices. They are made by the editor or the editor or with the director or producer. The speed of computer-assisted editing will enable creative decisions to be arrived at more quickly than earlier editing technology, but it will not make the creative decisions. Here then lie a number of fallacies about nonlinear editing.

A second issue that devolves from the new technology is that it will yield new forms of storytelling, new levels of interactivity, and a more democratic relationship between storyteller (film- or videomaker) and audience. Although much progress has been made in video games, and on the compact disc entertainment and education fronts, for the most part that work to date has not been particularly interesting nor creative. It has been game-oriented and youth-oriented. This may change but the promise of interactivity has yet to be fulfilled.

On the other hand, just as the invention of the printing press did not necessarily lead to a proportional increase in writers, but rather to a spread in ancillary effects—secularization, rationality, democratization via communication, so the result of the digital revolution is the growth of the Internet and its impact on communication, democratization and, hopefully, rationality. These changes may or may not have an impact on storytelling.

On a more positive note, there is no question that nonlinear editing and digital technology will have positive impacts on the editing process and on the outcome of that process, the screen story. In technical terms, time is money and the speed of nonlinear systems should have a positive impact on post-production budgets. So too will the capacity for the editor to build up his own tracks and mix them down on his nonlinear systems. The capacity to work in a more complex way with sound and picture can only help the post-production process and budget. Digital technology also helps in the creation of special effects. The famous shots of Gary Sinise legless in the second half of *Forrest Gump* (1994) were produced in a digitized set of images reconstituted frame by frame to eliminate his legs from each frame. Equally possible today is the removal of any portion, small or large, of the image. This same technology can be used in film or sound restoration as well.

☐ THE AESTHETIC OPPORTUNITIES

To begin to understand the aesthetic opportunities of the nonlinear digital age, we should begin by stating that, to date, interactive technology has had a more profound impact on video games and on making available art and photographs for specific educational goals than upon mainstream film and video. Consequently, its impact has been relegated to special effects and animation. That is not to say that these special effects in *Terminator 2: Judgement Day* (1991) or in *Jurassic Park* (1993) were not spectacular in aiding the dynamism and credibility of the story. What it does mean, however, is that those stories, *Terminator 2* and *Jurassic Park*, remained conventional screen stories, neither challenging old forms nor old ideas. The special effects simply made the films more sensational for their audiences.

Are there aesthetic opportunities in the digital technologies? Yes and no. Certainly the capacity to tell stories whose scale or expanse was not previously possible could add to the range of filmic experience. Stories such as Dostoyevsky's *Crime and Punishment* and Coetzee's *Foe* might focus on the interior life of the characters, thereby bringing two wonderful psychological novels to film in the richest manner rather than as plotted narratives flattened by the current conventions of filmic narrative. There are far less aesthetic opportunities where linearity as a dramatic shaping device dominates. And since the linear story, the plot-driven story, today reigns supreme, the likelihood is that digital technology will be used in support of linear tales rather than to subvert or emend the narrative conventions of today.

☐ THE NONLINEAR NARRATIVE

Nonlinear storytelling has been a factor at least since Luis Buñuel's *Un Chien d'Andalou* (1929). Although unusual and the exception to the rule, it is by no means unimportant, as a film such as Orson Welles's *Citizen Kane* (1941) attests. However, to understand the notion of nonlinearity, it is important to first define the linear narrative.

One feature of the linear narrative is its reliance on plot and upon our involvement with the main character.

A second equally important feature of the linear narrative is its dramatic shape. Whether one describes that shape as restorative three-act structure[1] or as the marriage of goal-directed characters and resolution-oriented plotting, the outcome is the same, a linear narrative arc. This linearity transcends story form and links film and video narratives to the Aristotelian equivalents in theatre and in the novel.

The consequence of the linear narrative is the fulfillment of a particular style of experience for an audience. In spite of surprising twists and turns in the plot, the audience knows at the outset the kind of resolution to anticipate. It in essence expects and experiences a predetermined outcome that we associate with linear narrative. That is not to say that linear narrative is boring or blasé; often it is exciting and satisfying. But it is always satisfying within predictable parameters.

The nonlinear narrative may not have a resolution; it may not have a single character with whom to empathize and identify; it may not have characters who are goal-directed; and it may not have a dramatic shape driving towards resolution. Consequently, the nonlinear narrative is not predictable. And here lies its great aesthetic potential, because of that unpredictability, it may provide an audience with a new, unexpected experience. This is the potential aesthetic upshot of nonlinearity—new, unpredictable experiences. This will never happen, however, if nonlinearity remains a technological fact rather than a philosophical and aesthetic attitude.

□ PAST RELIANCE ON LINEARITY

In the period where film and video narratives were popular cultural forms intended for the largest mass audiences on an international as well as national level, linearity as a narrative principle was critical. The codes of linear narrative—the goal-directed main character, the antagonist so superior in his counter-goal as to make a hero of the main character, the linear plot veering from point to counterpoint with an accelerating speed, and, of course, the inevitable resolution which justified all that had proceeded it—are portable, moving from one story to another, transported form one country to another, and from one medium to another. This is the system of storytelling is necessary in a period of mass audiences.

But what happens when the audience fractures? What happens when there are films and videos produced for particular age groups, particular interest groups, gender groups, educationally levelled groups, corporate culture groups, media-suspicious groups? In the digital age, with many channels (500-plus), the audience will fragment into a large number of specialty audiences. Under these circumstances, modes of storytelling also can be modified to take into account the pattern of desire, thought, and belief of these subgroups. In this new environment, the opportunity to move away form linear narrative, and to experiment with narrative styles is simply a fact of the digital age. If the makers don't experiment with new styles, they may find the audiences taking the means of production into their own hands. The accessibility of the means of production in the digital age will force filmmakers to reach out and to define those means with their audience. This very impulse lies at the heart of the success of Quentin Tarantino, Mary Harron, and Spike Lee. They have fashioned a style that helps them define and communicate with their audience.

Linearity served its purpose. It will not disappear, but nonlinearity will now assert itself more aggressively. The digital age demands new narrative styles for the new but fragmented audience of the age.

□ A PHILOSOPHY OF NONLINEARITY

Perhaps the most useful way to suggest a philosophy on nonlinearity is to begin with an operating principle related to expectations. Just as nonlinear editing has been called random access editing, sourcing shots, scenes, and sounds on an as-needed basis, we can view the narrative style of the nonlinear narrative as having an equally random quality. A does not follow B; cause is not followed by effect. The result is an altered narrative shape sufficiently unpredictable as to create a spontaneity or artifice that alters meaning.

A second characteristic of nonlinearity is the use of opposites to propose the different narrative shape. Opposites, because of their nonfluid relationship to what had proceeded them, undermine expectations. The opposite may be used as a counterpoint, clearly related to its predecessor, or may in fact be more random.

A third characteristic of nonlinearity is the break away from character identification. This may be achieved through the use of an ironic character. It may be achieved through the focus on a place or event rather than the experience of the character. It may be achieved by overbuilding the secondary characters at the price of the main character.

A final characteristic is the replacement of linear plot by elevated incident, set pieces over developmental narrative, feeling-state scenes over expository scenes. This approach undermines the notion of plot and of main character-driven narrative.

The nonlinear narrative is intuitive rather than purposeful, random rather than developmental, and feeling over action. When added to a group of characters, the nonlinear narrative embraces politics over psychology and aesthetics over ethics. The experience of the nonlinear narrative os also less susceptible to the gestalt of Aristotelian dramatic principles.

□ THE ARTISTS OF NONLINEAR NARRATIVE

The contributions of Porter, Griffith, and Vidor to the history and practice of film editing is that they created a series of editing choices that underpinned linear narratives—the close-up to articulate clearly the goal of the main character, a cutaway to provide an analogy for what the character was thinking about, and pace to provide an emotional rhythm for the clash of the main character's goal with the barriers to that goal. All these choices, including extreme long shots, camera placement, and camera movement, provided the code for the linear narrative.

It was the work of the Russian Revolutionary filmmakers, particularly Eisenstein, Pudovkin, and Dovshenko, who clarified the nonlinear possibilities. Images could be juxtaposed and, although random, the juxtaposition and sometimes the clash of images created new ideas and perceptions of narrative. The presence of nature—flowers, apples, cows—acts as a counterweight to the death of a patriarch in Dovshenko's *Earth* (1930); the playful camera/eye of the cinematographer as a character in Vertov's *The Man with a Movie Camera* (1929); Eisenstein's stylized executions near the beginning of *Alexander Nevsky* (1938); and the casual introduction of the character Nevsky acts as a visual counterpoint to those executions. Each example illustrates how thinking in terms of juxtaposition opens up the story to new interpretations. The result is greater than the parts (shots) in each case.

Perhaps no filmmaker took this principle of nonlinearity as far as Luis Buñuel, who in his work with Salvador Dali, set as his primary goal to destroy linear narrative and the restorative resolution it implies. There is no peace of mind for the audience when they view *Un Chien d'Andalou*. There is only the unpredictable sense while watching the film, that anything can happen next. Whether Buñuel wishes to launch an attack on the Parisian bourgeoisie or to create an anarchy of experience, his images of sexuality, death, and horror are provocative and unforgettable. The totality of the experience of *Un Chien d'Andalou* is a true nonlinear experience. There had been vestiges of such an experience in Eisenstein's *Strike* (1924) and in Dovshenko's *Earth*, but no film experience was as devoted to a nonlinear experience as Buñuel's film. He was to continue this pattern of narrative experience through *Belle de Jour* (1967) and *The Discreet Charm of the Bourgeoisie* (1972).

Other filmmakers have digressed from linear narrative: the Shakespeare performance sequence in Ford's *My Darling Clementine* (1946), the closing sequence in Antonioni's *L'Eclisse* (*The Eclipse*) (1962), the introduction of a second but different story and genre in Woody Allen's *Crimes and Misdemeanors* (1989). More often when the intention was a nonlinear narrative, filmmakers have found an orderly approach to the issue—the multiple narrators in Welles's *Citizen Kane*, and Kurosawa's *Rashomon* (1951)—or the overreliance on rituals and time in Davies's *Distant Voices, Still Lives* (1988). In the evolution of nonlinear narrative, however, few filmmakers have been as bold as Humphrey Jennings.

In his documentary *Listen to Britain* (1942) (see Chapter 21), Jennings achieves a remarkable film that is notably nonlinear. A war documentary that emphasizes the survival capacity of the British Isles against the Axis threat, would, in a linear narrative, highlight the Battle of Britain, focus on a single character or place at a particular time, or use of a political figure such as Winston Churchill as the unifying voice. Jennings does none of these. Instead, he uses music—orchestral, dance hall, pianists, guitar-strumming soldiers—to unify the film. Music is not war-like, but it does create a counterpoint sound and idea in the light of the sights and sounds of war.

Jennings sidesteps the single character, but shows many characters at work, at leisure. Again, the counterpoint is to people at work for war and people at leisure from war. Jennings creates an attitude rather than an act, and the consequences are powerful and moving.

Another dimension of his nonlinear approach is that he moves geographically from place to place, from time to time, in a random fashion. There is no obvious cause and effect here. Instead the geography, whether urban or rural, is a unity rather than a specific place. Trafalgar Square is as important as a beach looking out to the English Channel and the North Sea. Time is managed rather than being viewed as a dramatic end game of fighting the war. The cause and effect relationship between time, place, and history is sidestepped, undermined, and thus Jennings can step away from the actual event and present an attitude that, in the end, will persevere and assure Great Britain's allies that she will triumph.

The result of Jennings nonlinear approach to the subject is a film as fresh and innovative today as it was in 1942.

The next figure that is critical in nonlinear narrative is Jean-Luc Godard. Although others in the New Wave were interested in genre subversion (François Truffaut in *Shoot the Piano Player*, 1962) and expansion of the interplay between the past and the present and how memory defines one and redefines the other (Alain Resnais in *Last Year at Marienbad*, 1961), no one was as radical about narrative as Jean-Luc Godard.

Whether using essay as a formal structure (*Two or Three Things I Know About Her*, 1966), or a polemic (*La Chinoise*, 1967), or a musical (*Tout Va Bien*, 1970), Godard would always subvert that narrative invention with another. The result was to move us away from character towards ideas. His overriding concern with the journey in *Weekend* (1967) is subverted by his shifts in time from one place to another, leading us to question meaning in *Weekend*. An early scene, the leave-taking on the journey, is a farce; a middle scene, the Leonard character, meditates on history, academia, and the future; in a late scene, a husband in the traditional family considered the breadwinner, is actually consumed by his wife. He is "bread" rather than the breadwinner. These radical shifts take us away from the literal meaning of content (so often the core of the linear narrative) toward a experimental, almost explosive, set of new narrative ideas. As with nonlinear narratives already highlighted, the key to this new perception is to undermine the relationship between the audience and the main character. The jump cut, the overuse of the long shot, and the long take underscore our distance from the character.

In Great Britain, Lindsay Anderson (*O Lucky Man!*, 1973) was the greatest proponent of a nonlinear style. His use of music interludes as well as outrageous set pieces moving away from the narrative action line highlighted an anarchistic style that was in part nonlinear. In Germany, Wim Wenders (*The Goalie's Anxiety at the Penalty Kick*, 1971, and *Alice in the Cities*, 1974) best exemplify the nonlinear impulse. In the former Yugoslavia, Dusan Makavejev fuses documentary and drama, psychology and politics in *WR: Mysteries of the Organism* (1971), creating a disorderly portrayal of the life and ideas of Wilhelm Reich. Here too the nonlinear overwhelms the linear.

But in order to see the nonlinear aesthetic fully flower, we have to move beyond the experiments and flirtations of Arthur Penn (*Little Big Man*, 1970), Peter Brook (*Marat/Sade*, 1966), and Nicholas Roeg (*Don't Look Now*, 1973). When we approach the recent work of Quentin Tarantino (*Pulp Fiction*, 1994), Milcho Manchevski (*Before the Rain*, 1994), and François Girard (*Thirty-two Short Films About Glen Gould*, 1993), we see the nonlinear aesthetic in full bloom. Single character–driven stories are abandoned in both *Pulp Fiction* and *Before the Rain*. Although *Pulp Fiction* has a series of main characters who are criminals wrestling with an ethical question or problem, the affiliation of main characters in Manchevski's film are much looser. All are Macedonian and all are in love, but there the similarity ends. Age, education, geography all differentiate the characters from one another. In both cases, the multiple characters undermine the opportunity for identification. Although *Thirty-two Short Films About Glen Gould* clearly has a single main character, that character is posing in each film in such a way as to preclude identification. He distances himself from us and so no ongoing identification is possible.

A second dimension of these films is that the dramatic shape is subverted. In *Pulp Fiction*, we expect the gangster story to proceed according to tradition—crime, rise, fall—this doesn't happen. The crime section is undermined by a debate between the two main characters—Travolta and Jackson. The extent of the discussion/debate, its philosophical nature, undermines any developing sense of anxiety related to what these men are going to do—kill people. Similarly, the dramatic arc of each story in *Before the Rain*—tales of intrareligious conflict—is undermined by a love story or the aftermath of a love relationship. This introjection of a relationship into a tense and probably violent conflict between Muslims and Christians is a counterpoint that actually makes more powerful the final outcome of each of the stories.

A third dimension of these films is that each scrupulously avoids a cause and effect relationship in their stories. In both *Pulp Fiction* and *Before the Rain*, the time line is violated. In *Pulp Fiction*, we join the story in midstream and return to the same point later in the narrative. In *Before the Rain*, we begin in one story only to rejoin the late phase of that story at the end of the third narrative. In both cases, we did not know this until a visual cue, or repetition presents the return to the earlier time to us.

In *Thirty-two Short Films About Glen Gould*, we loosely follow a standard linear chronology of Gould's life, but the prologue and the epilogue may be a vision of Gould in a kind of Arctic heaven, speaking to himself and, in his fashion, to us, or it may be a metaphor for his status as visionary vis-à-vis the rest of us. In either case, these scenes frame the film in a way that subverts the chronological line of his life and of the organization of the films about his life. This nonlinear approach is deepened by using documentary films, abstract films, and dramatized narratives. The mix of styles further subverts the time line and any remaining linearity. Radical shifts in tone between the absurd and the studied or formal also act as a counterpoint to our impulse to organize the material so we can understand it in a linear fashion.

This latter brings us to the final dimension of nonlinearity—feeling over exposition. In these very abbreviated insights into Glen Gould, the filmmaker goes with a feeling—his perfectionism in the playing of a record in his hotel room in Germany, his eccentricity in the film about the Truck Stop. What Gould hears illustrates the extent he tuned out of the kind of observation we associate with such a casual experience (eating breakfast at a diner). When the most obvious becomes surprising, when a recording session isn't about the recording but rather the sense of ecstacy of the artist, we, the viewers, face a different kind of experience. This is the true possibility of the non-linear revolution, the opportunity to give us a new, surprising experience. Godard, Tarantino, Manchevski understand that to do so means not only creative risk, but the subversion of the linear expectation of the audience.

But just as the more media-experienced audiences grow, the opportunity of accessing specialty audiences via satellite and multi-channel television will encourage filmmakers to continue to experiment with new narrative styles to reach them. Here lies the true potential for a nonlinear aesthetic. The future is here. The technology is available. Filmmakers need only take the risk.

□ NOTE/REFERENCE

1. Ken Dancyger and Jeff Rush, *Alternative Scriptwriting* (Second Edition) (Boston: Focal Press, 1995), Chapters 2, 3, and 4.

31

Nonlinear Editing and Digital Technology II

∎

In the last chapter we introduced the notion that there is a tradition of nonlinear storytelling and that the technological shift to nonlinear editing has accelerated the consideration that this alternative approach to story is a viable option. As an option, however, it proceeds differently regarding shot selection and pace principally because the audience no longer experiences the narrative through a single main character; nor is the audience following the experience of that character from crisis to resolution.[1] Indeed we may be following multiple main characters, and there may or may not be a resolution. The conventional story arc, with its implications for editing, may simply not be relevant in the nonlinear narrative.

In order to understand the different editing choices made in nonlinear narratives, we will look at 4 nonlinear films. To explore those choices in detail and to highlight their differences from the classic narrative, we will use the following framework.

☐ THE FRAMEWORK

If there is no main character, no resolution, what are the goals of the editing of the nonlinear film? The first goal must be to assure that the narrative coheres, that it holds together. Each of the narrative tools of character, structure, genre, and tone may be used, but it is structure that is most critical in a macro sense.[2] The structural option most directly applicable to the nonlinear film is a shaping device. The murderous career of Mickey and Mallory is the shaping device in *Natural Born Killers* (1994); the battle for Guadalcanal is the shaping device of *The Thin Red Line* (1998); identity crises are the shaping device in *Pulp Fiction* (1994); an Atlantic island off of Georgia is the geographical shaping device and the day of migration is the temporal shaping device in *Daughters of the Dust* (1991). Whether the shaping device is an event, a place, a time, that device is the most general structural tool that helps the narrative cohere.

The second macro device is the voice of the filmmaker. As we saw in Chapter 1, Buñuel's narrative goal was to subvert narrative, and this dialectic highlighted his voice. Godard undermined the narrative to introject his political views through the narrative. The Coen brothers use irony to loosen us from our genre expectations in their work. Voice is the second important device that makes clear how we should experience the nonlinear narrative.

On a more detailed or micro level the nonlinear filmmaker has to concern him or herself with the issue of energy. Every narrative, linear or nonlinear, must engage the audience in an energetic experience. In the linear narrative this is far easier. The goal-directedness of the main character, the barrier of the antagonist, and the barrier of plot, provides a structure that keeps the dramatic arc moving from the critical moment of entry into the narrative and on to the culmination and resolution of the narrative. Each device implies the critical role that pace and camera movement and placement will play in energizing the narrative. The filmmaker and editor know that the close-up punctuates the most important events of the narrative.

Because the filmmaker has opted for a nonlinear narrative does not mean she can sidestep the energy issue.

What is removed from the narrative approach must be compensated for elsewhere, as an example will illustrate. The gangster film gains enormous energy from its plot: the rise and fall of the main character, the gangster. The gangster's career is in essence the plot of the film. In *Pulp Fiction*, however, which is a nonlinear narrative, the first thing we notice is that it has very little plot. In fact, the major plot is concentrated in the second of three stories that make up the narrative. Those stories occur out of chronological order, thereby taking temporal momentum out of the structural mix as a potential source of energy. Instead, the energy in *Pulp Fiction* comes from its dialogue, from the conflictual and conflicted nature of the characters. It also comes from considerable camera movement. It does not come from the traditional narrative source, the plot.

Filmmakers must replace the energy that would be more easily generated in the linear narrative. Here is an important role for the filmmaker and editor in the nonlinear edit—to find new sources to energize the narrative.

The issue for us then is to look for and to highlight those macro and micro editing strategies that make the nonlinear film connect with its audience. We turn now to our case studies.

□ THE CASE OF *THE ICE STORM*

Ang Lee's *The Ice Storm* (1997) takes place in upper-middle-class suburban Connecticut. The time is 1974 just prior to Nixon's resignation. The narrative focuses on two families, the Hoods and the Carvers. Both have two teenaged children. The families are dysfunctional in the sense that no one seems to be able to help one another. Consequently Ben Hood and Janie Carver are having an affair; their children Wendy Hood and Mikey Carver are trying to echo their "parental units." The others in the couples, Helena

Hood and Jim Carver, fluctuate between depression and a search for escape—into spirituality, into work, anywhere except the battleground of family life. The other children, Paul Hood and Sandy Carver, also look for escape—into violent fantasies in the case of Sandy. Paul Hood makes do with sexual fantasies. Sexuality as currency ties all these characters to one another: sexuality as power, as a weapon, as compensation for the sense of loss or failure, is felt by each of these characters.

The ice storm of the title refers to the storm that takes place in the last third of the narrative. The event is a natural expression of the despair of these characters. Because of the storm, an electrical wire fractures and kills Mikey Carver. But his death is as much a result of emotional neglect. He is out of it and does seem drugged out, but Mikey suffers from parents who can't help him or satisfy themselves and consequently they are disconnected from the lives of their children. Mikey is a casualty of materially rich, spiritually despairing America. His death punctuates a narrative filled with desperation and unhappiness. In this sense the sexual arc that runs through the narrative is compensatory rather than empowering its characters.

In terms of shaping devices, Ang Lee relies on one critical week in the life of the characters. It is significant that the week includes Thanksgiving, the most meaningful secular family holiday. The narrative focuses on how separate the members of two families can be, and the shaping event implies the opposite—togetherness. The dramatic conflict that runs through the narrative is generated out of this ironic paradox.

The second shaping device is to focus on two families, both with socio-economic goals and status in common. They both have two teenagers, and they both are tied to each other by adultery and desire. Both families also have one parent who is aggressive and the other who is intelligent and marginalized within the family.

The third shaping device is behavioral. The characters all are upstanding members of the community but all become transgressive in their behavior. The most obvious transgressors are Ben Hood and Janie Carver. Both are involved in adultery. They are not alone—the concluding social event in the film is a neighborhood post-Thanksgiving party. The focus of the party is organized adultery: a key-swapping lottery for a new partner for the night. But adultery isn't the only transgression. Early in the narrative Wendy Hood steals cosmetics from the local pharmacy. Later her mother, Helena, does the same and is caught. Sandy Carver indulges in violence, blowing up his toys and fantasizing about blowing up his teacher and classmates. Even the innocent Paul Hood drugs a friend to eliminate a sexual rival. Transgression unites these characters as much as their unhappiness and socioeconomic status.

In terms of voice Ang Lee is both genre specific and distinctly authorial in *The Ice Storm*. The dysfunctional American family was the subject of two satires that followed Lee's film, *Happiness* (1998) and *American Beauty* (1999). Lee, on the other hand, opted to treat *The Ice Storm* as melodrama.

All 8 characters in *The Ice Storm* are treated as the main character in a melodrama would be treated: as a powerless person attempting to secure power from an intractable power structure. As a result Lee invites us to empathize at one point or another with each of these characters. Even in the most extreme cases, Janie and Sandy Carver, Lee gently pokes fun at them but not so much that we can't see their pain. To feel their pain is to be with them. The other characters are easier to relate to, and they too display their vulnerability to us. Consequently, the dominant tone of *The Ice Storm* is realistic, and we are invited to care about each of these characters.

I have written elsewhere about Ang Lee's capacity to be inclusive of characters who too often occupy the margins of society or whose actions justify our contempt.[3] This sense of inclusiveness is the voice of Ang Lee. The issue from an editing point of view is how that voice is established. The most direct path to inclusiveness is to care about the characters. Aside from the content of the shot—we do see Ben Hood totally break down in tears near the end of the film—the issue is the use of close-ups. Lee does not go overboard in his use of close-ups, but he does use them strategically. When he wants to tell us that Sandy is sexually aroused by Wendy he uses a close-up and point-of-view shot. The two are performing in the high school band, but the shot is of Sandy looking not at the conductor but rather at Wendy's exposed underwear, which is visible as he looks down at her (she is seated to play her instrument while he stands to play his). When Lee wants us to feel for the characters he will resort to a close-up. When the agitated Sandy is confused and overwhelmed by the straightforward Wendy's exhibitionist sexual proposal, Lee simply holds on Sandy's face as desire turns to terror and confusion and anger. We understand Sandy and feel his emotional confusion. It would have been far easier to treat Sandy broadly and stereotypically as an unprepared teenager. Lee instead opts to stand with Sandy rather than against him. Consequently we stand with him as well. This is a pattern Ang Lee follows with all the characters.

Lee also uses context to tell us more about the characters and their feeling states. When Helena Hood is stealing from the pharmacy, we see in the security mirror above her the reflection of the pharmacist observing her while she perpetrates the theft. When Wendy Hood steals, an older woman glares at her implying that she will be caught, but Wendy glares right back ignoring the guilt implicit in her earlier actions. By providing a social context, Lee suggests that these characters are not isolated from their society. They are simply transgressive, regardless of the views of society.

Context also provides clues to the aspirations of the characters. When Helena bumps into Reverend Phillip Edwards, a man clearly interested in her as a woman, they chat over books that are being sold in the foreground, but in the background the community church looms. Helena's search for spiritual values is highlighted, as much as her quest for freedom is highlighted by the open road before her and behind her as she rides her bike in search of the feeling of freedom she associates with her daughter more than with her own desires.

Ang Lee also uses deep focus or contextual shots to suggest power. The closer he places the camera to a character, the more powerful they are. The image of Janie Carver, foregrounded in bed with Ben Hood in the background, implies who has the power in this relationship. So too in the case of the relationship of children to adults. Very often the adults are fore-grounded with the children in the background. When Lee wants to render a character even more powerless, the camera is placed farther from the character. In the last shot the Hood family is waiting for Paul Hood to get off the train. They, the adults and Wendy, are on the same plane, and the camera is far from them. The parents here are virtually equivalent to the children in their powerlessness, in their inability to help one another. The voice of Ang Lee is clear and powerful in the choice of these visuals.

As to the issue of energy, Lee uses a dual strategy to create energy in *The Ice Storm*. As mentioned earlier, he has adopted as one strategy the genre of melodrama. This realist approach, however, is broken intermittently by irony—an exaggeration strategy that breaks away from a connection with the characters. A scene between Ben Hood and Janie Carver makes the point. The couple has made love and Ben speaks obsessively about his antagonism toward a colleague at work, a colleague who is besting him on the golf course. Whether this is an expression of Ben's more general aggressiveness or insecurity about the implications of a rival in the workplace, Janie's response is boredom. She tells him she already has a husband, implying the boredom of the state of marriage. The aggressive humor puts Ben in his place, and for that instant the two characters are unjoyous adulterers. Although we quickly move back into realist mode, and consequently an engagement with the characters, this tonal shift unsettles as well as ener-gizes our experience of the narrative. Similar scenes are initiated with Paul Hood, Sandy Carver, and the friends and colleagues of the Hoods and the Carvers.

A second strategy Lee uses to generate energy in the narrative is more expected. He places the camera close to the characters. His use of deep focus assures a context for the actions of these characters, and he will use point of view to create energy, as well as cutaways and strategic close-ups. A good example is the scene where Paul drugs his sexual rival for Libitz, the girl of his dreams. There they are in her empty apartment, but the plan goes awry when Libitz also drinks a drugged drink. Rather than the night on the town Paul expected, he ends up with Libitz asleep in his lap. The desirable goal looks promising, even visually; the only problem is that she is asleep. Thwarted by his own clever plan, Paul ends up as he began, alone.

□ THE CASE OF *HAPPINESS*

Todd Solondz's *Happiness* (1998) is a portrait of a suburban family, the Jordans. The story focuses on the parents, Mona and Lenny Jordan; their adult daughters, Joy, Helen, and Trish; Bill Maplewood, a psychiatrist, and the husband of Trish Jordan; Billy, the son of Bill and Trish Maplewood; Andy, Joy's boyfriend; and Allen, a patient of Bill Maplewood. The prism for the narratives is relationships—love relationships, relationships of desire, parent-child relationships, and sibling relationships. The experience of the film suggests the irony of the title: the relationships are doomed by the self-absorption of the participants and by the imbalance between the pleasure and pain principles as they operate in the lives of these characters. In other words, this is a deeply neurotic set of characters.

The film is structured initially as a number of set pieces fluctuating between the obsessive goal of one of the characters and the indifference of the character to whom they look for help. In the second half of the film the momentum of three sexual obsessions is the focus: the lust of Joy, Bill, and Allen. In each case the relationship is transgressive. Joy has an affair with a married Russian cabbie, a student in the English as-a-second-language class she teaches. Bill pines for Johnny, his 11-year-old son Billy's friend. In fact, Bill, drugs and rapes the boy. And Allen is obsessed with Helen. When she responds positively to his obscene phone call, he is frightened into the arms of an obese neighbor, Kristina, who has in turn murdered and mutilated the building's doorman for attempting to rape her. At best the relationships are exploitative, and in the case of the child rape at the hands of a pedophile psychiatrist, the result is obscene and abusive. Ironically, this is the relationship that Solondz treats with the greatest empathy.

The narrative as I've described it doesn't fully capture the shaping devices Solondz relies upon to pull this nonlinear story together. The primary shaping device is to follow the course of a number of sexual relationships. We don't enter those relationships at the same point. Where they are more conventional relationships, a marriage or a male-female relationship of equals, we see only a fragment of the relationship and the emphasis is on its failure.

A second shaping device is to look at power relationships: a parent-child relationship, a therapist-patient relationship, a teacher-student relationship. In each case the more powerful character crosses the line, thereby exploiting the relationship.

A third shaping device is the tone that assumes the ironic position so often associated with satire. This tone permeates character, dialogue, and narrative structure.

Although I have addressed the issue of voice elsewhere in my work, it requires elucidation in this chapter as well. Todd Solondz exhibits a very distinctive voice in *Happiness*.[4] He is ironic and humorous about the Jordan sisters. The most-likely-to-fail sister, Joy, is the character who dominates screen time. The other sisters, Trish and Helen, have what might appear to be privileged lives. Trish has a husband and a family, and Helen has beauty and job success. But their surface successes belie a husband who is a pedophile and, in Helen's case, a dangerous promiscuity that implies failure rather than success. Both Trish and Helen are treated ironically; only Joy is allowed to become real for the audience. She has ironic moments, the relationship break-up with Andy, for example, or the kitchen conversation with Trish about happiness, but eventually Solondz relents and allows Joy moments of deep feeling—her created song, "Happiness," and her sexual relationship with the cabbie, are both treated with real feeling.

The same can be said for the male characters. Allen, the patient, is excessive and ironic, and although the treatment of Bill the psychiatrist may be ironic, the treatment of Bill as father and as sexual predator is treated more realistically. These shifts in tonal expectations imply that irony and empathy can coexist in the same narrative. Surprise and satire are both narrative goals for Solondz, and both go to the heart of his voice in the narrative. He heaps scorn on conventional people and on conventional behavior, but his empathy for the outsider is constant, and that empathy can be generated from the behavior of a character or from a group reaction to the behavior of a character.

The fact that Solondz uses sexuality as the currency for relationships as well as an expression of power that allows us to assess the behavior of a character only intensifies our response. By viewing Bill and Andy as sexual predators, and by viewing Kristina and Helen as castrating females, Solondz is demythologizing the notion of romantic love and bringing relationships down to the level of rough sex and abusive exploitation. But this does not dim the desire of any of these characters; rather it creates a self-absorbed context that sets up a new paradigm—sex without love, love of self over love between two individuals, and finally instant gratification over a lasting commitment to a relationship. This is the destination to which Solondz's narrative and voice take us.

A great deal of energy is generated in the narrative in the conflictual shifts in tone from irony to empathy. Although Solondz sidesteps pace, using classical editing strategies such as faster pace to generate energy, he does shift from one character to another. As an episode ends with Joy and Trish, for example, another begins with Bill and his son Billy. The dissonance between scenes generates a sense of narrative conflict. Within each scene another level of conflict is generated. In the scene between Trish and Joy, the conflict is sibling rivalry focused on Joy's unhappy state. In the next scene, the conflict emanates from Billy's state of sexual ignorance. As he punishes himself for that ignorance, his father, Bill, tries to assure him that all will be well. Bill, a psychiatrist, plays sexual scientist and plies his son with information. All the while we know Bill to be a sexual predator, and his questions to his son take on a distinct ironic edge. Although the focal point of the energy in these scenes is the dialogue, the complication of the subtext for one character in each scene raises the meaning of the dialogue and the conflict level. The energy that is usually generated from pace is nevertheless a powerful dimension of these scenes; only the source of that energy differs.

Solondz also uses the contrast of fantasy and reality to energize *Happiness*. Allen's verbal sexual fantasies, which are aggressive and abusive, give way to his telephone search for Helen. When he eventually finds she is his neighbor, he is petrified by her positive response to his abuse. Her sadomasochistic disposition in fact meshes well with his sadomasochistic fantasies. But the reality is too much for him. He cannot succeed with the reality of Helen and he retreats to the less threatening Kristina.

Allen's psychiatrist, Bill, also has destructive fantasies, such as a walk through Central Park with an M16. His violent fantasies have many victims but a positive dimension—at least he doesn't kill himself. Here too the mix of fantasy and reality generates energy in the narrative.

Finally, the inclusion of the MTV style yields considerable energy. In the opening scene of Joy and Andy in a restaurant, for example, he proposes marriage, but she then rejects his proposal, which in turn leads him not to offer her the friendship gift he would have given to the woman who loves him—all of which is presented with the quality of a TV sitcom being filmed before a live audience. There are few shots, but the lengthy sequence is the story of an entire relationship. In intention the scene is reminiscent of the breakfast scene in *Citizen Kane*: an entire relationship of 5 years is spun out in 5 minutes. And in its flat TV style, filmed as if the viewer sat in a live audience in front of the two characters, the scene has an intensity and a feeling level that isn't shared by what follows. It is in effect an MTV movie unto itself.

This MTV pattern, which Solondz follows in the first half of the film, gives each scene a powerful intensity. The MTV style generates the energy that ordinarily proceeds via identification with the main character in a linear story.

□ THE CASE OF *THE THIN RED LINE*

Terry Malick's *The Thin Red Line* (1998) is a war film about the battle for Guadalcanal. War films, whether they focus on a battle, a war, or a patrol that is a minor piece of a war, have a beginning, middle, and end. The end or resolution addresses whether the main character survived or did not. The tone of such films usually varies, ranging from patriotic films such as *Guadalcanal Diary* (1942) to the antiwar polemic of films such as *Too Late the Hero* (1970), a Pacific war film made while the United States was fighting the war in Vietnam. Forty-five years after the event, Malick's film is quite different from either of these extremes. In addition, rather than having a beginning, middle, and end, it is nonlinear in its presentation.

The film's nonlinearity is defined by its conscious attempt to sidestep linear structure. If the film were linear it would follow a land-on-the-island, battle-for-the-island, and win-the-island structure. Instead, Malick opens the film on a soldier, Private Witt, who has gone AWOL to another Pacific island. There he and a few army friends collude with the natives. They try to be part of the native community as opposed to that of the U.S. soldiers. When they are taken by U.S. Forces, we have no idea how much time passes before they are shipped to Guadalcanal. Certainly this soldier's outfit is shipped to Guadalcanal for the upcoming conflict. His sergeant, Ed Welsh, reluctantly takes him back into the company. From here the narrative progresses not on a time line but rather through a series of incidents: the landing; the first encounter with the enemy; the struggle to take an enemy bunker high atop the American position; the departure from the battlefield; the capture of a native village occupied by the Japanese; a patrol on which Private Witt sacrifices his life to save his patrol. But these incidents focus on the inner thoughts of a variety of soldiers in the company as well as their behavior. It's as if these inner thoughts create the private world of these characters. Rather than deal with the battle and the camaraderie that battle forges, their inner thoughts fragment the sense that the company is a unit. Instead it becomes a collection of individuals with distinct and differing goals.

Colonel Gordon Tall, who commands the company, is concerned only with the injustice of having commanding officers who are younger than he. For him the battle is an opportunity to secure the promotion that for too long has eluded him. Captain Staros, who answers to the colonel, is totally different. He is consumed by guilt and responsibility toward his men and their well-being. Captain Gaff, who is also responsible to the colonel is not racked by anything but doing the job that needs to be done. He is brave to the point of foolhardiness. Moving down the chain of command, Sergeant Welsh, who works most directly with the soldiers of the company, is survivalist and cynical. He has been disappointed in his superiors and consequently works to help his men deal with the threat of the enemy as well as the threat of the chain of command. Above all he wants to live, and he wants to help his men live.

The film focuses on three privates in the company, Private Witt, whom we meet at the opening of the narrative and who dies at its close. Witt is concerned about his place in the world. He feels he belongs in the outfit and has a responsibility to his fellow soldiers, as well as to his family at home and to the natives he meets on the Islands. This is a man looking to define his place in the universe. Another soldier, Corporal Fife, has a narrower field of focus: he looks beyond himself only to look at death in the universe. He is fearful and obsessed by the meaning of death. Yet another, Private Jack Bell, thinks only about home, specifically about his wife. He yearns for her, reveling in memories of his recent marriage, bathed in the recollection of the aliveness of her sexuality. Unfortunately, his feelings are not shared by his wife. Late in the narrative he receives a letter from her; she writes that she is leaving him for another man, an available States-side man.

Each man acts as a narrator, giving voice to his inner thoughts. The multiple points of view push the experience of the film as a nonlinear discontinuous experience. Together with an episodic structure, *The Thin Red Line* in fact becomes an impressionistic tone poem rather than a polemic putting forward a particular position on a particular battle in a particular war.

In order to give the film shape Malick poses a series of relationships, keying in on those relationships to break down the geography and the chronological progress of a significant World War II battle. Private Witt in the company relates to humanity in general, as we have seen. He relates to the native islanders as he does to his own comrades; he relates to them as people, as a part of humanity rather than as the enemy separated out of humanity. He even relates to the enemy, who in the end will kill him. Private Bell, on the other hand, relates more to the home front than he does to his comrades or to his presence on the island. American soldiers are not the only relationships Malick explores. Enemy soldiers when captured express the pain, the unbearable pain of losing their comrades. This particular scene humanizes the enemy just as the later death scene of Private Witt humanizes Witt as well as the enemy. Throughout the narrative Malick humanizes and individualizes so that the soldiers become individuals and people rather than soldiers. Each of the relationships portrayed mitigates against the solidarity of viewing the company of man as a war machine. Malick views the enemy, the U.S. soldiers, and the natives as individuals, as human beings. But humans are nothing more than part of the natural order, a part of the natural world. Consequently, his film nature, whether it be birds or bats or overgrown fields and outsized trees, plays an omnipresent role, as if to say that nature will endure, whatever man does to his fellow man. This is the voice of Terrence Malick. Relationships are the vehicle for this meditation. The war story is the genre he has used to explore these ideas about man and nature.

Voice can be genre specific, but many filmmakers challenge genre expectations in order to strengthen their voices. The Coen brothers, for instance, use satire to undermine the expected realism of the police story in *Fargo* (1996). Martin Scorsese uses a dark hyper-realism to undermine the heroism of the sports film in *Raging Bull* (1980). War films tend to realism, although Agnieszka Holland has used satire to make *Europa Europa* (1990), a child's nightmare come true. In *Come and See* (1985), Elem Klimov also takes the point of view of an adolescent's experience of war, but he creates a more intense nightmare. Terry Malick sees war differently, more philosophically. The tone he chooses for *The Thin Red Line* is poetic, stirring, and yet never nationalistic or patriotic. Malick is interested in questions of life and death, questions of friendship and of love. He is also concerned with man's place in the natural world. Consequently he doesn't see the battle for Guadalcanal in political, military, or economic terms. The result is an unhurried meditation on human behavior as well as of human behavior during unnatural events such as war. If there is antagonism here, it is also philosophical—what is death? What is life? What does it mean to help another or to empathize with another? These questions consume the narrative, influence behavior, and generally drive the shape of the narrative. This is a war film, but Malick had made it the most unusual of war films—a meditation rather than a melodrama. This is Malick's unique voice in *The Thin Red Line*.

Malick has supported that voice by changing the balance between plot and character layers in *The Thin Red Line*. For the most part the war film is a genre dominated by plot. The patrol to find Private Ryan in *Saving Private Ryan* (1997), the attack on the Ant Hill and its aftermath in *Paths of Glory* (1957), the attempted escape through the sewers of Warsaw in *Kanal* (1957), are all plot-driven narratives. That is not to say that the character layer isn't important in the war film, as it is in all the above-mentioned films. But plot dominates the war film. *The Thin Red Line* is an exception. Malick raises the character layer of all characters thereby downgrading the importance of plot. How this works is that the plot of the attack on the bunker, for example, is undermined by the elevation of the relationship stories of the Captain Staros and the Colonel Tall. The colonel will sacrifice any relationship to advance his ambition. His unwillingness to provide water for the company attacking the bunker supports his lack of care for others. The captain on the other hand, refuses to send his men into battle. He cares too much. In both of these cases, the scenes highlight the nature of each character, as opposed to the progress of the battle.

A similar result is created in the attack on the village on Guadalcanal. Rather than detailing the progress of the attack, Malick focuses on the feelings of the captives, the Japanese, their pain, their sense of loss with regard to dead comrades, their fear about their own fates. Instead of demonizing the enemy, Malick humanizes the enemy, thereby undermining the sense of victory for the main characters. This upgrade of character layer and downgrade of plot undermines genre expectations and accentuates Malick's voice.

Besides changing the balance between the plot and character layers, Malick uses narrative detail that pushes voice forward is his emphasis on two extreme states: living and dying. Particular sequences engender both phenomena. Movement through the tall grass convey the awareness that in one instant you are totally alive but in the next instant you could be dead. Living soldiers came upon the dead, or at least parts of the dead. The sequence of moving through the fog has a similar feeling—a heightened sense of the danger that brings death. During the battle for the bunker, Sergeant Keck falls on a grenade that accidentally explodes. Malick lingers over his dying. So too the death of Private Witt, who dies to save his patrol. But here Malick moves away from the moment of death to the elements of life dear to him: nature, the island natives, and animal life. These elements live on while he dies.

In this latter scene we see a recurring theme for Malick—the natural order. Although there are war films that embrace technology, such as *Full Metal Jacket* (1987) and *Apocalypse Now* (1979), Malick's narrative seems the opposite. It is environmental in its concerns rather than nationalistic or technological. It should come as no surprise that he ends the film with three shots of nature rather than of characters or machines.

Malick also uses narration to give voice to his philosophical concerns. "Who's killing us, robbing us of life and light?" "Is this darkness in you too?"

"You are like my sons. My dear sons. I'll carry you around wherever I go."
"War turns men into dogs. It poisons the soul." These words are spoken by
a variety of characters who probe for meaning. They are both personal and
poetic. These are the deep issues that Malick associates with war.

Malick's nonlinear approach to the narrative means giving up the natural strengths that plot and a main character yield: involvement. To do so
means finding other means to energize the experience of the narrative. What
alternative technologies does Malick use to energize the narrative? The first
strategy Malick uses is to provide contrast between sequences. As mentioned
earlier the sequences are not organized in a progressive or linear fashion.
Although they generally follow the time line of an invasion, neither the
proportion of film time spent on each sequence nor the narrative approach
to those sequences, builds progressively to a climax. Indeed, the focus in
the scenes will vary from pain and loss among the enemy in the taking of
the village to the opposite goals of a captain and a colonel as they face the
challenge of capturing a hill dominated by an enemy bunker. The contrast
at times is so great that the viewer is faced always with the unexpected.

More conventionally but no less effectively, Malick relies on the moving
camera, particularly in the military movement through the fog, the advance
through the overgrown fields, and the attack on the bunker as well as the
village. Subjective movement places us with the soldier Corporal Fife as
he advances. The anticipation and the anxiety are captured by the moving
camera. As much as possible the pace of the movement simulates human
movement, resulting in an identification with the feeling level of the soldier
in each case.

Malick also relies on close-ups to intensify the emotion and the energy
in particular scenes. Sergeant Welsh talking to his men, whether it is about
belonging to the company or carrying morphine to a dying man on the battlefield, is presented in close-up. So too is Private Bell, who is obsessed with
his wife at home. When the flashbacks occur they contain movement as well
as off-center framing, as if the soldier struggles to contain the memory and
also to possess the sexuality, the life force, he associates with his wife. Close-
ups intensify his desire to hold on to those memories and to that desire.

Finally, Malick uses cutaways to remind us that there is a world beyond
the battlefield—a world with families and with children, and a world where
nature not only exists but where it prevails. Again and again Malick cuts
away to images of that natural world, the context for his soldiers' story.

☐ THE CASE OF *MAGNOLIA*

Paul Thomas Anderson's *Magnolia* (1999) functions as a nonlinear drama
but, as in the case of Anderson's other films, it also functions as a movie
about moviemaking (a constructed reality), or more broadly the media. In
the case of *Magnolia*, the prologue consists of narration. A skeptical nar-

rator describes in detail 3 remarkable coincidences from the past. Each is framed as a past "how-done-it" as opposed to a who-done-it. Each incident ends in a death: the first a murder, the second an accident, and the third a suicide. Then Anderson proceeds to question, and in the case of the last incident prove, that it was something else: a murder rather than a suicide. Each case is a puzzle that is deconstructed to challenge or alter the first impression. The prologue also implies that the media creates illusions and that we, the viewers, should be skeptical about such constructed realities. Stories are told in the media but they can be reconfigured to alter their impact and meaning. Anderson uses pace and detailed close-ups to make the experience of the 3 stories of the prologue exciting. They leave us winded, not having had enough time to digest and process the visual and aural information.

Using the same sense of dynamic pace he launches us into the multiple stories of the main body of the narrative. What proceeds are the stories of 8 characters who will participate in essentially 3 story lines. By coincidence each story will link to the others. The first story is the story of the Partridge Family. The son, Jack, is now known as Frank Mackie, a media phenomenon. Frank is the voice for men being aggressive toward women, but his version of aggressiveness is as close as possible to rape just shy of being charged with a crime. His program is, needless to say, called "Seduce and Destroy." Frank (Jack) is alienated from his father Earl, who is dying. Before he dies, Earl would like to reconcile with his son, whom he deserted when he discovered that his wife Jack's mother was dying of cancer. Earl's new wife, Linda, who married him for his money, is now disintegrating because the man she's come to love is dying, and she is overwhelmed by the knowledge that she will lose him.

The second story is the story of Jimmy Gator, a famous TV game show host. Professionally, he is immensely popular; personally, he is dying of cancer and wants to reconcile with his daughter, Claudia. Claudia is a promiscuous coke addict who hates her father for sexually abusing her when he was drunk. Jim is a police officer who is earnest about his work. He is called to Claudia's apartment because of a complaint about noise from the stereo. Jim, rather than charging Claudia, falls in love with her. Their relationship rescues her from the self-destructive arc of her life.

The third story is that of Donnie, an adult child star made famous on an earlier TV game show. Today he has ruined his work life and his love life is even less successful. Stealing money from his current employer seems to be the solution to all his problems. It's not. Parallel to this story is the story of Stanley, a contemporary child star on Jimmy Gator's TV show. He is so knowledgeable that his 2 child teammates depend upon him to win. But Stanley is driven to win by a relentless, cruel father. When Stanley has to go to the bathroom no one on the show is empathetic, and when he finally urinates in his pants, his father goes ballistic. Stanley refuses to "play" genius for television or for his father. He just wants to be treated like the child he is.

All these stories are linked because Earl Partridge owns the TV game show, the setting for parts of two of the stories. In addition, Jim from the second story rescues Donnie from becoming a thief in the third story.

The best way to frame the stories is to consider each of the 8 characters as a character in crisis. Anderson for the most part treats the stories realistically. The dramatic arc of the stories leads the characters to help each other. Jim and Claudia help each other, and Jim helps Donnie return the stolen funds. One event or coincidence that is notable is that the narrative occurs in the late stages of each story. We can correlate the moment at which Anderson enters the narrative to the point of deepest despair for Jack, for Claudia, for Jimmy, and for Donnie. At this moment, during an intense storm, the rain is replaced by frogs falling from the sky. This event, analogous in tone to the plagues Moses called forward to punish Egypt for retaining the Jews as slaves, has a shocking, surreal quality, although Anderson treats the storm of pests realistically. After this event, reconciliation and recovery begin. Stanley tells his father that he wants to be considered as a child. Jack (Frank) cries for his father. And Jim helps Donnie return the stolen money. The film closes with Claudia breaking out in a smile. All of these signals of hope for the despairing characters seem to pivot on this act of God, the storm of pestilence. The storm and its character, together with the prologue, shifts *Magnolia* from the melodrama that it appears to be to a moral fable, a hyper-drama.[5]

The principal shaping device Anderson uses is the notion of three inter-connected narratives. As in stories told in the prologue, each can lead to death. In the first Earl Partridge will die, probably never forgiven by the son he deserted. In the second story Jimmy will certainly die of cancer, but his daughter Claudia may also die, given the level of her self-destruction. In the third story, it is the dignity of the character that is being destroyed: both Donnie and Stanley are being destroyed by their dependency upon the fame television has brought them. And in each case divine intervention or its equivalent, profound empathy for the other, saves the character from what appears to be their inevitable fate.

A second shaping device is the state of despair shared by so many of these characters. Even Frank Mackie, who was Jack Partridge in a former life, seems to be overwhelmingly defensive in his aggressive "Seduce and Destroy" posturing. We discover that he has never gotten over the wound of being abandoned by his father. He speaks of caring for his sick mother, but he has been abused by his father no less than Claudia has been by hers. Donnie longs for a lost past as much as he longs for the local muscular bartender. Stanley despairs for a lost childhood, and Earl despairs for his past sins, principally abandoning the wife, who died of cancer, a woman he loved deeply.

A third shaping device is the presence of the media in all these stories. Its presence provides a public-private forum to consider each of the characters. In the first story, Earl is a public success, for he owns successful television shows; but privately, as a husband and father, he is a failure. His son Jack (Frank) is a media star, a man's man, but privately he is a posturing, defensive boy, fearful of his deepest feelings. In the second story, Jerry is the most long-lasting TV game show host. Publicly, he is a star; privately, he is a failed father and a failing husband. In the third story, Stanley is the most brilliant child contestant on the Jimmy Gator show, but privately he is a young boy who wants to go out and play—to be a boy, rather than to be "a star," the role his father clearly needs him to be.

Anderson for the most part treats these stories realistically as we would expect in a melodrama. The result is that we become emotionally engaged with the characters, thereby masking voice as a key shaping device.[6] On the other hand, Anderson's use of the prologue together with the narrative intervention of the pestilence late in the narrative provides a constructed overlay to the realism of the narrative. It is here in the narration, in the skepticism about coincidence and the implicit skepticism about the manipulative capabilities of what we think we see (i.e., a construction, an anecdote, or a movie), that Anderson's voice is given its freest rein. By implying that a filmmaker can construct and alter perception, Anderson is alerting us to the power he yields in the film. Consequently, what we will watch is also a construction, albeit a powerful one. The dissonance between the prologue, the pestilence intervention, and the stories of these 8 desperate characters allows us to be involved with their stories but also to remember we are watching a film, a construction, an intentional coincidence. In this way Anderson allows us to have a powerful film narrative experience as well as his voice—which cautions that what we are watching is a construction, as all films are.

The energy in *Magnolia* comes from rather classical sources. The most important is pace. Anderson uses, and even overuses, pace, as early as the prologue. The cutting is so rapid that we can barely keep up with the 3 stories of coincidence. That breathless sense of pace carries on as he introduces all of the characters. Not only does Anderson introduce them quickly via rapid cross-cutting, but within each of the individual stories he also uses rapid camera motion and intense close-ups. This is a pattern he will use throughout the narrative: motion, close-up motion, and cutting on movement. Whatever the mood, the pace raises the energy level in the presentation of each of the stories.

Whenever Anderson wants to make an important point, however, he will hold on a shot to register that point. When Donnie realizes that he is trapped, he says: "The past is not through with us." When Frank is caught up in a lie about his past (about caring for a dying mother, or about growing up locally), he glares at the documentary reporter who has thrown his past back at him. Each of these scenes works with the notion of reversing the pace that has prevailed in the narrative, and Anderson's point is made.

Anderson also generates energy from the proximity of the camera to the characters in the different stories. A created song for the film, "It's Not Going to Stop Until You Rise Up," is sung by all of the characters. Anderson cuts from character to character as the song proceeds, each taking his or her turn singing the words. This artifice links each to the other and to the notion that they are each characters in a film as well as performers for a film.

Just as the film begins with a prologue, it ends with an epilogue. The epilogue is about confession, about characters revealing themselves, and states, "Sometimes people need to be forgiven."

□ NOTES/REFERENCES

1. Identification and the goal-directedness of a main character have particular editing implications, with respect to the use of the close-up, subjective camera placement, and movement and pace. Each of these editing choices creates a more emotional or dramatically meaningful experience. This classic approach to editing has less relevance in the nonlinear narrative.
2. See Ken Dancyger, *Global Scriptwriting* (Boston: Focal Press, 2001), Chapter 1 for definitions of each narrative tool.
3. Ibid., 77.
4. Ibid., 161–163.
5. Patricia Cooper and Ken Dancyger, *Writing the Short Film* (Boston: Focal Press, 1999), Chapter 14.
6. As a relationship between the character and the audience takes hold, that identification masks voice. The opposite is the basis for the clarity of the voice of the filmmaker: distance from character and structure reveals voice.

32

Conclusion

■

This book covers the theory and practice of editing from the beginning to the 1990s. We have far surpassed the skepticism that Rudolph Arnheim expressed when he said that technological changes such as sound could add nothing to the advancement of the silent film. Sound is now an artful addition to the repertoire of the film experience. This is also true of video.

Although they are different technologies, film and video have begun to merge. Movie screens are now smaller and television screens are larger than they once were, and the film audience is increasingly viewing films on a video format. Films that were once shot and edited on film are now shot on film and edited on video. Television shows that were once shot on video using three-camera studio techniques are now shot on video using single- camera filmic techniques. They are edited on tape, but have the look of a filmed show. The editing styles of films and taped television shows are becoming indistinguishable.

Much is different today from Alfred Hitchcock's time. Today's emphasis on technology—whether sound, image, or special effects—has placed a premium on sensation. On one level, the sensation of sound and image is what editing is about.

Because of its power, editing without an ethical dimension can only further the trend to use it to further sensation over more complex responses to film. This is the dangerous point at which we find ourselves today. In a sense, it places the artfulness of all that we have discovered—the power of film and television—in a spiritual vacuum.

When Eisenstein, Welles, and Buñuel created their works, they aimed to move the minds and emotions of their audiences. They used editing in a manipulative way, and yet their works had an ethical foundation. They deployed their creativity in a world of ethical choices. The music video—the apogee of sensation—encourages sensation with contextual reference but seems to have no ethical goals beyond the stimulus of the sound and image.

Eisenstein, Welles, and Buñuel did not live in a less difficult time than we do today. They managed to create works that speak to us vividly about ethics as well as aesthetics. The same is true for Truffaut and Antonioni and Kurosawa.

When I look at today's work, I see the height of technological achieve-ment in such films as *Terminator 2*. I am entertained, but I am not moved to consider the ethics of violence or technology or relationships. The sensa-tions of ear and eye are everything. Is that all there is? It seems to be. The post-modern world has arrived.

Here is the challenge. We have learned a great deal *from* and a great deal *about* the greatest art of this century. How do we want to use our knowledge?

Appendix A

Filmography

■

Addams Family, The (1991), Barry Sonnenfeld, United States
Adventures of Dolly, The (1908), D. W. Griffith, United States
Age d'Or, L' (1930), Luis Buñuel, France
Aguirre: The Wrath of God (1972), Werner Herzog, West Germany
Alexander Nevsky (1938), Sergei Eisenstein, USSR
Alfie (1966), Lewis Gilbert, Great Britain
Alice in the Cities (1974), Wim Wenders, Germany
Aliens (1986), James Cameron, United States
All About Eve (1950), Joseph Mankiewicz, United States
All That Jazz (1979), Bob Fosse, United States
All the President's Men (1976), Alan Pakula, United States
America, America (1963), Elia Kazan, United States
American Beauty (1999), Sam Mendes, United States
American Graffiti (1973), George Lucas, United States
American in Paris, An (1951), Vincente Minnelli, United States
An Affair of Love (2000), Frederick Fonteyne, Belgium
And Now For Something Completely Different (1972), Ian McNaughton, Great Britain
Andrei Rublov (1969), Andrei Tarkovsky, USSR
Apartment, The (1960), Billy Wilder, United States
Apocalypse Now (1979), Francis Ford Coppola, United States
Applause (1929), Rouben Mamoulian, United States
Armageddon (1997), Michael Bay, United States
Arrivée d'un Train en Gare, L' (Arrival of a Train at the Station) (1895), Louis Lumière and Auguste Lumière, France
Avventura, L' (1960), Michelangelo Antonioni, Italy
Back-Breaking Leaf (1959), Terence McCartney-Filgate, Canada
Bad Day at Black Rock (1955), John Sturges, United States
Ballad of Cable Hogue, The (1970), Sam Peckinpah, United States
Ballad of Ramblin' Jack, The (2000), Aiyana Elliott, United States
Bandit Queen (1994), Shekhar Kapur, India
Barry Lyndon (1975), Stanley Kubrick, United States
Battle of Algiers, The (1965), Gillo Pontecorvo, Italy
Battle of Culloden, The (1965), Peter Watkins, Great Britain

Beach Red (1967), Cornel Wilde, United States
Bear, The (1989), Jean-Jacques Annaud, France
Before the Rain (1994), Milcho Manchevski, Macedonia/United Kingdom
Belle de Jour (1967), Luis Buñuel, France/Italy
Ben Hur (1959), William Wyler, United States
Best Years of Our Lives, The (1946), William Wyler, United States
Bicycle Thief, The (1948), Vittorio de Sica, Italy
Big Chill, The (1983), Lawrence Kasdan, United States
Big Parade, The (1925), King Vidor, United States
Billy Liar (1963), John Schlesinger, Great Britain
Billy the Kid (1930), King Vidor, United States
Bird (1988), Clint Eastwood, United States
Birds, The (1963), Alfred Hitchcock, United States
Birth of a Nation, The (1915), D. W. Griffith, United States
Black Robe (1991), Bruce Beresford, Canada/Australia
Black Stallion, The (1979), Carol Ballard, United States
Black Sunday (1977), John Frankenheimer, United States
Blackmail (1929), Alfred Hitchcock, Great Britain
Blood and Fire (1958), Terence McCartney-Filgate, Canada
Blood on the Moon (1948), Robert Wise, United States
Blue Steel (1989), Kathryn Bigelow, United States
Blue Velvet (1986), David Lynch, United States
Body and Soul (1947), Robert Rossen, United States
Body Snatcher, The (1945), Robert Wise, United States
Bonnie and Clyde (1967), Arthur Penn, United States
Born on the Fourth of July (1989), Oliver Stone, United States
Boxing Bout, A (1896), unknown, United States
Braveheart (1995), Mel Gibson, United States
Brazil (1985), Terry Gilliam, Great Britain
Breathless (1959), Jean Luc Godard, France
Bridge on the River Kwai, The (1957), David Lean, Great Britain
Bridges of Madison County, The (1995), Clint Eastwood, United States
Brief Encounter (1945), David Lean, Great Britain
Bring Me the Head of Alfredo Garcia (1974), Sam Peckinpah, United States
Bringing Up Baby (1938), Howard Hawks, United States
Broadcast News (1987), James Brooks, United States
Broken Blossoms (1919), D. W. Griffith, United States
Bullitt (1968), Peter Yates, United States
Burden of Dreams (1983), Les Blank, United States
Cabaret (1972), Bob Fosse, United States
Cabinet of Dr. Caligari, The (1919), Robert Wiene, Germany
Candidate, The (1972), Michael Ritchie, United States
Carnal Knowledge (1971), Mike Nichols, United States
Catch 22 (1970), Mike Nichols, United States
Caught (1949), Max Ophuls, United States

Celebration, The (Festen) (1998), Thomas Vinterberg, Denmark.
Champion (1949), Mark Robson, United States
Chant of Jimmy Blacksmith, The (1978), Fred Schepsi, Australia
Chien d'Andalou, Un (An Andalusian Dog) (1929), Luis Buñuel, France
Chinatown (1974), Roman Polanski, United States
Cinderella (1899), unknown, France
Citizen Kane (1941), Orson Welles, United States
City Lights (1931), Charlie Chaplin, United States
City, The (1939), Willard Van Dyke, United States
Clerks (1994), Kevin Smith, United States
Clockwork Orange, A (1971), Stanley Kubrick, Great Britain
Clueless (1995), Amy Hockerling, United States
Cobweb, The (1955), Vincente Minnelli, United States
Come and See (1985), Elem Klimov, USSR
Conformist, The (1971), Bernardo Bertolucci, Italy
Conversation, The (1974), Francis Ford Coppola, United States
Cows (1991), Julio Medem, Spain
Cries and Whispers (1972), Ingmar Bergman, Sweden
Crimes and Misdemeanors (1989), Woody Allen, United States
Crimson Tide (1995), Tony Scott, United States
Crooklyn (1994), Spike Lee, United States
Cross of Iron (1977), Sam Peckinpah, United States
Crossing Delancey (1988), Joan Micklin Silver, United States
Crouching Tiger, Hidden Dragon (2000), Ang Lee, United States/Taiwan
Crowd, The (1928), King Vidor, United States
Culloden (1964), Peter Watkins, Great Britain
Dances with Wolves (1990), Kevin Costner, United States
Daughters of the Dust (1991), Julie Dash, United States
Day after Day (1965), Clement Perron, Canada
Day of the Jackal, The (1973), Fred Zinnemann, United States
Day the Earth Stood Still, The (1951), Robert Wise, United States
Days of Heaven (1978), Terence Malick, United States
Dazed and Confused (1993), Richard Linklater, United States
Dead Calm (1988), Phillip Noyce, United States/Australia
Dead End (1937), William Wyler, United States
Dead Ringers (1988), David Cronenberg, Canada
Deer Hunter, The (1978), Michael Cimino, United States
Desert Fox, The (1951), Henry Hathaway, United States
Desert Victory (1943), Roy Boulting, Great Britain
Design for Living (1933), Ernst Lubitsch, United States
Desperately Seeking Susan (1985), Susan Seidelman, United States
Diary for Timothy (1945), Humphrey Jennings, Great Britain
Diary of a Lost Girl (1929), G. W. Pabst, United States
Die Hard (1988), John McTiernan, United States
Dirty Harry (1971), Don Siegel, United States

Discreet Charm of the Bourgeoisie, The (1972), Luis Buñuel, France
Distant Voices, Still Lives (1988), Terence Davies, Great Britain
Diva (1982), Jean-Jacques Beineix, France
Divide and Conquer (1943), Frank Capra/Anatole Litvak, United States
Divorce—Italian Style (1962), Pietro Germi, Italy
Do the Right Thing (1989), Spike Lee, United States
Doctor Zhivago (1965), David Lean, United States
Dodes' Ka-Den (1970), Akira Kurosawa, Japan
Dogs of War, The (1980), John Irvin, United States
Don't Look Now (1973), Nicholas Roeg, United States
Double Indemnity (1944), Billy Wilder, United States
Dr. Jekyll and Mr. Hyde (1932), Rouben Mamoulian, United States
Dr. Strangelove (1964), Stanley Kubrick, Great Britain
Draughtsman's Contract, The (1982), Peter Greenaway, Great Britain
Dreamlife of Angels, The (1998), Erick Zonca, France
Drifters, The (1929), John Grierson, Great Britain
Duel in the Sun (1946), King Vidor, United States
Earth (1930), Alexander Dovshenko, USSR
East of Eden (1955), Elia Kazan, United States
Eclisse, L' (1962), Michelangelo Antonioni, Italy
Edvard Munch (1974), Peter Watkins, Norway
8½ (1963), Federico Fellini, Italy
El Cid (1961), Anthony Mann, United States
Elizabeth (1998), Shekhar Kapur, Great Britain
Empire of the Sun (1987), Steven Spielberg, United States
Enfant Sauvage, L' (The Wild Child) (1970), François Truffaut, France
Enigma of Kaspar Hauser, The (1974), Werner Herzog, West Germany
Enoch Arden (1908, 1911), D. W. Griffith, United States
E.T. the Extra-Terrestrial (1982), Steven Spielberg, United States
Europa, Europa (1991), Agnieszka Holland, France/Germany
Every Day Except Christmas (1957), Lindsay Anderson, Great Britain
Excalibur (1981), John Boorman, Great Britain
Exodus (1960), Otto Preminger, United States
Exorcist, The (1973), William Friedkin, United States
Exotica (1994), Atom Egoyan, Canada
Eyes Wide Shut (1999), Stanley Kubrick, United States
Faces (1968), John Cassavetes, United States
Fall of the Roman Empire, The (1964), Anthony Mann, United States
Family Life (Wednesday's Child) (1972), Ken Loach, Great Britain
Farewell to Arms, A (1957), Charles Vidor, United States
Fast, Cheap and Out of Control (1998), Errol Morris, United States
Fast Times at Ridgemont High (1982), Amy Heckerling, United States
Father (1966), Istvan Szabo, Hungary
Fellini Satyricon (1970), Federico Fellini, Italy
Fighter (2000), Amir Bar-Lev, United States

Fireman's Ball (1968), Milos Forman, Czechoslovakia
Fires Were Started (1943), Humphrey Jennings, Great Britain
Fish Called Wanda, A (1988), Lewis Gilbert, Great Britain
Fitzcarraldo (1982), Werner Herzog, Germany
Five Fingers (1952), Joseph Mankiewicz, United States
Flashdance (1983), Adrian Lyne, United States
Fly, The (1986), David Cronenberg, Canada
For the Boys (1991), Mark Rydell, United States
Foreign Correspondent (1940), Alfred Hitchcock, Great Britain
Forrest Gump (1994), Robert Zemeckis, United States
400 Blows, The (1959), François Truffaut, France
French Connection, The (1971), William Friedkin, United States
Frenzy (1972), Alfred Hithcock, United States
From the Life of the Marionettes (1980), Ingmar Bergman, Sweden
Front Page, The (1931), Howard Hawks, United States
Full Metal Jacket (1987), Stanley Kubrick, Great Britain
Funny Face (1957), Stanley Donen, United States
Funny Thing Happened on the Way to the Forum, A (1966), Richard Lester, Great Britain
Gattopardo, Il (The Leopard) (1963), Luchino Visconti, Italy
General, The (1927), Buster Keaton, United States
Get Shorty (1995), Barry Sonnenfeld, United States
Getaway, The (1972), Sam Peckinpah, United States
Gimme Shelter (1970), The Maysles Brothers, United States
Gladiator (2000), Ridley Scott, United States
Gloria (1980), John Cassavetes, United States
Glory (1989), Ed Zwick, United States
Goalie's Anxiety at the Penalty Kick, The (1971), Wim Wenders, Germany
Gold Diggers of 1933 (1933), Mervyn LeRoy, United States
Gold Rush, The (1925), Charlie Chaplin, United States
Golden Boy (1939), Rouben Mamoulian, United States
Goodfellas (1990), Martin Scorcese, United States
Good, the Bad, and the Ugly, The (1967), Sergio Leone, Italy
Graduate, The (1967), Mike Nichols, United States
Grass (2000), Ron Mann, Canada
Greaser's Gauntlet, The (1908), D. W. Griffith, United States
Great Dictator, The (1940), Charlie Chaplin, United States
Great Expectations (1946), David Lean, Great Britain
Great McGinty, The (1940), Preston Sturges, United States
Great Race, The (1965), Blake Edwards, United States
Great Train Robbery, The (1903), Edwin Porter, United States
Guerre Est Finie, La (1966), Alain Resnais, France
Guilty by Suspicion (1991), Irwin Winkler, United States
Gunga Din (1939), George Stevens, United States
Hail the Conquering Hero (1944), Preston Sturges, United States

Hallelulah (1929), King Vidor, United States
Hands Up (1965), Jerzi Skolimowski, Poland
Happiness (1998), Todd Solondz, United States
Hard Day's Night, A (1964), Richard Lester, Great Britain
Having a Wild Weekend (1965), John Boorman, Great Britain
Heaven and Earth (1993), Oliver Stone, United States
Heaven Can Wait (1977), Warren Beatty, United States
Hell in the Pacific (1968), John Boorman, United States
Help! (1965), Richard Lester, Great Britain
High Noon (1952), Fred Zinnemann, United States
High School (1968), Fred Wiseman, United States
Hiroshima, Mon Amour (1960), Alan Resnais, France
His Girl Friday (1940), Howard Hawks, United States
Hobson's Choice (1954), David Lean, Great Britain
Home of the Brave (1949), Mark Robson, United States
Hook (1991), Steven Spielberg, United States
Hospital (1969), Fred Wiseman, United States
Hospital, The (1971), Arthur Hiller, United States
How the West Was Won (1962), Henry Hathaway/John Ford/George Marshall, United States
Husbands (1970), John Cassavetes, United States
Hustler, The (1961), Robert Rossen, United States
I Want to Live! (1958), Robert Wise, United States
I Was a 90-Pound Weakling (1964), Wolf Koenig/George Dufaux, Canada
I Was a Male War Bride (1949), Howard Hawks, United States
Ice Storm, The (1997), Ang Lee, United States
If-.-.-.-(1969), Lindsay Anderson, Great Briatain
In the Mood for Love (2000), Wong-Kar Wai, Hong Kong
In Which We Serve (1942), David Lean, Great Britain
Indiana Jones and the Last Crusade (1989), Steven Spielberg, United States
Into the Arms of Strangers (2000), Mark Jonathan Harris, United States
Intolerance (1916), D. W. Griffith, United States
Invitation to the Dance (1957), Gene Kelly, United States
Isadora (1969), Karel Reisz, Great Britain
Jaws (1975), Steven Spielberg, United States
Jazz Singer, The (1927), Alan Crosland, United States
Jesus of Montreal (1990), Denys Arcand, Canada
JFK (1991), Oliver Stone, United States
Judith of Bethulia (1913), D. W. Griffith, United States
Jules et Jim (1961), François Truffaut, France
Jungle Fever (1991), Spike Lee, United States
Junior Bonner (1972), Sam Peckinpah, United States
Jurassic Park (1993), Steven Spielberg, United States
Killing of a Chinese Bookie, The (1976), John Cassavetes, United States
Kind of Loving, A (1962), John Schlesinger, Great Britain

Kiss Me, Stupid (1964), Billy Wilder, United States
Kiss of Death (1947), Henry Hathaway, United States
Kiss, The (1896), Thomas A. Edison, United States
Koyaanisqatsi (1983), Godfrey Reggio, United States
Kundun (1997), Martin Scorcese, United States
La Chinoise (1967), Jean-Luc Godard, France
La Femme Nikita (1990), Luc Besson, France/Italy
La Jetee (1962), Chris Marker, France
Lady Eve, The (1941), Preston Sturges, United States
Lady from Shanghai, The (1948), Orson Welles, United States
Lady in the Lake (1946), Robert Montgomery, United States
Last Laugh, The (1924), F. W. Murnau, Germany
Last Tango in Paris (1973), Bernardo Bertolucci, France/Italy
Last Year at Marienbad (1961), Alain Resnais, France
Laughter in the Dark (1969), Tony Richardson, Great Britain
Lawrence of Arabia (1962), David Lean, Great Britain
Lesson in Love (1954), Ingmar Bergman, Sweden
Letter to Three Wives, A (1949), Joseph Mankiewicz, United States
Life is Beautiful (1998), Roberto Benigni, Italy.
Life of an American Fireman, The (1903), Edwin Porter, United States
Life of Brian (1979), Terry Jones, Great Britain
Lineup, The (1958), Don Siegel, United States
Listen to Britain (1942), Humphrey Jennings, Great Britain
Little Big Man (1970), Arthur Penn, United States
Little Foxes, The (1941), William Wyler, United States
Lives of a Bengal Lancer, The (1935), Henry Hathaway, United States
Lola Montes (1955), Max Ophuls, France
Lonedale Operator, The (1911), D. W. Griffith, United States
Loneliness of the Long Distance Runner, The (1962), Tony Richardson, Great
  Britain
Lonely Boy (1962), Wolf Koenig/Roman Kroiter, Canada
Lonely Villa, The (1909), D. W. Griffith, United States
Long Good Friday, The (1980), John MacKenzie, Great Britain
Long Goodbye, The (1973), Robert Altman, United States
Long Way Home, The (1997), Mark Jonathan Harris, United States
Look Back in Anger (1958), Tony Richardson, Great Britain
Lost Honor of Katharina Blum, The (1975), Volker Schlondorff/Margarethe
  von Trotta, West Germany
Louisiana Story (1948), Robert Flaherty, United States
Loved One, The (1965), Tony Richardson, United States
Lust for Life (1956), Vincente Minnelli, United States
M (1931), Fritz Lang, Germany
Mad Max 2 (The Road Warrior) (1981), George Miller, Australia
Madigan (1968), Don Siegel, United States
Magician, The (1959), Ingmar Bergman, Sweden

Magnificent Ambersons, The (1942), Orson Welles, United States
Magnolia (1998), Paul Thomas Anderson, United States
Mahabharata, The (1989), Peter Brook, France
Major Dundee (1965), Sam Peckinpah, United States
Malcolm X (1992), Spike Lee, United States
Man Bites Dog (1992), Remy Belvaux, Belgium
Man in the Gray Flannel Suit, The (1946), Nunnally Johnson, United States
Man of Aran (1934), Robert Flaherty, Great Britain
Man Who Knew Too Much, The (1956), Alfred Hitchcock, United States
Man with a Movie Camera, The (1929), Dziga Vertov, USSR
Manchurian Candidate, The (1962), John Frankenheimer, United States
Manhattan (1979), Woody Allen, United States
Marat/Sade (1966), Peter Brook, Great Britain
Marianne and Julianne (1982), Margarethe von Trotta, West Germany
Marnie (1964), Alfred Hitchcock, United States
Marriage Circle, The (1924), Ernst Lubitsch, United States
McCabe and Mrs. Miller (1971), Robert Altman, United States
Mean Streets (1973), Martin Scorsese, United States
Medium Cool (1969), Haskell Wexler, United States
Memorandum (1966), Donald Brittain, Canada
Mephisto (1981), Istvan Szabo, Hungary
Meshes in the Afternoon (1943/1959), Maya Daren, United States
Midnight Cowboy (1969), John Schlesinger, United States
Midnight Express (1978), Alan Parker, United States
Minnie and Moskowitz (1971), John Cassavetes, United States
Miracle of Morgan's Creek, The (1944), Preston Sturges, United States
Mo' Better Blues (1990), Spike Lee, United States
Modern Times (1936), Charlie Chaplin, United States
Momma Don't Allow (1955), Karel Reisz/Tony Richardson, Great Britain
Mon Oncle (1958), Jacques Tati, France
Mon Oncle d'Amerique (1980), Alain Resnais, France
Monkey Business (1952), Howard Hawks, United States
Monte Walsh (1970), William A. Fraker, United States
Monty Python and the Holy Grail (1975), Terry Gilliam/Terry Jones, Great Britain
Moonstruck (1987), Norman Jewison, United States
More the Merrier, The (1943), George Stevens, United States
Morgan: A Suitable Case for Treatment (1966), Karel Reisz, Great Britain
Mother (1926), Vsevolod Pudovkin, USSR
Mr. Death (2000), Errol Morris, United States
Mr. Deeds Goes to Town (1936), Frank Capra, United States
Mr. Hulot's Holiday (1953), Jacques Tati, France
Mr. Smith Goes to Washington (1939), Frank Capra, United States
Muriel (1963), Alain Resnais, France
My Best Friend (1999), Werner Herzog, Germany

My Darling Clementine (1946), John Ford, United States
Nanook of the North (1922), Robert Flaherty, United States
Napoleon (1927), Abel Gance, France
Nashville (1975), Robert Altman, United States
Natural Born Killers (1994), Oliver Stone, United States
Navigator, The (1988), Vincent Ward, Australia
Nevada Smith (1966), Henry Hathaway, United States
Night and Fog (1955), Alain Resnais, France
Night Mail (1936), Basil Wright, Great Britain
Night of the Hunter, The (1955), Charles Laughton, United States
Night Porter, The (1974), Liliana Cavani, Italy
Ninotchka (1939), Ernst Lubitsch, United States
Nixon (1995), Oliver Stone, United States
No Way Out (1987), Roger Donaldson, United States
North by Northwest (1959), Alfred Hitchcock, United States
Northwest Mounted Police (1940), Cecil B. DeMille, United States
Nosferatu: The Vampyre (1979), Werner Herzog, Germany
Notorious (1946), Alfred Hitchcock, United States
O Lucky Man! (1973), Lindsay Anderson, Great Britain
Occurrence at Owl Creek, An (1962), Robert Enrico, France
October (1928), Sergei Eisenstein, USSR
Odds Against Tomorrow (1959), Robert Wise, United States
O'Dreamland (1953), Lindsay Anderson, Great Britain
Oliver Twist (1948), David Lean, Great Britain
Olivier, Olivier (1992), Agnieszka Holland
Olympia (1938), Leni Riefenstahl, Germany
Once Upon a Time in America (1984), Sergio Leone, United States
One Flew Over the Cuckoo's Nest (1975), Milos Forman, United States
Open City (1946), Roberto Rossellini, Italy
Opening Night (1977), John Cassavetes, United States
Ordinary People (1980), Robert Redford, United States
Our Daily Bread (1934), King Vidor, United States
Pale Rider (1985), Clint Eastwood, United States
Panic in the Streets (1950), Elia Kazan, United States
Parallax View, The (1974), Alan J. Pakula, United States
Paris, Texas (1984), Wim Wenders, West Germany/France
Passage to India (1984), David Lean, Great Britain
Passion of Joan of Arc, The (1928), Carl Dryer, France
Paths of Glory (1957), Stanley Kubrick, United States
Pawnbroker, The (1965), Sidney Lumet, United States
Performance (1970), Nicolas Roeg, Great Britain
Personal Best (1982), Robert Towne, United States
Petulia (1968), Richard Lester, United States
Pink Panther, The (1964), Blake Edwards, United States
Pirate, The (1948), Vincente Minnelli, United States

Place in the Sun, A (1951), George Stevens, United States
Plainsman, The (1936), Cecil B. DeMille, United States
Platoon (1986), Oliver Stone, United States
Plow That Broke the Plains, The (1936), Pare Lorentz, United States
Point Blank (1967), John Boorman, United States
Point Break (1991), Kathryn Bigelow, United States
Potemkin (1925), Sergei Eisenstein, USSR
Pour Construire un Feu (1928), Claude Autant-Lara, France
Prelude to War (1942), Frank Capra, United States
Prince of the City (1981), Sidney Lumet, United States
Privilege (1967), Peter Watkins, Great Britain
Promises (2001), Justine Shapiro and B. Z. Goldberg, United States
Proof (1991), Jocelyn Moorhouse, Australia
Providence (1977), Alain Resnais, France/Switzerland
Psycho (1960), Alfred Hitchcock, United States
Pulp Fiction (1994), Quentin Tarantino, United Sates
Punchline (1989), David Seltzer, United States
Purple Rose of Cairo, The (1985), Woody Allen, United States
Quo Vadis (1912), Enrico Guazzoni, Italy
Radio Days (1987), Woody Allen, United States
Raging Bull (1980), Martin Scorsese, United States
Raiders of the Lost Ark (1981), Steven Spielberg, United States
Raising Arizona (1987), Joel and Ethan Coen, United States
Ramona (1911), D. W. Griffith, United States
Ran (1985), Akira Kurosawa, Japan
Rashomon (1951), Akira Kurosawa, Japan
Reality Bites (1994), Ben Stiller, United States
Rear Window (1954), Alfred Hitchcock, United States
Red and the White, The (1967), Miklós Jancsó, Hungary.
Reine Elizabeth, La (Queen Elizabeth) (1912), Louis Mercanton, France
Requiem for a Dream (2000), Darren Aranofsky, United States
Reservoir Dogs (1992), Quentin Tarantino, United States
Ride the High Country (1962), Sam Peckinpah, United States
Rififi (1954), Jules Dassin, France
Rio Bravo (1959), Howard Hawks, United States
River of No Return (1954), Otto Preminger, United States
River, The (1937), Pare Lorentz, United States
Robe, The (1953), Henry Koster, United States
Robo Cop (1987), Paul Verhoeven, United States
Roger and Me (1989), Michael Moore, United States
Romeo Is Bleeding (1993), Peter Medak, United States
Rope (1948), Alfred Hitchcock, United States
Rosemary's Baby (1968), Roman Polanski, United States
Rosetta (1999), Luc and Jean-Pierre Dardenne, Belgium

Round-up, The (1965), Miklós Jansçó, Hungary.
Run Lola Run (1999), Tom Tykwer, Germany
Runaway Train (1985), Andrei Konchalovsky, United States
Running, Jumping and Standing Still (1961), Richard Lester, Great Britain
Ryan's Daughter (1970), David Lean, Great Britain
Sacrifice, The (1986), Andrei Tarkovsky, USSR
Sad Song of Yellow Skin (1970), Michael Rubbo, Canada
Salesman (1969), The Maysles Brothers, United States
Salvador (1986), Oliver Stone, United States
Sand Pebbles, The (1966), Robert Wise, United States
Saturday Night and Sunday Morning (1960), Karel Reisz, Great Britain
Saving Private Ryan (1997), Steven Spielberg, United States
Scarface (1983), Brian De Palma, United States
School Daze (1988), Spike Lee, United States
Searchers, The (1956), John Ford, United States
Second Awakening of Christa Klages, The (1977), Margarethe von Trotta, West Germany
Seconds (1966), John Frankenheimer, United States
Secrets of a Lost Soul (1926), G. W. Pabst, United States
Sense and Sensibility (1995), Ang Lee, Great Britain
Serpent's Egg, The (1978), Ingmar Bergman, United States/West Germany
Serpico (1973), Sidney Lumet, United States
Set-Up, The (1949), Robert Wise, United States
Seven Beauties (1976), Lina Westmüller, Italy
Seven Days in May (1964), John Frankenheimer, United States
Seven Samurai, The (1954), Akira Kurosawa, Japan
Seventh Seal, The (1956), Ingmar Bergman, Sweden
Seventh Sign, The (1988), Carl Schultz, United States
Shane (1953), George Stevens, United States
Sherman's March (1986), Ross McElwee, United States
She's Gotta Have It (1986), Spike Lee, United States
Shoot the Piano Player (1962), François Truffaut, France
Singin' in the Rain (1952), Gene Kelly, United States
Sink or Swim (1990), Su Friedrich, United States
Skirt Dance (1898), Cinematograph, Great Britain
Slacker (1991), Richard Linklater, United States
Slap Shot (1977), George Roy Hill, United States
Solzhenitsyn's Children Are Making a Lot of Noise in Paris (1979), Michael Rubbo, Canada
Some Like It Hot (1959), Billy Wilder, United States
Somebody Up There Likes Me (1956), Robert Wise, United States
Something Wild (1986), Jonathan Demme, United States
Song of Ceylon (1934), Basil Wright, Great Britain
Sons and Lovers (1958), Jack Cardiff, Great Britain

Sorcerer (1977), William Friedkin, United States
Sortie de l'Usine Lumière, La (Workers Leaving the Lumière Factory) (1895), Auguste and Louis Lumière, France
Specter of the Rose (1946), Ben Hecht, United States
Speed (1994), Jan de Bout, United States
Spellbound (1945), Alfred Hitchcock, United States
Stand by Me (1986), Rob Reiner, United States
Stop Making Sense (1984), Jonathan Demme, United States
Strangers on a Train (1951), Alfred Hitchcock, United States
Straw Dogs (1971), Sam Peckinpah, United States
Streetcar Named Desire, A (1951), Elia Kazan, United States
Strike (1924), Sergei Eisenstein, USSR
Sullivan's Travels (1941), Preston Sturges, United States
Summertime (1955), David Lean, Great Britain
Sunday in the Country, A (1984), Bernard Tavernier, France
Sunrise (1927), F. W. Murnau, Germany
Sunset Boulevard (1950), Billy Wilder, United States
Swept Away-.-.-.-(1975), Lina Wertmüller, Italy
Swing Time (1936), George Stevens, United States
Tampopo (1987), Juzo Itami, Japan
Ten Commandments, The (1923, 1956), Cecil B. DeMille, United States
Tequila Sunrise (1988), Robert Towne, United States
Terminator 2: Judgement Day (1991), James Cameron, United States
Terminator, The (1984), James Cameron, United States
Terminus (1960), John Schlesinger, Great Britain
Terra Trema, La (1947), Luchino Visconti, Italy
Thelma & Louise (1991), Ridley Scott, United States
Thin Blue Line, The (1988), Errol Morris, United States
Thin Red Line, The (1998), Terence Malick, United States
39 Steps, The (1935), Alfred Hitchcock, Great Britain
Thirty-Two Short Films about Glen Gould (1993), François Girard, Canada
This Sporting Life (1963), Lindsay Anderson, Great Britain
Three Brothers (1980), Francesco Rosi, Italy
Three Faces of Eve (1957), Nunnally Johnson, United States
Three Musketeers, The (1973), Richard Lester, Panama
Time Code (2000), Mike Figgis, United States
To Be or Not to Be (1942), Ernst Lubitsch, United States
Tom Jones (1963), Tony Richardson, Great Britain
Too Late the Hero (1970), Robert Aldrich, United States
Tootsie (1982), Sydney Pollack, United States
Top Gun (1986), Tony Scott, United States
Touch of Evil (1958), Orson Welles, United States
Tourist, The (1992), Rob Moss, United States
Tout Va Bien (1970), Jean-Luc Godard, France

Track 29 (1989), Nicolas Roeg, Great Britain
Train, The (1965), John Frankenheimer, United States/France/Italy
Trip to the Moon, A (1902), Georges Méliès, France
Triumph of the Will (1935), Leni Riefenstahl, Germany
Trouble in Paradise (1932), Ernst Lubitsch, United States
Twelve Monkeys (1995), Terry Gilliam, United States
Twentieth Century (1934), Howard Hawks, United States
Two or Three Things I Know About Her (1966), Jean-Luc Godard, France
2001: A Space Odyssey (1968), Stanley Kubrick, Great Britain
Unconquered (1947), Cecil B. DeMille, United States
Under Capricorn (1949), Alfred Hitchcock, Great Britain
Unforgiven (1992), Clint Eastwood, United States
Unstrung Heroes (1995), Diane Keaton, United States
Valmont (1989), Milos Forman, United States
Variety (1925), E. A. Dupont, Germany
Vertigo (1958), Alfred Hitchcock, United States
Very Nice, Very Nice (1961), Arthur Lipsett, Canada
Victor/Victoria (1982), Blake Edwards, United States
Wages of Fear, The (1952), Henri-Georges Clouzot, France/Italy
Waiting for Fidel (1974), Michael Rubbo, Canada
Walkabout (1971), Nicolas Roeg, Great Britain
Wall Street (1987), Oliver Stone, United States
War Game, The (1967), Peter Watkins, Great Britain
Warrendale (1966), Alan King, Canada
Weekend (1967), Jean-Luc Godard, France/Italy
Werner Herzog Eats his Shoe (1980), Les Blank, United States
West Side Story (1961), Robert Wise, United States
What's Up, Doc? (1972), Peter Bogdanovich, United States
White Dawn, The (1974), Phillip Kauffman, United States
White Heat (1949), Raoul Walsh, United States
Whore (1991), Ken Russell, Great Britain
Why We Fight (series) (1943–1945), Frank Capra, United States
Wild Bunch, The (1969), Sam Peckinpah, United States
Wild One, The (1954), Laslo Benedek, United States
Wild Strawberries (1957), Ingmar Bergman, Sweden
Winter Light (1962), Ingmar Bergman, Sweden
Wiz, The (1978), Sidney Lumet, United States
Wizard of Oz, The (1939), Victor Fleming, United States
Woman Under the Influence, A (1974), John Cassavetes, United States
Woodstock (1970), Michael Wadleigh, United States
Working Girls, The (1986), Lizzie Borden, United States
Wonderful, Horrible Life of Leni Riefenstahl, The (1995), Ray Muller, Germany
Woyzek (1979), Werner Herzog, Germany

WR: Mysteries of the Organism (1971), Dusan Makavejev, former Yugoslavia
Wrestling (1960), Michelle Brault, Marcel Carrier, Claude Fournier, and
  Claude Jutra, Canada
Year of the Dragon (1985), Michael Cimino, United States
You're a Big Boy Now (1966), Francis Ford Coppola, United States
Z (1969), Constatin Costa-Gavras, France

Glossary

A-B rolls The process used to create optical effects such as dissolves in film and videotape. Two rolls are used alternately. The A roll contains the first shot, and the B roll contains the second. The two rolls overlap for the length of the dissolve.

academy leader Film that precedes the first picture or sound. It contains synchronizing marks and countdown information used by the film lab for processing the composite print.

analog A form of electronic signal composed of varying voltage levels. Analog signals are of lower quality than digital signals.

anamorphic An image that is squeezed laterally so that the width-to-height ratio drops.

answer print The first lab print of a completed motion picture.

aspect ratio The proportion of picture width to height. For television and 16-mm film, the aspect ratio is 1.33:1; wide-screen 35-mm, 1.85:1; wide-screen 70-mm, 2.2:1; 35-mm anamorphic, 2.35:1.

assembly A rough cut; the organization of shots in rough order according to the script.

asynchronous Sound that is not synchronized to the picture being presented.

automatic dialogue replacement (ADR) The process of recording new dialogues. If the original dialogue recording has picked up too much ambient noise (such as an airplane), the dialogue is rerecorded in a studio under controlled conditions.

back lighting Light directed from behind the subject toward the camera. The effect is to soften the impression of the subject.

back projection The projection of an image, film, or television show on the rear of a translucent screen to be viewed from its front surface.

base For film or videotape, the flexible support on which a photographic emulsion or magnetic coating is carried.

batch number Identification number of a quantity of product that has been manufactured at one time and has uniform characteristics, particularly raw stock.

Betacam Sony's trade name for a broadcast-quality videotape recorder (VTR) system that uses half-inch tape with component recording of luminance and chrominance on separate tracks. The high-speed recording results in a higher quality image on the videotape.

Beta format The tape used in the Betamax system.

bias In audiotape recording, an ultrasonic signal applied to the record head to reduce distortion.

bidirectional microphone A microphone with equal sensitivity to sound arriving from the front or the rear.

bridging shot A shot used to cover a jump in time or another break in continuity.

broadcast standard In video practice, the highest quality of recording and reproduction; video capable of meeting the stringent requirements of broadcasting organizations.

burn-in The addition of visible time code numerals to a videotape recording.

butt splice A splice in a film or tape in which the two ends are not over-lapped.

camera angle The angle of view created by the position of the camera vis-à-vis the subject. The positioning results in a composition that has particular characteristics as a result of the angle.

cement Cellulose solvent used for joining pieces of film.

character generator A device used to issue the signals needed to form alphanumeric characters on a cathode-ray tube. Such characters are used to create time code numbers for establishing edit points and to display letters or graphics used in titles.

cheat shot A shot in which part of the subject or action is excluded from view to make the part that is recorded appear different from what it actually is. Cheat shots are often used in action sequences to create the illusion of danger or disaster.

chroma key An electronic matting process for combining two or more video images into a credible composite form.

CinemaScope A system of anamorphic wide-screen motion pictures that makes use of a horizontal compression-expression factor of between 2:1 and 2.5:1.

cinema verité See **direct camera**.

clapboard Sometimes referred to as *clapper board, clapper,* or *slate.* In motion picture photography, a board with a hinged arm used to identify the correct synchronization of picture and sound at the beginning or end of a scene. The clapboard yields a sharp sound that can be matched to the visual action of the clap.

clean edit list An off-line edit list that has had discrepancies, overrecord-ings, or redundancies resolved, preparing it for efficient on-line editing.

click track A prerecorded timing track that consists of recorded clicks and is used for dubbing music with precise timing. The click track is generally produced after all of the visual editing decisions have been made.

close-up A tight shot of a person's head and shoulders. An extreme close-up might include a part of the face or a hand, for example.

commentary   See **narration**.

control track   In videotape, a track used for servo information, synchronization, and scanning rate.

credits   Acknowledgments given in titles at the beginning or end of a film or television production, that list the cast, technicians, and organizations involved.

creeping sync   In film recording, a progressive error of synchronization between picture and sound track; the steps taken to correct this error.

cross-cut   Sometimes referred to as intercutting or *parallel editing.* The intermingling of shots from two or more scenes. An alternating of scenes sometimes implies an eventual relationship between them.

crystal sync   A method of synchronizing an audio magnetic tape recorder to a motion picture camera.

cut   An instantaneous change from one scene to another.

cutaway   Also known as an insert shot. A noncritical shot used to break or link principal action in scenes.

cutter   An editor.

cutting print   Sometimes called the *work print.* The positive print that the editor works with in the editing process. Once complete, the print is used to edit the negative for the printing of the film.

dailies   Also referred to as *rushes.* The first prints made from the newly processed picture or sound negative, which are used to check content and quality.

depth of field   Distance between the nearest and farthest points from the camera at which the subject is acceptably sharp.

digital   An electronic signal system composed of voltages that are turned on or off. Data in digital form may be copied many times with virtually no loss of quality (degradation) because the data are not altered or distorted as they go through the electronic system.

direct camera   Also referred to as *cinema verité.* A style of filming real-life scenes without elaborate equipment. The result is less intrusion into the activities of the subject being filmed than with standard techniques.

dissolve   A gradual merging of the end of one shot into the beginning of the next, produced by the superimposition of a fade-out onto a fade-in of equal length.

Dolby   A noise reduction system for magnetic and photographic sound recordings.

dolly   A movable platform on which a camera may be mounted so that action in front of the camera may be followed. See also **tracking shot**.

double system   In cinematography, the system in which picture and sound are recorded on separate films or on film and tape. This system allows greater flexibility in working with sound than a single system in which original sound and picture are recorded simultaneously on the same piece of film.

dub Also referred to as *dupe*. In television, to copy a videotape. In film, to mix and compose audio sound tracks from several elements by balancing them for level, proportion, and equalization.

edge coding Sometimes called *edge numbering* or *footage numbers*. A coding system for numbers printed on motion picture film raw stock by the manufacturer. They are included once every foot on 35-mm film and once every 20 frames, or every 6 inches, on 16-mm film. These letters and numbers are used by the film negative cutter to match a work print film frame to its corresponding negative original. Time code, an electronic form of edge numbers, serves a similar purpose on videotape.

edit controller A keyboard or mouse used to communicate edit commands to the computer and the electronic editing system, including VCRs, VTRs, video switchers, and audio switchers.

edit decision list (EDL) The time code information defining each edit in a sequence. The list may be constructed for use on a computerized editing system.

edit point The position on the tape where two scenes are joined to create an edit. The end of one scene is joined by means of a splice to the beginning of the second scene.

effects track The composite or single track that is reserved for the sound effects to be used with the pictures.

electronic editing A method of electronically transferring pictures and sound from one videotape to another. This new, or edited, copy is regarded as a second-generation copy.

electronic field production (EFP) Remote, as opposed to studio production, techniques that use television cameras and portable video recorders.

electronic news gathering (ENG) The fast and portable electronic photography used in news reporting or in educational or industrial applications.

establishing shot Usually a long shot used near the beginning of a scene to establish the interrelationship of details to be shown subsequently in nearer shots.

fade-in The beginning of a shot that starts in darkness and gradually lightens to full brightness.

fade-out The beginning of the shot starts in full brightness and gradually darkens to black.

fine cut Also called *final cut*. An editor's last cut of the edited work print after all of the changes have been made and the program is ready for the conforming process.

first generation The original videotape used to record the production. Each subsequent copy loses one generation.

flashback A scene that takes place at an earlier time than the scene it follows.

flash frame An extra frame of film, usually seen at an edit point. It appears as a momentary flash.

focus pull The shift of the subject in focus from the foreground to the background or vice versa.

footage   The length of film measured in feet.

format   In videotape, there are various systems: half-inch, three-quarter inch, one inch. Tape can be Beta, VHS, super VHS, 8-mm, etc. Each has different characteristics and is used in different geographical regions. Various formats also reflect amateur or consumer purposes as well as professional broadcast uses.

frame   A single image of film is the still visual composition.

frame rate   The rate at which film or video proceeds through a camera or projector. The American standard is 24 frames per second; the European standard is 25 frames per second. For television, the NTSC standard is 30 frames per second; the PAL and SECAM standard is 25 frames per second.

freeze frame   At a chosen point in a scene, the effect of freezing the action. It is accomplished by repeatedly printing a particular frame.

full shot   A shot in which an entire person or object is visible within the frame.

generation   Each copy of the original videotape. A deterioration of quality results from the process of copying.

genlock   Short for *generator lock*. A method of synchronizing or electronically locking several video sources together so that they are in electronic time.

guide track   A speech track recorded with too much background noise that serves as a guide for the actor to repeat the speech in a studio.

high-definition television (HDTV)   A television system that contains 1125 horizontal scan lines per frame. Conventional television displays 525 lines per frame. The screen aspect ratio of HDTV is 1.78:1, as opposed to 1.33:1 for standard television.

insert shot   See **cutaway**.

intercut   See **cross-cut** and **parallel cut**.

interlock   A method of connecting a separate sound track and picture by means of electronic or mechanical links between devices such as ATRs, VCRs, and film projectors. Interlock is used in the transfer of film to videotape.

iris   An adjustable diaphragm of metal leaves over the lens aperture that controls the amount of light passing through the lens. In the early days of film, the stopping down of the iris was used to fade out on the subject in the center of the frame. The effect was cruder than today's light-to-dark fade-out, which affects the entire frame.

iris in, iris out   A decorative fade-in or fade-out in which the image appears or disappears as a growing or diminishing oval. This effect was used often in the silent cinema era.

jump cut   A cut that breaks the continuity of time by jumping forward from one part of an action to another that is obviously separated from the first by an interval of time.

key lighting (high or low)   A high-key image has a characteristic all-over lightness achieved by soft, full illumination on a light-toned subject with light shadows and background.

lap dissolve   See **dissolve**.

leader   A length of film joined to the beginning of a reel that is used for threading the film through the camera or projector.

library shot   A shot used in a film but not recorded specifically for it. Often, newsreel footage is stock, or library, footage filmed previously but copied and used for another film or television show. Journalistic films often rely extensively on library shots.

lip synch   The accurate synchronization of a sound track with its corresponding picture. The phrase in *lip synch* means that the sound matches the picture.

long shot   A wide, long-distance shot generally used to establish the scene and give the audience a reference point for subsequent shots.

loop   A short length of film joined together at its ends to form an endless band. It can be passed through a projector to give a continuous repetition of the subject. Loops are used to rerecord dialogue and particular sound effects.

magnetic film   A strip of magnetically coated or striped material that has perforation similar to that of photographic film for transport and synchronization. Original audiotape sound is transferred to magnetic film for editing.

magnetic tape   A thin plastic or Mylar material coated with a formula of magnetically responsive ferrous oxide that records and preserves electronic signals.

M and E tracks   Separate music and sound effects tracks.

married print   The composite of optical sound track and a positive print of the complete film. The final laboratory step of printing the film includes the sound track. The synchronization is correct for projection.

mask   A shield placed before the camera to cut off some portion of the camera's field of view.

master shot   A single shot of an entire piece of dramatic action designed to facilitate the assembly of the closer, detailed shots from which the final sequence will be created.

match cut   A cut in which the end of one shot leads logically and visually to the beginning of the second shot. An example is the cut from a character exiting frame right to the character entering frame left.

match dissolve   A dissolve in which one object is seen in different settings but occupies the same position on screen throughout the dissolve.

medium close shot   A shot with a looser frame than a close shot. A medium close shot of an actor, for example, includes everything from the waist up. A close shot includes only the actor's face.

medium shot   For the human figure, a shot from the waist up.

mix   To combine the various separate sounds on location or to combine various sound tracks to make a smooth composite.

monitor   A video display screen. A monitor usually does not include a tuner.

montage   A compilation of images.

MOS   Silent shooting (no sound recorded at the time).

Moviola   The trade name for a portable editing machine. It is based on the same technical concept as a motion picture projector. Sound is run separately from picture, to allow for editing of each sound or picture individually or of both together.

multiple exposure   Repeated exposures made on a single series of film frames.

multitrack   A technique of sound recording that uses a separate track for each source to permit subsequent mixing and blending.

narration   Also called *commentary*. Descriptive dialogue accompanying a film. Voice over serves as a bridging device between sequences. Voice over can also be used to clarify the narrative intentions of the visuals.

negative   Refers to the originating material, film and videotape, used to record images. Tone and color values are the reverse of the original.

negative cutting   Editing the original negative film from the positive working copy used during the editing. Once the negative cutting is complete, the film is printed from the negative, or an interpositive is printed from the negative.

nonlinear editing   Editing videotape out of sequence. It allows the editor to build or switch segments in any manner.

NTSC   The North American television standard: a 525-line system that scans 30 interlaced television frames per second.

off-line edit   Editing video material using low-cost equipment to produce rough cut before using expensive broadcast-standard equipment for the final work.

one light   A film print made using the same exposure for every scene and take on a roll without any color correction.

on-line edit   The last stage of videotape editing, which results in a final master tape. Time-coded off-line edit decisions are used to create the master tape.

optical   Any effect carried out using an optical printer. Opticals are usually performed in a laboratory. Dissolves, fades, and wipes are examples of opticals.

optical printer   A high-quality film projector and motion picture camera that are mechanically interlocked so that both synchronously advance the film one frame at a time. Fades, dissolves, and other special effects are recorded on an optical printer.

optical track   The sound track mixed from magnetic track onto a magnetic master mix, then transferred to an optical track so that it can be combined with the visuals on a composite print.

original   The film exposed in the camera after processing; the first video recording prior to copying or editing.

outtake   A shot or scene discarded in the process of editing.

PAL   The European color television coding standard: a 625-line, 50-Hz television transmission system.

panning shot   A shot in which the camera moves along a horizontal axis. A panning shot is often used to establish location or to follow action.

parallel action   A device of narrative construction in which the development of two pieces of action is represented by alternately showing a fragment of one and then a fragment of another. See also **cross-cut**.

parallel cut   See **cross-cut**.

perforation   Holes along the edge of a strip of film used for its transport and registration.

post-production   The editing of prerecorded material, including the use of special effects and audio dubbing.

print   A photographic copy of a film, usually with a positive image.

random-access editing systems   Nonlinear electronic video editing equipment allows the editor to build a segment out of sequence without having to modify material on either side of a shot or sequence. The shot and sound information are stored in computer memory, and when needed, picture and sound are switched from one camera to another.

reaction shot   A cut to a performer's face to capture an emotional response.

release print   A motion picture positive print that includes picture and sound and is made for general distribution and exhibition.

retake   The repetition of a take.

reversal film   A special type of direct positive film.

rewind   An apparatus for rewinding film.

rushes   See **dailies**.

shooting ratio   The amount of film or tape exposed or recorded in production compared to the amount actually used in the final edited program.

single system   A method of film or videotape recording or editing in which the picture and sound are located on the same piece of film or videotape.

slate   A device used in front of the film or television camera to display production information such as scene number, take number, date, and other pertinent information. The clapboard, which also provides a simultaneous sound cue for editing, is one type of slate.

slave   A unit designed to function only as ordered by a master unit, for example, a videotape recorder that is controlled by another VTR.

slow motion   A movement or shot that takes place more slowly than it did in reality.

sound track   A narrow path that normally runs along one side of cinematographic sound film in which sound is recorded in the form of a light trace varying in its light transmission.

special effect   A general term for scenes in which an illusion of the action required is created by the use of special equipment and processes.

splice   A physical joining in film or tape.

stock shot   See **library shot**.

superimpose   To add one picture on top of another. Usually, both continue to be visible. To add a caption or graphic over a picture.

sync   To match sound and picture.

synchronizer An apparatus that facilitates the mechanical operation of synchronizing two tracks.

synchronous sound Sound that has been synchronized with the picture.

take A single recording or a shot.

tilt To move the camera on a vertical axis: from up to down or from down to up.

time code A coding system, usually binary, recorded on audiotape, videotape, and sometimes on film for subsequent synchronization and editing. It denotes hours, minutes, and seconds and allows frames to be identified.

time code generator An electronic clock that generates and assigns to each video or audio frame a unique identification number of eight digits.

time code reader A device that reads and visually displays the eight-digit SMPTE time code.

track A defined part of the recording medium, photographic or magnetic, that carries discrete information.

tracking shot Also known as a *trucking shot*. A shot taken when the camera is in motion on a truck, dolly, or trolley.

trim The portion of a shot remaining after the selected material has been used in an edit.

trolley A wheeled device on which the camera can be moved while taking a shot.

two-shot A shot framing two people, usually from the waist up.

U-matic The trade name for a videocassette system that uses three-quarter-inch tape.

videocassette A cassette containing video recording tape with separate supply and take-up spools.

videotape Magnetic tape specifically designed for use as a video recording medium.

videotape recorder (VTR) A device used to record and replay television pictures and sound on magnetic tape.

wide-angle lens A lens of short focal length that has a wide angle of view and great depth of field.

wide screen A screen with a ratio greater than 1.33:1.

wild shooting Shooting the picture of a sound film without simultaneously recording the sound of the action.

wild track A sound track recorded independently of the picture with which it will subsequently be combined.

wipe A transition from one shot to another in which a line appears to travel across the screen, removing one shot and revealing another.

work print See **cutting print**.

zoom To magnify a chosen area of the image by means of a zoom lens (a lens with a variable focal length). The camera appears to move closer to the subject.

SELECTED BIBLIOGRAPHY

■

Anderson, Gary. *Video Editing and Post-Production: A Professional Guide.* New York: Knowledge Industries, 1984.

Andrew, Dudley. *Concepts in Film Theory.* New York: Oxford University Press, 1984.

———. *The Major Film Theories.* New York: Oxford University Press, 1976.

Arijon, Daniel. *Grammar of the Film Language,* 2d ed. Los Angeles: Silman-James Press, 1991.

Aruheim, Rudolph. *Film.* London: Faber and Faber, 1933.

Baddley, Hugh. *The Technique of Documentary Film Production.* Boston: Focal Press, 1963.

Balio, Tino, ed. *The American Film Industry.* Madison: University of Wisconsin Press, 1976.

Barsam, Richard Meran, ed. *Nonfiction Film: A Critical History.* New York: E. P. Dutton, 1973.

———. *Nonfiction Film: Theory and Criticism.* New York: E. P. Dutton, 1976.

Bazin, André. *What Is Cinema?* Vols. I, II. Berkeley: University of California Press, 1971.

Belenky, Mary Field, Blythe McVicker Cliachy, Nancy Rule Goldberger, and Jill Mattuck Torule. *Women's Way of Knowing. The Development of Self, Voice and Mind.* New York: Basic Books, 1986.

Bordwell, David, Janet Staiger, and Kristin Thompson. *The Classical Hollywood Cinema.* New York: Columbia University Press, 1985.

Bordwell, David, and Kristin Thompson. *Film Art: An Introduction,* 3d ed. New York: McGraw-Hill, 1990.

Burder, John. *The Technique of Editing 16-mm Films.* London: Focal Press, 1975.

Cameron, W. Evan. "An Analysis of 'A Diary for Timothy.'" *Cinema Studies,* Vol. no. 1 (Spring 1967):68.

Carringer, Robert L. *The Making of Citizen Kane.* Berkeley: University of California Press, 1985.

Chatman, Seymour. *Antonioni, or the Surface of the World.* Berkeley: University of California Press, 1985.

Cook, David A. *A History of Narrative Film.* New York: W. W. Norton, 1990.

Crittenden, Roger. *The Thames & Hudson Manual of Film Editing.* London: Thames and Hudson, 1981.

Dancyger, Ken, and Jeff Rush. *Alternative Scriptwriting,* 2d. ed. Boston: Focal Press, 1995.

Dmytryk, Edward. *On Film Editing.* Boston: Focal Press, 1985.

Dovzhenko, Alexander. *The Poet as Filmmaker.* Cambridge: MIT Press, 1973.

Eisenstein, Sergei. *Film Form.* New York: Harcourt Brace Jovanovich, 1977.

———. *The Film Sense.* New York: Harcourt Brace Jovanovich, 1975.

———. *Notes of a Film Director.* New York: Dover Publications, 1970.

Elsaesser, Thomas. *Early Cinema.* London: British Film Institute, 1950.

Erikson, Erik. *Identity: Youth and Crisis.* Yew York: Dutton, 1968.

Freud, Sigmund. *Beyond the Pleasure Principle.*

Gottesman, Roger, ed. *Focus on Citizen Kane.* Englewood Cliffs, N.J.: Prentice-Hall, 1971.

Happé, Bernard, ed. *Dictionary of Image Technology.* London: Focal Press, 1988.

Henderson, Brian. *A Critique of Film Theory.* New York: E. P. Dutton, 1980.

Innsdorff, Annette. *François Truffaut.* Boston: Twayne Publishers, 1978.

Jacobs, Lewis. *The Movies as Medium.* New York: Farrar, Strauss and Giroux, 1970.

———. *The Rise of the American Film.* New York: Harcourt, Brace and Company, 1947.

Jung, C. G. *Memories, Dreams, Reflections.* New York: Pantheon, 1963.

Katz, Steven. *Film Directors Shot by Shot.* Boston: Focal Press, 1991.

Kernberg, Otto. *Severe Personality Disorders: Psychotherapeutic Strategies.* New Haven: Yale University Press, 1984.

Konigsbertg, Ira. *The Complete Film Dictionary.* New York: New American Dictionary, 1987.

Kracauer, Seigfried. *Theory of Film.* New York: Oxford University Press, 1965.

Leyda, Jay. *Kino.* London: George Allen and Unwin, 1960.

Lovell, Alan, and Jim Hillier. *Studies in Documentary.* London: Martin Secker and Warburg, 1972.

Lundgren, Ernest. *The Art of the Film.* London: George Allen and Unwin, 1948.

MacCann, Richard Dyer. *Film: A Montage of Theories.* New York: E. P. Dutton, 1966.

Mast, Gerald, and Marshall Cohen. *Film Theory and Criticism*, 3d ed. New York: Oxford University Press, 1985.

Mayer, David. *Eisenstein's Potemkin.* New York: Da Capo Press, 1972.

McBride, Jim. *Orson Welles.* London: Martin Secker and Warburg, 1972.

Mellen, Joan. *The World of Luis Buñuel: Essays in Criticism.* New York: Oxford University Press, 1978.

Michaelson, Annette, ed. *Kino-Eye: The Writings of Dziga Vertov.* Berkeley: University of California Press, 1984.

Monaco, James. *Alain Renais.* New York: Oxford University Press, 1975.

———. *How to Read a Movie.* New York: Oxford University Press, 1977.

———. *The New Wave.* New York: Oxford University Press, 1976.

Nelson, Thomas Allen. *Kubrick: Inside a Film Artist's Maze.* Bloomington: Indiana University Press, 1982.

Nichols, Bill, ed. *Movies and Methods: An Anthology.* Berkeley: University of California Press, 1976.

Nilsen, Vladimir, *The Cinema as Graphic Art.* New York: Hill and Wang, 1936.

Pudovkin, V. I. *Film Technique and Film Acting.* London: Vision Press, 1968.

Rabiger, Michael. *Directing the Documentary*, 2d ed. Boston: Focal Press, 1992.

Reisz, Karel, and Gavin Millar. *The Technique of Film Editing*, 2d ed. Boston: Focal Press, 1968.

Rosenblum, Ralph, and Robert Karen. *When the Shooting Stops-.-.-.-*New York: Da Capo Press, 1986.

Sarris, Andrew. *The American Cinema.* Chicago. The University of Chicago Press. 1968.

Schneider, Arthur. *Electronic Post-Production Terms and Concepts*. Boston: Focal Press, 1990.

Sussex, Elisabeth. *The Rise and Fall of British Documentary*. Los Angeles: University of California Press. 1975.

Swann, Paul. *The British Documentary Film Movement, 1926–1946*. Cambridge: Cambridge University Press, 1989.

Tudor, Andrew. *Theories of Film*. London: Martin Secker and Warburg, 1974.

Vardac, Nicholas A. *Stage to Screen*. Cambridge: Harvard University Press, 1949.

Weis, Elisabeth, and John Belton, eds. *Film Sound: Theory and Practice*. New York: Columbia University Press, 1985.

Wollen, Peter. *Readings and Writings*. London: Versa, 1982.

———. *Signs and Meaning in the Cinema*. London: Martin Secker and Warburg, 1969.

Wood, Robin. *Hitchcock's Films Revisited*. New York: Columbia University Press, 1989.

Index

■

Jordan, Neil, 401

journey as narrative form, *Paris, Texas* example, 170–171

Judith of Bethulia, 7

Jules et Jim, 133–134

Julius Caesar, 378

jump cut
    defined, 453
    and discontinuity, 131–134
    MTV style and, 185

Jungle Fever, 171, 173–174

Junior Bonner, 159

Jurassic Park, 410

Kahlo, Frida, 191

Kahn, Nathaniel, 344

Kanal, 427

Kapur, Shekhar, 243, 244–248

Karen, Robert, xviii

Kar-wai, Wong, 196, 206–207, 213

Kasdan, Lawrence, 398

Kaufman, Philip, 392–393

Kazan, Elia, 82, 115–116, 153, 232, 260

Keaton, Buster, 40, 72, 74, 82, 273–276, 278, 279, 293, 297

Keaton, Diane, 82

Kelly, Gene, 75

Kerensky, George, 20

Kern, Jerome, 75

key lighting defined, 453

Killing, The, 238

Kind of Loving, A, 156

King, Allan, 126

King Arthur, 219, 407

Kingdom of Heaven, 258

King Is Alive, The, 260

King Kong, 255, 256

Kingsley, Sidney, 76

Kino-Eye, 25

Kinski, Klaus, 330–331

Kiss, The, 3

Kiss Me, Stupid, 297

Kiss of Death, 269

Klimov, Elem, 249–251, 426

Koenig, Wolf, 123, 126, 393

Komeda, Christopher, 398

Konchalovsky, Andrei, 394

Kopple, Barbara, 328

Koyaanisqatsi, 322

Kragh-Jacobsen, Søren, 234

Kroitor, Roman, 123, 126, 393

Kubrick, Stanley, xx, 95, 119–120, 164–167, 238–240, 279, 294, 349–350, 351, 361, 366, 379–380, 400

Kuleshov, Lev, 15–16, 53

Kundun, 240–242

Kureishi, Hanif, 153

Kurosawa, Akira, xv, 121, 129–131, 189, 190, 211, 214–215, 269, 350, 366, 393, 413, 433

La Chinoise, 414

Lady Eve, The, 298–300, 303

Lady from Shanghai, The, 128

Lady in the Lake, 97–98

La Femme Nikita, 187, 188

L'Age d'Or (The Golden Age), 34, 35–37, 185

La Guerre Est Finie, 137

Land and Freedom, 260

Land without Bread, 329, 330

Lang, Fritz, 46–49, 79, 128, 400

Langdon, Harry, 40, 74, 293

Langlois, Henri, 131

Lanza, Mario, 149

lap dissolve. *See* dissolve

La Promesse, 261

La Reine Elizabeth (Queen Elizabeth), 7

Las Hurdes (Land without Bread), 329

La Sortie de l'Usine Lumière (Workers Leaving the Lumière Factory), 3

Last Laugh, The, 14, 237, 239

Last Year at Marienbad, 414

La Terra Trema, 121

Lauffer, Bernard. *See Memorandum*

Laughter in the Dark, 154

Laughton, Charles, 82

Laurel and Hardy, 293

L'Avventura, 120

Lawrence of Arabia, 90, 91, 92, 95–96, 202, 243, 244, 269

Leacock, Richard, 328